Latin American Frontiers, Borders, and Hinterlands: Research Needs and Resources

SALALM Secretariat
General Library
University of New Mexico

Latin American Frontiers, Borders, and Hinterlands: Research Needs and Resources

Papers of the Thirty-Third Annual Meeting of the
SEMINAR ON THE ACQUISITION OF
LATIN AMERICAN LIBRARY MATERIALS

University of California, Berkeley
and Stanford University

Clark Kerr Conference Center
University of California, Berkeley

June 6-10, 1988

Paula Covington
Editor

SALALM SECRETARIAT
General Library, University of New Mexico

ISBN: 0-917617-24-X

Contents

Part Three. Publishing Patterns and Acquisitions Methods

I. Frontier, Border, and Hinterlands Resources: Case Studies

II. Regional Organizations: Documents and Other Publications

Part Four. Meeting the Automation Challenge

Preface

The choice of "Frontiers, Borders and Hinterlands" as the theme of SALALM's thirty-third annual conference is a logical outgrowth of several factors. First, it was prompted by the increased attention given to Latin American border issues in recent years. Evidence of this surging interest includes the creation of new border institutes, the accelerating pace of publishing in this area, the creation of bibliographic databases on borders, and the growing demand for information on a wide range of border topics. Second, the choice of California as our meeting site made this topic appropriate because of the opportunity to focus on issues relating to the Mexico–California border. Third, concentrating on the concept of frontiers seemed especially appropriate because the Bolton school of frontier historians originated at Berkeley.

The topic surfaced during discussions at the SALALM conference held in Berlin. In that historic city, we climbed steps to view the imposing bulk of the Berlin Wall, with its heavily guarded towers. The deserted patch of land dividing peoples was in sharp contrast to the constant flow that characterizes even our hemisphere's most heavily regulated, that between Mexico and California. In projecting the importance of the conference theme in the 1980s and thinking about the important changes in the role of international boundaries, none of us could have imagined that in three years the Berlin Wall would come down and Berliners would climb it and embrace. The rapidly changing concept of borders has become an even more significant topic internationally than we could have foreseen.

"Frontier" is not a simple, nor a single, concept. Alastair Hennessey in his work, *The Frontier in Latin American History*,[*] outlines many frontiers in Latin America: the frontiers of religious sects, Indian frontiers, Amazonian frontiers, cattle frontiers, mining frontiers, ethnic, cultural, and economic frontiers. In the history of the

---

[*] Alastair Hennessey, *The Frontier in Latin American History* (London: Edward Arnold, 1978).

United States, the frontier was the region between settled and unsettled land, and it moved continuously westward. By contrast, in Latin America, frontier settlement was a slow "filling in" process of adapting to peoples and environment, beginning with the gold expeditions into the interior. It was not a frontier moving westward with waves of European immigrants—as it the United States; it was—and is—a mobile, ever-changing space with multiple identities and shifting settlements. Even now, the gold mining boom in the frontier of Amazonia threatens the survival of Indian groups and the environment.

Thinking about borders and frontiers thus involves far more than issues of boundaries and geopolitical conflict. Frontier concerns range from contemporary government colonization schemes on the frontier to questions concerning the survival of civilizations and environment, as depicted in the film about the Amazon frontier, *The Emerald Forest*. The papers reflect this broad range of concerns, addressing the frontier from historical, geographical, and literary perspectives. Perceptions of the frontiers in Latin American history, both mythological and concrete, are explored by several historians: frontier culture, bandits and cowboys are discussed, as are the changing frontiers of colonial Brazil. Contemporary frontiers in Latin America and along the United States–Mexico border are examined from a geographical perspective, and Fernando Alegría, the well-known Chilean poet, and Luis Leal, noted literary critic and poet, engage in a dialogue about the frontier in literature.

Publishing and acquiring materials outside traditional publishing centers can be viewed as collecting from the frontier. Librarians from the Library of Congress's Field Office in Rio de Janeiro discuss the problems of acquisition and the nature of publishing in the Amazon. Several panels and workshops review publishing from secondary centers and collecting at the regional and subnational level. A panel of law librarians surveys Latin American transborder problems and the documentation of regional organizations.

As is traditional at SALALM conferences, the goal was to achieve a balance between scholarly and bibliographic programs. The papers in Part One provide an overview of principal issues and trends in border studies scholarship by scholars in a wide range of disciplines, as mentioned above. The diversity of resources, publishing patterns, and problems of acquisition are discussed by academics, librarians, and Latin American vendors in the sections that follow. The conference provided the opportunity for a dialogue between academics and librarians of Latin American collections on how these research needs are being met, both in terms of accessing information and availability of resources.

The other balancing act in conference planning is to provide the right mix of thematic and functional programs. Included in the proceedings are the papers of a number of nonthematic panels, several of which deserve special mention. One is an outgrowth of a colloquium organized by Barbara Robinson at the University of Southern California to aid in the development of the Latin American collection there. Experienced Latin American bibliographers define and present the criteria and approaches for building Latin American collections, for cooperating in their development, and for assembling research collections with unique complementary resources. The panel was organized in the hope that SALALM will begin to develop a series of standards and criteria for Latin American research collections.

In another panel, catalogers of Latin American library collections discuss new approaches for improved cooperation and access. A further panel appraises the impact of automated systems on Latin American collecting from the perspectives of the bibliographer and the book dealer. Several panels assess the experiences of various libraries in identifying and collecting nonmainstream resources from Latin America, such as the Library of Congress's effort to document Brazil's political and social movements through collecting "marginalized" literature.

As part of SALALM XXXIII, a "town meeting" was held to present and discuss a medium-range agenda for the organization, particularly in the areas of collections and cooperation. This session underscored the need for members to strengthen cooperation in several areas: developing needed reference works and databases, enhancing access to collections, and seriously working toward national-level cooperative collection development.

All of the programs highlight the need for SALALM members to work together so that the collections of member institutions will not only grow stronger individually but also complement one another more coherently. The continuing cooperation we have developed through SALALM is essential to the future of our collections and will shape the nature of Latin American scholarship in the years to come.

Paula Covington

Acknowledgments

These proceedings are the result of the work of the conference participants, panel chairs, and members of SALALM involved in the planning of the meeting. Thanks go to the host institutions—University of California, Berkeley, and Stanford University—and their representatives, Dan Hazen and Jim Breedlove; members of the Executive Board and Larry Lauerhass, who served on the Conference Planning Committee; and the "West Coast" Local Arrangements Committee. I would particularly like to thank Dan Hazen for his Herculean efforts as Chair of Local Arrangements and for his many valuable suggestions for participants from the host institutions.

Part One

The Frontier Concept: Its Past, Present, and Future Influence

I. Historical Perspectives of the Frontier

1. Historical Frontier Imagery in the Americas

Richard W. Slatta

Introduction

The literature on the frontier in the United States is as extensive as it is pervasive. Since Frederick Jackson Turner "created" the study of the frontier for the nation in 1893, it has become a dominant interpretive theme and political symbol. But we also find important roles and images assigned to the frontier in other countries of North and South America. This paper compares many threads of frontier imagery in the Americas, with special attention to Argentina, Brazil, the United States, and Canada. I examine frontier definitions and types, and the putative frontier attributes of machismo, violence, opportunity, and democracy. I conclude with a look at the conflict between ranching and farming frontiers and with some thoughts on the closing and significance of the frontier. Most of the examples come from cattle frontiers and their prototypical figure, the cowboy.

The stimulus given to the frontier concept by Frederick Jackson Turner is too well known to bear repetition. Several subsequent generations of scholars have taken up and often extended Turner's themes. The works of Ray Allen Billington refine, clarify, and defend much Turnerian thought. In his 1931 presidential address to the American Historical Association, Herbert Eugene Bolton called for the comparative study of Western Hemisphere frontiers. Whether we accept the interpretation or not, we must admire the breadth of vision in Walter Prescott Webb's *The Great Frontier*. Alistair Hennessy surveys many types of frontiers in his overview of *The Frontier in Latin American History*. [1]

A number of writers have focused specifically on cattle frontiers. Glenn R. Vernam surveys changing equestrian equipment in *Man on Horseback*. Robert M. Denhardt includes valuable information on equestrian life in *The Horse of the Americas*. Edward Larocque Tinker's pioneering works, *Horsemen of the Americas* and *Centaurs of Many Lands*, compare the lives, literature, and legends of several cowboy types. David Dary points out the many Hispanic influences on America's *Cowboy Culture*. My own recently completed monograph,

Cowboys of the Americas, compares the lives and mythology of cowboys in six areas of North and South America as well as in Hawaii. [2]

Types and Definitions

Frontier definitions are as abundant as they are vague. Is a frontier a place, a process, or both? Do we categorize them by type or economic activity; hence mining, ranching, and farming frontiers? In describing Brazilian frontiers, for example, Martin T. Katzman combines geographical and economic categories, such as the São Paulo coffee frontier and the Amazonian rubber frontier. Does the frontier modify or override the "germs" of European culture carried across the Atlantic? From the Latin *fronteria*, the term as used in Europe indicated a national boundary. Usage in the United States through most of the nineteenth century followed this definition. By the late nineteenth century, however, one dictionary defined a "frontiersman" as someone living "beyond the limits of a settled or civilized region." [3]

American usage of the term "frontier" since Turner's time has combined elements of place and process into a broad definition indicating "open" or vacant land beyond settled areas. The many attributes (some discussed below) imputed to frontier regions by Turner became part of the definition. In one of his most famous phrases, Turner described the frontier as "the meeting point between savagery and civilization." [4]

Turner's vision of the frontier as the juncture of savagery and civilization is both anticipated and echoed in Latin America. In Argentina and Chile (as in the United States), the frontier generally represented a moving line separating European settlement from "vacant lands," that is, areas still controlled by Indians. The arrival of "civilized" institutions and settled, white populations generally heralded the closing of the frontier. Various Indian chieftains (caciques) capably held Spanish expansion outward from Buenos Aires and Santiago at bay for centuries. Many Indian groups, from the Nez Perce and Apaches of North America to the Araucanians of South America, resisted domination until nearly the twentieth century. In contrast, Canada features a seeming anomaly in its western territories, a "civilized" frontier where legal and political institutions preceded significant European population. [5]

While not as prevalent as in the United States, frontier images have played a role in Brazilian historiography. A number of Brazilian scholars, including Caio Prado Júnior, Gilberto Freyre, and J. F. Normano, have pondered the nature of frontier characteristics and influences. In Brazil the frontier region is generally defined as the *sertão*, the rugged interior plains or "backlands" of the country lying between the narrow coastal plain and the Amazonian Basin. Brazilians employ the Portuguese word *fronteira* to mean a national boundary, usage also customary in Europe. [6]

Part of the diminished significance of the frontier in Brazil is attributable to its coastal settlement pattern. Exploration and settlement began in 1550 on the northeastern "hump" and crept slowly southward to Rio de Janeiro, São Paulo, and Rio Grande do Sul. The sharp escarpment that rises from the coastal plain, a dearth of navigable rivers outside the Amazon Basin, and hostile, nomadic Indians inhibited Portuguese expansion inland. Thus Brazil developed a coastal settlement fringe around an interior, "hollow frontier." The inland sertão and the Amazon remained largely unpopulated by Europeans. Yet despite the difference in frontier development between the United States and Brazil, imagery not unlike that employed by Frederick Jackson Turner also appears in Brazil. [7]

The southern plains of Brazil, the *campanha* of Rio Grande do Sul with its cattle ranches worked by *gaúchos*, would seem an ideal place for the growth of strong frontier imagery. In addition to being a traditional cattle-raising region, southern Rio Grande also constitutes a frontier in the European sense. The state's southern border is a boundary between the nations of Brazil and Uruguay. The gaúcho becomes an important regional symbol but does not achieve the national significance of the American cowboy or the Argentina gaucho. John Chasteen, of Bates College, recently completed a dissertation on the ranching frontier borderland of southern Brazil and northern Uruguay. The work, titled "Twilight of the Lances: The Saravia Brothers and Their World," traces the fortunes of a Brazilian borderlands family, the Saravias, across several generations. In terms of popular values and material life, the gauchos of Uruguay and the gaúchos of southern Brazil share a common, equestrian folk culture. But the national boundary did create two different political climates. [8]

Neither the gaúcho of southern Brazil nor the *vaqueiro* cowboy of the northeastern sertão, becomes the archetypal frontiersman. It is rather the *bandeirantes* of São Paulo, mestizos who trekked into the interior in search of Indians to enslave. These slave-hunting expeditions, sometimes involving thousands of men and lasting for years, depopulated many Jesuit Indian missions of Brazil and Paraguay. But Brazilian mythology created an admirable figure very different from that of history. Throughout the Americas, myth-making accompanies frontier expansion. [9]

Civilization and Barbarism

Despite substantial differences in frontier definitions across the Americas, Turner's image of the frontier as "the meeting point between savagery and civilization" is widespread. The long sweep of writing about frontiers in the Americas shows the strong stamp of a parallel construct, "civilization and barbarism." This construct depicts fundamental frontier social categories and ideological values that have been used by dominant, conquering groups to subjugate others.

The term "barbarian" has a long history. The Greeks and Romans popularized the distinction between themselves and "barbarians" and spread the distinction across Europe and Asia. Yet the concept is not limited to Western culture. From the twelfth through the nineteenth centuries, Japanese military rulers carried the official title "Barbarian-subduing Generalissimo." [10]

"Civilization" and "barbarism" became common categories used by western European nations in the last third of the eighteenth century. Lucien Febvre traces the first use of *civilisation* in French to the year 1766. The French invariably contrasted their civilization with the barbarity or savagery of "less advanced" cultures. The ideas underpin the great burst of Western imperialism that culminates in the headlong race for empire in the nineteenth century. Social Darwinism and Positivism both feed on the metaphor. In 1896, the jingoistic *New York World*, trying to goad President William McKinley to take action against the Spanish in Cuba, asked "is there any *barbarism* known to the mind of man that will justify the intervention of a *civilized* power?" Shortly thereafter, Theodore Roosevelt interjected the metaphor into the Latin American policy of the United States. His Corollary to the Monroe Doctrine warned Latin American nation that their wrongdoing "may ultimately require intervention by some *civilized* nation." Not surprisingly, Roosevelt declared that nation to be the United States. [11]

When applied to frontier regions, the categories of "civilized" and "barbaric" have usually included a racial component. In general, white people have pronounced nonwhites to be barbarians. But this means of conceptualizing the frontier involves more than white racism. It can carry a religious component that divides people into heathens and believers. Recall that the unchurched gauchos of the Argentine plains referred to themselves as "Christians" to distinguish themselves from Indians whom they called "savages." Europeanized elites in Argentina in turn defined themselves as civilized and the lowly gauchos as the barbarian. The construct can involve multiple levels of definition. [12]

In addition to the forces of race, religion, and nationalism, geography enters in. Social groups have been declared barbarian based upon their location. Perhaps the most famous example of this is Rome's division of humanity into Romans and others. But more often rural frontier regions have been pressed into the barbarian category by urban-based conquerors. Strains of telluricism and environmental determinism appear in the nineteenth-century writings that divide up the world geographically and culturally. [13]

But we find another side to the coin of dominance and racism. Frontiersmen, those labeled "barbarians," frequently hold outsiders, even their conquerors, in contempt. One unlettered gaucho of the nineteenth century complimented a European visitor to the Argentine plains: "He is a foreigner, true, but very civilized." To the gaucho, this meant that the man could ride a horse well—the gaucho's hallmark of civilization. It is the views of frontiersmen, including indigenous societies, that are needed to round out our social description of these regions. [14]

Many Latin American writers have taken up various aspects of the "civilization and barbarism" motif. The most influential formulation came in 1845, when Domingo Faustino Sarmiento published his famous attack on the dictatorship of Juan Manuel de Rosas, called *Facundo* or *Civilization and Barbarism*. Written in exile from Santiago, Chile, the book portrays Argentine history as a struggle between urban, European, civilizing forces and the rural frontier barbarity of gauchos and caudillos. Some Argentines today continue to view their society through a similar lens, substituting Juan Perón for Rosas and the "shirtless" masses of Peronism for yesterday's gaucho. [15]

In 1902 Euclydes de Cunha cast Brazilian history in similar terms in another classic of Latin American literature, *Rebellion in the Backlands (Os sertões)*. The author based his work on conflict between frontiersmen and government forces at the Canudos uprising in 1896-97. Followers of a messianic figure named Antonio Conselheiro lost the fight against central control. But, like Sarmiento, da Cunha finds much to admire in the frontiersman. Nevertheless, both concluded, in da Cunha's words, that "we are condemned to civilization. Either we shall progress or we shall perish." Admirable traits of a "noble savage" are sometimes attributed to "barbaric" frontiersmen. But ultimately, the frontier savage, whether Indian or mestizo, must yield to the press of civilization. [16]

The plains frontier of Venezuela gave rise to another important novel of civilization and barbarism. Rómulo Gallegos makes the battle between these forces the central motif of his powerful work, *Doña Bárbara*. Civilization triumphs over barbarism, but at the cost of revealing the close ties between the two. As with most other Latin

American writers, Gallegos presents a frontier of wild, dangerous, powerful forces that must ultimately succumb to civilizing influences. [17]

Machismo and Violence

Frontiers have generated images of an exaggerated machismo, probably because of the population imbalance between men and women. As male domains, frontiers developed norms and behaviors different from societies where women participated more fully. Much of what is defined as macho in American popular culture can be traced to putative traits of the Old West. In addition, the role of women in frontier regions has been ignored by frontier historians. In his more than 2,000 published pages, Turner devotes only a paragraph to women. His disciple Billington likewise ignores women in his writings on the frontier. Thus both frontier demography and subsequent scholarly sexism have limited our knowledge of women on the frontier. [18]

A few women could be found in some frontier locations, such as ranches, taverns, and military outposts. Saloons offered many activities to attract customers and to generate additional profits. Prostitution provided a natural adjunct to liquor and gambling. Richard Erdoes notes that "Westerners divided women into two categories—good ones and bad ones." Men outnumbered women and young men in particular outnumbered women their age on the frontier. The sexual imbalance toward males in frontier regions dictated that often men could socialize with "bad ones" or none at all. An even more skewed sex ratio was likely found in Latin American frontier regions. [19]

For example on the Argentine pampa the demands of ranch work as well as powerful, negative pressures from the landed elite condemned most gauchos to enforced bachelorhood, or, at best, serial concubinage. Some ranchers discouraged or even prohibited women from living on their land. Women were thought to arouse jealousy and fighting among the men. The requirements of ranch work and desire to escape military conscription forced gauchos to live nomadic lives. With little hope of owning land, gauchos had few opportunities for a stable home life. [20]

In contrast, macho violence was less frequent on the Canadian ranching frontier. Ranchers attempted to replicate English country life and seemingly accorded a greater role to the influence of women. According to the diaries of ranch women, Canadian cowboys would exhibit a high degree of chivalry and respect to the rancher's wife. They would even bow to some attempts to impose a degree of "civilization" on their lives. The "squirearchy" of the Alberta ranching frontier transplanted English "civilization" insofar as was possible to the range. They might have to substitute coyotes for foxes in the hunt, but British tradition and culture persisted on the frontier. [21]

But violence seems to have been commonplace in most frontier regions, Alberta excepted. Cowboys and the expanding livestock industry came into conflict with Indians throughout the Americas. Argentina's lengthy confrontation with various Indian groups of the pampas extended from the sixteenth century to nearly the end of the nineteenth. Only a massive military mobilization and superior technology applied by Julio A. Roca in the "Conquest of the Desert" finally defeated the Indians. Bandit gangs operated with impunity and even controlled many rural areas of Latin American well into the twentieth century. Pillage, extortion, rape, rustling, theft, murder, and kidnapping victimized inhabitants of such bandit-infested areas. [22]

Gauchos of the Río de la Plata engaged in ritualized, but nevertheless bloody knife duels. The traditional goal of such duels was simply to mark an opponent's face with the long, dangerous gaucho knife (facón). But drunken fights often went far beyond simple marking. One Argentine rancher suggested (with some exaggeration) that 99 percent of homicides, injuries, and disorders occurred at pulperías, combination general stores and taverns frequented by gauchos. Police and judicial records are full of cases in which knife duels ended in wounding or death. The perpetrator usually fled to other, more remote areas of the frontier. Some passed through the "cultural membrane" of the frontier and took up a new outcast life amongst Indian raiders. [23]

Officials and gauchos took very different views of such frontier violence. Gauchos considered the killing of someone in a drunken duel to be a desgracia—an unfortunate accident. In the eyes of his peers, the killer deserved sympathy, not blame. Police viewed the incident as murder. In many other instances, the perspective of the frontiersman and those seeking to extend their domination over the frontier diverged widely. [24]

Interpersonal violence often marred frontier life. Frontiersmen gathered to drink and gamble at saloons and at the Latin American equivalents, pulperías, pulquerías, boliches. While popular media have exaggerated and stereotyped frontier fighting, the real incidence was significant. Temporary bonds of male communal drinking often gave way to macho contests of dominance, competition, and conflict. Rousing, furniture-smashing fistfights ("dogfights") were largely creations of the Western movies. Cowboys disdained fisticuffs. As one old-timer remarked, "If the Lord had intended me to fight like a dog,

He'd a-give me longer teeth and claws." But a cowboy did not hesitate to fight with a knife and gun. The mining frontier apparently rivaled the cattle frontier for boisterous behavior. Elliott West found high levels of homicide in saloons of Rocky Mountain mining towns. [25]

In the Canadian West, Mounted Police established the rule of law (and a monopoly over firearms) before significant numbers of settlers reached the prairies in the late nineteenth century. Indians were, for the most part, secured on reservations, so that the "cowboy and Indian" battles, popularized in American movies and television, did not occur in Canada. As Pierre Berton well documents, *Hollywood's Canada* included many distorted elements grafted in from the mythology and folklore of the American Old West. But the reality, as usual, was far different from the cinematic images. [26]

Opportunity and Democracy

Turner's critics have long questioned whether the frontier experience stimulated American democracy. Many have expressed doubt that the frontier offered a "safety valve" of enhanced opportunity for the common man. It appears that frontiers of both North and South America offered neither greater democracy nor more opportunity than more settled regions. For example, Canada's western land lease policy, developed in 1881, favored large, corporate ranches. With leases awarded up to 100,000 acres in size, considerable capital investment was required. Large ranchers summarily evicted squatters with the temerity to try to graze animals on their holdings. The lease laws and the expenses of getting started in ranching meant that few Canadian cowboys had an opportunity to gather a small herd and become ranchers themselves. As in Latin America, a few mighty ranchers controlled the land, animals, and labor. [27]

Turnerian frontier mythology in the United States emphasizes the frontier as a place of opportunity, a social safety valve for oppressed urban workers. But on the cattle frontier, cowboys for the most part had only the opportunity to work long hours for low pay. Few enjoyed upward mobility into the ranks of landholders. Laws in several Latin American nations imposed sharp restrictions on the rural population. Latin American governments attempted to curtail and control their unruly rural populations through legal and extralegal means. The burden of restrictions fell with special force on horsemen, who might form an impromptu cavalry for a threatening caudillo.

Neither did frontiers promote democracy. To be sure, a small rancher and his one or two hired hands might develop a familial, egalitarian relationship. But in general the livestock industry replicated and sometimes magnified class distinctions from society at large. Race, wealth, and culture determined one's standing. Whites looked down on nonwhites, as in society at large. And whites controlled frontier resources, just as they controlled opportunity and assets elsewhere in society. In the Canadian West, racial divisions played a minor role on the cattle frontier, because virtually all ranchers and cowboys were white. But little frontier leveling occurred, and a "squirearchy" not unlike that of rural England became established in Alberta. [29]

In Brazilian mythology, the sertão frontier is a place of racial and social democracy. João Capistrano de Abreu (1853-1927) was one of the first Brazilians to take up the frontier theme. Indeed, his nationalism and "New Worldism" invite comparison with Turner. Inspired by the writings of João Capistrano de Abreu, others, including Cassiano Ricardo, Gilberto Freyre, and Euclydes da Cunha, came to believe that the miscegenation characteristic of the nation gave rise to more democratic race relations. The mestizo bandeirantes, residents of colonial São Paulo who hunted Indians to enslave them, became the heroes of this myth. Ricardo depicted the slavers as explorers who successfully bridged the cultural and racial gap between the Portuguese and indigenous cultures. The mythical bandeirante becomes the moral equivalent of Turner's hardy frontiersman, an archetype of Brazilian national identity, and a force in cementing Brazilian national unity. The bandeirantes explored and expanded the national territory (at the expense of Spanish America) and stimulated the economic development and settlement of the frontier. The reality of the rapacious, brutal, plundering bandeirante raids was quite different from this mythology. [30]

Farming *versus* Ranching

The advent of the farmer's frontier is generally associated with the decline of the ranching frontier. But the relationship between farming and ranching frontiers varied widely across the Americas. In general, the wealthy landed elites of Latin America preserved special prerogatives for cattle ranching. Under Spanish law and customs, it fell to agriculturists, often Indian peasants, to protect their crops from marauding livestock. This bias coupled with labor shortages retarded agricultural development in some plains areas of Latin America for centuries. Most often, Indian agriculture suffered as Spanish livestock-raising expanded.

But little rancher-farmer conflict occurred in either Chile or Argentina. Agriculture had always coexisted with ranching in the fertile Central Valley around the capital of Santiago, because a few wealthy landowners controlled both grazing and farm lands. Sharecroppers worked the land, supplemented by migrant labor during the harvest and roundup seasons. In neighboring Argentina, the landed elite controlled the expansion of agriculture in the late nineteenth century by maintaining ownership of the land. Spanish and Italian immigrants farmed as sharecroppers on three- to six-year contracts. Farming only became established where it complemented or did not compete directly for land with livestock-raising. [31]

In Chile and Argentina, European immigration is closely tied to the expansion of agriculture. The Chilean and Argentine elites looked down on their native rural population. Leaders worked assiduously to replace it with "superior" immigrant blood. Chilean officials even evicted Chilean squatters and gave the land over to immigrants. As a result of such policies, the Chilean rural landless ended up working for foreigners in the countryside. Southern Chile became a virtual German colony during the late nineteenth century. Chile's discrimination against its rural poor spurred Chilean migration to the southern Argentine frontier in Patagonia. Faced with a growing foreign population on its soil, Argentina took belated interest in developing the southern Patagonia frontier. In 1895 only 300 of 24,000 inhabitants of the border territory of Neuquen were Argentine. Argentines remembered that earlier Chilean immigration to Bolivia and Peru fueled Chilean expansionism. Argentina did not wish to see the War of the Pacific (1879) repeated in Patagonia. [32]

English herd laws, in contrast with those of Spanish America, assigned to cattlemen the responsibility for damage to agriculture. Not surprisingly, we see law and the political climate favoring the expansion of agriculture at the expense of open-range ranching in the United States and Canada. In both societies, the extension of farming represented the coming of "civilization" to the frontier. It was not only the "sins" of the cattle industry, such as overstocking the range, that led to its decline. The inexorable movement of the plow across the western plains played a large role in closing the cattle frontier. [33]

Conflict between farmers and ranchers existed in Alberta just as it did south of the border in the United States. But disputes generally did not erupt into violence. Once gain, the Canadian frontier showed itself less violent than its counterpart to the south. Disputes generally ended through the judicial process, not in gunplay. But many ranchmen found little to admire in the wave of agricultural immigrants that engulfed them. In 1910 Mounted Police Superintendent Richard Burton Deane received a complaint of horse theft. The victim, an immigrant Mormon farmer from the United States named Roueche, lost two animals to men who worked for him for a few days. Farmers, "having been too careless and too indolent to take reasonable care of their horses, they now showed they were too careless and too indolent to make reasonable attempt to recovery their property. The Western prairie," complained the superintendent, "is swarming with useless settlers of this calibre." [34]

Cowboys often did not accept the advent of the farmer's frontier gracefully. A mock will, penned in 1919 by a Saskatchewan cowboy, vents frustration against "sodbusters." The cowboy wished to "create a fund, to be ultimately used for the extermination of that class of vermin, commonly known as farmers." He added a clause three years later. "I leave to each and every *Mossback* my perpetual curse as some reward to them for their labors in destroying the *Open Range*, by means of that most pernicious of all implements, the plow." Ranch workers from Alberta to Argentina shared this disdain of the farmer. [35]

Closing of the Frontier

Other forces in addition to the expansion of agriculture precipitated the decline of ranching frontiers. Indeed, the closing of the frontier in the Americas came for widely different reasons. For the llanos of Colombia and Venezuela, decline came during the first half of the nineteenth century as a result of generalized political violence. Ranching declined precipitously on the llanos during the independence and civil wars, lasting from 1810 through the 1850s. Warfare decimated herds, drained manpower, and interrupted market routes. Bandit gangs proliferated, many claiming to fight for some political cause. Similar, but shorter-lived disruptions hit Chile and Uruguay. We can date the decline of Mexican ranching with precision to the violent Revolution that swept the nation from 1910 to 1920. [36]

The independence wars that swept Chile in 1817 and 1818 had similar negative effects. Livestock and agricultural production, particularly in the southern part of the nation, suffered. Livestock production during the 1820s fell to less than half of what it had been during the first decade of the century. Taking advantage of the turmoil, Indians in the south pushed the frontier of European settlement back further to the north. Like the llaneros, Chile's cowboys (*huasos*) found themselves fighting as cavalrymen rather than working on ranches. Civil wars in Uruguay during the 1840s also disrupted rural production and uprooted gauchos there. [37]

Argentina was buffered from the direct ravages of the independence wars. But during the nineteenth century, the nation experienced a combination of political violence and socioeconomic changes that reshaped life on its plains. From the 1820s on, elites ruling from the port city of Buenos Aires waged military and political war against the frontier gaucho population. They passed a plethora of restrictive laws. Internal passports, working papers, military conscription, and vagrancy laws curtailed the movements of gauchos. Elite policy used the gaucho to fight against another "barbarian" threat, plains Indians. Governmental oppression, massive immigration, new technology, and rural economic changes ended open-range ranching and the traditional livelihood of the gaucho. [38]

On the Anglo cattle frontiers in the United States and Canada frontiers closed from a combination of natural and economic factors, not because of political conflict. Farmers began pushing against the edges of the cattle kingdom within a few years after the Civil War ended. The harsh weather of the mid-1880s delivered the coup de grace to open-range ranching. But changing settlement patterns in many areas, such as Kansas, had already impinged on the cattle frontier. The growing population of Kansas farmers had already lobbied successfully for restrictions on the Texas cattle trade and on open-range grazing before the disastrous winters hit in 1885 and 1886. With the Anglo-American prejudice on behalf of agriculture, cattlemen were viewed as holding back civilization. Thus culture, weather, demography, and unwise range practices all combined to eclipse the open-range cattle industry. [39]

The golden age of Canadian ranching was even briefer than in the United States. Former mounted policemen and other pioneer ranchers began modest herds in the mid-1870s. A decade later, large corporate ranches had established control of the best ranges. By the early twentieth century, the Alberta range experienced many of the changes that hit the American West a little earlier. Farmers, encouraged by government policy and frontier mythology, quickly crowded out the big herds and the cowboys who tended them. The heyday of the Canadian cowboy lasted only from about the mid-1880s until the harsh winter of 1907. [40]

Weighing Frontier Significance

Economic significance is often related to historical visibility and cultural importance. Regions, frontier or other, that lacked economic consequence rarely loom large in a nation's historiography or culture. But this argument only partly explains the relative significance attached to cattle frontiers of the Americas. Ranching played a secondary, regional role in the economic development of Canada, Brazil, Venezuela, and Chile. Agricultural or mineral development overshadows the livestock economy. And in these nations, the cowboy figure remains of regional, not national, significance.

In contrast, the cattle industry played the central economic role in Argentina and Uruguay until the late nineteenth century. The gaucho became a prominent topic for writers, historians, and politicians in both countries. But the economic argument breaks down for the United States. The ranching industry in the United States was ephemeral (circa 1865 to 1885) and was far overshadowed by the rise of industry during the same period. Yet the cowboy and the frontier loom large in the nation's written history. Clearly, forces beyond economic development are at work in shaping the significance of frontier imagery in a nation's history.

Taking inspiration from Turner, Walter Prescott Webb, and David Potter focused on frontier *abundance* as a key historical force. According to Webb, the silver, gold, and new lands of the Americas fueled a four-century economic boom for Europe. New World natural riches created Old World wealth. In Potter's variant of the frontier riches thesis, resources and open lands in the American West helped shape the national character. The frontier remained an important historical force until industrialization and urbanization opened other avenues to abundance. [41]

By drawing on Turner, Webb, and Potter, we might argue that differential abundance accounts for some differences between Spanish and Anglo frontiers. The Spanish found more readily accessible sources of wealth in Latin American than the British did in North America. As Webb emphasized, precious metals in Mexico and Peru fueled fortunes for some. More importantly, the Spanish harnessed massive numbers of Indians to labor for them in a wide range of enterprises. "Red Gold" in the form of Amerindian labor began the economic boom of Latin America. Black slaves, imported from Africa, quickly augmented the labor pool.

The Spanish also "seeded," often inadvertently, several plains regions with livestock. In but a few decades after initial Spanish exploration, herds of wild cattle and horses flourished in plains regions from the Río de la Plata to northern Mexico. In terms of gold, silver, labor, and livestock, the Spanish enjoyed tremendous riches in their frontier regions.

Brazil's frontier seems to fit midway between the readier abundance of Spanish America and the niggardliness of North America. In the early sixteenth century, Portuguese explorers encountered only hostile Indians and stands of wood suitable for making red dye. No major mineral deposits were found until the very end of the seventeenth century. Sporadic gold and diamond strikes have occurred since, but for the colonial period, "the mining industry in Brazil never went beyond a fleeting venture." Neither did Brazilian planters subdue large numbers of Indian laborers. They had to import black slaves from Africa instead. Most Indians who remained avoided direct conquest except for those enslaved by the marauding bandeirantes. Plentiful herds of cattle did develop in Minas Gerais and Rio Grande do Sul. But Brazilian ranches mostly produced for local markets and did not develop the large export capacity that characterized ranching in Argentina. [42]

The Anglo-American frontiers of the United States and Canada lacked easily extracted sources of wealth. British North America did not include large concentrations of Amerindians suitable for impressed labor. The Aztec and Incan empires in Spanish America had already organized and concentrated the work force. With the conquest, the Spanish took over governance from indigenous rulers. Nothing comparable to these vast Amerindian empires of Latin America existed in the British colonies. In British North America, this slower, more difficult path to riches gave rise to a society of settlers, not conquistadors.

If the economic role is not an absolute guide to frontier significance, then perhaps the duration of the frontier phase is related to its subject importance. But again no clear relationship exists. The llanos of Colombia and Venezuela, for example, began experiencing Spanish exploration by the midsixteenth century. Cattle-raising and the expansion of missions to convert there Indians quickly followed. For a variety of reasons, the llanos remained a "static, permanent" frontier into the twentieth century. The region experienced little of the modernizing changes that altered the livestock industries of Argentina, Canada, and the United States. But despite the persistence of a traditional cattle frontier over centuries, llanos imagery has less significance in Venezuelan and Colombian national life than the ephemeral Western cowboy does in the United States. [43]

The heyday of open-range ranching in the United States was very short-lived by comparison with the llanos or with the pampas of Argentina. In the span of a single generation, ranching moved from a burgeoning frontier to a big business, complete with managers, foreign investors, fences, and work rules. Yet this brief period of American history, from about 1865 to 1885, looms large in the national consciousness. A frontier's economic and real historical life is no measure of the significance ascribed to it. Clearly, cultural and ideological factors enter into the weight given to frontier images and influences.

Frontier as Cultural Membrane

As we have seen, frontier imagery has been rife with mythology and symbolism at variance with historical reality. One problem is that our vision of the frontier has been dominated by one side, the conquering white society. Ethnohistorians have rightly criticized Turner for an insensitivity to indigenous populations in frontier regions. Researchers today have extended their vision to the "other side" of the frontier to examine indigenous societies. I have focused on mestizo and white horsemen—cowboys—for many examples. But the horse also was a very important part of many frontier indigenous societies. Several studies detail the impact on Indian cultures of the horse, including Don Worcester, *The Spanish Mustang*, Elizabeth Atwood Lawrence, *Hoofbeats and Society*, John C. Ewers, *The Horse in Blackfoot Indian Culture*, and LaVerne Larrell Clark, *They Sang for Horses*. [44]

Indian-white race relations and the Indian policies of various nations have also come under examination. John Hemming critically examines Brazilian governmental policy in *Red Gold* and in *Amazonian Frontier*. Equally critical of Argentina's "final solution" against the Indians of the pampa are Julio Aníbal Portas, *Malón contra malón*, and Kristine L. Jones in her dissertation "Conflict and Adaptation in the Argentine Pampas." For the United States, Ray Harvey Pearce (*The Savages of America*), Richard Drinnon (*Facing West*), Brian M. Fagan (*Clash of Cultures*), Francis Jennings (*The Invasion of America*), and others have examined the Indian Frontier. Olive Patricia Dickason (*The Myth of the Savage*) does likewise for French Canada. [45]

If we extend the corrective vision of recent ethnographic research, frontiers might well be viewed as membranes separating indigenous and European cultures. Influences pass in both directions, but the dominant pressure on the membrane is from the European side. White, European values meet and mix with indigenous cultures on plains frontiers. The two societies compete for and fight over access to natural resources. Frontiersmen often blended the language, equipment, and values of both European and Amerindian cultures. [46]

Frontiers have at times been analyzed in isolation from the cultures that gave rise to them. Disciplines of Frederick Jackson Turner went too far in trying to establish the primacy of frontier forces over European roots. In the case of the Canadian ranching frontier, English roots are clearly in evidence. English and Canadian ranchers in Alberta transplanted cultural values to the frontier. Those values and practices changed very little in the face of frontier influences. Metropolitan values, notably a respect for law and order, were established as a matter of policy in the Canadian West. British cultural values and class attitudes accompanied the ranching elite to Alberta. [47]

Spanish cultural values likewise penetrated to frontier regions in Latin America. The *hidalgo* role model of medieval Spanish Catholic culture carried a stigma against manual labor. Spaniards avoided manual trades, if at all possible. Much work was left to mestizos, blacks, and Indians. As in the antebellum American South, slaves tended cattle in many ranching areas of Latin America, including southern Brazil, the llanos, and the Argentine pampas. Spanish colonies languished where labor was in short supply. Sharp lines of class, culture, and race stratified Spanish colonial society. The Spanish carried over these prejudices to frontier society where virtually no social leveling took place. [48]

Marvin Mikesell has shown that British settlers in North America created frontiers of exclusion that sharply divided whites and Amerindians. Despite their racial biases, the Spanish and Portuguese mixed with indigenous societies to create a new mestizo race. In Latin America, much more so than in Anglo-America, Amerindian influence complemented and modified Hispanic tradition. The gaucho, for example, got his most formidable weapon, the bolas, and his favorite beverage, maté, from indigenous cultures. The vocabulary of the gaucho and the llanero, the cowboy of the tropical plains of Venezuela and Colombia, is heavily peppered with indigenous terms. There is virtually no indigenous element detectable in Anglo-American cowboy life. The Anglo-American frontier of exclusion and the reservation system isolated Amerindians from Anglo settlement. In Canada, the *métis*, French-Indian mestizos, also became something of an outcast class. [49]

Despite a large body of criticism, the frontier concept and many of its Turnerian images retain a compelling power. Clearly the idea of the frontier will not die. But further refinement is necessary. William Norton, a Canadian geographer, has laid out a number of suggested directions. He suggests viewing the frontier from many perspectives, as "a zone of land competition, ecological imperialism, recent settlement, contact, transfer, acculturation, or a cultural region." Further comparative questioning, such as that done nearly thirty years ago by Dietrich Gerhard, is also needed. Comparative works in agricultural history, like those of Donald Denoon and John Fogarty, offer useful research models. [50]

A wide range of frontier attributes and images, real and imagined, has developed in both North and South America. This historical imagery is still relevant. Frontier images remain potent symbols today. Ronald Reagan captured the imagination of many with homely but popular frontier images of covered wagons and rugged individualism. More than any recent politician, he succeeded in reviving the mythology of the frontier. We speak of the remaining frontiers of undersea and space exploration. Brazil created an inland capital, Brasilia, in 1964 to promote the settlement of its frontier. Argentina plans to follow suit with a march south to its Patagonian frontier. Thus frontiers, real and imagined, remain compelling forces in the Americas today.

NOTES

1. Herbert Eugene Bolton, "The Epic of Greater America," *American Historical Review* 38:3 (April 1933), 448-474. Ray Allen Billington was a prolific scholar. Especially germane to this paper are *America's Frontier Heritage* (New York, NY: Holt, Rinehart and Winston, 1966), *The Frontier Thesis: Valid Interpretation of American History?* (Huntington, NY: Robert E. Krieger, 1966, 1977), and *Land of Savagery; Land of Promise: The European Image of the American Frontier in the Nineteenth Century* (New York, NY: Norton, 1981); Walter Prescott Webb, *The Great Frontier* (Austin: University of Texas Press, 1951, 1979), and "The Western World Frontier," in Walker D. Wyman and Clifton B. Kroeber, eds., *The Frontier in Perspective* (Madison: University of Wisconsin Press, 1957), pp. 111-126; Alistair Hennessy, *The Frontier in Latin American History* (Albuquerque: University of New Mexico Press, 1978). See also Jack D. Forbes, "Frontiers in American History," *Journal of the West* 1:1 (July 1962), 63-73; Frederic L. Paxon, "A Generation of the Frontier Hypothesis: 1893-1932," *Pacific Historical Review* 2:1 (March 1933), 34-51; Ray Allen Billington, "The American Frontier" in Paul Bohannan and Fred Plog, eds., *Beyond the Frontier: Social Process and Cultural Change* (Garden City, NY: Natural History Press, 1976). Criticism of the Turner hypothesis has been gathered into a single convenient volume, Richard Hofstadter and Seymour Martin Lipset, eds., *Turner and the Sociology of the Frontier* (New York, NY: Basic Books, 1968).

2. Glenn R. Vernam, *Man on Horseback: The Story of the Mounted Man from the Scythians to the American Cowboy* (Lincoln, NE: Bison Books, 1964, 1974); Robert M. Denhardt, *The Horse of the Americas*, rev. ed. (Norman: University of Oklahoma Press, 1947, 1975); Edward Larocque Tinker, *Horsemen of the Americas and the Literature They Inspired*, 2d ed. (Austin: University of Texas Press, 1952, 1967), and *Centaurs of Many Lands* (London: J. A. Allen, 1964); David Dary, *Cowboy Culture: A Saga of Five Centuries* (New York, NY: Knopf, 1981).

3. On the general definition of the frontier, see Owen Lattimore, "The Frontier in History," in *Studies in Frontier History: Collected Papers, 1928-58* (New York, NY: Oxford University Press, 1962); Fulmer Mood, "Notes on the History of the Word Frontier," *Agricultural History* 22:2 (April 1948), 78, 80-81; Lucien Febvre, "Frontière: The Word and the Concept" in Peter Burke, ed., K. Folca, trans., *A New Kind of History from the Writings of Lucien Febvre* (London: Routledge and Kegan Paul, 1973), pp. 208-209; Martin T. Katzman, "The Brazilian Frontier in Comparative Perspective," *Comparative Studies in Society and History* 17:3 (July 1975), 275-281.

4. Frederick Jackson Turner, "The Significance of the Frontier in American History," 1893, reprinted in Billington, ed., *Frontier Thesis*, p. 10. Useful frontier bibliographies include Roger L. Nichols, ed., *American Frontier and Western Issues: A Historiographical Review* (Westport, CT: Greenwood Press, 1986); and Rodman W. Paul and Richard W. Etulain, comps., *The Frontier and the American West* (Arlington Heights, IL: AHM Publishing Corp., 1977).

5. On the frontier in Canadian history, see Michael S. Cross, ed., *The Turner Thesis and the Canadas: The Debate on the Impact of the Canadian Environment* (Toronto: Copp Clark, 1970); David H. Breen, "The Turner Thesis and the Canadian West: A Closer Look at the Ranching Frontier," in Lewis H. Thomas, ed., *Essays on Western History in Honour of Lewis Gwynne Thomas* (Edmonton: University of Alberta Press, 1976), pp. 147-156; Morris Zaslaw, "The Frontier Hypothesis in Recent Historiography," *Canadian Historical Review* 29:2 (June 1948), 153-167; J. M. S. Careless, "Frontierism, Metropolitanism, and Canadian History," *Canadian Historical Review* 35:1 (March 1954), 1-21.

On the frontier in Latin America, see Victor Andrés Belaunde, "The Frontier in Hispanic America," *Rice Institute Pamphlet* 10:4 (October 1923), 202-213; Bolton, "The Epic of Greater America"; Silvio Zavala, "The Frontiers of Hispanic America," in Wyman and Kroeber, eds., *The Frontier in Perspective*; Isaiah Bowman, *The Pioneer Fringe*, ed. G. M. Wrigley (New York, NY: American Geographical Society, 1931); Richard J. Morissey, "The Shaping of Two Frontiers," *Americas* 3:1 (January 1951), 3-6, 41-42; Katzman, "Brazilian Frontier," pp. 266-285; Jorge Mañach, *Frontiers in the Americas: A Global Perspective*, Philip H. Phenix, trans. (New York, NY: Teachers College Press, 1975); Mary Lombardi, "The Frontier in Brazilian History: An Historiographical Essay," *Pacific Historical Review* 44:4 (November 1975), 437-457; Hebe Clementi, "National Identity and the Frontier," *American Studies International* 19:3-4 (1981); 36-44; Silvo Duncan Baretta and John Markoff, "Civilization and Barbarism: Cattle Frontiers in Latin America," *Studies in Comparative Society and History* 20 (October 1978), 587-620; Hennessy, *The Frontier in Latin American History*.

6. Lombardi, "Frontier in Brazilian History," pp. 441-442, 447-448; Febvre, "Frontière," pp. 209-211.

7. Lombardi, "Frontier in Brazilian History," pp. 444, 456.

8. John C. Chasteen, "Twilight of the Lances: The Saravia Brothers and Their World," Ph.D. diss., University of North Carolina, Chapel Hill, 1988. See also Moises Vellinho, *Brazil South: Its Conquest and Settlement* (New York, NY: Knopf, 1968).

9. Lombardi, "Frontier in Brazilian History," pp. 453-454. See also Richard M. Morse, ed., *The Bandeirantes: The Historical Role of the Brazilian Pathfinders* (New York, NY: Knopf, 1965); and Clodomir Vianna Moog, *Bandeirantes and Pioneers* (New York, NY: George Braziller, 1966).

10. William W. Savage, Jr. and Stephen I. Thompson, "The Comparative Study of the Frontier: An Introduction," in Savage and Thompson, eds., *The Frontier: Comparative Studies*, vol. 2 (Norman: University of Oklahoma Press, 1979), p. 13 (the notes to this essay, pp. 19-24, offer an excellent guide to literature on comparative frontiers); Kristina L. Jones, "Conflict and Adaptation in the Argentine Pampas," 1750-1880 (Thesis, University of Chicago, 1984), pp. 376-379, 405; Francis Jennings, *The Invasion of America* (Chapel Hill: University of North Carolina Press, 1975), pp. 6-7.

11. Lucien Febvre, "Civilisation: Evolution of a Word and a Group of Ideas," in Burke, *New Kind of History* pp. 220-221; Fernand Braudel, *On History*, Sarah Matthews, trans. (Chicago, IL: University of Chicago Press, 1980), p. 180; *New York World*, May 17, 1896; Theodore Roosevelt, "Annual Message of 1904," reprinted in Thomas L. Karnes, ed., *Readings in the Latin American Policy of the United States* (Tucson: University of Arizona Press, 1972), pp. 143, 190, italics added.

12. Ricardo Rodríguez Molas, *Historia social del gaucho* (Buenos Aires: Marú, 1968), p. 136; Daniel Granada, *Reseña histórico-descriptiva de antiguas y modernas supersticiones del Río de la Plata* (Montevideo: Barreiro y Ramos, 1896); Richard W. Slatta, *Gauchos and the Vanishing Frontier* (Lincoln: University of Nebraska Press, 1983), pp. 11-13.

13. See Louise K. Barnett, *The Ignoble Savage: American Literary Racism, 1790-1890* (Westport, CT: Greenwood Press, 1975), and Billington, *Land of Savagery*.

14. Quoted in José Antonio Wilde, *Buenos Aires desde setenta años atrás (1810-1880)* (Buenos Aires: EUDEBA, 1966, 1977), p. 78.

15. Domingo F. Sarmiento, *Life in the Argentine Republic in the Days of the Tyrants: Or, Civilization and Barbarism*, Mrs. Horace [Mary] Mann, trans., 1868, reprint (New York, NY: Hafner, 1971).

16. Euclydes da Cunha, *Rebellion in the Backlands (Os sertões)*, Samuel Putnam, trans. (Chicago, IL: University of Chicago Press, 1944), p. 54.

17. Rómulo Gallegos, *Doña Bárbara* Robert Malloy, trans. (New York, NY: Peter Smith, 1931, 1948).

18. Richard Jensen, "On Modernizing Frederick Jackson Turner: The Historiography of Regionalism," *Western Historical Quarterly* 11:3 (July 1980), 316-317.

19. Julie Roy Jeffrey, *Frontier Women: The Trans-Mississippi West, 1840-1880* (New York, NY: Hill and Wang, 1979); Richard Erdoes, *Saloons of the Old West* (New York, NY: Knopf, 1969), p. 182; John C. Hudson, "The Study of Western Frontier Populations," in Jerome O. Steffen, ed., *The American West: New Perspectives, New Dimensions* (Norman: University of Oklahoma Press, 1979), pp. 44-45.

20. Martínez Estrada, *X-Ray of the Pampa*, Alain Swietlicki, trans. (Austin: University of Texas Press, 1971), p. 205. On the many barriers to gaucho family life, see Slatta, *Gauchos*, pp. 58-60.

21. Patrick A. Dunae, *Gentlemen Emigrants: From the British Public Schools to the Canadian Frontier* (Vancouver and Toronto: Douglas and McIntyre, 1981); Monica Hopkins, *Letters from a Lady Rancher* (Calgary: Glenbow Museum, 1981); Mary Ella Inderwick, "A Lady and Her Ranch," *Alberta Historical Review* 15:4 (Autumn 1967), 1-9; Moira O'Neill, "A Lady's Life on a Ranche," *Blackwood's Edinburgh Magazine* 163 (January 1898), 3-16.

22. On the Argentine Indian frontier, see Roberto H. Marfany, *El indio en la colonización de Buenos Aires* (Buenos Aires: Comisión Nacional de Cultura, 1940); Juan Carlos Walther, *La conquista del desierto*, 2d ed. (Buenos Aires: Círculo Militar, 1964). On frontier banditry, see Richard W. Slatta, ed., *Bandidos: The Varieties of Latin American Banditry* (Westport, CT: Greenwood Press, 1987).

23. Buenos Aires Province, Comisión de Hacendados del Estado de Buenos Aires, *Antecedentes y fundamentos del proyecto de código rural* (Buenos Aires, 1864); letter from Mauricio Díaz, Bahía Blanca, March 6, 1850, juez de paz de Azul 9-4-4; reports of juez de crimen 1872, 38-4-313; Archivo Histórico de la Provincia de Buenos Aires "Ricardo Levene" (La Plata, Argentine); police reports of March, June, July 1852, Policía 1852, Archivo Histórico Municipal de Tandil (Tandil, Argentine).

24. Slatta, *Gauchos*, pp. 12-13, 118-119.

25. Richard Slotkin, *Regeneration by Violence: The Mythology of the American Frontier, 1600-1860* (Middletown, CT: Wesleyan University Press, 1973); quote from Ramon F. Adams, *Western Words: A Dictionary of the American West* (Norman: University of Oklahoma Press, 1968), p. 96; see also pp. 39, 190; Elliott West, *The Saloon of the Rocky Mountain Mining Frontier* (Lincoln: University of Nebraska Press, 1968), pp. 19-21.

26. Pierre Berton, *Hollywood's Canada: The Americanization of Our National Image* (Toronto: McClelland and Stewart, 1975).

27. Hofstadter and Lipset, *Turner and the Sociology of the Frontier*, pp. 15-42, 120-151, 172-200; Breen, "Turner Thesis," pp. 151-152.

28. See Morrisey, "Shaping of Two Frontiers," pp. 3-6, 41-42.

29. Breen, "Turner Thesis," pp. 156; Zavala, "Frontiers of Hispanic America," pp. 45, 56; Dunae, *Gentlemen Emigrants*.

30. Clementi, pp. 40-41; Lombardi, pp. 444, 449-451.

31. Brian Loveman, *Chile: The Legacy of Hispanic Capitalism* (New York, NY: Oxford University Press, 1979), pp. 123-124; James R. Scobie, *Revolution on the Pampas: A Social History of Wheat* (Austin: University of Texas Press, 1964), pp. 53-54; 58-60, 162.

32. Solberg, "Discriminatory Frontier Land Policy," pp. 125-127, and *Immigration and Nationalism: Argentina and Chile, 1890, 1914* (Austin: University of Texas Press, 1970), p. 24; David Rock, *Argentina, 1516-1987: From Spanish Colonization to Alfonsín*, rev. ed. (Berkeley: University of California Press, 1987), p. 179; Charles C. Griffin, "Francisco Encina and Revisionism in Chilean History," *Hispanic American Historical Review* 37:1 (February 1957), 1-28. On changing Chilean and Argentine attitudes toward immigration, see Solberg, *Immigration and Nationalism*.

33. Dary, *Cowboy Culture*, pp. 310-311; David H. Breen, *the Canadian Prairie West and the Ranching Frontier, 1874-1924* (Toronto: University of Toronto Press, 1983), pp. 51, 70; Craig Miner, *West of Wichita: Settling the High Plains of Kansas, 1865-1890* (Lawrence: University Press of Kansas, 1986), pp. 176-177.

34. Richard Burton Deane, "A Horse-stealing Case," in "Reminiscences of a Mounted Police Officer" (Glenbow Archive, M 311); Breen, *Canadian Prairie West*, pp. 64, 67, 74.

35. Quoted in Breen, *Canadian Prairie West*, p. 168.

36. Miguel Izard and Richard W. Slatta, "Banditry and Social Conflict on the Venezuelan Llanos," in Slatta, ed., *Bandidos*, pp. 40-45. See also Robert P. Matthews, Jr., "Rural Violence and Social Unrest in Venezuela, 1840-1858: Origins of the Federalist War," Ph.D. diss., New York University, 1974; Miguel Izard, *El miedo de la revolución: La lucha por la libertad en Venezuela, 1777-1830* (Madrid: Tecnos, 1979); Manuel A. Machado, Jr., *The Northern Mexican Cattle Industry, 1910-1975: Ideology, Conflict, and Change* (College Station: Texas A&M University Press, 1981), pp. 7-28.

37. Loveman, *Chile*, pp. 142-143. José Pedro Barrán, *Apogeo y crisis del Uruguay pastoril y caudillesco, 1839-1875*, vol. 4, *Historia uruguaya*, 2d ed. (Montevideo: Banda Oriental, 1975), pp. 50, 131-132.

38. On repressive laws, see Buenos Aires Province, *Registro oficial* (Buenos Aires, 1822), pp. 69, 170, 277; Benito Díaz, *Jurgados de paz de la campaña de la Provincia de Buenos Aires, 1821-1854* (La Plata: Universidad Nacional de La Plata, 1959), pp. 105-106; 202-203; Slatta, *Gauchos*, pp. 106-125, 141-160.

39. Miner, *West of Wichita*, pp. 176-177.

40. Breen, *Canadian Prairie West*; Simon M. Evans, "The Passing of a Frontier: Ranching in the Canadian West, 1882-1912," Ph.D. diss., University of Calgary, 1976; Edward Brado, *Cattle Kingdom: Early Ranching in Alberta* (Vancouver: Douglas and McIntyre, 1984).

41. Webb, *Great Frontier*, pp. 8-28; David M. Potter, *People of Plenty: Economic Abundance and the American Character* (Chicago, IL: University of Chicago Press, 1973), pp. 124, 155-165.

42. Caio Prado Júnior, *The Colonial Background of Modern Brazil*, Suzette Macedo, trans. (Berkeley: University of California Press, 1971), pp. 197, 213-241.

43. Jane M. Rausch, *A Tropical Plains Frontier: The Llanos of Colombia, 1531-1831* (Albuquerque: University of New Mexico Press, 1984).

44. Don Worcester, *The Spanish Mustang: From the Plains of Andalusia to the Prairies of Texas* (El Paso: Texas Western Press, 1986); Elizabeth Atwood Lawrence, *Hoofbeats and Society: Studies of Human-Horse Interaction* (Bloomington: Indiana University Press, 1985); John C. Ewers, *The Horse in Blackfoot Indian Culture* (Washington, DC: Smithsonian Institution Press, 1969); LaVerne Harrell Clark, *They Sang for Horses: The Impact of the Horse on Navajo and Apache Folklore* (Tucson: University of Arizona Press, 1966).

45. John Hemming, *Red Gold: The Conquest of the Brazilian Indians* (Cambridge, MA: Harvard University Press, 1978), and *Amazonian Frontier: The Defeat of the Brazilian Indians* (Cambridge, MA: Harvard University Press, 1987); Julio Aníbal Portas, *Malón contra malón: La solución final del problema del indio de la Argentina* (Buenos Aires: La Flor, 1967); Ray Harvey Pearce, *The Savages of America: A Study of the Indian and the Ideal of Civilization* (Baltimore, MD: Johns Hopkins University Press, 1965); Richard Drinnon, *Facing West: The Metaphysics of Indian-Hating and Empire-Building* (Minneapolis: University of Minnesota Press, 1980); Brian M. Fagan, *Clash of Cultures* (New York, NY: W. H. Freeman, 1984); Jennings, *Invasion of America*; Olive Patricia Dickason, *The Myth of the Savage and the Beginnings of French Colonialism in the Americas* (Edmonton: University of Alberta Press, 1984).

46. Forbes, "Frontiers in American History," pp. 63-73; Jack D. Forbes, "Frontiers in American History and the Role of the Frontiers Historian," *Ethnohistory* 15:2 (Spring 1968), 203-235; David J. Weber, "Turner, the Boltonians, and the Borderlands," *American Historical Review* 91:1 (February 1986), 81; Baretta and Markoff, "Civilization and Barbarism," pp. 593-595.

47. Carl Berger, *The Writing of Canadian History: Aspects of English-Canadian Writing, 1900-1970* (Toronto: Oxford University Press, 1976), p. 175; Breen, "Turner Thesis," p. 149; Robin W. Winks, "Frontier, Canada," in Howard R. Lamar, ed., *The Reader's Encyclopedia of the American West* (New York, NY: Crowell, 1977), pp. 416-418; Dunae, *Gentlemen Emigrants*.

48. Weber, "Turner, the Boltonians, and the Borderlands," pp. 70, 73; John Francis Bannon, *The Spanish Borderlands Frontiers, 1513-1821* (New York, NY: Holt, Rinehart and Winston, 1970), p. 5; Herbert Eugene Bolton, *The Spanish Borderlands: A Chronicle of Old Florida and the Southwest* (New Haven, CT: Yale University Press, 1921), pp. 233-234.

49. Marvin W. Mikesell, "Comparative Studies in Frontier History," *Annals of the Association of American Geographers* 50:1 (March 1960), 62-74; Slatta, *Gauchos*, pp. 7-8, 78-80, 87; Félix Coluccio, *Diccionario folklórico argentino*, 2 vols. (Buenos Aires: Luis Lasserre, 1964); José Antonio de Armas Chitty, *Vocabulario del hato* (Caracas: Universidad Central de Venezuela, 1966).

50. William Norton, "The Cultural Landscape of the Historical Frontier," *Journal of Cultural Geography* 3:2 (September 1983), 119; Dietrich Gerhard, "The Frontier in Comparative Perspective," *Comparative Studies in Society and History* 1 (March 1959), 205-229; Donald Denoon, *Settler Capitalism: The Dynamics of Dependent Development in the Southern Hemisphere* (New York, NY: Oxford University Press, 1983); John Fogarty, "Staples, Super-Staples, and the Limits of Staple Theory: The Experience of Argentina, Australia and Canada Compared," in D. C. M. Platt and Guido di Tella, eds., *Argentina, Australia and Canada: Studies in Comparative Development, 1870-1965* (London: St. Martin's, 1985), pp. 1-18.

2. Frontiers in Colonial Brazil: Reality, Myth, and Metaphor

A. J. R. Russell-Wood

Historiography

Historiography on the frontier in the Americas is richer than for any other continent. Pivotal was Frederick Jackson Turner's 1893 essay "The Significance of the Frontier in American History," which spawned its own historiography on his interpretation, on the meaning of the frontier to the United States, and on geographical frontiers such as the Far West frontier and the borderlands frontier. For Turner there was direct linkage between American democracy and the frontier, and how the frontier experience formed the American ethos and character and forged a national covenant in American historical writing. [1] In part, because of a different historical development and, in part, because of geography, the frontier as a topic is less prominent in the historiography of Canada or of Hispanic and Portuguese America with two exceptions: Argentina and Brazil. The purpose of this essay is to examine the concepts and realities of the frontier in colonial Brazil, 1500-1822. [2]

The historiography of the frontier in colonial Brazil is essentially a nineteenth-century creation. Early Jesuit writers had described the land, flora, and fauna, and the Indians of Brazil. General histories by Pero de Magalhães Gândavo (1576), Vicente do Salvador (1627), Samão de Vasconcelos (1663), and Sebastião da Rocha Pitta (1730) focused on the coastal regions, as, too, did the *Descriptive Treatise* of Gabriel Soares de Sousa, whose detailed description which he had taken to Lisbon in 1584 had been a captaincy-by-captaincy account of the coastline and a detailed description of Salvador and the captaincy of Bahia—this from a traveler to the upper valley of the Rio Salitre. [3] An exception to this reticence to discuss the frontier was the Jesuit André João Antonil who resided in Bahia from 1681 to 1716 and whose *Cultura e Opulencia do Brasil* (1711) described the major economies of the colony. Of particular interest are his descriptions of cattle raising in the *sertão* (backlands; interior) and the perceptive observation on the importance of cattle trails in linking three regions and three economies of early eighteenth-century Brazil, namely the sertão, Bahian littoral, and Minas Gerais, and cattle, sugar, and gold, respectively. Pedro Taques de Paes Almeida Leme (1714-1777) and Gaspar da Madre de Deus (1715-1800) not only exalted the *paulista* (inhabitant of São Paulo de Piratininga, often white or mixed white and Amerindian) role but, more importantly, considered Brazil from the perspective of the Plateau of Piratininga rather than the coast, and from a nativist rather than Portuguese outlook. [4]

In João Capistrano de Abreu (1853-1927), Brazil found its Frederick Jackson Turner. Capistrano de Abreu's studies responded to the suggestion by German Karl Friedrich Philipp von Martius that the history of the sertão merited closer attention (mercifully without drawing comparisons between *bandeirantes* [members of a group of pioneers and explorers] and Spanish *conquistadores*, as suggested by von Martius). Abreu emphasized the importance of the sertão in the historical development of Brazil, dwelling on exploration and settlement of the interior. Abreu was the first Brazilian historian to integrate people (Indians and Portuguese), geography, economy, transportation, and cultural factors in the move to the west. He took up Antonil's theme of the importance of trails and fluvial routes in integrating disparate parts and peoples of Brazil. He expressed the view, revolutionary for the 1870s, that the "real" Brazil lay in the interior and that coastal settlements were but extensions of European civilization. It was in the sertão that Abreu placed the locus for independent thought and action, the rejection of colonialism, and embryonic Brazilian nationalism. In short, Abreu shared the perspective of Pedro Taques and Gaspar da Madre de Deus and wrote a history of Brazil and not a history of Portuguese America. The Brazilian historian, Sérgio Buarque de Holanda (1902-1982) broke with the traditional patriotic glorification of the past, emphasizing the Indian contribution and demythifying the bandeirantes. Central to his writings was the theme of the move from the littoral to the interior and the break with seigneurial traditions and continental Portuguese antecedents. Buarque de Holanda rejected the applicability of the Turner thesis and North American historiographical interpretations to Brazil and argued that, if the frontier notion were to be applied to Brazil (a course he clearly did not favor), this be solely and rigorously within the Brazilian context. Other Brazilian scholars have heeded this admonition only in part, if at all. The sociologist Gilberto Freyre and the historian Caio Prado Júnior have adopted the concept of moving frontiers. Other historians have signaled important differences between North American and Brazilian frontiers, the former sustained whereas the latter was characterized as being a "hollow" frontier. [5]

Of "frontier peoples" in the colony, the bandeirantes have dominated the historiography. Afonso d'Escragnole Taunay set a high scholarly standard and essentially monopolized the term for the paulistas. The bandeirantes have been portrayed variously as social renegades, negative and unstable forces, and bloodthirsty opportunists, or as culture heroes epitomizing democracy and an independence of thought and action which became part of the national character. A characteristic of "frontiersmen" was their facility for mixing with other races. [6] Euclides da Cunha (1866-1909) in *Os sertões* (1902) drew attention not only to the deplorable conditions of *sertanejos* but to their being what he refers to as the "bedrock of our race." By this, he was not referring to the pure Caucasian, Indian, or Negroid, nor even the products of miscegenation, but to that final stage of racial crossings when individual strains were no longer apparent and had been absorbed into the true "bedrock of our race," for Euclides, the human epitome of Brazilian nationality. In his high opinion of the sertanejo, he was echoing the words of Henry Koster who had come from England to Brazil in 1809 for reasons of health. Koster traveled through the sertão, and was a keen observer of its inhabitants, whose generosity and hospitality he championed. [7] Obsession with the bandeirantes and with their association with the frontier has detracted from frontier attention due other frontiersmen in colonial Brazil (*vaqueiros*, *capitães do mato*, *tropeiros*) and even missionaries, soldiers, and crown representatives. More serious has been the ink spent on the exploits of the likes of Fernão Dias Pais and Domingos Jorge Velho at the expense (until recently) of seeing the frontier as the inter-penetration between different cultures and peoples rather than in geographical terms.

The term "frontier" presents a methodological challenge, and the meaning attributed to it may depend on the discipline. To the geographer, it is a topographical feature or boundary; to the anthropologist, it is a geographical region whose inhabitants exhibit certain shared characteristics; to the historian, it carries the politico-geographical connotation of being that part of a country fronting another, or whose extremities are conterminous with those of another. [8] The temptation to present a typology of frontiers and frontier types in Latin America has proven irresistible: mission frontier, Indian frontier, Maroon frontier, mining frontier, cattle frontier, agricultural frontier, political frontier; and, for colonial Brazil, *tropeiros* (drovers), *buqueiros* (hunter of Indians; derogatory term), *capitães do mato* (hunters of runaway slaves), *faisqueiros* (gold-mining prospectors), *garimpeiros* (illicit diamond prospectors), *calhambolas* (small groups of runaway slaves), and bandeirantes. I treat the word "frontier" in two senses. The first is to regard the frontier as a serial boundary or line associated with a geographical region. Inherent to such a notion is a political component of ownership and territoriality. This notion may well be subjective, nationalistic, or ethnocentric. The second is to regard it as that area where there occurs interaction or interpenetration between hitherto separate societies or cultures or where one group extends itself beyond its host society to such a degree as to form its own nucleus with its own identity. Let us examine the geographical, economic, political, and jurisdictional frontiers of colonial Brazil.

The Linear Frontier

Geographically, Brazil has been described as being bounded by the Atlantic to the east, by the Amazon to the north, by the Rio de la Plata and riverine systems to the south, and by the Andes to the west. Closer scrutiny suggests that, with the exception of the Atlantic, Brazil lacks true frontiers, if one accepts frontiers in the sense of impassable barriers such as deserts or mountain ranges. But there are geographically definable feature which are obstacles to horizontal movement; the sertão to the west; the *selva*, or forest, of Amazonas; the Amazon and its tributaries to the north; the Serra de Mantiqueira.[9] Such frontiers could be, and were overcome in the colonial era. Such obstacles did not, for the most part, coincide with the demarcation of political frontiers, nor were they necessarily on the peripheries of the political entity which was Portuguese America. If they did form a frontier of sorts, it was irregular in shape and was not continuous. There were topographical features forming islands or even archipelagoes of obstacles which impeded movement and defied settlement. Some were peripheral to areas of greatest human or economic concentration, but others impinged substantially on the economic and social life of the colony. A bird's-eye view of Portuguese America would have revealed that, even for the later colonial period, fluvial and terrestrial movement of peoples and transportation of goods were dictated largely by topography. Indeed, until the end of the colonial period and beyond, travel between most of the cities of Brazil was easier by water than by land, the exception being São Paulo and Mariana.

Topography, climate, and soil conditions also formed frontiers and determined economic potential and its limits and, consequently, settlement patterns. The combination of soil and climate created conditions essential to thriving hardwood trees whose wood produced a dye that was the first major revenue to the Portuguese crown from

Brazil. The Bahian Recôncavo well illustrates how different soil conditions determined economic activity: *massapé*, organically rich, thick, claylike soil, was ideal for sugar cane, giving as many as twenty harvests without replanting or fertilizing; *salão* was sandier but still viable for cane; whereas *areia*, a light sandy soil, was suitable for the cultivation of tobacco and food crops such as manioc. Thus, soils influenced the distribution of agricultural activities around the Bay of All Saints: sugar on the north side; tobacco around Cachoeira and the Paraguassú; subsistence farming to the south. [10] The Pernambucan counterpart to the Recôncavo was the Várzea, where massapé encouraged cane planting in the flood plain. The Recôncavo and Várzea had originally formed part of the *zona da mata*, a forested strip along the Atlantic coast which was to be substantially destroyed by agricultural development and cutting of lumber for construction. Beyond the Recôncavo and the Várzea was the bare and rocky transition zone of the *agreste*, which soon gave way to the sertão, whose expanses of scrub and cactus were suitable only for cattle ranching.

The capital investment essential for a plantation and the labor intensity of sugar production had social and economic repercussions for the colony. These lie beyond the purview of this paper except to point out that the allocation of the best lands for cultivation of export crops and land grants (*sesmarias*) created latifundia, denying small farmers access to lands in some coastal regions and essentially forcing them toward a frontier of marginally cultivatable land where they engaged in subsistence farming and especially the growing of manioc. Depending on the crop, modes of production ranged from plantations to farms, to smallholdings; so, too, did the color of agriculturists from predominantly white plantation owners to mulattoes and free blacks with smallholdings, with a corresponding decline in number of slaves from as many as one hundred for a sugar plantation, to twenty for a tobacco farm, and one or two for a manioc grower.

Although sugar was cultivated in Minas Gerais in the eighteenth century, there was no radical dislocation or redistribution or development of new areas of export agriculture in the colonial period. Amazonian cacao was short lived as an economic cycle (c. 1720-1759) and by its mode of collection did not constitute a new frontier. Farms and smallholdings came into being along the slowly developing network of roads to the interior, and mining communities in Minas Gerais, Goiás, and Mato Grosso were to have their own food-production areas. There was not a moving agricultural frontier in colonial Brazil, but rather the creation of isolated nuclei of agricultural or commercial activity. A classic example is cotton in the Maranhão which developed from a local market to an export commodity in the late eighteenth century. [11] Livestock production, initially in the borderlands beyond the Recôncavo and Várzea, did expand north from Pernambuco to Paraíba and Rio Grande do Norte and along the São Francisco river in the late sixteenth and early seventeenth centuries. By the eighteenth century, the expansion had pushed northward from Piauí into the Maranhão and westward as far as Goiás to meet the demands of new and intensified domestic and export markets. [12] That colonial Brazil had limitless lands for cultivation and cattle ranching and was a land of unbridled opportunity was true, but only in part. *Senhores de engenho* (owners of a sugar mill or sugar plantation) and *fazendeiros* (owners of ranches or farms), the latter counting such dynasties as the Guedes de Brito of the Casa da Ponte and the Dias d'Avila of the Casa da Tôrre with vast landholdings in the sertão, took good care to ensure that their privileges as holders of sesmarias were observed and refused to countenance cultivation of even unused or marginal lands by their retainers (*agregados*).

The designation frontier is most commonly applied to colonial Brazil in the context of gold. Alluvial gold had been found from Paranaguá to Pernambuco in the first two centuries of settlement, but only in the 1690s and the early 1700s was there to be a flurry of confirmed strikes from Rio das Velhas, Serro do Frio, Itocambiras, Rio das Contas, and Espírito Santo. By 1720, no part of Minas Gerais had been spared exploitation. Waves of speculators pushed inland from coastal enclaves. Mining encampments of Minas Gerais became townships and served as bases for further movements inland to Mato Grosso where gold was discovered on the rivers Coxipó and Cuiabá (1718-19), and further northward on the rivers Guaporé (1734) and Arinos (1745). Gold had been found in paying quantities on the Rio Vermelho in Goiás in 1725. By 1750 all major strikes that were to be made had been made but minor discoveries continued in Pernambuco, Goiás, Sergipe, and Espírito Santo. The unpredictability of the industry, rampant speculation, and the willingness of people to uproot themselves on the strength of rumor alone led to this experience being characterized by instability with the desertion of communities for secondary and tertiary "rushes" and reverse migration for the disillusioned. [13]

These strikes illustrate fundamental aspects of the historical development of Brazil and are critical to our understanding of frontiers. New land routes to the interior were developed, from Rio de Janeiro and São Paulo to Minas Gerais, and a second network of roads from the sertão of Bahia along the Rio São Francisco. By the 1740s

land routes had been developed to Vila Boa de Goiás from Rio das
Velhas, from the northeast, and from Mato Grosso. Such routes did
not in themselves constitute a frontier, but they did mean that new
hubs were established: Arraial de Mathias Cardoso on the
São Francisco for travelers to Minas Gerais from Pernambuco, Ceará,
Piauí and the Maranhão; Jacobina as the point of convergence for
routes from the northern captaincies to the Rio São Francisco, to Rio
das Contas, and to Salvador; Vila Rica and other mining communities
in Minas Gerais. Of equal importance in the move to the west was the
pioneering use on a large scale of rivers. Despite cataracts at Paulo
Afonso, this had occurred on the São Francisco. For access to Mato
Gross, travelers exploited the network of the rivers Tietê, Paraná,
Pardo, Anhanduí, Aquidauna, Coxim-Taquarí, and Paraguay.

The second aspect that bears on our discussion of frontiers lies in
the nature and repercussions of the gold rushes and subsequent
developments. In the newly discovered gold-bearing regions, mining
encampments developed into townships. These were either totally
isolated from one another or were accessible to one another to permit
formation of a definable collective entity. An example of the former is
Serro do Frio; examples of the latter are Vila Rica, Sabará, Vila do
Carmo (later Mariana), São João del Rei, and São José. These did
become population and commercial nuclei and were bases for further
movement. But such townships did not in themselves represent a
frontier. They were pivotal to westward movement but they were not
at the frontier of a sustained line of demographic, economic, or
agricultural development. [14]

The mining experience typifies the broader phenomenon of what
has come to be termed the "hollow frontier" in Brazil. Be it in the far
north, the south, the west, or even along the coast, the historical
development of Brazil was characterized by the establishment of a
series of what were essentially outposts: missions, fortresses, trading
posts, and even towns and cities. Rarely was there established an
unbroken nexus between them such as to be considered even a limited
linear frontier; ever more rarely was there the demographic,
administrative, or commercial development for the sustained backup
necessary to make them part of a moving frontier. A map of the
colony prior to 1822 reveals a series of isolated communities or
archipelagoes of loosely connected demographic or commercial centers.
Had it not been for the potential for interaction afforded by water
transport along the Atlantic seaboard, the major cities of Brazil would
have been even more isolated than they were from one another, and
certainly from those on the northwest coast. The conclusion is

inescapable that access to Europe or Africa may have been easier than to some coastal enclaves, let alone the interior, of Brazil. During the colonial era there was no true geographical, agricultural, mining or settlement frontier in Brazil, if by frontier is meant an unbroken line at the leading edge of sustained demographic and commercial development.

It is remarkable how little the national frontier of Brazil has changed since 1500. It took the diplomats negotiating the Treaty of Tordesillas (1494) to assign to Portugal a westerly limit to its jurisdiction, but this was essentially mathematical and had no basis in topography. In the next two and a half centuries, territorial expansion and Portuguese settlements were so to infringe upon the terms of the treaty that it became virtually meaningless. During the "factory period" (1502-1534), no attempt was made to define boundaries and it was only with the proprietary settlements that there was the first demarcation territorially in the colony. Fifteen lots of varying sizes were demarcated to the west by the line of Tordesillas and to the east by the ocean. Two centuries were to elapse until, by the Treaty of Madrid (1750), Spain and Portugal formally demarcated frontiers in the Americas on the principle of *uti possidetis*, thereby establishing what were essentially the boundaries of modern Brazil. [15] This is not to say that within that territory which was Portuguese America there were not to be jurisdictional changes. On two occasions (1572-1578 and 1608-1613) the southern captaincies (Espírito Santo, Rio de Janeiro, São Vicente) formed an entity separate from the jurisdiction of the governor-general in Salvador. From 1621 to 1774 the Estado do Maranhão had its own captain-general, was separate from the Estado do Brasil, and was dependent on Lisbon.

In establishing new jurisdictions, the crown was responsive to changing colonial realities. The crown created captaincies other than the original donatory captaincies. These new captaincies did not in themselves define a new frontier but did represent recognition by the crown of the difficulties of enforcing government and imposing law and order. They were the crown's attempt at grappling with the problem of attempting to extend the frontier of effective crown administration. During the later sixteenth and early seventeenth centuries, Portuguese radiated northward from Bahia and Pernambuco predominantly and the crown created new captaincies in Ceará, Pará, and Maranhão. But it was the eighteenth century that was to witness the greatest economic and demographic dislocation spurred by the discovery of gold in Minas Gerais in the 1690s and subsequent strikes in Mato Grosso and Goiás. New captaincies were carved out of the sprawling and undefined territories that had fallen under the governor of Rio de Janeiro: first the captaincy of São Paulo e Minas do Ouro (1709), and then subdivision of this (1720) into the two captaincies of São Paulo and Minas Gerais. The more westerly regions were slower in gaining royal attention: Goiás in 1744 and Mato Grosso in 1748, both carved out of the vastnesses of the captaincy of São Paulo.

The crown also responded to the challenge of attempting to bring a degree of stability to the colony. The prime instrument of this policy was the township or *vila* which represented stability, a degree of self-determination at the local level, and a crown presence. [16]   A royal order (1693) permitted the governor-general to establish vilas in the hinterland, if they would assist in the introduction of law and order. During the next fifty years, communities that met the basic criteria of substantial numbers of people, military and strategic importance, and potential for economic growth were accorded the status of vila. Inducements were offered to new settlers, revenues for the fledgling townships were generated by authorized taxes on commodities and rents from municipal lands, and civic pride was instilled in what had previously been unstable and anarchic communities.   These inducements were moderately successful in cutting crime and serving as points of departure for expeditions to the interior, but they were too isolated to serve as an administrative frontier.   Much the same can be said of the crown's creation of new judicial districts (*comarcas*) and new bishoprics. Human failings—lack of accountability, corruption, and avarice— undermined the royal intentions, but the single most critical obstacle lay in the sheer physical phenomenon of distance.

Perhaps it was officialdom—be it embodied in individuals such as successive monarchs and their representatives in Brazil or in institutions such as the Overseas Council, the Treasury, the Board of Conscience and Orders, and the Church—which alone had a frontier mentality toward Brazil as reflected in a series of treaties. Certainly, with Portugal as the reference point, Brazil was indeed the frontier conceptually and in reality.   Monarchs viewed Brazilians as being distinct from Portuguese (to the detriment of the former), imputed to Brazilians lesser moral and physical fiber, and considered the territory and its native peoples as exotic and uncivilized.   The New World enterprise was tolerated and encouraged initially only insofar as Brazil was a source for raw materials and revenues which sustained the metropolis. Certainly, monarchs did aspire to create a frontier which would be continuous and unbroken and which could withstand foreign incursions. The crown also aspired to create an administrative frontier, supported by effective and continual backup, to provide continuity of administrative control from the coastal cities to the interior. Neither aspiration was to be fulfilled. There were numerous penetrations by foreigners of the frontiers of Brazil, in large part attributable to the sheer impossibility in terms of manpower and resources of effectively patrolling the longest combined coastal and inland frontier of any European colony in South America. The vicissitudes of the Colônia do Sacramento, an isolated outpost on the Rio de la Plata combining military and commercial (horning in on the contraband trade with Buenos Aires) objectives, was a classic example of misplaced priorities. Nor did the crown come close to creating an effective administrative frontier within the colony. If anything, the administrative frontier was even more hollow and disjointed than had been the commercial or demographic. Throughout the colonial period, there was an administrative no-man's-land between the administrative centers themselves and between these and the peripheries of Portuguese America.

The Portuguese had attempted to secure their richest colony from foreign attack by putting in place in the seventeenth century forts and fortresses along the coast from São Vicente in the south to Presépio and Garuá at the mouth of the Amazon. By the late seventeenth century, the Amazon itself counted, inter alia, forts and fortresses of São José da Barra do Rio Negro, Obidos, Santarém, Santo Antonio de Gurupá, Santo Antonio de Macapá, and Araguari. The building of Sacramento on the northern bank of the Rio de la Plata (1680) had been intended to protect Portuguese interests in that strategic region. The eighteenth century, during the reign of Dom João V and during the administration of the Marquis of Pombal, witnessed further defensive works in the Amazon Valley and, on the western front, forts Coimbra, Ladário, and Miranda, and the garrisons of Albuquerque and Vila Maria. To the Far West were the ramparts of the Fort Príncipe da Beira on the Guaporé River begun in 1774. [17] The colonial era (1500-1822) was to witness numerous incursions, and even occupations, by Europeans: French attempts at an "Antarctic France" in Rio de Janeiro (1555-1567), an "Equinoxial France" in the Maranhão (1612-1615), invasion and occupation of Rio de Janeiro (1711); English corsairs along the coast, with a short-lived settlement on the Lower Amazon in the early seventeenth century; Dutch occupation of a substantial part of the Northeast from the River São Francisco to the Maranhão from 1630 to 1654; and continual hostilities with the Spanish in what would come to be Southern Mato Grosso, Guaíra and, most seriously, in the hard-fought hostilities in the 1770s over the Debatable Lands of the Platine region and Rio Grande do Sul. [18] Such defensive positions—impressive though they were—were too far apart and the intervening territories too porous to constitute an effective military frontier. Four factors contributed to this situation. First, sheer distance and the nature of the terrain made communications, transportation, and the movement of troops or munitions difficult. Second, especially to the south of São Paulo and to the west, a Portuguese presence was established and upheld in the absence of regular soldiers by bandeirantes, often acting without official sanction and beyond the effective control of a royal representative in the colony. Third, the predations of the Dutch West Indian Company had not been limited to Brazil but included the Portuguese settlements in West Africa. São Jorge da Mina, Luanda, Benguela, São Tomé. The Dutch presence on both sides of the Portuguese south Atlantic served to drive home the lesson that the eastern frontier of Portuguese America lay not solely on the American continent but on the west coast of Africa. Fourth, such incursions by foreigners underlined the fact that Brazil was vulnerable not only to the ebb and flow in its changing relationship to the metropolis but to the impact on Portugal of altering configurations of political relationships among the European powers. The importance of forts and fortresses transcended the purely military to become highly visible symbols of Portuguese claims to eminent domain on the peripheries of Brazil. [19]

The Frontier as Metaphor

The second part of this essay adopts a very different approach to the frontier: to see the frontier as metaphor and to see in the term "frontier" that area of interaction between different cultures. As a figure of speech, as good a place to start as any lies precisely in the realm of lexicography.

Elsewhere in the Americas the frontier has been associated with points of the compass (*el sur* in Argentina as celebrated in the short story of Jorge Luis Borges; the west in the United States). That was not the Brazilian experience. As in Argentina (*las pampas*), the United States (The Great American Desert), or Australia (Outback), in colonial Brazil one topographical feature and one word expressing perceptions as much as realities was paramount. [20] The most common word is sertão or sertões. To the geographer, the sertão is that area beyond the agreste where the land becomes higher and more arid, the climate drier, and where scrub and cactus predominate. But to inhabitants of the colony, the sertão was less precise. A key aspect of the sertões was that they were infinite and boundless. No matter how far man entered the sertão, there was ever more with the vague designation of *o interior do sertão*. The sertão was not continuous, nor could it be harnessed, nor was there a precise beginning or ending. It was not a frontier in a political or geographical sense, but rather a state of mind.

Sertão was not a neutral word. Context and use of adjectives show that sertão carried certain connotations. Sertões were regions not normally inhabited by Portuguese. The sertão came to be seen as the embodiment of a disruptive, potentially dangerous force. It was barbarous, chaotic, unchristian, uncivilized, and hostile to those values and tenets—justice, Christianity, orderliness, stability, good governance—which the Portuguese held dear. It was a region forsaken by God and unknown to civilized man. In short, civilization and orthodoxy stopped where the sertão began. The concept was essentially ethnocentric, the conceit of colonial administrators, Catholic missionaries, and colonists who prided themselves as representatives of civilization as understood by the Portuguese. Whites did not merely travel to the sertão, they penetrated it or made entries (*entradas*). Such penetrations were associated with conquest or suppression and not with the notion of expanding frontiers.

The natural inhabitants of a sertão were savages (*gentios*) who were untamed (*bravos*) and committed atrocities (*barbaridades*). On this there was universal agreement, among white settlers at least. From the sixteenth century through to the nineteenth, these native Americans were perceived as a threat. Portuguese reaction was to subdue, baptize, catechize, and "civilize" them. Often the result was mass genocide, both systematic and by happenstance, of the aboriginal population. Two other categories of persons associated with the sertão were not native to the area. They were moved by one of two motives, which were often interrelated: namely, refuge and opportunity. The sertão was a place of refuge for those who rejected, or were rejected by, society or who were fugitives from the church, from justice, or from oppression. They included persons fleeing the visitations of the Inquisition, those avoiding civil or criminal proceedings, and runaway slaves or persons of African or mixed descent. Some of them might come to find in the sertão a land of opportunity, but this had not been their primary motivation. To the second category belonged the bandeirantes who, from the sixteenth century, penetrated inland from Bahia, Pernambuco, and São Paulo in search of profit, be it in the form of Indians to be enslaved and sold, gold, or land. If there were to be a single type associated with the sertão it was the *poderosos do sertão*, the powerful men of the backlands whose capital was mostly in cattle, who lived and acted as they pleased, terrorized with their henchmen and private armies, and defied authority. But, neither the Indians nor the men of the latter two categories were frontiersmen in the sense that they had sought out this region consciously in order to be on the frontier or beyond it. For some Indians, the sertão was their homeland. For the other categories, they might become backwoodsmen, versed in survival in a hostile environment, but they did not see themselves—nor were they seen by others—as being on the frontier in the sense that the term came to be used in the United States. They became at one with the sertão. One such was Domingos Affonso, a paulista and backwoodsman, who added the surname Sertão to become Domingos Affonso Sertão, owner of plantations and cattle ranches in the sertão. [21]

Because of the metaphorical nature of sertão and the disparate nature of persons associated with it, it is difficult to talk of a frontier culture in colonial Brazil. The only common ground was that all lived beyond the frontier of effective civil or ecclesiastical jurisdiction. The effectiveness of their refuge and their chance of opportunity lay essentially in their inaccessibility because of distance and topography to representatives of crown government. They were transfrontiersmen in that they lived beyond mechanisms of social or legal control. [22] This was well illustrated by those runaway slaves who inhabited the loosely federated villages known as Palmares in Pernambuco and who resisted some twenty Dutch and Portuguese attacks between 1602 and 1694. [23] Typical of the breed was the group of blacks and mixed-bloods who, in the 1730s, roamed through the interior under a leadership of a self-anointed Prince of Brazil. A constant thorn in the side of the Portuguese crown was the poderosos do sertão who committed lèse majesté a thousand times over, faced down royal representatives sent to curb them, paid taxes as they pleased (usually not), and yet who—in a curious way—maintained a degree of stability in the sertão. In the eyes of officialdom and of many colonialists, the sertão was not associated with any democracy of spirit but rather with anarchy and violence. [24]

If there was a sertão culture, to the fore were three characteristics. A continuous theme running through the history of the sertão was violence: entradas (lit., entries) to kill, enslave, and violate Indians or to appropriate tribal lands; Indian offensive or retaliatory raids on such intruders; predations of powerful men of the backlands leading to arson, massacre, and torture; razzias against runaway slaves by blood-hungry capitães do mato or paulistas; raids by runaway slaves on isolated farmsteads or communities. The second characteristic was evasion. Inhabitants or transients in the sertão engaged with virtual impunity in contraband, tax evasion, and cattle rustling. The third characteristic was religious unorthodoxy. In the sertão there were few constraints on individual or collective manifestations of religious beliefs and practices, be they Catholic, shamanistic, or animistic and of African, European, or Native American provenience, or hybrids derived from syncretism of these three cultures. Paralleling this religious syncretism were superstitions derived from popular Portuguese, African, and Indian traditions revering the supernatural and giving great weight to portents and divination. Sorcery and magic were part of the portfolio of those who held sway over the sertão. Here was a region confusing and threatening to many Brazilians because of this culture of unorthodoxy, even though rare would be the Brazilian who had not been exposed to deviations from the Catholic canon and superstition even in the populous and sophisticated port cities. But the sertão was perceived as a crucible of beliefs so unorthodox as to be idolatrous and superstitions so intense and so unbridled as to threaten the stability of domestic, collective, and individual existences and, by extension, the state.

It is in the context of frontier as metaphor that we can approach the interpretation among the three cultures that came together in Portuguese America. Two of these cultures—the African and the European—had had extensive contact dating back to classical times and receiving fresh impetus with the unloading at Lagos in southern Portugal of 235 blacks in 1444. In the century between 1444 and the introduction of plantation slavery into Brazil, such contacts had intensified. But neither Europeans nor Africans had prior contact with the aboriginal peoples of the Americas until the landfall of Pedro Alvares Cabral in 1500 or, in the case of Africans, some thirty years later. For the Indians, there had been mutual isolation vis-à-vis Europeans and Africans and total absence of exposure to any racial group other than their own.

For Brazil, the physical frontier opened with the arrival of Pedro Alvares Cabral and the conceptual frontier with the first letter from Portuguese America penned by Pero Vaz de Caminha on May 1, 1500, to the king Dom Manuel. Caminha rhapsodized about the "dark brown and naked," "ingenuous," and "innocent" Indians. But there were ominous undertones with references to possible gold and silver deposits, how the country was so well favored that it needed only to be cultivated properly, and—most ominous of all—that the natives were lacking only in understanding to be converted to Christianity. [25] It has been estimated that in 1500 the Indian population of Brazil was 2,431,000. The modern population is some 100,000. Many native peoples were depleted after independence but, by the end of the colonial period (1822) many had fallen victim to mass genocide and ethnocide. [26] The Portuguese failed to establish total hegemony over Indian peoples but succeeded in more important regions. The nineteenth century witnessed open warfare between Indians and settlers in the Maranhão and Mato Grosso, and the Botocudo were to resist European intrusions until the 1890s. A remarkable aspect of Brazilian historiography is the imbalance between the extensive literature on Portuguese-African contacts and the meager offerings on Indian-Portuguese and Indian-African contacts. Indian-Portuguese contacts fall primarily into three categories: labor, missionary, hostility.

In the early years European-Indian relations were cordial with fraternization. [27] In the dyewood industry—totally dependent on Indian labor—voluntary labor gave way to barter. As Indians became sated with metal axes, knives, and manufactured goods, there was the transition from barter to enslavement directly or through the intermediary of intertribal wars whose prisoners were turned over to the Portuguese. This transition was exacerbated by the labor requirements of the sugar industry. The Portuguese experimented with various forms of Indian labor on the sugar plantations of the northeast. Enslaving Indians ran contrary to Portuguese laws of 1570 and 1587 guaranteeing Indians their liberty, and to Christian and humanist doctrine, but concepts of "extreme necessity" (condoning slavery as an alternative to death) or of "just war," and the reality of open hostility provided loopholes that led to open season on enslaving Indians. Raiding/trading expeditions to enslave Indians were regularized in the 1570s. Bahians and Pernambucans (such as the half-caste Tomacaúna), and not the paulistas, were to the fore. For the latter part of the sixteenth and early seventeenth centuries Amerindians and Africans worked together on plantations with the scales tilting to Africans as the preferred labor source, in part because of royal opposition to enslavement of Indians but more practically because of susceptibility of the latter to disease and low productivity. This was not the end of Indian forced labor. The arrival of the Portuguese on the Amazon and opening up of Maranhão and Pará in the early seventeenth century created a new demand for labor. Extending from the lower reaches of the Amazon in the 1620s to the Upper Amazon by the 1660s, "ransom" raids had caused havoc from Belém to the Solimões. European firearms exterminated whole tribes; others were "ransomed" and enslaved; "free" Indians were sent to Jesuit mission settlements called *aldeias*. Indians of mission villages became the main labor pool for settlers and the crown in seventeenth- and eighteenth-century Maranhão and Pará (1680, 1686 legislation on use of mission labor).

In the Amazon, Indian and not African labor was the norm for much of the eighteenth century. The gold rush to Cuiabá created a new demand for Indian labor leading to the massacre of the Paiaguá, enslavement of the passive Parecís, enslaving or taming of the Caiapó and co-option of the Bororó. Anarchy ruled in Mato Grosso but in their missions in the Amazon the Jesuits imposed their own brand of labor, which was longer lasting. Expulsion (1759) led to secular administration of the Indians by the Directorate (1757-1798) and a strenuous effort to incorporate Indians into the economy as free laborers. [28] For those "tame" Indians, neither products of the missionary villages nor victims of forced labor, there was always a place in the free labor force, most notably in the North and Northeast. In Belém, Indians of both sexes worked in the dockyard and at specialized tasks—some calling on native skills—such as the making of cordage from vegetable fibers or as sailmakers. The whaling factory on the island of Itaparica in the mideighteenth century counted at least two Indians on the labor force. Indians also worked on cattle ranches of the Northeast and in mining in Mato Grosso and Goiás.

The best-documented aspect of European-Indian contacts concerns missionary activities in general, and of the Society of Jesus in particular. Cardim's *Dialogue about the Conversion of the Heathen* (1556), Nóbrega's letters, and Anchieta's Tupí grammar testified to Jesuitical enthusiasm. [29] These Jesuits and others brought zeal and organizational skills to establishing missions in Bahia and northern Brazil and in São Paulo and São Vicente in the south. From the end of the sixteenth century until 1759 the Jesuits virtually controlled Indians under Portuguese rule. Initially, this was a mutually over-enthusiastic love affair: the Jesuits saw the Indians as innocents prime for mass conversions and baptism; the Indians saw in the black robes protection against the colonists. Aldeias were filled with coastal Indians and additional aldeias were established to the north and south. Mutual euphoria gave way to mutual disillusionment. Indian materialism and reluctance to abrogate tribal customs and behavioral mores were disturbing to the Jesuits. The decision to "reduce" the Indians was critical, creating an unholy alliance between the missionaries and government forces which was to be abused, especially on the Amazon. Force had been seen initially as a last resort but became acceptable on the grounds that the end justified the means. Aldeias placed Indians totally under Jesuit tutelage and were most plentiful and successful in the Maranhão and Pará and in Guaira. Indian hierarchies of authority, sexual distribution of labor, mobility, and hunting practices were abolished. For the first time, Indians faced the imposition of physical frontiers represented by the containing area of the aldeia. Casual labor had been replaced by structured labor which, while not slavery, was coerced. In terms of cultural interaction, mutual exposure did not result in greater understanding. The failure of native ordinations led the Jesuits at an early stage to drop any pretense at meaningful intellectual exchange and the academic program was based on rote learning. The enthusiasm of the Indians for music and ceremonies was unabated. John Hemming characterizes the Indians of the aldeias as "pious domesticated congregations." The Jesuits were unbending, and it is not clear whether the attitudes and practices of the French Capuchins, more tolerant of Indian customs, led to greater mutual understanding. [30]

The third area of contact was conflict. The establishment by the king of the donatary system of land grants signaled Portuguese intent to stay in Brazil and initiated three centuries of warfare between Indians and whites. The aggressive nature of the Tupí and their intertribal rivalries, and European aspirations, made war inevitable. The eating of the first lord-proprietor (donatário) of Bahia and of the first bishop by the Caethé set the scene for savage reprisals by Mem de Sá who virtually wiped out the coastal Tupinambá. There were complex and changing alliances, based on mutual self-interest rather than cultural relations, forged between different European nationalities and Indian tribes. The Tupí-speaking peoples were fragmented into many tribes at war with one another and quite prepared to exploit European hostilities to further their own ends. Europeans—French, English, Portuguese, Dutch, and Spanish—who enlisted Indian help may have been totally unaware of an ally's hidden agenda. On the other hand, European friendship could be devastating, as illustrated by the fate of the Tamoio around Rio de Janeiro in the 1550s, whose alliance with the French led to their decimation by European diseases and loss of life in wars against the Temimino and Waitacá to which they were incited by the French. To facilitate access to brazilwood of the Rio Paraiba and antagonize further the Portuguese, the French allied themselves with the Potiguar who were hostile to Portuguese expansion along the east-west coast north of Pernambuco. But in the 1580s the Portuguese won over the Tobajara by a marriage alliance and by exploiting their hatred for the Potiguar and forced surrender on the Potiguar in 1601. The Portuguese then used them against the Aimoré. In Pernambuco the alliance between the Caethé and French was devastating to Igaraçú and Olinda. The Caethé were enemies of both Portuguese and Tupinambá. Despite intertribal wars, through the 1560s many tribes still held their own against the Portuguese, but by the turn of the century native resistance by coastal tribes had been virtually suppressed. Especially fearsome were the Aimoré whose all-out warfare contrasted with the more elegant style of the Tupí. John Hemming has suggested that if the Aimoré and other Tapuia tribes had not been driven from the coast by the Tupí before the arrival of the Portuguese, European settlement would have been more difficult. In the seventeenth century the Portuguese moved northward culminating in the massacre of the Tupinambá war of 1616-1619 and subsequent annihilation of the Indians in Pará and the Maranhão. In the seventeenth century, inroads were made against the Tapuia and Janduím in the cattle country of Ceará, Rio Grande, and the Maranhão. The gold rush to Cuiabá brought Portuguese into conflict with those superb horsemen who were the Guiacurú and the canoeists who were the Paiaguá. If the Paiaguá resisted and were killed, the Bororó tried the different tack of allying themselves with the Portuguese to fight against other tribes, especially their rivals the Caiapó. Whether the Indians manipulated the Europeans or were manipulated, whether they signed treaties, formed alliances through marriage, resisted enslavement, or were passively enslaved, the results were the same: massacre of native peoples and destruction of their cultures. Against this changing backdrop of campaigns and incursions from the Upper Amazon and Mato Grosso to the coast was the constant of the adversarial relationship between paulistas and Indians. By the 1580s Indians around São Paulo were extinct and the paulistas extended their predatory activities, reaching as far as the headwaters of the Tocantins. These activities paled against the brutal attacks and massacres committed by the paulistas against the Jesuit provinces of Guaira, Tapé, Uruguay, and Itatín between 1616 and midcentury. [31] Despite this violence, the greatest scourge was disease which destroyed whole tribes in an ongoing process as they were exposed to European intruders.

Finally, how much acculturation was there? After initial encounters and fraternization, European Edenic visions and fantasies about "noble savages" gave way to more materialistic and exploitative assessments of the Indians. The idyllic life of Caramurú in Bahia or of João Ramalho in Piratininga with extended families in the early sixteenth century was short-lived. Cannibalism gave the Europeans the moral high ground and justified exploitation and enslavement. European offensives forced Indians to retreat from tribal lands to avoid further contacts. This was an ongoing process of retreat to the more remote reaches of the sertão or forest. The reward was preservation of independence and cultural integrity. But the struggle was continual as

illustrated by those Tupinambá who had marched from coastal Bahia to
the lower Amazon in the late sixteenth century only once again to be
accosted by Europeans as French and Portuguese expanded into the
Amazon in the early seventeenth century. What culture contact there
was depended on European rather than Indian initiatives. The most
thorough and sympathetic early reports came not from the Portuguese
but from ethnographically inclined French missionaries such as Jean de
Léry and André Thevet. [32]   And it was the French who, of all
European nationalities in Brazil, enjoyed the most cordial relations
with Indians, actually lived with the Indians and served as interpreters,
and tried to understand the perspective of the vanquished by describing
Indian reactions to Europeans and translating or reporting Indian
speech.   Several French interpreters shared fully in tribal activities,
including cannibalism.   And yet Villegagnon was hostile to the
Tupinambá of Antarctic France in 1555.   But this was exceptional,
breaking with the usual French practice of not establishing settlements,
in counterdistinction to the Portuguese. Later in the Maranhão, there
was adoption by the Tupinambá of some French practices, including
fencing, but this appears to have been more mimicry than cultural
assimilation.   French, Portuguese, and English brought back to
sixteenth-century Europe Indians as part of the exotica of the New
World. Within Brazil, French and Portuguese mated with Amerindian
women freely in the early stages of culture contact. Later this was less
common as Indians retreated, died, or were held under strict
surveillance by the Jesuits.   By the end of the sixteenth century
miscegenation between Europeans and native Americans had been
replaced by European-African sexual relationships. Contacts became
limited to those Indians who made the effort to come to the European
towns or European traders who visited Indian villages. In the latter
case, alcohol and firearms were objects of exchange with disastrous
consequences for the Indians.
     Jesuits, paulistas, and cattlemen had most sustained contacts with
Indians, and we may examine how these fared. [33] The aldeias were the
most lasting and intensive experiment in coexistence, but neither the
detribalized Indians nor the Jesuits were capable of more than
superficial culture contact and there was exposure but not interaction.
The result was the creation of a unique subculture rather than
acculturation.   Early Jesuit attempts at working through chiefs and
even adopting some native practices of communication were soon
abandoned.   Tribal marriage customs were suppressed, communal
longhouses were replaced by huts, and the Indians' culture was
destroyed. At least the missionaries learned Indian languages and tried

to understand their beliefs and customs, if only to alter them. For their part, governors rarely differentiated between tribes when issuing orders for entradas. The paulistas were the other group to have most contact with Indians. They were the products of mating between Portuguese men and Indian women on the plateau of Piratininga, and so rapidly did their numbers grow that *mameluco* became synonymous with paulista. They learned Tupí from their mothers, had a knowledge of survival lore, were conversant with herbs, and were skilled trackers. And yet it was precisely the half-caste sons of Ramalho whose resentment for Jesuit strictures against polygamy and slaving led them to use their own prestige to turn the Tupiniquin against the Jesuits. This was not the last time that Indians would be duped into trusting such mamelucos and consenting passively to "descent," as forced relocation from the interior to the proximity of white settlements was euphemistically known, and enslavement. Subsequent paulistas activities were directed to enslaving and killing rather than acting as intermediaries between two cultures. Their skills as backwoodsmen made them sought after by governors for guerrilla tactics against the Dutch, against *quilombos* (communities of runaway slaves), and against Indians in just and not-so-just wars. The third group were cattlemen whose move away from the zona da mata to the sertão of Bahia and Pernambuco had started in the sixteenth century and continued unabated into Ceará, Piauí, and the Maranhão. Indian tribes were displaced, subdued, or extinguished, and yet cattle ranching had a place for Indian skills as cowboys and for Indian women as sexual partners and was one economy where Indians and Europeans coexisted reasonably amicably. Within the colonial period, there were some areas of cultural exchange which were more lasting: cultivation and preparation of manioc (cassava) and cultivation of pumpkins, gourds, and beans by Europeans; especially with the conquest of the Amazon many more spices and medicinal herbs became available; and it was the Europeans who imitated the Indians in smoking tobacco. Despite such bloodshed and violence, Portuguese noted with pride Indian ancestors in their genealogies.

An area of exchange which has scarcely raised a ripple on the historiographical surface concerns Indian-African cultural inter-penetration. [34] The context in which the two are most frequently mentioned together is slavery. The irrationality of enslaving Africans ostensibly to free Indians reveals the very different attitudes, laws, and behavior by Portuguese toward Indians and Africans. There may have been contacts when blacks fled and lived in Indian villages, or when Indians were in quilombos, but they were sporadic and rare. Hemming notes some black blood among surviving tribes of Brazilian Guiana and Indian blood among blacks on the northern rivers, but more often there was hostility on the part of Indians who feared such intruders as carriers of disease. Marriage between Africans and Indians was discouraged by church, state, and colonists. A 1755 law declaring the enslavement of Amerindians illegal specifically excluded Amerindian-black offspring born of black slaves. Pombaline legislation promoting marriages between Amerindians and white settlers denied benefits or concessions to Amerindians who married blacks. Despite such opposition, random references show that Church-sanctioned and stable relations did occur, but probably in small numbers. Persons of African descent in such unions would probably have as their nonnegroid partners *mestiços* rather than Indians, in part because of the unavailability of the latter. Should the female partner in such unions be Amerindian and the male a slave, by law the offspring was born free. In reality, both mother and child were virtually enslaved if they were not to be separated from their husbands or father, respectively. Nor is there evidence from the colonial period of the interpenetration of religious or superstitious practices, divination, wearing of charms, or how much the extensive herbal knowledge of both Africans and Amerindians for medicinal and other purposes became intertwined. Certain objects may have had ritual significance for both cultures.

The study of European-African relations and cultural interpenetration requires numerous volumes. It cannot be overemphasized that Europeans and Africans shared in being intrusive elements into the Americas. Second, demographics alone made unavoidable far more extensive contact than had been the case before either Europeans or Africans and indigenous populations. From 1500 to 1810, it has been estimated that some two and a half million persons were brought from Africa to Brazil to be slaves. [35] The pattern of Portuguese migration favoring single males over families or married couples, especially in the first two centuries, made miscegenation inevitable. The result was a growing and increasingly influential mulatto population. Another characteristic of colonial demography was a black majority in many regions, especially those of greatest economic intensity. Economic opportunity and miscegenation, singly and in combination, were the context for increasing incidences of manumission and the significant presence of a free population of persons of African descent.

Demography had major implications for cultural interpenetration. First, new arrivals provided a constant revitalization of African cultures in Brazil. Second, because slaves had been drawn from different places of origin, they were the transmitters of, and heirs to, widely differing

African cultural traditions; the sequitur was that for many Africans cultural interpenetration with fellow Africans occurred only in the New World. Indeed, of all New World peoples, Africans were the possessors of more cultural diversity than were native Americans despite tribal differences and than were Europeans despite national and religious distinctions. Third, with the exception of the distinction between Old Christians and New Christians among Catholic Caucasians, no ethnic group was legally divided as was the negroid, viz into slaves and freedmen. With the possible exception of gypsies and suspected Judaizers, no group was the object of such sustained official attempts to suppress cultural mores, beliefs, and values.

The context for most contacts between Europeans and Africans was the institution of slavery. The prime occupations of slaves were in agriculture, in gold and diamond mining, as artisans, and in domestic labor. There were variants within the institution: at one extreme were slaves working in the large-scale gold-mining operations known as *lavras* or in the diamond washings who were under constant and rigorous supervision; at the other were day workers (*jornaleiros*) and slaves available for hire (*escravos de ganho* or *escravos de aluguel*) who had reached mutually beneficial understandings with owners and who enjoyed substantial mobility and freedom from supervision. Within the institution of slavery in Brazil, there was substantial room for accommodation. [36] To view relationships in a series of polar dichotomies (big house-slave quarters, owner-slave, black-white), is to misrepresent the nuanced nature of many economic and social relationships in Brazil and the high potential for individual or even collective accommodations. An extreme example of this potential was the settlement negotiated and the treaty signed between runaway slaves and their owner in the late eighteenth century. Finally, free blacks and mulattoes contributed substantially to the social, cultural, and economic life of the colony and had become a major demographic presence in urban areas by the eighteenth century. Against this background of constant physical, social, and economic, interaction, I turn to interpenetration between Portuguese and African cultures. [37] My purpose is not to enter the vexed question of African survivals or examine the adaptive capacity of persons of African descent, both within and without slavery, to the New World, or to pinpoint characteristics irrefutably of African provenance, but rather to focus on boundaries between European and African cultures under four headings: kinship and naming practices; technology; religion; the arts.

Kinship was important within African and European cultures. This could be consanguineal or fictive. In the latter case, for persons of African descent it could take the form of a shared experience; transportation on the same ship; membership of the same *quilombo*, or work in the same household or plantation. To be of the same "nation" could be tantamount to kinship. Within the Portuguese community, ritual kinship was expressed either by godparenthood (*padrinazgo*) or co-parenthood (*compadrazgo, compadrio*). This could be within the context of Catholic baptism or marriage, but might be wholly secular. In both cultures, forms of ritual kinship were used to extend the family beyond the bounds of consanguinity and affinity. That ritual kinship was an integral part of the black experience in colonial Brazil was confirmed by correspondence from the governor of Minas Gerais in 1719. The Count of Assumar noted that at baptisms and marriages, blacks chose as godfathers (*padrinhos*) other blacks who had attained positions of prominence and respect within the black community in Brazil, were of the same 'nation," or had been members of ruling families in Africa. Preferred were those not already blood relatives. Personal qualities and descent-line of the honoree were more important than distinctions of legal status, viz slave or free. The governor alleged that slaves gave their earnings to godparents rather than to their owners, that godparents abused their authority by inciting such kin to flight, and that aspiring leaders had used godparenthood as a stepping stone to positions of authority in the black community and in quilombos. By godparenthood, slaves and freedmen were reinforcing ties crossing time and space, asserting African origins predating the initial enslavement of ancestors or their own ethnic backgrounds. Whether Africans by so doing were continuing to the New World an institution well entrenched in African societies, or whether they saw in compadrazgo an institution—both secular and religious—acceptable to Portuguese and used this as a cover for what might otherwise have been prohibited practices, or whether Assumar was simply finding in Portuguese the nearest equivalent for an African institution, is not known. But the bottom line was that by their choices of godparents, Africans were reinforcing their *africanité*. But there was also an exclusively New World context for secular and fictive kinship precisely in the manner in which this had been understood and practiced by Portuguese in Europe and thence in Brazil. In the context of slavery, slaves preferred free persons as godparents. This choice was wholly pragmatic and had no ethnic or religious component. It was prompted by recognition of a godparent's potential as sponsor and protector. When slaves chose as godparents whites or free persons of color, they were exercising vertical choice. Padrinhos could intervene to prevent physical abuse, forced separation of slave families, or miscarriages of justice, serve as mediators in manumission proceedings, or provide protection against highhanded and over-zealous law enforcers or draconic edicts. [38]

A parallel situation may also apply to naming practices, although they have yet to be studied systematically for colonial Brazil. Some persons of African descent sought, by their choice of names, to establish a linkage to a place in Africa, to an African cultural or ethnic legacy, to a shared experience, or to their forefathers, in short, to meet the psychological need of transplanted persons to seek self-identification by a point of reference. Such names were African. But other names were clearly Portuguese or American: an owner's surname, a Christian name, or the Portuguese name for a place or plantation. The motivation may have been the same, or attributable to vanity, an owner's influence, desire to climb the social ladder, or to express identification with the New World. Rare are examples from colonial Brazil of hybrid naming practices as occurred in Saint-Domingue, viz the addition of an African name to identify a slave, for example, "The Congo Diane, called in her country Ougan-Daga," although occupations and places of origin were used to identify more specifically a slave (e.g., João sapateiro [John Shoemaker] or Pedro Cabinda). [39]

Technology transfer is another instance of cultural boundaries in colonial Brazil. Two such areas were sugar processing and gold mining. [40] Persons of African descent had no previous knowledge of the processing of sugar cane. The Jesuit Antonil had noted (1711) the use of unskilled and skilled and slave and free labor in the processing of sugar. Even placing the cane into the rollers required skill, but the truly skilled occupations were in boiling to keep the correct temperature and knowing when to add lime, ash, or water and how to skim, and in the purging house where there were separating and drying. Supervisors were often freedmen of African descent. In contradistinction, when it came to mining for gold it was the Africans who had the technical knowledge. Few Portuguese migrants or entrepreneurs had prior knowledge or experience of gold mining, and throughout the colonial period, mining technology was most rudimentary. This was apparent in an overdependence on alluvial mining and the inability to exploit veins. The crown refused to dispatch skilled miners from Hungary or Saxony for fear that their knowledge of the mineral riches of Brazil might be put at the service of hostile powers. But slaves from the Costa da Mina came from regions where gold mining and metallurgy were highly developed. In the Akan states gold dust was the internal currency and shaft mining and alluvial washing were commonplace. Other slaves came from iron mining and smelting regions. Within Benin City, blacksmiths and bronze casters were highly sophisticated and had an excellent knowledge of constituent metals in the casting of bronze and brass. The result was that African slaves were the possessors of highly valued technical knowledge which was a boon and a bane (as shown in their proven skills in debasing gold by mixing the dust with silver, copper, and iron filings).

Religion was both a boundary and a bridge between cultures. At first sight, practitioners of Catholic orthodoxy and of fetishistic African religions would appear to have little in common. However, as Laura de Mello e Souza has reminded us in her pioneering study of witchcraft in colonial Brazil, there was an abyss between the erudite and the popular in the understanding of dogma and in the practice of Catholicism in Brazil. She introduces the notion of an "imperfect" Catholicism, already a hybrid of the profane and the sacred in Portugal, and further hybridized in the colony. The same could have held true for religions brought by Africans to the New World. In colonial Brazil, there took place the syncretism of religions which had already undergone hybridism in Europe and Africa respectively. For their part, African antecedents dictated a wide variety of sects, liturgies, and ceremonies, with Dahomans of the Gege group (Ewe, Fon), and Yoruba (Nago, Egba, Ketu) well represented in Brazil. Religious beliefs included the worship of gods and goddesses who were personifications of natural phenomena and worship of ancestors. [41] This aspect of African life is scarcely documented, in part because the major tenets were passed from father to son by word of mouth, in part because of official suppression, and also because religion was vested in secrecy. The participation by slaves and freedmen in the public religious life of the colony is, however, well documented. Persons of African descent established their own brotherhoods, built chapels and even churches, participated in Corpus Christi and other civic spectacles, were present at funerals, and were models of decorum and institutional stability. At death, they left bequests for the saying of masses for their souls, for dowries, and for charitable applications. Two allegations that should be put to rest are that brotherhoods of slaves and freedmen of color assisted runaways and were fronts for the clandestine practice of African religious rites. There is no evidence to support such allegations of illegal activities. Indeed, of all the regions of the far-flung Portuguese empire in which the essentially Catholic and European institution of the brotherhood was to be adopted, nowhere was it to be so wholeheartedly adopted by a non-European population as in colonial Brazil. [42]

If there was one area where Europeans and Africans, free men and slaves, joined culturally, it would be in the building and decorative arts. Free and slave blacks and mulattoes were involved in the construction and decoration of secular and religious buildings throughout the colonial period and nowhere more conspicuously than those churches and chapels built during the "golden age" of Brazil in Bahia and Minas Gerais. The best-known mulatto architect was Antonio Francisco Lisboa, son of a Portuguese master carpenter and architect and his slave. He received instruction in draftsmanship, architecture, and sculpture and probably in painting and design. His attributable works include masterpieces of the baroque in Minas Gerais such as the Third Order of St. Francis in Vila Rica and in São João del Rei, delicately carved Madonnas and saints, and the Old Testament prophets and Way of the Cross at Congonhas do Campo. Even more spectacular in social terms was the achievement of Manuel da Cunha (1737-1809), a slave who showed such artistic promise that he was sent to Lisbon for further training. On return to Brazil he was bought out of bondage and went on to execute masterpieces of religious art in churches and chapels of Rio de Janeiro. But his real claim to fame is that he was the first artist in Brazil, and among the first black artists in the Americas, to distinguish himself as a portraitist. What is so remarkable about the thousands of nameless African artists who built, decorated, painted, and furnished secular and religious, private and public, buildings in colonial Brazil, was that they adhered so precisely to the canon of European art and, to the best of my knowledge, nowhere is there evidence in such works of an African decorative arts tradition such as one finds for Indian artisans in the Spanish colonial buildings of Quito or La Paz. [43]

In our examination of frontiers among the cultural traditions of Europe, Africa, and America, as they interpenetrated in colonial Brazil, music and language are two areas where these three cultures continue to interact today. Although little documented for the precolonial or early colonial period, limited evidence and ethnographic analogy suggest that Indians had a wide variety of musical instruments with a preference for wind instruments such as flutes. Jesuits testified to the superb choral qualities of Indians but their music itself seems to have been rather limited with monotonous repetition of a single refrain or of a few rhythms derived from bird songs and nature. The Jesuits recognized Indian aptitude for music but, instead of allowing them to develop their own culture, used music as an instrument to achieve control. They introduced them to new European instruments such as the harpsichord and taught them chants in Latin and Portuguese. The result has been that Indian musical traditions have survived only away from the centers of Portuguese activities, although in the nineteenth century Carlos Gomes turned to Indian sources for inspiration for his opera *O Guaraní* as too did the composer Heitor Vila-Lobos in the twentieth century. Anthropologists and ethnographers have shown that this tradition is still alive and that music and dance accompany every important event and transition in the lives of those native Americans who have survived genocide and ethnocide. [44]

Africans may not have had a richer musical tradition than native Americans, but their sheer numbers and constant replenishment led to its perpetuation in the New World. Unlike the Indian, African music tends to be polyrhythmic, and percussion instruments, drums in particular, are prominent; but it shares with Indian music a penchant for repetitive chanting. To divide African music into religious and secular may be to perform the disservice of imposing a Western concept of dividing the religious from the profane and ignoring the more holistic quality of non-Western cultures where lines between art, religion, music, and medicine are blurred, if they exist at all. But, in general terms, there was music associated with African religions and later Afro-Brazilian cults of which we have so little evidence prior to the nineteenth century. It is reasonable to assume, on the basis of African and of nineteenth- and twentieth-century Brazilian evidence, that also in the colonial period there were songs and rhythms associated with each god or goddess. In fact, one may speculate that some of the music associated with Afro-Brazilian ceremonies in Brazil today may represent a fossilized form of earlier music which has subsequently become modified or totally changed during the cultural development in West Africa since the end of the slave trade. In contrast to the secrecy surrounding such religious music, the profane *batuques* (black hoedowns) were as public as they were scandalous to infuriated colonial administrators who made them the subjects of their reports and went to great lengths to try to eradicate this cultural tradition. Today, this legacy is readily apparent in the variety of percussion instruments in any Brazilian orchestra or band, in the strong emphasis on rhythm in Brazilian music, in dance, and in a manner of singing clearly distinguishable as African.

There is another aspect to the African contribution to Brazilian music which is less well publicized but better documented. Persons of African descent were prominent in musical pageants, theatrical performances, operatic presentations, mimes and dances which were essential parts of celebrations of royal marriages, birthdays, the arrival of a high court judge, or the installation of a governor or bishop.

Apart from these essentially amateur performers and dancers, there was a school of professional colored musicians and actors in Minas Gerais in the late eighteenth century. These counted singers, instrumentalists, composers, and conductors. Reconstitution of their works suggests that there was true talent, and several mulattoes at the end of the eighteenth century revealed themselves to be masters of the music of the baroque in Brazil. Two of the better known were José Joaquim Emerico Lôbo de Mesquita and Inácio Parreira Neves. Lôbo de Mesquita, organist in the church of Sto. António in Arraial do Tijuco, was a composer rated by Curt Lange as being on a par with his leading European contemporaries; Inácio Parreira Neves was chorister, composer, and conductor in Vila Rica and composed and directed the funeral music on the death of Dom Pedro in 1787. In short, not only did persons of African descent preserve African musical traditions in the New World but they also elaborated on them to create a new musical tradition; furthermore, they mastered certain aspects of an exclusively European musical tradition. This was their contribution, unique to Africans alone, among the interpenetration of three cultures in colonial Brazil. [45]

Finally, I turn to the languages of Brazil and examine the boundaries among them. The Portuguese were, for the most part, unique among the three groups in being monolingual. The only exceptions were those missionaries who learned African or Indian languages and the bandeirantes, many of whom were bilingual in Portuguese and Tupí-Guaraní. The Indians had innumerable local dialects, tribal languages, and more general linguistic families. Under the linguistic umbrella of Tupí-Guaraní, which in Eastern Brazil alone included the Gê, Tapuya, Botocudo, and Bororó. Africans were also polyglots, speaking as many as three or four African languages and adapting to Portuguese in varying degrees of fluency. It should be emphasized that in this Babel, there were some Africans who did not speak Portuguese and there were instances of Africans whose native language was not intelligible even to their fellow Africans. Gilberto Freyre has pointed out the vacuum that existed in Brazil between written Portuguese and the spoken language, and between the erudite language as spoken by judges, graduates, civil servants, and ecclesiastics and the popular língua do povo. It is reasonable to assume that Portuguese of the sertão absorbed into their language Indian words or phrases. Indian names still predominate for topographical features such as rivers and mountains, for flora and fauna, and for fishes and birds. Freyre has pointed out the influence of Africans on the reduplication of the tonic syllable, on the soft final syllables, and on personal names. Alexander Caldcleugh, a visitor to Brazil in the early nineteenth century, noted distinctive differences between the Portuguese of Brazil and that of the metropolis, although it would be too much to attribute to African influence alone differences in syntax between Portuguese and Brazilian. Today, especially in the northeast, African words are part of everyday spoken speech and carry certain connotations absent from their less-expressive Portuguese counterparts. [46]

Conclusion

Examination of the realities and concepts of frontiers in the context of colonial Brazil alerts us to the very real dangers of transposing to a different culture—with a different rate and intensity of historical development—notions derived from another culture. These notions have given rise to a historiography and to interpretations that are not applicable, except with severe reservations, beyond that physical and cultural milieu in which they were originally conceived. It has been shown that, for colonial Brazil, the linear concept of the frontier had little applicability other than in narrowly mathematical terms and as a political characterization related to territoriality and imperialism.

What is so exceptional in the Brazilian case is that, notwithstanding the prevalence of what has been characterized as a "hollow frontier," an archipelagic quality, and difficulties imposed by deficit communications and transport, the colony exhibited a remarkably high degree of socioeconomic and political unity. The ambiguity inherent in the word "sertão"—at one and the same time a no-man's-land and yet a region whose habitation by certain groups considered marginal to, or marginalized by, society was deemed to be acceptable—may provide the key to the alternative approach, namely to examine the frontier as metaphor. [47] Here the word "frontier" is understood in the context of a boundary between cultures: this approach is more revealing, and more in keeping with, the unique blending of cultures which was an inherent part of historical development in the colonial period and is an ongoing and no less evident phenomenon of modern Brazil.

NOTES

    1. Frederick Jackson Turner, "The Significance of the Frontier in American History," *American Historical Association Annual Report* (Washington, DC, 1893), pp. 199-227. The "Turner thesis" has spawned a literature of its own. Good starting points are: R. A. Billington, ed., *Selected Essays of Frederick Jackson Turner: Frontier and Section* (Englewood Cliffs, NJ: Prentice-Hall, 1961), and *The Frontier Thesis: Valid*

Interpretation of American History? (New York, NY, 1966); Richard Hofstadter and S. M. Lipset, eds., *Turner and the Sociology of the Frontier* (New York, NY, 1968). See also Vernon E. Mattson and William E. Marion, *Frederick Jackson Turner: A Reference Guide* (Boston, MA, 1985). For an interesting interpretation based on the idea of incarnation as an organizing principle of American self-consciousness, see Myra Fehlen, *American Incarnation: The Individual, the Nation and the Continent* (Cambridge, MA, 1986).

2. A general survey of the frontier in Latin America is Alistair Hennessy, *The Frontier in Latin American History* (Albuquerque, NM, 1978); see also Sílvia Zavala, "The Frontiers of Hispanic America," in Walker D. Wyman and Clifton B. Kroeber, eds., *The Frontier in Perspective* (Madison, WI, 1957), pp. 35-58; and the essays of Emilio Willems and Martin Katzman in David H. Miller and Jerome O. Steffen, eds., *The Frontier: Comparative Studies* (Norman, OK, 1977), pp. 259-273 and 275-296. For Canada see W. J. Eccles, *The Canadian Frontier, 1534-1760* (Albuquerque, NM, 1976); A. I. Silver, "French Canada and the Prairie Frontier, 1870-1890," *Canadian Historical Review* 50:1 (March 1969), 11-36; M. Zaslow, "The Frontier Hypothesis in Recent Canadian Historiography," *Canadian Historical Review* 29:2 (June 1948), 153-167.

3. Pero de Magalhães Gândavo, *História da província Sancta Cruz a que vulgarmente chamamos Brasil* (Lisbon, 1576), translated as *The Histories of Brazil*, John B. Stetson, Jr., trans., 2 vols. (New York, NY, 1922); Frei Vincente do Salvador, *História do Brasil* (Lisbon, 1627); Simão do Vasconcelos, *Chrónica de Companhia de Jesus do Estado do Brasil* (Lisbon, 1658); Sebastião da Rocha Pitta, *História da América portugueza* (Lisbon, 1730); Gabriel Soares de Sousa, *Tratado descriptivo do Brasil em 1587* (Rio de Janeiro, 1851). For survey of this literature and editions, see José Honório Rodrigues, *História da história do Brasil. Vol. 1, Historiografia colonial,* 2d ed. (São Paulo, 1979). A useful introduction in English is Mary Lombardi, "The Frontier in Brazilian History: An Historiographical Essay," *Pacific Historical Review* 44:4 (November 1975), 437-457.

4. André João Antonil (It: Giovanni Antonio Andreoni), *Cultura e opulencia do Brasil por suas drogas e minas* (Lisbon, 1711) has not been translated into English; an excellent French translation is available in the meticulous edition of André Mansuy (Paris: Institut des Hautes Études de l'Amérique Latine, 1968). Pedro Taques de Almeida Paes Leme, *Nobiliarchia paulistana, histórica e genealógica* (Rio de Janeiro, 1912) and *História da Capitania de São Vicente* (Rio de Janeiro, 1847); Gaspar da Madre de Deus, *Memórias para a história da Capitania de São Paulo* (Lisbon, 1797). See Rodrigues, *História*, pp. 129-141 and 142-151, and Alan K. Manchester, "Some Brazilian Colonial Historians," *Bulletin of the Pan-American Union* 68 (September-October 1934), 634-647 and 698-707.

5. João Capistrano de Abreu, *Capítulos de história colonial* (Rio de Janeiro, 1907), and *Caminhos antigos e povoamento do Brasil* (Rio de Janeiro, 1930); Sérgio Buarque de Holanda, *Monções* (Rio de Janeiro, 1945), and *Caminhos e fronteiras* (Rio de Janeiro, 1957); Gilberto Freyre, *Brazil: An Interpretation* (New York, NY, 1945), *New World in the Tropics* (New York, NY, 1959); Caio Prado Júnior, *Formação do Brasil contemporâneo* (São Paulo, 1942), available in English as *The Colonial Background to Modern Brazil* (Berkeley and Los Angeles, 1969), and *História econômica do Brasil* (São Paulo, 1945).

6. Afonso d'Escragnole Taunay, *História geral das bandeiras paulistas*, 11 vols. (São Paulo, 1924-1950). A selection of writings on the *bandeirantes*, with a useful introduction, is by Richard M. Morse, ed., *The Bandeirantes: The Historical Role of the Brazilian Pathfinders* (New York, NY, 1965); Jaime Cortesão, *Raposo Tavares e a formação territorial do Brasil* (Rio de Janeiro, 1958). More interpretive are: Vianna Moog, *Bandeirantes and Pioneers* (New York, NY, 1964) and Ricardo Cassiano, *Marcha para Oeste: a influencia da "bandeira" na formação social e política do Brasil*, 2 vols. (Rio de Janeiro, 1959). For individuals, see Manuel da Silveira Soares Cardozo, "The Last Adventure of Fernão Dias Pais, 1674-1681," *Hispanic American Historical Review* 26:4 (November 1946), 467-479, and Virginia Freehafer, "Domingos Jorge Velho: Conqueror of Brazilian Backlands," *The Americas* 27:2 (October 1970), 161-184.

7. Euclides da Cunha, *Os Sertões* (1902), translated as *Rebellion in the Backlands* by Samuel Putnam (Chicago, IL, 1957); Henry Koster, *Travels in Brazil* (London, 1816); see also João Guimarães Rosa, *Grande sertão: Veredas* (1956), translated as *The Devil to Pay in the Backlands* by Joseph Taylor and Harriet de Onis (New York, NY, 1963).

8. Lucien Febvre, "Frontière," in Peter Burke, ed., *A New Kind of History: From the Writings of Febvre* (New York, NY: Harper and Row, 1973); Fulmer Mood, "Notes on the History of the Word "Frontier," *Agricultural History* 22:2 (April 1948), 78-83. The introduction by Howard Lamar and Leonard Thompson, eds., to *The Frontier in History: North America and South Africa Compared* (New Haven, CT, and London, 1981) provides an interesting theoretical framework.

9. Excellent starting points are: Harold Blakemore and C. T. Smith, eds., *Latin American Geographical Perspectives* (London, 1971); Preston E. James and C. W. Minkel, *Latin America*, 5th ed. (New York, NY, 1986). For Brazil, see: M. Katzman, "The Brazilian Frontier in Comparative Perspective," *Comparative Studies in Society and History* 17:3 (July 1975), 266-285.

10. This is based on Stuart B. Schwartz's superb *Sugar Plantations in the Formation of Brazilian Colonial Society* (London and New York, NY, 1985), pp. 75-97, 106-107.

11. For a modern perspective on the agricultural frontier, see M. W. Nicholls, "The Agricultural Frontier in Modern Brazilian History: The State of Paraná, 1920-1965," in *Cultural Change in Brazil: Papers from the Midwest Association of Latin American Studies* (Muncie, IN, 1969). A historical overview is C. R. Boxer, *The Golden Age of Brazil, 1695-1750* (Berkeley and Los Angeles, CA, 1962). A miscrostudy is William Fredric Harrison's "The Struggle for Land in Colonial Brazil: The Private Captaincy of Paraíba do Sul, 1533-1753" (Ph.D. diss., University of New Mexico, 1970).

12. On ranching and cattlemen specifically, see: Rollie E. Poppino, "Cattle Industry in Colonial Brazil," *Mid-America* 31 (October 1949), 219-247; Spencer Leitman, "Slave Cowboys in the Cattle Lands of Southern Brazil, 1800-1850," *Revista de História* 51:10 (January-March 1975), 167-177; Mario José Maestri Filho, *O escravo no Rio Grande do Sul: A charqueada e a génese do escravismo gaúcho* (Porto Alegre, 1984); Luiz R. B. Mott, "Fazendas de gado do Piauí, 1697-1762," *Anais do VIII simpósio nacional dos professores universitários de história* (São Paulo, 1976), and "Estructura demografica das fazendas de gado do Piauí colonial; um caso de provoamento rural centrifugo," *Ciência e Cultura* 30 (1978), 196-210; a contemporary perspective is provided by P. Riviere, *The Forgotten Frontier: Ranchers of Northern Brazil* (New York, NY, 1972).

13. A. J. R. Russell-Wood, "Colonial Brazil: The Gold Cycle, c. 1690-1750," in Leslie Bethell, ed., *The Cambridge History of Latin America*, vol. 2, *Colonial Latin America* (London and New York, NY, 1984), esp. pp. 547-559.

14. For studies of the "move to the west,"and to the fringes of colonial Brazil, see: Bernardo Pereira de Berredo, *Annaes históricos do Estado do Maranhão* (Lisbon, 1749); H. C. Palmatory, *The River of the Amazonas: Its Discovery and Early Exploration, 1500-1743* (New York, NY, 1965); Walter N. Breymann, "The Opening of the Amazon, 1540-1640" (Ph.D. diss., University of Illinois, 1950); David G. Sweet, "A Rich Realm of Nature Destroyed: The Middle Amazon Valley, 1640-1750" (Ph.D. diss., University of Wisconsin, 1974); David M. Davidson, "Rivers and Empire: The Madeira Route and the Incorporation of the Brazilian Far West, 1737-1808" (Ph.D. diss., Yale, 1970) and "How the Brazilian West Was Won: Freelance and State on the Mato Grosso Frontier, 1737-1752," in Dauril Alden, ed., *Colonial Roots of Modern Brazil* (Berkeley and Los Angeles, CA, 1973), pp. 61-106; Lewis A. Tambs, "Brazil's Expanding Frontiers," *The Americas* 23:2 (October 1966), 165-179. For the southern expansion of Brazil, see Moysés Vellinho, *Brazil South: Its Conquest and Settlement*, translated by Linton Lomas Barrett and Marie McDavid Barrett, preface by Erico Veríssimo (New York, NY, 1968). See also James Lockhart and Stuart B. Schwartz, *Early Latin America* (Cambridge, MA, 1983), pp. 253-304. The most effective syntheses are: Basílio de Magalhães, *Expansão geográphica do Brasil colonial*, 2d ed., (São Paulo, 1935) and *História geral da civilização brasileira*, Tomo 1, *A época colonial*, Vol. 1, introdução geral de Sérgio Buarque de Holanda (São Paulo, 1960), pp. 257-379.

15. Luís Ferrand de Almeida, *A diplomácia portuguesa e os límites meridionais do Brasil*, Vol. 1, *1493-1700* (Coimbra, 1957); Jaime Cortesão, *Alexandre de Gusmão e o Tratado de Madrid (1750)*, 10 vols. (Rio de Janeiro, 1952-1963); an excellent summary is José Carlos de Macedo Soares, *Fronteiras do Brasil no regime colonial* (Rio de Janeiro, 1939); Guillermo Kratz, *El tratado hispano-portugués de límites de 1750 y sus consecuencias* (Rome, 1954). On the 1855 boundary conference and supporting documentation, see *Protocoles de la conférence su la délimitation des Guyanes française et brésilienne* (Rio de Janeiro: Typ. Universelle de Laemmert, 1857). A cornucopia of bibliographical knowledge is the catalog by Dagmar Schäffer for the exhibition, *Portuguese Expansion to the West and the Formation of Brazil, 1450-1800* (Providence, RI: The John Carter Brown Library, 1988).

16. Nestor Goulart Reis Rilho, *Evolução urbana do Brasil, 1500-1720* (São Paulo, 1968); Edmundo Zenha, *O município no Brasil* (São Paulo, 1948); Russell-Wood, "Local Government in Portuguese America: A Study in Cultural Divergence," *Comparative Studies in Society and History* 16 (March 1974), 187-231; Richard M. Morse, "Brazil's Urban Development: Colony and Empire," in Russell-Wood, ed., *From Colony to Nation: Essays on the Independence of Brazil* (Baltimore, MD, 1975), pp. 155-181. A different perspective is provided by Roberta Marx Delson, *New Towns in Colonial Brazil: Spatial and Social Planning of the Eighteenth Century* (Ann Arbor, MI, 1979).

17. *Real Forte Príncipe de Beira*. With an essay by José Maria de Souza Nunes; cartography and iconography by Isa Adonias (Rio de Janeiro: Spala Editora, Ltda., 1985); this is the most comprehensive study of a single fortress. There is nothing for colonial Brazil to compare with that available for Portuguese East and West Africa: C. R. Boxer and Carlos de Azevedo, *Fort Jesus and the Portuguese in Mombasa, 1593-1729*

(London, 1960), or A. W. Lawrence, *Trade Castles and Forts of West Africa* (London: Jonathan Cape, 1963).

18. Mario Rodriguez, "Colonia do Sacramento: Focus of Spanish-Portuguese Rivalry in the Plata, 1640-1683" (Ph.D. diss., University of California, Berkeley, 1953); Dauril Alden, *Royal Government in Colonial Brazil, with Special Reference to the Administration of the Marquis of Lavradia, Viceroy, 1769-1779* (Berkeley and Los Angeles, CA, 1968). See also José C. Canales, "Rio Grande do Sul in Luso-Spanish Platine Rivalry, 1626-1737" (Ph.D. diss., University of California, Berkeley, 1959). For disputes on Brazil's northern frontier, see Raul d'Eça, "A History of the Conflict and Settlement of Boundaries between Brazil and the British, Dutch and French Guianas," (Ph.D. diss., George Washington University, Washington, DC, 1936).

19. The Bahian historian Sebastião da Rocha Pitta (*História da America Portugueza* [Lisbon, 1730]) employed a variety of words with quite specific connotations: *fronteira* to designate a frontier such as that represented by the Camon fort on the frontier with French Cayenne; *demarcação* to designate the territorial limits of the colony; *continente* to designate the total territoriality of Brazil. Other words were *selva*, associated with jungle, and *mato*, which had a specific meaning as a type of undergrowth but was devoid of any sense of frontier.

20. Maps of the colonial period do not employ these terms; furthermore, the designation *sertão* is invariably accompanied by an ethnographic qualifier, e.g., "sertão dos tapuias." On maps as historical sources, see Jaime Cortesão, *História do Brasil nos velhos mapas*, 2 vols. (Rio de Janeiro, 1965-1971).

21. For European-Indian contacts on the "frontier," see John Hemming, "Indians and the Frontier in Colonial Brazil," in Leslie Bethell, ed., *The Cambridge History of Latin America*, vol. 2 (Cambridge, MA, 1984), pp. 501-545. A systematic study of *poderosos do sertão* has yet to be made: for one example of the species, see Russell-Wood, "Manuel Nunes Viana: Paragon or Parasite of Empire?" *The Americas* 87:4 (April 1981), 479-498. See also Billy Jaynes Chandler, *The Feitosas and the Sertão dos Inhamuns: The History of a Family and a Community in Northeast Brazil, 1700-1930* (Gainesville, FL, 1972).

22. A term coined by Philip D. Curtin in the 1960s (personal communication); see his *The Rise and Fall of the Plantation Complex: Essays in Atlantic History* (Cambridge, MA, 1989), pp. 92-96.

23. R. K. Kent, "Palmares: An African State in Brazil," *Journal of African History* 6:2 (1965), 161-175; see also Stuart B. Schwartz, "The Mocambo: Slave Resistance in Colonial Bahia," *Journal of Social History* 3:4 (Summer 1970), 313-333.

24. For a North American point of comparison, see John Stilgoe's fascinating *Common Landscape of America, 1580-1845* (New Haven, CT, and London, 1982), esp. pp. 7-21.

25. An Englished version of this letter is available in E. Bradford Burns, *A Documentary History of Brazil* (New York, NY, 1966), pp. 20-29.

26. These estimates are based on John Hemming, *Red Gold: The Conquest of the Brazilian Indians, 1500-1760* (Cambridge, MA, 1978), pp. 487-501. For the colonial and later periods, *Red Gold* should be read in conjunction with Hemming's *Amazon Frontier: The Defeat of the Brazilian Indians* (Cambridge, MA, 1987), on which much of the following account is based. Edward H. Spicer, *Cycles of Conquest: The Impact of Spain,*

Mexico, and the United States on the Indians of the Southwest, 1533-1960 (Tucson, AZ, 1962) provides a basis for comparison to the Brazilian experience.

27. The classic study of Indian-Portuguese relations in the early period remains Alexandar Marchant, *From Barter to Slavery: The Economic Relations of Portuguese and Indians in the Settlement of Brazil, 1500-1580* (Baltimore, MD, 1942). On Indian labor, see Stuart B. Schwartz, "Indian Labor and the New World Plantations: European Demands and Indian Responses in Northeastern Brazil," *American Historical Review* 57:1 (February 1977), 69-81; Colin MacLachlan, "The Indian Labor Structure in the Portuguese Amazon, 1700-1800," in Alden, ed., *Colonial Roots*, pp. 199-230. For a broader discussion of Indian rights, see Mathias C. Kieman, O. F. M., *The Indian Policy of Portugal in the Amazon Region, 1614-1693* (Washington, DC, 1954). A controversial interpretation is Georg Thomas, *Die portugiesische Indianerpolitik in Brasilien, 1500-1640* (Berlin, 1968). "Just War" and differing Portuguese attitudes and policies toward persons of African descent and Native Americans are discussed by Russell-Wood, "Iberian Expansion and the Issue of Black Slavery: Changing Portuguese Attitudes, 1440-1770," *American Historical Review* 83:1 (February 1978), 16-42.

28. Colin MacLachlan, "The Indian Directorate: Forced Acculturation in Portuguese America (1757-1799)," *The Americas* 28:4 (April 1972), 357-387, and Hemming, *Amazon Frontier*, pp. 40-61.

29. Simão de Vasconcelos, *Chrónica da Companhia de Jesu do estado do Brasil . . .* (Lisbon, 1663); Fernão Cardim, *Tratado do clima e terra do Brasil* and *Do princípio e orígem dos indios do Brasil . . .*; Manoel da Nóbrega, *Cartas do Brasil do Padre Manoel da Nóbrega (1549-1560)* (Rio de Janeiro, 1931); José de Anchieta, *Arte da grammática da lingua mais usada na costa do Brasil* (Coimbra, 1595). See Rodrigues, *História*, pp. 256-272. Of these, only Cardim is available in English. Samuel Purchas, *Hakluytus Posthumus or Purchas His Pilgrimes* (1625), 20 vols. (Glasgow, 1905-1907), vol. 16, pp. 417-517.

30. A useful general survey in English is Magnus Mörner, *The Political and Economic Activities of the Jesuits in the La Plata Region: The Hapsburg Era* (Stockholm, 1953); see Hemming, *Red Gold*, pp. 97-118, 419 ff.

31. Dauril Alden, "Black Robes versus White Settlers: The Struggle for 'Freedom of the Indians' in Colonial Brazil," in Howard Peckham and Charles Gibson, eds., *Attitudes of Colonial Powers toward the American Indian* (Salt Lake City: University of Utah Press, 1969), pp. 19-45.

32. The dearth of Portuguese accounts and iconography for Brazil has yet to be explained, contrasting with the ethnographic interest shown by other Europeans in both Amerindians and Africans in the New World. Three contemporary accounts, each of whose authors brought a different religious perspective, with much of ethnographic interest, are: Hans Staden, *Warhaftige Historia und Beschreibung einer Landtschafft der wilden, nacketen grimmigen Menschenfresser Leuthen in der Newenwelt America gelegen* (Marburg, 1557); André Thevet, *Les singularités de la France Antartique, autrement nommée Amérique* (Paris, 1557); and Jean de Léry, *Histoire d'un voyage fait en la terre du Brésil autrement dite Amérique* (La Rochelle, 1578). All are available in English translations.

33. Hemming's two volumes, *Red Gold* and *Amazon Frontier*, should be read in conjunction as a chilling chronicle of inhumanity, exploitation, and exchange.

34. Russell-Wood, *The Black Man in Slavery and Freedom in Colonial Brazil* (London 1982), pp. 173-178, 184-186.

35. Philip D. Curtin, *The Atlantic Slave Trade: A Census* (Madison, WI, 1969); Maurício Goulart, *Escravidão africana no Brasil* (São Paulo, 1949); Herbert S. Klein, *African Slavery in Latin America and the Caribbean* (New York, NY, 1986); Robert E. Conrad, *World of Sorrow: The African Slave Trade to Brazil* (Baton Rouge, LA, and London, 1986).

36. Russell-Wood, *The Black Man in Slavery and Freedom*, pp. 50-66, 104-127; Mary C. Karasch, *Slave Life in Rio de Janeiro, 1808-1850* (Princeton, NJ, 1987), pp. 185-213; for an unusual, possibly unique, documented act of accommodation, see Stuart B. Schwartz, "Resistance and Accommodation in Eighteenth-Century Brazil: The Slaves' View of Slavery," *Hispanic American Historical Review* 57:1 (February 1977), 69-81.

37. Volumes have been written on African slavery and race relations in Brazil. Excellent starting points are: Carl Degler, *Neither Black nor White: Slavery and Race Relations in Brazil and the United States* (New York, NY, 1971); the classic works of Gilberto Freyre, *Casa-grande e senzala* (1933), translated as *The Masters and the Slaves: A Study in the Development of Brazilian Civilization* by Samuel Putnam (New York, NY, 1946) and *Sobrados e mucambos* (1936) translated as *The Mansions and the Shanties*, Harriet de Onis, ed. (New York, NY, 1963); also available in English translation is Katia M. de Queirós Mattos, *To Be a Slave in Brazil, 1550-1888* (New Brunswick, NJ, 1986).

38. Stephen Gudeman and Stuart B. Schwartz, "Baptismal Godparents in Slavery: Cleansing Original Sin in Eighteenth-Century Bahia," in Raymond Smith, ed., *Kinship Ideology and Practice in Latin America* (Chapel Hill, NC, 1984), pp. 35-58; Russell-Wood, *Black Man in Slavery and Freedom*, pp. 187-190.

39. Russell-Wood, *Black Man in Slavery and Freedom*, pp. 187-190.

40. For the technology of sugar processing, see Schwartz, *Sugar Plantations*, pp. 98-159; on mining, see Russell-Wood, "The Gold Cycle," pp. 579-584, and *The Black Man*, pp. 104-127; Francisco Vidal Luna, *Minas Gerais: Escravos e senhores, 1718-1804* (São Paulo, 1981); W. L. von Eschwege, *Pluto Brasiliensis*, 2 vols. (Berlin, 1833).

41. Laura de Mello e Souza, *O diabo e a terra de Santa Cruz* (São Paulo, 1987). On African religions, see Pierre Verger, *Note sur le culte des Orishá et Vodoun à Bahia, la Baie de tous les saints au Brésil et l'ancienne Côte des Esclaves en Afrique* (Dakar, 1957); Roger Bastide, *O Candomblé da Bahia* (São Paulo, 1961), *African Civilizations in the New World*, Peter Green, trans. (New York, NY, 1971), and *The African Religions of Brazil: Toward a Sociology of the Interpretation of Civilizations*, Helen Sebba, trans. (Baltimore, MD, 1978); Juana Elbein dos Santos and Deoscorides dos Santos, "Ancestor Worship in Bahia: The Egún-Cult," *Journal de la Société des Américanistes* 58 (1969), 79-108, and Juana Elbein dos Santos, *Os Nagô e a morte: Padé, Asese e o culto Egún na Bahia* (Petropolis, 1976).

42. Russell-Wood, "Black and Mulatto Brotherhoods in Colonial Brazil," *Hispanic American Historical Review* 54:4 (November 1974), 567-602; Patricia Mulvey, "The Black Lay Brotherhoods of Colonial Brazil" (Ph.D. diss., City College of New York, 1976); Julita Scarano, *Devoção e escravadão. A irmandade de Nossa Senhora do Rosário dos Prêtos do Distrito Diamantino no século xviii* (São Paulo, 1976).

43. Germain Bazin, *Aleijadinho et la sculpture baroque author Brésil* (Paris, 1963); Nair Batista, "Pintores do Rio de Janeiro colonial: notas bibliográficas," *Revista do Património Histórico* 3 (1939), 103-121.

44. Hemming, *Red Gold*, pp. 124, 141, 194, 202, 262, 264, 375, 395, 423 for numerous examples. For a comprehensive account, see David P. Appleby, *The Music of Brazil* (Austin: University of Texas Press, 1983).

45. Francisco Curt Lange, *Archivo de música religiosa de la Capitania Geral das Minas Gerais, Brasil, siglo xviii: hallazqo, restauración, y prólogo* (Mendoza, 1951); "La música en Villa Rica: Minas Gerais, siglo xviii," *Revista Musical Chilena* 102-103 (1967-1968). José Ferreira Carrato, "O povoamento e a música religiosa em Minas Gerais no século xviii," *Revista de história de São Paulo* 31:64 (October-December 1965), 415-426.

46. Two studies which may be read in conjunction are: David Miller Driver, *The Indian in Brazilian Literature* (New York, NY, 1942), and Raymond Sayers, *The Negro in Brazilian Literature* (New York, NY, 1956). On African languages, see Yeda Pessoa de Castro, *Os falares africanos na interação social do Brasil colonia*, Centro de Estudios Baianos, no. 89 (Bahia: Universidad Federal da Bahia, 1980). Alexander Caldcleugh, *Travels in South America during the Years 1819-20-21 Containing an Account of the Present State of Brazil, Buenos Aires, and Chile*, 2 vols. (London, 1825).

47. I am indebted to Professor Janaína Amado of the Department of History of the Federal University of Goiás for stimulating discussion on frontiers and the notion of ambiguity in the word *sertão*.

3. Themes and Sources for Missionary History in Hispanic America

David Block

The Spanish mission has long been a staple of Latin American colonial history. While the profession often points to H. E. Bolton's 1917 address describing the mission as a frontier institution as beginning its organized study, historical work on the missions reaches back to the age of their operation. [1] This paper summarizes my reading of the historical sources in preparing an essay on the Jesuit Moxos reductions in colonial Charcas, an area located in what is now southern Bolivia. Those familiar with the contours of the historiography of Latin America will find my presentation predictable. Because of long-term interest in the missions, their study provides a chronicle of trends in the field. Nevertheless, the extension and variety of the mission enterprise offers a challenge to their summary. The historical record reveals Dominicans in Baja California and in the interior llanos of Venezuela and Colombia; Augustinians in southern Chile, Apolobamba, and the Meta; Mercedarians in Mainas, Chiloé, and Puntamayo; Capuchins on the Caribbean coast of South America; and Franciscans and Jesuits everywhere. And the activities of these missionary orders are documented in an extensive, growing literature. For instance, the 1986 volume of *HAPI* cites missionary studies in at least nineteen of its headings, ranging from "Acculturation" to "Serra, Junípero." In fact, the most significant lacuna in mission studies to date is synthesis, even of the sort that Max Moorhead gives us for the presidio. And while I cannot claim to succeed where others have feared to tread, I can try.

Contemporary Accounts

The first historians of Hispanic missions were the missionaries themselves. Because of the circumstances accruing on the frontier, missionaries' accounts often stand as the only surviving version of events critical to the reconstruction of mission history. The long-term interest in the missions, in the activities of missionary religious orders, and—most recently—in the history of former frontier regions in the

Americas has led to the systematic collecting, editing, publishing, and translating of these accounts.

Work on these primary documents from the American Southwest is well developed. The histories and correspondence of men such as Miguel Venegas, Andrés Pérez de Ribas, Eusebio Kino, and Junípero Serra have been published several times, and all since 1983.[3] Contemporary accounts also appear in monographic series such as the Jesuit-sponsored Monumenta Missionum Societatis Iesu and its subseries Monumenta Mexicana and Monumenta Peruana, in the Consejo Superior de Investigaciones Cientificas's *Biblioteca Missionalia Hispánica* (now apparently complete in 27 volumes), and in the newly launched *Monumenta Amazónica*, which has produced two titles since its inauguration in 1987.

Although not as well known as their northern counterparts, contemporary accounts of the Amazonian, Orinoco, Rio de la Plata, and Araucanian missions are available for consultation in research libraries. The works of Joseph Gumilla on the llanos of Venezuela, of Manuel Biedma for the Peruvian montaña, Alonso de Ovalle for Chile, and Pedro Lozano for Paraguay have all appeared in modern editions.[4] Josep Barnadas's recent transcription of the manuscript history of a Hungarian Jesuit from Moxos stands out as an example of the scholarship that often accompanies the publication of missionary texts. In translating to Spanish the Latin original of Francisco Xavier Eder's *Description provinciae moxitarum in Regno Peruano*, Barnadas appends a biography of the missionary and a substantial essay on the history of the Moxos missions under Jesuit rule.[5]

The contemporary accounts—as their most recent editors remind us—are not histories in the modern sense. The missionaries, and even the official historians of the orders, chronicled the events of their lifetimes. Their works are often discursive, always ethnocentric, and sometimes misleading. The sources speak, in the Rankeian phrase, but with heavy accents. Yet the publication and republication of these accounts continue unabated, and as well they should since this activity makes valuable primary sources available to researchers and to the general reading public.

Administrative-Institutional Studies

As professional historians began to examine the missions, they demonstrated the need to integrate activities on the frontier with those of the Spanish empire. Bolton and his students brought this approach to the missions of North America, but a full list of practitioners is longer than the number of missionary enterprises. The administrative-institutional historians stress the foundation, expansion, and decline of mission systems, normally limiting their focus to a particular geographic area or missionary order.

Bolton's 1915 work, *Texas in the Middle Eighteenth Century*, which he subtitled *Studies in Spanish Colonial History and Administration*, stands as a prototype of this approach. [6] Bolton demonstrates the importance of missionary foundations as a counter to the expansion of European rivals in the Americas and the often-strained interplay between missionary and secular objectives.

Following Bolton's lead, and often his direct inspiration, a number of North Americans wrote histories of missionary systems on their continent. Representative of these works are studies of the Dominicans in Lower California by Peverel Meigs, of the Jesuits in northern Mexico by Peter Masten Dunne, and of the Franciscans in Coahuila and Texas by Michael McCloskey and in Florida by Maynard Geiger. [7] These regional studies, all completed in the 1940s and 1950s, delineate the profound differences among the missions systems of the Spanish borderlands. While the authors do not make comparisons themselves, their works demonstrate important differences in the location of stations (i.e., propinquity to sources of supply), in the cultures of the native people approached by the missions, and in the ways in which the missionary orders approached their tasks.

Administrative studies from the last two decades expand the themes of missionary history and extend their geographic focus beyond the borderlands. In his book, *A Spanish Frontier in the Enlightened Age*, Kieran McCarty examines the transition of the Jesuit missions of Sonora and Arizona to Franciscan control after 1767. [8] In describing the Franciscan takeover, McCarty broadens the traditional administrative approach to include a useful examination of the economic state of the missions. A second work that expands the themes of mission studies in the borderlands is Father Charles Polzer's *Rules and Precepts of the Jesuit Missions of Northern New Spain*, which examines the internal structures of one prominent mission order through the codes of conduct written to govern priests' activities on the frontier. [9] Polzer provides a number of insights into the patterns of Jesuit mission governance and how the Society's concerns for both ascetic and administrative matters were reflected in its rules and precepts.

In South America the eminent priest-historians Guillermo Furlong Cardiff, José del Rey Fajardo, and Lino Gómez Canedo have studied the important Jesuit and Franciscan systems in Paraguay, Moxos, and Venezuela. [10] All present solid research on the missions and on the missionaries' role in opening frontier regions to European penetration. These historians' command of the religious sources, including access to religious materials sometimes denied other researchers, makes their works especially valuable for biographical data on the missionaries.

Unlike the borderlands where Jesuits and Franciscans effectively dominated the mission fields, South America saw a wider religious participation on the frontier. Buenaventura de Carrocera's studies of the Capuchin missions on the coastal llanos of Venezuela and Guayana offer an interesting contrast to the activities of the more active missionary orders. [11] In Cumaná some thirty mission sites were staffed by less than a dozen Capuchin priests for much of the eighteenth century. And the order's strict observance of its vow of poverty forced the missionaries to divide their time between conversion and begging for alms in Caracas. Fernando del Campo Pozo's *Los Agustinos en la evangelización de Venezuela* and Pedro Nolasco Pérez's *Historia de las misiones mercedarias en América* offer well-researched presentations of the efforts of other "lesser" missionary orders in South America. [12]

Administrative studies provide the basic framework for understanding the mission experience. Their presentations of chronologies, personalities, and events introduce the generalist reader to the historical significance of the missions and give scholars a springboard from which to apply additional analysis. Despite the longevity of this approach, valuable administrative studies have appeared in this decade, and some important mission areas still await definitive capture of the basic events of their history. For instance, there are no modern treatments for the important Jesuit reduction system of Chiquitos.

Historical studies of the missions have not escaped the ascendancy of social and economic methodologies. Although precursors of these approaches appeared as early as the 1930s, historians trained in the boom (and postboom) years have begun to examine the missions as centers of culture change and foci of economic activity. Their work relies on primary materials produced by the missionaries and central religious bureaucracies but emphasizes the importance of group behavior over individual action. A benchmark of the emergency of these new directions is the appearance of the journal *Cuadernos para la Historia de la Evangelización en América Latina* (1986—) which takes its place beside the long-running *Missionalia Hispanica* as an organ for missionary studies.

Social History

For lack of a better organizer, I suggest "ethnohistory" as a term to order one set of recent social histories of the missions. Those who practice this approach stress the importance of reconstructing the life patterns of the Indian in the missions. S. F. Cook's *Population Trends among the California Indians* foreshadowed this trend toward ethnohistory by nearly thirty years. [13] Using mission censuses held in the University of California Bancroft Library at Berkeley, Cook carefully pieced together a compendium of vital statistics for Indians under mission rule. He established the now familiar patterns of high death and low fertility rates and of mission populations dependent on new immigrants to maintain their numbers. More important for the future directions of Native American demographic history, Cook suggested the wave of steep decline, stabilization, and slow recovery of an Indian population which he would later reiterate for central Mexico in his collaboration with Professor Woodrow Borah. Succeeding studies of frontier mission Indians, and here I include my own work and Mardith Schuetz's "The Indians of the San Antonio Missions, 1718-1821," have verified Cook's demographic models for other systems. [14]

In addition to demography, ethnohistorians have examined the Indians' participation in the missions. The missionaries' success in attracting neophytes has been attributed to two basic factors: continuities between aboriginal culture and missionary approaches and the systematic use of European goods as incentives. In his study of the Franciscan missions among the Guaraní, Louis Necker argues that the priests succeeded in assuming the traditional native role of shaman-chief. [15] Other studies have stressed the importance of continuities between aboriginal caciques and those who held office in the model cabildos introduced by the missionaries. Alfred Métraux's stimulating essay, "The Revolution of the Ax," highlighted the importance of missionary-introduced tools to native peoples of the tropical forest. Following Métraux's lead, recent students of the missions have pointed to the irresistible appeal of food, tools, and baubles provided in the missions. [16]

Ethnohistorians have also begun to reexamine mission Indian social structure. Evidence from San Antonio, Paraguay, and Moxos overturns any surviving notions of mission communism and suggests the existence of populations differentiated by inherited political positions and by occupational specialization as well as by age and sex. Moxos's eighteenth-century censuses divided the native peoples into two broad categories that segregated those engaged in European arts and offices, such as musicians and smiths, from those who performed subsistence activities. [17]   And David Owens's thesis on the Jesuit reductions shows that the new system created niches for widows and orphans, states that did not exist in aboriginal society. [18]

The increasing attention to mission societies is not limited to their Indian populations. The missionary staffs have also undergone scrutiny for patterns of birthplace, training, and service records. The multinational character of Jesuit priests and brothers has been examined by Josep Barnadas and the creole-peninsular rivalries that took place within the all-"Spanish" Franciscan missions of Peru by Antonine Tibesar. [19]   Pedro Borges Morán's extensive research into the background of European missionaries departing for the Indies shows that colonial demands for personnel resulted in increasingly younger and less-trained men entering service. [20]   Other interesting observations emerge from commentaries on the missionaries' service records published by Geiger for the California Franciscans, Block (Moxos Jesuits), Francisco Morales (Mexican Franciscans), and Jay F. Lehnertz (Franciscans of the Peruvian central montaña). [21]   These studies show remarkable disparities in length of service between long duration in California and Moxos and very short in the montaña, a statistic with obvious implications for continuity in the missions.

The daily activities of the missionaries remain to be explored by social historians. A part of this lacuna is the lack of documentation in areas that lacked Spanish functionaries such as judges and notaries. Theodore Treutline's thesis, a revealing examination of German missionaries' travel diaries, gives glimpses of the priests' lives, unfettered by the need to impress donors, religious superiors, or secular officials. [22]   But such studies are few and far between and accurate reconstructions of the missionary *vida cotidiana* remain an obvious gap in our knowledge.

Economic Studies

Despite long awareness of mission resources such as the Pious Fund of the Californias, exegesis of the sinews of mission support is largely the result of the past ten years of research. Treutline again proved ahead of his time as his "The Economic Regime of the Jesuit Missions in the Eighteenth Century in Sonora" provides an account of symbiosis between mines and missions in northwest Mexico. [23]   Evelyn Hu-DeHart reiterates Treutline's points in her study of the Yaqui under Spanish colonial rule. And Cynthia Radding's *Estructuras socioeconómicos* goes even further, insisting that by the end of the colonial period the missions served much as modern suburbs do, furnishing a hearth for workers who commuted to their work, in this case to neighboring mines and haciendas. [24] Radding's conclusions would be even more stimulating if they were supported by detailed evidence from archives in the Spanish settlements showing the Indians' economic roles and patterns of migration. Finally, Robert Archibald has published an extensive investigation, *The Economic Aspects of the California Missions*, which covers those stations' cottage industries in some detail. [25]

Magnus Mörner's work on the Jesuit mission economics in Rio de la Plata opened the broad theme of Jesuit mission support. Even though he concluded that the Jesuit presence in the Plata region was exceptional, Mörner introduced the components of a Jesuit economic system which united activities as diverse as the Guaraní's gathering of yerba maté and the Córdoba and Salta colegios' extensive participation in transport and the Potosí mule trade. [26] The discussion of Jesuit economics has assumed a life of its own, with Nicholas Cushner's works on the Argentine, Ecuadorian, and Peruvian systems adding to knowledge gained from the histories of Mexico and New Granada. [27] All concur that extensive investment in agricultural properties and the use of specialists to manage land and capital fueled Jesuit activities, including the missions.

My work on Moxos links the Jesuit missions there to the economic system directed out of Lima. Moxos had haciendas and *censos* dedicated to its support. [28] It was this income, generated at the core, which brought the tools and trade goods so attractive to Indian neophytes and furnished the mission churches in a way that can only be described as sumptuous. The Capuchin practice of interspersed conversion and begging has already been cited, and studies of Franciscan systems, such as those in San Antonio and the Peruvian montaña, describe mission support only in terms of Crown donations and trade with local Spanish communities. [29] As with a number of themes raised in this paper, the comparative significance of these diverse mission economic systems remains unexplored.

In commenting on the themes of mission history prior to 1917, Bolton was almost contemptuous. He cited "chronicles of the deeds of the Fathers, polemic discussions by sectarian partisans, or sentimental effusions with literary, edifying, or financial intent." The passage of seventy years has expanded historical treatment of the missions, removed most of the sectarian and sentimental, and perhaps added a leavening of permissiveness as well. For if this resumé of the mission literature reflects an ongoing evolution of themes and paradigms, it also points out the enduring contributions of methodologies no longer in vogue. The principal task before us now lies in uniting often divergent streams of research, generalizing episodes within them, and loosening them from their documentary contexts.

NOTES

1. Herbert Eugene Bolton, "The Mission as a Frontier Institution in the Spanish American Colonies," most recently published in *Bolton and the Spanish Borderlands*, John Francis Bannon, ed. (Norman: University of Oklahoma Press, 1964).

2. *Hispanic American Periodicals Index* (Los Angeles, CA: UCLA Latin American Center, 1988).

3. Eusebio Francisco Kino, *Crónica de la Pimería Alta: favores celestiales*, 3d ed. (Hermosillo: Gobierno del Estado de Sonora, 1985). Junípero Serra, *Escritos de Fray Junípero Serra*, Jacinto Fernández-Largo, ed., 5 vols. (Petra, Mallorca: [S. Vicedo], 1984). Miguel Venegas, *Obras californias del padre Miguel Venegas, S.J*, W. Michael Mathes, ed., 5 vols. (La Paz: Universidad Autónoma de Baja California, 1979-1983). Andrés Pérez de Ribas, [*Historia de los triumphos de nuestra santa fe*]. *Paginas para la história de Sonora: Triumphos de nuestra santa fe*, 3d ed. (Hermosillo: Gobierno del Estado de Sonora, 1985).

4. Joseph Gumilla, *El Orinoco ilustrado y defendido* (Caracas: Academia Nacional de Historia, 1963). Manuel Biedma, *La conquista franciscana del Alto Ucayali* (Lima: Milla Batres, 1981). Alonso de Ovalle, *Histórico relación del reino de Chile* (Santiago: Editorial Universitaria, 1979). Pedro Lozano, *Historia de la conquista del Paraguay, Río de la Plata y Tucumán*, 5 vols. (Buenos Aires: Caca Editora "Imprenta Popular," 1873).

5. Francisco J. Eder, *Breve descripción de las reducciones de Mojos*, Josep M. Barnadas, trans. and ed. (Cochabamba: Historia Boliviana, 1985).

6. Herbert Eugene Bolton, *Texas in the Middle Eighteenth Century: Studies in Spanish Colonial History and Administration* (Berkeley: University of California Press, 1915).

7. Peveril Meigs, *The Dominican Missionary Frontier of Lower California* (Berkeley: University of California Press, 1935). Peter Masten Dunne, *Pioneer Jesuits in Northern Mexico* (Berkeley: University of California Press, 1944) and *Pioneer Black Robes on the West Coast* (Berkeley: University of California Press, 1940). Michael Brendan McCloskey, *The Formative Years of the Missionary College of Santa Cruz of Querétero, 1683-1733* (Washington, DC: The Catholic University of America, 1937).

8. Kieran McCarty, *A Spanish Frontier in the Enlightened Age: Franciscan Beginnings in Sonora and Arizona, 1767-1800* (Washington, DC: Academy of American Franciscan History, 1981).

9. Charles W. Polzer, *Rules and Precepts of the Jesuit Missions of Northwestern New Spain* (Tucson: University of Arizona Press, 1976).

10. Guillermo Furlong Cardiff, *Misiones y sus pueblos de Guaraníes* (Buenos Aires: Imprenta Balmes, 1962). José del Rey Fajardo, *Misiones jesuíticas en la orinoquía* (Caracas: Universidad Católica Andrés Bello, 1977). Rubén Vargas Ugarte,

Historia de la Compañia de Jesús en el Perú, 4 vols. (Burgos: Imprenta de Aldecoa, 1963-1965). Lino Gómez Canedo, *La provincia franciscana de Santa Cruz de Caracas*, 3 vols. (Caracas: Academia Nacional de Historia, 1974).

11. Buenaventura de Carrocera, *Misión de los Capuchinos en Cumaná*, 2 vols. (Caracas: Academia Nacional de la Historia, 1972) and *Misión de las Capuchinos en Guayana*, 3 vols. (Caracas: Academia Nacional de la Historia, 1979).

12. Fernando del Campo Pozo, *Los Agustinos en la evangelización de Venezuela* (Caracas: Universidad Católica Andrés Bello, 1979). Pedro Nolasco Pérez, *Historia de las misiones mercedarias en América* (Madrid: [Revista Estudios], 1966).

13. S. F. Cook, *Population Trends among the California Indians* (Berkeley and Los Angeles: University of California Press, 1940).

14. David Block, "In Search of El Dorado: Spanish Entry into Moxos, A Tropical Frontier, 1550-1767" (Ph.D. diss., University of Texas, 1980). Mardith K. Schuetz, "The Indians of the San Antonio Missions, 1718-1821" (Ph.D. diss., University of Texas, 1980).

15. Louis Necker, *Indiens Guaraní et chamanes franciscains: les premiers réductions du Paraguay (1580-1800)* (Paris: Editions Anthropos, 1979).

16. Alfred Métraux, "The Revolution of the Ax," *Diogenes* 25 (1959), 28-40. For instance, see Ignacion del Río, *Conquista y aculturación en la California jesuítica 1697-1768* (México, D.F.: UNAM, 1984).

17. Block, "El Dorado," pp. 301-303.

18. David James Owens, "A Historical Geography of the Indian Missions in the Jesuit Province of Paraguay: 1609-1768" (Ph.D. diss., University of Kansas, 1977).

19. Josep Barnadas, "Introdución," to Eder, *Breve descripción*. Antonine Tibesar, "The Alternativa: A Study in the Spanish-Creole Relations in Seventeenth Century Peru," *The Americas* 11 (January 1955), 229-283.

20. Pedro Borges Morán, *El envío de misioneros a América durante la época española* (Salamanca: Universidad Pontifica, 1977).

21. Maynard Geiger, "Biographical Data on the California Missions," *California Historical Society Quarterly* 44:4 (December 1965), 291-310. Block, "El Dorado," pp. 260-266. Francisco Morales, *Ethnic and Social Background of the Franciscan Friars in Seventeenth Century Mexico* (Washington, DC: Academy of American Franciscan History, 1973). Jay F. Lehnertz, "Lands of the Infidels: The Franciscan in the Central Montaña of Peru, 1709-1824 (Ph.D. diss., University of Wisconsin, 1974).

22. Theodore Treutline, "Jesuit Travel to America (1678-1756) as Recorded in the Travel Diaries of German Jesuits" (Ph.D. diss., University of California, Berkeley, 1934).

23. Theodore Treutline, "The Economic Regime of the Jesuit Missions in the Eighteenth Century in Sonora," *Pacific Historical Review* 8:3 (September 1939), 289-300.

24. Evelyn Hu DeHart, *Missionaries, Miners, and Indians* (Tucson: University of Arizona Press, 1981). Cynthia Radding, *Las estructuras socio-económicas de las misiones de la Primería Alta, 1768-1850* (Hermosillo: Instituto Nacional de Antropología e Historia, Centro Regional del Noroeste, 1979).

25. Robert Archibald, *The Economic Aspects of the California Missions* (Washington, DC: Academy of Franciscan History, 1978).

26. Magnus Mörner, *The Political and Economic Activities of the Jesuits in the La Plata Region: The Hapsburg Era* (Stockholm: Victor Petersens Bokindustri, 1953).

27. Nicholas P. Cushner, *Farm and Factory* (Albany, NY: State University of New York Press, 1982), *Jesuit Ranches and Agrarian Development in Colonial Argentina, 1650-1767* (Albany, NY: State University of New York Press, 1983), and *Lords of the Land* (Albany, NY: State University of New York Press, 1980). Herman Konrad, *A Jesuit Hacienda in Colonial Mexico* (Stanford, CA: Stanford University Press, 1983). Germán Colmenares, *Haciendas jesuitas en el Nuevo Reino de Granada, siglo xviii* (Bogotá: Universidad Nacional de Colombia, 1969).

28. David Block, "Links to the Frontier: Jesuit Supply of its Moxos Missions, 1683-1767," *The Americas* 37:2 (October 1980), 161-178.

29. See Schuetz, "Indians of San Antonio," and Lehnertz, "Lands of Infidels."

4. Sons (and Grandsons) of Bolton: The Development of Borderlands Historiography

Peter Stern

The Spanish borderlands stretch from deep in the heart of north-central Mexico almost to the Canada prairies, and from the Pacific in the west to the Atlantic shoes of the Carolinas in the east. This enormous expanse of territory has been since the turn of the century an endlessly fertile ground for the work of historians, anthropologists, geographers, and other social scientists. But what constitutes the borderlands or borderlands history? What are the geographical, the chronological, the disciplinary boundaries that define borderland studies? How did borderlands history arise, and how has it developed since its inception at UC Berkeley early in the twentieth century?

Scholars can agree on a core area of what might be defined as the Spanish borderlands: the northern states of Mexico and the greater southwest of the United States, northward to the Great Salt Lake and eastward to the forests of western Louisiana. The Spaniards also controlled Florida and organized missionary settlements in Georgia. A peace treaty in 1765 gave them control of the Mississippi Valley, and on one occasion they projected their military power as far north as Michigan. The borderlands run southward as well into contentious territory; from the moment the Spaniards leveled Tenochtitlan and looked beyond the Aztec ruins, the borderlands lay always to the north of the Central Valley of Mexico. First the frontier lay beyond Zacatecas; then missionaries and soldiers marched north and west to Culiacán and Sinaloa. A daring leap into the unknown brought them into the valley of the Río Grande as New Mexico was conquered and Santa Fe was established a thousand isolated miles from the capital of Mexico City. Still later they moved northeastward into Texas as foreign rivals began to penetrate south and west into territory the Spaniards claimed in search of the silver of New Spain.

It is clear that social scientists have in the borderlands an area of almost infinite boundaries in which to work. Some borderlands historians have confined themselves to what is today United States territory; others would argue that the northern tier of Mexican states must be added. But there are some who have urged even vaster territorial boundaries, suggesting that the "Greater Borderlands" include Central America, the Caribbean, and Gulf peripheries, together with all of "aridamerica."[1] Clearly we must delineate between a vast area that Spain claimed as its own and a much smaller area that was effectively Hispanic in language, culture, and religion. But if we argue about what composes the borderlands geographical, we can pinpoint with certainty the genesis of what we call borderlands history.

In 1893 a man delivered a paper at the American Historical Society that constitutes an "Origin of Species" for borderlands scholars. Oddly enough, he was not a Mexicanist, and he was speaking not of Spanish but of American (more properly United States) history. Frederick Jackson Turner's "The Significance of the Frontier in American History" opened a fruitful new territory for the history and formulated a thesis against which all frontier historians can compare their own areas and theories.[2] Whether one agrees with or dissents from Turner's viewpoint that the frontier significantly shaped the formation and development of American democracy (not to mention takes umbrage with Turner's definition of the frontier as the meeting point between savagery and civilization), we must acknowledge that his essay stimulated much historical speculation about what frontiers were or were not, and what effect they might have upon the development of societies.[3]

It has been argued that the effect of Turner's thesis upon Spanish borderlands scholarship has never been significant;[4] nevertheless, Herbert Eugene Bolton's earliest works upon the borderlands were to some degree affected by Turner. This is hardly surprising, considering Bolton earned his master's degree at the University of Wisconsin, and proudly called himself one of Turner's "boys." After Bolton arrived at Berkeley in 1911 he developed a course entitled "The History of the Americas," which asked the question, "Do the Americas Have a Common History?" Bolton answered in the affirmative, even if others did not.[5]

With Herbert Eugene Bolton we have the birth of borderlands history. But it is crucial to remember that Bolton was by training a U.S. historian, not a Latin Americanist; he was also a Hispanophile, a partisan of institutions and prominent men. "Heroic figures and the high drama of explorations and international rivalry captivated him," and he clearly saw the mission and presidio as institutions of supreme importance in the extension, holding, and "civilizing" of the frontier.[6]

Nevertheless, Bolton's contribution to borderlands historiography is impressive in both the number and breadth of his scholarly publications. His essay on the mission as a frontier institution is a

definitive work of institutional history and revealed his deep interest in
and profound respect for the work of Spanish missionaries. His book
on the Spanish borderlands, which he subtitled "a chronicle of Old
Florida and the Southwest," his works on the missionaries of the
Pacific Rim, his epic tale of Coronado ("knight of pueblo and plain"),
his two-volume compendium of the correspondence of Athanase de
Mézières—these set the standards for his own students and the
borderlands historians who succeeded him. [7]

At the same time we admire Bolton, we can make the evaluation
that Bolton's work is by today' standards rather old-fashioned history.
His deeply romantic and Hispanophile sentiments led him to paint a
one-dimensional and decidedly ethnocentric picture of borderlands
history: a struggle between the Catholic, European forces of light and
the darkness of aboriginal savagery. To Bolton, Coronado was a knight
of the plains; if one reads Jack Forbes or Elizabeth John, writing some
forty years later, one has the impression of a war criminal of the
foulest deeds. [8] Four decades later, ethnocentricity and Hispanophile
tendencies have given way to a more balanced assessment of Indian-
Spanish relations (not altogether unaffected by an abiding sense of
European guilt).

Bolton was a pioneer. Not only did he write a large number of
works on the borderlands, he trained an entire generation of graduate
students, and sired a new generation of fronteristas—the sons of
Bolton. [9]

The works of this second generation follow many of the same
paths that Bolton pioneered. Jesuits like Peter Dunne and John
Francis Bannon continued exploring the missionary frontier in Sonora,
Baja and Alta California, and the Tarahumara country. [10] Indeed,
Bannon not only became Bolton's dedicated historiographer, but also
wrote the first and, so far, only general synthetic work on the Spanish
borderlands. [11] Dunne and Bannon have been characterized as
apologists for the Spanish missionaries, but the work of early mission
chroniclers should not be judged by the sensibilities of the 1960s and
later decades.

Alfred Barnaby Thomas wrote a series of superb books that
border on administrative history, explorations of Spanish imperial
policy in the complex Indian situation of the frontier; Thomas's
excellent volumes of translated documents from the Spanish and
Mexican archives trace the evolution of the Spanish equivalent of "the
great game," a delicate minuet of war and bribery between warring
Indian nations. [12] (So prolific and important were Thomas's
contributions to borderlands historiography that he himself was

honored with a festschrift.) [13] Another great historian, Max Moorhead, epitomized the Boltonian institutional scholar; his work on the presidio remains the standard, indeed virtually the only, close examination of the other critical borderlands institution, the ally of and sometimes obstacle to the Spanish missionary enterprise. [14]   Other notable borderlands scholars trained or influenced by Bolton include Woodrow Borah, George Hammond, Lawrence Kinnaird, John Caughey, J. Lloyd Meechum, and John Tate Lanning.

At the same time that Bolton's sons were spreading their gospel in the United States, a small number of Mexican works were emerging on the borderlands.   It cannot escape notice that the overwhelming majority of borderlands histories have been written by scholars in the United States. Indeed, the term "borderlands" and the concept of the borderlands as a separate region are the product of *norteamericanos*—a fact that has been commented upon with some degree of asperity by borderlands historian, José Cuello. [15]   Cuello, a scholar of colonial Saltillo, laments that "borderlands history has mysteriously lagged behind the study of colonial Mexico's central regions since the end of World War II.   Only in recent years have we been able to catch a glimmer of demographic, economic or social history amidst the boundless desert of adventure stories, missionary chronicles, and institutional narratives for which borderlands history is known." [16]

I would like to second José Cuello's suggestion that Mexicanists lay claim to borderlands history as a legitimate field of Latin American, as opposed to United States, studies. With the sons and grandsons of Bolton Mexicanists reclaim from the United States the study of the north of colonial Mexico, the farthest reaches of the Spanish empire. Studying the borderlands as a microcosm of colonial Spanish society, an extension of Hapsburg and Bourbon America, is distinctly different from studying the area as a temporary appendage of Spain or Mexico, soon to be rightly gathered into the Anglo-Saxon fold as part of the manifest destiny of the United States.

Undeniably, borderlands history has lagged behind the study of the Mexican core area in the United States; it has done so to an even greater extent in Mexico among Hispanic historians.   Three early exceptions were Lino Gómez Canedo, Vito Alessio Robles, and Luis Navarro García. All wrote excellent regional histories: Alessio Robles on Coahuila; Navarro García on Sonora and Sinaloa; and Canedo on Texas. Furthermore, Navarro García's massive work on José de Gálvez and the office of *comandante general* of the *provincias internas* is everything one could wish of a carefully documented institutional history. [17]   But there is little doubt that the same tendency to concentrate investigation on central and southern Mexico, to the detriment and even belittlement of the far north, was a tendency even more marked among Mexican than among North American historians— although why this should be so is a matter that should be vigorously discussed by both groups.

Other scholars who are sons or heirs of Bolton and his legacy include Odie B. Faulk, Jack Holmes, Donald Cutter, Cleve Hallenbeck, Noel Loomis, Abraham Nasatir, Oakan L. Jones, Donald Worcester, Philip Wayne Powell, and Robert West.[18] These historians helped give borderlands history a much-needed legitimacy in the 1950s and '60s as a separate focus of study within both Latin American and United States historiography.

The first generation of Boltonians tended to concentrate on institutes or the actions of significant individuals. They are in the main Hispanophile or ethnocentric, often ignoring or denying the cultural validity of the indigenous societies transformed and finally destroyed by the Spanish, French, and North American intrusions. The grandsons and great-grandsons of Bolton reflect the changing currents of historiography, bringing to their work and appreciation for geography, ecology, demography, epidemiology, economics, sociology, anthropology, and even feminist history. Although these currents have occasionally produced bogus, trendy, or shamelessly simplistic scholarship,[19] they have also brought a necessary sense of balance to borderlands studies, reminding us, in the words of Jack Forbes, "that every frontier is actually two: the frontier of those who are advancing and the frontier of those who are being advanced upon."[20]

A seminal work which has set the standard for ethnohistorical writing since its appearance in 1962 is Edward Spicer's *Cycles of Conquest*. Spicer's sweeping, yet thoroughly researched and conceptualized narrative explored the acculturation of half a dozen Indian groups in the southwest Sonoran-Arizonan borderlands over a period of centuries. His sympathies are apparent throughout, although his objectivity is equally so.[21]

Two other works from the sixties went far in redressing the neglect of indigenous cultures in borderlands studies. Jack Forbes, himself a Native American, chronicled the interactions of Spaniards, Apaches, and Navajos in the first century after contact with a pen dipped in acid; indeed, so bitter and clear an indictment of the Spaniards does he draw that one is left with the impression that only a Nuremburg-style trial would begin to redress the injustices suffered by the Indians at the hands of Coronado and his men.[22] Elizabeth A. H. John's massive (800-plus pp.) work, *Storms Brewed in Other Men's*

Worlds, is a narrative chronicling the entire spectrum of relations between Pueblo, Apache, Comanche, and *norteño* tribes of Texas and the Spanish and French intruders and settlers over a period of two hundred and fifty years.   Throughout, her primary focus is on the shattering changes forced upon native societies through war, conquest, trade, and biological and cultural invasion.

At the same time that borderlands history was growing into an area of inquiry with an identity and legitimacy of its own, scholars were returning to examine and amplify, even to dispute the original ideas of Turner and his disciples.   James Leyburn, a sociologist, identified four types of frontiers, and attempted to characterize varying historical and geographical frontiers by economic and social criteria.   Leyburn moved away from the absolute dichotomies of the Turnerian frontier, writing that, "It is a region, it is a process, it is even a state of mind." [23] Marvin Mikesell, a geographer, criticized Turner and his followers for failing to make comparative studies.   After analyzing the American, Canada, Australian, and South African frontier experiences, Mikesell theorized that frontiers could be either inclusive (or assimilationist), or exclusive; he also suggested distinctions between static and dynamic frontiers. [24] Louis Hartz even revived the Germanic "germ" theories of historical development which Turner had opposed in the 1890s.   He proposed a fragment theory of development, in which each colonial society began as an imitation of the parent society; in spite of economic, demographic, and social growth and development, the colonial society will continue to model itself on its parent metropolis. [25]

The growing tendency toward comparative and interdisciplinary approaches is apparent in contemporary borderlands history. Borderlands studies has become more specialized and at the same time narrowly focused.   Like other branches of the discipline, it has become regionalized, cliometric, and ideological.   Current work on the borderlands tends to be social history.   Some of its most significant areas of research are Indian-Spanish relations (now examined from a neutral, if not aggressively anti-Spanish, viewpoint), regional history (micro populations in a macro context), institutional history (cabildos, *intendencias*, and missions), or economic and demographic changes in a frontier context.   Although the art of synthesis seems to have been lost, the borderlands historian is thriving.   The 1988 Latin American Studies Association Congress, for example, included a panel on northern Mexican regionalism, in which three historians examined political and economic issues in narrowly focused regional studies. [26]

Works like Michael Swan's on colonial Durango and Alicia Tjarks's on San Antonio de Béjar now seem to be the rule rather than the exception. [27] Indeed, demography has joined economics, sociology, anthropology, agricultural economics, religious studies, military history, urban studies, and many other disciplines as an acceptable focus for borderlands studies. [28]

Broad, sweeping narratives covering the frontier as a whole have given way to narrowly focused regional economic and social studies; [29] at the same time historians are examining race and class and the marginalization of frontier peoples in the borderlands. [30] Institutional histories have not disappeared: there are studies of the *mesta* and Spanish ranching as an institution and economic activity as important to borderlands studies as the mission and presidio. [31] Studies of the mission and the missionary continue to appear: notable names include Charles Polzer, Kieran McCarty, John Kessell, and Cynthia Radding de Murieta. [32] Examinations of Indian-Spanish relations, sometimes self-consciously free from ethnocentric bias, at other times clearly anti-Spanish, have added immeasurably to our conception of the borderlands from a non-Hispanic viewpoint: a few notable names are Elizabeth John, Evelyn Hu-deHart, and John Kessell again. [33] Cultural geographers like Michael E. Swan and Peter Gerhard continue in the tradition of Carl Sauer, the Berkeley-based scholar whose work exemplified the interdisciplinary approach to historical inquiry. [34] This interdisciplinary approach is most apparent in works that examine Indian mission history from social, economic, demographic, and acculturational perspectives. [35]

At the same time that borderlands history has been accepted as a subfield within Latin American (as opposed to U.S.) history, Hispanic historians have rediscovered the frontier as part of Spanish colonial history (although a "lost territories" literature has long existed as part of Mexican national history). Ignacio del Río Chávez and José Luis Mirafuentes Galván have written on Pimería Alta and Baja California Indian populations from a demographic and acculturational perspective; [36] María Carmen Velázquez Chávez has written institutional studies on both mission and *provincias internas*. [37]

The impression of a booming borderlands academic industry is reinforced by the appearance of both a journal and a database exclusively devoted to study of the frontier. The Association of Borderlands Scholars publishes *The Journal of Borderland Studies*, which first appeared in 1986. Barbara Valk, editor of the *Hispanic American Periodicals Index* (*HAPI*), has established a database called BorderLine. BorderLine is based at UCLA; dial-up access through the

UCLA online library catalog, ORION, puts the file of 9,000 records on the U.S.-Mexican border at the disposal of the researcher. [38] The data also appear in published form under the title *BorderLine: A Bibliography of the United States-Mexico Borderlands*. [39] There are also several specialized reference works for borderlands scholars: *The Borderlands Sourcebook*, a guide to the literature of northern Mexico and the Southwest, and an eminently useful research guide assembled by Charles Polzer and others at the University of Arizona. [40] Indeed, the Documentary Relations of the Southwest (DRSW) project at the University of Arizona, under the direction of Father Charles Polzer, is a bold step into the age of electronic scholarship, with the construction of a documentary database, not of bibliographic references but of unpublished primary source materials.

We may then ask where is borderlands history heading? It is clear that the pioneering institutional or heroic narrative of Bolton and his heirs has evolved into a wide range of specialized and narrowly focused studies over a wide spectrum of disciplines. The studies contribute to a deeper understanding of the borderlands throughout the colonial and independence eras; it appears to some that we now have a multitude of bricks that comprise a wall, but no one is standing back to view the structure as a whole anymore. Most significantly, borderlands history has taken its place among the field of borderlands studies, which ranges from the *maquiladoras* of border towns, to the demographics and economics of illegal migration from Mexico to the United States, and from the growth and development of border communities to water disputes and agribusiness in the border regions.

David Weber, in an excellent article paying tribute to John Francis Bannon and borderlands historiography, [41] lamented what he saw as the marginalization of borderlands history, and the scarcity of serious borderlands work, even as he listed an impressive number of monographs and articles on the same region. I believe Weber to be unduly pessimistic; borderlands history has passed from what Weber calls "The Bolton-Bannon construct" into a broader, if more amorphous, realm. Bolton and Bannon saw the borderlands as a process as well as a place—a shifting frontier on the edges of the Spanish empire in North America. They conceptualized that process in terms of the colony and its institutions, and so for them the process stopped in 1821 with the end of Spanish hegemony on the continent. [42] The borderlands is still for many scholars in many fields a process as well as a place. The United States and Mexico share a border that is still a frontier of acculturation, assimilation, and interchange on economic, linguistic, religious, political, and cultural levels.

Geographical and political boundaries have been fixed for a moment, but the dynamic interchange that began in the sixteenth century will never stop; as long as that is the case, borderlands history and borderlands studies will continue to flourish. [42]

NOTES

1. Howard F. Cline, "Imperial Perspectives on the Borderlands," in *Probing the American West*, K. Ross Toole et al., eds., (Santa Fe: Museum of New Mexico, 1962), p. 173.

2. Frederick Jackson Turner, "The Significance of the Frontier in American History," in *The Turner Thesis: Concerning the Role of the Frontier in American History*, George Rogers Taylor, ed., 3d ed. (Lexington, MA, 1972), p. 3-28.

3. See Walter Prescott Webb, *The Great Frontier* (Boston, MA: Houghton Mifflin, 1952) for an application of Turnerian ideas to world history as a whole; the foremost proponent of Turner's thesis is Ray Allen Billington, *The Genesis of the Frontier Thesis: A Study in Historical Creativity* (San Marino, CA: Huntington Library, 1971); see also his *The American Frontier Thesis: Attack and Defense* (Washington, DC: American Historical Society, 1971).

4. David J. Weber, "Turner, the Boltonians, and the Borderlands," *The American Historical Review* 91:1 (February 1986), 66-81.

5. Lewis Hanke, ed., *Do the Americas Have a Common History? A Criticism of the Bolton Theory* (New York, NY: Knopf, 1964).

6. Weber, "Turner," p. 68.

7. A Bolton festschrift (*Greater America: Essays in Honor of Herbert Eugene Bolton* [Freeport, NY: Books for Libraries Press, 1968]) contains a lengthy bibliography of Bolton's historical writings.

8. See Jack D. Forbes, *Apache, Navajo, and Spaniard* (Norman: University of Oklahoma Press, 1960), and Elizabeth A. H. John, *Storms Brewed in Other Men's Worlds: The Confrontation of Indians, Spanish, and French in the Southwest, 1540-1795* (College Station: Texas A&M University Press, 1975).

9. A near-contemporary of Bolton was Charles W. Hackett. His three-volume collection of Spanish documents relating to New Mexico and Nueva Vizcaya was one of the first transcribed, translated collation of borderlands documents made available to scholars: *Historical Documents Relating to New Mexico, Nueva Vizcaya, and Approaches Thereto, to 1773*, collected by Adoph F. A. Bandelier and Fanny Bandelier, Publication no. 330, 3 vols. (Washington, DC: Carnegie Institution of Washington, 1923-1926).

10. See Peter Dunne, *Pioneer Black Robes on the West Coast* (Berkeley and Los Angeles: University of California Press, 1940), *Pioneer Jesuits in Northern Mexico* (Berkeley and Los Angeles: University of California Press, 1944), *Early Jesuit Missions in Tarahumara* (Berkeley: University of California Press, 1948), and *Black Robes in Lower California* (Berkeley: University of California Press, 1952).

11. John Francis Bannon, *The Spanish Borderlands Frontier, 1513-1821* (New York, NY: Holt, Rinehart and Winston, 1970). For a bibliographical exploration of Bannon's work, see David J. Weber, "John Francis Bannon and the Historiography of the Spanish Borderlands: Retrospect and Prospect," *Journal of the Southwest* 29:4 (Winter 1987), 331-363. Weber himself is working on a new general history of the borderlands; like Bannon's book, his will be a synthesis, primarily of secondary scholarship.

12. Alfred Barnaby Thomas, *Forgotten Frontiers: A Study of the Spanish Indian Policy of Don Juan Bautista de Anza, Governor of New Mexico, 1777-1787* (Norman: University of Oklahoma Press, 1932), *After Coronado: Spanish Exploration Northeast of New Mexico, 1696-1727* (Norman: University of Oklahoma Press, 1935), *The Plains Indians and New Mexico, 1752-1778* (Albuquerque, NM, 1940), and *Teodoro de Croix and the Northern Frontier of New Spain, 1776-1783* (Norman: University of Oklahoma Press, 1941).

13. *Militarists, Merchants and Missionaries: United States Expansion in Middle America: Essays Written in Honor of Alfred Barnaby Thomas,* Eugene R. Huck and Edward H. Moseley, eds. (University: University of Alabama Press, 1970).

14. Max L. Moorhead, *The Apache Frontier: Jacobo Ugarte and Spanish-Indian Relations in Northern New Spain, 1769-1791* (Norman: University of Oklahoma Press, 1968), and *The Presidio: Bastion of the Spanish Borderlands* (Norman: University of Oklahoma Press, 1975).

15. José Cuello, "Beyond the 'Borderlands' is the North of Colonial Mexico: A Latin-Americanist Perspective to the Study of the Mexican North and the United States Southwest," in *Proceedings of the Pacific Coast Council on Latin American Studies,* Kristyna P. Damaree, ed. (San Diego, CA: San Diego State University Press, 1982), pp. 1-24.

16. Ibid., p. 3.

17. Vito Alessio Robles, *Coahuila y Texas en la época colonial* (Mexico: Editorial Cultura, 1938); Luis Navarro García, *Sonora y Sinaloa en el siglo xvii,* Publicaciones de la Escuela . . . 176) (Seville: Escuela de Estudios Hispano-Americanos de Sevilla, 1967), and *José de Gálvez y la Comandancia General de las Provincias Internas del norte de Nueva España,* Publicaciones de la Escuela . . . 2d ser., 148) (Seville: Escuela de Estudios Hispano-Americanos de Sevilla, 1964); Lino Gómez Canedo, *Primeras exploraciones y poblamiento de Texas, 1686-1694* (Monterrey, 1968), and *Evangelización y conquista: experiencia franciscana en Hispanoamérica* (Mexico: Editorial Porrua, 1977).

18. To name some of their significant works: Odie B. Faulk, *The Last Years of Spanish Texas, 1778-1821* (The Hague: Mouton, 1964); Donald Cutter, *Apache Indians I [-XII-],* American Indian Ethnohistory: Indians of the Southwest (New York, NY: Garland Publishing, Inc., 1974); Cleve Hallenbeck, *The Journey of Fray Marcos de Niza* (Dallas, TX: Southern Methodist University, 1987), and *Spanish Missions of the Old Southwest* (Garden City, NY: Doubleday, Page and Company, 1926); Donald Worcester, *Instructions for Governing the Interior Provinces of New Spain* (Berkeley, CA: Quivara Society, 1951); Noel Loomis and Abraham Nasatir, *Pedro Vial and the Roads to Santa Fe* (Norman: University of Oklahoma Press, 1966); Oakan L. Jones, *Los Paisanos: Spanish Settlers on the Northern Frontier of New Spain* (Norman: University of Oklahoma Press, 1979); Philip Wayne Powell, *Soldiers, Indians and Silver: The Northward Advance of New Spain, 1550-1600* (Berkeley: University of California Press, 1952), and *Mexico's Miguel Caldera: The Taming of America's First Frontier, 1548-*

1597 (Tucson: University of Arizona Press, 1977); Robert C. West, *The Mining Community in Northern New Spain: The Parral Mining District*, Iberoamericana, 30 (Berkeley: University of California Press, 1949).

19. Some "Indian studies" have been particularly guilty of these historiographical excesses. See Dee Brown, *Bury My Heart at Wounded Knee: An Indian History of the American West* (New York, NY: Holt, Rinehart and Winston, 1971), and Vine Deloria, *Custer Died for Your Sins: An Indian Manifesto* (New York, NY: MacMillan, 1969). For a splendidly entertaining revisionist essay on one controversial aspect of Indian-European relations, see James Axtell, "The Unkindest Cut: Or Who Invented Scalping," in *The Indian and the European: Essays in the Ethnohistory of Colonial North America* (New York, NY: Oxford University Press, 1981), pp. 16-35.

20. Jack Forbes, *Frontiers in American History and the Role of the Frontier Historian*, Preprint series, no. 21 (Reno: Desert Research Institute, University of Nevada, 1966), pp. 6-7.

21. Although Spicer wrote a number of distinguished works, his two outstanding contributions to ethnohistory are *Cycles of Conquest: The Impact of Spain, Mexico, and the United States on the Indians of the Southwest, 1533-1960* (Tucson: University of Arizona Press, 1962), and *The Yaquis: A Cultural History* (Tucson: University of Arizona Press, 1980).

22. Forbes, *Apache, Navajo, and Spaniard*, and *Warriors of the Colorado: The Yumas of the Quechan Nation and Their Neighbors* (Norman: University of Oklahoma Press, 1965). In later years Forbes became involved with DQ University, a Native American institution near Sacramento, California.

23. James G. Leyburn, *Frontier Folkways* (New Haven, CT: Yale University Press, 1935), pp. 1-2.

24. Marvin Mikesell, "Comparative Studies in Frontier History," *Annals of the Association of American Geographers* 50 (March 1960), 62-74.

25. Louis Hartz, *The Founding of New Societies: Studies in the History of the United States, Latin America, South Africa, Canada, and Australia* (New York, NY: Harcourt, Brace and World, 1964), p. 3.

26. "Roots of Revolt: Regionalism and Rebellion in Northeast Mexico to 1836," Latin American Studies Association XIV International Congress, March 17-19, 1988, New Orleans. The panel participants were: José Cuello (Marquette University), "The Colonial Roots of Regionalism in Northeast Mexico"; Jesús F. de la Teja (General Land Office of Texas), "Rebellion on the Frontier: San Antonio, Texas, in the Mexican War of Independence"; Ricki S. Janicek (Tulane University), "Federalism in Northeast Mexico: The Uneasy Union of Coahuila y Texas."

27. Michael M. Swan, *Tierra Adentro: Settlement and Society in Colonial Durango* (Boulder, CO: Westview Press, 1982); Alicia V. Tjarks, "Comparative Demographic Analysis of Texas, 1777-1793," *Southwestern Historical Quarterly* 77 (January 1974), 291-338, and "Demographic, Ethnic and Occupational Structure of New Mexico," *The Americas* 35 (July 1979), 45-88.

28. See Weber, "John Francis Bannon," pp. 356-358.

29. See José Cuello, "Saltillo in the Seventeenth Century: Local Society on the North Mexican Frontier" (Ph.D. diss., University of California, Berkeley, 1981); also Leslie Scott Offutt, "Urban and Rural Society in the Mexican North Saltillo in the Late Colonial Period" (Ph.D. diss., University of California, Los Angeles, 1982).

30. See Robert McCaa, "*Calidad, Clase* and Marriage in Colonial Mexico: The Case of Parrall, 1788-90," *Hispanic American Historical Review* 64:3 (August 1984), 477-501. For an examination of marginal peoples in frontier society, see Peter Stern, "Social Marginality and Acculturation on the Northern Frontier of New Spain" (Ph.D. diss., University of California, Berkeley, 1984).

31. See Richard Morrisey, "The Northward Expansion of Cattle Ranching in New Spain, 1550-1600," *Agricultural History* 25 (July 1951), 115-121; William M. Dusenberry, *The Mexican Mesta: The Administration of Ranching in Colonial Mexico* (Urbana: University of Illinois Press, 1963); and Jack Jackson *Los Mostenos: Spanish Ranching in Texas, 1721-1821* (College Station: Texas A&M University Press, 1986).

32. See Charles Polzer, *Rules and Precepts of the Jesuit Missions of Northwestern New Spain* (Tucson: University of Arizona Press, 1976); John L. Kessell, *The Missions of New Mexico Since 1776* (Albuquerque: University of New Mexico Press, 1980); Kieran McCarty, O.F.M., *A Spanish Frontier in the Enlightened Age: Franciscan Beginnings in Sonora and Arizona, 1767-1770* (Washington, DC: Academy of American Franciscan History, 1981); Cynthia Radding de Murieta, *Las estructuras socio-económicas de las misiones de la Pimería Alta, 1768-1850* (Hermosillo: Instituto Nacional de Antropologia e Historia, Centro Regional del Noroeste, 1979).

33. See Evelyn Hu-DeHart, *Missionaries, Miners and Indians: Spanish Contact with the Yaqui Nation of Northwestern New Spain, 1533-1820* (Tucson: University of Arizona Press, 1981), and *Yaqui Resistance and Survival: The Struggle for Land and Autonomy, 1821-1910* (Madison, WI: University of Wisconsin, 1984); John L. Kessell, *Mission of Sorrows: Jesuit Guevavi and the Pimas, 1691-1767* (Tucson: University of Arizona Press, 1970), *Friars, Soldiers, and Reformers: Hispanic America and the Sonora Mission Frontier, 1767-1856* (Tucson: University of Arizona Press, 1976), and *Kiva, Cross, and Crown: The Pecos Indians and New Mexico, 1540-1840* (Washington, DC: National Park Service, U.S. Department of the Interior, 1979).

34. Works by Carl Sauer which deal with the borderlands are *Colima of New Spain in the Sixteenth Century* (Berkeley: University of California Press, 1948) and *Sixteenth-Century North America: The Land and the People as Seen by the Europeans* (Berkeley: University of California Press, 1971). For modern historical geography, see Swan, *Tierra Adentro*, and Peter Gerhard, *The North Frontier of New Spain* (Princeton, NJ: Princeton University Press, 1982).

35. See Robert Jackson, "Causes of Indian Population Decline in the Pimería Alta Missions of Northern Sonora," *Journal of Arizona History* 24:4 (1983), 405-429, and "Demographic Change in Northwestern New Spain," *The Americas* (Academy of Franciscan History) 41:4 (1985), 462-479. See also Peter Stern and Roberto Jackson, "*Vagabundaje* and Settlement Patterns in Colonial Northern Sonora," *The Americas* (Academy of Franciscan History) 44:4 (1988), 461-481.

36. See Ignacio del Río Chávez, ed., *Descripción de la antigua California, 1768* (La Paz: H. Ayuntamiento de La Paz, 1975), and "Aculturación e integración socio-económica de los chichimecas en el siglo xvi," *Humanitas* (Mexico) 22 (1981), 255-268; José Luis Mirafuentes Galván, *Movimientos de resistencia y rebeliones indígenas en el norte de Mexico (1680-1821)* (Mexico: Archivo General de la Nación, 1975).

37. María Carmen Veláquez Chavéz, *La decentralización administrativa y el pago de los sínodos a las misiones norteñas del siglo xviii* (Guadalajara: Librería Font, 1974), *El marqués de Altamira y las provincias internas de Nueva España* (Mexico: Colegio de

México, Centro de Estudios Históricas, 1976), and *Establecimiento y perdida del septentrión de Nueva España* (Mexico: Colegio de México, 1973).

38. BorderLine was developed by the UCLA Latin American Center. The references are in standard bibliographic format, and include material on history, economics, labor, commerce and industry, communications and mass media, language and linguistics, anthropology, religion, literature, and art. Physical formats on BorderLine include monographs, serial titles, journal articles, chapters and sections of books, government documents, conference proceedings, theses, unpublished papers, maps, slides, films, phonograph records, video cassettes, etc.

39. Barbara Valk, ed. (Los Angeles: UCLA Latin American Center and University of California Consortium on Mexico and the United States, 1988).

40. *Borderlands Sourcebook: A Guide to the Literature on Northern Mexico and the American Southwest*, Ellywn R. Stoddard, Richard L. Nostrand, and Jonathon P. West, eds. (Norman: University of Oklahoma Press, 1983); Thomas C. Barnes, Thomas H. Naylor, and Charles W. Polzer, *Northern New Spain: A Research Guide* (Tucson: University of Arizona Press, 1981).

41. Weber, "John Francis Bannon and the Historiography of the Spanish Borderlands: Retrospect and Prospect."

42. Ibid, p. 348.

43. This essay has only skimmed the surface of the vast bibliography of borderlands writings extant; for excellent historiographical essays, see Weber, "Turner, the Boltonians, and the Borderlands," and "John Francis Bannon and the Historiography of the Spanish Borderlands: Retrospect and Prospect."

5. Commentary

Woodrow Borah

Two preceding papers that I think are models of bibliographical work are those by David Block and Peter Stern. I try to follow research on the mission, and I confess that I found two topics new to me in Dr. Block's paper. I assume that he knows how to manipulate the computer much better than I and has had access to it somewhat longer since I am an old fogey, who comes to it very reluctantly. Both of these papers give rise to significant questions that go far beyond the papers themselves. For example, Dr. Block's paper omits the Portuguese missions in Brazil and the French missions in Canada. A consideration of these would be needed for comparison of purposes and methods, and so a broader understanding of the Spanish missions. He does not take up what is an important part of Maynard Geiger's works, oddly enough, namely a series of monographs on the lives of Franciscans in California, which Geiger wrote in his somewhat sullen retirement in Santa Barbara. Sherburne F. Cook's most important work, in the opinion of many scholars, is the four volumes in the Ibero-Americana series on the California Indian and white civilization , which have been reprinted in a single volume. [1] This is a brilliant, provocative analysis that for many years led Franciscans to start meetings on Franciscan history in California with a "we hate Cook" session. Cook simply showed that the Spanish mission in California had many aspects, not all of them kind to the Indians.

Both of these papers demand consideration of certain aspects of the mission. It was an instrument of European imperialism. Quite simply, the missionaries made no bones about the fact that they served two majesties, the divine and the terrestrial (whether the terrestrial was the King of Spain, the King of France, or the King of Portugal). Beyond that lies a vexing and very difficult concept: cultural relativism. It is both a tool of illumination and one of great destructive power. I have watched anthropology and sociology descend into near conceptual chaos by accepting cultural relativism too wholly and uncritically so that they lost all standards of reference. They have been a long time recovering. Actually, no one can be neutral. To think that you can is an illusion. Objectivity, a somewhat different quality, demands that you take other and opposing factors into account and that you adhere to evidence, but you still have a point of view. The instant you have a point of view, you have adopted a stand. There is simply no way of getting around the problem. We're fallible human beings, not God. Perhaps God can manage neutrality or a truly compassionate overview; we trust He can. What I have said covers ethnocentricity, of course.

Beyond these questions, we have a problem that is far more serious for scholars than most, except philosophers and theologians, have realized: the age-old dilemma of the cosmic process as against human ideas of justice. You will find it expounded with considerable brilliance in the Book of Job. But the Book of Job ends by the Lord's telling Job to shut up and stop questioning; it does not solve the problem at all. The poetry of that is magnificent, but may I say that the philosophical resolution comes to nil, except perhaps that it truly describes the human condition. Whether we like it or not, the world has been and is going through a long process of consolidation. In the course of it, groups have been annihilated, subjugated, and absorbed in simple or complex ways. The European conquest of America and the consequent Europeanization of America are simply one in a long series of similar processes that have taken place. We may declare them vile and unjust, and demand that scholars subject them to judgment in a sort of Nuremberg trial. I must admit that I do not know what good a postmortem does in such cases. If Coronado and Cortés were villains, they have both been dead for more than four hundred years. Moreover, they were actors in a cosmic process that was inevitable. Father Ernest Burrus has raised what is basically the same question in a book on the Jesuit missions of Baja California. [2] Were the missions something which had to be or which should not have been? Burrus comes to the conclusion that European penetration was inevitable and that the missions were perhaps the most lenient way of carrying out the unavoidable opening of contact with Europeans. He may well be right. Europeans or Asians would have come to the Americas. They would have brought diseases. Whether at that time or later, long-range navigation was continuing unification of the globe as an inevitable process. It continues today. I may add as a private comment that neither in the past, the present, nor the future has it been nor will it be always benevolent and strictly in accord with our ideas of human justice.

Our ideas of human justice hold today that one must have concern for Indian interests; one must not intrude upon others; one must not seize their possessions; nor should one assimilate them to one's culture.

Most recently, we have witnessed a new French concept: ethnocide. The assimilation of a minority or of a neighboring people means the destruction of their culture; that is ethnocide. But all great states of the world and many smaller ones, that is, the nation-states as we know them, are founded on ethnocide, not just the United States. France, for example, has suppressed the Bretons, the Alsatians, and the Basques, and others. Other sinners are Germany, Britain, Italy, China, the Soviet Union; indeed, all countries. That is cosmic process as against human ideas of justice. Is it good, bad, indifferent? So you come to a standard of judgment—the historian or scholar as judge. But the historian or scholar as judge is hardly impartial. He repeats his own prejudices, his own predilections, and those of his generation. Another aspect of cosmic process dictates that no matter what is done, it will be assimilated into the fabric of what is to come. In perhaps unpredictable ways, very much of the injustice—injustice as we understand it—will be mitigated. Philosophers will recognize the Hegelian triad, but that recognition is no comfort to the sufferer of human injustice.

Let me take up one illustrative point. Dr. Stern, in his "Sons (and Grandsons of Bolton)" discusses Jack Forbes, a so-called Native American. If the term means that the American Indians were here when the Europeans arrived, they are indeed natives. If it means a claim that they were autochthonous, the term is nonsense, for man did not originate here. They are simply the earliest immigrants. But Jack Forbes is only partly American Indian. He is a mixture of Indian and white, in other words, a mestizo, living essentially in a European or Europeanized culture. Only by assimilating and operating within the white man's norms is he able to do anything for the Indians. He's a fine anthropologist, by the way. He gave up a promising career as an anthropologist to pursue his hope of an independent Indian university and Indian culture. I suspect that it is a mirage since a large part of the American Indians today live in cities, where increasingly they intermarry and blend into the common European culture. If not, they remain divided by many tribal cultures. The national Indian movement is another white-inspired creation with a great deal of the Hollywood ideas of Indians in it. I at least recognize the puzzling business of a relentless cosmic process.

In the matter of frontiers, let me say in the first place that there was more than one scholar at Berkeley studying the so-called borderlands, but Carl O. Sauer inspired another group to a great extent in opposition to the ideas of Bolton. Sauer, Lesley Byrd Simpson, and Alfred Louis Kroeber formed an interdisciplinary group which did a great deal of fine work in history. Robert West, who was cited by

Peter Stern, is a student of Sauer's.   One of the best books on the
southwest is by Meinig, a geographer. [3] In fact, geographers have been
among the more brilliant ethnohistorians produced in the United
States and Europe.   Somehow, when discussing ethnohistory, the
anthropologists and historians never get around to talking about
geographers.

The largest omission in Peter Stern's paper is, I think ,the
existence of schools in Spain, studying aspects of the frontier.   There
are really two Spanish foci: the study of missionary personalities and
activities, centered in two institutes in Madrid, and the study of other
aspects, centered in the Archivo General de las Indias in Sevilla.   A
long list of distinguished scholars is associated with these institutes;
they have their journals, especially the *Anuario de Estudios Americanos*,
Missionalia Hispánica, and the *Revista de Indias*.   Virtually all these
scholars tend to have a Spanish imperial focus, partly because of their
own ethnocentricity, but partly also because the materials they use out
of the Spanish archives are the imperial records.   Their point of view
essentially holds that the Spanish conquest and settlement of America
meant that Spain carried out a benevolent civilizing mission, the results
of which are to be seen in the many Europeanized nation states, all
having a common tongue and similar culture, that have risen in the
former Spanish territory in America.

The eccentricity of the cosmic process from the human point of
view is illustrated by the fact that Spanish studies of America were
relatively poor in quality until Franco's triumph in the Civil War,
something most of us deplore.   Franco, however, reorganized Spanish
scholarly studies.   He brought into existence many institutes that gave
the impetus to Spanish scholarship.   I am not happy with this event;
my personal preferences are on the other side; but I am forced to
recognize the simple fact that standards of scholarship in Spain have
risen steadily and that Spain today is a very real force in studies of
America.

The point of view to be applied in studies of the Spanish missions,
settlements, and political administration in America is very difficult for
Spanish scholars to come to terms with.   For them, what Spain did did
not merely advance Spain's own interests but also brought civilization
and Christianity to the American Indians.   They may recognize some
negative aspects which make them uncomfortable but hold that they
are far outweighed by what they would call the positive aspects.   Any
other view they hold to be the Black Legend, inspired by envy and
hatred of Spain.   An opposite point of view deplores everything that
the Spanish did.   Indeed, some would demand restitution for the

Indians, not merely from Spain but from the United States as well. True restitution would require that the Indians be returned to their situation in 1492 or whenever the Europeans appeared on their territory. But such a requirement is impossible to implement today. In the United States most Indians are either an imitation of the white man or isolated on reservations. Many are partly or wholly dependent on federal funds. In Mexico, equally, the amalgamation of races and cultures would render impossible any restitution based on race.

Let me give one more illustration from the history of California. Hispanic founders of civilization pressed up from the south to bring the light of the gospel and European culture to the Indians as California pioneers crossed the Rockies and came by sea to establish a new state. The California Indians sickened from the diseases the intruders brought, and died in droves. More were slaughtered or perished from oppressive treatment. Were the missionaries and pioneers monsters or saints? Frankly, I would say that if you are not God, you'd better avoid judgment. Was the Spanish mission a great and noble institution? Well, it was, in many ways. Was it a terrible engine of destruction? It was, in many ways. If you look in the treatise of Tacitus on Britain, you will find a speech put in the mouth of a British chieftain—a long and bitter statement about the Romans. The Chieftain finally summarizes, "They make a desert and they call it peace." That is one appreciation, and a true one, of "the glory that was Rome." On the other hand, the grandeur of the Roman empire and Roman civilization is still remembered after nearly two millennia. It brought about the Latinization of the western half of the Mediterranean basin, the northern part of which still speaks tongues derived from Latin. The problem of judging what Spain and Portugal did in the New World is similar. A large part of the Americas today speaks Spanish and Portuguese, in fact, more people than speak English. They form part of Iberian civilization. The costs of this accomplishment are also very real. I am sorry to say that I can't solve the dilemma for you because I, too, am stuck with it.

NOTES

1. *The Conflict between the California Indian and White Civilization*, Ibero-Americana 21-24, 4 vols. (Los Angeles and Berkeley: University of California Press, 1943).

2. Ernest J. Burrus, ed., *Jesuit Relations, Baja California, 1716-1762* (Los Angeles, CA: Dawson's Book Shop, 1984).

3. Donald William Meinig, *Southwest: Three Peoples in Geographical Change, 1600-1700* (New York, NY: Oxford University Press, 1971).

II. Geographic Perspectives

6. Cartographic and Image Resources for Research on the United States-Mexico Borderlands

Ronald J. Wasowski and Norman J. W. Thrower

Introduction

Throughout its history and particularly in recent years, the Seminar on the Acquisition of Latin American Library Materials has appropriately emphasized textual materials, whether descriptive, analytical, or statistical. Maps and aerial images are becoming increasingly important information resources, to both geographers and nongeographers, and are especially important information research resources to consider at this particular conference, given its theme.

As the title of this paper suggests, the thoughts and examples presented here derive from research involving one particular border region, viz. that between Mexico and the United States. Even though traditional types of textual resources were consulted extensively for this research, Landsat satellite MultiSpectral Scanner (MSS) images (supplemented by limited fieldwork) and maps were considered to be the fundamental information resources. Despite the emphasis on the United States-Mexico border, we believe that the general principles, the map and image sources, and the textual resources presented here are viable and valuable for all of Latin America.

The United States-Mexico Borderlands Project

Many researchers have long recognized that the states of Baja California in Mexico and California in the United States have many effects upon each other, some subtle and others quite profound. About 1980, several experts from various University of California campuses began discussing the possibility of organizing and coordinating extensive new research efforts dealing with these crossborder interrelationships. These Californians also recognized that many crossborder interrelationships followed the international boundary all the way to the Gulf of Mexico. As a result, the United States-Mexico Borderlands Project was formalized to include all nine campuses of the University of California system (as well as additional experts from both sides of the border). Because there is a very strong geographic component to most crossborder phenomena, it was decided that the results would be published as a series of thematic atlases on a wide variety of topics including a satellite imagery overview, history, physical geography, politics, natural resources, natural hazards, vegetation, and cities (with special emphasis on border twin cities).

Some Comparisons between Cartographic and Image Resources

Before the advent of photography and airplanes, mapping depended upon tedious field surveys with very limited perspectives. Especially in the early days of European exploration and settlement of the Americas, maritime logbooks and terrestrial surveys were typically short on detail. Frequently, the precise location, size, shape, and even name of features were known only vaguely. As a result, cartographers had to estimate, extrapolate, or simply guess before putting pen to paper. This is well illustrated by a map of New World territories attributed to Matthew Seutter (1725?), annotated entirely in Latin and focused upon Mexico and the Florida territories. Even a cursory examination reveals major inaccuracies, among them: Lake Huron is labeled "Michigane Lac," while Lake Michigan is labeled "Lacus Ilinois"; the geographic details of many lakes and rivers are far from accurate, such as one mapped "Nicaragua Lac Sive Granada" instead of the actual separate lakes Managua and Nicaragua; the Florida and Yucatan peninsulas have seriously distorted shapes. Nonetheless, Seutter's and other similar maps contain extremely valuable information about early perceptions and misperceptions of these areas that no textual source could possibly provide.

By the end of the nineteenth century, geographic knowledge of most of the world had greatly improved. This is well illustrated by the map of Mexico in *The Century Atlas of the World* (Smith, 1897, No. 64). Not only are shapes and sizes far more accurate than on Seutter's map, but enough demographic information was available to permit the cartographers to indicate the approximate population of each mapped city. In fact, so many place-names are included on the *Century Atlas* map of Mexico that it is quite difficult to read the map.

Contemporary maps provide additional improvements, not so much in accuracy of shapes and sizes as in readability. Depending in part upon intended application, these maps may be greatly simplified by including only the largest cities, using shaded relief instead of hachures, and using color to indicate approximate elevation (U.S. Central Intelligence Agency, 1978).

Each of the three maps described in and of themselves present valuable information. But examined as a coherent time series of information resources, they add an extremely useful spatiotemporal perspective that could be obtained in no other way.

In the last half-century, an intimate relationship has developed between maps and aerial images. Virtually all modern maps are produced from aerial images. This has significantly changed the process of map production because field data have been supplemented or replaced by images that contain far more information than can be represented in traditional map formats. One new product that has resulted is the orthophotomap (Thrower and Jensen, 1976), in which a geometrically adjusted aerial photograph is used as the map based upon which selected features such as mountains, rivers, cities, and roadways are annotated (e.g., United States Department of the Interior Geological Survey, 7.5 Minute Series Orthophotomap [Topographic], 1982, *Lake Lucero SE Quadrangle, New Mexico*). The spatial resolution and geometry of modern satellite images is improving to the extent that some experts speculate that map accuracy standards can soon be met at scales as large as 1:24,000. Techniques are already well developed that permit the automated production of both topographic and thematic maps from digitized satellite imagery. In addition, rapid automated entry of these image-derived maps into computerized databases called Geographic Information System (GIS) is now possible. Since geocoded textual and statistical information is usually also included in the GIS, direct spatial comparisons can be quickly made between any combination of information "layers," with results easily presented in both tabular and map formats.

Despite the intimate relationship between maps and images just described, there are also distinct differences that can result from cultural structures. Just as researchers primarily interested in textual or statistical resources can encounter difficulties because of crossborder language or procedural differences, so too researchers interested primarily in spatial information can face problems. Consider the following:

a. Just as with statistical resources, maps are often produced by governmental agencies and thus treat national boundaries as if nothing existed beyond (United States U.S. Department of the Interior Geological Survey, 7.5 Minute Series [Topographic], 1965, *Camel Mountain Quadrangle, New Mexico*)! This was also the case with the first satellite image-based map produced for the Mexico-United States borderlands (Thrower, 1970). Because this UCLA project was under the auspices of the U.S. Geological Survey, the finished photomap was not permitted to include any Mexican territory, even though the hyperaltitude photographic coverage, like nature, knew no boundaries.

That early borderlands imagery research planted the seed for a satellite imagery overview of the entire borderlands; the crossborder prohibitions intensified the resolve to include analysis and display of both sides of the international border.

   b.   Topographic maps in Mexico are produced at a scale of 1:50,000, cover 15 minutes of latitude and 20 minutes of longitude, and express contours in meters. Equivalent maps in the United States are at a scale of 1:24,000, cover 7.5 minutes of both latitude and longitude, and express contours in feet.

   c.   Single maps compiled from two disparate data sources may have confusing discontinuities where the two data sources abut. Various approaches are possible: the Lang Canyon provisional map stops the metric contours a small distance below the international border, while the Guadalupe Pass provisional map brings the metric contours right to the border (United States Department of the Interior Geological Survey, 7.5 Minute Series [Topographic] Provisional Edition, 1983c *Lang Canyon Quadrangle, New Mexico-Sonora-Chihuahua*, and 1983b *Guadalupe Pass Quadrangle, New Mexico-Sonora*).

   d.   Adjoining crossborder thematic maps such as those for geology frequently do not correlate, either because rock unit names or because classification criteria differ.

   Until recently, the situation was not fundamentally different with aerial photographs obtained for mapping purposes. Great care was usually taken to insure that an absolute minimum of photography crossed the international border. For those photos that do overlap the border, the crossborder areas might be artificially masked out. A major exception to this pattern is satellite imagery. Following upon the "Open Skies Policy" first proposed by President Eisenhower, it has become customary international law that satellite imagery of any one nation's territory may be obtained and distributed to any entity in any other nation without obtaining prior permission from the imaged nation. The issue of nondiscriminatory image dissemination has been debated for nearly two decades in the United Nations Committee on the Peaceful Uses of Outer Space (Wasowski, 1978). Nonetheless, the existence and widespread acceptance of commercial remote sensing satellite systems in the United States (the Landsat system with continuous imagery available beginning in 1972) and in France (the SPOT system with continuous imagery available beginning in 1986) demonstrate that real needs exist for such information resources. The Soviet Union has also recently entered the satellite remote sensing market, offering photography obtained from their manned space station. In June 1988, three cosmonauts were launched to rendezvous with the second-generation Soviet Mir space station.

Even though the satellite imagery itself is available without restriction, the philosophy of product production can vary considerably. For example, the two versions of the first satellite photomosaics of the contiguous United States are neatly cropped at both the Canadian and Mexican borders (National Geographic Society, 1976). At the other extreme is *Escena de Casas Multicolores* (Larson, 1977), a Landsat MSS color infrared photomosaic of Mexico that shows extensive areas of the United States in order to fill out the chosen rectangular format. We and many other observers prefer the latter approach, which permits the primary area to be seen within its physiographic context.

Where distinctive crossborder cultural differences affect the landscape, as in the vicinity of the border twin cities Calexico and Mexicali, the international boundary can be easily identified on the Landsat MSS imagery. But most of the time the landscape is continuous in every observable way, so the actual border is invisible. Regardless of border visibility, either photovisual or computer analyses of the images may be conducted without hindrance from artificial restrictions or compilation criteria. In addition, digital multispectral satellite remote sensing images are multipurpose information resources: one and the same database might be used for rapid, economical, synoptic assessments of the quality of surface waters, vegetation type and extent, geologic structure, logging and mining practices, erosion and natural hazard potential, urban sprawl, and unregistered airfields that might be used for illegal activities.

Specific Cartographic Resources

Without doubt, maps present for our appreciation special information regarding both the perception and the reality of the world (Thrower, 1972). Even though the quality of both art and design involved in producing maps can provide a wide variety of valuable information such as property boundaries, perception of space and environment (especially across political boundaries), variations in place and feature names with passage of time, and visual display of numerical information.

Most major libraries contain a section devoted to maps and atlases. These can range from general purpose maps designed for use by motorists to highly detailed thematic maps displaying information about phenomena such as population characteristics or natural resource availability.

The University of Notre Dame Hesburgh Memorial Library houses a small map collection, limited almost entirely to maps produced by U.S. government agencies. The UCLA Henry J. Bruman Map Library has one of the largest map collections in the United States, housing more than 500,000 maps with good to excellent collections on certain areas of Latin America. Many of those maps were invaluable for our research along the Mexico-United States border.

Topographic Maps

The UCLA Map Library serves as a repository for all regional maps produced by the United States Geological Survey (U.S.G.S.), including all areas of the United States adjacent to the border with Mexico. The great majority of these are topographic maps, in two basic series: the original 15-minute quadrangles (usually at a scale of 1:62,500) and the current 7.5-minute quadrangles (usually at a scale of 1:24,000). Because the 7.5-minute maps are produced and updated from aerial photographs, they not only record elevational and vegetational details but also cultural features such as cities, reservoirs, transportation routes, and mines. Successive editions of the same map are excellent sources of information regarding the physical expansion or contraction of such features, information that may not be readily available from any other source. Comparable topographic maps are also available for Mexico, with the basic series produced at a scale of 1:50,000.

Color Image Maps

In the late 1970s, the U.S. Customs Service of the Department of the Treasury, in cooperation with the U.S. Geological Survey, initiated a very significant cooperative map project with Mexico. Initially concerned with the border crossing ares, the Color Image Map Series uses orthophotographic versions of color infrared (CIR) photos acquired and provided by Mexico. All map production is done in the United States, yet the topographic contours are in meters, the scale is 1:25,000, and the landscape format more closely resembles Mexican than U.S. topographic maps.

Analysis of these photomaps is quite instructive. The standard U.S. Geological Survey 7.5-minute topographic quadrangle map of *Calexico (1957)* is quite stark and shows nothing south of the border. By contrast, the *Calexico Port of Entry* color photo map *(1979a)* richly details the border twin cities of Calexico and Mexicali (even differences in street-paving materials) and clearly illustrates the designed proximity of the All American Canal to the artificial linear international border. This differs from the *El Paso Port of Entry* color photo map (*1982a*), where the international border follows an irregular natural feature and is therefore less evident. Of particular note is the locator map, indicating that the orientation of individual map sheets is determined by the border trend rather than by the compass. Different still is the border delineation in the *Nogales Port of Entry* color photo map (*1982b*), where a lighter tone resulting from heavier grazing in the southwestern quadrant of the photomap is considerably more obvious than the border within the twin cities.

Comparison of the standard U.S. Geological Survey 7.5-minute topographic quadrangle maps of *Presidio East* and *Presidio West* (*1979a* and *1979b*) with the color photo maps of *Presidio East* and the *Presidio Port of Entry* (*1982c* and *1982d*) illustrates how rapidly certain sections of Ojinaga have developed in just three years. For the most part, however, the landscape is continuous and the border invisible.

General Image Resources

Since the 1960s, the process of acquiring and recording data and/or information about the electromagnetic radiation characteristics of an area has been called "remote sensing." Eyesight acquires information in the visible light portion of the electromagnetic spectrum (EMS) but is technically not remote sensing because no precise, permanent record is produced. Both camera and electronic scanner images have been developed for remote sensing in four contiguous wavelength regions of the EMS referred to as "bands": the ultraviolet, the visible plus reflected infrared, the thermal infrared, and the radar (or microwave) bands.

The ultraviolet (UV) band of the EMS is particularly useful for monitoring thin-film oil spills on open-water surfaces. Virtually invisible by all other observational techniques, the thinnest part of an oil spill is most readily affected by wind and therefore can be used to predict where thicker parts of the oil spill are likely to move. The UV band is also useful for monitoring those wild animal breeding populations for which the fur of adults and newborns reflects ultraviolet light very differently. The major difficulty with UV imagery is that it employs a very short wavelength that is strongly scattered by the atmosphere, especially water vapor, and thus is effective only on very clear days and from very low altitudes.

The visible plus reflected infrared bands of the EMS are usually considered together because of their use in the ubiquitous color infrared imagery. Considered by subunits also referred to as bands, the visible portion of the EMS contains blue (0.4 to 0.5 μm wavelengths), green (0.5 to 0.6 μm wavelengths, and red (0.6 to 0.7 μm wavelengths) bands; the reflected infrared includes the wavelengths between 0.7 μm and 3.0 μm. A wide variety of spectral band combinations are possible, but there are four common ones, two monochrome and two color.

  a. Panchromatic images combine the green and red visible bands (thus the alternate name "minus blue" imagery) and represent them in shades of gray. Panchromatic images commonly are used for aerial mapping.

  b. Natural color images use the blue, green, and red bands and represent them in those same colors to mimic what the human eye sees. Because they use visible blue light, natural color images are best for monitoring shallow underwater features.

  c. Panchromatic infrared images use only the reflected infrared band, represented in shades of gray. Because healthy vegetation reflects infrared very strongly and water absorbs infrared almost completely, vegetation is very bright and water very dark in panchromatic infrared images.

  d. Color infrared (CIR) images use the green, red, and reflected infrared bands, representing them as blue, green, and red, respectively. Because healthy vegetation reflects about three times as much infrared as green light, areas with different types and amounts of vegetation are distinctive shades of red on CIR images. Very silty water appears light blue, whereas clear water appears black. Thus, CIR images are excellent for monitoring vegetation and for delineating land/water boundaries.

  The thermal infrared (TIR) band of the EMS is usually limited to the subbands of 3.0 to 5.0 μm and 8.0 μm to 14.0 μm, because all other portions of the TIR are almost completely absorbed by the Earth's atmosphere. Whereas panchromatic and CIR images record portions of sunlight reflected by features, TIR records electromagnetic radiation emitted by features. TIR images are records of the radiant temperature of features. The 3.0 μm to 5.0 μm subband is best used for monitoring "hot" features such as wildfires and geothermal sites. The 8.0 μm to 14.0 μm subband is best used for monitoring "cool" features such as cloud patterns over the entire Earth.

  The radar (or microwave) band of the EMS includes wavelengths from 3.0 mm to 30 m. Because most of those wavelengths are reserved for uses such as broadcast radio and television or aircraft and weather monitoring, few subbands are actually used for imaging. The most common wavelengths are 3.2 cm and 23.5 cm. Unlike all other imaging technologies, radar is an "active" system because it produces its own illumination of the Earth's surface and records the reflection as the image. The longer the radar wavelength, the less it is affected by clouds. Thus radar is the only imaging possibility for regular monitoring of perennially clouded regions, including vast areas of Latin America. Aircraft radar system were thus the first to provide an image mosaic of the entire Darien Province in Panama, from which the first generalized geologic map could be produced. Similarly, project RADAM was the first to produce detailed maps of virtually the entire Amazon basin.

Specific Image Resources

The Landsat satellite overview of the Mexico-United States borderlands needed thirty-five Landsat scenes to cover the entire region. A total of sixteen satellite orbital paths were needed to cover the entire border, fourteen of these with same-date north/south image pairs, two with image triplets, and a single image for metropolitan Los Angeles. Because cloud-free images were essential, images acquired over several years were selected. After requesting computer searches for existing imagery, black-and-white transparencies at a scale of 1:1,000,000 were purchased of each of the three spectral bands (green, red, and second-infrared) needed to produce CIR images. The discussion that follows is but a brief sample of the types of information that can be interpreted from such images. The examples progress from east to west (all references are to Wasowski entries in Imago-bibliography).

The Landsat Path 28, Rows 41 & 42 images are of the Brownsville/ Matamoros vicinity along the coast of the Gulf of Mexico. Acquired February 2, 1976, this scene pair well illustrates the excellent discrimination of land/water boundaries same well as of turbidity difference in different areas. Variations in the vegetation cover are quite evident, especially with the darker polygons near the top which are indicative of recently plowed land.

The Landsat Path 29, Rows 41 & 42 images are of the area just west of the previous scene pair. Acquired three years earlier on March 17, 1973, the brilliant red color indicates very healthy vegetation cover. The Falcon Reservoir on the Rio Grande and the Presa Marte R. Gómez to the south are very obvious, as is the fact that the southern lobe of the latter is receiving considerably more sediment than the northern and western lobes. The border twin cities of Laredo and Nuevo Laredo are evident as the pale blue area northwest of the Falcon Reservoir.

The Landsat Path 30, Rows 40 & 42 images are of the area just west of the previous scene pair. Acquired five years earlier on April 24, 1978, the pale cyan color provides a striking contrast to the adjacent scene pair and indicates very poor vegetation cover. The border twin cities of Laredo and Nuevo Laredo are about one-third of the way up the right edge of the scene pair but nearly invisible. Together with the previous scene pair, the value of time series images is abundantly clear.

The Landsat Path 35, Row 37 image is of the White Sands, New Mexico region. Acquired on April 11, 1978, it exhibits as much diversity as can be expected of any inland region: the bright white of White Sands, the deep black of the elongated lava flow to the north, the forested mountains to the east, and the barren ridges to the west.

The Landsat Path 39, Rows 37 & 38 images are of the Phoenix/ Lukeville/Sonyoita area. Acquired on May 21, 1978, it shows the diversity of this area from large reservoirs, metropolitan and agricultural areas, to scattered mining operations "rivers of blood": riparian vegetation along ephemeral desert stream courses.

The Landsat Path 40, Rows 37 & 38 images are of the Gila River valley and Gran Desierto area just west of the previous scene pair. Acquired on April 3, 1977, both coastal and inland detail can be readily interpreted from these images, and quite dramatic changes can be observed from one season and year to the next.

The Landsat Path 44, Row 36 image is of the metropolitan Los Angeles region. The location of the San Andreas and Garlock faults, as well as of many other smaller ones, illustrates yet another application of such satellite imagery. Indeed, previously unrecognized geologic faults have been recognized on such imagery around the world. Of particular interest are localities where two or more fracture zones intersect, because the probability of mineralization is higher there than elsewhere.

Image Sources

Image resources can provide important information because of both the overview perspective as well as the objectivity and permanence of the image. Images yield more information per unit area than any other data source, yet with minimal output of time and money.

From the beginning of the United States manned space program, cameras have been on board. Virtually every one of those manned missions had handheld cameras which were used to obtain unsystematic coverage of the Earth and its atmosphere. A number of the manned missions had Earth photography as a specific objective, and these provide somewhat more systematic (although intermittent) photographic coverage. Two classes of U.S. manned space missions produced large numbers of photographs: Skylab and the Space Transportation System (better known as the Space Shuttle). All of these photographs are archived and cataloged and can be obtained at modest cost through the EROS Data Center in Sioux Falls, SD.

Far more systematic and consistent is the imagery that has been produced by the U.S. series of five Landsat satellites, beginning in 1972 and continuing to the present. The two major Landsat imagery systems are the Multispectral Scanner (MSS, on all five satellites) and the Thematic Mapper (TM, on only the last two satellites). Both produce digital rather than photographic images that are transmitted to receiving stations on Earth. The images can be purchased in either digital or photographic formats and can be in a researcher's possession as little as two weeks after acquisition. The MSS acquires images covering an area of 185 km by 185 km, in four spectral bands (green, red, and two reflected infrared), with a spatial resolution of 80 meters. The TM acquires images also covering an area of 185 km by 185 km, in seven spectral bands (blue, green, red, three reflected and one thermal infrared) with a spatial resolution of 30 meters. Four Landsat receiving stations acquire imagery for all of Latin America:

Comision Nacional de Investigaciones Especiales (CNIE), Centro De Procesamiento, Avenue Dorrego 4010, 1425 Buenos Aires, Argentina;

INPE-DI, Caixa Postal 01, Cachoeira Paulista, SP, CEP 12630, São Paulo, Brazil;

CLIRSEN (In operation beginning August 1989), Edificio Instituto Geografico Militar, Quito, Ecuador;

Earth Observation Satellite Corporation, 4300 Forbes Boulevard, Lanham, MD 20706, U.S.A.

Another very important source of satellite images is SPOT (Systeme Probetoire pour Observation de la Terre). SPOT-1 was launched in 1986 and acquires images covering an area of 60 km by 60 km, in three spectral bands (green, red, and reflected infrared) with a spatial resolution of 20 meters or in one panchromatic band with a spatial resolution of 10 meters. SPOT images can be purchased from SPOT Image Corporation, 1897 Preston White Drive, Reston, VA 22091-4326, U.S.A.

Satellite images with poor spatial resolution of 1.1 km by 1.1 km but with daily coverage useful for preparing very large estimates of green leaf area index (GLAI, or standing green biomass) are produced by the Advanced Very High Resolution Radiometer (AVHRR) on several U.S. Oceanic and Atmospheric Administration (NOAA) satellites. These images can be purchased from United States Department of Commerce, National Oceanic and Atmospheric Administration, National Environmental Satellite, Data, and Information Service, Page Building 2, Room 288, 3300 Whitehaven Street, NW, Washington, DC 20235.

Some radar imagery is available from the Seasat satellite and from the two Shuttle Imaging Radar (SIR-A and SIR-B) missions. Information can be obtained from National Space Science Data Center, Code 633.4, Goddard Space Flight Center, Greenbelt, MD 20771.

Specific Text Resources

As mentioned, even though maps and images were considered the primary information resources for our research on the Mexico-United States border, textual resources were extensively consulted. They were found in three distinctly different catalogs: traditional textual resources, cartographic text resources, and remote sensing textual resources.

Traditional textual resources are simply mentioned as important to our research on the Mexico-United States border, relative to our emphasis on map and image resources. Some of these textual resources are historical, aiding in understanding the exploration and definition of various border segments that can be seen on the satellite images (Emory etc.). Other textual resources provide numerical and/or statistical information concerning visible features (Amistad & Falcon Reservoirs). Still other textual resources are essentially descriptive, presenting anecdotal information that put a more human and down-to-earth perspective on selected borderland areas (border visits). One particularly helpful new source is the *International Guide to Research on Mexico*. This annual publication contains a separate heading for Border studies (Estudios fronterizos), but it is not definitive because keyword selection is made by the researchers rather than by the volume compilers. As a result, it is essential for interested researchers to consult other potentially fruitful keyword or topical listings.

Cartographic textual resources include a wide variety of books and periodicals that report completed research. Certain periodicals are particularly helpful, among them: *The American Cartographer Cartographia, The Cartographic Journal*.

Remote sensing textual resources represented the third category. Locating reports of remote sensing research conducted within approximately 60 kilometers of the border was the least fruitful aspect of textual library searches. One of the major problems is that remarkably few remote sensing projects have been undertaken for these borderlands. Nonetheless, a number of helpful remote sensing textual resources were found. Several relatively generalized books contain brief examples or sections covering the Mexico-United States borderlands (National Geographic Society, 1985; Sheffield, 1981 and 1983). Each of these same general sources also have examples covering other parts of Latin America. Professional remote sensing journals occasionally have articles on Latin American areas. The most promising journals include *Photogrammetric Engineering and Remote Sensing*, *Remote Sensing of Environment*, and *Canadian Journal of Remote Sensing*. Related to yet distinct from the professional journals are proceedings of several remote sensing meetings and symposia, which typically include the full text (rather than simply abstracts) of the papers as presented. Among them are:

a. *Proceedings of the Annual Joint Meeting of the American Society for Photogrammetry and Remote Sensing and the American Congress on Surveying and Mapping* (American Society for Photogrammetry and Remote Sensing, Falls Church, VA, U.S.A.);

b. *Proceedings of the Fall Technical Meeting of the American Society for Photogrammetry and Remote Sensing* (American Society for Photogrammetry and Remote Sensing, Falls Church, VA, U.S.A.);

c. *Proceedings of the International Symposia on Remote Sensing of Environment* (Environmental Research Institute of Michigan, Ann Arbor, MI, U.S.A.)

d. *Proceedings of the Thematic Conference on Petroleum Exploration* (American Society for Photogrammetry and Remote Sensing, Falls Church, VA, U.S.A.).

Because of the relative lack of remote sensing research projects in progress and completed for the Mexico-United States borderlands specifically, and Latin America generally, those interested in particular aspects of any region that might be effectively examined using aircraft or satellite images would do well to search the remote sensing literature by topical keywords as well as by area. This would both clarify what might be expected of remote sensing research and suggest possible design strategies.

Summary and Conclusions

This paper presents an overview of ways in which map and image resources were used as the fundamental information resources for a geographic overview and examination of the entire extent of the Mexico-United States borderlands. It also proposes the thesis that such resources can be valuable in many ways for research relating to all parts of Latin America, whether in frontiers and borderlands or entire nations or regions.

REFERENCES

It is customary to list the research materials cited in a professional paper. With very rare exception, this bibliography contains only textual materials. As this presentation attempts to make clear, it is often important, appropriate, and even essential to refer to cartographic and image research materials. Listings of maps cited have long been accepted as valid and distinct, described by the term "cartobibliography." Because of the importance of maps for our Mexico-United States borderlands research, we have included a cartobibliography after the traditional bibliography. But because satellite images in particular were even more fundamental to our research, we came to realize that a third (apparently unnamed) type of listing was essential. We suggest the term "imagobibliography" to describe the listing of images used and cited in scholarly research reports. Acknowledging that one purpose of such a listing of citations is to allow other researchers to duplicate and verify the research, an imagobibliography should if at all possible include:

Name of the acquiring agency

Image identification number assigned by the acquiring agency

Date and time of image acquisition, if not coded in the identification number

Recording technique (e.g., photographic or scanner, analog or digital)

Name(s) of the researcher(s) who produced the final image

Spectral band(s) used to form the final image

Processing procedures used for the final image (e.g., the colors assigned to each image in a color composite) including the map projection used, if any

Publication forum, if any.

BIBLIOGRAPHY

Center for U.S.-Mexican Studies
    1987   *International Guide to Research on Mexico.* San Diego, CA: Center for U.S.-Mexican Studies, University of California, San Diego.

Dent, Borden D.
    1985   *Principles of Thematic Map Design.* Reading, MA: Addison-Wesley.

Francis, Peter, and Pat Jones
    1984   *Images of Earth*. Englewood Cliffs, NJ: Prentice-Hall.
Greenwood, David
    1964   *Mapping*. Chicago, IL: University of Chicago Press.
National Geographic Society
    1985   *Atlas of North America: Space Age Portrait of a Continent*. Washington, DC: National Geographic Society.
Neri Vela, Rodolfo
    1986   *El Planeta Azul: Mision 61-B*. México, D.F.: EDAMEX.
Parry, R. B., and C. R. Perkins
    1987   "Mexico," in *World Mapping Today*. London, Boston: Butterworths, 1987. Pp. 179-183.
Ryder, Nicholas G.
    1981   *Ryder's Standard Geographic Reference: Satellite Photo-Atlas of the United States of America*. Denver, CO: Ryder Geosystems.
Sheffield, Charles
    1981   *Earthwatch: A Survey of the World from Space*. New York, NY: Macmillan.

    1983   *Man on Earth: How Civilization and Technology Changed the Face of the World—A Survey from Space*. New York, NY: Macmillan.
Short, Nicholas M., Paul D. Lowman, Jr., Stanley C. Freden and William A. Finch, Jr.
    1976   *Mission to Earth: Landsat Views the World (NASA SP-360)*. Washington, DC: National Aeronautics and Space Administration.
Short, Nicholas M., and Locke M. Stuart, Jr.
    1982   *The Heat Capacity Mapping Mission (HCMM) Anthology (NASA SP-465)*. Washington, DC: National Aeronautics and Space Administration, Scientific and Technical Information Branch.
Smith, Benjamin E.
    1897   *The Century Atlas of the World*. New York, NY: Century.
Tarragó, Rafael E.
    1988   "Buying in the Latin American Marketplace," *Access: News from to University Libraries at Notre Dame* 35 (April), 1,4.
Thrower, Norman J. W.
    1966   *Original Survey and Land Subdivision: A Comparative Study of the Form and Effect of Contrasting Cadastral Surveys*. Washington, DC: The Association of American Geographers.

    1970   "Land Use in the Southwestern United States: From Gemini and Apollo Imagery," *Annals—Association of American Geographers* 60:1 (March), 208-209, plus color Map Supplement Number 12.

    1972   *Maps and Man: An Examination of Cartography in Relation to Culture and Civilization*. Englewood Cliffs, NJ: Prentice-Hall.
Thrower, Norman J. W., and John R. Jensen
    1976   "The Utility of the Orthophoto and Orthophotomap: Characteristics, Development and Application," *The American Cartographer* 39:3.

Wasowski, Ronald J.
 1978 "The Legal and Political Implications of Natural Resource Satellites."
 M.A. thesis, University of California, Los Angeles.

Williams, Richard S., Jr., and William D. Carter, eds.
 1976 *ERTS-1: A New Window on Our Planet*, U.S. Geological Survey
 Professional Paper 929. Washington, DC: U.S. Government Printing
 Office.

CARTOBIBLIOGRAPHY

Seutter, Matthew
 1725(?) *Mappa Geographica Regionem Mexicanam et Floridam*; 47.6 cm x
 57.6 cm; 1:10,000,000.

United States Central Intelligence Agency
 1978 *Mexico*; 1:5,500,000.

United States Department of the Interior Geological Survey, 7.5 Minute Series
(Topographic)
 1950 *Lake Lucero SE Quadrangle, New Mexico-Otero Co.*; 1:24,000.

 1955; photorevised 1967 and 1973 *Fort Bliss SE Quadrangle, Texas-El Paso Co.*,
 AMS 4747 IV SE-Series V882; 1:24,000.

 1957 *Calexico Quadrangle, California-Imperial Co.*; 1:24,000.

 1965 *Camel Mountain Quadrangle, New Mexico*, AMS 4547 IV SE-Series
 V881; 1:24,000.

 1979a *Presidio East Quadrangle, Texas-Chihuahua*, DMA 5143 III SE-Series
 V882; 1:24,000.

 1979b *Presidio West Quadrangle, Texas-Chihuahua*, DMA 5143 III SW-Series
 V882; 1:24,000.

 1981 *Nogales Quadrangle, Arizona-Sonora*, DMA 3846 IV SW-Series V898;
 1:24,000.

 _____. (Topographic) Provisional Edition.
 1983a *Cabin Wells Quadrangle, New Mexico-Chihuahua*, 31108-E2-TF-024;
 1:24,000. Mexico portion copied from DGG 1:50,000-scale map *Los
 Moscos*, H12B29, 1978.

 1983b *Guadalupe Pass Quadrangle, New Mexico-Sonora*, 31108-C8-TF-024;
 1:24,000. Mexico portion copied from DGG 1:50,000-scale map *Rancho
 Nuevo*, H12B37, 1981.

 1983c *Lang Canyon Quadrangle, New Mexico-Sonora-Chihuahua*, 31108-C7-
 TF-024; 1:24,000. Mexico portion copied from DGG 1:50,000-scale map
 Rancho Nuevo, H12B37, 1981.

 1985 *Guzmans Lookout Mountain Quadrangle, New Mexico-Chihuahua*,
 31107-G2-TF-024; 1:24,000. Mexico portion copied from DGG 1:50,000-
 scale map *Nuevo Cuauhtemoc*, H13A23, 1981.

 _____. Orthophotomap (Topographic)
 1982 *Lake Lucero SE Quadrangle, New Mexico-Otero Co.*; 1:24,000.

United States Department of the Interior Geological Survey, Department of the Treasury, U.S. Customs Service Color Image Map

1979a   *Calexico Port of Entry, California-Baja California*, Sheet 11; 1:25,000.

1979b   *Camel Mountain, New Mexico-Chihuahua*, Sheet 80; 1:25,000.

1979c   *Guzman's Lookout Mountain, New Mexico-Chihuahua*, Sheet 81; 1:25,000.

1979d   *La Lesna Mtns., Arizona-Sonora*, Sheet 39; 1:25,000.

1982a   *El Paso Port of Entry, Texas Chihuahua*, Sheet 86; 31106-F3-PI-025; 1:25,000.

1982b   *Nogales Port of Entry, Arizona-Sonora*, Sheet 50; 1:25,000.

1982c   *Presidio East, Texas-Chihuahua*, Sheet 115; 29104-D3- PI-025; 1:25,000.

1982d   *Presidio Port of Entry, Texas-Chihuahua*, Sheet 114; 29104-E4-PI-025; 1:25,000.

IMAGOBIBLIOGRAPHY

General Electric Company

1976   *Space Portrait U.S.A.: The First Color Photomosaic of the Contiguous United States.* Washington, DC: The National Geographic Society. Color infrared and pseudo-natural color versions.

Larson, Carl W.

1977   *Escena de Casas Multicolores* (A Landsat multispectral scanner color infrared photomosaic of Mexico). Kirkland, WA: The California Institute of Earth, Planetary and Life Sciences.

Wasowski, Ronald J. Landsat Multispectral Scanner color infrared image.

Path 28, Row 41, 2 February 1976; positive photographic print on Cibachrome (Pearl Surface) by successive pin-registered contact printing of 1:1,000,000 scale positive transparencies: Red = E-2376-16172-7; Green = E-2376-16172-5; Blue = E-2376-16172-4.

Path 28, Row 42, 2 February 1976; positive photographic print on Cibachrome (Pearl Surface) by successive pin-registered contact printing of 1:1,000,000 scale positive transparencies: Red = E-2376-16175-7; Green = E-2376-16175-5; Blue = E-2376-16175-4.

Path 29, Row 41, 17 March 1973; positive photographic print on Cibachrome (Pearl Surface) by successive pin-registered contact printing of 1:1,000,000 scale positive transparencies: Red = E-1237-16381-7; Green = E-1237-16391-5; Blue = E-1237-16381-4.

Path 29, Row 42, 17 March 1973; positive photographic print on Cibachrome (Pearl Surface) by successive pin-registered contact printing of 1:1,000,000 scale positive transparencies: Red = E-1237-16383-7; Green = E-1237-16383-5; Blue = E-1237-16383-4.

Path 30, Row 40, 24 April 1978; positive photographic print on Cibachrome (Pearl Surface) by successive pin-registered contact printing of 1:1,000,000 scale positive transparencies: Red = E-21188-16062-7; Green = E-21188-16062-5; Blue = E-21188-16062-4.

Path 30, Row 41, 24 April 1978; positive photographic print on Cibachrome (Pearl Surface) by successive pin-registered contact printing of 1:1,000,000 scale positive transparencies: Red = E-21188-16064-7; Green = E-21188-16064-5; Blue = E-21188-16064-4.

Path 35, Row 37, 11 April 1978; positive photographic print on Cibachrome (Pearl Surface) by successive pin-registered contact printing of 1:1,000,000 scale positive transparencies: Red = E-21175-16330-7; Green = E-21175-16330-5; Blue = E-21175-16330-4.

Path 39, Row 37, 21 May 1978; positive photographic print on Cibachrome (Pearl Surface) by successive pin-registered contact printing of 1:1,000,000 scale positive transparencies: Red = E-21215-16580-7; Green = E-21215-16580-5; Blue = E-21215-16580-4.

Path 39, Row 38, 21 May 1978; positive photographic print on Cibachrome (Pearl Surface) by successive pin-registered contact printing of 1:1,000,000 scale positive transparencies: Red = E-21215-16583-7; Green = E-21215-16583-5; Blue = E-21215-16583-4.

Path 40, Row 37, 3 April 1977; positive photographic print on Cibachrome (Pearl Surface) by successive pin-registered contact printing of 1:1,000,000 scale positive transparencies: Red = E-2802-17102-7; Green = E-2802-17102-5; Blue = E-2802-17102-4.

Path 40, Row 38, 3 April 1977; positive photographic print on Cibachrome (Pearl Surface) by successive pin-registered contact printing of 1:1,000,000 scale positive transparencies: Red = E-2802-17105-7; Green = E-2802-17105-5; Blue = E-2802-17105-4.

Path 44, Row 36, 6 May 1975; positive photographic print on Cibachrome (Pearl Surface) by successive pin-registered contact printing of 1:1,000,000 scale positive transparencies: Red = E-2104-17495-7; Green = E-2104-17495-5; Blue = E-2104-17495-4.

7. The United States-Mexico Border Region in Comparative Human Geographic Perspective

Lawrence A. Herzog

Territorial borders are quite meaningless for science and economic interdependence crosses political borders not occasionally, but as a general rule.

N. Luhman

The boundary that divides the United States and Mexico has gained increasing attention in recent years, as foreign policy issues such as immigration and narcotics smuggling have placed the borderlands under greater hemispheric scrutiny. It is no longer sufficient to think of the nearly 2,000-mile border as merely a corridor separating two disparate cultures; the boundary today is both a functional and symbolic meeting place between the First and Third worlds, between the United States and Latin America. Our success in resolving common concerns along this border will set the tone for U.S.-Mexican and U.S.-Latin American relations more generally.

Perhaps the most noticeable characteristic of the late twentieth-century borderlands is that they have become increasingly populated. The proliferation of cities and dynamic industrial and service economies along the U.S.-Mexican border raises a host of new questions for scholars and researchers in Latin American studies, U.S.-Mexican studies, and related fields of the social sciences and humanities. In this paper I outline several salient features of the human geography of this border region. I begin by describing, more generally, a context for thinking about the changing significance of borders. Second, I briefly address some of the elements of the demographic transformation of the borderlands. Third, I describe three levels of comparative settlement geography along the border: economy, spatial form, and political systems. I conclude with a few comments on library collections and future research.

On the Meaning of Boundaries

The partitioning of the earth's surface into formal political geographic units (nation-states) has unfolded for several hundred years,

111

yet in the last few decades social scientists have begun to challenge the notion that the world system is dominated by nation-states. Wallerstein (1974) has postulated the notion of a single world market fused by capitalist relations of production that have their origins in sixteenth-century Europe. Other writers have posited a global political economy in which the forces of corporate power, aided by technological developments in communications, transport, and industrial production, operate on a worldwide basis that, over time, has altered the traditional meaning of the "nation-state" (Strange, 1984). As one study states,with reference to the managers of multinational corporations: "What they are demanding in essence is the right to transcend the nation-state, and in the process, to transform it" (Barnet and Müller, 1974, p. 16).

The territorial implications of global interdependence within the changing world system have received little attention from scholars. Political geography (and geography more generally), with a few noteworthy exceptions, has been slow to respond to the ideas of Wallerstein and other social scientists studying the world system. Gottmann (1973) is one of the few important voices in political geography emerging in the last two decades to address the subject of territory and international political economy. Territory, he argues, now carries with it a "social function" that is derived from a complementarity of interests between the nation-state and the international community. The uses of national territory are tied into an international network of reciprocal relations. The artificial borders that once strictly divided national political space no longer have the same impact.

Let us look to the past for a moment. The need to enclose and control territory seems to be one of the fundamental characteristics of sedentary civilizations. Mesopotamian, Roman, and medieval cities were rimmed by walls. Although some cultures rejected the notion of the walled town, most notably the Greeks and the Incas, in general, physical boundaries represent a political act taken to assert control over the environment. In a more complex sense, boundaries represent, in the modern era, a manifestation of nation-state actions to make political power real and explicit by linking it directly to territory (Sack, 1983). Yet geographer Ellen Semple's (1911, p. 204) advice that "nature abhors boundaries" suggests one of the ironies of human territorial behavior that continues to haunt the world. The examples of Chernobyl, the Rhine River spill, Canadian-U.S. border acid rain, and U.S.-Mexican border sewage spills remind us of the nonconformance between ecological system and man-made political borders.

The concept of a territorial boundary linked to one culture or nation of peoples did not clearly emerge until the modern period of Western history, beginning in the sixteenth century, when the conditions leading to the evolution of nation-states three centuries later were first implanted in Western Europe. Most scholars, however, agree that the idea of the territorial frontier can actually be traced back to the Roman Empire (Lapradelle, 1928). During the period of the Roman Empire (first to fifth centuries A.D.), and during the Middle Ages, territory was divided up into "kingdoms" or "empires"; the "nation-state," a form of modern political partitioning of space, would not emerge until the nineteenth century. Some writers view the Roman walls constructed in Scotland and along the Rhine and Danube rivers as evidence that Roman politicians and bureaucrats were concerned about defining and protecting the limits of the empire (Lapradelle, 1928; Prescott, 1965; Tagil, 1982). Scholars have identified two kinds of territorial lines: *limes imperii*, the fortified or functional boundaries of the empire, and *fines*, the legal borders of the Roman state (Lapradelle, 1928).

During the late nineteenth century, the formal production of knowledge about boundaries and frontiers began. Friedrich Ratzel (1897), often called the "father of political geography," initiated this body of work with his pioneering book, *Politische Geographie*. In it he proposed a set of "geographic laws," which explained patterns of world political power on the basis of locational and spatial relationships among nation-states. On the subject of nation-state boundaries, Ratzel offered the analogy of the state as a living organism. The boundary, like the epidermis of animals and plants, was the "skin" of the living state. It served to defend the nation-state against undesirable forces while allowing healthy exchanges, such as commerce and cross-border travel, to occur.

Ratzel's view of the boundary illustrates the dominant thrust of much of the early research about political boundaries. Boundaries were analyzed principally in terms of their role as political and military dividing lines between nation-states. The dominant paradigm of political geography at the beginning of the twentieth century was that territorial political power was negotiated by controlling the "landpower setting" (Cohen, 1975). Boundaries served to delimit territorial power in a world in which nation-states were the critical unit of negotiation. During the twentieth century, a large body of legal thinking would evolve, placing the concern of land boundaries into the field of international law.

Boundaries and Space in the Twentieth Century

During the twentieth century, the functions of boundaries within the world political system have undergone considerable transformation. National borders have proven to be highly vulnerable to changing social, economic, and political developments within and between nations. The statement, "Back of a boundary are not only national interests and ambitions, but a philosophy of international relations" (Boggs, 1940), hints at the context that has defined the meaning of boundaries in this century. Two periods can be identified in characterizing the role of boundaries in the twentieth century: (*a*) 1900 to 1945; and (*b*) 1945 to the present.

In the first half of the twentieth century, nation-states negotiated their land-based spheres of influence, often through military confrontation. Two world wars were fought during this period. Border scholars emphasized the defensive, military character of nation-state political boundaries. Spykman (1942), for example, studied the relationship between boundaries and national security. He traced the successive use of earthen walls, brick, masonry, steel plates, and reinforced concrete in the construction of barriers along national borders, especially in Western Europe. Equally, Boggs (1940), while giving attention to broader questions about the nature of boundaries across time and space, emphasized the global military and strategic importance of boundaries.

Western Europe has been an important arena for the challenging and testing of the relation between boundaries and national defense. Both world wars fought on the European continent reflected instances in which the "shelter function" (Gottmann, 1973) of national borders was threatened. Boundaries provided functional lines of defense between countries during a period of territorial expansion and redefinition of the limits of nation-states. An excellent example of the symbolic military importance of borders is the construction of the Maginot Line on the French side of the Franco-German border prior to World War II, and the corresponding construction of the Siegfried line on the German side. With both nation-states regarding military invasion as a real threat, what Prescott (1965) has termed the "border landscape" became a zone of military fortification.

Since 1950, the functions of international boundaries have continued to evolve in response to changing global economic and political trends. The shelter function of boundaries, so vital to the power struggles that characterized world political geography between the two world wars, has begun to lose sway. Gottmann (1973) attributes the "demise of the shelter function" of territorial boundaries to a combination of technological, socioeconomic, and political factors.

Technology has transformed the world political map. New forms of military technology, particularly the development of air power, rocketry, and nuclear power, have changing the rules of territorial competition. Armed confrontation is no longer exclusively land-based. With the advent of nuclear weapons, land-oriented territorial sovereignty has diminished. The possibility of global war and large-scale human loss make boundaries between nation-states far less vital than before. Other technological shifts have contributed to the decline in the "barrier" functions of boundaries. Satellite communications, radio, and television allow for rapid transfer of information at a scale that easily transcends political borders. Sophisticated forms of transportation have allowed for frequent and high-volume movements of people and goods across boundaries. Large-scale migrations and the gradual internationalization of trade markets have been important technology innovations in the second half of the twentieth century.

International Boundaries in the Late Twentieth Century: Demographic Transformation

Transnational economic relationships have altered the scale and nature of global political geography. Nation-states have sought to create organizations and policies to respond to these changes. International organizations like the United Nations, World Bank, and International Monetary Fund have produced institutional responses to these changing conditions. Some scholars have observed the effects of interdependence on border regions and the policy opinions open to the nation-states affected by these processes (Anderson, 1982). Others speak of "trans-border regimes" and other innovative forms of governance around borders under conditions of complex inter-dependent association (Duchacek, 1986; Martinez, 1986). Western Europe is at the leading edge of discoveries and experiments, particularly within the European Economic Community and the Council of Europe, organizations whose existence is based on the recognition that cross-border interdependence requires a relaxation of national sovereignty in favor of regional cooperation.

In the late twentieth century, the boundaries of Western Europe and the United States-Mexico borderlands have been transformed from isolated buffer zones into highly urbanized regions with formidable concentrations of resources, capital, economic activities, and institutional mechanisms for further growth. Metropolitan border regions that have grown in Western Europe include Lille (935,000 population in 1980), the Basel agglomeration (766,117), Geneva (335,000), Strasbourg (373,000) and Liege-Maastrict-Aachen (824,000). This proliferation of urban settlement clusters has typically been accompanied by an increase in sets of transboundary spatial and economic linkages, including commuter worker flows, trade, and exchange of capital and technology.

The U.S.-Mexican border region offers an even more striking example of boundary demographic transformation. During the period 1950-1980, it was one of the fastest growing regions in the world. Important emerging population centers included San Diego-Tijuana (2.4 million population in 1980); El Paso-Ciudad Juarez (1.2 million); Calexico-Mexicali (460,000); McAllen-Reynosa (604,000); Laredo-Nuevo Laredo (386,000); and Brownsville-Matamoros (450,000). The implications of U.S.-Mexican border urbanization are clearly distinct from those in Western Europe. Substantial differences in levels of economic development and culture, as well as a history of borderlands conflict mark the region (Friedmann and Morales, 1984). The philosophy of European integration that led to the formation of the European Economic Community does not have a counterpart in North America. The emergence of a symbol of cities in the U.S.-Mexican borderlands region illustrates how this region has moved from a nineteenth-century frontier zone at the margin of national territory to a twentieth-century area of economic dynamism. The appearance of cities on the landscape of the border region is a barometer of the transformation of the region's economy. The borderlands urban system, as it grew and spread over the territory of the U.S. Southwest and Northern Mexico, has displayed increasing integration, both within the United States and Mexico and across the international boundary. The strengthening of interregional ties can be correlated with the gradual improvement and diversification of the regional economy and the region's expanding importance to the hemisphere.

On both sides of the political boundary, mean annual growth rates have far surpassed the national average. In the United States, during the decade of the 1970s, growth rates for the largest U.S. border cities were three to four times greater than the national average. Obviously, this growth figure did not entirely result from proximity to the border, particularly in the cases of San Diego and Tucson, cities with diversified economic bases. Still, it remains significant that growth rates were abnormally high on the U.S. side. Along the northern Mexican border, growth rates in the decade 1960-1970 were one-and-a-half to two times as large as the national average in most of the region's principal border cities. Between 1970 and 1983, this growth continued. It is quite likely that the Mexican population estimates may be undercounted for two reasons: first, many new immigrants to the Mexican border cities live on property that is not registered by the government and thus may be excluded in census population counts; second, there is a substantial population of border residents that migrates seasonally to employment opportunities north of the border and therefore may be missed by census takers. In any case, it seems clear that border cities have become an important part of Mexico's national population picture. Of the fifteen largest cities in Mexico, eight are cities located along the border. By comparison, the importance of border region cities in the United States to the larger national urban system is far weaker than in Mexico. Only three U.S. cities out of the top fifteen lie in border states, and of these, none is a border city.

Comparative Human Geography Elements of the Borderlands

Economic Base and Income

One crucial barometer of the changing settlement patterns along the border is the regional economic base. As the border zone rapidly establishes economies that are regionally and nationally competitive, traditional activities such as agriculture are being replaced. In the Mexican states, one sees that the manufacturing, commerce, and service sectors employ more workers than the national averages, a reflection of the propensity in border states for economic activity in *urban* areas. Nearly all of the manufacturing activities in the Mexican border states are derived from the assembly-plant program, which allows foreign corporations to utilize Mexican labor to assemble products that are then shipped to their final market destinations outside of Mexico.

On the U.S. side of the boundary, according to the Secretaria de Industria y Comercio, México, manufacturing represents a lower percentage of employment in the border states (16.9) than in the remainder of the United States (22.1). Yet the construction, trade, and services sectors all employ higher than the national averages. One must also acknowledge the lower proportion of agricultural works in the U.S. border states (1.2 percent) as compared to Mexico (47.7 percent). Yet, even the Mexican proportion will continue to decrease as more people leave the rural towns for jobs in industry and services in the cities.

The economic base of U.S.-Mexican border cities is as complex as the various subregions that divide the two-thousand-mile border region. On the Mexican side of the border, a number of cities display growing manufacturing sectors, most notably Tijuana, Piedras Negras, and

Nuevo Laredo, whereas agriculture continues to be an important source of employment especially in Mexicali, Ensenada, and the Lower Rio Grande Valley cities of Reynosa and Matamoros. In these cities, agriculture continues to account for more employment than industry, contradicting prevailing theories of urban growth, which typically assume that industry replaces agriculture as the driving force of the settlement economy.

Another important characteristic of the economic base of border cities is the dominant role of the tertiary sector. It is now clear that retail/wholesale trade, government, education, and services are becoming the dominant economic activities of the border cities. Neither industry nor agriculture alone has established locational attractiveness for capital and labor migration to the border cities. Rather, it is the strategic importance of activities such as tourism, retail trade, construction, and specialized services that have increasingly fueled these urban economies. On the Mexican side of the border, the sum of tertiary activities for most border settlements (construction + retail/ wholesale trade + services + government) far surpasses the national figure of 31.3 percent (Secretaria de Industria y Comercio, 1976). In most cases, these activities, taken together, represent more than half of the total employment in these cities. Some, such as construction and personal services, are simply concomitants of urban growth, yet others reflect the penetration of U.S. markets by Mexican border cities. In addition, there exists a large category of service and commercial employment that goes unrecorded—the informal or street economic activities, typified by vendors of goods and services who work periodically at different locations.

On the U.S. side, the tertiary economy has become equally important, although for different reasons. The retail trade sector has grown, with some linkages to Mexican markets. Services such as real estate, finance, and insurance represent a large proportion of the tertiary growth in border settlements, as does tourism, which attracts both a regional and a national market because of the climate, physical amenities of the Sunbelt, and the proximity of Mexico. Construction activities, education, and real estate are concomitants of high urban growth rates. In many cases employment in government far out-distances any national urban figures, owing to the location of large military bases and operations along the border near cities like Las Cruces, El Paso, Yuma, and San Diego. Some of these cities also employ large numbers of civilians in activities that support military base operations (e.g., ship repair, construction and manufacturing contracts, food and other services).

Perhaps the most striking characteristic of the border cities is the economic asymmetry at the boundary. In Mexico in 1960, for example, border municipalities averaged about $640 (U.S.) in per capita income per year, approximately one-fifth the average income in the U.S. for the same year. Still, the Mexican figure represented more than twice the average per capita income of other cities in Mexico, suggesting that Mexican border cities are prosperous relative to the rest of the nation. Proximity to Mexico, however, appears to bring down the per capita levels in many U.S. border cities. Wage levels in 1977 for border towns such as Calexico, Eagle Pass, Laredo, and Brownsville tended to represent only one-half the average wage levels for the respective states. As one moves away from the border (El Centro, Yuma, or Tucson), or in cases where cities have a more diversified economy (San Diego), per capita incomes rise substantially.

The spatial distribution of urban per capita incomes presents an interesting set of patterns. In Mexico, per capita income is relatively homogeneous across the boundary region, with the exception of Tijuana (where it is higher). Mexican spatial variation has a north-south orientation, rather than an east-west one. As one moves into the interior, per capita incomes decrease. In the United States, the opposite is true. As one moves away from the border, incomes tend to rise, except in cities where a higher proportion of Mexican American workers live, such as San Antonio. In addition, per capita incomes rise as one moves from east (Texas) to west (California). Hansen (1981, p. 75) has noted that much of this urban income pattern is correlated with ethnicity. A strong negative correlation between income levels and Hispanic settlement can be documented in U.S. towns and cities across the two-thousand-mile border.

The economic asymmetry between the two nations does not end at the boundary—it spills over into the United States and, with a few exceptions, leaves a belt of socioeconomically depressed areas (relative to the rest of the United States) along the immediate border on the U.S. side. Ironically, on the Mexican side, the ability to earn U.S. dollars in service activities such as tourism, auto repair, or entertainment has created a belt of prosperous border towns just south of the boundary. The coexistence of these two sets of settlements with contrasting characteristics reflects one of the important peculiarities of borderlands settlement space at the international political line.

Comparative Spatial Structure: The San Diego-Tijuana Region

The politic boundary not only separates the United States and Mexico jurisdictionally, it sharply divides the urbanization processes that have led to the growth of large cities along the border. National culture is a critical determinant of urban spatial formation, even when two urban places share an international boundary. Although some boundaries serve to bring cultures together, the United States-Mexico boundary does not entirely perform such a function. The wealthy North and developing South clash at the meeting place of two contrasting societies. More generally, the cross-border relationships constitute a microcosm of bilateral relations.

One measure of the clash between U.S. and Mexican culture at the boundary can be found in both the divergent structures and the visual landscapes of border cities. Over time, cultures produce cities that reflect the underlying values, priorities, and meaning attached to location and urban form on each side of the border. Cultures also produce different architectural styles, although I do not attempt to analyze those here. Regional and national economic and political dynamics in each country are partly responsible for shaping different city morphologies. Thus even in areas of high interdependence, such as a border region, neighboring cities reflect the pull of national politics and culture, which generate distinct built environments and spatial structures. Using one twin city border region—San Diego-Tijuana— these distinctions can be briefly outlined.

Tijuana in 1950 was a concentrically shaped urban nucleation, concentrated within a settled sphere three to four kilometers from the central business district. In many ways, it resembled the classic "pedestrian city" of the United States a century earlier. Although some of its compact structure is attributable to the historical importance of the downtown, two other explanations can be posed: first, economically, it is less expensive to provide neighborhood services in areas closer to the urbanized core; second, limited private automobile ownership made access by road impractical for the majority of residents, although this pattern has changed in the last decade. Still, it will take some time before the morphology is reshaped to accommodate the car.

Between 1950 and 1980, the city experienced a large-scale diversification of industry and the growth of an enormous tertiary economy. Massive population expansion took place. Population grew by 1,000 percent in three decades. By 1980, the boundaries of the urbanized portion of the region reached 12 to 14 kilometers (7.5 to 8.75 miles) to the southeast (along the road to Tecate), with peripheral growth along the coast and in the southwestern quadrant of the urban area, where many of the squatter communities are located. Despite these centrifugal settlement patterns, Tijuana in the early 1980s still displays a relatively concentrated morphology, with important locations clustered in the central portion of the city, either downtown or along the one important development corridor represented by the River Zone, and its parallel commercial corridor along Aguas Calientes Boulevard, and along the highway to Tecate.

San Diego, on the other hand, displays a far more decentralized, sprawling spatial form. In physical area, the San Diego urbanized region is probably three to four times larger than the Tijuana region. By 1970, most of Tijuana's development was concentrated within 3.75 miles of downtown; San Diego's growth pattern, however, was heavily concentrated on the periphery. The urbanized area extended to the north as far as Oceanside (30 miles from downtown), to the south to San Ysidro (12 miles), and east to El Cajon (14 miles). From 1970 to 1985, although much of Tijuana's growth amounted to infilling within 7.5 miles of the city, San Diego's growth was channeled toward exurban and rural towns lying 18 to 20 miles from the central business district. San Diego was able to develop its periphery because of, first, an extensive streetcar system and, later, the construction of a wide-ranging freeway network, opening up suburban locations for housing to the north, east, and, to a lesser extent, the south.

Comparisons of the use of land in the two cities are equally revealing. San Diego allocates nearly twice as much land for industry as does Tijuana. One possible inference is that Tijuana is several decades behind the average U.S. city in terms of establishing rational controls over urban space. It suffers from a shortage of land for large industry tracts as well as from an abundance of industry sites that are incompatible with surrounding land uses. In addition, the *city* of San Diego has more of its land devoted to streets and to public uses (parks, military), whereas Tijuana has a slightly higher percentage of land in commercial activities. Tijuana has more vacant and unusable land than San Diego, a topographic feature that has made land-use planning even more challenging. More than one-third of Tijuana's land is owned by the government, principally the federal and state government, indicating the dominant role of government in the urban development process.

These differences have been exacerbated by the contrasting degrees of intraurban mobility in the two cities. San Diego's freeway system is far larger and more developed than Tijuana's highway network. Not only does San Diego's freeway system extend outward to wider areas of influence, it can accommodate much larger volumes of traffic, is more sophisticated in design and materials used, and covers more miles of terrain. Unlike San Diego's extensive and modern six-to eight-lane freeways, Tijuana's highway network consists of two- and four-lane roads, many unfinished or in need of repairs. The highways intersect more regularly with collector roads and arterials and therefore do not allow for high-speed intraurban automobile travel to the extent that San Diego's freeways do.

There are also important differences in the distribution of social classes in urban space on either side of the border. In Tijuana, strategic locations are established by the historical value attached to the downtown and the elite spine running to the southeast along the river. High-status locations concentrate along that spine and around the central business district. Only recently have high-status neighborhoods emerged along the coast in the Playas zone. In general, residential ecology orients toward the traditional central business district and its recent companion business district—the River Zone. Elite dwellings continue to be built around these development districts, and real estate values here have skyrocketed in the last decade. In general, social class varies inversely with distance from the central business district (CBD) and River Zone. One exception to this spatial principle is that marginal housing can also appear in canyons or on other harsh land surfaces that the wealthy or middle classes do not occupy. Thus, one finds pockets of low-income housing tucked into elite neighborhoods near the center of the city.

San Diego's residential ecology contrasts dramatically. The CBD has an effect almost directly opposite to that of Tijuana. The CBD and its commercial spine (El Cajon Boulevard and University Avenue running to the east) are low-status locations—some of the lower-income areas of the city lie near them. There is a direct correlation between distance from the city center and social prestige. In San Diego, residential locations derive value not only from their proximity or distance from the CBD but from a range of locational attributes that enhance or detract from exclusivity, privacy, environmental beauty, and refuge from the high-density elements of the city. There appears to be a high correlation between residential wealth and semirustic, rural locales. Some of the wealthiest areas of the city lie in highly remote settings on the outer edge of the urbanized region or in areas of great physical beauty (e.g., Point Loma, La Jolla, and Coronado Island).

Political Systems

There are vast differences between the political systems that manage urban settlements on either side of the border. Let me briefly contrast these differences.

Local Politics and Planning in Mexico

To begin, one cannot divorce the question of local politics in Mexico from the Mexican political system more generally. The Mexican system is one that places a number of constraints upon the ability of local government to operate autonomously. Principal among the barriers to local autonomy is an enormous shortage of public revenue to build infrastructure, distribute vital services and provide other urban development projects. Local governments lack the ability to control their own destinies. This condition is reinforced by the political process.

One element of Mexican politics that works against effective local political organization and planning is the cyclical nature of the political system. Virtually all Mexican political issues revolve around the six-year presidential terms of office (*sexenios*). Every six years, when a new president is chosen, large-scale shifts in personnel and in the organizational structure of the ministries take place. This bureaucratic reorganization tends to be structured around the camarilla relationships established during the previous sexenio. Because of the specter of personnel realignment, there is a tendency toward conservatism in government. Bureaucrats tend not to want to take risks by pursuing controversial policy questions; local (municipal) politicians are not likely to jeopardize their chances of moving up the political ladder. At the same time, it has been observed that some politicians, recognizing the inevitability of political turnover, favor implementing highly visible policies such as the building of public monuments, parks, or other civic improvements. *Plazismo*, as some have labeled this behavior (Fagen and Tuohy, 1972), unfortunately occurs at the expense of badly needed social infrastructure (e.g., water, sewerage, drainage, street lighting and paving, schools), especially in large metropolitan areas.

Thus, there are a number of structural features in the Mexican political system that impede the local political process. This discussion can only lay bare a few irregularities in the complex fabric of Mexican politics. It must be emphasized that most elements of Mexican government—the one-party system, the monolithic power of the President, elite bargaining arrangements, client-patron relationships, and the six-year rotations of office—are unified through a dramatic centralization of political power, both geographical and hierarchical. The result is that local government is severely limited as an agency of policy-making and change, and has very little impact on such matters as urban development and planning.

It is ironic that the local jurisdiction in Mexico is referred to as *municipio libre* (free municipality), because it is anything but free.

Mexican law guarantees that municipal governments will be controlled by state and federal authorities—the law states that no one is obliged to pay local taxes not approved by the state government, and that all local transactions and revenue sources just be reported monthly (Fagen and Tuohy, 1972). Local governments have very little income anyway. In February 1983, a Constitutional amendment strengthening municipal government was approved by the Mexican Congress. Article 115 of the Constitution was aimed at strengthening municipal finances and political autonomy. Such an objective is laudable, but the actual decentralization of finances will require a majority dislocation of political power from central to local government. Judging from past history, it is unlikely that such a change will occur in the short term. To date, the restructuring of the public financing system seems to consist mainly of rhetoric. The reality is that the public monies remain at the federal level, and to a lesser extent at the state level.

As a result of both the hypercentralization of monies and the hierarchical imbalance of political authority, a patronage system has emerged in Mexico. It has its most pernicious influences on local government. For example, funds for local projects are often mishandled. Because local political appointments are seen as a stepping stone to higher political office, politicians may use their time to build a power base, establish camarilla relationships, and please specialized constituencies, rather than carry out development projects or service-provision programs tuned to the needs of the local population. I have already alluded to the plazismo syndrome—the implementation of visible political programs that enhance the image of the local politician. That is one way in which local governments, being on the wrong end of the public-financing hierarchy, tend to misspend monies needed for vital services and development projects. Because the political system rewards success by moving professionals up the status ladder, the best politicians and bureaucrats never stay in local government: they end up in the state capitals or in Mexico City, the seat of the federal government.

A brief comment can be made on the nature of urban planning in Mexico. Up until the mid-1970s, urban planning was virtually nonexistent as a practice in government. Mexico, like most Latin American countries, has had a tradition of economic (sectoral) planning, directed from the federal government. Not until 1976, with passage of the Law of Human Settlements, did the government formally recognize city planning as a public sector priority. Shortly thereafter, the Ministry of Human Settlements and Public Works (SAHOP) was created, and a national urban plan initiated.

Still, there have been many obstacles to effective urban planning. For one, even though a federal ministry was created to administer the planning process, "planning" still essentially followed the rationale of the economic sectors, rather than a spatial or regional logic. Furthermore, SAHOP was never given the funding to implement the national urban plan—that task fell to the powerful economic planning agency, the Ministry of Budget and Planning (SPP). Following the Lopez Portillo administration (1976-1982), De la Madrid reasserted the priority given to *economic* over physical planning.   De la Madrid, himself, was a former minister of SPP.   His administration quickly disbanded SAHOP, replacing it with an entirely reorganized Ministry of Urban Development and Ecology (SEDUE), an agency that observers agree has accomplished little since 1983 (Ward, 1986). Although urban planning was finally recognized as a legitimate activity of the state in the mid-1970s, it was never given the resources and political clout to achieve its objectives.   In addition, the two federal urban planning agencies mainly established policies at the macro level—there was limited urban planning within cities. For example, far more research and analysis of national and state urban system have been undertaken since 1976 than studies dealing with *intraurban* problems such as transportation, sewage, housing. The exception to this is Mexico City, which has been studied extensively.   However, most other municipalities did not even have comprehensive development plans until the mid-1980s.   Planning may have finally appeared on the scene because the government recognized that it could legitimize its actions under the guise of planning.   Ward (1986) labels this "political mediation"—state policies that serve to maintain social control.   Given the enormous migration of rural populations to the cities in the three decades following World War II, the problems of cities became paramount among the social pressures applied to the Mexican state. "Plans" gave the impression that government was responding to urban problems.   They provided a cushion for politicians to safely repel public criticism that urban infrastructure was failing to meet the needs of the population.   Whether the plans actually achieved social improvement is a question that can only be examined on a city-by-city basis.

Local Politics and Planning in the United States

As a result of legislatively induced changes in political organization and in financing mechanisms, municipalities in the United States today possess abundant resources for providing services to their constituents. Few countries in the world can match their fiscal and decision-making powers. The severe Depression of the 1930s was an important stimulus for the gradual evolution of the machinery of local public management. The Depression put local governments in a weakened financial state. In order to provide services and other local needs, they began borrowing heavily. This set the stage for the development of expertise and interest in local financing mechanisms. After the 1930s, local governments would gain access to legal powers that allowed them to become powerful and autonomous units of government. For example, they acquired the "police powers" to plan and zone land within their boundaries, the right to obtain and sell property, the authority to provide services and enforce regulations (such as building codes, housing ordinances, and zoning laws), and, most importantly, the power to raise revenue by imposing charges, or by collecting taxes. Today, U.S. local governments operate under the "corporate city" principle derived from English feudal law, whereby the crown granted charters to local towns to make them independent from landed gentry. Local governments use their corporate powers to operate in a manner similar to higher levels of government. They tax and collect fees to allow themselves to carry out a vast array of service activities, ranging from police and fire protection, sewerage, public welfare, education and housing to management of airports, parks, utilities, and hospitals. By 1975, municipal governments were generating one half of their income through local property taxes, local sales taxes, and other locally created income transfer techniques (Yeates and Garner, 1980, p. 422). "Planning" in the United States has a long tradition that dates back to the colonial era. Yet many consider it only partly successful in reaching the social classes that need it the most. In the end, planning is a tool to rearrange the spatial structure of urban areas to allow for the most efficient and profitable circulation of goods and services. That these elements may be at variance with the needs of communities for adequate housing, healthy environments, transportation, services, and community facilities is one of the ongoing dilemmas that city planning faces in the United States.

Conclusion: Research Resources and Library Collection Development

The Western Hemisphere has entered a new dimension of greater human geography interdependence. The boundary separating the United States from Mexico and the remainder of Latin America is becoming an important place to measure how well the North and South manage their growing integrated lives. What I have underscored in this paper is that, despite the functional, ecological, and cultural overlap between societies along the U.S.-Mexican boundary, the political line continues to separate two very different cultures and political systems.   I believe the cross-cultural analysis of the borderlands may be one of the most important research perspectives over the next two decades.   Let me offer a few thoughts on the implications for library collections and research resources.

1.   There will be a need for better indexing of information pertinent to specific international borders like the United States-Mexico case.   Indexing of library of catalogs and published bibliographies on border topics tends to be very narrow, and often follows archaic boundary matters only, such as boundary line disputes, redrawing of boundaries, and so forth.   Modern boundary issues need to be clarified.   For example, the following should appear under indexes on boundaries and borders: assembly plants, peso devaluation, environmental pollution, smuggling.

2.   The availability of statistical data must be both upgraded and reorganized to allow for better comparative cross-boundary research.   It is very difficult to find comparable demographic data aggregated to units of analysis convenient to border research.   For example, simply finding income, population growth or employment for states, counties, and municipalities on both the U.S. and Mexican sides of the border is difficult.   Mexican units are measured differently, the categories of data collection vary from those in the United States, and some data are simply not available.

3.   Transborder economic and spatial data are difficult to find within the border region.   Information on transborder flows such as commerce, pedestrian and auto travel, and tourism expenditures for subregions of the U.S.-Mexican borderlands is scarce.   This information needs to become regularly available and disaggregated at the level of cities, subregions, and states.

4.   Better map collections for both the U.S. and Mexican sides of the border are needed.

5.   Comparative sources of archival information must be upgraded.   For example, there are still limited newspaper and magazine computer databases for Mexican sources.   This again hinders cross-border research.

REFERENCES

Anderson, M.
    1982   "The Political Problems of Frontier Regions," *West European Politics* 54:1-17.

Barnet, Richard J., and Ronald E. Müller
1974 *Global Reach: The Power of Multinational Corporations.* New York, NY: Simon and Schuster.

Boggs, Samuel W.
1940 *International Boundaries: A Study of Boundary Functions and Problems.* New York, NY: Columbia University Press.

Cohen, Saul B.
1975 *Geography and Politics in a World Divided.* New York, NY: Random House.

Duchacek, Ivo D.
1986 *The Territorial Dimension of Politics Within, Among, and Across Nations.* Boulder, CO: Westview.

Fagen, Richard, and Williams S. Tuohy
1972 *Politics and Privilege in a Mexican City.* Stanford, CA: Stanford University Press.

Friedmann, John, and Rebecca Morales
1984 "Transborder Planning: A Case of 'Sophisticated Provocation'?" Paper presented at the Conference on Borderlands Study, Tijuana, B.C., Mexico.

Gottmann, Jean
1973 *The Significance of Territory* (Charlottesville: The University Press of Virginia.

Hansen, Niles M.
1981 *The Border Economy: Regional Development in the Southwest.* Austin: University of Texas Press.

Lapradelle, P.
1928 *La Frontière* (Paris: Editions Internationales.

Luhman, N.
1982 "Territorial Borders as System Boundaries." In R. Strassoldo and G. Delli Zotti, eds., *Cooperation and Conflict in Border Areas.* Milan: Franco Angeli Editore. Pp. 235-244.

Martinez, Oscar, ed.
1986 *Across Boundaries: Transborder Interaction in Comparative Perspective.* El Paso: Texas Western Press.

Murty, T.
1978 *Frontiers: A Changing Concept.* (New Delhi: Palit and Palit.

Prescott, J. R. V.
1965 *The Geography of Frontiers and Boundaries.* Chicago, IL: Aldine.

Ratzel, Friedrich
1985 *Politische Geographie.* Munich: Oldenbourg.

Ricq, C.
1982 "Frontier Workers in Europe," *West European Politics* 5:98-108.

Sack, Robert D.
1983 "Human Territoriality: A Theory," *Annals of the Association of American Geographers* 73:55-74.

Semple, Ellen C.
 1911   *Influences of Geographic Environment.* New York, NY: Holt.
Spykman, Nicholas J.
 1942   "Frontiers, Security and International Organization," *Geographical Review* 32:436-447.
Strange, Susan, ed.
 1984   *Paths to International Political Economy.* London: Allen and Unwin.
Tägil, Sven
 1982   "The Question of Border Regions in Western Europe: An Historical Background," *West European Politics* 5:18-33.
Taylor, Peter J.
 1985   *Political Geography: World-Economy, Nation-State and Locality.* London: Longman.
Turner, J.
 1894   "The Significance of the Frontier in American History," *Annual Report of the American Historical Association.* Reprinted in Roger Kasperson and Julian Minghi, eds., *The Structure of Political Geography* Chicago, IL: Aldine, pp. 132-139.
Wallerstein, Immanuel M.
 1974   *The Modern World-System* New York, NY: Academic Press.
Ward, Peter M.
 1986   *Welfare Politics in Mexico: Papering over the Cracks.* (London: Allen and Unwin.
Yeates, Maurice H., and Barry J. Garner
 1980   *The North American City.* New York, NY: Harper and Row.

8. "Nose-to-Nose in Nowhere": Organizing to Study the Penetration of South America's Empty Borderlands

William H. Bolin

It is an honor for me to participate in this look at borderlands with the most distinguished organization gathering information about Latin America. I am, after all, a freshman academic surrounded here by real pros in Latin American scholarship.

Upon associating with the University of California, Los Angeles four years ago, when I was asked what I thought was the set of evolving events that represented the most strident and understudied inter-disciplinary phenomenon in Latin America, I said immediately that it was South America's empty spaces. I was referring to the unnoticed miles along borders between very different nations—frontiers that, historically, have seen very little border trade, very little cross-border movement of people, and very little conflict, compared with many other borders in the world.

Having been of no importance for centuries, why should those empty spaces now attract attention? It's because many are filling up at an astonishing rate—with transport facilities, communications, agricultural, industrial, and mining production and—above all, with people. The contacts between peoples on South American borders have grown by leaps and bounds in just the few decades that I have been visiting them personally, observing the new economic opportunities and the new possibilities for friction growing each day.

There is a remarkable contrast between the history of international affairs among the independent nations of South America and the roughly same number of countries occupying Western Europe since the end of the Napoleonic Wars. Notwithstanding many more miles of boundaries, the South American countries have developed surprisingly little economic interdependence compared with post-Napoleonic Europe. The reasons must go far beyond linguistic or tribal differences among European peoples, compared with the basically two-language South American continent. There are even greater cultural differences, we all know, between the largely indigenous population of Bolivia and the European-descended Argentines than there are between any two

130

European countries. The contrasts between largely black northern Brazil and mainly mestizo Venezuela are almost as great.

While Europe was torn by over a century of wars costing millions of lives, in comparative terms South America has had infrequent skirmishes, the War of the Pacific in the 1880s and the Chaco War of the 1930s being the only exceptions. More people died at Stalingrad alone in World War II.

Whereas intra-European trade and European economic inter-dependence have grown amazingly in spite of major European wars every generation or so, South American countries with few exceptions do not trade with or invest in each other very much. [1] It is important to understand why South American countries have felt so few threats and seen so few opportunities in their thousands of miles of shared boundaries, because many of those frontiers are in the midst of rapid change.

Immense population grown, economic development, and technological changes during the past forty years now have pushed the South American peoples together as never before. The historic "unresolved border questions" of the continent are not withering. [2] On the contrary, as each previously uninhabited forest or desert or offshore island becomes more populated or has its resources developed, that boundary becomes more important as an economic and political issue. (It is worth noting that nitrate in the empty Atacama and possible oil in eastern Bolivia were significant elements in the Pacific and Chaco wars previously mentioned.)

Meanwhile, the skies are full of radio, video, and electronic data signals, which, with airplanes and roads, daily bring more South Americans nose-to-nose intellectually as well as physically, in various places historically thought about as "nowhere."

To give you a little more personal flavor of what is going on along some South American borders now, let me share some quotations from individuals with whom I have had conversation over the last few years on various borders, some of which I had observed on and off for three decades.

Listen to a U.S.-educated Venezuelan junior executive in a government development organization on the lower Orinoco. While passing the air force base on the way into Ciudad Guayana in 1986 he observed: "When the new air base is finished at Tumaremo, we hope to have some fighter aircraft there. After all, this has now become Venezuela's most important single strategic target." (Tumaremo lies on the new road south from the lower Orinoco leading to the Brazil border.) He was of course referring to the huge Guri Dam, the port facilities, and the growing new factories in the area.

On the same visit to Venezuela in September 1986, a Jesuit university professor just returned from Tumaremo said, "There are more than 10,000 people mining gold clandestinely on the river leading into Guyana from the new highway to the Amazon between the Ayuán-Tepuí and Roraima. There is every nationality: Venezuelan, Brazilian, Australian, American, Guayanese. There are practically no laws or order or public health facilities. People are standing side-by-side among mosquitoes in the river sluicing gold with mercury, which all goes down the river into Guyana."

In the same week, I talked in Caracas with Dr. Aroldo Gabaldon at the National University, the same Gabaldon who bravely led the near extinction of malaria in the Orinoco Valley nearly forty years ago. He confirmed those observations. "There is no question that malaria is back in the area in its most virulent form, along with dengue and schistosomiasis. It is a question of uncontrollable population movements in many mosquito-filled areas."

Those discussions also made me remember a hot dirty day in 1980 visiting Itaipú to observe again the largest dam in the world under construction in the jungle-surrounded site on the Brazilian-Argentine-Paraguayan border. I was approached by a salesman offering shares in a new country club development for future corporate executives, complete with golf courses, swimming pools, and surrounding luxury houses.

In November 1987, a small rancher in Patagonia, just barely inside Argentina and only thirty minutes by good road from Puerto Natales, Chile, explained that, instead of shipping his cattle to a packing house in Puerto Natales, he must truck the animals three hundred miles to Río Gallegos on the Argentine Atlantic coast near the Strait of Magellan. No wonder he is tempted to smuggle them across into Chile in spite of the AFTOSA regulations. By the way, the television in his little house was tuned to a Chilean station, and it can't receive Argentine broadcasts.

On the same 1987 trip I visited the new oil concessions just concluded as joint ventures between the Argentine private companies ASTRA and BRIDAS, along with Occidental Petroleum of Los Angeles, French TOTAL, and others for offshore and onshore oil production near the Strait of Magellan. My transportation having been delayed a day by a strike, I sat on the beach on the Argentine side of the Strait and watched thousands of nesting penguins, apparently undisturbed by a new Argentine government oil well being drilled a quarter-mile away, beyond which I could see, just inside the Strait of Magellan, the closest Chilean government offshore well. These oil and gas fields are even more important to Chile, which extracts over 40 percent of its fuel needs from the Strait area. [3] An engineer with an international geophysical company (doing work in both countries) described to me the continuing successful cooperation between the two national oil companies regarding the exploitation of a gas field that lies directly under the Strait of Magellan and spans the border between Argentina and Chile—countries that nearly went to war in the area a few years ago.

These kinds of contacts have made real the data on border growth and cultural impact, and have convinced me that an understanding of the frontier situations of South America is important to any analysis of the long-term outlook for continental peace and economic development.

Scholars have long recognized borders as pressure points. The pertinence of frontier strains worldwide in foreign affairs was reflected in a series of lectures at UCLA in 1940 as the European war began to be felt in its full dimensions. [4] The lectures were published in 1941, a few months before Pearl Harbor, and they are worth noting now, because they could as well have been written this morning by a group in UCLA's faculty.

Malbone Graham, who chaired the lectures, writing the preface to their publication on July 19, 1941, said it very clearly: ". . . it is precisely in proportion as states become integrated, rub shoulders more closely, that frontiers rise in importance because they are the media through which and across which the modern world passes." [5]

Roland Hussey, writing specifically on the frontier questions of the Americas, looked forward from 1940 and concluded, "There is probably no method which will assure the avoidance of the dangers of frontiers. But at least we of the Americas may thank our fates for space in which still to grow. . . . " [6]

One has only to overlay a population map of South America in 1940 on a topographic map of the continent to see what Professor Hussey had in mind. In cultural and economic terms South America had been an archipelago of "population islands" separated by deserts, jungles, mountain ranges or, often, just plain emptiness. South American peoples have not fought or traded much largely because they were not in touch with one another. Navigable waters would have connected them more than their borders, which run through empty land spaces.

As we all know, those spaces were really not impenetrable even in 1940. In the few decades since then, the spaces have indeed been penetrated at an accelerating pace. Roads—from high-speed highways to dirt roads for truck and bus routes—now link every major city in South America with every other. A large part of the Amazon jungle, the Andes, the Chaco, and Patagonia—nearly all of the huge regions historically perceived as remote—now can be reached to an incredible extent by scheduled bus, truck, or airplane service. Agricultural land has been created (or used more intensively). Hamlets and trading posts of the 1940s are turning into towns with Rotary Clubs and Chambers of Commerce. Some have become major cities. Dams and factories have been erected and, above all, people are settling in frontier areas that hardly anyone on either side of the border even noticed a few decades ago.

Exactly to what degree and where has Dr. Hussey's "Space still to grow" been filling? With what economic, political, social, and ecological impact? With what new opportunities and what new threats for peace, development or cultural progress of a quarter-billion people? What lessons can be drawn from other frontier situations that have been more extensively studied? What are the implications of these phenomena for U.S. policy and U.S. welfare?

A project has been undertaken at UCLA to research, analyze, document, and report on these and related questions raised by the rapid development of frontier areas of South America.

The essence of the program is the examination of interplay between events occurring within the scope of a variety of disciplines, so as to understand not only the events within each field of scholarship but also the manner in which they affect one another. The study, it is hoped, will have participation of scholars in the fields of anthropology, ecology, economics, history, geography, information management, law, political science, public health, and sociology over a period of years.

Universities in California are uniquely equipped to undertake this far-reaching research effort. For the past decade, various University of California campuses have been managing studies of unprecedented depth and detail concerning the border region between Mexico and the United States, some of them in cooperation with Stanford University. Fine work has been done at San Diego State and elsewhere. Various techniques and processes for interdisciplinary border studies have been developed. An important bibliographic tool for future research has been created by scholars from several campuses, under the leadership of Barbara Valk, in the form of the UCLA BorderLine database on the

Mexico-United States frontier. The database was published as a bibliography in June 1988. [7]

A new, broader project on South American borders has the potential to build significantly the base of knowledge about similar rapidly evolving frontier phenomena on our neighboring southern continent. Richard Wilkie's *Latin American Population and Urbanization Analysis* [8] showed (among many other lessons) the recent high percentage growth rates of many formerly empty border provinces. Such study can have very important implications for future U.S. public and private policy.

We have evolved some fifty potential, reasonably measurable indicators or indexes of either economic growth or cultural contact in previously empty frontier areas. These indicators include topics as diverse as population, number of telephones, reported border trade, agricultural products, number of automobile club members, number of schools, number of scheduled buses per week, number of post offices, and the like. They follow the pattern of *Statistical Abstract of United States-Mexico Borderlands* edited by Peter Reich, [9] but the list is longer because the availability of data varies greatly from one border to another, and also it includes some "leading indicators" of new penetration. Trends in various indicators need to be tracked in the statistics of about sixty border provinces, territories, or states in a manner capable of being arranged into matching pairs—such as Amazonas Territory, Venezuela, bordering on Roraima Territory in Brazil, or Zone XII in Chile bordering on Santa Cruz Province in Argentina, as done in the Reich United States-Mexico data.

Like Mexico and the United States, most South American countries gather data by states or provinces for later consolidation into the national statistics that are passed on to the World Bank, CEPAL, IMF, and so on. Tracking a large number of indexes of growth in bordering provinces for the past four decades would allow construction of a statistical matrix of border areas with various indicators of growth or contact, in an effort to answer more precisely the question of exactly where and to what degree frontiers are being filled most rapidly by human activity or contact, and thus provide a more precise sense of priority.

Among the twenty-odd places in South America that were really "nowhere" forty year ago and now have potential for risks or rewards, I have concentrated especially so far on four areas, where the pace of change—with its opportunities and threats—has been most evident to me in personal visits over several decades.

The first region of great interest is the lower Orinoco Valley—
opened to development by the spectacular conquest of malaria when
DDT became available after World War II—an area that had been
basically closed to development by that disease in spite of immense
resources long known to exist there.

This public health conquest accelerated the development of one of
the world's richest iron ore deposits upstream on the Orinoco (and,
later, of important bauxite deposits).   Vast amounts of cheap
hydroelectric power have been created on the Coroní River leading up
from the Brazilian border to the Orinoco. New steel mills, aluminum
factories, and a wide range of secondary producers are in full
operation, all monitored by a multistory computer center. There are
huge plantings of pine forest on previously unusable lands, all on top
of a major natural gas and oil field and arranged around an ocean port.
Puerto Ordaz consisted of an iron ore dock and a camp for mine
workers near a small village of some 4,000 persons at San Felíx when I
first saw it in 1949. These both now merge with the new industrial
complex of Ciudad Guayana to form an urban population on the lower
Orinoco estimated in 1986 to be in excess of 400,000, complete with
supermarkets, theaters, world-class hotel, and a university.

Meanwhile, that huge jump in population and that surge in
productivity have caused roads and communication systems to be built
all the way down to the Brazilian border through a zone that could not
even be visited without a special permit from the authorities as recently
as ten years ago when I lived in Venezuela. Now, in the dry season,
you can take a bus from Manaus on the Amazon through Boavista on
the Rio Branco and Tumaremo to Ciudad Guayana on the Orinoco
and then on to Caracas passing within fifty miles of Mount Roraima
where Conan Doyle had the setting of his 1912 novel *The Lost World*,
and less than that distance from Indian tribes whose exact location and
cultures were unknown in 1940.

Another frontier in process of accelerating change is the Itaipú
area on the Paraná River system where Argentina, Brazil, and Paraguay
meet. Here, over the past fifteen years, there have been built the
world's largest hydroelectric project, at a place where previously there
were only a couple of sleepy towns and two hotels for the few tourists
who managed to get there to view the famous Iguassú Falls. Just the
building of the dam contributed new highways through southern Brazil
and Paraguay, accelerating the linkage of Paraguay to the Atlantic
Ocean, thus relieving Paraguay's dependence on the unpredictable
Paraná-La Plata River system, which historically inhibited its exports.
These and other new transport and communication facilities have

turned Paraguay and southwest Brazil into one of the world's leading sources of soybeans. The dam is now functioning and, as its steadily increasing availability of cheap power has its effect, a series of industrial projects are planned and being executed in the manner of the lower Orinoco. Little Puerto Stroessner, on the Paraguayan side of the Paraná, became a boomtown. The movement of people back and forth across the river now seems essentially without control, as is the movement of goods—with attendant public health problems, smuggling, and lawlessness. Those problems will continue to grow as productivity in the region rises, if not given specific attention. Meanwhile, further down the Paraná, in Argentina's "Misiones" Province, over 200,000 tons a year of wood pulp began to be produced in 1985, and new forest plantings continue. [10]

The control of the flow of water in the Paraná River system has, of course, been a major issue in the planning and construction of the dam from the standpoint of river transport, flood control, ecological impact, etc., with various real and potential tensions (and opportunities) abounding all the way to Buenos Aires. [11]

Another obvious zone of development and tension is the "Far South"—in Patagonia, on the Strait of Magellan, on Tierra del Fuego, and on the Beagle Channel—where dangerous international tension already has been a product, in part, of increased development. Only a few years ago, Argentine and Chilean tanks were lined up facing each other on the low saddle over the Andes at Río Turbio—to the alarm and astonishment of local residents on both sides who, when they were very few, got along together remarkably well for more than a century. Behind those tensions, to a significant degree, was the very rapid development of resources of oil, gas, coal, fish, wood products, and chemicals all around the southern tip of the continent, plus programs of conscious industry and trade development to populate the Far South of both countries. Such government programs created over thirty small factories on Argentine Tierra del Fuego and a commercial-industrial "free zone" on the outskirts of Punta Arenas, Chile.

The development continues. Between Puerto Natales and Punta Arenas there is a new open-pit coal mine, which began to produce only last October—at the rate of over 800,000 tons a year. Local commercial use of natural gas doubled from 1947 to 1986 in Chile's Region XII. The world's largest methanol plant, dedicated entirely for export and based on steadily increasing natural gas availability, opened in June 1988 on the Strait of Magellan north of Punta Arena. Exported forest products tripled from 1974 to 1986. [12]

Seafood exports from the Puerto Montt-Chiloe area have expanded immensely, including, now, cultivated fresh chilled salmon. Registered seafood shipments from the extreme south of Chile (Zone XII) doubled from 1980 to 1986. No one knows the amount of open-sea fish being taken offshore by the huge Russian, Asian, and Norwegian factory ships that refuel regularly at Ushuaia on the Beagle Channel. The Territorial Governor there told me last December that there is almost always one of those ships refueling at the Ushuaia dock.

The total population of the four most southern cities of Chile grew from 77,000 to 119,000 from 1970 to 1982, according to official sources. On the Argentine side, in 1987 conversations, informed local government and business people estimated the growth of population as follows: Rio Gallegos (Santa Cruz Province), "From 42,000 to 75,000 since 1980." Ushuaia and Rio Grande (Tierra del Fuego), "15,000 to 50,000 since 1980." There is no way now to verify these estimates and there will not be until the next census, but evidence of rapid growth is on all sides, in new construction and in signs of strain on local infrastructure. Also, regarding Tierra del Fuego, they roughly match recent Chilean government estimates.

Finally, a fourth area of extraordinarily rapid development along a previously empty border is the often-rich alluvial plain on the eastern slope of the Andes leading down into the Amazon Basin and the Chaco. Santa Cruz de la Sierra had one semipaved street and no buildings over two stories high forty years ago. It was linked to Cochabamba and La Paz by a new highway, progressively improved since then. Bolivia thus opened a major new zone of cattle, cotton, and food production in an organized effort to create a new and more productive life for the Indians living on the bleak, worn-out lands of the Andean Altiplano. Similar efforts in reaching roads over the Andes in Peru and Ecuador have sought similar lands (and also oil and gas), and all this has carried populations into areas that were previously almost empty, near the Brazilian border. Brazil, meanwhile, in a major national program has pushed its own roads and communications and agricultural development—some planned, some unplanned—westward to its frontiers.

I hope these brief comments will give you some feel for the reasons that these phenomena have attracted the interest of scholars at UCLA. Naturally, we started out first to discover what might have already been done to look at the matter in an integrated, inter-disciplinary way. After nearly a year of that, we came to the conclusion that the answer was, in fact, very little—although some worthwhile attention has been given to particular situations by the O.A.S., by ECLA, and by the Inter-American Development Bank's Institute for Latin American Integration in Buenos Aires. [13] Small groups in the capital cities of Venezuela, Colombia, Brazil, Chile, and Argentina also have done some work. Military schools naturally have been interested. [14] Finally, there has been new interest in Washington in recent years about drug-related events in these areas.

A natural early element in approaching the subject was to begin building a bibliography, taking care to do it in such a way that it can be used readily across disciplines and be easily accessed by computer, to meet the interdisciplinary needs of the project. Sylvia Mariscal and Jorge Reina-Schement, with their library data-management background at UCLA, have made important contributions to a prototype bibliographic database. This is conceived as a comprehensive interdisciplinary tool, so far, all on IBM PC "Notebook" format, so as to be readily accessible, and have the capability to receive suggested contributions from a wide variety of disciplines in a wide variety of locations. Ideally, users could be contributors, from their own terminals, through a central quality-control point, using computer mail to expedite personal contact without necessarily getting together in one room, thus confronting one practical mechanical problem of inter-disciplinary study.

The intention of this interdisciplinary project and bibliographic database is: to create mechanisms for expediting continuous communications across academic departments; to provide a continuous sense of overall proportion and direction in the trend of many interactive events; to develop more techniques and generate new resources for the particularly difficult problems of study about areas that span national boundaries and historically have been of marginal national importance; and, finally, to draw the attention of key people in the United States and especially in the capital cities of South America, where I have found many to be amazingly unaware that their own populations every day are meeting nose-to-nose, more-and-more, out there in "Nowhere."

NOTES

1. In spite of major efforts to increase them, intraregional Latin American exports as a percentage of total exports rose only from 12.6 percent in 1965 to 17 percent in 1975 and appear not to have grown since then. James W. Wilkie and Adam Pertal, eds., *Statistical Abstract of Latin America*, Vol. 24 (Los Angeles, CA: UCLA Latin American Center Publications, 1986), table 2605.

2. Gordon Ireland, *Boundaries and Conflicts in South America*, (Cambridge, MA: Harvard University Press, 1938); and Robert Burr, "The Balance of Power in Nineteenth-Century South America: An Exploratory Essay," *Hispanic American Historical Review* 35 (February 1955), provide good perspective on historical border disputes and their origins.

3. *Geografía XII Region de Magallanes y de la Antárctica Chilena* (Santiago, Chile: Instituto Geográfico Militar, 1987), p. 321.

4. Malbone W. Graham, ed., *Frontiers of the Future* (Berkeley: University of California Press; London: Cambridge University Press, 1941).

5. Ibid., p. viii.

6. Ibid, p. 139.

7. *BorderLine: A Bibliography of the United States-Mexico Borderlands*, Barbara G. Valk, ed. (Los Angeles and Riverside: UCLA Latin American Center and University of California Consortium on Mexico and the United States, 1988).

8. Los Angeles: UCLA Latin American Center Publications, 1984.

9. Los Angeles: UCLA Latin American Center Publications, 1983.

10. "A Harvest of Cellulose on the Paraná River," *IBD News: Monthly Newsletter of the Inter-American Development Bank* (July 1986), 4-5.

11. Problems and opportunities of the La Plata Basin were the subjects of extensive studies by the Organization of American States, Office of Regional Development, directed by the Comité Intergubermental Coórdinador de la Cuenca del Plata (C.I.C.), published in Washington by the O.A.S. General Secretariat in 1985. (The studies also produced new maps of the Basin's population distribution, geology, hydrology, electrical facilities, agricultural usage, natural resources, transport, soils, and natural vegetation, drawing on data from five countries as well as international organizations.)

12. Chile. Secretaría Regional de Planificación Coordinación, XIIa Region, Magallanes y Antártica Chilena, *Exposición de Intendente Mayor Generál Don Claudio Lopez Silva a S.E. El Presidente de la República Capitán Generál Don Augustino Pinochet Ugarte* (Punta Arenas, Chile: The Secretaría, 1987), p. 22.

13. "La frontera como factor de integración," *Integración Latinoamericana* 118, Special Issue (November 1986).

14. General (R.) Julio Londoño, *Geopolítica de Suramérica* (Bogotá: Imprenta y Publicaciones de la Fuerzas Militares, 1977) is a representative military study and provides a short bibliography of studies at military institutes of other Latin American countries.

III. Literary Perspectives

9. Unos cuantos frailes y unos pocos burros

Fernando Alegría

¿Por qué será que cuando ciertos anticlericales blasfeman, en lugar de salirles sapos y culebras por la boca les sale un homenaje tan enternecedor y rendido a la Santísima Trinidad?

Este ilustre amigo mío quería borrar de una plumada la gesta heroica de los franciscanos en California. Era la suya plumada de capitán de coraceros, a fondo, sangrienta, y no pudiendo más de indignación y menosprecio, se preguntó en alta voz:

"¿Y las Misiones qué fueron?"

Y se contestó con resonante frase:

"Unos cuantos frailes . . . y unos pocos burros."

La ofensa se convirtió en elogio, el desprecio en admiración. Porque todos nos quedamos pensando en que, ciertamente, eso había sido la conquista española de Oeste norteamericano; una magna empresa llevada a cabo por unos cuantos frailes y unos pocos burros. Estos burros y esos frailes convirtieron la alucinación de los buscadores de oro en realidad. Le dieron forma de dorado adobe y verde hortaliza a la fantástica hechicería de Cíbola y sus lucientes ciudades; reemplazaron los fosos, las troneras, almenas, torres y atalayas, por suaves estructuras de lodo y paja; y al patio de piedra donde el caballo golpeaba sobre la humedad sangrienta del indio vencido, le dieron la esbelta serenidad de un atrio y lo rodearon con el calor fermentado de los establos. Frente al caballo blanco pusieron la cabra arisca y la apacible vaca. Echaron a correr gallinas entre las espuelas de plata. Sobre el altar floreció el vino, y sobre viejas maderas, la leche. Moviéronse los frailes a lo largo de la escarpada costa californiana, entre bosques de pino y manzanita, siguiendo al burro sabio y tenaz. California, la agrícola, la morena organización de chácaras y aserraderos, creció fortalecida por los vientos marinos y purificada por el cristal de sus cordilleras. En el pecho se puso una cruz; cruz de palo, franciscana. A la espalda—como tan bien dijo nuestro amigo—, la sombra de unos cuantos burros ye de un fraile, en particular: Junípero Serra.

El 6 de diciembre de 1749 llegó al Puerto de Veracruz, a bordo del *Villasota*, un destacamento de franciscanos reclutados en España para llevar adelante el trabajo evangélico de las misiones en tierras al norte de México. Entre ellos venía un padrecito de diminuta estatura, de ojos oscuros y expresión iluminada; la piel curtida por los vientos de cien días de navegación: hombre-niño de ademanes bruscos; se llamaba Junípero Serra.

A los 36 años de edad, el Padre Serra podía vanagloriarse de haber alcanzado la cúspide de una carrera eclesiástica dedicada a la enseñanza y a la propagación de la fe. Cinco años antes se le había confiado la primera cátedra de Teología Scotista (Duns Scotus) en la Universidad de Palma de Mallorca. Su portentosa sabiduría, la vehemencia y el vuelo de sus sermones le habían merecido la admiración de los mallorquines; pronto se convirtió en uno de los predicadores más solicitados de la isla. El pequeño padre hablaba con voz de tremenda resonancia y asumía en el púlpito una actitud de combatividad tal, que hacía temblar al auditorio. Triunfador en un ambiente de difíciles jerarquías, venerado y temido, con un brillante futuro en el mundo eclesiástico y académico, ¿qué más podía ambicionar el joven franciscano? Y, sin embargo, lo abandonó todo, lanzándose, de improviso y a ciegas, en el abismo de la conquista del Nuevo Mundo.

Antes de emprender el viaje y respondiendo a las preguntas de sus amigos, confesó con lágrimas en los ojos que su conciencia estaba llena de remordimientos por no haber zarpado antes, distraído, como se hallaba, en "estudios académicos". Su vocación despertó así, con un ardor y un celo súbitos.

A poco de llegar al Colegio de los Fernandinos en México, partió a propagar la fe en la Sierra Gorda, primero, y en California, después. Desde 1750 hasta su muerte en 1784, realizó una de las empresas más heroicas y de mayores consecuencias históricas en la conquista de América. Al mando de un puñado de frailes, desarrapados e iluminados como él, sin más arma que un crucifijo ni otra consigna que el "Amar a Dios" de sus salutaciones, arreando vacas, cabras, puercos, gallinas, barajando las flechas envenenadas con la bendición apostólica, protestando, sin rebelarse, de los abusos de jefes militares, el Padre Serra convirtió las soledades de California en una especie de huerta mallorquina con muchas voces, berridos, ladridos, relinchos, cencerros, mucha cal y mucho sol al borde del océano. Donde hacía poco disputaban tribus caníbales, los franciscanos de Serra, en menos de cincuenta años, establecieron una república comunal que llenó de asombro a los europeos del siglo XVIII.

Con toda razón comenta Omer Englebert, en *The Last of the Conquistadors* [1]: "En un libro de fama universal publicado en 1516, Thomas More formuló esta pregunta: ¿Cuál es el sistema político ideal y que puede garantizar la felicidad humana? Se contestó él mismo, diciendo con Platón: el régimen comunal. Sin embargo, antes de publicar su libro tuvo el cuidado de titularlo *Utopia*, para mostrar claramente que se trataba de un sueño y que él consideraba impracticable el sistema. Del testimonio citado, ¿no tenemos razón al creer que por lo menos una vez, gracias al genio y la santidad del Padre Junípero Serra, este ideal imposible se logró, y que la utopía de Thomas More llegó a realizarse?" (Págs. 337-338).

Englebert se olvida de los jesuitas del Paraguay, tan comunizantes como el Padre Serra, pero su observación no por eso deja de ser justa, aunque limitada. La gesta del Padre Serra, con todos su sacrificios, sus renunciamientos y su violento afán de sembrar la paz tenía que tentar a novelistas, poetas y dramaturgos, y no es extraña coincidencia, entonces, que en 1956 aparecieran tres libros directa e indirectamente relacionados con su vida. Hasta hoy la fuente primordial de información había sido la obra de su colega y amigo inseparable Francisco Palou titulada *Relación histórica de la vida del V. P. Fray Junípero Serra* (1787). A esta biografía viene a agregarse el libro del Abate Omer Englebert, publicado primero en francés.

El Abate Englebert ha hecho uso de documentos nuevos y, aunque su obra es una exégesis del Padre Serra, rehuye la glorificación y deja que los hechos, portentosos en sí mismos, reemplacen a los adjetivos y exclamaciones. Hay en su libro algo de ese estilo con que San Francisco de Asís se dirigía a los zorzales. Sin argumentar ni esforzarse por hacer razones de sinrazones, expresa su convencimiento de que en algunos actos del Padre Serra se reconoce un hálito sobrenatural. A la muerte del franciscano, sus compañeros—marinos, soldados, monjes, artesanos—se pusieron a cortar pedacitos de tela de su hábito para fabricar escapularios y, muy pronto, Serra empezó a hacer milagros. El abate de cuenta de estas cosas sin comentarios. Ni se asombra.

He aquí, se dice, un hombre poseído por el amor de Dios y de sus semejantes, que descubre el verdadero e íntimo sentido de su vocación apostólica y sale a los caminos del mundo a probarla. Los libros académicos cayeron una vez más en el pozo de la sabiduría. En adelante no será ya con silogismos como se ordenará su vida. Al frente de sus rebaños buscará el misionero la dirección de los vientos, las fuentes y riachuelos, escondidos, los humores de la tierra; escalará montañas, vadeará ríos, se embarcará en minúsculas fragatas buscando las tierras heladas de los "rusos"; atravesará desiertos y, con la intuición del auténtico conquistador, escogerá los sitios privilegiados para fundar sus misiones y establecer sus comunidades indígenas. Sus escritos estarán llenos de alusiones a ganados, semillas, monturas y herramientas. Combatirá fieramente por la fanega de trigo que salvará del hambre a sus feligreses. Apenas llegado a Veracruz, sufre una infección en una pierna que lo deja inválido para el resto de su vida. Durante 35 años recorre el inmenso territorio de sus misiones arrastrando su pierna ulcerada. Diferentes gobernadores se le oponen en su camino y luchan por aplastarlo. El Padre Serra, sabio como la serpiente y manso como la paloma, los derrota siempre, y a pesar de las demoras y la falta de elementos, levanta misiones, siembra, construye, pelea y sigue.

Pero ¿cuál fue la naturaleza íntima del heroísmo que inspiró su vida? ¿Qué efecto produjo en los hombres que compartieron su hazaña? ¿En qué opinión se le tuvo en la Península, en México, en América? De las páginas del Abate Englebert no siempre se saca una impresión completa de las encontradas influencias que el Padre Serra ejerció en su época y, en especial, de las reacciones que provocó. Su libro es testimonio de veneración: humilde, pero parcial. El espíritu franciscano pone luces donde hay equívocos. Otros aspectos en el carácter del Padre Serra, sin embargo, exigen una interpretación más compleja y terminante. El Padre Serra tuvo enemigos implacables en el ejército y dentro de la Iglesia. ¿Por qué? Sus enemigos jamás dudaron de su santidad y de buena gana le hubieran canonizado. Algo le censuraban, no obstante, algo que en el libro del Abate Englebert nunca se aclara. Puede ser que el diminuto franciscano pareciera un exaltado activista ante los ojos de directores eclesiásticos muy encumbrados en México: tenaz pero obstinado, dogmático, voluntarioso, impaciente hasta el punto de cegarse y no oír e imponer su criterio sin reconocer peligros ni obstáculos. Algo tenía el Padre de ese empecinamiento suicida del líder que ha dejado en la huella su astucia y su poder de adivinación; como si en la fuerza gastada se le hubieran borrado también los propósitos primeros, los reales, los únicos que debieron contar, y la visión de su guerrilla se le hubiese enturbiado, volcándose hacia adentro, confundiendo seres, cosas y ambientes, y tomando el clamor de la batalla por una manifestación de fuerzas interiores ya incontrolables. El Padre Serra indudablemente cargó, al fin, la balanza hacia su lado: defendió el poder absoluto; desconfió, se fue secando, y el celo evangélico encontró los muros que habían de ahogarlo.

Cuando un Gobernador le llamó la atención sobre los peligros de fundar tan precipitadamente sus misiones y le recomendó prudencia—¡largas esperas!—, el Padre Serra no ofreció reparos, pero siguió adelante con sus planes. Y los indios le destruyeron la Misión de San Diego y masacraron a toda su comunidad. Y cuando Felipe de Neve trató de implantar el gobierno municipal a cargo de los indios, el Padre Serra se opuso y no descansó hasta desbaratar los planes de reforma. ¿Por qué lo hizo? ¿Pensó que los indios caerían en manos de manipuladores diabólicos No le interesan estas preguntas al Abate Englebert; tampoco explica la rivalidad entre dominicos y franciscanos.

Por otra parte, el Abate Englebert muestra cierta falta de tino al referirse a la historia contemporánea de México. Por supuesto, no es el único cronista que, por explicar apresuradamente hechos contradictorios en la sociedad mexicana, prefiere hacer uso de simplificaciones y generalizaciones. Tal cosa se revela, por ejemplo, en las páginas en que describe la ruina y decadencia de las misiones durante el siglo XIX. Si le fuéramos a creer al Abate, México marchó sobre el paraíso del Padre Serra con paso de ganso y garras de lobo, desbaratando su obra en pocos años de abusiva autoridad. Pero ¿era México la única fuerza política y económica que buscaba entonces expansión hacia el oeste? ¿Fueron sus gobernantes los únicos interesados en acabar con la tradición hispanofranciscana y en apoderarse de las tierras de los indios?

Por supuesto, no se debe culpar al Abate Englebert por no considerar problemas que no atañen directamente al plan de su libro. Ni creo justo exagerar estas objeciones. *The Last of the Conquistadors* es un libro de reconcentrada fuerza espiritual, una lección de optimismo y de fe, de tenacidad y valor ante lo imposible. Escrito con candor, sólidamente documentado, de sus páginas sale un sorprendente Padre Serra: cojo, enjuto, luminoso adelantado, fiero andarín, angélico albañil, agricultor empecinado y fecundo.

En comparación con esta obra, las otras dos publicadas en 1956 acerca del Padre Serra no tiene mayor significación. En su novela, *The Road to Glory*, Darwin Teilhet teje una trama que sólo indirectamente concierne al franciscano. Trata de las aventuras de Hugo O'Connor, un aprendiz de conquistador del siglo XVIII, con algo de caballero y mucho de pícaro. Don Hugo, comisionado para establecer los linderos entre la ciudad de San José y las misiones franciscanas, se ve envuelto en líos con una partida de contrabandistas, pelea con dientes y muelas, miente como un condenado, se enamora de una emigrante gallega y, al fin, descubre el verdadero sentido de sus esfuerzos bajo la tutela del Padre Serra. Es un personaje sintético. Las aventuras que le suceden han sido cocinadas en el horno sobrecalentado de las novelas por entrega. ¡Hay aquí cada coincidencia! Pero así son los folletines y Teilhet no hace más que usar la receta con entusiasmo. En cambio, sus descripciones, ¡ah! en ellas Teilhet se luce. Quien haya recorrido la costa, los valles y la sierra de California admirará los apartes en que el autor goza evocando los bosques de pinos gigantes, la manzanita audaz y retorcida, la fragancia de los valles de lechugas y tomates, el humo de los atardeceres, las Rápidas neblinas de la costa, los temblores, los aludes. Teilhet tiene ojo de arriero cuando mueve a sus personajes por los senderos de la primitiva California. No se le escapa detalle del paisaje y todo lo envuelve en un ambiente virilmente poético.

Pero todo no puede ser descripción en esta novela. Los personajes hablan. ¡Y qué mal hablan! ¿Hay en la literatura moderna algo peor que ese afán de ciertos novelistas norteamericanos de imitar el lenguaje español en inglés? Para Teilhet el problema es aún mayor porque sus personajes deben hablar un español del siglo XVIII. La mezcolanza resulta fascinante. A esto agréguese un buen número de gazapos: Mr. Teilhet dice Hugito, aguardiente pura, oyédme, empañada (por empanada), rasqueado, indígenes, jovenito, soldados de cuerra (traducción de *leatherjackets*). Las latinazgos llegan a doler. Los nombres de los personajes, digamos de paso, dan retorcijones. ¿Cómo puede llamarse Marica una heroína? ¿Y Roderigo un coronel? ¿Y Borrego un galán? Bueno, lo importante es que Mr. Teilhet pone al Padre Junípero Serra en el camino de su don Hugo y el franciscano gana terreno en el camino de su glorificación.

En cuanto al libro de Mackinley Helm, pero *Fray Junípero Serra, The Great Walker*, puede decirse que es una especie de poema dramático en el cual, por medio de largas recitaciones en prosa y verso, se intenta exaltar las virtudes del Padre Serra para la consideración del Vaticano en el proceso de su canonización. Desgraciadamente, Helm no cala tan hondo como un Paul Claudel, ni tiene el genio para tejer coronas de epítetos líricos de un Pablo Neruda. Además, la historia del Padre Serra debe ser contada en prosa. Poesía, le sobra. Engalanada por mano barroca, desmerece. El altar del Padre Serra es de madera antigua, apolillada pero dura, chorreada de cera, la misma que aún resiste el tiempo en San Diego, Santa Bárbara, Carmel y San Francisco, madera chicana, morena, quemada, olorosa, picante como el hábito del cura que, en pedacitos, sigue haciendo milagros.

NOTE

1. Harcourt, Brace and Company, New York, 1956.

10. La frontera: imágenes literarias y realidad social

Luis Leal

El contacto de la cultura mexicana con la norteamericana a lo largo de la frontera, o mejor dicho la contigüidad de la zona norte de México y el Suroeste de los Estados Unidos, ha dado origen a una original cultura fronteriza. En esas regiones se ha modificado no sólo la lengua, sino también las costumbres, las artes y las letras, y hasta se podría decir que el carácter de los habitantes también ha sufrido cambios.

Es por esa razón que podemos hablar de una literatura de frontera. Este estudio, sin embargo, lo vamos a dedicar al examen de algunas obras de la literatura chicana que tratan de temas y asuntos fronterizos.

Los críticos chicanos, al hablar de la cultura fronteriza, sólo enfocan las diferencias que existen entre la cultura mexicana y la chicana, esto es, lo que distingue a los mexicanos de acá y de allá. O mejor dicho, no abordan el problema de las diferencias entre las dos grandes culturas, a la manera de un Octavio Paz o un Carlos Monsiváis. Es necesario, sin embargo, al deslindar la naturaleza de esas literaturas, señalar los términos que distinguen la literatura chicana no sólo de la mexicana, sino también de la norteamericana, ya que la literatura chicana de frontera se caracteriza por ser el producto de las dos culturas, según lo manifiestan el estilo (uso del inglés y/o el español), los temas y asuntos, los conflictos raciales y culturales y sobre todo la presencia de imágenes biculturales y de realismo mágico.

Entre los escritores chicanos que escriben sobre la frontera, el uso de los dos lenguajes lo vemos mejor que en ningún otro autor en la poesía de Alurista, sin duda el escritor chicano que más se ha valido de ese recurso literario. Pero también lo han utilizado José Montoya, Abelardo Delgado, Nephtalí de León, Jesús Maldonado, Juan Felipe Herrera y tantos otros. El conflicto racial-cultural entre representantes de ambas culturas lo documentan varios novelistas que escriben en español, entre ellos Aristeo Brito, Miguel Méndez, Tomás Rivera, Alejandro Morales y Rolando Hinojosa-Smith; y entre los que escriben en inglés, José Antonio Villarreal y Arturo Islas.

Si bien la literatura chicana fronteriza es una literatura que se escribe ya en inglés, ya en español, el uso de ambas lenguas en la misma obra es frecuente. El autor que escribe en inglés se vale del español con el propósito de crear una visión realista de la vida y la cultura de los chicanos que viven en la frontera, y el autor que escribe en español usa el inglés con el mismo fin.

El uso de las dos lenguas facilita la creación de imágenes biculturales, esto es, imágenes compuestas por elementos pertenecientes a las dos culturas, la mexicana y la angloamericana. La yuxtaposición o amalgama de elementos dispares, para crear imágenes biculturales, es lo que da a la literatura chicana su originalidad. A través de la imagen literaria, ya sea de origen mexicano, angloamericano o chicano, esto es, bicultural, el escritor fronterizo ha podido expresar los problemas sociales y los conflictos raciales, lo mismo que sus preocupaciones, esperanzas y anhelos. La mayor parte de las imágenes que aparecen en sus obras son el resultado del diario contacto entre los dos pueblos, cuyos discursos literarios no pueden ser separados por una imaginaria línea divisoria. El poema de Abelardo Delgado, "El Río Grande", termina con estos versos, dirigidos al mismo río:

> un día tus fuerzas,
> como las fronteras,
> se van a acabar . . . [1]

Uno de los recursos más frecuentes en la literatura chicana, como hemos dicho, es la intercalación de palabras o frases en inglés, si la obra está escrita en español, y palabras o frases en español, si el autor escribe en inglés. La palabra intercalada puede ser un simple nombre propio, como lo hace Abelardo Delgado en el poema "Los huelguistas de farah":

> bajo el sol de el paso tejas
> échenle pleito a farah
> y denle luz a mis quejas [2]

Para captar la imagen es necesario que el lector recurra a la realidad social, ya que Farah es una compañía que utiliza trabajadores mexicanos en la recolección de la basura en la mayor parte de las ciudades fronterizas y contra la cual los trabajadores se han declarado en huelga varias veces.

Los desproporcionados niveles económicos entre los miembros de los dos grupos culturales los expresa Nephtalí de León en su "Himno dedicado a los comercios chicanos" utilizando imágenes antagónicas que se convierten en símbolos de la riqueza y la pobreza. La siguiente

escena es típica de la realidad social entre los campesinos que el poeta
supo captar con imágenes sacadas de ambos ambientes:

> y Ford y Chrysler
> nunca nunca
> llegaron a comer taquitos fríos . . . [3]

En la cultura fronterizo existe un personaje, el vaquero, que los
westerns (novelas y películas) han mitificado, no como vaquero
mexicano, sino como *cowboy* americano. El poeta Alurista se queja de
esa injusticia y de la caracterización del indígena como antihéroe; el
concepto lo capta haciendo uso del inglés y el español, técnica que ha
perfeccionado:

> and we've played cowboys
> —as opposed to Indians
> when ancestors of mis charros abuelos
> indios fueron
>
> if we must
>   cowboys play
>
> let them have the cheek bones
> de firmeza y decisión
> of our caballeros tigres. [4]

El uso de la imagen mítica "caballeros tigres", nos lleva al
problema del uso de elementos reales y ficticios en una obra literaria.
Las relaciones entre la historia (lo real) y el mito (lo ficticio) es un
tópico que ha preocupado tanto al filósofo como al historiador y al
crítico literario desde la antigüedad. En nuestros días el historiador
Arnold Toynbee ha dicho, "History, like drama and the novel, grew out
of mythology, a primitive form of apprehension and expression in
which . . . the line between fact and fiction is left undrawn." [5]

Y si es verdad, como dice Toynbee, que la historia no puede
prescindir totalmente de elementos ficticios (los caballeros águila, por
ejemplo, son una invención de los cronistas españoles), también es
verdad que la ficción no puede prescindir de los elementos históricos y
los recursos técnicos del historiador. Por último, Toynbee añade:

> The drama and the novel do not present fictions, complete fictions and
> nothing but fictions regarding personal relationships. If they did, the
> product, instead of deserving Aristotle's commendation that it was "truer
> and more philosophical than history," would consist of nonsensical and
> intolerable fantasies. [6]

Como dijimos, en la literatura chicana predomina la historia sobre
la ficción. Y por historia en la ficción entendemos el conjunto de
datos, motivos e indicios realistas que estructuran la obra.

En los escritores chicanos la técnica consiste, más bien, en dar profundidad y complejidad a la obra injertándole imágenes míticas o de realismo mágico. Las imágenes realistas imparten la verosimilitud necesaria en toda obra, y las imágenes irreales, mágicorrealistas o míticas aportan la identidad metafórica. En general, se podría decir que las imágenes míticas que predominan en la literatura chicana son aquellas procedentes de las culturas prehispánicas, sobre todo la nahua y la maya. Y las mágicorrealistas son el producto de la sobrevivencia de tradiciones heredadas de las culturas populares.

Con el uso de esas imágenes Jesús Maldonado logra integrar, en el tiempo y el espacio, la vida del campesino chicano a la de sus antepasados. Aquí la imagen en inglés, "on pavement ground", simboliza lo duro de la vida del campesino, que es atosigado por el sol de sus antepasados, ya presente en la imagen titular, "Under a Never Changing Sun"; el poema dice, en parte:

> El algodón cae
> torpe
> on pavement ground
> Y mi espalda
> arde
> under hot Aztec sun [7]

Las diferencias culturales, en la literatura de la frontera, son tema recurrente, y que en ese espacio geográfico la proximidad hace resaltar lo dispar y, al mismo tiempo, atenuar lo semejante. En el poema "Homenaje a los padres chicanos" Abelardo alude a una costumbre americana que, aunque celebrada también por chicanos y mexicanos, no es precisamente igual. Aquí el poeta se vale de la duplicación de imágenes en ambas lenguas para captar la realidad lingüística del chicano:

> padre, papá, apá, jefito, dad, daddy . . . father
> como acostumbremos llamarte, eres el mismo.
> la cultura nuestra dicta
>   que el cariño que te tenemos
> lo demostremos poco
>   y unos hasta creemos
> que father's day
>   es cosa de los gringos [8]

En el poema "Quetzalcóatl" Juan Felipe Herrera asocia el mito tolteca al destino del chicano y lo hace con imágenes ricas en elementos míticos:

Quetzalcóatl
plumed heart
of struggle

Quetzalcóatl
rising spiral árbol
tule de vida
ramas de luz
fruto de raza
dulzura in tloque in nahuaque

razamilpa
milparraza
glowing heart fifth sun [9]

Si es verdad que la imagen mítica aparece con frecuencia en la poesía chicana, es en la novela donde verdaderamente predomina. Veamos primero *Peregrinos de Aztlán* de Miguel Méndez, [10] cuya acción se desarrolla en una ciudad fronteriza, Tijuana, en la época contemporánea. El mundo que allí encontramos es un mundo imaginado compuesto por personajes ficticios que actúan en escenas fingidas. Por lo tanto, la interpretación de la realidad social fronteriza no tiene valor antropológico. Sin embargo, la novela es una metáfora de esa sociedad y como tal podemos hacer observaciones sobre la crítica que de ella se hace. Además, el mismo autor ha dicho que lo que pinta en la novela es lo que observó en Tijuana. "En la década de los 60", nos dice, "fui a Tijuana, nada más que a observar ese mundo y me condolí mucho de tanta gente tan buena y tan sufrida que vive allí". [11]

En la obra resaltan las imágenes míticas yuxtapuestas a escenas de un crudo realismo. El título mismo de la novela, sin embargo, introduce el mito de Aztlán, mito heredado de la cultura azteca por el chicano. Aztlán no era solamente el lugar de origen de los aztecas, sino también el paraíso abandonado para ir en busca del lugar prometido por los dioses. Así, el tema de la novela es el deseo de recobrar ese mundo ahora convertido en un verdadero paraíso terrenal por medio de la tecnología. La realidad social que encuentran los peregrinos ficticios de Méndez, y en realidad miles de inmigrantes, es muy distinta. Los yaquis que han sido arrojados de sus tierras en México se dirigen al norte, sólo para encontrar la pobreza y la miseria.

El mito se enfrenta a la realidad en la zona fronteriza. El niño Chalito es caracterizado con imágenes realistas: se gana la vida dando bola, esto es, lustrando los zapatos de los turistas en las calles de Tijuana. El protagonista de la novela, el anciano yaqui Loreto, cuyo apellido, Maldonado, es simbólico, es un ser marginado por la sociedad urbana. Sin embargo, lleva en el alma el mundo mítico de sus antepasados. Cuando estos dos personajes, el niño y el anciano, se encuentran, se entabla un significativo diálogo compuesto de imágenes míticas y realistas:

—¿Cómo te llamas, chamaquito?
—Chalito, señor.
—¿Cuántos años tienes?
—Siete.
—¿Has ganado mucho dinero hoy dando bola?
—No, señor, apenas cuatro pesos, me canso, el sol me hace daño. [12]

Al escuchar la palabra "sol", la mente de Loreto automáticamente se transporta al mundo mítico, y le refiere a Chalito el mito del astro, mezclando las imágenes míticas y realistas:

El sol no es malo; pobrecito, trabaja tanto . . . tiene que alumbrar durante el día; como también se cansa, en la noche le dice a su mujer, la señora luna. ¿La conoces, Chalito? Es blanca, con manchas de paño en la cara. Le dice: tú alumbrarás mientras yo duermo. Ella le contesta: —Tengo mucho miedo. —Para que no temas, mi amada luna, te guardará un ejército de estrellas. [13]

La imagen con la cual se caracteriza a la luna, "manchas de paño en la cara", nos remite a las representaciones de Coyolxauqui en la escultura azteca, donde la diosa lunar aparece con la cara amedallada. Al decir Méndez que el sol, como Chalito, también se cansa, le da a la narración un significado tanto cósmico como social.

Méndez es, al mismo tiempo, el defensor del yaqui y su cultura y por lo tanto presenta los hechos, como en el caso de Loreto, el protagonista yaqui, desde su perspectiva y con su psicología, como lo habían hecho durante los años treinta los novelistas mexicanos que practicaban el indigenismo. En la poesía, Alurista, en nuestros días, ha continuado también esa tradición indigenista.

En la novela de Aristeo Brito, *El diablo en Texas*, [14] donde predomina la realidad histórica, también encontramos elementos fantásticos, legendarios, mágicorrealistas, y míticos. El diablo es un personaje importante en la novela, no tanto desde la perspectiva estructural, sino también como agente maléfico. El antiguo fortín del pueblo de Presidio, donde se desarrolla a la acción de la novela, es un edificio del siglo diecisiete, especie de castillo encantado en las márgenes del Río Grande donde los espíritus y los diablos espantan a los habitantes. "Los incrédulos lo niegan diciendo que son mitotes, pero lo cierto es que la historia se intuye. Las leyendas de la gente son las páginas de un libro que se arrancaron y se echaron a la hoguera". [15] Según esa cita, el proceso al cual se refiere Toynbee, los orígenes míticos de la historia, es aquí invertido: la historia se ha convertido en leyenda.

Intercalada entre dos escenas realistas —la historia de los deportados durante la Gran Depresión económica de los años treinta, y la historia del pueblo de Presidio— encontramos una escena mágicorrealista (un diálogo con un personaje muerto) en la cual se describen las voces que se oyen en el fortín como los llantos de los inmigrantes que quieren cruzar el río. Al mismo tiempo, el pueblo de Presidio, frente a Ojinaga en México, se describe como si fuera el infierno. Ni la barca de Carón hace falta, sólo que aquí el barquero es más humano: se llama Lorenzo.

A continuación encontramos otra escena fantástica donde se personifica a la luna y al conejo se le dan características humanas. Trátase, por supuesto, de una recreación del conocido mito azteca del conejo en la luna. Brito, sin embargo, le da un significado social, la lucha entre el fuerte y el débil, el cazador y su víctima.

Otro elemento mítico lo forma el relato cosmogónico en el cual se interpreta la creación del universo y el hombre según la versión bíblico. [16] El realismo lo encontramos en el marco dentro del cual se cuenta el mito, esto es, por boca del cuentero Leocadio el cacarizo, quien usa el lenguaje de la frontera para narrar los hechos míticos. Brito sabe combinar hábilmente las dos imágenes, la social y la mágicorrealista, como vemos en esta corta descripción de un accidente observado y contado por uno de los personajes, un muchacho de doce años, pero ya experto campesino: "Había volado el avión patrullero muy bajito, hasta nivel de cabeza y zas. El señor a caballo había perdido la cabeza muy finito. Quesque por la noche la anda buscando todavía". [17]

En la novela de Arturo Islas, *The Rain God*, [18] sobresalen las imágenes sociales. Aunque muy vivas, esas imágenes son el resultado de la memoria del narrador, quien ya formado reconstruye la vida de su familia, de ascendencia mexicana, en un pueblo fronterizo inmediato al desierto.

Por el título ("El dios de la lluvia", esto es, Tlaloc en la mitología náhuatl) se pensará que la novela es una obra de estructura mítica. Todo lo contrario. *The Rain God* es una novela que tiene más elementos naturalistas que míticos. En verdad, el dios de la lluvia sólo se menciona en un poema de Nezahualcóyotl que se cita a propósito del destino del hombre en el universo, esto es, a lo perecedero de la existencia y de la materia. Todo es destruido y lo único que queda es su recuerdo en la palabra escrita. "Vanished are the glories. . . . Nothing recalls them but the written page". [19]

Sin embargo, la novela termina con una escena realista donde la familią Angel rodea a la abuela, Mamá Chona, que agoniza. Y en ese preciso momento irrumpe la imagen mítica. Miguel Chico, "felt the Rain God come into the room". [20] La imagen de Tlaloc en el desierto simboliza el triunfo de las ideas nuevas sobre las ideas caducas, representadas por Mamá Chona; el triunfo de la renovación sobre la tradición, de la vida sobre la muerte.

En conclusión, diremos que en la literatura chicana de frontera predominan las imágenes de la realidad social urbana típica de la región. Esa es la impresión que recibimos al leer por primera vez las novelas de tema fronterizo. Sin embargo, si las analizamos con cuidado, descubrimos que en casi todas ellas se encuentran los elementos irreales que no han desaparecido de la cultura chicana. Esa presencia, especie de realismo mágico, da a la literatura chicana de frontera una nueva dimensión, que la distingue de la literatura angloamericana y, a la vez, la une a la literatura de la América Latina.

NOTAS

1. Tino Villanueva (compilador), *Chicanos: Antología histórica y literaria* (México, D.F.: Fondo de Cultura Económica, 1980), p. 274.

2. Ibid., p. 277.

3. Ibid., p. 310.

4. Ibid., p. 245.

5. Arnold J. Toynbee, *A Study of History* (New York: Oxford University Press, 1947), p. 44.

6. Ibid., p.45.

7. Villanueva, p. 317.

8. Ibid., p. 276.

9. Ibid., pp. 296-297.

10. Miguel M. Méndez, *Peregrinos de Aztlán* (Tucson, AZ: Editorial Peregrinos, 1974).

11. Méndez, p. 10.

12. Méndez, p. 104.

13. Ibid.

14. Aristeo Brito, *El diablo en Texas* (Tucson, AZ: Editorial Peregrinos, 1976).

15. Ibid., p. 36.

16. Ibid., pp. 60-63.

17. Ibid., p. 70.

18. Arturo Islas, *The Rain God* (Palo Alto, CA: Alexandrian Press, 1984).

19. Ibid., p. 162.

20. Ibid., p. 179.

Part Two
Resources

I. Building Research Collections

11. Introduction

Barbara J. Robinson

In the fall of 1985, I joined the staff of the University of Southern California Library System as their first curator for Iberian and Latin American collections. My charge was the exciting yet somewhat awesome task of developing a new Latin American research collection in a library where none had existed before. This collection and its adjacent research center, the Boeckmann Center for Iberian and Latin American Studies, honoring the major donors Mr. and Mrs. Herbert F. Boeckmann II, are now housed in the Doheny Memorial Library.

On March 20-21, 1987, the Boeckmann Center hosted a colloquium on Latin American research collections, drawing on the experience and expertise of SALALM colleagues. This colloquium was an integral part of the Library's planning process for USC's newly dedicated Boeckmann Center and collections.

In creating the agenda for the colloquium, I was mindful of the specific concerns of USC's emerging research collection as well as more universal problems associated with defining what constitutes a Latin American research collection and tangential support from the institution. The mix of formal presentations and informal discussion covered philosophical and pragmatic issues such as historical and current trends; existing criteria; acquisitions and collecting methods; selection of various types of materials; budget support; technical services support; preservation and binding; cooperation between libraries; and the relationship of the Library of Congress to major academic collections.

The papers selected for the panel "Building Latin American Research Collections" were chosen from among the papers presented at the USC colloquium and focus primarily on collection development issues. Many unanswered questions remain about the building of a Latin American research collection which, very appropriately, require SALALM's response. What are valid and acceptable criteria for defining Latin American research collections? Is size the sole relevant measure or are there other more timely measures? What are the present trends and future needs for these collections? Which library collections meet these criteria?

As President of SALALM 1988-89, I have proposed the creation of a task force that will shape our organization's response to these and other pertinent questions. This task force should dedicate its work to defining minimum standards for developing and maintaining our Latin American research collections beyond the twentieth century. I envision it also as a forum for encouraging dialogue among bibliographers, catalogers, administrators, acquisition librarians, and public service librarians from various types of Latin American research collections. Through such collaboration we can develop a management tool for approaching our administrators, and thus attain stronger institutional commitments.

This task calls for a unity of effort among Latin Americanists in all areas of our libraries, not just those charged with collection development. It is not enough, nor even realistic, to know individually what needs to be done and to act unilaterally. Difficult as it may be, SALALM must begin to document a response in a coherent and concerted way. Strong and relevant Latin American research collections in the next century require this present effort.

My hope is that the papers of this panel on "Building Latin American Research Collections" prove stimulating and useful as initial background reading for a SALALM task force and serve as a springboard for its creation. They should also assist us in the interim to gain a clearer understanding of what support and collaboration are required now for our major research collections on Latin America.

12. Latin American Collections: Criteria for Major Status

Carl W. Deal

How many collections with major status are there in the United States and where are they located? What does a major status collection include? Why are they located where they are? How do we know they are major (i.e., by what standards or criteria can we judge that)? What mix of services characterizes a collection of major status, and how have they been affected by automation? These are questions to which I was charged to respond in a symposium on Latin American research collections which was held at the University of Southern California in May 1987.

What should a collection of major status include? Briefly, it requires a comprehensive collection of bibliographies, an across-the-board reference collection for all social science and humanities disciplines, of statistical information from each country, including materials published by government agencies and national banks, the works of major authors and representative works of secondary authors of each country, and a selection of the most important official publications. The cream of publishing in each country (institutional, university, and commercial presses included) should be aggressively sought. The leading journals in addition to all titles appearing in the *Hispanic American Periodicals Index* (*HAPI*) should be in the collection. In accomplishing this a library will require a full-time acquisition staff of three or four persons to select, process, and maintain such a collection.

The major collections, excluding those of the Library of Congress and the New York Public Library, are held by Cornell, Yale, Virginia, University of California, San Diego, Harvard, Columbia, Florida, Tulane, Texas, New Mexico, University of California, Los Angeles, Stanford, Pittsburgh, University of California, Berkeley, Kansas, Wisconsin, Indiana, and Illinois. The Latin American Collections at Texas and Berkeley exceed 500,000 volumes. At Illinois and Yale they exceed 300,000 volumes, and at Wisconsin, Arizona, Columbia, Kansas, Miami, North Carolina, University of California, Los Angeles, Indiana, Tulane, Cornell, Pittsburgh, Virginia, and New Mexico Latin American

Collections are reported to exceed 200,000 volumes. Collections at Stanford, Florida, Wisconsin-Milwaukee, Pittsburgh, Princeton, and Vanderbilt contain more than 150,000 volumes. There may be other collections which are in the above ranges of size.

Is size, then, a major criteria for measuring a collection's research value? I believe it is a reasonably reliable measure. Of the twenty-three academic collections I mentioned as having 150,000 or more volumes, eleven are in the top fifteen ARL libraries holding the most volumes. All of these eleven institutions, except Harvard and Indiana, have had Title VI National Resource Centers. Those two which have not served as National Resource Centers have had traditionally powerful acquisitions programs, as is the case of Harvard, or exceptional outside funding, as at Indiana where Lilly Foundation and Ford Foundation grants provided some years of real glory.

What else do these collections have in common? Most are on campuses that have two or more Title VI National Resource Centers. This indicates there has been a strong campus and library priority for International Studies. The coexistence with other strong programs on the same campus suggests the research libraries that serve those centers are strong havens for those same programs in the future.

There is a nationally recognized need for major library programs on Latin America and other world areas which can be counted on to sustain present priorities even in hard times. The Report of the President's Commission on Foreign Language and International Studies (1979), the report *Education for Global Affairs* of the International Education Project (1972), and the well-known Lambert Report (1973) all call for an adequate number of major library collections to offer more comprehensive coverage, thereby permitting smaller collections to use more limited resources to concentrate on more specific and better-defined collection goals. In that way, and this really makes sense in the present world of growing resource-sharing, all collections can benefit by avoiding unnecessary duplication. We may want to discuss the status of our knowledge about Latin American collections across the country. This is a topic that is still inadequately studied in both a quantitative and qualitative sense.

There are number of reasons why these larger collections are located where they are: (1) They have been included within traditional across-the-board strengths of their libraries; (2) the location of some has been dictated by the geographical location of the institution; (3) they have resulted in part from the influence of major scholars; (4) they have benefited from a special campus priority. The institution that best fits the category of traditional strengths in all areas is

Harvard. Geography has certainly had a major impact on Florida's Caribbean focus, Tulane's Central American focus, Miami's Cuban focus, and Texas's Mexican focus. The heavy influence of major scholars like Carl Sauer at Berkeley and William Spence Robertson at Illinois nurtured library budgets for many years at those institutions. Campus priorities may have been established or driven by special programs as happened at Kansas where a faculty exchange program with the University of Costa Rica has resulted in a Central American library program of amazing vitality.

Finally, resources are attracted to resources. Texas's acquisition of the Genaro García collection could not help but attract greater resources. The Bancroft Library has had the same impact on Berkeley's collection, and the acquisition of the Gates collection at Tulane has affected that program.

One final thought on size: should libraries with new or emerging interests attempt to create comprehensive collections? The answer is no in most cases. First, the expense is prohibitive. What was purchased with $100,000 twenty years ago at $5 per title would cost three to four times that much today. Second, the existence of major collections of serials and prior monographic sets are no longer readily available. Latin America is fast becoming sold out in key retrospective materials. Finally, with our improved bibliographic access to other collections, there is really no need to duplicate holdings; to do so would be squandering resources for the wrong purposes. With ready access to other resources, it is possible that our way of thinking about the importance of major collections may now be changing. Smaller and specialized collections are assuming greater importance in serving national research needs with a more limited, but more highly specialized, geographical, disciplinary, and linguistic focus.

Apart from size and scope, how do we define further a major collection? The most important measure for me is the library's permanent materials allocation as well as the amount allocated for the Latin American collection. The larger the institution's permanent allocation basis, the greater are the opportunities for other collection development activities to influence and enrich the core Latin American collecting effort.

In terms of an annual allocation for maintaining a major Latin American collection, any library spending under $100,000 annually is aspiring to a collections goal that is fast becoming impossible to maintain. Collecting current monographs from Argentina, Mexico, and Brazil alone on a wide but selective basis will cost a major collection $30,000 to $35,000 per year. Dr. Nettie Lee Benson years ago noted a comprehensive collection at that time would require 600,000 to 800,000 volumes, a level no library outside of the Library of Congress today would claim to have achieved.   SALALM recommended to the President's Commission in 1979 that major national repository libraries be supported and that they have a minimum of 150,000 volumes. My own view is that Dr. Benson's definition must be scaled down by one half in order for us to claim today a number of moderately comprehensive collections in the 300,000 plus range.   I believe the surge in cooperation, bibliographic access, and resource sharing makes the smaller comprehensive collection more satisfactory for scholars than in earlier years.   For example, with the NEH grant for Latin American Serial documents soon to make materials cooperatively available through CRL, who needs to duplicate those disintegrating collections we will have on film? I shudder to think that everything we buy from Latin America on poor paper is also purchase of a preservation problem.

Patterns of allocation for major collections are now changing. This is being forced by the inability of libraries to provide adequate price increases, not to speak of their inability to meet the desires of faculty and students who wish to find locally everything they need. Today owing to the existence of LAMP, CRL, and the emphasis on improved access through interlibrary loan, allocations may be distributed somewhat differently than in years past.   In fact, in evaluating a library program we can no longer ignore the existing resources available readily through interlibrary loan or in nearby libraries. In an area as rich in resources as Los Angeles, New York, or the Bay Area, for example, cooperation can have a much greater payoff than the continual amassing by libraries in the same area of more and more of the same resources.   While cooperation through shared acquisition responsibilities is obviously an avenue to be exploited, librarians fear the possible disadvantages like the inability of an institution to continue a cooperative agreement, or a change in local programmatic focus which could upset a collecting equilibrium upon which other institutions may have come to depend.

Another important measure of a collection's major status is the adequacy and expertise of its professional and support staff.   Every Latin American collection of importance needs a curator, librarian, or bibliographer who has leadership responsibility in the selection of materials and collection development, and who oversees all service aspects of that collection.

Major collections require adequate professional expertise for cataloging, for providing full reference service, and for bibliographic instruction. How that staff is identified will vary among institutions. In a separate collection, like Texas or Tulane or Florida, such identification is easier. Staffing patterns are different, however, in an integrated collection like the one at Illinois.   There, holistic librarianship is well developed and the Latin American collection, which is taking in some 8,000 volumes annually, has an estimated total backlog of some 8,000 titles.   At Illinois, a well-automated and decentralized system which is heavily profiting from OCLC production has eliminated much larger backlogs, and original cataloging, although it is the main responsibility of the Latin American unit, is spread throughout the system.   Cataloging production, then, is another criterion for assessing a major program and collection, and it has always been a major problem for Latin American collections. I heard this at my first SALALM meeting in 1963, and we continue to hear it today.   Be it performed in a traditional setting of a Cataloging Department or in a more decentralized system, cataloging must be done to the satisfaction of the library and its users. Numbers of staff to do this, then, really are only relative, as results are dependent upon the degree to which the library is automated or to which cataloging responsibilities are dispersed within the system.

Most, if not all of the major collections have set up significantly large blanket order plans. At Illinois, our experience has been that one clerical position has been required to receive and process a blanket order plan that acquires 5,000 titles annually. Obviously the blanket order should only aspire to collect the cream of publishing, leaving room for individual selection of other materials. My experience has been that buying trips have been another excellent source to acquire material which is not in the commercial trade, especially official and institutional publications. At Illinois, such trips often result in setting up exchanges outside of the library's normal or centralized exchange program, and maintaining these exchanges now requires at least a one-half time graduate student.

Let me in closing dwell a moment on access and automation, drawing again from my own experience. I have seen access in my own library enormously improved by automation in the past ten years. Not only can any public or academic library in the State of Illinois now access our collections via our computerized online catalog for 48-hour delivery service, even individuals from out of state may search our online catalog from their own personal computers and dial the University of Illinois through their interlibrary loan operation for the loan.

That kind of automation virtually has turned our library into a state lending library by tying its collections into a statewide database which includes more than 10 million titles held by 30 academic libraries. Dial-up access to these expanded resources has allowed the University of Illinois Library to become a net borrower in spite of its having more than 7 million volumes. This experience, expanded to a larger regional or national scale, it would seem, is inevitable and is occurring elsewhere. The national plan for acquisitions of SALALM, once libraries can handle the cataloging and access issues, then will be successfully exploited for resource sharing.

What are some of the issues that will have an impact on our major Latin American collections in the future? Let me be bold and suggest a few possibilities.

1. The SALALM National Plan for Acquisitions and Cataloging will become fully operational. Its present organization by country will be subdivided in some fashion by topical, disciplinary, and regional responsibilities. This will be influenced by the growth of the North American Collection Inventory Project (NCIP).

2. NCIP, which is based on the RLG Conspectus, will be widely expanded within ten years, and all of the major collections will have input their data for the 700 plus subject categories now in the RLG Latin American Conspectus.

3. CD ROM or other new technology will be exported abroad so that the *Hispanic American Periodicals Index (HAPI)* and the *Handbook of Latin American Studies* will have their information supplemented by other automated abstracting and indexing services produced in Latin America.

4. Books and serials will be produced in such quantity and will have become so expensive in Latin America to acquire in the next ten years as to have made cooperation, vastly facilitated by improved information access through automation, not only desirable but a requirement for every Latin American collection. Such cooperation will facilitate heavier specialization in some areas by many larger and smaller collections which is not possible without a cooperative arrangement.

13. Methods of Collecting Latin American Library Materials

Thomas Niehaus

Blanket Order Plans

A good blanket order plan is one of the best ways to develop a collection of Latin American materials. The book trade in Latin America is labyrinthine, and requires that someone in the country keep up constantly with the changing patterns in publishing. Much of this is attributable to economic issues that cause publishers to change their plans, such as when public agencies lose their funding.

It is not unusual for the size of a printing to be 1,500 copies in Latin America, and there are many that are only 500. This is an additional reason for having someone in the country, like a blanket order dealer, to obtain books before the small editions are exhausted.

When the librarian reviews a blanket order shipment, additional information on existing titles can be found in the books themselves. Many books list all the titles in the same series or they list the publisher's latest titles. One use for these lists is to check the quality of the coverage of your blanket order. If you have had your blanket order for several years, has your dealer sent you the other titles in the series over the years?

Such publishers' lists could also generate titles for a desiderata list. One very efficient way to create and manage such a list is to construct a bibliographic database on a personal computer using a software program such as Procite, which is designed specifically to manage bibliographies. The entries can be tagged by country in the Index field, and then sorted by country, printed out, and sent to a dealer.

In the last fifteen years the quality and quantity of dealers in Latin America have increased considerably. For example, before the late 1970s Central America was a very difficult area from which to obtain books. There were very few good dealers in Central America who were interested in selling books to foreign libraries. Around 1980, five Latin American bibliographers in the United States attempted to organize themselves and form a group in order to share in the work of regular trips to Central America to buy books. But in the early 1980s the appearance of two or three blanket order dealers in California solved the problem.

Gift and Exchange Programs

Many major U.S. libraries receive gift books from Latin American governmental agencies and universities because there is a standard way of distributing publications. But over the years many agencies have wanted to receive something in return, so exchange programs were set up.

The first U.S. library to set up an exchange program with Latin American institutions was the University of Texas at Austin. In the 1940s or 1950s Nettie Lee Benson, head of the Latin American Collection at Texas, had little money for acquisitions but did have free postage at the university. So she wrote letters to many Latin American governmental agencies and universities to request their free books in exchange for Texas publications and duplicates that she could send them.

One major reason for the importance of an exchange program for Latin American acquisitions is that many publications in Latin America are not for sale, but are only obtainable "free," on the understanding that something is sent in exchange. Typical examples would be the census and statistical publications by Latin American governmental agencies. Until recently the pattern was that they could not sell these publications, but would accept other books in exchange for them. Many times the agency's books were free, but there was no postage money available to send them. The problem of finances has increased over the years.

When I arrived at Tulane in 1977, there was no exchange program, so I initiated one. We now have about 125 exchange partners in Latin America. The program is our main source of Cuban publications, since the United States government does not allow us to spend dollars in Cuba. I estimate that 10 percent of our materials are acquired by exchange. We now use a computer to make our lists of books available on exchange. Almost all of them are duplicates. Each year we send four lists to our Latin American exchange partners. Each list contains about 250 items. It is possible to run such a program on 12-15 hours per week of work by someone who can write original letters in Spanish. Often a graduate student can perform this function, but it is necessary to have a regular library staff member supervise it so that continuity exists.

A good source of agencies and addresses is the directory of exchange sources published by the Seminar on the Acquisition of Latin American Library Materials (SALALM).

Exchange lists received from Latin America are also a good source for learning about new publications, new series, new publishers, and new serials.

Selection from Catalogs

Selection from catalogs is an essential supplement to a blanket order plan. Considering the large amount of lists issued by U.S. and Latin American dealers, it is becoming increasingly difficult to build a collection using only lists without also having blanket order plans. Of the top fifteen U.S. research libraries in the Latin American field, I know of only one that orders exclusively from lists and uses no blanket orders.

The use of dealers' lists of new titles for sale does not warrant much comment, but the use of catalogs of out-of-print books brings up some interesting reflections. Not all libraries are inclined to order many OP titles owing to the higher costs and limited budgets. But when a library specializes in a fairly well-defined subject area, it is possible and necessary to buy OP titles to fill in gaps in the collection. In the Tulane Latin American Library we fit this pattern. Our specialty is Mexico and Central America, and we buy from OP catalogs for those regions. Over the years the fun of OP catalogs at Tulane has been the friendly competition we engage in with our colleagues across the country for the one copy of certain OP books listed for sale. When an OP catalog on Central America arrives at Tulane, we often have a team of people joining in to search the catalog as soon as possible and call in our reserves before someone else beats us to the items we want. The staff has a feeling of accomplishment when they hear that we got all or almost all of the items we called to reserve.

Book-Buying Trips

A library that is serious about its Latin American collection needs to send its bibliographer on book-buying trips to Latin America periodically. There are obvious reasons for this, and also some not so obvious. The reasons usually cited are: (1) to discover and purchase publications that would otherwise not be obtained by the library; (2) to reaffirm current exchange agreements and find new sources for exchange; and (3) to obtain books given by publishers and other contacts during the trip. On a recent trip to Mexico City, as I worked from contact to contact, I obtained some $3,700 in free books for

Tulane. In one sense it was a little embarrassing. I was coming from
the rich country to the poor country, and was getting so many things
free. But the key to success is contacts, and the ability to work from
one to another until one finds the books one needs.

One of the less obvious reasons for buying trips is their function
as learning trips for the bibliographer. It is understood that no
bibliographer could ever rely only on buying trips to build a collection.
The trips are used as a way to inform oneself about the following:
(1) the structure of the book trade; (2) the difficult conditions under
which the blanket order dealer works; (3) new publishing trends;
(4) the importance of contacts; and (5) ways of using trips to advantage
in one's own library.

To elaborate on these somewhat, I can make the following
comments:

1.   The structure of the book trade in Latin America is
something only fully understood when one sees the system firsthand.
You learn that books are sometimes found in places where a North
American would never think of looking. For example, on a trip one
can see firsthand that the Central Bank in a given country is one of the
largest publishers. For example, there is no substitute for going to
Quito, Ecuador, and seeing the six-story building that the Central Bank
uses exclusively for its cultural activities: book publishing, archives for
historical manuscripts and photographs, the bank's art collection, and
so on. One also learns that the Central Bank finances and administers
the country's public library system of some twenty libraries located in
various cities in Ecuador.

2.   The difficult working conditions encountered by blanket
order dealers is something that the bibliographer needs to see firsthand
in order to understand why certain items can be obtained easily and
why some others require much more work and, therefore, cost more.
A bibliographer who has never gone on a buying trip may be short on
patience when certain items are priced high owing to the extra legwork
performed by the dealer.

3.   New publishing trends are something the bibliographer
encounters constantly on a trip. There may be a new labor union that
is publishing books, or perhaps a newly formed women's organization
that is printing pamphlets. If the government has changed recently,
there may be new agencies that are producing books that can be
obtained on exchange. Faculty members in one's own institution are
often excellent sources of information on these new agencies.

4.   The importance of contacts in Latin America is often cited as
a key cultural characteristic. It is one thing to read this in a history

book, but something else again to engage in it on a buying trip. One must take calling cards to affirm one's identity, and move confidently from contact to contact. Some days there are few rewards. But in the process one is building up a list of names and addresses that will turn into new exchange sources. There is also the list of new serial titles that are discovered in these contacts. Then, every once in a while, a big discovery comes. On one trip a contact told me to go to a bookbinding firm that had some free books available for persons who represented major U.S. research libraries. I was taken to a small showroom at the bindery. It was lined with shelves of books in fine bindings, and I was told to select what I wanted. After doing so, more books from the warehouse were brought in, and I selected what I wanted. All were limited editions in fine bindings. In a period of just two hours I had obtained over $3,000 worth of free books. An amazing experience.

    5.   There are various ways of using trips to advantage in one's own library. At the very least, it is necessary to counteract the attitude by others in the library that the bibliographer's trips are wonderful vacations and little else. One good tactic is to stage a "show and tell" session after the book packages arrive home. Spread them out on tables and leave boxes of them around the rest of the room. Tell some of the stories of how they were obtained. Describe the complicated task of figuring out the Latin American system. Show them the bargains you have obtained, and, if possible, give figures that show that the value of free books obtained more than paid for the cost of the trip. Include catalogers in such meetings so that they understand the Latin American field better and develop a greater appreciation of the materials you are collecting for the library.

Creative Methods of Collecting

    The difficulty of collecting Latin American materials leaves open many opportunities for creative ways of obtaining publications. The following are three examples of how we use creative methods at Tulane.

    We have had difficulty obtaining some newspaper subscriptions from Central America. Newspapers from Honduras arrive daily in New Orleans on the airlines from that country. A Honduran man has invented a job for himself by meeting the planes, obtaining the free newspapers, and selling them to various grocery stores in New Orleans. We give them a deposit of $200 and they save a copy of each day's newspaper for us. Once a month we pick them up.

Since New Orleans is a port, we have a variety of Latin American consulates. Over the years I have visited the Consuls to obtain any publications they might have received from their governments. One year when a new Brazilian Consul General arrived, he decided to clean out the office of all unneeded publications, and we received about forty boxes of books. For some ten years the Argentine consulate provided us with their copies of the newspaper *La Nación*, which we picked up monthly.

On a buying trip to a Latin American country I went to the office of a newspaper and paid $60 cash for a subscription. Nothing ever arrived. So I decided to ask for the help of our dealer in the country. He asked a little old lady who ran a kiosk to save two copies of the newspapers each day for two U.S. libraries. Once a month he went to collect the newspapers and mail them to us. This was the only way I could get the newspaper regularly.

Conclusion

In sum, these are some of the major collecting methods we use: (1) blanket orders that have made our jobs a lot easier in the last ten years; (2) exchange programs that produce materials that we cannot buy; (3) dealers' OP catalogs that we rip apart so that more than one person can search them and we can call in the reserves before someone else buys the books; (4) buying trips that are learning trips; (5) creative methods that include little old ladies at a kiosk saving newspapers for us.

The payoff in personal satisfaction comes when a patron comes in and asks for information on Panama, and you say that it is in the Panama City phone book. As you hand him the book, you say: "You know how I got that? I was on a buying trip in Panama City and saw a boy delivering phone books. I asked him for one, explaining that I was collecting for my library in the U.S. He said that the book was only for persons who had a phone. So I thought for a second and whipped out my calling card from Tulane and pointed to the phone number on it. 'There's my phone number,' I said. And he gave me the phone book."

14. Exploring the Third Bank of the River: Deciding What to Collect for a Research Library

Ellen H. Brow

In order to explain how I came to have the arrogance to presume to make suggestions to other librarians as to how they might decide what to collect when building a collection about Latin America, I need to explain that for the last thirty years I have been a migrant academic. I used to be a bibliographer responsible for the collection of materials from and about Latin America. Both as a student and as a librarian, I was always at state universities. Five years ago, following an earthquake, a bombing and the 28th SALALM Conference, I gave all that up and became, instead, a book selector at Widener Library, the social science and humanities research library of the College of Arts and Sciences at Harvard University. On a superficial level, the responsibilities remained the same. But my focus changed from "How does one build a good collection?" to "How can I possibly maintain this collection?" Even knowing what was in the collection was, and is, a problem. After five years, I tell myself that I am beginning to understand; but I make new discoveries every day. There have been many surprises. Much of what I have to say about collecting for a research library will come from my inward and outward struggle with the question of what should be collected, what should be ignored, what should be discarded at Harvard—all considered in the light of what I had learned at the University of California at Davis, San Jose State, and the Universities of Wisconsin, New Mexico, and Kansas in the previous twenty-nine years.

Arriving at Harvard, I began to discover what seemed to me to be the Mother Library. Getting to know Widener is a little like dissecting the DNA of American libraries. "So that's where that idea came from" is my most frequent conversation with myself, just after "Where did I leave my glasses?" This recognition should not have surprised me, since the same process occurred in other areas as universities spread westward across the United States. Traditionally, what has been considered to be appropriate matter for academic investigation began in the United States at Harvard. Mercifully, other scholars, other influences, have diluted the mix; but the realization of the dominant influence of the Mother Institution first became clear to me when I began to work at Widener. As an undergraduate at Davis, I had thought it was cute that the accreditation committee had criticized the university for having too many faculty with Harvard degrees. But now I understand in a much deeper fashion the elitism, the stiffness, and the formality that so frightened and offended me as an undergraduate. Similar to Harvard, Davis did not "spoon-feed" its students in the 1950s, even though it is a state institution with a land-grant mission of service to the population at large. San Jose, by contrast, was all wrapped up in the teaching process, the library as a place for learning, an openness and a focus on discovery that, in retrospect, seems very different.

What I would like to suggest is that all of us carry within ourselves a model Latin American collection, a Platonic ideal, based mostly on our first love—probably the library where we did graduate work in Latin American studies. For me that library is Wisconsin; for others, it may well be UCLA, Texas, Florida, or any one of the many excellent collections represented in SALALM. We go out like Johnny Appleseeds and begin to re-create replicas of the Mother Library.

Although there are good things about that process, I would like to suggest that as collection builders, we are an important link in what ends up becoming history. We are not particularly responsible for what has happened, but we do influence what is known about what has happened. Therefore, the biases with which we approach the process of selection can have important long-term consequences. If we disregard certain formats, certain ideas, certain social groups, simply because we have been programmed by our previous training to consider those formats to be junk, or that social group to be unworthy of regard, we risk skewing future views of reality with our laboriously learned biases.

It is important to clear our minds and attempt a fresh view; to look at our part of the world with new eyes; to take the initiative and ask if there are not obvious realities in front of our noses that need to be represented in our collections. We need to conscientiously set out to create collections that are unique and that will show the scholar of the twenty-first century an accurate aspect of the world as it was up to this moment and as it is at this moment.

So the irony is that in order to take this fresh view, in order to build a collection that best reflects "your" reality, the first rule should be that you should not listen to someone from Harvard. Rather, we should all create unique collections that are responsive to our local situations and opportunities. Having, I hope, proved that what I have to say is not needed, I would now like to propose some dilemmas or hard choices that I believe it is important to consider when trying to ferret out our imbedded biases.

When we are faced with a conflict between current faculty and student requests and long-term collection building, the answer is easy. We should take it for granted that we will satisfy faculty and student requests, either through acquisition of the hard company, purchase of the film, or prompt attempts at interlibrary loan. Sometimes they ask for things that cannot be acquired, things that never existed, or materials totally beyond the library's collecting policy. In those cases, it is important that you are on their side in any standoff. Do everything you can to assist, even though what they need is for their aged grandmother or their son's science project. You must always be an ally of the patron's right-to-information. Otherwise you destroy confidence. Usually, they only ask for modest amounts of material. Remember that if a faculty member read one book every day for the whole year, that would only be 365 books; if he or she read ten books every day, that would be 3,650 books. They are not a threat, and we don't have to worry that their research appetites will consume our salary raises for the next five years. My experience has been that we need to worry that they don't place enough demand on the library, that they don't have enough time to read broadly and deeply, and that they aren't bringing us the questions that would ensure that the library is in touch with the work of the faculty and the students. Graduate students and faculty can be our best allies in building collections because they have the time and the need to specialize. We do not. If we tell a researcher that she doesn't need statistics on hog mortality in the altiplano, or if we throw away the publications on hog mortality in the altiplano, we become, in effect, book burners. I find it helpful always to assume that a "yes" will override a "no" when considering what to add and what to discard. "When in doubt, keep it."

Second, there is the question of local vs. global constituency. When you set out to rethink reality, to predict the needs of the twenty-first century, to turn history upside down and look at its underbelly, it is important to build upon the local base or local enthusiasms. Make sure you give high priority to collecting and treasuring your own local publications and ephemera. If you are contemplating that mysterious concept, the Conspectus, and trying to pick an area for which you will attempt a level five (what has been called the vacuum cleaner approach), be sure that there is local interest and a local constituency. There are numerous examples of these types of collections in the United States. There is the Basque collection at the University of

Nevada where that local connectedness with the Basque population is very apparent, the Cuban collection at the University of Miami, and border studies at San Diego State, to name a few of the more obvious examples. If a collection has a strong constituency, it need never worry about support.

If you are going to collect at a level five for some subject area, make sure that your institution is really willing to do so. Most librarians abhor level five. Many don't even see the point of level four, probably because the model library that they carry in their head was limited to basic curriculum support. At Harvard, the Judaica Collection is probably the only level five collection. It includes bus schedules, T-shirts, bumper stickers, stamps, and junk mail to name just a few of the formats that have startled me. Once the material has been acquired, there is still a need to see that it is processed, housed and cared for, and appreciated for its worth. If you collect an elephant, be prepared to catalog it, feed it, house it, and eventually stuff it, should you outlive it.

The dark side of selection is de-selection, also known as weeding. It means discarding. Nothing gives librarians quite as much satisfaction as confidently knowing that something has outlived its usefulness or never had any and can be thrown away. The same biases that have little to do with the actual value of the publication are often the determining factors when publications from Latin America are thrown out: print type, paper quality, general appearance, age, general disregard for the significance of the area, size of the publication, or other arbitrary judgments based on factors other than content and eventual utility.

At this point, I would like to entertain you a bit with a few horror stories. In New England we love horror stories. They keep our blood circulating in January and February.

Horror Story No. 1: A nuclear physicist tried to look up data on the particular type of reactor used at Chernobyl at the time of the accident; but his university library had discarded those materials because they were out of date.

Horror Story No. 2: A scholarly librarian in Portugal at the time of the 1974 coup collected a sizable amount of material from off the streets—mostly pamphlets. Since it could not be processed immediately, it was placed in a vertical file. Several years later when he tried to use it, the collection could not be found. Rumor has it that it was discarded.

Horror Story No. 3: A university of distinction weeded its developmental biology collection when developmental biology was out of fashion.   Now, when there is renewed demand, the collection is gone.

Horror stories are, of course, fictional.   Or are they?   They are close enough to our own experience to cause all of us to remember others.   I would like to suggest that weeding is an activity that is better left to the campus gardeners.   Collection policies should tend toward the inclusive rather than the exclusive.   As soon as you categorically exclude some type of publication or subject, you will be hit with a massive research project that will require that you go back and acquire, at ten times the cost, all the publications that you tossed out last year.

There are other dilemmas that a bibliographer faces: fat books or skinny books; monographs or serials; hard copy or microfilm; new books or old; cheap vs. expensive; and what I describe as symbol vs. content.   Let me continue this laundry list of hard choices by making a case for the importance of acquiring serials.   Serials are the oxygen of the collection.   Without them our libraries are brain dead.   As we fear the insatiability of faculty demands, so we fear serial subscriptions as if they were costly drug addictions.   Remember, we collect from Latin America where the serials mortality rate has to be among the highest in the world.   While subscriptions have increased in price everywhere, the big problems are with science subscriptions and with U.S. and European subscriptions, not with Latin American subscriptions.   Our problem is acquiring the elusive creatures and then keeping them coming.   To cancel an active and live subscription from a Latin American country because the Dutch or the Germans have raised the price of their periodicals makes about as much sense as shooting ourselves in the foot because our ear aches.

If we have a choice between a fat book and a skinny book, librarians inevitably opt for the fat book.   Unless a book is fat enough, it can't even get cataloged in some libraries.   This, of course, is a problem when you are trying to build a collection for Belize, Guyana, or some of the Caribbean countries where hardly anything is very fat.   If a publication is worth acquiring, then it should be worth cataloging.   It should be worth binding and cherishing.   The reason for this bias against the skinny books is obvious.   Cost accounting and a production mentality tend to weigh cataloging productivity by the pound.   Luckily, it is becoming easier to microfiche pamphlets as an alternative to those diabolical devourers of skinny books, the vertical file and massive microfilming projects without cataloging.

When we have to choose microfilm or microfiche over hard copy, it is usually a matter not of film or hard copy but rather of film or nothing—either because the hard copy is not available or because the hard copy has become very soft and is about to vaporize. Sometimes even new books arrive in need of either filming or Xeroxing because they have been printed on newsprint. We are faced with the dilemma of taking time to become what feels like publishers. We have paid ten dollars for a new book; two dollars for postage; taken the trouble to order and receive it; and now we must literally remake it if it is to last more than a few years. The same can be true of old books available on the market today. Which brings me to the dilemma of new vs. old. It makes sense to systematically acquire all appropriate new publications when they are published; but sometimes it makes more sense to buy old books. One of the best ways to acquire old books is through the purchase of collections. Most established research collections avoid buying a private collection because of the duplication. However, because of the manner in which private collectors and academic scholars work, these collections almost always contain unique and unusual titles that add to the depth and quality of the main collection.

Another area of choice is free vs. expensive, and everything in between. The middle ground is where we all do a reasonably good job. Most of us take some satisfaction in being economical or at least not being extravagant. We cannot bring ourselves to subscribe to a newsletter that comes out twelve times per year, is eight pages long, and costs $500 per year. But we tend not to bother with lots of very inexpensive or free publications, either. I don't have to tell you what will be rare in twenty years.

If we collect things that look dubious to other librarians, particularly catalogers, we must be prepared not just to defend the acquisition of that material, but to inspire enthusiasm. It's not good enough to tell a cataloger who questions the utility of the hog mortality statistics that "God will get us if we don't add the hog mortality statistics." We should give others the means to be enthusiastic about these publications. Much of that can be learned from faculty who generously share their vision of reality. But in those places where we go beyond the faculty vision, it can be difficult to sound convincing. "Prof. X uses this material in this or that manner," is convincing. "Humanity will need to know this someday," or "Trust me, I know what I'm doing," fall flat. Where you have a live patron waiting for the material, the library is being *re*-active. We should have had the publications yesterday. But when you collect for the future, you are attempting to predict how research will be done in the future and what questions will be asked. We must believe in the process and the ability of the publications to speak for themselves if they are allowed to survive.

This brings me to the last of the hard choices that I consider in this paper: symbolic vs. content material. Symbols are things that help us to capture an idea without knowing much about the details. Needless to say, hog mortality statistics don't make good symbols. At the Museum of Natural History at the University of Kansas, there is an exhibit that includes Comanche, General Custer's horse. Comanche is stuffed. Things like this make me nervous because I think, should I be collecting Ché's bandanna? Daniel's designer glasses? But the Museum of Natural History is the most popular tourist attraction in the State of Kansas. Lots of people come to the University of Kansas to see Custer's horse. So Comanche is a symbol that people can relate to. Libraries need more of them. But it helps to realize that they are not the content of the collections. Content will look more like the hog mortality statistics. I worry that the U.S. society will become pure symbol with no content; nevertheless, it is a consideration we cannot ignore—a tool we cannot disparage.

Last, I would like to explain the metaphor that I used in the title of this paper, "The Third Bank of the River." It is the title of a short story by João Guimarães Rosa, published in 1962 by José Olympio in a collection of Rosa stories entitled *Primeiras estorias*. An English translation was published by Knopf in 1968 which used this particular short story as the title of the book: *The Third Bank of the River and Other Stories*. The narrator tells a curious story about his father. The father builds a canoe, takes it out on the river, and never returns. He doesn't go away. He just stays out on the river. And the family endures this problem over the years and finally drifts away to other parts of the country. But the son stays. Daily, he leaves food on the riverbank for his father, but never does he have any word from his father, nor any explanation of why he is doing this. Finally, one day, the son waits until his father is in view and yells to him: "Father, you're getting old, you've done your part. . . . You can come back now, you don't have to stay any longer. . . . You come back, and I'll do it, right now or whenever you want me to; it's what we both want. I'll take your place in the canoe!" And, of course, the father hears the son, gets to his feet in the canoe, and begins to paddle toward the shore. But the son panics and flees.

As with all of Guimarães Rosa's work, there are many ways to interpret the story. Since Rosa is dead and can't contradict us, there are no limits to the exaggerations to which we can subject this fragile little story. The Holy Trinity, God the Father, the Son and the Holy Ghost; duty, faith, responsibility; guilt and remorse are all there. But considering the intriguing boundary problems that are the focus of this conference, the story can be seen as a parable for librarians. Every once in a while, an individual or an institution with a unique view of reality takes on a collecting activity that makes it seem a little nutty to normal folk. For it to succeed, those of us who come after need to keep the faith—to be willing to climb into the canoe and go out onto the river. We may be willing, but frequently we panic, run from the loneliness, the pain, and the cold; or, more concretely, from a long-term commitment to the hog mortality statistics. Deciding what to collect for the scholars of the twenty-first century has elements of this agony, and it seems to me, as I contemplate what looks like a leaky canoe, that this might have been the sort of thing Rosa was trying to describe when he conceived of the third bank of the river.

15. Cooperative Development of Latin American Collections: The Stanford/Berkeley Experience

James M. Breedlove

I want to share with you my experience in working over the years toward bringing about an effective cooperative and coordinated Latin American collection development policy and practice between the Stanford University Libraries and the libraries of the University of California at Berkeley. I am speaking for myself and not for my colleagues at Berkeley, nor, for that matter, at Stanford. I believe, however, that they might agree with much of what I am going to say.

First, the questions: "Why cooperate?" and "What do I mean by cooperative collection development?" The answer to the first seems obvious: we're in the business of providing scholars with what they need to do their work in Latin American studies—this is why that first group of Latin Americanist librarians got together in Florida back in 1956, the group that developed into SALALM. We've been first-rate cooperators, we members of SALALM, ever since. Our first efforts were directed toward getting the materials. This led us to cooperation in trying to identify what we needed to collect. Within a short time we began, through LACAP, to work together to acquire Latin American materials. Over the years since 1956 we've cooperated with one another in every way: sharing information, creating bibliographies, actually buying for one another, consolidating serials collections for filming. No one library could take on all this work alone. Over the past few years it has become clear that no one library can collect it all. In order to fulfill our individual goals of providing users of our individual libraries with what they need, we've had to figure out ways of providing them with what we sometimes don't have. The need to share our resources with one another is a practical need, not a response to a moral injunction. Our need has the do with enlightened self-interest.

This brings me to the answer to my second question, "What do I mean by cooperative collection development?" In my answer I focus on acquisition planning, retrospective and current, rather than other necessary components such as bibliographic access, preservation, and document or text delivery. These latter components, however, are essential, indeed prerequisite, to the possibility of cooperation in collection building—by which I mean planning together what we won't collect in the context of continuing to do what we already do well. If we decide not to get certain materials at Stanford then I must be reasonably sure that some other library, easily accessible to Stanford users, will get those materials. I believe it continues to be my job to see the Stanford scholar as coming first.

So, having said all this, let me tell you some of the conclusions I have come to from our attempts to draw up and then implement over time a joint collection development policy statement. My first conclusion, or really my observation, is that in making our current agreement for cooperative collection development between Stanford and Berkeley, we were incapable of being seers into the future. Implementing the agreement has not been all that successful nor easy. Some of the components necessary to success were in place in 1982, and still are, but others which I now see as essential did not exist at the time and, indeed, are still in the planning stages. In describing each of these categories my conclusions are obvious. In my view, all the components I list are necessary, whether or not they currently exist. Our experience since 1982 is not that we have failed but that we have come to more clearly understand what we need to do. It is experience that has been very fruitful in forming current plans for overall cooperation between the Stanford and Berkeley libraries.

At this point, I set the context for and give you some of the history of our 1982 agreement. The combined Latin American collections in the Stanford and Berkeley libraries offer an extraordinary intellectual resource of major research value, not only to Stanford and Berkeley users but to the Latin American scholarly community in general. The collections at Berkeley have been consistently developed for almost a century and are particularly strong in archaeological and ethnographic materials, art, drama, education, law, literature, and religion. Berkeley's Bancroft Library is renowned for its holdings on colonial Spanish America, on Mexico, and on Central America. The Berkeley libraries maintain a collection of over 530,000 monograph volumes, 3,385 periodical titles, and 1,625,000 manuscripts on Latin America. The retrospective strengths of the Berkeley collections complement the large Latin American collections at Stanford, which are the result of efforts concentrated in the past two decades. The general emphasis at Stanford has been on materials on the nineteenth and twentieth centuries, with particular attention to Brazil and to the social sciences. The collections are strongest in political, social, and economic changes since World War II throughout Latin America. Stanford has directed collecting efforts to post-1810 histories of

Argentina, Bolivia, Chile, Colombia, Guatemala, Peru, and Mexico, in addition to a broad emphasis on Brazilian history. In recent years we have built particularly strong holdings in linguistics, the history of women in Latin America, and in travel literature. The Hoover Institution's holdings on contemporary Cuba enjoy an international reputation and are supplemented by extensive holdings on other Latin American countries in the twentieth century. In all, the Stanford Latin American collections contain well over 200,000 monographs and over 1,600 periodical titles. The Stanford and Berkeley collections have been strongly supported by the two centers for Latin American studies and by grants from the Andrew Mellon Foundation and from the federal government.

In the mid 1970s Gaston Szokol, who was Don Hazen's predecessor as Latin American librarian at Berkeley, and I began discussing the logic and possibilities of cooperating closely in the development of our Latin American collections. As was true for all Latin American bibliographers at the time, it was becoming increasingly clear to Gaston and me that, in spite of the continued and increasing scholarly need for research materials in our universities, no single institution could do it all. Given the strengths I've already described and the proximity of our campuses, it made sense to explore the idea that we could help one another out and serve our users' needs even better.

So, beginning some ten years ago we began a series of evaluations of our collections to determine their adequacy to support research and curricula, and to provide data for drafting sound acquisitions policies that would take into account the strengths and weaknesses of each library's holdings. A little later the Government Documents Departments of the two institutions began similar discussions.

During the same years the Stanford University libraries and the Berkeley libraries agreed to cooperate on a broader basis. The elements of this agreement were: (1) a shared catalog data file; (2) regular exchange of serials records; (3) a telephone link at each campus enabling them to get rapid and direct catalog and reference information; and (4) the extension of direct borrowing privileges to faculty and graduate students at both universities. Further, we established a daily bus service between the two libraries to transport both users and materials, making rapid interlibrary loan possible. Finally, Stanford became a full member and participant in the nine campus University of California Shared Purchase Program. Support for these activities, both on the wider library system level and specifically for the Latin American efforts, came variously from the

Andrew Mellon Foundation, the Title II program, the Alfred Sloan Foundation, the Bonsall Fund at Stanford, and the Department of History at Berkeley.   There was significant funding from the two campuses' Centers for Latin American Studies as well.

In 1981, the federal government funded the establishment of the Joint Stanford-Berkeley National Resource Center for Latin American Studies. An important element in the original and subsequent funding of this joint center was and is support for and encouragement of the cooperative efforts and activities of the libraries.

In 1982, in the context of and as a result of all these events, programs, and activities, Gaston Szokol and I drew up a collecting agreement for Latin America. We knew we were entering unexplored territory and saw the agreement as experimental; in retrospect, I've come to view it as a pilot project from which we learned a lot, as much about what not to do as about what to do. With all the discussions this week at SALALM about the successes and shortcomings of cooperative efforts, I believe the Stanford/Berkeley agreement points up the care that needs to be taken in formally allocating responsibilities between two libraries. In 1982, we made such allocations both by country and by type and provenance of publication. For any of you interested in the details I refer you to a 1982 brochure describing our plan which was published by the Joint Center and distributed at the 1982 SALALM/LASA meeting in Washington. In addition to the agreement, the two Government Documents Departments made a similar agreement in 1983.

There have been some real problems in implementing our 1982 arrangement. I summarize them in no particular order of importance:

1.   Parts of the overall infrastructure I described functioned well, other parts didn't, particularly in the area of access to technical processing information—Stanford's access to Berkeley's online acquisitions records and catalog data files is incomplete.

2.   Soon after 1982 there was a personnel gap in the Berkeley library. A considerable amount of time passed before Gaston Szokol's retirement and Dan Hazen's appointment as Latin American Librarian.

3.   There are real problems in the way we allocated and defined our different collecting responsibilities. We made an honest and rational attempt to look at Latin American materials in a certain way, but experience has shown me that we were incorrect. Country division with further subdivision by type and provenance of materials is not the practical way to go. What looks good conceptually and on paper doesn't always reflect acquisitions and collecting realities. Furthermore, subsequent cooperative activities in Latin American

collection development and management suggest other more practical avenues toward success. These are, to name a few: the recent proposal and grant to support online reconversion of card catalog files on Latin America at six major Latin American collections; the RLG Geology Project on Latin America, which we heard described at the 1988 SALALM town meeting; and the recently formed ICCG plans on Cuban acquisitions. There are also other discussions which have taken place this year at SALALM in workshops on cataloging and on official publications.

4.   Another factor affecting the success of any agreement between Stanford and Berkeley is that some of the most important resources at each campus are housed in libraries with very limited access compared with other libraries, namely the Hoover Institution Library and the Bancroft Library.

5.   Finally, the nationwide erosion of support for collection development, an erosion affecting libraries' priorities, an erosion of acquisitions funds and of the level of staff support, has had a negative effect on the ability to implement the 1982 agreement.

In that agreement we stated, "The agreements will be subject to periodic review and revision." I believe the time has come for such a review. We continue to have institutional support, and indeed at Stanford we have an institutional mandate for cooperation with Berkeley. A document called "Stanford-Berkeley Cooperative Program: Collection Development Proposal" was recently brought to Stanford University Libraries' Collection Development Group by Michael Ryan, Stanford's Collection Development Officer. It states:

The Stanford-Berkeley cooperative library program reflects a rare relationship between two major research institutions. This relationship has become a symbol and a paradigm of interlibrary cooperation. The goals of the present proposal are to expand and enrich cooperative collection development arrangements currently in place as well as to begin new initiatives for the purpose of creating a more broadly based program of coordinated collection development and management. This enriched program will create a singular partnership among major academic libraries, and it will include not only collection development policy but cataloging, preservation, and access. Moreover, it will be formally integrated with academic programs at both institutions through respective faculty-library committees and joint departmental relationships.

The proposal covers eight areas; revision of collection development policy statements, continued collection evaluations, cooperative cataloging, cooperative preservation, enhancements of our local bibliographic communities, access to information, building on current strengths, and publicizing the program.

So, there are continued developments for the Stanford/Berkeley Latin American collections in several overlapping contexts: that of the two institutions themselves as reflected in their libraries and in the Joint Center for Latin American Studies; that of SALALM's new directions in cooperative programs; and, finally, the context of our experience in the past six years. Drawing upon all these and having given you a brief description of them, I'd like to conclude with a simple list of what I believe are the essential elements of success in cooperative development, planning, and management of collections in any area studies field. This list isn't entirely my own; it draws upon the experience and wisdom of other members of SALALM and also upon discussions held at a small roundtable on Latin American collections which Barbara Robinson hosted at USC in 1987. The key elements are:

1. Trust that each institution will meet its commitments. Cooperation is sometimes a fragile enterprise because local collecting focuses change without notice.

2. Technical capacity—online access to bibliographic records, ideally including acquisitions records, e-mail connection between key personnel—is essential.

3. The larger cooperative structure between the libraries involved must be in place.

4. At each institution there must be internal communication among its various libraries.

5. The bibliographer at each institution must have wide, if not full, authority for selection decisions for the areas and languages affected by the agreement.

6. We need to define in a flexible, nonrestrictive way what a core Latin American collection is in order to understand the context, boundaries, and goals of any agreement.

There may be other elements which I've missed and, clearly, I haven't elaborated on all of the ones listed; but these are the crucial ones that come to mind. Cervantes wrote, *"Entre dicho y hecho hay gran trecho."* For many years and in many ways SALALM has proven Cervantes wrong—we have done what we have dreamed about and talked about since 1956. I'm confident that we will continue to do so.

II. Cataloging and Institutional Cooperation

16. No Bibliographer Is an Island: Cataloging and Collection Development of Latin Americana

Gayle Ann Williams

At first glance, the title of my paper may seem flippant or facetious. In all fairness, perhaps "Neither Bibliographer nor Cataloger Is an Island" would have been a more judicious phrase since my intention here is to explore the relationship between collection development and the cataloging of Latin American materials.

It may appear curious to declare an interest in what could be viewed as a fairly cut and dried work flow. In an academic library that emphasizes the collection of materials from and about Latin America, a subject bibliographer is responsible for the processing of that same material so that it ends up in the stacks at the library users' disposal. It is additionally obvious that each librarian faces respective complexities. Budgets are never quite plentiful. Certain materials demand more effort to acquire. Bibliographers also provide many public service duties. Backlogs of material requiring original cataloging build up. Cataloging rules and accompanying practices are in a constant state of change. Meeting the standards involved in participation in a national cataloging database is coupled with increasing demands for local automation needs.

Within this generalized pattern I see both cooperation and isolation. Successful collection development of Latin Americana requires a supportive cataloging environment (cooperation). The emphasis on this cooperative work flow becomes heightened when the bibliographer perceives that local collection building also signifies participation within national resource-sharing programs. Cataloging on OCLC and RLIN provides built-in national level participation, although other factors can also jeopardize such an assumption (isolation).

There are considerations regarding how different librarians view their respective roles. For the bibliographer, is the purview of collection development suspended during the period certain materials are in the backlog awaiting processing? Should the cataloger have the same commitment to local collection building that is meant to tie into a national cooperative framework? As a librarian who has for some time been involved in both cataloging and collection development, I view my particular responsibilities in each area as equal halves of the same whole rather than two separate functions. I remain aware of factors within libraries that do not make this attitude a comfortable one. I do not suggest that in general Latin American catalogers have not dealt with these issues. In fact, a review of past cooperative cataloging efforts can provide more insight into these concerns.

Cooperation and resource sharing have been key words involved in the business of building Latin American collections. They generally relate to projects dealing with acquisitions or collection development. The Farmington Plan, the Latin American Cooperative Acquisitions Plan (LACAP), the Center for Research Libraries, the Latin American Microform Project, and the RLG Conspectus are all pertinent examples here. The notion of cooperation also extends to Latin American cataloging through the efforts of SALALM.

SALALM's initial venture in cooperative cataloging came about in 1964 owing to the LACAP project. [1] The cataloging project actually expanded a prior exchange agreement between the University of California, Los Angeles and Cornell University for cataloging copy of Peruvian and Colombian imprints received through their respective LACAP blanket orders. At the ninth SALALM meeting held in St. Louis, Missouri (June 1964) an ad hoc committee created a plan in which ten libraries (Cornell, Duke, Florida, Illinois, Kansas, North Carolina, Stanford, Texas, University of California, Los Angeles, the University of Southern California) eventually provided main entry cards for the country or area of responsibility assigned. Between September 1964 and October 1966 the libraries supplied cataloging for 7,497 titles. This project was discontinued when the Library of Congress's National Program for Acquisitions and Cataloging began providing cataloging for LACAP blanket orders until the demise of LACAP in 1972.

The growing implementation of OCLC for a national database of shared cataloging encouraged further interest in cooperative cataloging by SALALM in the mid 1970s. The Subcommittee on Bibliographic Technology surveyed selected libraries to identify their anticipated participation in OCLC, willingness to enter into a formal agreement on cooperative cataloging, and a possible country or area assignment. [2] The resulting Ad Hoc Cooperative Cataloging Group (formed in 1977) established the goal of each member providing cataloging for its assigned area into OCLC as quickly as possible. The actual level of activity of this group is uncertain. Citing the switch of four of the original eight members from OCLC to RLIN, the increased availability of Library of Congress cataloging for certain countries, lack of success in the recruitment of new participants as factors, the committee officially disbanded in 1981. [3]

Subsequent interest in cooperative cataloging was explored with the modified Farmington Plan, but does not appear to have taken hold. A 1987 survey on cataloging practices for Latin Americana also suggests that the establishment of cataloging priorities is based more on local needs than on adherence to any formal cooperative cataloging agreement. [4]

The differing outcomes of the 1964 and 1977 projects indicate that the potential to unite collection development and cataloging exists but cannot be taken for granted. The 1964 project was clearly enhanced by its connection to LACAP which had already been in operation for a few years. Expectations that cooperation would carry over from acquisitions to cataloging would have been readily fostered under the circumstances. The fact that the 1977 project did not get off the ground in spite of taking place in a period when we often expect library automation to solve all our problems is a reminder of why I am dealing with cooperation and isolation.

The Latin American cataloger and bibliographer obviously share a common goal, although their duties differ. They often possess similar qualifications with respect to language expertise and subject degrees. Consultation usually takes place between the two to establish priorities and solve particular problems. Earlier, I brought up questions that relate to my own perception of cataloging and collection development. The factors that may isolate the two processes are those that particularly affect catalogers. Two broad areas I consider significant here are the institutional organization of cataloging and the status of the cataloger.

The Latin American cataloger ultimately reports to a department head in cataloging with respect to accountability and supervision. The nature of departmental expectations may determine whether or not an individual cataloger has a hand in following through with a special project, such as a cooperative cataloging assignment. Often, there is a perception that it is not especially significant to focus on one specific country when the larger overall backlog will still exist. The Latin American backlog is either prone to being warehoused or threatened with minimal level cataloging when these options are viewed by the library administration as the most expedient solutions. Libraries that have developed online catalogs at great expense have also developed a tendency to introduce local minimal-level entries that bypass sharing that data with OCLC or RLIN. Under such circumstances it is

understandable that Latin American catalogers (or any cataloger, for
that matter) may feel that their responsibilities have less to do with
fulfilling collection development goals than with responding to these
pressing issues.

The perception of catalogers as a particular class of librarian
further limits the role that they can play in collection development.
The view that catalogers do boring work that involves technical
application of minor details, and their own obsession with doing it all
perfectly, still haunts us.   One must consider instead that most
librarians employ a certain amount of technical expertise, whether it is
applying correct MARC codes to original cataloging, following
specified search structures in an online database, or explaining how to
use *Psychological Abstracts* for the third time in one day!   If it is
perceived that catalogers simply wind up with the lion's share of
repetition of certain details, using it for faultfinding serves no
constructive purpose.   It is possibly easier to criticize what catalogers
do since our work is on constant display, leaving errors (despite our
merciless quest for perfection) and misunderstood practices for those
who use them for complaints.

Given that the last few years have evidenced concerned discussions
about the lack of catalogers to fill sorely needed vacancies and the
acknowledgment that OCLC and RLIN have not diminished the need
for experienced original catalogers, the long-held misconceptions
pertaining to catalogers can be seen to hold less and less weight.   In
their place should follow stronger support for what catalogers should
be doing. Support to insure a steady pool of catalogers for the future
is equally critical.   The boring part of a cataloger's job that I will
ascribe to is in the very fact that all most catalogers do is catalog.
Even an enjoyable occupation becomes limiting.   The assignment of
cataloging in combination with some other responsibility provides a
means in which catalogers can stay charged to following larger goals.
This is especially meaningful for the Latin American cataloger. I am a
cataloger with the rare opportunity of also being able to have subject
selection assignments.   My interests as a cataloger have been
immeasurably bolstered by becoming familiar with the needs of faculty
and students.   Not all catalogers find it necessary to broaden their
scope of duties, but institutions would be well advised to retain a
flexible attitude toward combined assignments whether in reference,
collection development, or other library operations in which the
cataloger has interest or expertise. Other librarians would be equally
well advised to take on cataloging assignments in order to have a
clearer perspective of unfamiliar territory!

Understanding the challenges that a cataloger faces is essential in order to maintain a cooperative spirit that overcomes departmental boundaries. In this day and age it may well be that cooperative cataloging will be more fulfilled by engaging in cataloging for our national bibliographic utilities than by limiting it to a local system.

NOTES

1. Carl Deal, "Cooperative Cataloging of Latin American Materials," *Thirteenth Seminar on Latin American Library Materials: Final Report and Working Papers*, vol. 2 (Washington, DC: Pan American Union, General Secretariat, Organization of American States, 1969), pp. 259-263 passim.

2. Susan Russell, "Cooperative Cataloging of Latin American Materials: A SALALM Response." *Twenty Years of Latin American Librarianship: Final Report and Working Papers of the Twenty-first Seminar on Latin American Library Materials* (Austin, TX: SALALM Secretariat, 1978), p. 253.

3. "Cooperative OCLC Cataloging Group," *SALALM Newsletter* 9:1 (September 1981), 7.

4. Richard F. Phillips and Peter T. Johnson, "Cataloging Questionnaire," *SALALM Newsletter* 15:1 (September 1987), 15.

17. Innovations in Cataloging at Princeton University

Richard F. Phillips

In a survey of major Latin American library collections carried out in spring of 1987, returned questionnaires revealed that the great majority of these national-resource collections were saddled with large cataloging arrearages. They ranged in volume as high as 75,000 items (as reported by one institution in the Midwest). Virtually no respondents stated that they were trying any alternative means of cataloging that would alleviate their backlogged holdings.

This is not to say that there are no Latin American catalogers at these institutions. The opposite is true. Of the sixteen respondents to the survey all but one institution indicated the presence of at least one FTE doing Latin American monographic cataloging. Only two reported not having a Latin American serials position (either FTE or partial). So, SALALM is blessed with a number of catalogers. And their production is rather good, in my opinion. Again, looking at the sixteen respondents, only one indicated not performing any original cataloging. That should put to rest the old myth that catalogers across the nation sit on backlogs waiting for someone else to make a move on Latin Americana. Survey respondents averaged about 1,000 original cataloging records yearly.

Therefore, the conclusion should be that production is not keeping pace with acquisitions. Obviously, as the literacy rate in Latin America continues to rise, [1] as political events intensify, as literature is further read and appreciated, as the world grows more and more financially interrelated, book production in and about Latin America has increased. [2] But, cataloging approaches and the size of cataloging staffs seem to stay the same. Whether or not we have hit "organizational dry rot," as it is called in the literature, remains to be seen. [3] But, as stated, virtually none of the survey respondents indicated they were looking for or trying alternative means of cataloging to deal with their sizable arrearages.

Princeton seems to be one exception to this. It has taken an aggressive posture in Technical Services that cuts across the spectrum of cataloging. It is the leading nonfederal contributor to the National

Coordinated Cataloging Operations (NACO) project and is the leading component of the LSP project. It has for the past several years promoted its "Modified Cataloging" to other SALALM members as a possible path to cutting down backlogs. Princeton was innovative in its Pamphlet Collection Cataloging Project, funded by a Title II-C grant from NEH. And, last, Princeton has undone the barriers and walls that for so long slowed Technical Services and has introduced a real "hands-on involvement" of its professional staff.

Before I go into details, allow me to reflect a bit on institutional commitment to cataloging. I do so by comparing cataloging operations in terms of staffing ratios. A hypothetical library might have 90 professional positions in its organization. [4] I use this number after having examined statistics from some 118 ARL members and from personal observations. Princeton has about the same number of professional positions. The hypothetical model has a good-sized staff in its cataloging department—45 staffers (both professional and non-professional). Princeton again has a similar number—about 45 positions—but here differences emerge. At the hypothetical model, of the total 45, some 15 librarians are carrying the entire load of original and member-copy cataloging as well as authority work, training, revision, and the like—for all subjects and languages. Princeton, however, has some 27 professionals staffing its cataloging operation—almost double the number of professional catalogers than the hypothetical library. I would like to ask the members of SALALM to reflect upon their own staff makeup in this regard.

Carrying this comparison further reveals the following: the model (with its ratio of one professional to every two nonprofessionals) is overwhelmed with backlogs—7,000 items just in the area of Latin Americana alone was the most common response given in the survey we did in 1987. This is not to say that the hypothetical model we have created is not a productive institution; just the opposite could be true. Viewed in light of the results of our survey, they could rank among the leaders. However, the elements of the staffing equation in that hypothetical organization (and maybe in many real organizations) have evolved in a manner that has undersupported their needs for many years, in terms of their division's skill mix.

To go further with this one must return to the situation at Princeton. It has no backlog as backlogs are traditionally defined. That is one key measure of success. But that gives only a yardstick to determine quantity. To measure quality, let's look at other elements. Princeton is a national leader in NACO, a status that carries huge responsibilities. Its headings are there for everyone else to use. This status was given them only after heavy scrutiny and training by the Library of Congress (LC). One answer to why they have both quantity and quality is definitely in the staff makeup. Simply put, a higher level of staffing in cataloging, as used by them, means that individuals are on hand to make the difficult decisions that only a professional can make and that so many Latin American materials require.

A good number of published items from Latin America (and elsewhere) are from the large publishing houses we are all familiar with and recognize. They carry ISBNs, are quite uniform in nature, and are from well-known personal authors and corporate bodies. They are routinely picked up by LC within a year or so and given full cataloging by them. However, a sizable amount of material is peripheral in nature and most definitely requires professional judgment in any ARL Technical Services before it can be cataloged and classified in proper fashion. Each of these would take time.

In the past five years, the cataloging teams at Princeton handled nearly as many or more non-LC items, meaning original and member copy, than LC AACR2 copy. In the years 1978-1982, however, LC supplied some 70 percent of the copy Princeton used and Princeton's pattern of staffing in cataloging was more similar to the model than it is currently. The Library of Congress suffered a drastic production shortfall following the introduction of AACR2, and it has lately been saddled with budgetary limitations which prevented it from recovering the momentum of the 1970s. Also, the increasing use of minimum level cataloging by LC and a lack of timeliness in its record creation have rendered much of LC's copy for non-English materials only marginally satisfactory. Without more professionals to make the judgments that non-LC demand and MLC necessitate, a good number of these materials would quickly have become backlogged (see Appendix 1). In the mid-1980s Princeton moved to alter its cataloging staff ratio, concluding that reliance on LC was not proving wise. As nonprofessional lines were vacated by attrition or even by transfer, they were converted into professional positions. Often the cost difference was insignificant. Overall, it has given the Catalog Division great flexibility since professionals are not usually limited by restrictive job descriptions, union regulations, shortcomings in initiative, and the lack of judgment-making creativity developed by collegiality.

What are these judgments I speak of? First, there is the descriptive portion of each record which must be created, in the case of original cataloging, or which must be verified, in the case of member-contributed copy. For member copy, Princeton has bibliographic assistants to help its professionals with some preliminary verification such as checking spelling, series form, and treatment, as well as tagging. For original cataloging, only professionals take on the responsibility of creating the record.

Subject analysis and classification are areas of work only professionals should be doing. At the ARL level, I would like to believe that the individuals performing original cataloging have backgrounds in the field upon which to base their judgments. I may be forced to conclude otherwise from the lack of catalogers that attend SALALM, since few collections are ever represented on a regular basis.

Actual record entry is done by Princeton's professional catalogers. They are the ones with the language abilities and often, prior to online work during precataloging searching and verification, they discover important details that clerks would only quickly pass over. At Princeton each cataloger has several hours of online time scheduled daily. Entries are checked against the national authority file for strict adherence to AACR2. Headings not established are "nacoed."

Indeed, authority control is another high skill area in cataloging. AACR2 and its rule interpretations demand a constant monitoring of entries to remain in agreement with national standards. This is especially true when headings are locally created at an institution at a certain date only to be overridden by LC at a later date. Princeton, having reached a point in catalog maintenance where the cost of record correction was becoming unbearable, decided to put the resources up front with a total commitment to "naco" all headings its catalogers came across which were not fully established in the national authority file. It has grown to be an enormous yet manageable undertaking given the staff ratio and skill mix employed by Princeton's Catalog Division. There are 1.5 professional positions overseeing the authorities operations of our library. It includes the local public catalog database as well as our NACO/LSP work. FY 1987 saw Princeton create and enter some 10,000 headings into the national authority file, which is what made Princeton the largest nonfederal contributor to the NAF. That figure represents more than double the second contributor's total. The figures in Appendix 2 document the NACO project, in its eleventh year of operation nationally, and in its eighth at Princeton at this writing.

In regard to Modified Cataloging and the Pamphlet Project, past SALALM conferences have been venues for promotion of these alternative cataloging strategies. Princeton does not claim that these are panaceas promising quick relief from institutional ailments that are results of years of underfunding and understaffing. Used in conjunction with sound managerial policies and procedures, however, modified cataloging and collection treatment of pamphlets can keep an organization from sinking into the morass of the uncontrolled and hopelessly backlogged.

Detailed narratives of these programs as implemented at Princeton are in Appendixes 3 and 4. As in all Princeton cataloging, headings not fully established in the national authority file are entered by Princeton catalogers via the LSP procedure. As outlined in the most recent *SALALM Newsletter*,[5] some 7,000 pamphlets have been cataloged in collection fashion between 1986 and 1988.

In conclusion, the future of cataloging at Princeton seems to be projected as one readying itself for a world with less LC AACR2 copy and less LC authority work. Continued conversion of nonprofessional lines into professional cataloging positions seems inevitable. Greater direct involvement of professionals in actual record verification, creation, and production will remain. The key is not necessarily the absolute number of Technical Services staff; rather, it will be the skill levels of the staff. The ratio of individuals making decisions and exercising professional cataloging judgment must improve nationally if we are to keep the information flow in Latin American studies from becoming stagnant.

NOTES

1. *Educación en América e informaciones estadísticas* (Washington, DC: OAS, 1986—), I, 16.

2. *New Book of World Rankings* (New York, NY: Facts on File, 1984), pp. 410-411.

3. "How to Prevent Organizational Dry Rot," in *Management Strategies for Libraries* (New York, NY: Neal-Schuman, 1985), pp. 406-412.

4. *ARL Statistics, 1985-1986* (Washington, DC: Association of Research Libraries, 1987), pp. 52-54.

5. *SALALM Newsletter* 15:3 (1988), 12-13.

BIBLIOGRAPHY

Getz, Malcolm, and Doug Phelps, "Labor Costs in the Technical Operations of Three Research Libraries," *The Journal of Academic Librarianship* 10:4 (September 1984), 209-219.

Godden, Irene P., ed. *Library Technical Services, Operations and Management.* Orlando, FL: Academic Press, 1984.

Schauer, Bruce P. *The Economics of Managing Library Services.* Chicago, IL: American Library Association, 1986.

Appendix 1.   Selected Cataloging Statistics at Princeton University
1976/77-1986/87

Fiscal Year	New Titles Cataloged	LC Copy		Non-LC Copy		Original	
		Number	Percent-age	Number	Percent-age	Number	Percent-age
76/77	51,535	36,931	72	7,792	15	6,812	15
77/78	58,645	37,982	65	13,178	22	7,485	13
78/79	50,886	32,117	63	12,094	24	6,675	13
79/80	57,098	34,693	61	15,323	27	7,082	12
80/81	46,763	29,743	64	10,229	22	6,991	14
81/82	33,559	19,699	59	8,244	25	5,616	18
82/83	63,465	32,204	52	19,415	31	11,846	19
83/84	62,100	30,259	49	19,969	32	11,602	19
84/85	53,863	26,655	49	15,009	28	12,199	23
85/86	61,844	31,498	51	16,508	27	13,838	22
86/87	65,850	34,349	52	18,136	27	13,365	21

Appendix 2.   Cataloging Records Processed Through National
Coordinated Cataloging Operations (NACO)

Library	Date Joined	Items Completed FY86	FY87	Totals to Date

I. Numbers of authority records contributed by participating institutions, arranged by dates of entrance into NACO, to LC's automated files

   A.   Records authenticated (processed via NACO or the separate divisions)

      1.   Name of authority records

Library	Date Joined	FY86	FY87	Totals to Date
U.S. Government Printing Office Library	10/77	2,283	3,670	63,865
Texas State Library	02/79	252	236	2,275
University of Texas at Austin	01/80	948	631	5,421
University of Wisconsin, Madison	01/80	154	294	2,720
Northwestern University	02/80	739	858	4,740
Minnesota Historical Society	03/80	507	765	3,501
University of California, Berkeley	08/80	820	663	6,815
Princeton University	09/80	3,985	9,993	16,719
University of Michigan	11/80	710	1,036	4,358
Montana State Library	12/80	96	64	1,503
New York State Library	02/81	181	264	1,568
Yale University	04/81	651	762	3,208
University of California, Los Angeles	06/81	722	1,557	4,897
National Library of Medicine	06/81	7,228	5,540	20,646
University of Washington	06/81	61	46	752
Harvard University	11/81	2,383	2,549	12,412
Indiana University	11/81	5,788	2,725	26,531
U.S. Department of the Interior	12/81	1,040	1,754	8,509
University Microfilms International	12/81	202	59	1,288
Louisiana State Library [1]	02/82	185	0	1,666
Washington State Library	02/82	230	187	1,996
North Carolina State Library	04/82	283	656	2,555
South Dakota State Library	04/82	0	4	227
University of Chicago	07/82	3,197	4,608	24,527
Eighteenth-Century Short Title Catalog/ North America	03/83	603	848	3,742
American Antiquarian Society	06/83	1,782	1,618	5,075

---

[1]   Participation discontinued.

Library	Date Joined	Items Completed FY86	FY87	Totals to Date
University of Illinois, Urbana/Champaign	12/83	2,319	979	7,226
National Agricultural Library	02/84	1,954	1,196	5,547
State Library of Ohio	05/84	99	182	1,550
South Carolina State Library	05/84	61	71	280
University of Wisconsin—Milwaukee	07/84	291	294	1,705
Cornell University	01/85	303	854	1,431
Utah State Library	01/85	51	57	127
Stanford University	04/85.	731	863	1,760
Wyoming State Library	06/85	139	103	285
Saint Louis University School of Law	09/85	1,633	1,264	3,019
Ohio State University	10/85	425	298	723
University of Maryland	05/86	182	2,666	2,848
University of Pittsburgh	05/86	297	574	871
University of California, San Diego	08/86	40	787	827
Center for Research Libraries	10/86	0	751	751
Louisiana State University	02/87	0	97	97
Total name authorities		43,555	52,423	260,563

2.   Series authority records [2]

Library	Date Joined	Items Completed FY86	FY87	Totals to Date
Harvard University			255	255
National Library of Medicine			151	151
Northwestern University			81	81
Princeton University			222	222
University of California, Berkeley			64	64
University of Chicago			321	321
University of Illinois, Urbana/Champaign			2	2
U.S. Department of the Interior			136	136
U.S. Government Printing Office Library			1,363	1,363
Yale University			173	173
Subtotal series authorities			2,768	2,768
Total authority records authenticated		43,555	55,191	263,331

---

[2]   Series authority records were included under Section I.A.1 above, prior to 1987.

Appendix 3.   Subject: Modified cataloging (monographs)
                (Cataloging Procedure 21a, May 18, 1987,
                Rev. June 29, 1987)

General

This procedure sets forth the guidelines, general and specific, to be followed in the creation of original catalog records for monographs at modified standard. Selection of items for modified treatment is normally the province of the selector/bibliographer whose fund was used to purchase such items. This procedure may also be invoked by the cataloger in specific instances where full original cataloging is not possible, e.g., in accommodating monographs in languages beyond the Division's currently available resources. In cases where a selector has designated an item as a candidate for modified treatment but the cataloger judges it equally easy to provide full standard cataloging, the cataloger is free to upgrade the cataloging to full standard.

This procedure meets or exceeds RLG standards for base-level cataloging in all its particulars.

The intent of modified cataloging is to provide a set of guidelines which permit original cataloging to proceed at a quicker and easier pace than would pertain if full standard cataloging were employed. Catalogers should apply these guidelines with this intent in mind. Thus, whereas the guidelines below specify that one general subject heading is permissible where two more specific headings would normally have been given if full standard cataloging was in effect, if it is in fact quicker and easier for the cataloger in a given case to provide two specific headings rather than one general heading, then this is what the cataloger should do.

Cataloging

Supply fields and data as indicated below. Fields not listed are not required. Fields marked "(S)" pertain to SCORES. Fields marked "(R)" pertain to RECORDINGS.

Control Fields

EL:	7
CC:	955_
BLT:	am (BKS), cm (S), or im (R)
DCF:	a
CSC:	d
SCO:	Format of music (S)
PTS:	Existence of parts (S)

CP:	Country of publication code
L:	Language of text code
PC:	Publication date code
PD:	Publication date(s)
MMD thru BSE:	MICROFORM phys. desc. fields
RMD thru RC:	RECORDINGS phys. desc. fields (R)

Variable Fields

010:	LC card no.	Required if on item.
020:	ISBN	Required if on item.
024:	Standard recording number (R)	Required if on item.
028:	Publisher number for music (S)	Required if on item.
040:	Catalog source code	
043:	GAC	
1XX:	Main entry	Refer to ENTRY below.
245:	$a Title proper	
	$h GMD	Required for MICROFORMS and RECORDINGS
	$b Other title info.	
	$c Statement of respons.	
	$n Dependent title number	
	$p Dependent title	
250:	$a Edition statement	
254:	Musical presentation area (R)	
260:	$a Place of publication	Only the first place listed on the item is required.
	$b Publisher	Only the first publisher listed on the item is required.
	$c Publication date(s)	
300:	$a Extent of item	
	$c Size of item	
4XX:	Series statement	Refer to SERIES below.
511:	Participant or performer note (R)	Required if applicable for RECORDINGS.
533:	Photoreproduction note	Required if applicable.
6XX:	Subject headings	Refer to SUBJECTS below.
7XX:	Added entries	Refer to ENTRY below.

Entry

Only <u>personal</u> name entries are provided, and only for authors, editors and compilers (and illustrators when applicable). Choice and form of entry is determined in accordance with AACR2 standards.

All entries are verified, established, and provided with authority work in accordance with current cataloging policies and procedures.

For SCORES and RECORDINGS, 773 (Host item entry) is mandatory if applicable.

Any other entries (corporate names, uniform titles, added (740) titles) may be provided at the cataloger's discretion, but are never required and should be avoided unless the cataloger deems they are absolutely necessary.

Series

Series statements (4XX) are recorded in accordance with AACR2 standards.

Normally, series are not verified in SCL2 and are not traced. Series which are established as ANALYZED or CAS constitute the one exception to this rule. For the most part, the ORDER TYPE on the acquisition record will inform the cataloger if an ANALYZED or CAS situation pertains to the series on the item in hand. However, the cataloger should check SCL2 regardless of the ORDER TYPE indicated if he/she deems that an ANALYZED or CAS series could be involved (e.g., a numbered series entered under personal author). If in doubt whether it is worthwhile to check SCL2 or not, *do not check*.

Subjects

Normally, only one subject heading is required. In some cases, the heading assigned may represent a more general level of subject analysis than would have been applied to full standard cataloging. In other cases, the heading may represent the main aspect of the work with secondary aspects being ignored. If the content of the work has a geographic emphasis, the heading chosen may represent a higher jurisdictional level or broader regional level than would have been appropriate to full standard cataloging, unless the local jurisdiction or feature is a prominent one (i.e., one you would expect to have already been well established; if in doubt, use the more general term).

Classification

Class numbers assigned may follow the guidelines for subject analysis, i.e., a more general number may be selected than would otherwise have been the case if full standard cataloging were being provided.

Appendix 4. Princeton's Title II-C Latin American Microfilming Project

I. Significance of the Project

Primary sources form the qualitative core of any research library. For Latin American collections these should include monographs, manuscripts, government documents, and a selected array of pamphlets, serials, broadsides, and posters. Publications forming this last category are especially important for documenting the socioeconomic and political life of Latin America. Pamphlets have a long history of existence in Latin America, where they are recognized as a standard format which is unlikely to disappear. The perspective offered in pamphlet literature generally is one from the microlevel of society, for it is here that the evolution of leadership begins amidst the large and small problems confronting society. To understand how Latin Americans individually and collectively respond to the challenges of their society one must be able to read the literature of groups at the microlevel in sufficient quantities for patterns to emerge. Only then will the dynamics behind the transitions within society be correctly identified. The popular reaction to dictatorships and the process of power transitions involving autocratic and democratic regimes which result in competitive politics figure centrally in the prior sources frequently not collected or organized by research libraries.

During the French and Mexican Revolutions, the U.S. Suffrage Movement, and a variety of social causes, pamphlet literature provided one of the best mediums for expression of the community interests and the leaderships' positions. This too is true for Latin American political parties, ethnic groups (especially Blacks and Indians), labor unions, women's and feminist groups, human rights associations, the church, and also for such issue-oriented activities as agrarian reform, migration, and political protest. These and other areas account for a significant proportion of the primary sources essential for understanding the base levels of Latin American society today as well as in the future. Because of the economic and political realities present in most Latin American countries, groups publishing these pamphlets usually flourish for relatively short periods. But when viewed collectively over the long term, definite patterns emerge which indicate the ferment of ideas and actions among non-elite groups. The challenge for research libraries is to identify and acquire in a timely fashion their publications and then to organize them adequately for use.

The Princeton University Library's collections from such groups begin with nineteenth century imprints and increase substantially from

1952 (the Bolivian Revolution) to the present. By focusing upon the instigators of change at the microlevel, these collections document various aspects of the organizing efforts and debates which elude the official or commercial presses. Indeed, the insights to be gained from these pamphlets, journals, monographs, and broadsides can reverse existing scholarship which by necessity is based upon the readily available trade publications supplied by Latin American bookdealers. Only with extensive field work and consistent collecting efforts is a counterbalance feasible. It is precisely this other perspective of reality among Latin America's women, political opposition, human rights advocates, Blacks, revolutionary movements, and the poor which Princeton University Library is qualitatively collecting through special arrangements in Chile, Peru, Colombia, Argentina, Brazil, Uruguay, and Nicaragua. Thanks to a Title II-C grant for 1986-87, a small amount of this material at Princeton is being organized for microfilming and being made available through fully standard cataloging at the collection level in the RLIN database.

Important today for social scientists in many areas of studies, these works will provide the basis for historical research much as pre-twentieth century pamphlets do for Europe and the United States. Political scientists, anthropologists, sociologists, historians, economists, and geographers require the facts and opinions expressed in this form of literature in order to interpret the development of society and to analyze the causes for change within it. Clearly the collection has an appeal broader than Latin American studies, with its focus on issues relevant in comparative studies such as women, Blacks and other minority groups, labor unions, political parties, revolutionary and clandestine groups, and human and civil rights groups.

It is known that these pamphlets are not being systematically collected elsewhere, even by the issuing organizations or by the Library of Congress. Further, often mimeographed and/or on paper of newsprint quality, most are destined to crumble. Unless collected in significant quantity they are difficult to organize in a meaningful fashion, and the cataloging of them often has low priority, given the numbers of commercial publications on hand. As an example of the uniqueness of these works, it is estimated that 50% of the names encountered in the cataloging of these pamphlets require original authority work. The majority of the time is being spent in organizing and cataloging pamphlets heretofore unavailable on any level. The intention of the project is to begin to add a complete component to scholarly research that before this time has been only partially done. Included will be current imprints (1980s) and retrospective ones to the early 19th century, and entire groups such as the demographic pamphlets held by the Office of Population Research Library, labor pamphlets and serials in the Industrial Relations Library and the bound country pamphlet volumes in the general library collections. Short-lived 20th century serials in the social sciences and the humanities will serve as a prototype for continued cataloging of newly acquired pamphlet material, for both this and other research libraries.

The intention of the project is to disseminate information on these materials at meetings of a wide variety of scholarly and professional groups as well as through the newsletters of these groups. Given the frequent discussions about the difficulties of managing pamphlet materials, we would expect broad interest in this project from Latin Americanists, and descriptive articles will appear in the *SALALM Newsletter* as well as in the *LASA Forum*, the newsletter of the Latin American Studies Association. Although we do not now plan to issue a catalog of these works, the project provides two means of doing so in the future. The cataloger provides the Latin American bibliographer with an RLIN printout of each collection record, including a listing of the authors and titles of the individual pamphlets, which could be arranged by collection and reproduced for distribution. In addition, the project flags each RLIN record in such a way that these records could be extracted from our RLIN tapes and sorted by collection, individual authors and titles, and subject to form a comprehensive catalog.

II. Plan of Operation

The project involves personnel from three areas of the library. From Collection Development, the Bibliographer for Latin America, Spain, and Portugal, Peter T. Johnson, and students in the Latin American Studies Program organize the materials. They sort them first by country of origin, and then by the issuing corporate body. If the collection contains only a small amount of material by an issuing body, it may be grouped together with other such corporate bodies which fall into the same broad subject area and country. On the other hand, if a particular corporate body's output is large, it may be subdivided based on subject.

Materials held by departmental libraries in subject or country files are reviewed for consistency of topic and reorganized as necessary to conform with the project's guidelines. Bound pamphlets, all of which carry a distinctive local classification number, are evaluated for appropriateness of inclusion. Ceased serials of runs less than 6 years are filmed providing that the title does not already exist in microformat and the run is complete or lacks so few issues that obtaining these numbers would be easy through interlibrary loan. The Collection Development staff makes a table of contents for each collection and Peter Johnson assigns a collective title to it.

The collection is then sent to Luisa Paster, Database Management Librarian, who reviews the table of contents and the collection title from a cataloging point of view. After any changes are made, in consultation with Peter Johnson, the title page is typed, and Waldina Zullo, Senior Bibliographic Specialist, does the descriptive portion of the cataloging online in RLIN. This cataloging includes title or author/title added entries for each major item or serial in the collection and broad subject entries as required, often assigned from a preselected Latin American subset of LC subject headings. Thus the film will be accessible by its own collection title, by the names of each major corporate body involved, by the title of each major item in the collection, and by overall subject content. Accession numbers are used for call numbers, and the films will be assigned accession numbers according to the already established sequences for master preservation negatives, master printing negatives, and service copies.

The cataloging is reviewed by Luisa Paster for accuracy and thoroughness. She revises subjects as necessary for greater breadth or specificity. She reviews the corporate body headings, doing both local authority work and authority work required for submittal of the heading to NACO. Acceptance of these headings by NACO will make them available for use by the Library of Congress and by all libraries which use Library of Congress authority work.

When the review is complete, she orders catalog cards and magnetic tape output through RLIN. The record is added to the Princeton Online Catalog via the RLIN tape. The materials are sent to be filmed in the Princeton University Library Photographic Services Department and testing is done to ensure that quality standards are met. Two 35 mm Kodak microfilming cameras are used. The table of contents is the first frame of the reel. Care is taken to organize the materials in such a way that the collection can be added to, if appropriate. The films are housed with the Library's Master Negative Collections. A printout of the catalog record is sent to Peter Johnson for possible future use in compiling a catalog of these records. The original pieces will not be retained by the Library but will be sent on exchange to appropriate Latin American academic libraries, thus furthering international availability of these documents. Copies of the film will be available to other libraries at cost.

WORKFLOW

Collection Development	Database Management		Administrative Services
Peter Johnson with student assistance	Luisa Paster	Waldina Zullo	Photoduplication

Collection Development — Peter Johnson with student assistance

1. Sort materials.
2. Assign collective titles.
3. Make table of contents.

Database Management — Luisa Paster

4. Approve groupings and collective titles in consultation with Peter Johnson.

Database Management — Waldina Zullo

5. Type table of contents.
6. Catalog proposed film online, including all added entries and subjects.
7. Assign accession number and make temp. card for shelflist.

Luisa Paster

8. Review cataloging, including subjects.
9. Do authority work for corporate bodies (local & for NACO submittal).

Waldina Zullo

10. Produce record.
11. Send materials to be filmed with printout as a target.

Administrative Services — Photoduplication

12. Film materials and target.
13. Develop film.
14. Test film with densitometer and methylene blue.
15. Box film and prepare labels.
16. Send film to Binding and Preservation.
17. Send materials and printout of record to Binding and Preservation to be sent to Peter Johnson.

Collection Development

18. Send materials to Latin American Libraries.

III. Guidelines for Cataloging

    A.   Fixed Fields

        1.   CC - Use 994 for substandard cataloging, due to the changes in fixed field coding, the unusual 300 field, the numerous added entries, etc.

        2.   CP and PC/PD - Use the place and the date(s) of publication of the original materials. In this way, the limiting search capabilities of RLIN and Princeton's Online Catalog may be used effectively.

        3.   Microform Fixed Fields - A separate line is required for the Master preservation microfilm, the Master printing microfilm, and the service copy.

    B.   Descriptive Cataloging

        1.   245 field - If only one title is being cataloged (e.g., a bookset or a serial) use the appropriate title from the piece. If the item is a collection, invent a title that covers the subject area of the collection. Use a General Material Designator "microform." Use a subtitle such as "pamphlets," "campaign literature," etc. if appropriate and if it helps clarify the title.

        2.   260 field - Use the lowest geographical level that is accurate for the majority of the items in the collection. This is usually a city or a country. Use a specific publisher if it is common to all the items in the collection. Otherwise use the phrase "various publishers." Use dates inclusive of the publication dates of all the items in the collection.

        3.   300 field - For a single title use a standard collation. For a collection state the number of individual items and the presence and type of illustrations. If the collected items vary in size, leave out any size indication.

        4.   Notes - If the collection contains a variety of types of material, include a note (e.g., "Includes pamphlets, broadsides, photographs, campaign advertising"). If some items are in a language other than that of the country of publication,, mention that in a note (e.g., "Some items in English"). Use other explanatory notes as necessary.

        5.   Microfilm note - Use a standard microfilm note in the 533 field. In the holdings segment use "Also In" notes for the three locations, and notes to identify the

Master Preservation microfilm and the Master Printing microfilm.

6. Subject headings - Use all inclusive topical subject headings which cover the general topic of the collection. They will almost always have a country as a geographical component. For source materials add "History—Sources" or "Sources" as appropriate.

7. Added entries - Make added author, author/title, or title entries for the following:

   a. Corporate bodies which have issued various individual items in the collection. This is true for all political parties in collections of election campaign materials.

   b. Important personal authors represented by various individual items in the collection.

   c. Separate individual items that are important because of their impact or rarity. Choose author/title entry or title entry as appropriate.

   d. Serials that are important because of their impact or rarity. If the name of a corporate body appears prominently on the serial and the serial title is not distinctive, make an added entry for the corporate body instead. Include the number(s) of the issue(s) of the serial in the collection.

In most cases prefer corporate body author entries to other types if doubt exists. Judge importance by the impact of the item on the society, its rarity, its usefulness for current research, and its probable usefulness for future research.

18. Sweeping Out the Bibliographic Closet: Cataloging the Arrearage at Arizona State University

Sheila A. Milam

In June 1986 Arizona State University had more than 16,000 books that had been received from Latin American countries sitting in a storage room. These books had been purchased by the University, but their existence was unknown to the library users. By June 1988 all of that backlog had been searched and had been cataloged or was waiting to be worked into the cataloging work flow. Most of the books still awaiting cataloging were scheduled to be cataloged by fall 1988.

At the beginning of 1987, the Latin American arrearage comprised more than 42 percent of all arrearages at ASU. It was the fastest-growing arrearage, perhaps because blanket orders suffered less than firm orders in the book budget crunch. There were several good reasons to lobby for the cataloging of this arrearage to be top priority. First, there was the fact that it was the largest single arrearage. Patrons of the Latin American collection were being denied access to a great number of books. Second, that arrearage was the fastest growing of them all and the problem of what to do with it would continue to get worse. Third, some of the materials in storage had not been searched even once before being sent to the bibliographic hinterlands. Many of them would have records in OCLC, making their cataloging less expensive and less time-consuming than the original cataloging required for those without OCLC records. A sample search conducted of 20 books per receipt year showed that 89 percent of them had either LC or member records in the database. Fourth, the space that had been lent to store the arrearage was now needed by its rightful owner, and it would be difficult to find another available space. The fifth reason, and the most important—although it disregards the realities of staffing in academic libraries—was that these materials must be important to the collection or they would not have been acquired in the first place. They were of no use to library users as long as there was no bibliographic control. If an item is important enough to be acquired, it is important enough to be cataloged. The best collection development plans are rendered useless when the existence of the acquired materials is unknown to the patrons.

In December of 1986, the Latin American area specialist, Pamela Howard, and I, the Latin American catalog librarian, decided to present a proposal to the heads of the two departments which were responsible for the cataloging of materials. We searched a random sample of 20 books per receipt year in OCLC (1983-1986). There were records for 89 percent of the items searched, with 60 percent of them having Library of Congress records and 29 percent having member records. That was a hit rate that would support a plan to pull the books and search them because it pointed to a good return on the searching time. So, Ms. Howard and I met with the department heads (after having provided them a written copy of the proposal days beforehand) and we presented a united front that gave the proposal added strength. Then we waited for the proposal to go through proper administrative channels and for the department heads to determine the impact of cataloging this collection on the present work flow.

Timing was an important factors in this story. Six months earlier, in July of 1986, the Technical Services Division at ASU was reorganized. For our purposes here, it is important to know that the department of Catalog Service was split into two separate departments: (1) Bibliographic Records and (2) Original Cataloging and Special Languages. Until then, there had been an OCLC unit within Catalog Service that searched books in OCLC and cataloged those having LC copy or member copy which had a call number suitable to our collection. Now, Bibliographic Records was structured to include Tier I, where books were first searched and where those with LC copy would be cataloged on the spot by a Library Assistant I, and Tier II, which received books for which Tier I did not find LC copy. Tier II would research them and catalog those having member copy with call numbers. The fallout—books with no LC copy, with member copy but no call number, or with problem copy—would travel on to Original Cataloging. This new work flow meant that books with LC copy would be cataloged promptly, and the random search of the Latin American arrearage had shown 60 percent of the items having LC copy. So, there was a strong indication that a great deal of the Latin American arrearage could be processed within a short period of time and without a large investment on the part of higher level paraprofessional or of professional catalogers.

Another pertinent change had taken place as of July 1, 1986. With the reorganization of Technical Services and of its work flow, the arrearages had been closed in order to disallow further growth. Books received after July of that year would go to holdings areas. The difference between an arrearage and a holdings area is that while an arrearage is more of a storage area without a timetable for cataloging, a holdings area has a designated timetable for searching and cataloging of the items depending on the hit rate in OCLC and on the work load. For example, when the holdings area for Latin American books was set up, the deferment time was six months, then it was increased to nine, then to twelve months, owing to the hit rate in OCLC. Now, the holding time is shortening again because Tier I has time to work more of these in. This cataloging plan is the kind that begs the accusation of shirking national responsibility. It is a plan that takes into consideration the staffing realities of a library. We would all like to do more original cataloging but must work within certain limitations that we don't control.

So, in July the arrearages were closed and there was a statement that they would be cataloged, but there was no definite plan. Right then, the Latin American librarians came along with the proposal to make the Latin American section the first priority. Then the head of Technical Services and the department heads of that division drew up a document listing cataloging priorities for the arrearages. The first to be cataloged would be the English language and the Latin American arrearages, done simultaneously. (This agrees with the recommendation of an ad hoc committee on cataloging priorities of the arrearages formed in Original Cataloging soon after our proposal had been made, and of which I was a vocal member).

After the document on cataloging priorities of arrearages was written and approved, the process could begin. One condition set for the cataloging of the Latin American arrearage was that a workshop be given to provide useful Spanish and Portuguese language tips to those in Tier I and II who would be handling so many Latin American items. Ms. Howard and I presented a two-hour workshop for the library staff which provided information useful to their encounter with the languages. It covered vocabulary commonly found in the areas of a catalog record—statement of responsibility, imprint, series, and so on, the structure of personal names, and LC's treatment of editions and printings. The workshop was well received, and the participants left with a packet of materials designed to answer on-the-spot questions they might have while cataloging an item.

The pulling of the Latin American arrearage began in April of 1987. The number of books searched per month varied greatly, depending on the number of priority receipts to be cataloged. Tier I catalogers would start each week cataloging the English language receipts and other first priority items. Then when those were finished, they would search and catalog arrearage materials. This part of the process went smoothly. The bottleneck occurred at Tier II. Even before the arrearage came along, Tier II was receiving more items than could be cataloged in a timely manner. When the bottleneck would get too tight, arrearage items with member copy would go back to the shelves to await the day Tier II could catalog them. Books without OCLC copy or with member copy but no call number traveled on to Original Cataloging. Most of these books (1,000 titles) are sitting behind my desk, awaiting cataloging. Tier I has enough time to research them and to catalog those with LC copy. The ones found to have member copy or with no copy during this second search will have to wait their turn behind the higher priority cataloging. During the first months of pulling from the arrearage, some of the books intended to travel on to Original Cataloging were returned to the storage shelving owing to a breakdown of communication. As of June 1988, there were approximately 3,500 books which were searched once and which need Tier II or original cataloging. They are being research now and are cataloged by Tier II or go to Original Cataloging. The goal is to have all of the arrearages at ASU cataloged by fall before Hayden Library extends into a connected underground building. Needless to say, this is an ambitious goal if original cataloging is included, and is more attainable if it is left out.

And that brings us up to June 1988 with ASU's Latin American arrearage. In summary, there were approximately 16,000 volumes in the arrearage at the end of June of 1986. A sample search in OCLC found copy for 89 percent of them (60 percent LC copy, 29 percent member copy). In April of 1987, the books began to be searched and cataloged. All have been cataloged except 4,500 which have been searched and have no OCLC copy, have member copy with no call number, or have member copy and are awaiting Tier II's attention. All of these are being researched now and those with OCLC copy will be cataloged in the coming months.

Some of the significant factors in this case follow:
1. The fact that many of the books had not been searched before going to the arrearage increased the likelihood they would have copy in OCLC. Our staff that catalogs books with LC copy can have a shorter waiting period than staff doing member copy cataloging or original cataloging.
2. The reorganization of Technical Services Division to include a unit that is dedicated to searching and cataloging with LC copy allowed a high percentage of the books in the arrearage to be cataloged and on the shelf within a short period of time.

3.   Timing was in our favor. The arrearages were officially closed and
     the administration had committed to cataloging them. With work
     flows being changed, the system was flexible to allow new
     elements to be introduced.
4.   Agreement and cooperation between the Latin American library
     for public services and collection development and the Latin
     American librarian for technical services were more convincing
     than either one alone. Also, we had done enough work before
     talking with the people involved that the scope of the project was
     known without them having to do it. Initiative paid off.

Every library has its own set of circumstances within which it
operates. Perhaps knowing about the cataloging of the Latin American
arrearage at Arizona State University will be of some use to other
libraries trying to offer their users the best access possible to the
collection.

19. An Administrator Looks at Cooperative Cataloging

Judy Ganson

Libraries have been functioning in an era of cooperative cataloging since 1901, when the Library of Congress began selling its catalog cards. Since then, there have been a number of programs designed to share cataloging records among groups of libraries: the National Union Catalog; the Shared Cataloging Program, sponsored by the Library of Congress, the Latin American Cataloging and Acquisitions Program; OCLC; RLIN; UTLAS; and the new Coordinated Cataloging Program. Some other such efforts include programs established under the aegis of the Research Libraries Group, informal arrangements among libraries that have purchased larger microform sets, and various consortia formed for a variety of cooperative programs. Among the languages of subject specialists, East Asian catalogers in several California libraries shared catalog cards for a period of time.

From an administrative viewpoint, such programs have the benefit of establishing some reasonable predictability in locating usable cataloging copy. This known availability is an important factor in the planning process: a catalog department's organizational structure, work flow, staffing level requirements, and bibliographic utility costs are predicated on estimates of quantity and quality of copy available. Overall processing costs are dependent, in part, on the volume of copy that can be purchased rather than created locally as original cataloging.

Within the environment of a bibliographic utility, the predictability of copy available in the database can only be determined within a broad range of factors:

1. First, and in many ways the most important, the cataloging priority process at the Library of Congress. For Latin American and Spanish-language material, the priority is currently a very low one.

2. Collection development policies among member libraries. For Latin American materials, available copy is dependent on the number of major collections among the libraries, the countries and languages collected for those collections, and the depth of collections.

3. Cataloging practices and staffing in member libraries. Do the majority of libraries wait for LC copy, do they contribute original cataloging in languages and subjects needed locally, and what is the perceived quality of the original cataloging which is done?

The initial proposal for a cooperative cataloging project between Stanford University and the University of Southern California was presented by the Latin Bibliographers in those institutions. Both libraries have current approval plans for the majority of Latin America, in some instances with the same vendors, and both are members of the Research Libraries Group, contributing cataloging to the same database—RLIN. While this effort is still in a very preliminary discussion stage, I found the idea worth pursuing because USC has recently begun an effort to develop a significant research collection in Latin American and Iberian materials; because it would be a project with another RLG library within California; and because it would increase the availability of cataloging records to an identifiable group of materials. In this interim period between proposal and implementation, there has been time to identify the necessary elements of a successful cooperative program.

Planning a successful cooperative with another library of libraries would include the following:

1. There must be a commitment to such a project, regardless of its scope or size, at all levels within the organizations, particularly by the heads of cataloging and technical services administrators to insure that resources are available to the catalogers assigned to the project. Time must be allocated for cataloging, searching, and inputting staff to give these materials priority processing. In large academic libraries, the commitment of staff may well be a matter of time rather than position, but when staff turnover occurs, or when priorities for the library as a whole change, a cooperative program should be given a high priority in the internal planning process. Collection development personnel must also have a commitment to cooperative programs, as cataloging priorities might have to be reevaluated to allow an individual library to focus on the cataloging of a specific category of materials. The effect of specific projects on general cataloging priorities should be known throughout the library.

2. A written "contract" or project agreement should be prepared to formalize any cooperative project. The agreement would include a statement of language and/or subject assignments accepted by the participants, schedules for providing cataloging and the means for

provuding records to participating libraries, and description of a reporting mechanism for the review of problems, progress, and changes in the program.

3. Participating libraries should provide each other with reasonably detailed information concerning cataloging practices and policies followed in each library; specifically on classification and subject heading practice, series and serials cataloging policies. Commonality of practice in cataloging is critical to any cooperative project, and differences need to be identified in advance to insure acceptance of cataloging produced by the participants.

4. Frequent conversation among collection development and technical services personnel will be needed to identify any change in collection focus and acquisitions methods, to insure that assumptions about the project remain the same, and to review current progress and future plans.

5. The project plan must be equitable to all parties, not necessarily in volume of cataloging reports provided, but in terms of performance. One library might be willing to provide a greater number of records in one language or subject area in exchange for another library's cataloging in a narrower subject area or language specialty which may not be available otherwise. In a broader meaning, however, equitable should be defined as all participants meeting agreed upon schedules and commitments. All parties should be benefiting from such a project or it will cease to be a cooperative effort and will probably just cease.

6. There should be an easy means of dissolving the agreement for any or all parties. Institutional priorities may change, staff turnover may result in a library's temporary or long-term inability to continue its participation, or any number of reasons may occur to require a library to withdraw; participants should be in a position to do so without penalty. If this condition does not exist and participation becomes a burden on any of the libraries, the project will cease anyway, and all parties will lose the benefits that might derive from expansion or temporary suspension.

Cooperative cataloging programs that have been started with the best of intentions have succeeded or failed for any number of reasons; even the support of the Library of Congress has not always been sufficient to keep some of these programs viable. Those that have succeeded have shared characteristics of organization, planning, and commitment on the part of participants. Programs that have failed also share certain characteristics:

1. Programs drawn and agreed upon by library directors. They are almost guaranteed to fail, not because the programs are not well intentioned, well documented, but simply because library directors have other issues requiring their attention and because commitments to such programs need to be agreed upon throughout the library organization.

2. Programs drawn and agreed upon by collection development librarians. Unless they have cataloging assignments as well, they are not in a position to make the commitment of staff time and resources to participate in shared cataloging programs.

3. Programs that focus on materials that are not mainstream to the needs of library users in a participating library. Priorities for use of existing staff and other resources focus on the research and teaching needs of a library's known and regular patron group. Diverting resources to process materials that might have some value in the national scholarly community has a nice philosophical and professional ring to it, but most libraries have backlogs of needed materials to process and insufficient resources to stay current. Realistically, budgeting agencies are not likely to respond to the trumpet of ultimate good.

4. Programs that are too generally defined, e.g., series analytics for specific series. Such a program is difficult to manage and to maintain despite the usefulness of such a project.

In summary , as an administrator, I find much to value in shared cataloging programs that are well planned and coordinated. The predictability of records known to be available is attractive to planning generally, and is more cost-effective than locally created cataloging. Saving limited funds can be a viable reason to pursue any such project.

III. Cooperation: Sharing Knowledge and Resources

20. The "Strange Career" of Latin American Librarianship in the United States

Mark L. Grover

A few years ago my local city government was approached by developers with a plan for a new ski resort. They came with the usual promises of riches, in part because they proposed to build not only winter recreational facilities but also something to attract summer visitors. They wanted to build a Polynesian village that would use local college students from the Pacific islands as entertainers, cooks, and guides. Their logic was that this type of project had worked well in Hawaii so it would obviously make money in Utah. It didn't seem to bother them that Utah is mountainous without an ocean close by, that it has pine and not palm trees, or that it gets cool in the evenings even in the middle of August.

There was little support in the community for an establishment so ecologically out of place. Possibly the only residents in favor of the project were the mosquitoes of Utah Lake who looked forward to the increase of feeding areas spawned by the costumes on the Polynesian dancers.

There are times when I walk into sections of the library that include a high percentage of books from Latin America and I wonder if we are not creating Polynesian villages in library environments similar to pine forests. The unbound volumes from Latin America display a wide variety of colors whereas the surrounding books published in the United States are mostly in subdued blues, greens, browns, and black. The volumes published in the United States tend to be of similar sizes and number of pages whereas the Latin American volumes are for the most part smaller and published in a variety of shapes and sizes. I have heard my English-speaking-only colleagues, in subdued tones, question the need for these books in the collection as they hurriedly pass through the area to get to a more familiar and comfortable English-language area of the library.

In 1964, Richard Morse, Yale professor of history, published an article entitled "The Strange Career of Latin American Studies" that criticized the study of Latin America in the United States. In this article he acknowledged the explosion of research on Latin America but questioned its direction. Morse felt that the research was not resulting in an improved understanding of Latin America but only in an increase in the quantity of publications. The emphasis on Latin America by the educational establishment in the United States was detrimental to an understanding of the area because it was based on a negative view of Latin America. [1]

Morse attributed the difficulties to a "fundamental alienation between the two Americas." A historical split between the two cultures that had its genesis in the sixteenth-century European conflict between Catholicism and reformational Protestantism had sent each down very different and opposing paths. The variations in mindset that developed between the two areas of America was so significant that, without considerable efforts to bridge the philosophical differences, little appreciation or understanding would result from contact. [2]

Morse's concern was that American academic Latin Americanists, primarily young Ph.D. candidates, were going to Latin America with so little understanding or appreciation of the culture that they developed little respect for the intellectual accomplishments of the area. Consequently, their view of Latin America was tainted, often subconsciously, by an arrogant and patronizing attitude. Americans wrote negatively about Latin America and saw the area only in terms of "problems" for which the solutions were to be found outside of the society in which they originated. Morse felt that the questions American researchers examined were not related to an attempt to understand the Hispanic Catholic mindset or social system but more commonly "How can agricultural extension services in Iowa be adapted for Highland Peru?" [3]

Although Morse has received considerable criticism for his negative assessment of Latin American studies in the United States, he touched a nerve that is still a major concern for Latin Americanist scholars today. Morse's ideas are also important questions librarians in North America should consider. How has our profession reacted and responded to Latin America? Have we been affected by the basic cultural antagonism between the two Americas and responded negatively and patronistically toward Latin America?

Perceptions of the Role of the U.S. Library

Morse felt that the only area where North Americans had made a positive contribution to the study of Latin America was in the area he called "services" (i.e., bibliographic compilation, research aids development, and library collections growth). Had he looked closer he would have recognized similar problems in our profession.

The development of Latin American studies in the United States was in part the result of the growth of the United States into a world power. As part of this development, our educational establishment believed we had to become knowledgeable about the entire world. Area studies programs were established on campuses across the country to focus education on the world. The role of libraries in this development was to build collections that included copies of all the important books published anywhere in the world.

With money, influence, and specialized bibliographers our libraries set up extensive international acquisition systems to buy new books, collections, out-of-print items, and manuscripts. Libraries needed extensive collections to support the worldwide research of faculty and students. Unfortunately, librarians have only occasionally examined the questions of cultural patrimony and the right of a country to keep their intellectual national treasures, including the right to write their own history. We have justified the growth of our collections in part by claiming to protect manuscripts and books that would face possible destruction if left in Latin America. This perception is an example of the sometimes patronizing view we as librarians often have of Latin America. [4]

Perception of Latin America

Librarians' perceptions of Latin America have often followed the lines suggested by Dr. Morse. In the record of SALALM over the past thirty-three years, the Latin American book trade and library world has not been treated kindly. American librarians and book dealers have seen the Latin American book trade and libraries as underdeveloped, antiquated, difficult to understand, and plagued by "problems." We have seen the Latin American book trade as something to live with until it can be changed and developed in large measure by the introduction of modern U.S. and European ideas and technology. In the first SALALM held in 1956, our librarians complained about the lack of national bibliographies, the problems of responsiveness of publishers and bookstores to our requests, and the complicated nature of Latin American society. Only one paper, that of Emma Simonson, was upbeat and offered a positive view of Latin America. She did not whitewash the Latin American book trade but focused on American adaptability and understanding rather than on the need for changes in Latin America. Presentations such as Simonson's have been made at SALALM seminars, but they are definitely in the minority. [5]

What has been our answer to the perceived "problems" of the Latin American book trade? We have in large measure been able to ignore it by encouraging the development of a highly efficient cadre of Latin American book dealers who accept our dollars in exchange for a supply of books arriving at our doors on a regular basis. I have nothing against those who provide this invaluable service. My concern is over what we as librarians miss by not being required to become involved with the book trade and library world in Latin America. Many of us are now able to ignore that part of Latin American society with which we should be more familiar. Most of us can now avoid buying trips that place us in Latin America where we can learn and understand. Those who still take buying trips very quickly become aware of the value of those experiences.

Our avoidance of Latin America is somewhat analogous to a political science professor writing a book on poverty in rural Brazil. He has completed his research and written his study primarily in the United States. His time in Brazil was limited to two months spent in Brazilian research centers in Rio, São Paulo, and Brasilia. He only briefly visited those areas of Brazil that are the object of his research. One cannot understand poverty in rural Brazil without spending time walking the trails and streets, eating the food, and observing how people survive in nonurban Brazil. It is those observable activities that never become part of the published statistics that American researchers need to experience.

One of the recurring issues in SALALM since 1956 has been that of defining the purposes and goals of the organization. That question has almost always surfaced when the issue of Latin American participation in SALALM is examined. We somehow feel that if librarians from Latin America become involved in SALALM, the topics of our meetings and the goals of the organization will have to change. Although there may be some justification for this concern, I don't believe it is a serious issue and is, in actuality, a smoke screen hiding another issue.

Latin American participation is important for our organization but not in terms of the value it provides them; we need to have their input. There are issues and questions in our libraries that could use suggestions from different perspectives. We have since the beginning of SALALM requested assistance in the area of acquisitions. There are, however, other areas where their expertise is needed. For example, how do Latin American librarians provide reference service and what sources do they use? It is disturbing to realize that the most heavily used reference books in our libraries dealing with Latin America are published in the United States. [6] Is it because their reference books are inferior, or that we do not know how to use their sources? Do they use different sources because the type of reference service they provide is different? Can we improve the reference service we offer by understanding way Latin American librarians provide reference? They have had more experience with Latin America reference than most of us have.

A second are of concern is that we, as librarians, generally do not see Latin America as a place for possible answers to our own library concerns. Most American librarians see Latin America as a place of problems and not solutions. We are presently confronting problems of bibliographic access and cataloging backlogs. Latin Americans have faced these issues often and have come up with solutions. Have we ever tried to find out how they have reacted to similar situations? Could their solutions help us? There are any number of issues in our profession for which we could use the influence and experience of our colleagues in Latin America. We need their presence much more than they need ours.

In making these suggestions I am not implying that Latin Americans will have answers that are better or more feasible than our own. What I am suggesting is that our profession is based on Latin America and the products of the Latin American intellectual environment. The ideas and books we deal with were produced there. It is imperative that we appreciate and understand the system in which those ideas were created.

Conclusion

In conclusion, as librarians involved in the development of collections outside of Latin America, we should always maintain a certain degree of discomfort in our position. This discomfort will result in part from the inherent difficulty of developing large collections outside the place of origin. It will also occur because we work on a daily basis with the history, culture, and intellectual products of an area we do not regularly personally experience. As librarians we should be constantly aware of what Richard Morse described as a fundamental alienation between North and South that has the potential for negatively distorting our understanding and appreciation of Latin America. We must make a concentrated effort to avoid these potential problems by increasing, as much as possible, our own activities in Latin America itself, and encouraging, in all ways, Latin American participation in SALALM. If successful, our results will be rewarding.

NOTES

1. Richard M. Morse, "The Strange Career of Latin-American Studies," *Annals of the American Academy of Political and Social Sciences* 356 (November 1964), 106-112.

2. For an expanded explanation of his views, see Richard M. Morse, *El espejo de próspero: un estudio de la dialéctica del Nuevo Mundo* (Mexico: Siglo vientiuno, 1982). See also Kenneth F. Woods, "Latin American History and the United States Historian," *Western Explorer* 4 (Spring 1966), 26-28, and Julio de Mesquita Neto, "O Encontro da poesia com a política," *O Estado de São Paulo*, May 26, 1985, sec. *Cultura*, pp. 1-6.

3. For other articles on the same theme by Morse see, "The Care and Grooming of Latin American Historians or: Stop the Computer, I Want to Get Off," in *Latin America in Transition: Problems in Training and Research*, Stanley R. Ross, ed. (Albany: State University of New York Press, 1970), pp. 27-40; "Cultural Differences and Inter-American Relations," *Yale Political* 2 (April 1963), 16, 38-40; "The Two Americas: Musings of a Gringo." *Encounter* 25 (September 1965), 90-95; "The Latin American Boom," *The Times Literary Supplement*, July 28, 1966, pp. 683-684; "The Challenge for Foreign Area Studies," *Bulletin of the National Association of Secondary-School Principals* 51 (January 1967), 18-33; and *Brazilianists, God Bless'em! What in the World Is to Be Done?* (Stanford, CA: Stanford-Berkeley Joint Center for Latin American Studies, 1983).

4. Charles Gibson, "Latin American and the Americas," in *The Past Before Us: Contemporary Historical Writing in the United States*, Michael Kamman, ed. (Ithaca, NY: Cornell University Press, 1980), pp. 187-202; and Magnus Mörner, "The Study of Latin American History Today," *Latin American Research Review* 8 (Summer 1973), 75-93.

5. Emma Crosland Simonson, "Purchase of Latin American Books through Bookstores, Publishers, and Dealers," *Final Report of the First Seminar on the Acquisition of Latin American Library Materials, Chinsegut Hill, Brooksville, Florida, June 14-15, 1956* (Gainsville: The University of Florida Libraries, 1956).

6. Edwin S. Gleaves, "The Most Useful Reference Sources on Latin America: Results of a Survey of Those Who Use Them Most," *The Reference Librarian* 17 (Spring 1987), 203-234.

21. Cooperation among Libraries: A Mexican Proposal

Helen Ladrón de Guevara Cox

For a long time now, the subject of cooperation among libraries has been under examination. In and of itself, there is little new about the subject. What is noteworthy is the fact that, in spite of efforts made by librarians, institutions, and other organizations that have made advances in library development in Latin America, grave problems still persist, and they need to be explored again in the search for solutions.

There is a great deal in the literature about the level of cooperation being accomplished by inter-American, international, national, and governmental organizations, library associations, foundations, libraries, archives, and others. I believe that what has been done in the past was valid for its time. Some projects achieved their goals and went on to new modes: others perished owing to obstacles that arose. As an example of the former, I cite the case, in Mexico, of the Network of Library Systems of the Universities of the Central Area (RESBIUC) [1]; among the latter, the Network of Mexican Libraries (REBIMEX), consisting of more than thirty university libraries, was a fascinating attempt at cooperation that failed from the lack of economic resources. [2]

There still persist echoes of the great library work done by the Latin Americanists Marietta Daniels Shepard, Nettie Lee Benson, Josefa Emilia Sabor, Maurice A. Gelfand, and William V. Jackson, as well as others, many of whom are active members of SALALM. The uninterrupted work of SALALM, its founders, and the past generations of librarians stands out in the literature on library cooperation.

The specialized literature on library cooperation with Latin America has covered the following areas: (1) library education and training in centers of higher education, and courses in professional training; (2) documentary services, and services for the collection and translation of specialized papers for publication and distribution in the

---

Editor's Note: This paper was sponsored by SALALM's Enlace/Outreach Committee.

library field; (3) technical counseling by expert librarians for the implementation, expansion, and improvement of services in libraries and information centers; and (4) national bibliographical activities in areas of bibliographic control, bookselling, and exchange of publications.

In these areas, the work of the OAS stands out. Its objectives have been to stimulate "active collaboration with national and international associations of librarians, with foundations, international organizations, and national agencies engaged in the improvement and expansion of library and bibliographic services and the increase in the number of libraries." [3]

Despite these attempts at cooperation, however, a problem lies in the countries that have not reached a high level of development in library science. Perhaps what is needed is a present-day "total study that combines the experience of everyone, sums up criticism, and comes to valid conclusions that can give direction to future international action in this field," as Josefa E. Sabor indicated some time ago. [4]

As for Mexico, there are concrete programs for cooperation, some better than others. Cooperative arrangements have been made, many based on geographical or functional considerations, in which the institutions try to complement each other. This has resulted in a wide range of cooperative mechanisms: agreements, accords, networks, and so on. A heavy impetus for cooperation was provided by the Integrated Program for the Development of Higher Education (PROIDES), which includes in its subproject 7.4 the encouragement of library services, with the object of "consolidating the library's function as a fundamental support for the achievement of higher levels in the work of research and teaching." [5]

There is currently a second great national project for library services of the country which requires great coordination. I refer to the National Program for Public Libraries, [6] instituted in 1983 and to the General Library Law decreed on December 21, 1987, which supports it. [7]

The factors that do or do not make for the success of any cooperative project are numerous, and "although cooperation will not be the answer to all our problems, the pooling of resources and ideas may provide needed assistance in meeting the challenge of the 1980s," which is now reaching its close. [8]

The following are recommendations for improving cooperation:

1. An international committee should be formed which includes representatives of the national library associations of Latin America to determine the state of the art of the libraries in the

various regions, with the object of identifying areas for strengthening library cooperation within Latin America and with the United States. The Outreach Committee of SALALM and the OAS would participate.

2. The international organizations should promote, with the ad hoc national institutions or organs, the strengthening and establish-, ment of a great number of programs for the teaching of and training in library science in Latin America.

3. Inter-American organs like the OAS and the national and international library associations should facilitate, together with the Latin American universities and other appropriate institutions, library research with the dual purpose of (1) accelerating advancement on the subject in Latin America and (2) generating publications.

4. Organs such as the OAS, UNESCO, and SALALM should formulate agreements with Latin American library institutions or related institutions, for the translation of papers on library science into English, or vice versa.

5. A proposal should be made to the Mexican Library Association that it set aside in its budget a fund for the support of programs for library cooperation to include the exchange of specialized information, looking ahead to the formation of a data bank, and bilateral interchange for the updating of skills of library personnel, between Mexico and foreign countries.

6. Forums such as the International Book Fair in Guadalajara should be utilized for presentations on international library cooperation. [9]

NOTES

1. Juan Voutssás et al., "Estudio acerca de la estrategias planteadas sobre las redes de bibliotecas y su posible desarrollo: documento preliminar." Documento presentado en la V Reunión Nacional de Responsables de los Sistemas Bibliotecarios de las Universidades Públicas Estatales, Tampico, Tamaulipas, mayo 1988, p. 23 (fotocopia).

2. Ibid., p. 22.

3. Marietta Daniels Shepard, "Inter-American Program of Library and Bibliographic Development," in *Round Table on International Cooperation for Library and Information Services in Latin America: Final Report and Documents: Washington, D.C., September 30-October 2, 1965*, v. 2 (Washington, DC: Pan American Union, 1966), p. 6.

4. Josefa Emilia Sabor, "La cooperación internacional en la formación de los bibliotecarios," *Boletín de la UNESCO para las Bibliotecas* 19:6 (noviembre-diciembre 1965), 296.

5. Voutssás et al., p. 1.

6. México, Ley general de bibliotecas, *Ley general de bibliotecas: texto y debate parlamentario* (México: SEP, Dirección General de Bibliotecas, 1988), pp. 7-8.

7. México, Ley general de bibliotecas, "Ley general de bibliotecas," *Diario oficial,* 21 enero 1988, pp. 14-16.

8. Laura Gutiérrez-Witt, "Latin American Library Collections in Public Academic Institutions: A Perspective of the 1980s," in *Library Resources on Latin America, New Perspectives for the 1980s: Final Report and Working Papers of the Twenty-Fifth Seminar on the Acquisition of Latin American Library Materials*, University of New Mexico, Albuquerque, New Mexico, June 1-5, 1980 (Madison, WI: SALALM Secretariat, 1981), p. 235.

9. The first Guadalajara International Book Fair (FIL '87) was held in Mexico's second largest city. It will be repeated annually. The goals of FIL are to encourage reading and to strengthen the publishing industry through international cooperation and self-help. Furthermore, the intention is to provide a forum for professionals from all over the Americas.

22. La Biblioteca Nacional de Chile y sus colecciones patrimoniales

Ursula Schadlich Schönhals

Primeros años de la Biblioteca Nacional

La Biblioteca Nacional de Chile nació casi junto al Gobierno que asumió la autoridad luego de los acontecimientos que, en 1810, pusieron fin al período colonial. La preocupación por la educación, la cultura y el desarrollo de la nacionalidad emergente, cristalizó en la proclama publicada en *El Monitor Araucano* el 19 de agosto de 1813 que creaba la primera biblioteca pública y hacía un ferviente llamado a los ciudadanos para contribuir con donaciones de libros a enriquecer los ejemplares ya reunidos por el Gobierno con este fin. [1] El aporte de los ciudadanos fue magro, ya que existía una real escasez de impresos en el país, y, por otro lado, las obras emprendidas por los patriotas despertaban la reticencia y desconfianza de partes de la sociedad chilena cuyas costumbres y modos de vida se veían alteradas por ellas. [2]

Entre las obras recolectadas figuraron obras valiosas para la época, entre ellas dos incunables que aún figuran entre las existencias. El grueso de la biblioteca lo aportó la colección que perteneció a la orden de los Jesuitas confiscada con motivo de su expulsión en el año 1767. Esta pasó primero a la Universidad de San Felipe y de allí a la Biblioteca Nacional en 1813. Compuesta por los libros del Colegio de San Miguel (Santiago), que sumaban más de 6.000, y los depositados en otros establecimientos y residencias de la Orden a través del país, representaron una colección valiosa si bien no siempre apta para la consulta y lectura del público general. La Biblioteca no terminaba aún su organización cuando se produjo la reconquista del poder por partes de los realistas en 1814 y se ordenó su clausura.

El 5 de agosto de 1818, ya consolidada la Independencia, un decreto del Director Supremo Bernardo O'Higgins dispuso la reapertura de la Biblioteca Nacional. [3] Manuel de Salas fue su primer Director y Bernardo O'Higgins autorizaba partidas de presupuesto para la adquisición de libros. [4] También en esta oportunidad se apeló a la generosidad pública que hizo sus aportes, entre los que figuran colecciones pertenecientes a militares extranjeros que habían combatido junto a las tropas chilenas en las últimas batallas en la lucha por la independencia nacional.

Posteriormente, la Biblioteca se enriqueció mediante la incorporación de colecciones completas pertenecientes a particulares que las habían formado as través del tiempo. En ellas figuraron muchos impresos adquiridos especialmente en Lima y en Europa durante los viajes de sus dueños al continente. Entre las bibliotecas que ingresaron pueden destacarse especialmente la de Mariano Egaña, estadista y jurisconsulto (1846), la de Ignacio Víctor Eyzaguirre, la de Andrés Bello, la de Benjamín Vicuña Mackenna, más adelante las de Diego Barros Arana, de José Toribio Medina y de Guillermo Feliú Cruz, además de otras menores que sería largo de enumerar. [5]

La antigüedad de las ediciones de los libros que sirvieron de base a la Biblioteca Nacional —deplorada por Diego Barros Arana— es la que hizo la riqueza de que hoy se enorgullece y que los bibliógrafos aprecian. En cierto modo, marcó sendas para la Biblioteca Nacional, que siempre se mantuvo alerta en la recopilación y conservación de colecciones aunque no respondieran a sus necesidades inmediatas.

La Biblioteca Nacional en su carácter de biblioteca pública

La ausencia de bibliotecas escolares y públicas para satisfacer la demanda de los establecimientos educacionales y de los sectores favorecidos con los programas de educación impulsados por los sucesivos gobiernos nacionales, obligaron a la Biblioteca Nacional el asumir, también, el rol de biblioteca pública y escolar. Satisfacía estos requerimientos, atendiendo en su propio local, asistiendo a las bibliotecas que iban formándose y aún remitiendo por vía postal los títulos que le eran solicitados desde provincia. La Biblioteca Nacional cumplía así el destino que habían soñado para ella los impulsores de la Independencia: ser el centro cultural de la nación, conservando los testimonios del pasado y proporcionando a las nuevas generaciones materiales actualizados en las distintas disciplinas.

Preciso, sin embargo, es reconocer que esta doble función representó una pesada carga para la Biblioteca, al punto de impedirle, en ocasiones, cumplir sus funciones esenciales. De hecho, sufrió la mutilación, destrucción y pérdida de colecciones bibliográficas valiosas debido a un uso y manejo inadecuado, derivado de esta doble función. Algunas medidas se tomaron para paliar esta situación, las que fueron, globalmente consideradas, insuficientes. En 1886, se creaba el Museo Bibliográfico de la Biblioteca Nacional, con el fin de sustraer a la consulta pública los volúmenes más antiguos. La formación de una colección separada para ser facilitada a domicilio obedeció al mismo propósito (en 1887 se creó el Servicio de Lectura a Domicilio). La creación de bibliotecas públicas igualmente apuntó a liberar a la Biblioteca Nacional de una responsabilidad para la que no contaba con recursos humanos, financieros y materiales para realizarla.

En este momento existen en la Región Metropolitana de Santiago 44 Bibliotecas Públicas distribuidas a través de las distintas comunas. [6] De la Biblioteca Nacional propiamente tal, depende la Biblioteca Pública N° 4 Luis Montt M., con una dotación de 100.000 volúmenes que atiende estudiantes entre 14 a 18 años, y la Biblioteca Pública Infantil N° 7, que atiende niños entre 5 a 13 años. Ambas constituyen las principales bibliotecas públicas a que tienen acceso el estudiantado y el público general.

Las colecciones patrimoniales de la Biblioteca Nacional

A pesar de la carga y responsabilidad que representaba para la Biblioteca Nacional llenar la ausencia de bibliotecas escolares y públicas, no descuidó su obligación de conservar el patrimonio impreso nacional. Las colecciones que fueron integrándose a medida que se adquirían por compra y donación de las bibliotecas de los principales estudiosos y coleccionistas del país, se constituyeron en valiosos recursos para la investigación histórica y bibliográfica.

Las bibliotecas de próceres y estudiosos incorporadas tienen en común la característica de ser extraordinariamente ricas en obras relativas a la historia americana y en primeras ediciones chilenas, fascículos y proclamas diversas que, de no haber sido coleccionadas por ellos, difícilmente habrían llegado hasta nuestros días. Nombraremos las principales:

La Biblioteca Egaña. Aparece individualizada en un catálogo impreso y durante años contó con una sala especial para ella. Actualmente es conservada, en bóveda, en Sección Chilena. [7]

Biblioteca de Víctor Eyzaguirre. Cuenta con catálogo impreso, adicionado con explicaciones para proporcionar mayores detalles de cada una de las secciones en que se divide.

La Biblioteca Americana de Don Benjamín Vicuña Mackenna. En 1861 se adquirió parte de esta colección, compuesta por las obras de más mérito y más escasas. Se confeccionó un catálogo que daba cuenta de 1.606 volúmenes con numerosas notas explicativas relativas a cada una de las secciones en que se divide la colección. [8]

Biblioteca de Don Andrés Bello. Pocos años más se adquirió la colección de educador y jurisconsulto venezolano Andrés Bello, autor del Código Civil Chileno.

Diego Barros Arana fue el autor de un minucioso inventario, adicionado de referencias bibliográficas del que aun existen dos copias, una en el Museo Bibliográfico y otra en la Biblioteca Central de la Universidad de Chile.

Biblioteca Diego Barras Arana. Sin duda alguna, el mayor historiador chileno, el lugar más indicado para conservar su valiosa colección fue considerada la Biblioteca Nacional por su hija Josefina la que hizo entrega de ella en 1920. Los ejemplares referidos a la historia chilena y americana en general, se depositaron en la sala que lleva su nombre. Otras obras de contenido más general, se incorporaron a distintas secciones de la Biblioteca Nacional. No existe catálogo impreso de esta colección, sino solamente en fichas.

Biblioteca de José Toribio Medina. Bibliófilo y bibliógrafo connotado, en vida dispuso el traspaso de su valiosa Biblioteca a la Nacional. El Decreto N° 8.253, de 11 de diciembre de 1925, aceptaba la donación y se ordenaba la apertura de una sala especial con el nombre de José Toribio Medina para contener los libros y documentos del sabio. Conservador de ellos fue nombrado don Guillermo Feliú Cruz. La producción intelectual de Medina no se circunscribió al ámbito de la historia americana. La biblioteca Medina refleja las inquietudes de quién fue su dueño que incursionó en la numismática, la etnografía, el derecho, la crítica literaria, la lingüística y la arqueología, versatilidad representada en libros, folletos y documentos de la colección.

Biblioteca Guillermo Feliú Cruz y Archivo Sergio Fernández Larraín

Entre las últimas importantes colecciones integradas a la Biblioteca Nacional, no podemos dejar de mencionar la Biblioteca de don Guillermo Feliú Cruz (11.087 volúmenes) en 1974, incorporada a la Sala Medina y el Archivo de Sergio Fernández Larraín en 1976. Este archivo está compuesto de más de 42.000 piezas de gran relevancia para la investigación del pasado chileno, americano y europeo. Cuenta con una sección propia encargada de su conservación e investigación de sus fondos.

Otras colecciones

Pero no sólo los conjuntos bibliográficos antiguos e importantes como los citados tienen valor de colección patrimonial para la Biblioteca Nacional. Ejemplares de esta característica se encuentran también en otras secciones. La sección de periódicos chilenos y la hemeroteca son especialmente ricos en colecciones únicas.

La Sección Periódicos. Esta Sección de la Biblioteca Nacional posee un acervo bibliográfico de 30.000 volúmenes de diarios y periódicos, es decir 8.510 títulos diferentes que se guardan en una extensión de 3.000 metros lineales de estantería. Su colección incluye la mayor parte de la producción periodística chilena del siglo pasado y la actual, además de algunas piezas extranjeras, incluso del siglo XVIII.

La Dirección del Servicio, conjuntamente con las autoridades de la Biblioteca Nacional, preocupadas de la conservación del acervo bibliográfico de periódicos, ha iniciado durante el año 1987 un proceso de microfilmación de los periódicos del siglo XVIII y XIX, llevando a cabo durante este año la filmación de aproximadamente 1.160 títulos diferentes, los que equivalen a 374 volúmenes de periódicos y diarios. La microfilmación de periódicos de esta Sección se ha complementado con la adquisición de una máquina lectora —impresora de microfilmes de 35 mm. y microfichas.

De lo anterior se desprende que en el futuro se podrá guardar las colecciones originales, para así poder ser restauradas apropiadamente, y facilitar en préstamo las reproducciones fílmicas. Durante el año 1988 se continúa con el proceso de microfilmación de diarios y periódicos existentes en esta Sección, para lo cual se está en proceso de selección de aquellos títulos que en esta etapa ameritan su procesamiento de filmación.

La Sección Revistas. Las colecciones de la Sección Revistas están formadas por revistas chilenas y extranjeras que abarcan todas las áreas del conocimiento. Comprende 7.000 títulos, 48.365 volúmenes y 49.849 tomos. La importancia de sus colecciones radica en que por su contenido y volúmenes es la más grande existente en el país. De las revistas chilenas se destacan *Anales de la Universidad de Chile*, revista científica y literaria, y *Revista Católica*, revista de la Iglesia Chilena. Ambas se empiezan a editar en el año 1843, siendo a la fecha las más antiguas de Hispanoamérica.

Otros Repositorios

La política coleccionista y el trabajo bibliográfico del personal de la Biblioteca Nacional, ha permitido formar, además, en la actualidad importantes archivos.

Sección Referencias Críticas. Compila el Archivo de Referencias Críticas (1968-) sobre autores chilenos e hispanoamericanos. Registra en forma sistemática la información que la prensa nacional dedica a los escritores chilenos, que recopila de los diarios y revistas de depósito legal que se ponen a su disposición. Tiene además bajo su tuición los siguientes archivos particulares:

Archivo de don Raúl Silva Castro, que contiene información literaria hasta el año de su muerte (1969).

Archivo de don Alfonso Calderón, sobre literatura chilena, sin determinación de tiempo.

Archivo de don Pedro Lastra, que posee la particularidad de integrar autores hispanoamericanos.

Archivo de don Joaquín Edwards Bello, de carácter misceláneo, contiene una amplia gama de materias que interesaban al autor para escribir sus crónicas.

Un antiguo catálogo, en fichas, perteneciente a don Emilio Vaisse, fallecido en 1935, que contiene información sobre escritores hasta 1920, aproximadamente.

Archivo del Escritor. El Archivo del Escritor es un departamento de la Biblioteca Nacional de Chile, creado por Decreto N° 13.541, del 18 de diciembre de 1969, con el propósito de reunir, conservar y organizar los originales autógrafos de obras publicadas e inéditas, epistolarios, iconografías y objetos personales de escritores chilenos e hispanoamericanos. Con el curso de los años sus colecciones se han incrementado considerablemente. A la fecha, ya suman algunos miles —alrededor de 5.000— los manuscritos, borradores, copias fotostáticas y otros que se conservan en sus bóvedas.

Entre sus autores es posible destacar, entre muchos otros, los nombres de Arturo Aldunate Phillips, Joaquín Edwards Bello, Julio Barrenechea, Juan Marín, Augusto D'halmar, Gabriela Mistral, Pablo Neruda, Enrique Gómez Carrillo, Roque Esteban Scarpa, Hernán Díaz Arrieta, Raúl Silva Castro, Miguel de Unamuno, Juan Ramón Jiménez y Rubén Darío.

Los archivos o fondos documentales que se conservan comprenden mayoritariamente originales autógrafos, borradores, originales dactilografiados, copias dactilografiadas y copias fotostáticas de obras literarias y epistolarios de connotados autores.

Archivo Iconográfico. Conserva fotografías originales, reproducciones, grabados, dibujos y otros de autores nacionales e hispanoamericanos. El archivo iconográfico reúne aproximadamente 3.000 piezas.

Colecciones o Archivos relevantes. Destacaremos aquí solamente tres:

Archivo de Gabriela Mistral reúne originales autógrafos y dactilografiados, copias dactilografiadas y copias fotostáticas de poesía, prosa y correspondencia que abarcan un período comprendido entre las años 1920 y 1940 aproximadamente. Incluye además 43 rollos microfilmados. N° de piezas 504.

Archivo de Hernán Díaz Arrieta reúne originales dactilografiados y manuscritos de crónicas, correspondencia, discursos, etc. Incluye 2 rollos con microfilmes. N° de piezas 14.

Archivo de Pablo Neruda reúne originales autógrafos de poesía, correspondencia y otros. N° de piezas 31.

Indudablemente que algunos de estos archivos constituyen piezas excepcionales; esto por el carácter de únicos en su género, así como por el contenido o materias tratadas por los autores.

Sección Música y Medios Múltiples. La Sección Música y Medios Múltiples, creada en 1969, está destinada a reunir y conservar nuestro patrimonio cultural, en los que se refiere al registro de voces y música. Para estos efectos, posee una colección de 10.000 partituras y 115.000 grabaciones musicales, a cuyo incremento ha contribuido generosamente la Asociación de Compositores de Chile con su valioso y permanente aporte.

La colección de partituras está formada principalmente por obras de compositores nacionales, de todo tipo de música, con obras editadas y obras manuscritas. Las grabaciones musicales comprenden fundamentalmente obras chilenas doctas y folklóricas.

La música universal también está presente con obras representativas, en partituras y grabaciones. Paralelamente a lo anterior, se conserva aquí el **Archivo de la Voz**, un registro sonoro con las voces de destacados intelectuales nacionales y extranjeros, especialmente de habla hispana. Poemas y textos de la literatura de todos los tiempos se encuentran también en la voz de locutores profesionales. Complementa estas colecciones un archivo documental que contiene recortes de prensa, programas, bibliografías e información sobre compositores e intérpretes nacionales.

Conclusión

Las colecciones patrimoniales de la Biblioteca Nacional de Chile constituyen indudablemente una valiosa fuente de información chilena y americana. El principal escollo para un mayor acceso a ellas y para una coordinación e integración con colecciones similares existentes en otras bibliotecas, radica en la falta de catálogos, tanto parciales, por materia y globales.

La Biblioteca Nacional ha iniciado medidas para superar estos inconvenientes dentro del marco de sus posibilidades, que son limitadas. Se mencionó ya la microfilmación de sus colecciones de periódicos y revistas chilenas del siglo XIX, lo que permitirá proporcionar, bajo ciertas condiciones, copias a bibliotecas. En cuanto a monografías, 150.000 títulos que corresponden a obras editadas a partir del siglo XVI y que constituyen importantes piezas bibliográficas, se presentó un proyecto que los incorpora al sistema automatizado de información de la Biblioteca para permitir su recuperación en línea por autor, título y materia. Este proyecto consiste en transformar parte de los ficheros manuales correspondientes al material bibliográfico antiguo de la Biblioteca Nacional en archivos mecanizados para su recuperación en tiempo real, abarcando parcialmente las secciones Fondo General y Chilena en sus colecciones más valiosas.

Otro medio destinado a acercar recursos bibliográficos valiosos al público, consiste en la investigación de sus fondos relativos a hechos o acontecimientos nacionales o americanos de relevancia, investigación que se materializa en las exhibiciones de la "Galería Azul" de la Biblioteca. Acompañamos algunos catálogos y desplegables que los documentan.

Por otro lado, la Biblioteca Nacional tiene programados —siempre en el contexto de la difusión de sus colecciones patrimoniales— los siguientes proyectos aún no financiados:

1. Creación de un Archivo Iconográfico para organizar, conservar y difundir las reproducciones iconográficas que se elaboran con distintos objetivos y que generalmente reproducen ilustraciones de valor. Este mismo Archivo conservaría un índice de reproducciones y grabados relevantes de las principales piezas bibliográficas de la Biblioteca Nacional.
2. Implementación de una infraestructura material que garantice óptimas condiciones de conservación y preservación de las piezas y colecciones más valiosas.
3. Instalación de talleres de restauración con el equipo técnico y el personal calificado para recuperar numerosos ejemplares afectados por un alto grado de deterioro.
4. Implementación de una línea permanente de publicaciones que consulte ediciones facsímiles, catálogos y reproducción iconográfica en vistas a difundir este excepcional patrimonio bibliográfico al grueso de la población.
5. Incrementar la habilitación de salas y recintos para exposiciones bibliográficas que cuenten con el más óptimo y moderno equipamiento para estas actividades.

Por último, la Biblioteca Nacional de Chile tiene un alto interés por vincularse con instituciones hermanas y otras cuyo objetivo gira también en torno al estudio, difusión, valoración, conservación y preservación de impresos importantes para la historia colonial y del centenario de vida independiente de las repúblicas americanas, basado en la calidad de sus colecciones y la contribución que puede aportar a la comunidad estudiosa de la realidad americana, sus raíces y proyecciones.

Hay que mencionar que la Biblioteca conserva gran parte de las obras relativas a nuestro país impresas en la época colonial, entre las que se cuentan magníficas y escasas ediciones de los primeros cronistas y viajeros que escribieron sobre Chile. De este modo, volúmenes con los textos de Alonso de Ercilla y Zúñiga, de Francisco Núñez de Pineda, de Alonso Ovalle, de Alonso de Góngora Marmolejo, de Juan Ignacio Molina, alternan con notables ejemplares de relaciones de navegantes y viajeros que pasaron por el Chile colonial, como Drake, Cavendish, Le Maire, Schouten, Spilberger, Brouwner, Anson, Frezier, La Perouse, Vancouver, Bouganville, D'Orbigny, Schmidtmeyer, Mary Graham y muchos otros.

Este caudal de volúmenes se acrecienta con los primeros textos que comenzaron a editarse en el país a partir de las postrimerías del siglo XVII, y que tienen su primera materialización en un diminuto pero importante impreso de dos hojas titulado *Modo de Ganar el Jubileo Santo*, con el cual comienza en 1776 la actividad tipográfica nacional.

De un modo muy particular, nuestra Biblioteca se distingue por la excepcional cantidad y calidad de los volúmenes y colecciones que se refieren a la historia de la América Colonial. Incluye ejemplares de los primeros libros editados en Europa, donde por primera vez aparecen menciones sobre el Nuevo Mundo como son, entre otros, los textos de Jacobo Phelipe Bergomense y Sebastian Munster, que vieron la luz, muy pocos años después del descubrimiento de Colón. A ellos se suman un número importante de obras que en los años posteriores se escribirán sobre América. Es así como en las diferentes secciones de la Biblioteca existen ediciones de los grandes historiadores y cronistas de aquel período: Antonio de Herrera, Las Casas, Cieza de León, Garcilaso de la Vega, Juan de Laet. Y también innumerables libros de autores, si se quiere, más modestos pero que por aquellos años alcanzaron una amplia difusión, contribuyendo a formar la imagen y el imaginario que se constituyó en torno al Nuevo Mundo. Tales libros en su conjunto son los que ahora cobran un renovado interés en la víspera del Quinto Centenario.

En ese sentido, iniciando las actividades de conmemoración de ese acontecimiento, la Biblioteca presentó en el mes de marzo en su Galería Azul, una exposición centrada en los tres primeros volúmenes de la monumental colección *Grandes y Pequeños Viajes*, editada por el célebre impresor flamenco Theodor de Bry a fines del siglo XVI. Como se sabe, esos tres primeros libros, con una deslumbrante iconografía, se refieren a los territorios de Virginia y Florida, en la América del Norte, y de Brasil, en la América del Sur, respectivamente. Similares exposiciones están programadas para ser presentadas de aquí a 1992.

De mayor trascendencia, incluso, resultan ser las valiosas colecciones de primeros impresos americanos que posee la Biblioteca Nacional. Ellos provienen de los principales y más antiguos centros impresores americanos del Nuevo Mundo como fueron ciudad de México, Lima, Puebla de Los Angeles y Guatemala. Una muestra selectiva de estos volúmenes tuvimos ocasión de exhibir el año pasado en una exposición sobre el Libro Religioso que se presentó en la Biblioteca Nacional, con motivo de la visita de Su Santidad Juan Pablo II a nuestro país.

En lo concerniente a literatura universal, nuestra Biblioteca posee un estimable patrimonio bibliográfico, constituido por ediciones de obras clásicas y una significativa cantidad de libros raros, entre ellos varios incunables, como es el caso de un ejemplar del célebre texto de Sebastian Brant *Salutifera Navis* (La nave de los locos) impreso en Italia en 1488, edición que consulta diversos grabados ejecutados por el propio Durero.

Hay que hacer notar, sin embargo, que este cuantioso y valiosísimo patrimonio bibliográfico requiere de urgentes programas de apoyo para su conservación, restauración y difusión.

NOTAS

1. *El Monitor Araucano* (Santiago, Chile), No. 57 (19 de agosto de 1813).

2. Sergio Martínez Baeza, *El libro en Chile* (Santiago: Biblioteca Nacional, 1982).

3. *Gaceta Ministerial de Chile*, T.I., No. 52, Colección de Leyes y Decretos desde 1810 hasta 1823, publicada por don Cristóbal Valdés (Santiago, 1846), p. 149.

4. Diego Barros Arana, *Historia general de Chile*, 16 vols. (Santiago: Rafael Jover Ed., 1884).

5. Martínez Baeza, p. 157 y ss.

6. Información, Oficina Estadística, Dirección de Bibliotecas, Archivos y Museos, Santiago, Chile.

7. *Catálogo alfabético y por materias de las obras que contiene la Biblioteca Nacional Egaña de Santiago de Chile* (Santiago: Imprenta de la Sociedad, 1860).

8. *Catálogo completo de la Biblioteca Nacional . . . , que posee don Benjamín Vicuña Mackenna* (Valparaíso: Imprenta y Librería del Mercurio de Santos Tornero, 1861).

23. Pooling Resources: The OAS Programs for Library and Archives Development in the 1980s

Susan Shattuck Benson

Introduction

The Organization of American States (OAS), headquartered in Washington, DC, is the oldest existing regional organization. It includes thirty-two member states from the Western Hemisphere. It was formerly called the Pan-American Union, which was created in 1889 to link the countries through improved telegraph communications and a network of railroads.

The OAS has both political and technical functions. This paper discusses only those technical activities related to development of libraries, archives, documentation centers, paper and photographic conservation, and mass media. Projects in these fields are managed primarily by the Executive Secretariat of Education, Science, and Culture (EDICICULT). Information in the paper is not comprehensive, but includes only examples of different kinds of cooperation that have been achieved.

During the Alliance for Progress, which was based on multilateral rather than bilateral assistance, the OAS grew and the Executive Secretariats of Education, Science, and Culture and of Economic and Social Affairs became important technical arms of what had been primarily a political organization.

In the 1980s the United States stressed bilateral assistance and reduced its support to international organizations. This is particularly difficult for the OAS, whose only affluent member is the United States. As a result the OAS is about to go through drastic program cuts that will be reflected in the 1990-91 biennium.

It is now evaluating what it has been doing for the past twenty years and setting priorities for the 1990s. If it continues to give technical assistance (and it may not), information will probably be among the priorities, and collaboration between countries and international organizations will be emphasized more than ever.

Trends in Assistance

In the 1960s and early 1970s the assistance was primarily vertical North-South. The Library Development Program (LDP) met the need for basic technical works to process information and promote standardization by producing at Headquarters a variety of milestone works and series such as the Cuadernos Bibliotecológicos, Inter-American Library Relations, Estudios Bibliotecología, the translation into Spanish of the *Reglas de catalogación angloamericanas I* (the OAS bestseller and most profitable of all its publications), and the *Lista de encabezamientos de materia*. Assistance to institutions at that time was largely given by the staff of the LDP and by U.S. librarians, although by the late 1960s Latin American librarians were playing a larger role. It was during this period that the OAS provided the first Secretariat for SALALM.

Emphasis was given to strengthening key institutions and the library schools of the region, specifically in Colombia, Mexico, Paraguay, Brazil, and Jamaica. Scholarships were given to send Latin Americans to these schools and four to five fellowships were given each year for graduate studies in the U.S. as well.

By the mid-1970s exchange of Latin American expertise began to be fostered to a greater extent.

Gradually, Latin American institutions took over the tasks of publication so that in the early 1980s such works as the Spanish translation of the *Autoridades: Un formato MARC* was published by the Consejo Nacional de Ciencia y Tecnología in coordination with UNAM of Mexico in 1982. The *Reglas angloamericanas de catalogación II* was revised by a team of Latin American librarians under the coordination of the Universidad Nacional de Costa Rica and made available in 1984. A lengthy project coordinated by the Instituto Colombiano para El Fomento de la Educación Superior brought together librarians from many different countries to update and expand the *Lista de encabezamientos de materia* originally developed by Carmen Rovira. The first thesaurus on children's literature in Spanish was produced in 1987 by the Banco del Libro of Venezuela, *El tesauro de literatura infantil*. Both it and the previous work are available on diskette and in print to allow both the computerized and noncomputerized centers to work together and share information. Related to the thesaurus are fourteen bulletins, prepared at local initiative in different countries on children's literature, as part of the inter-American network on children's literature fostered by the OAS. A series of more modest but no less important works were published by Latin American institutions on such topics as use of mass media for children, writing for new readers, records management, microfilming, and paper conservation.

The first comprehensive guides to cultural and information-communication institutions in Guatemala, El Salvador, Honduras, and Panama were prepared by teams of Central Americans from different fields to help planning and coordination.

From 1980 on, assistance and training have promoted national and regional information networks and systems. New fields that had been introduced in the late 1970s became more prominent in the program: popular communication, mass media, post-literacy, children's literature, and informatics.

A 1981 survey of the information systems in the member states found that the most developed sectoral information systems are in the fields of the sciences, economics, commerce, and related social sciences, in agriculture and education. Those in purely "cultural" fields (e.g., museums, folklore, music, art) are least developed. On the other hand, information systems for society as a whole ("information for culture") have received attention in the last decade, often in the form of legislation which has been only partially enacted.

Fostering Cooperation within Countries

One of the most important achievements of assistance can be the fostering within a country of interdisciplinary collaboration among different kinds of institutions and between the institutions that are advanced and those that are not. It is natural that a strong institution such as a central bank library or university library would be reluctant to work with less developed institutions. They often see this as a drag on their limited time and resources. The lack of strong professional associations is both a cause and effect of "noncollaboration." The tendency to have vast concentrations of expertise and facilities in a few metropolitan areas also hinders development of the information fields. Fortunately, planning agencies throughout the Hemisphere are beginning to emphasize decentralization as a key to development—strengthening of the provinces and seeking more equitable distribution of resources.

In the 1970s centralized and cooperative cataloging projects created teams of institutions working together to prevent duplication and establish standards in Chile, Colombia, Costa Rica, Mexico, and Paraguay. This laid the basis for subsequent automation in the 1980s.

Examples of more recent projects in the 1980s that have helped countries unite their own institutions that had not worked together before:

Ecuador: Participación Comunitaria en el Desarrollo de Bibliotecas Públicas Rurales was a project initiated by indigenous communities that either built or assigned space to an existing building for the library, elected a librarian and cultural promoter. The community representatives were trained in organization in skills for communicating with the authorities in the different ministries, while people in the Ministry of Education were trained in coordination and support skills and in communication with the low-income rural communities. It identified projects and foundations in Ecuador that had not heretofore worked with the Ministry, such as the Fundación Muñoz Hermanos and the community development teams in the Ministry of Agriculture, and brought them into the program.

Peru: Sistema Bibliográfica Nacional was a project that helped the Biblioteca Nacional work with provincial documentation centers to create a network to identify provincial publications (public and private) and enter them as a part of the national bibliography. It trained provincial documentalists and trained the National Library staff in coordination and computer use.

At the Seminario Nacional Sobre Información para El Desarrollo Cultural, Lima, December 1983, entities from all over the country that formed part of the Instituto Nacional de Cultura met. For the first time provincial centers were invited to present papers and suggestions to the metropolitan centers and a broad view was taken of what constituted cultural information. Discussions were held on public libraries, national bibliography, documentation and cultural information, archaeological, historic, and artistic patrimony, museums, cultural manifestations, archives, promotion of the book, promotion of reading, graphic design, social communication, and cultural development. As a result, a pilot project was developed in 1984 to develop a comprehensive information system in the province of Tacna. In November 1987 a meeting of several countries was held to look at the experience and to develop jointly national and regional information systems with the collaboration of the education, science, and cultural information sectors.

Saint Vincent and the Grenadines and Saint Lucia: The archives-records management program involves all ministries. Between 1984 and 1987 a study of their needs was made and legislation was recommended. The parliaments enacted the legislation. The program then provided advice on buildings and staff. Once the staff was in place the program provided both on-site training and in-service training abroad for many levels of staff from the clericals to the registrars to the first secretaries of the ministries.

What is interesting about the micro states (Saint Vincent and the Grenadines, Saint Lucia, Grenada, Dominica, Antigua and Barbuda, and Saint Kitts-Nevis) is that the public library is generally the only formal information institution in the country. It is in charge of all aspects of the national information service, including the archives. The demands on the librarians, who are frequently the only librarian in each country, are hard for anyone to comprehend—especially if one is accustomed to specialized libraries and to dealing with and through a network of colleagues with different specialties and who have access to recent professional literature. They have to do everything from adapting to computers, training staff, serving schoolchildren, government, and agricultural specialists, to working with a variety of international organizations.

The Central American countries had no comprehensive directories of institutions concerned with information or cultural extension. Ministries of Education and Culture had no idea of their own institutional constituency. OAS created interdisciplinary teams of people in each country (except Costa Rica) to prepare a descriptive directory for each. This has been done, and OAS provides tools for planning and networking not available before and has left behind a group of people from a variety of institutions that now see some advantage to interdisciplinary teamwork.

Honduras through its Programa Nacional de Casas de Cultura has trained Ministry staff and community leaders in communication, evaluation, and organizational skills and laid the basis for a national network of community-based centers assisted by the Dirección Nacional de Cultura. Institutions from rural and urban areas that had not collaborated are now doing so.

Colombia incorporated the LIBRUNAM database of Mexico into the systems of the Universidad del Valle and the Universidad de Los Andes to provide the basis of the Sistema Colombiano de Información Bibliográfica (SCIB), which is usable on different kinds of hardware and software. It has also incorporated what had been separate specialized databases created in Colombia into one national database. It has been adapted to include full-text legal information, for example. There are now at least seventy institutions participating in the system which represent many different levels of development. The more advanced institutions with computers are online; others get printouts of the information.

Although the project began as a service to higher education, it is now serving government and business as well.

Cooperation between Countries

Venezuela to Latin America: Through the Proyecto Interamericano de Literatura Infantil (PILI), Venezuela has assisted Latin American countries between 1981 and 1987 by: (*a*) providing in-service training of librarians and documentalists from other countries at its Banco del Libro; (*b*) sending its experts to all the Spanish-speaking countries to provide assistance; (*c*) mounting the Latin American exhibit at the annual Bologna children's book fair; (*d*) offering regional courses in writing and in illustrating children's books; (*e*) creating a thesaurus on children's literature and publishing and disseminating it to documentation centers in seventeen member states as well as to Spain and France; (*f*) establishing documentation centers in seventeen countries; (*g*) coordinating the Inter-American Network on Children's Literature; (*h*) publishing technical works on children's literature and sending them to these centers as well as to ministries and libraries throughout the region; and (*i*) providing training in evaluation and selection techniques.

The Instituto Autónomo Biblioteca Nacional has assisted both Latin American and English-speaking Caribbean countries through training, technical assistance, and technical manuals in the fields of paper conservation, automation of technical services, community information services, and publishing for new readers.

Mexico to Latin America: Through the Proyecto Adiestramiento de Investigadores en Bibliotecología it trained between 1985 and 1987 thirty-five library school professors from other countries in research techniques which had not been taught in any library school outside of Mexico. It amassed a research collection on librarianship, reading needs, the information sector, and informatics on Latin America which is the best to be found anywhere.

Through the Proyecto Interamericano de Transferencia de Información Bibliográfica Automatizado, 1978-80, CONICYT of Mexico pioneered assistance to other countries in automated bibliographical control and database creation.

Through Proyecto Medios de Comunicación Masiva para Niños Latinoamericanos (MECOM), the Secretaría de Educación Pública and the *Revista Chispa* are providing experts to assist the Central American and Andean countries develop and use magazines for children and radio and television programs with science content.

The Archivo General de la Nación is donating 600 copies of six manuals on conservation that it prepared for distribution throughout Latin America and will provide assistance in the field of paper chemistry to other countries.

Jamaica to the Organization of Eastern Caribbean States (OECS): Between 1982 and 1987 Jamaica has provided through Project Development of Integrated Information Systems in the English-speaking Caribbean (DISC) librarians who gave national courses in the other English-speaking countries. They had surveyed public library facilities in 1982, which helped determine course content.

One Caribbean Country to Another: Project DISC pools the expertise of the Caribbean and has fostered teamwork among the librarians. In the English-speaking Caribbean in the 1980s all national and regional projects in the information fields were coordinated. The librarians and archivists of the region met every two years to plan both national and regional projects together. Organizations such as IDRC, UNESCO, Caribbean Development Bank, the University of the West Indies, and CERLALC sent representatives so that their programs could be coordinated. These meetings involved not only planning but identification of resource people and centers of excellence in the region that could provide the training or assistance needed. The OECS countries have formed a public library working group within ACURIL.

Conservation Consortium: The Inter-American Center for Conservation and Microfilming of Books, Documents and Photographic material (CENTROMIDCA), which is an OAS Center, provided purely vertical cooperation until 1987, when it identified other centers of excellence in the field of conservation and at a meeting in September 1987 created a consortium so that assistance and training will henceforth be provided by the Latin American expert best qualified to give the help and the institution best qualified to give a particular kind of specialized training. They will also share publications and coordinate research. The countries in the consortium so far include the Dominican Republic, Mexico, Brazil, and Venezuela. At the same meeting the group formed the Asociación Interamericano para Conservación Documental which held its first meeting in Mexico in 1988.

United States to Latin America and the Caribbean: The following are examples of assistance provided by a variety of U.S. institutions through OAS projects since 1984:

Books for the World has given 18,000 new children's books in Spanish to the public libraries of Panama and is giving books to the public libraries of Guatemala and Honduras when the public libraries have completed the next phase of training and organization.

It may provide collections of children's books in English for the public libraries of the OECS countries.

U.S. National Archives gave a conservation seminar to Caribbean and Latin American archivists in 1987 which was followed by more advanced training in 1988.

American Library Association has taken over the cost of distributing the AACRII in Spanish published by the Universidad Nacional de Costa Rica and has established accounts in each country so institutions can pay with local currency. ALA gave the rights to the OAS for the translation.

Library of Congress has supported the OAS conservation program by providing training, experts, and technical publications. It and the National Archives provide training in a variety of other fields, for example, in development of folk archives and in management of audiovisual materials.

Colombia University, Graduate School of Library Services, is translating and duplicating documents and articles on paper conservation for Latin America as support to the consortium formed by CENTROMIDCA. It is also providing free technical assistance to Chile, Brazil, and Paraguay. They have also developed a graduate program on conservation to which they are recruiting Latin Americans and which will contain special courses for Latin American needs.

International Reading Association developed a booklet on writing for new readers jointly with the OAS and has cosponsored meetings on reading.

Cooperation with International Organizations since 1984

Most of the regional projects and many of the national projects in the information area are also assisted by other organizations.

The Friedrich Ebert Foundation of Germany has supported rural public library projects in Ecuador and Central America with experts in use of mini-media, communication, and project evaluation.

Radionederland has cosponsored planning meetings and research in Latin America and the Caribbean on radio and television production for children. It is cosponsoring research on children's interests and is producing a series of radio programs on New

World themes for the Quincentennial. It will work with OAS on a pilot program for use of computers with new literates and on desktop publishing for new readers in the near future.

UNESCO has supported project DISC by paying participants' costs in a Caribbean records management course and by providing computers to some of the public libraries involved in the project. It has supported CENTROMIDCA by sending experts there to help teach courses and paid for participants to courses there. It has supported the Venezuelan project PILI with travel funds for meeting participants, funding for publications, and in 1984 through CERLAL support for the PILI circulating exhibit of Latin American children's books.

Centro Interamericano de Educación Superior para America Latina (CIESPAL) has supported projects in the fields of popular communication and mass media for children by publishing the results of planning meetings, by providing experts for courses and technical assistance, facilities, and support for planning meetings.

International Development Research Council of Canada (IDRC) has worked in the Caribbean with national information systems, information services to governments, and national library development.

International Council of Archives (ICA) has cosponsored seminars and technical publications.

Other institutions that have provided experts include CARICOM, the University of the West Indies, the Association of Caribbean Research Institute Libraries (ACURIL), the Caribbean Development Bank, the International Board of Books for Youth, the Patiño Foundation of Switzerland, and the International Federation of Library Associations.

How to Get OAS Assistance

Fellowships

A U.S. citizen may apply for a grant for field research in Latin America for up to one year, with extension possible. This research can be for a book or for a doctoral dissertation.

People from other member states can get fellowships for graduate level study at institutions throughout the Hemisphere, except Canada, which is not a member. Once a person has been accepted for graduate work he/she can apply to the OAS for a fellowship. The forms are available from the OAS office in each country.

Projects

Regional projects are those involving many countries and may have been written at OAS Headquarters or have been written elsewhere and presented to the OAS by the countries. National projects are those which just involve one country and which are presented by the country. OAS can fund projects with private or public institutions, but the projects must have been presented by a country.

The OAS fiscal year begins in January and ends in December. Projects are funded by biennia. At the time of this writing we are in the 1988-89 biennium. By February of 1989 projects for 1990-91 should have been presented. They will be evaluated from the technical view and will then pass through the political bodies before the General Assembly approves the final budget at its annual meeting in November.

The Departments of Education, Science and Technology, Culture, and Fellowships provide a broad range of help in the information fields:

Department of Educational Affairs: Learning resource centers, university libraries, school libraries, library schools.

Department of Science and Technology: Science libraries and documentation centers and basic training in informatics.

Department of Cultural Affairs: Libraries (national, public, and specialized libraries in the fields of culture); archives, primarily national; paper and photographic conservation facilities; library schools; professional associations in the information fields; publishing and mass media for children and new readers.

Department of Fellowships and Training: Provides fellowships for graduate study and research in all fields, except medicine, plus a variety of short-term courses in different countries whereby OAS pays travel and the host country pays tuition and living costs.

The departments have independent budgets raised from voluntary contributions (as opposed to the regular budget financed by quotas based on GNP). What this means to anyone requesting help is that there is no competition among the different areas. For example a country can present a project for learning resource centers to Education, for support to the national library to Culture, and for a science information system to Science, without having to decide that one has higher priority than the others. On the other hand, if a country presents to Culture projects for the national archives, for a restoration laboratory at the national library, and for public library development they will be competing for the "same piece of pie."

Projects can include any or all of the following:

Training: Advanced (in-service treating, intensive short courses, or graduate education), basic and intermediate training through national and regional courses or in-service.

Technical Assistance: An expert sent to the country to advise, help plan.   (Frequently the greatest value to the outside expert is his/her ability to bring different institutions together to work toward common goals.)

Equipment or supplies: Purchase of basic bibliographical working tools and equipment such as microfilm cameras and microcomputers, which are necessary to help an institution advance.

Technical meetings: An institution may want to call a meeting on a particular technical subject (to promote collaboration within a subregion, to work on a common problem, such as on exchange of publications or development of a list of subject headings, or carry out the translation of a technical manual needed by a lot of institutions, or to attend SALALM, ACURIL, IFLA, or other international technical meeting whose theme is relevant to the country's development needs.

Research: For example, teach research techniques, do research needed for policy-making.

Technical Publications: Prepare technical manuals that might be needed locally or by many countries, or the results of meetings or research.

Cooperation of SALALM Librarians

When SALALM's secretariat was located at the OAS, Marietta Daniels Shepard developed an extensive human resources file of U.S. librarians who were interested in either working as consultants or in contributing time during sabbaticals.   Few of the people were used because there was generally a Latin American who not only had the skill needed but also the experience applying it in a Latin American context.

Many institutions have skilled staff but not enough staff to dig out of backlogs or to implement new systems.   Many Peace Corps librarians act as extra staff.   In Colombia, for example, one volunteer (Elizabeth Krakauer) found incunabula and other rare books in the general stacks. She took them out, cleaned and cataloged them, and formed the basis for what is now an important rare book collection.

Library schools need guest faculty for short workshops or for full semesters.   Research is needed as is teaching of research techniques on library and information impact and needs.   OAS would be able to provide information on a wide variety of institutions to those interested in working in Latin America or the Caribbean on sabbaticals, vacation, or during travel for research.

Gift and exchange programs are weak in most Latin American libraries and almost nonexistent in independent research institutions. SALALM members could provide a great service if they could help librarians in Latin America and the Caribbean understand that their government publications as well as a variety of pamphlets from public and private sources are considered research material by U.S. and European libraries and therefore valuable in exchange for publications they need.

Latin Americans have more trouble than U.S. librarians acquiring Latin American materials. They do not have the dollars to buy them with. They cannot travel to acquire materials. They do not have the bibliographic tools or distributors that are available in the United States. Any techniques SALALM members might have that would help them overcome these problems would be useful if published in Spanish.

Duplicates of library manuals and journals (as well as runs of technical journals) that are in good condition are in short supply and would be useful to both library schools and libraries. When SALALM members attempted a program with the OAS many years ago to provide duplicates to Latin America they could not get funds to mail them either to the countries or to the OAS which was willing to mail them abroad. If SALALM could overcome this problem OAS would still be ready to help.

If U.S. graduate schools of librarianship were interested in attracting Latin American and Caribbean students and were able to lower their tuition or provide other means of partial support, the OAS could spread the information and would look on requests for fellowships to these schools with interest. The Graduate School of Library Service of Columbia University is recruiting Latin American students to its graduate conservation program. It is helping the recruits apply for OAS fellowships and is looking for ways to adapt the curriculum to Latin American needs and to lowering the tuition. It is also providing assistance to institutions that are sending students and studying the conditions to which they will return.

A practical way for individual SALALM members to help is to figure out what they themselves need in terms of research or acquisitions and then work out an exchange with colleagues in Latin America and the Caribbean whereby each helps the other.

24. ARUDSI: Primera red de bibliotecas en México

Georgina Arteaga Carlebach

Introducción

Las universidades del noreste de México constituyen un núcleo cultural y académico que posee un carácter propio y una estrecha vinculación al contexto en que viven. Las características de este contexto son: (1) ser una región altamente industrializada y (2) estar geográficamente situada en la frontera con los Estados Unidos. Estas dos características han impactado en la formación y desarrollo de ARUDSI. La primera nos ha llevado a desarrollar servicios de información para dar soporte a la investigación científica y tecnológica que ha generado el desarrollo de la tecnología propia en el país. La segunda, nuestra situación geográfica, ha implicado el recibir una fuerte influencia en la planeación del desarrollo académico, de investigación e industrial.

En México, como en otros países, las universidades se han desarrollado a través del tiempo adaptándose a la ecología del lugar, adquiriendo así, características propias que les dan una identidad diferente y sus funciones mantienen una proyección hacia la comunidad en que están ubicadas y una dependencia de las condiciones de esa misma comunidad.

Si bien estas universidades del noreste cumplen con las tareas comunes a todas las universidades del país, el nivel de investigación que en ellas se realiza y su propia inquietud de un mejoramiento en el aspecto académico, que sea paralelo a la demanda del crecimiento industrial, las ha llevado a una serie de programas de cooperación, siendo uno de estos ARUDSI, sigla que resume el nombre de Acuerdo Regional de Universidades para el Desarrollo de Sistemas Inter-bibliotecarios, que representa a la red de bibliotecas universitarias, especializadas e industriales de la región noreste del país, misma que constituye la primera red de bibliotecas en México.

La experiencia mundial en materia de servicios de información ha establecido, sobre todo en los últimos veinte años, que les es imposible a las instituciones académicas reunir en cada una de ellas, el acervo total que dé acceso a toda la información que es necesaria a un buen trabajo de desarrollo académico y de investigación y que dé soporte al desarrollo tecnológico. Los problemas económicos propios del desarrollo del país refuerzan la necesidad de una acción cooperativa entre las instituciones de educación superior e investigación.

ARUDSI, a través de sus primeros años de vida, ha logrado una acción interna de organización, ha establecido las bases para los servicios interinstitucionales, ha procurado el desarrollo de los recursos humanos, ha realizado ya una primera reunión nacional de redes y cooperativas de bibliotecas, ha participado en programas nacionales en materia de sistemas de información y ha alcanzado así la madurez para plantearse así misma una segunda etapa de desarrollo que incluye una etapa de automatización.

Un sistema automatizado permitirá el procesamiento y servicio compartido de la información existente entre todas las bibliotecas, lográndose con esto que las bibliotecas participantes, a través de sus servicios de información y comunicación, sean verdadero soporte para elevar la acción académica y de investigación en calidad y eficiencia. Pero para su materialización se requiere aplicar la tecnología apropiada que permita el acceso directo a las fuentes de información, optimizándose así los recursos humanos y financieros de las bibliotecas de la región noreste de México.

Antecedentes de ARUDSI

En una reunión de información sobre sistemas y desarrollo de bancos y bases de datos con especialistas franceses y mexicanos sostenida en la Universidad de Monterrey en 1983 y a la cual asistieron rectores de universidades, directores de planeación académica e investigación y directivos de empresas públicas y privadas del estado de Nuevo León, se planteó la necesidad de comunicación e intercambio de información documental entre las bibliotecas de las diferentes universidades e industrias en el estado de Nuevo León.

Posterior a esta reunión, universidades y centros de investigación del estado de Coahuila solicitaron su integración al núcleo de bibliotecas del estado de Nuevo León y así desarrollar una cooperación a nivel, no sólo estatal, sino regional.

Al inicio, las bibliotecas de las instituciones participantes procuraron solamente el intercambio de materiales bibliográficos en un marco de préstamo interbibliotecario, pero muy pronto fueron descubriendo nuevos campos de trabajo, necesidades de una estructura simple y flexible, pero concreta y reconocida. Se analizaron necesidades de coordinación y como resultado se descubrieron las ventajas de una acción colectiva y cooperativa. Todo esta llevó a que en febrero de 1984 se firmara un acuerdo entre las instituciones participantes, creándose así oficialmente lo que pasaría a ser la primera red de bibliotecas en México, ARUDSI. Dicho acuerdo fue firmado entre universidades, institutos tecnológicos, centros de investigación e industrias de Nuevo León y Coahuila.

Por Nuevo León:

> Universidad Autónoma de Nuevo León (participan tres de sus bibliotecas, el Centro de Información y Documentación en Salud de la Facultad de Medicina; el sistema de bibliotecas de la Facultad de Ciencias Químicas y la biblioteca universitaria Capilla Alfonsina)
> Instituto Tecnológico y de Estudios Superiores de Monterrey
> Universidad de Monterrey
> Universidad Regiomontana
> Universidad de Montemorelos
> Instituto Mexicano del Seguro Social (participa con siete bibliotecas médicas)
> Tecnológico de Nuevo León
> Universidad Mexicana del Noreste
> Celulosa y Derivados (CYDSA/Industria)
> Pigmentos y Oxidos (PYOSA/Industria)

Por Coahuila:

> Centro de Investigación en Química Aplicada
> Universidad Autónoma de Coahuila
> Universidad Autónoma Agraria "Antonio Narro"

Al establecerse el acuerdo oficial se definió también el objetivo de la red, mismo que fue:

1. Intercambiar información sobre los acervos disponibles en las bibliotecas de las instituciones participantes.
2. Realizar procesos técnicos dirigidos a establecer bases de datos.
3. Planear nuevos servicios que complementen los ya existentes y faciliten el trabajo académico a profesores, investigadores y estudiantes.

Organización de ARUDSI

Durante el período de tres años, que comprendió 1985-1987, se avanzó en materia de:

1. Establecer una organización ágil y funcional.
2. Delimitar participación de los miembros.
3. Establecer políticas de membresía y permanencia en la red.

4. Establecer políticas y tarifas de servicios interinstitucionales.
5. Conocer el nivel de preparación del recurso humano existente en las bibliotecas participantes y desde ahí diseñar programas de capacitación que preparen a los bibliotecarios para el trabajo cooperativo.
6. Diagnosticar la situación de las bibliotecas participantes.
7. Recibir asesoría británica y canadiense en materia de planeación de redes de bibliotecas.

Lo antes enunciado permitió diseñar una organización flexible y funcional, estableciéndose una asamblea general con los representantes legales de las instituciones participantes que son los directivos de las bibliotecas o sus representantes y los representantes y participantes en los comités que se establecieron, mismo que están integrados por el personal intermedio de las bibliotecas.

La estructura de esta organización es la siguiente:

Consejo Administrativo

Organo legislativo formado por los directivos de las unidades de información (bibliotecas y/o centros de información y documentación) participantes para toma de decisiones, definición de política global y selección de cambios en los servicios bibliotecarios y de información de la región.

Asamblea General

Organo ejecutivo formado por personal intermedio de las unidades de información participantes.

Presidente de Asamblea

Electo por la asamblea, coordina la asamblea y canal de comunicación con el Consejo Administrativo.

Staff Administrador

Propuesto por el Consejo Administrativo y aceptado por la Asamblea, tiene responsabilidad para control administrativo de la red.

Comités

Formados por los Jefes de Areas de Procesos Técnicos, Servicios al Público, Comunicación y Extensión, etc. de las bibliotecas participantes, su función es ejecución de proyectos.

Segunda etapa de ARUDSI

Las bases y objetivos de ARUDSI forman la infraestructura que permite realizar un proyecto piloto en materia de automatización para bibliotecas universitarias y especializadas. La base central de ARUDSI es la cooperación entre bibliotecas de una región, que desean un mútuo apoyo en el uso y planeación del desarrollo de los servicios de información.

Los avances logrados hasta la fecha en la organización de la red, nos han llevado a determinar una segunda etapa en el desarrollo de ARUDSI, para lo cual el proyecto piloto en materia de automatización viene a procurar el cumplimiento de los siguientes objetivos:

1. Materializar en forma preliminar un aspecto de la segunda etapa del desarrollo de ARUDSI, a través de un proyecto piloto que permita verificar la factibilidad de una organización regional de bibliotecas a través de procesos automatizados.
2. Realizar los primeros ensayos en catalogación compartida formando una base de datos que permita obtener catálogos regionales en línea e impresos de los acervos de todas las bibliotecas miembros de ARUDSI.
3. Implementar un sistema que permita accesar esta información con los procesos y equipo técnico, necesarios para recuperar información en línea y producir ejemplares en diversos formatos.
4. Establecer controles y bases de evaluación de los servicios operados a través del sistema, como etapa de fundamentación a nuevos proyectos y programas de la red.

Bases del Proyecto

La realización de este proyecto piloto de ARUDSI estará fundamentado en las siguientes bases:

1. Las bibliotecas participantes establecerán estándares de normalización para el procesamiento de información bibliográfica, lo que permitirá la transferencia. Esto incluye la aplicación de normas de catalogación (AACR2) y el uso del formato MARC.
2. Se incluirán en este proyecto los acervos de las bibliotecas, que por su situación actual, puedan participar.
3. Las bibliotecas participantes en el proyecto en el aspecto de automatización, deberán contar con el personal suficientemente capacitado y en número necesario para cumplir con las tareas que el proceso técnico y su aplicación a los servicios requiere.
4. Las bibliotecas participantes en el proyecto de automatización, deberán contar con los recursos técnicos, administrativos y financieros que aseguren que la materialización y operación de la red funcione eficientemente.
5. Los miembros de ARUDSI, que participarán en esta primera etapa, requerirán de una adecuada demanda de consultas a este tipo de servicios que permita verificar la operacionalización del proyecto.

6. Los miembros de ARUDSI, y especialmente aquellos involucrados en este proyecto piloto, deberán continuar con trabajos que lleven a mantener actualizada la base de datos catalográfica.

7. El recurso humano de las bibliotecas participantes aplicado a la catalogación y clasificación de materiales bibliográficos deberá participar en todos los seminarios de capacitación sobre reglas de catalogación y uso del formato MARC.

Conclusiones

A través de sus primeros cuatro años de vida, ARUDSI ha demostrado que puede operar como red, que los bibliotecarios de las distintas bibliotecas participantes tienen la capacidad suficiente para adquirir el conocimiento requerido para desarrollar servicios cooperativos.

ARUDSI se ha podido desarrollar, tanto por las características de la región que ya se han mencionado al inicio de este trabajo, como por el hecho de contar con un grupo de bibliotecarios, que a diferencia de otras regiones de México, tiene la preparación profesional requerida en el campo de bibliotecología y administración de información.

Sin embargo, tenemos deficiencias aún y éstas son básicamente la falta de experiencia tanto en el desarrollo de redes de bibliotecas como en lo que respecta a implicaciones que conlleva la catalogación compartida; esta última nos representa un nuevo conocimiento a adquirir, por lo que la asesoría que hemos recibido y seguimos recibiendo en esta materia por parte de redes de bibliotecas que ya tienen varios años de experiencia hará nuestra labor más ágil y acertada.

Conocemos el incremento en la demanda de servicios de información que tendremos que enfrentar en los siguientes años y hemos considerado que sólo bajo mecanismos de cooperación podremos optimizar nuestros recursos humanos, tecnológicos, financieros y de información.

BIBLIOGRAFÍA

ARUDSI. Comité de Planeación. Proyecto de desarrollo; segunda etapa. Monterrey, N.L., octubre 1986.

_____. _____. Nueva organización de la red. Monterrey, N.L., noviembre 1986.

_____. Informe de actividades correspondiente a 1986. Monterrey, N.L., junio 1987.

_____. Proyecto de automatización. Monterrey, N.L., agosto 1987.

Part Three

Publishing Patterns and Acquisitions Methods

I. Frontier, Border, and Hinterlands Resources: Case Studies

25. Acquiring Publications from the Amazon: Issues and Sources

Carmen Meurer Muricy

Introduction

The Amazonian region is the largest of Brazil's geographic regions, covering four states—Acre, Amazonas, Pará, and Rondônia—and two federal territories—Amapá and Roraima. It represents about three-fifths of Brazil, two-fifths of South America, and a twentieth of the earth's surface.

The Amazonian basin, which extends over 60 percent of Brazil's territory, contains the most extensive continuous area of humid tropical forests in the world, an exuberant flora and fauna, and immense, largely unexplored mineral reserves.

The largest Brazilian region is also the least developed, least populated, and least explored in all of its potential. The magnitude and problems of this area are reflected in the difficulties the Rio Office of the Library of Congress has faced in acquiring material published from this region in the past twenty years. Acquisitions work is difficult as a result of the lack of a current bibliography for the area, poor distribution of publications, very small printings which are quickly exhausted, and the geographic position of the region, in some aspects still isolated from the rest of the country.

In the last twenty years a remarkable increase in economic activities has occurred in the Amazonia as a result of the implementation of government development policies for the area. The building of roads and dams, the establishment of colonization projects, the development of agribusinesses, and, above all, the large-scale exploration of forestry and mineral resources, have had a tremendous impact on the environment and on the local population. The implications and the results of this development policy have been widely discussed by intellectuals and politicians, by the press, and by the people, and the variety of opinions and reactions indicate the complexity of the subject.

The Book Trade

Bibliographic Control

Through the years the Library of Congress Rio Office has concentrated its efforts on the most critical problem in the whole acquisition process: the knowledge of what is being currently published and by whom. Years ago, the bibliographic sources were very few and poor. Most of the information was obtained from a newspaper clipping service the office subscribed to, which covered commercial publications, and from regular visits to the Rio bookstores, where books from other Brazilian states were rarely found. Bibliographic information from the north, for both commercial and noncommercial publications, was very scarce.

In recent years, however, the material available for bibliographic research has improved considerably in both number and quality, requiring a concentrated effort to keep abreast of what has been coming out.

Taking advantage of this improved situation, in July 1986 the Rio Office began a massive effort to examine the largest possible number of bibliographic sources. This continuing effort involves a group of nine people reviewing and checking bibliographic tools daily. As a result of this effort, there was a 145 percent increase in the number of new in-scope titles identified by the office (i.e., published, during 1987 and the preceding six years), an impressive twenty-seven new titles identified per working day in fiscal year 1984 (according to the Rio Office annual report for 1987).

Our regular research includes daily screening of the newspaper clipping service which provides nationwide press coverage relating to any type of publication (including music). Very little information from the north has been obtained through this service.

The second aspect of regular research is the systematic review of publishers' catalogs, dealers' lists, exchange partners' lists, library and accession bulletins, and all types of current bibliographies. Some government agencies in the north have been publishing catalogs or lists of their publications. Among them, the most important are those of the Emilio Goeldi Museum (Museu Paraense Emilio Goeldi, Belém), the State Council for Cultural Affairs (Conselho Estadual de Cultura do Pará, Belém), the Institute for Economic and Social Development of the State of Pará (Instituto de Desenvolvimento Econômico Social do Pará [IDESP], Belém), State Public Library (Biblioteca Pública Estadual "Arthur Viana," Belém), and Amazonas State Center for Development Center Planning and Technological Research (Centro de

Desenvolvimento, Pesquisa e Tecnologia do Estado do Amazons [CODEAMA], Manaus). However, many of the titles listed in such catalogs are not always available. The most common reasons are: restricted circulation (frequently the case with government documents), and titles are out of print before the catalog is published. Exchange partners' lists and library accessions lists deserve special mention. In the past, there were very few of these and they were poorly done, listing mostly noncurrent titles and foreign material. This has changed. The increasing number of libraries staffed by professional librarians has resulted in an improvement in these lists, which have become one of the best sources for keeping the Rio Office informed about regional publications. Since the number of pieces received from the libraries that issue the exchange lists has been relatively limited, we have adopted the following procedure: at the same time that we send a request to the library that is offering the list, we also send a letter to each publisher of the titles selected from that list. In 1987 the Rio Office received 150 exchange partner's lists. The library accessions bulletins from the Emilio Goeldi Museum, National Institute for Amazonian Research (Instituto Nacional de Pesquisas da Amazônia, Manaus), and the Center for the Incentive to Small and Medium-Sized Businesses (Centro de Apoio a Pequena e Média Empresa do Amazonas [CEAG]) have been very useful for identifying new titles published in the north region.

The third component in our ongoing acquisitions work is the continuing examination of all incoming materials, especially scholarly journals and monographs, newsletters, directories, and other reference tools. These materials are all possible sources of information on new titles for the program or provide new publishing sources to be contacted. The office carefully searches any promising source of information that falls into our hands, so as to identify potential new noncommercial publishers. Among the most useful sources are government directories, telephone directories, institutional lists, and university catalogs. For example: the *National Directory of Environmental Institutions: Cadastro nacional das institutções que atuam na área do meio ambiente* (3a. ed. Brasilia: Secretaria Especial do Meio Ambiente, 1987); the Pará labor union directory, *Catálogo de entidades sindicais* (Belém: Secretaria Especial do Trabalho do Pará, 1988); *Quem informa no Brasil: Guia de Bibliotecas, Centros e Serviços de Documentação e Informação* (Brasilia: IBICT, 1987, 195 pp.); the state government directory of Amazonas *Livro de autoridades* (1988, 236 pp.), which lists all government agencies, officers, addresses, and telephone numbers. The fact that we may not know whether or not the institution actually publishes does not prevent us from sending it a letter of inquiry to establish contact.

Scientific and technological information about the Amazonian region has been collected, organized, and disseminated by the network system Scientific and Technological Information System on the Amazonia (Sistema de Informação Cientifica e Tecnológica da Amazônia [INFORMAM]). It is made up of eight regional institutions which are responsible for collecting bibliographic information on the Amazonia and forwarding it to the central unit of the system, located in the Center for Advanced studies on the Amazonian Region (Núcleo de Altos Estudios Amazônicos [NAEA]) in the Federal University of the State of Pará. The cooperating units are the universities of Acre, Amazonas, Maranhão, Mato Grosso, Pará, and Rondônia, the Emilio Goeldi Museum, and the National Institute for Amazonian Research. They disseminate their bibliographic production through the bulletin *Alerta Amazônia* (formerly *Alerta Amazônia e Carajás* and *Alerta Carajás*), which covers areas of their emphasis such as Anthropology, Archaeology, Botany, Ecology, Tropical Medicine, Regional Planning, Forestry Resources, and Zoology, and material related to the Carajás area.

Publishers

The great majority of books issued in the north are published by the municipal, state, and federal governments, and by research institutions and universities in Belém and Manaus. There are no publishing houses, with the exception of *Edições CEJUP* (Centro de Estudos Jurídicos do Pará), established in Belém in 1980. Its catalog has eighty-nine titles, mostly in the area of law, but it also has some titles on history, economics, sociology, and literature. For example, Pasquale Di Paolo, *Cabanagem*, 2d ed. (1986), Manoel José de Miranda Neto, *O dilema da Amazônia*, 2d ed. rev., enl. (1986); Darcy Flexa Di Paolo, *Os estivadores do Pará no movimento sindical brasileiro: um estudo sociológico* (1986); Rodrigues Pinagé, *Obras completas (poesias) de Rodrigues Pinagé* (1987); Ricardo Borges, *Vultos notáveis do Pará* (2d ed. rev. (1986).

Many authors use local printers to issue their works, which they distribute themselves or place in the local bookstores on consignment. Most are in the area of literature, especially poetry, and have been acquired on a very selective basis by the Rio Office. Some good writers in the Amazonian area have their books published in the south.

The traditional printer Falongola (Gráfica Falangola Editora Ltda.) established in 1949 in Belém absorbs most of the printing work of the State of Pará (excluding the State government printing office and the university press). It operates most of the time as a printer but has also done some publishing work.

Booksellers

In Belém, the best place for acquiring books by writers of the State of Pará is the bookstore of the Municipal Department for Education and Culture (Secretaria Municipal de Educação e Cultura [SEMEC]). Another is Jinkings (R. A. Jinkings Com. e Representações, Rua Tamoios, 1592, 66.000, Belém, Pará), which has a small section of books by local writers. In Manaus there are no bookstores, but only multipurpose stores which sell a few local titles collected in a bookcase. The best ones are Livraria Acadêmica (Rua Henrique Martins, 167, 69.000, Manaus, Amazonas) and Livraria Nacional (Rua 10 de Julho, 613, 69.000, Manaus, Amazonas).

Noncommercial Publications

The government and local institutions have published extensively on the Amazonian region. In addition, a number of commercial and noncommercial publications about the area have originated in other parts of the country.

Government

The majority of publications acquired by the Rio Office from the four states and two territories of the north have come from governmental sources. Acquisition of this material has required a great deal of effort in view of the difficulties already mentioned.

Municipal government. The Library of Congress collects official publications at the municipal level on a very selective basis. Belém, the capital of the State of Pará, is one of the seven Brazilian cities whose documents the Library collects.

The two best sources for acquiring municipal publications are: The Company for the Development and Administration of the Metropolitan Area of Belém (Companhia de Desenvolvimento e Administração da Area Metropolitana de Belém [CODEM]), responsible for government plans, reports, and economic studies; and the Municipal Department for Education and Culture (Secretaria Municipal de Educação e Cultura [SEMEC]), an especially good source for local literature.

State government. The areas of economic planning, technical research, and agriculture are among the most active in the state government. Two important research institutes, which have been active for more than twenty years in the region, are the Institute for

Economic and Social Development of the State of Pará (Instituto de Desenvolvimento Econômico-Social do Pará [IDESP]) and the Amazonas State Center for Development Planning and Technological Research (Centro de Desenvolvimento, Pesquisa e Tecnologia do Estado do Amazonas [CODEAMA]).

The Cultural and Education Departments of the states of Pará and Amazonas publish educational plans, books on regional history, literature, and sociology.

In 1987, the Amazonas State Government created the Institute for Higher Studies on the Amazonian Region (Instituto Superior de Estudos da Amazônia [ISEA]), as a joint effort of the northern states to defend the Amazonian interests. Its headquarters are in Manaus.

In the 1960s a fiscal incentive program was established by the Brazilian Government through the creation of the Superintendency for the Development of the Amazonian Region (Superintendência de Desenvolvimento da Amazônia [SUDAM]) and the Bank of the Amazonia (Banco da Amazônia [BASA]), both in Belém, and the Superintendency for the Duty Free Zone of Manaus (Superintendência da Zona Franca de Manaus [SUFRAMA]).

Other special development programs were directed at the region, such as the POLAMAZONIA (Cattle Raising and Agromineral Program of the Amazônia) and the POLONOROESTE (Northwest Development Program). Many Brazilian and multinational corporations were attracted by these programs, with their tax incentives and offerings of federal land at bargain prices. One such example was the huge forestry and pulp project established in 1967 on the Jari River, covering parts of the Federal Territory of Amapá and the State of Pará, designed and controlled by the American entrepreneur Daniel Ludwig, which in 1982 was sold to a consortium of Brazilian companies.

Elsewhere in the Amazonian Region, considerable mineral deposits have been discovered in recent years, especially after RADAM satellite mapping of the region. In the area of the Carajás mountains, between the Araguaia and the Xingu rivers, one of the world's largest mineral deposits was discovered, containing enormous quantities of high-grade iron ore, as well as manganese, copper, bauxite, and other minerals. To develop this area, the Federal Government created the Greater Carajás Program (Programa Grande Carajás), an integrated mineral exploitation, railroad, and port operation. Earlier, in the 1970s, the construction of the Transamazonian Highway, although not considered by most observers to be among the more successful of the government's megaprojects, did promote integration of the region with the rest of the country. Other new highways have opened up this vast region to settlers who have come largely from the northeast of Brazil, Minas Gerais, and the south. The North-South Railroad, the Balbina Hydroelectric Project, and the Calha Norte Project are the latest programs launched by the Federal Government in this region.

These activities gave rise to a number of publications, many of which were intended for only the internal use of the involved agencies and are not readily available for public consumption. Aimed at the public is another type of publication, the illustrated brochure or propaganda pamphlet, such as the *Greater Carajás Program: A Challenge for all Segments of Brazilian Society* (Brasilia: Brazilian Interministerial Council of the Greater Carajás Program, n.d., 37 pp.); *Albrás: Aluminum in the Amazon* (Belém: Albrás, 1988, in English, 11 pp.); and *Jari* (Rio de Janeiro: Companhia do Jari, n.d.)

The Ministry of the Interior and the Ministry of Mines and Energy are the two federal agencies that have produced the largest number of titles dealing with this region.

Scholarly Publications

The most important research institutions in the north are the Emilio Goeldi Museum (Museu Paraense Emilio Goeldi) in Belém, responsible for the study of the flora and fauna as well as of man and his physical environment, and the National Institute for Amazonian Research (Instituto Nacional de Pesquisa da Amazônia [INPA]), both with a considerable number of titles published. In the area of agriculture, important research studies have been done concerning the rubber tree and African palm, cocoa growing, and humid tropical agriculture.

The Center for Advanced Studies on the Amazonian Region (Núcleo de Altos Estudos Amazônicos [NAEA]) is another prestigious research institution in the area, under the Universidade Federal do Pará.

To acquire all the titles published by the Pará Federal University it is necessary to make direct contact with each sector. One may try the Central Library (Biblioteca Central), which has an Exchange Section (Seção Intercâmbio) but does not have all the university titles available on exchange. They publish an exchange list *Lista de duplicatas* (irregular). The Gráfica e Editora Universitária do Pará is the only university press in the north. Its latest catalog lists sixty-seven titles that are sold at a bookstall, in the Central Library building, on the university campus.

The Universidade Federal do Amazonas has published very few titles. One of their most important titles recently copublished with Instituto Nacional do Libro was the facsimile edition of *Autos da devassa contra os indios Mura do Rio Madeira e nações do Rio Tocantins (1738-1739): Facsimiles transcrições paleográficas* (Brasilia, 1986), 186 pp.

Social and Popular Movements

The socioeconomic transformations caused by the implantation of the great development projects in the Amazonia have provoked some serious consequences, especially with respect to land tenure and the treatment of Indians.

For years the Indians have been suffering from the deforestation and occupation of their lands through the establishment of agri-business, construction of hydroelectric projects, mineral extraction, and road construction.

One of the more controversial cases of the moment involves the Calha Norte Project (PCN) and the Yanomami Indians. This project, the first stage of the Plan for the Development of Amazônia (PDA), began being implemented by the national government in late 1986. It is a defense and economic development program in the frontier area north of the Amazonas. Since the installation of this project, the local Indians have been invaded by an increasing number of construction workers and prospectors. The result from the point of view of the Indians has been the spread of contagious diseases, armed conflict, and death. With the support of a civic society founded by Brazilians in 1978, the Commission for the Creation of the Yanomami Park (CCPY), with its center in São Paulo, the Yanomami have been fighting to preserve their culture and survival through the creation of the Yanomami Indian Park and continued efforts to remove prospectors from this area.

Throughout the country several institutions have mobilized to defend the Indians' cause and to denounce these violations of human rights, calling for equal justice for the poor and assisting marginalized people in general.

The migration to the north has been spontaneous and has produced all sorts of conflicts, as between the *posseiros*, or squatters, who settle on unoccupied land and others who claim it. In the state immigration center at the Rondônia border town of Vilhena, for example, about thirty busloads arrive daily from southern states like Paraná and Minas Gerais, but there is no infrastructure to support the growing influx of immigrants.

In Porto Velho, a Center for Studies and Pastoral Work with Migrants (Centro de Estudos e de Pastoral dos Migrantes), a Catholic institution, promotes studies and defends the interest of the migrants in the region. Among others in the country, the Center for Research on Migration in São Paulo (Centro de Estudos Migratórios [CEM]) is very active, publishing pamphlets and the serial *Vai-vem*. The Library of Congress Rio Office has established contact with it and has received publications from twelve church and civic groups active in the human rights and Indian defense areas in the north. Recently, two new minority groups were identified in Belém: the Center for Studies and Defense of the Black in the State of Pará (Centro de Estudos e Defensa do Negro do Pará [CEDENPA]) and the Movement of Rural and Urban Women (Movimento de Mulheres do Campo e da Cidade). We are also obtaining publications from a very active and strong urban movement in Belém supported by the Commission of the Neighborhoods of Belém (Comissão de Bairros de Belém).

Field Trips to the Amazonian Region

Field trips are of vital importance for the success of the acquisitions program in Brazil. Through an annual schedule of trips planned based on the importance of the different publishing centers, we visit the principal capitals every two to four years. Contacts are renewed and new ones established during these trips. The frequent changes of address, staffing, and the structures of the institutions are learned only during personal visits. In view of the relatively small number of titles published in the region and the high cost of field trips, only Belém and Manaus are scheduled for a visit every two or three years. The remaining states and territories are visited less frequently, or not at all.

The latest trip to the north was in April 1988, when the Rio Office visited Belém and Manaus. In nine working days, the Rio Office acquired 814 titles and made 68 contacts. Of the pieces acquired, 606 were from Belém and 208 from Manaus. Eighteen new contacts were established, and fifteen new institutions were identified. We believe that some of the important titles received during this trip would never have reached the office through regular channels, such as correspondence or telephone calls. For instance, a comprehensive annotated bibliography of Pará, in four volumes, published in 1986, Denise Helena Farias de Souza, Maria de Nazareth Moreira Martins de Barros, and Luiza Castro das Chagas, eds., *Estado do Pará: Pesquisa histórico-bibliográfica* (edition sponsored by the Governo do Estado do Pará and the Universidade do Pará) was discovered during a visit to an institution in Belém. Already out of print, it was obtained only by means of a telephone call to one of the authors and by picking it up later at her residence.

BIBLIOGRAPHY

Aragón, Luis E., and Luc J. A. Mougeot, orgs. *Migrações internas na Amazônia: Contribuições teóricas e metodológicas.* Série Cadernos NAEA/UFPA, 8. Belém: Universidade Federal do Pará, Núcleo de Altos Estudos Amazônicos, 1986. 254 pp.

Autoridades brasileiras. 6a. ed. Brasília: Empresa Brasileira de Notícias/EBN, 1986.

Brazil. Secretaria de Modernização Administrativa/SEMOR. *Titulares e endereços.* 7a. ed. Brasília: SEMOR [1987]. 515 pp.

Enciclopédia Mirador Internacional. São Paulo: Encyclopaedia Britannica do Brazil Publicações Ltda., 1975. Vol. 2, pp. 427-442.

Hallewell, Laurence. *O livro no Brasil (sua história).* Tradução de Maria de Penha Villalobos e Lólio Lourenço de Oliveira. São Paulo: T. A. Queiroz; Editora Universidade de São Paulo, 1985.

Library of Congress. Library of Congress Office, Brazil. *Annual Report for Fiscal Year 1987.* Rio de Janeiro, 1987. 33 pp.

Mirando Neto, Manoel José de. *O dilema da Amazônia.* Belém: Edições CEJUP, 1986. 154 pp. Bibliography, pp. 138-154.

Monteiro da Costa, José Marcelino, coord. *Os grandes projetos da Amazônia: Impactos e perspectivas.* Série Cadernos NAEA, 9. Belém: Universidade Federal do Pará, Núcleo de Altos Estudos Amazônicos, 1987. 168 pp.

Perfil: Administrações estaduais: Norte. No. 12. São Paulo: Visão, 1981. (Includes Acre, Amapá, Amazonas, Pará, Rondônia, Roraima.)

Schmink, Marianne, and Charles H. Wood, eds. *Frontier Expansion in Amazonia.* Gainesville: University of Florida Press, 1984.

Silva, Aluizio Tadeu Marques da. *A política de desenvolvimento regional para a Amazônia, 1980/85.* Estudos Paraenses, 56. Belém: Instituto de Desenvolvimento Económico-Social do Pará, 1986. 30 pp.

26. Colombia (editorialmente), un país de fronteras en papel . . . y sin papel

J. Noé Herrera C.

Colombia está situada en el hemisferio occidental, formando el extremo norte-occidental de la América del Sur, que, a través del Istmo de Panamá, se une con la América Central, a pesar de Panamá, hoy de nuevo de moda en los medios internacionales de comunicación masiva.

Dueña de costas sobre el Océano Atlántico, en 1600 kilómetros, al norte y sobre el Pacífico, al occidente en 1300 kilómetros, Colombia tiene islas en el Mar Caribe, como San Andrés, Providencia, Santa Catalina, Barú y Tierrabomba, lo mismo que en el Mar de Balboa, como Malpelo, Gorgona y Gorgonilla. [1]

Según la medida o amplitud de zonas marítimas o aguas territoriales que se aplique (12 o 200 millas), Colombia tiene 30.896 o 514.976 kilómetros cuadrados de plataforma sobre el Atlántico y 25.103 o 418.418 kilómetros cuadrados sobre el Pacífico. [2]

Cubierta en parte considerable por la Cordillera de los Andes, que al penetrar el país por el sur se subdivide en la Cordillera Occidental, la Cordillera Central y la Cordillera Oriental, Colombia cuenta con un sistema montañoso que, no obstante haber constituido un obstáculo de la naturaleza al desenvolvimiento de las comunicaciones y del transporte y aún del ímpetu colonizador, también ha sido en alto grado crisol de la nacionalidad, núcleo genérico y propulsor del crecimiento demográfico y del desarrollo económico e, inclusive, factor determinante de las condiciones climáticas del país, a la vez que fuente de recursos hidrológicos y sobre todo hidroeléctricos del mismo.

Desde luego, en la geografía colombiana no son menos importantes las llanuras orientales, conformadas por la Amazonía y la Orinoquía, las planicies del Caribe y del Pacífico y las zonas isleñas, todas las cuales totalizadas constituyen más de la mitad del territorio nacional y que, con su paulatino y demorado desarrollo económico y social, han empezado a dejar de ser solamente reserva y han comenzado a convertirse en factores determinantes de la realidad colombiana.

Con una topografía que, aunque desde el punto de vista orográfico enriquece el país climatológica, hidrológica y geológicamente,

Colombia no ha sido capaz, sin embargo, de doblegar sus montañas, conquistar sus llanuras y utilizar adecuadamente sus recursos hídricos, para establecer un adecuado sistema de comunicaciones terrestres, fluviales y marítimas. Si bien debe anotarse que, en cambio, fue uno de los países pioneros de la aviación comercial en el mundo y cuenta hoy con un sistema bastante desarrollado de telecomunicaciones.

El país, por ejemplo, en 1984 solamente tenía 121.374 kilómetros de carreteras no siempre ni todas transitables, para una extensión de más de un millón de kilómetros cuadrados y una población cercana a los 30 millones. [3] Y mientras en 1985 el transporte aéreo nacional movilizó 5.942.969 pasajeros y 91.124.900 millones de toneladas métricas de carga, el transporte por ferrocarril en el mismo año fue de solo 1.445.317 y de 1.267.617 de toneladas métricas de carga.

No existen estadísticas sobre el movimiento o transporte interno de pasajeros y de carga por las vías terrestres, fluviales o marítimas. En cambio, se sabe que en 1985 [4] los colombianos hablamos por teléfono, con el exterior, durante 42.289.167 minutos, de ellos 62.1% con los Estados Unidos, el 9% con Venezuela, el 4% con Panamá y el 3,2% con el Ecuador.

Aún hoy somos un país más cercano del exterior que de nosotros mismos: Ir de Bogotá a Quito toma 80 minutos, a Panamá 85 minutos, a Miami 210 minutos, a Caracas 100 minutos; mientras que viajar, en avión desde luego, de Medellín a Leticia, de Ríohacha a Pasto o de Quibdó a Arauca puede tomar todo un día o más, si se tienen en cuenta las escalas que sería forzoso hacer en cada caso. Y conste que lo anterior sería por avión, pues, los ferrocarriles hace tiempo dejaron de ser el sueño de pioneros y quijotescos colonizadores parar convertirse en fortín de una burocracia zángana y corrupta. Y el tiempo, las horas que se necesitarían para recorrer por tierra las mismas distancias mencionadas asustarían a cualquiera, así tuviera alma de aventurero al estilo de Arturo Cova, el famoso personaje de *La Vorágine*.

Con extensas fronteras terrestres (6.342 kilómetros), con dos océanos que la circundan (en extensión de 2.900 kilómetros) y con muchos ríos navegables (Atrato, Cauca, Magdalena, Casanare, Meta, Vaupés, Vichada, Guaviare, Inírida, Apaporis, Caquetá, Putumayo), Colombia es un país un tanto incomunicado. No sólo por sus montañas que han operado hasta cierto punto como barreras internas y porque sus llanuras mismas, en vez de facilitar la interrelación regional y con los países vecinos, han permanecido inexploradas en su mayor extensión, sino también porque carece de puertos marítimos y fluviales, y aún de aeropuertos apropiados. Leticia, Cúcuta, Santa Marta,

Barranquilla, Cartagena, Turbo, Buenaventura e Ipiales no son aún las puertas de oro del país, como a una de ellas se le denominó, más poética que realísticamente.

Según el censo de 1985, la población de Colombia está distribuido así: [5]

Bogotá, D.E.	3.982.941
Región Atlántica	5.678.001
Región Oriental	5.214.400
Región Central	7.643.553
Región Pacífica	4.904.791
Intendencias Comisarias	443.640
Total	27.867.326

De los 27.867.326 habitantes, 18.737.547 son radicados en centros urbanos, y de estos, 12.498.193 residen en ciudades con más de 100.000 habitantes. [6]   Colombia es un país preponderantemente urbanizado (69,9%). [7]

Según el censo citado, entre 1982 y 1984 arribaron al país 698.806 viajeros internacionales.   Más de estos viajeros, 649.902 llegaron por vía aérea, 44.913 por vía terrestre, 2.477 por vía marítima y 1.516 por vía fluvial.   En el mismo período, 1982-1984, salieron del país 685.568 viajeros internacionales, discriminados así: 659.318 por aire, 31.072 por tierra, 2.178 por mar y 2.000 por río.

País de ciudades o, más exactamente, país con la mayoría de su población radicada en centros urbanos, Colombia concentra su población urbana en las ciudades citadas en el Cuadro 1.

Sin embargo, como se comprobará por los cuadros estadísticos que siguen, bibliográfica y editorialmente, Bogotá es la verdadera metrópolis de Colombia, sin desconocer la importancia que Cali y Medellín han adquirido en este como en otros campos de la actividad industrial, económica, política y social del país, al constituirse también en vigorosos y pujantes núcleos de desarrollo (Cuadros 2-6).

En las provincias, en las fronteras colombianas, no sólo se imprime poco, sino que lo impreso allí tampoco llega a la capital. ¿Por falta de una adecuada distribución, por carencia de un apropiado sistema de transporte?   Estas deficiencias, al parecer y en parte, desaparecieron con ocasión de la reciente Feria Internacional del Libro, celebrada en Bogotá, en la cual se demostró que en la provincia colombiana sí se está editando y que el principal problema de las publicaciones regionales colombianas radica en su falta de distribución o mercadeo.

Cuadro 1. Población Urbana

Departamento		Departamento	
Antioquia		César	
Medellín		Valledupar	192.049
1.909.664 [a]		Aguachica	48.824
Apartadó	44.661	Codazzi	39.621
Caldas	42.158	Córdoba	
Copacabana	40.309	Montería	224.147
Caucasia	39.190	Cereté	53.915
Rionegro	56.195	Lorica	75.578
Sonsón	39.117	Planeta Rica	44.267
Turbo	70.113	Sahagun	58.059
Yarumal	33.070	Tierralta	53.317
Atlántico		Cundinamarca	
Barranquilla	899.781	Factativá	51.639
Malambo	52.584	Fusagasugá	56.816
Sabanalarga	50.925	Girardot	70.076
Soledad	165.791	Soacha	109.051
Bolívar		Zipaquirá	53.370
Cartagena	531.426	Choco	
Carmen de Bolívar	61.448	Quibdó	75.524
Magangué	87.446	Huila	
Boyaca		Neiva	194.556
Tunja	93.792	Garzón	40.310
Chiquinquirá	35.807	Pitalito	51.107
Duitama	67.831	La Guajira	
Sogamoso	81.226	Riohacha	76.943
Caldas		Maicao	53.855
Manizales	299.352	Magdalena	
Chinchiná	43.684	Santa Marta	218.205
La Dorada	54.195	Ciénaga	120.253
Riosucio	42.877	Fundación	42.086
Salamina	23.511	Plato	62.126
Caquetá		Meta	
Florencia	79.515	Villavicencio	178.685
Cauca		Nariño	
Popayán	158.336	Pasto	244.700
Bolívar	46.882	Ipiales	69.894
Santander de		Samaniego	43.745
Quilichao	53.954	Tumaco	94.230

[a] Sin incluir a Bello, Envigado, Itagüí.

Cuadro 1. (Continuación)

Departamento		Departamento	
Norte de Santander		Valle (Continuación)	
Cúcuta	379.478	Buga	94.753
Ocaña	66.058	Candelaria	44.400
Pamplona	39.436	Cartago	97.791
Vailla del Rosario	63.615	El Cerrito	40.188
Quindio		Florida	42.853
Armenia	187.130	Jamundi	42.158
Calarcá	52.476	Palmira	214.395
Risaralda		Sevilla	50.825
Pereira	287.999	Tuluá	121.490
Dos Quebradas	101.480	Yumbo	50.263
Santa Rosa de		**Intendencia**	
Cabal	60.696	Arauca	
Santander		Arauca	21.279
Bucaramanga	352.326	Casanare	
Barrancabermeja	153.296	Yopal	23.169
Floridablanca	143.824	Putumayo	
Girón	50.070	Mocoa	20.235
Piedecuesta	48.286	San Andrés	
San Vicente de		San Andrés	32.282
Chucurí	50.078	**Comisaria**	
Sucre		Amazonas	
Sincelejo	135.857	Leticia	19.245
Corozal	46.096	Guania	
San Onofre	41.723	Inírida	9.214
Tolima		Guaviare	
Ibagué	292.965	San José del	
Chaparral	42.950	Guaviare	31.082
Espinal	54.805	Vaupés	
Líbano	43.063	Mitú	13.192
Valle		Vichada	
Cali	1.350.565	Puerto Carreño	8.081
Buenaventura	193.185		

Cuadro 2. Evolución institucional del mercado
editorial, 1959-1983

Ciudad	Editoriales existentes	
	1959-1960 [a]	1982-1983 [b]
Bogotá, D.E. [c]	64	146
Armenia	--	3
Barranquilla	6	18
Bucaramanga	10	20
Buga	--	2
Cali	8	33
Cartagena	4	8
Cúcuta	1	5
Florencia	--	1
Girardot	--	2
Ibagué	1	3
Manizales	5	23
Medellín	14	39
Montería	1	5
Neiva	1	3
Ocaña	--	2
Palmira	--	6
Pasto	6	5
Pereira	--	7
Popayán	4	8
Santa Marta	1	3
Tuluá	--	2
Tunja	--	5
Valledupar	--	4
Villavicencio	--	4

---

a Rubén Pérez Ortiz (compilador), *Anuario Bibliográfico Colombiano,
1959-1960* (Bogotá: Instituto Caro y Cuervo, 1961), pp. 197-221.

b Francisco José Romero Rojas (compilador), *Anuario Bibliográfico
Colombiano "Rubén Pérez Ortiz," 1982-1983* (Bogotá: Instituto Caro y Cuervo, 1986),
pp. 637-661.

c De acuerdo con el directorio telefónico de Bogotá, D.E., en 1988 existen en
Bogotá, en total, 115 editoriales, 40 imprentas y 55 litografías.

Cuadro 3. Evolución institucional del mercado
del libro, 1959-1983

Ciudad	Librerías existentes	
	1959-1960 [a]	1982-1983 [b]
Bogotá, D.E.	59	39 [c]
Armenia	--	2
Barranquilla	11	9
Bucaramanga	3	8
Buga	--	2
Cali	20	12
Cartagena	2	2
Cúcuta	--	3
Florencia	--	1
Girardot	--	1
Ibagué	--	3
Manizales	8	8
Medellín	27	27
Montería	--	6
Neiva	1	3
Ocaña	--	2
Palmira	--	3
Pasto	4	3
Pereira	--	5
Popayán	2	3
Santa Marta	--	1
Tuluá	--	2
Valledupar	--	3
Villavicencio	--	4

a Rubén Pérez Ortiz (compilador), *Anuario Bibliográfico Colombiano, 1959-1960* (Bogotá: Instituto Caro y Cuervo, 1961), pp. 197-221.

b Francisco José Romero Rojas (compilador), *Anuario Bibliográfico Colombiano "Rubén Pérez Ortiz", 1982-1983* (Bogotá: Instituto Caro y Cuervo, 1986), pp. 637-661.

c De acuerdo con el directorio telefónico de Bogotá, D.E., en Bogotá existen 85 librerías en 1988.

Cuadro 4. Distribución geográfica del mercado gráfico en 1988 [a]

Ciudad	Editoriales	Imprentas	Litografías	Tipografías	Librerías
Armenia	4	1	7	14	15
Barrancabermeja	1	2	1	2	5
Barranquilla	10	8	18	50	35
BOGOTÁ	115	40	55	105	115
Bucaramanga	8	10	13	41	30
Buenaventura	--	1	--	3	3
Buga	--	1	--	2	3
Calarcá	--	1	--	1	4
Cali	32	37	20	53	35
Cartagena	4	2	12	10	20
Cartago	--	1	1	6	7
Cúcuta	1	4	4	18	10
Florencia	--	1	1	3	6
Girardot	--	1	--	3	4
Ibagué	2	3	7	16	10
Manizales	8	5	3	19	12
Medellín	25	25	33	100	70
Montería	5	2	3	9	8
Neiva	1	3	4	22	13
Ocaña	3	--	--	5	5
Palmira	2	1	1	14	6
Pamplona	--	1	1	3	3
Pasto	2	2	3	6	10
Pereira	4	4	5	20	7
Popayán	2	3	2	5	10
Santa Marta [b]	--	--	--	--	--
Sincelejo [b]	--	--	--	--	--
Tuluá	1	1	1	4	4
Villavicencio [b]	--	--	--	--	--

a Estadística extractada de los directorios telefónicos de las ciudades mencionadas.

b Sin datos.

Cuadro 5. Realidad incuestionable: Bogotá, metrópoli
editorial de Colombia

Ciudad	Títulos editados	%
Arauca	1	
Armenia	5	
Barranquilla	66	
BOGOTÁ	3.045	77,31
Bucaramanga	17	
Buga	2	
CALI	182	4,62
Cartagena	3	
Cúcuta	6	
Chinchiná	1	
Choachí	1	
Florencia	1	
Girardot	2	
Ibagué	10	
Ipiales	1	
Leticia	1	
Lomalinda	4	
Manizales	63	
MEDELLÍN	461	11,71
Melgar	6	
Montería	2	
Neiva	4	
Palmira	7	
Pamplona	3	
Pasto	7	
Pereira	2	
Popayán	2	
Quibdó	1	
Rionegro	1	
San Andrés	1	
Tibaitatá	12	
Tunja	22	
Villavicencio	2	

Fuente: Francisco José Romero Rojas (compilador), *Anuario Bibliográfico Colombiano "Rubén Pérez Ortiz", 1982-1983* (Bogotá: Instituto Caro y Cuervo, 1986).

Las fronteras en general y las provincias en particular, pues, permanecen abandonadas, distantes, como si solamente tuvieran derecho a figurar en el papel, en el papel de los mapas, en las promesas de los políticos en busca de elección y en los mensajes o memorias de los gobernantes en plan de hacer olvidar lo que prometieron sin ser capaces de cumplir.

Somos, pues, editorial y bibliográficamente, un país de fronteras en papel . . . y sin papel!

NOTAS

1. *Colombia estadística*, vol. 1 (Bogotá: Departamento Administrativo Nacional de Estadística [DANE], 1987), p. 13.

2. *Colombia en el universo: atlas geográfico*; Banco de Datos, 4a ed. (Bogotá: Ediciones Cultural, 1986), p. 65.

3. *Colombia Estadística*, 1987, vol. 1, p. 679.

4. Ibid., p. 695.

5. Ibid., p. 52.

6. *XV Censo Nacional de Población y IV de Vivienda*, vol. 1 (Bogotá: DANE, 1986), p. 24.

7. *Avance de Resúmenes Preliminares del XV Censo Nacional de Población y IV de Vivienda*, diciembre de 1985 (Bogotá: DANE, 1986), p. 14.

27. Establishing Exchange Programs with Argentine Institutions

Gabriela Sonntag-Grigera

An exchange program is simply an arrangement between two institutions whereby materials are exchanged on a regular basis. The materials exchanged can either be duplicates of materials in the collection or extra copies of the material which the institution publishes. After a brief look at factors that influence exchange programs in Argentina, this paper examines exchanges from a different perspective and presents some guidelines to help establish a viable exchange program.

In Argentina, exchange programs exist on local, national, and international levels among all types of libraries in government agencies, universities and research centers, and large public libraries. There is considerable incentive to establish exchange programs within the country and especially with libraries in foreign countries. Most institutions have little or no acquisitions budget, their researchers need foreign publications, and they cannot import books since the laws that govern acquisitions are so complex that they inhibit the importation of books.

Opponents of exchange programs usually claim that the correspondence needed to maintain them is too time consuming. Sometimes they fear that the exchange will not be reciprocal. The cost of mailing also presents a problem; in many institutions no budget is allotted for this type of expense.

Nevertheless, exchanges have been in force for years. As far back as 1958 José María Martínez wrote on the status of exchange programs in Argentina.* He proposed the creation of a national exchange center that would coordinate exchanges. The difficulties he cited then are still valid today:

Lack of coordination among libraries.

---

*"Present Status of Exchanges in Argentina." Working Paper IIB. SALALM III, Berkeley, CA, July 10-11, 1958.

Lack of independence of libraries within the rigid organization of the
parent institutiocomplain

Need to convince authorities that exchange programs are the responsibility of the library.

Need for librarians to have input in the decisions of the editorial office.

Urgent need for fulfillment of international exchange conventions.

Need to centralize duplicate materials to avoid the alternative of
purchasing, which is especially costly in the case of periodicals.

Need for a librarian association to solve fundamental problems in a
systematic and effective manner.

In general, little has changed since then, and these factors
continue to hinder the development of exchange programs. The
effectiveness of the programs depends largely on the person responsible
for them but also, of course, on the availability of publications to
exchange.

Publications vary in content, title, format, or regularity as a
reflection of the changes within each institution. Very few research
institutions in Argentina function independent of government funding.
In the past few years the government has made adjustments and given
more attention to specific areas of research to the detriment of others.
Many institutions which did not previously receive financial support
from the government are suddenly favored and very active. Others
have had funds withdrawn and are no longer able to publish. Many
institutes, especially those within thc universities, encourage their
researchers to publish in foreign journals and even provide them with
the contacts to enable them to do so. The same articles may also be
published by the center, or separatas may be printed for local
distribution. In some cases, the center may decide to cancel its
publications program altogether.

Government agencies have also felt the winds of change. On the
one hand, many of them, like the Secretaria de Justicia, the Secretaria
de la Marina Mercante, Ministerio de Trabajo, and the Ministerio de
Obras y Servicios Publicos, have been instructed to discontinue
publishing annual reports but to submit them instead to a centralizing
agency which then publishes abstracts for very limited distribution and,
perhaps from our point of view, of very limited interest. On the other
hand, some agencies such as the Banco Central and the Secretaria de
Comercio Exterior have been encouraged and funded to publish a
bulletin or a series of research reports and articles.

The University in Argentina deserves special attention. In most
cases exchanges are established directly with the institutes and centers
of the university. They have suffered much the same change of focus

and lack of funds as the government agencies. The tendency now is toward the centralization of university administration, which has met with considerable resistance within the university and from the general public. But if the trend continues, exchanges will be made with both a centralizing agency in the university—be it a special exchange office or the university publishing office or the Rector—and the individual centers or institutes. The latter may refuse to hand over all their publications to the centralized office. They argue, perhaps justifiably, that the centralized agency knows nothing of exchanging materials, lacks knowledge of the kinds of publications needed by the institutes, and has no idea of what is involved in the exchanges that the institutes have worked so hard to establish and maintain through the years. This problem is compounded by the fact that few, if any, of the universities have a central library. But one can also see the positive aspect if, indeed, centralization takes place. The university would be in greater control of its publications, making it easier to ascertain what is published and if it is available. With only one office in charge of all university publications and exchange programs, correspondence would decrease, generally simplifying the exchange process.

I have stated that many institutions are no longer receiving maximum government attention, and the lack of funds has caused them to cease publication, but even so new publications of interest have appeared. But many factors other than economic ones can influence the success of an exchange program. Change in personnel deeply affects the functioning of the institution and its library and, thus, the effectiveness of an exchange program. The person responsible for the exchange program is very instrumental in its success. The institution continues to publish but the person in charge of the exchange program is gone. The new librarian is not a proponent of exchange programs or is not even aware that they exist in that institution. The new person may not be a trained librarian or may be there for just a short time, to be followed by a succession of others. Perhaps a certain institution has been publishing for some time and only now, with a new person in charge, as the institution redesigns its structures and functions, decides to exchange.

Knowing that exchange programs have been around for years, how can we view them as a frontier, a new field? The answer is that they should be seen as such because old ideas should be tossed out and old exchange ties should be considered from a new perspective.

The following procedure may be followed as a guide for establishing exchanges. First decide with whom to establish an exchange program irrespective of a knowledge of its publications.

Select a core group of institutions that specialize in the subject area of interest. Make contact with the institution by a letter that explains carefully (and preferably in Spanish) the exchange to be implemented. State clearly the objectives of your own institution in establishing the exchange program and what is expected in return. Perhaps include an explanation of how difficult it is to obtain information from Argentina and the need for a channel by which both partners can obtain information. It is useful to add a clause stating that exchanges will be considered active only as long as requests continue to be filled by both parties.

Ideally, the exchange of published materials is handled by the library of the institution. Thus, your initial contact should be made with the librarian. The librarian, however, is not involved in the publishing process when it is handled in another office. Even then, though, the librarian is the best point of contact because he/she is the best source of information on what is being published and where to get it. Further, all copies of what is being published for exchange are generally deposited in the library of the institution. Moreover, the library is the best source for information on research within the institution.

Chances are that if contact with the exchange partners is not fairly regular, the information on these exchanges becomes relatively outdated and the institution misses out on what is available through an exchange program. Contacts need to be maintained, nurtured and, of course, this involves much letter writing, a task facilitated by the use of a word processor.

First of all, the choice of the institution is most important. Perhaps the institution is very well known but does not publish, or if it does, publishes relatively poor works or merely issues separatas and reprints. The exchange is nevertheless desirable because of the institution itself. The exchange can be useful because of the prestige of the institution or its people.

Second, it is important to know what information is wanted and in what format. Knowing what is available is a considerable task, but not impossible. If publications exist, they can be identified with the aid of the librarian. A few institutions like to exchange databases, software programs, audiovisuals or photographic collections for other kinds of materials, an exchange worthy of consideration.

Still another consideration is how to motivate the exchange. Innumerable institutions publish a highly desirable bulletin or journal, but they have no library and no desire to exchange publications. The opposite is also true. An institution has a library which is known for its special collections or which is outstanding in some other respect. Yet it has no funding for publications and therefore leaves the library without any means for exchange despite an urgent need to do so. With such an institution it is possible to exchange your publications for their information, reference services, or computer searches. Through that kind of exchange program, contacts can be made to help keep us up to date on events and publications in the areas of interest. Given the general lack of bibliographic control in Argentina, these contacts can be the best source of information on current research trends and publications. Flexibility is essential. All options should be considered.

Unfortunately, usually when an exchange contact has been established one considers it over and done with and gives it only minimum consideration. For best results, personalize the exchange by putting a name and perhaps a face to the contact. Aim to choose a few important institutions, ask for their advice on an exchange program, and make sure the incentive to exchange is maintained. It is essentially our aim to ensure that the exchanging institutions develop a workable relationship that will last despite all the fluctuations and inconsistencies that characterize Argentine society.

28. Acquisitions and Exchanges on the Mexican Side of the United States-Mexico Border

Marta Stiefel Ayala

In one of his classic essays, "The Personality of Mexico," Carl Sauer,* the famous human geographer, defined northern Mexico as an area that has always received most of its cultural goods from the central states. Throughout the colonial period, the region was defined as a frontier, *provincias internas*, an area thought of more as a drain than as a contributing factor to Mexico's development. Presently, northern Mexico is still considered a peripheral region, an area that needs to be civilized. There is still a lack of understanding about northern Mexico on the part of many; *capitalinos* still believe that they need to bring "culture" and "knowledge" to the frontier. It is true that northern Mexico was a recipient of "Mexican culture" from the south since pre-Hispanic times and continued to be so through colonial and modern times. Almost everything of value, including books, was produced or originated in the central states and it trickled up the old colonial routes to northern Mexico. Very rarely did anything of national consequence originate in the northern Mexican states. The same can be said about the publishing industry. Again, rarely was anything of national impact published in the northern states of Tamaulipas, Coahuila, Nuevo León, Chihuahua, Sonora, Baja California, and Sinaloa. This has been changing gradually for the book publishing industry, as well as for every other aspect of production and development. As northern Mexico develops its own dynamic publishing industry, it has become less dependent on books from southern Mexico. Often development has occurred in cooperation with institutions from southern Mexico and from the U.S. side of the border: San Diego State University with Universidad Autónoma de Baja California; University of Arizona with University of Sonora; University of Texas with Universidad de Ciudad Juárez.

---

*In *Land and Life: A Selection from the Writings of Carl O. Sauer* (Berkeley: University of California Press, 1965).

During my internship at the Library of Congress, Hispanic Acquisitions Program, I compiled a list of sources of publications for northern Mexico. This assignment was of value to the Library of Congress because the contacts with the region had diminished, in spite of previous exchange agreements. Also, it was believed that the blanket order dealers in charge of providing books to the Library of Congress from Mexico had very limited contact with the publishing institutions in northern Mexico. Consequently, there was a gap in the acquisitions process for Mexico.

Later, Francisco Ayala and I did field acquisitions work for the Library of Congress. Subsequently, we have worked with the Institute for Border Studies of San Diego State University—Imperial Valley Campus. We discovered at firsthand the richness and vastness of the publishing industry in the border states of Mexico. The principal publishing institutions are university presses, university research centers, state government presses, city government presses, government-sponsored programs, and private presses. We have found 31 institutions in Baja California, 13 in Coahuila, 10 in Durango, 7 in Tamaulipas, 16 in Chihuahua, 13 in Nuevo León, 17 in Sonora, and 5 in Sinaloa which have some kind of publication program. Some, of course, are very organized and extensive, others more limited and sporadic.

Although the publishing industry is flourishing, it is not without its problems.

One of the major problems we find in Mexico is the lack of distribution and publicity program at the publishing and research centers for their publications and research findings. This occurs at the national level, within the state, or even within the institution. Often, one *escuela*, or college, does not know what the other *escuela* at the same university is publishing. The problem grows proportionately more acute at the more isolated regions of the states. One of the most rewarding aspects of the acquisition trips was that we were able to link some institutions that shared common interests by providing names, addresses, and information about each others' research or publication programs (e.g., the Instituto de Investigaciones Sociales at UABC and Universidad de Sinaloa).

Another problem in Mexico is its tendency to centralize: everything has to originate from the center of power and then be dispersed through the rest of the country. Even the people from the northern states believe this to be the way to operate. For example, many authors from the northern states, fearing that their works will not have the proper distribution if they are published in their home state, will go to Mexico City and pay very high prices to have their books published there. What it boils down to is that a book that is produced in the central states has a wide national, even international, distribution; a book that is published in the northern states has very limited distribution. The best example is Manuel Roja's *Joaquin Murrieta el Patrio*; another is the periodical *Calafia* published at Universidad Autónoma de Baja California.

A very discouraging aspect of the publishing industry in northern Mexico, and perhaps in other parts of Mexico as well, is the lack of lists or catalogs of publications available for sale or exchange. For example, we have been trying to persuade the editorial leadership of the UABC, for at least ten years, to produce a catalog of publications, without success. Almost every institution also lacks records of its bibliographic output. Frequently, they even lack archival copies of their own publications. Even the libraries within the institutions do not systematically collect all the publications of the entity and are not aware of what is being published under their own roof.

A major obstacle for the distribution of materials, by purchase or exchange, is the lack of a postage budget. We found several institutions, which supposedly had exchange agreements with the Library of Congress, with stacks of materials ready to be sent. They were unable to do so not only because of lack of postage money but also because of internal regulations that limit foreign mailings. And this problem, if anything, is getting worse.

Another very disruptive problem in Mexican institutions is the change in personnel which occurs whenever the administration and government change. One consequence of these personnel changes is that old policies, agreements, *convenios*, and the like, are no longer enforced or are forgotten. One then needs to start the negotiation process all over again. Many times, when the personnel changes, all files are destroyed or removed, so there is a tremendous lack of continuity.

As a consequence of personnel changes, there are frequently changes in goals and directions in the institution's publishing and research programs. They may change their focus or be eliminated altogether; therefore, many publications are discontinued, and new ones get started only to be abandoned when new changes occur. A case in point is the government publication program in the State of Sonora. During one administration, a huge effort was made to collect and publish everything of value about the state. As a result, at least one hundred books were published with tremendously valuable information about the history, geography, literature, and anthropology of Sonora.

The administration changed and the publications were discontinued, even those that were ready to be sent to press. Even more discouraging is that very few copies were printed and no plans have been made to reprint some of the more valuable works. Another problem is that, many times, the president of a university has the final say on what is published at that institution, overriding editorial decisions that had already been made.

Another consequence of these changes in personnel and direction is the uncertainty from one year to the next as to the continuity in programs. Therefore, many library directors and editors hesitate to establish agreements or make long-range commitments for fear of having to cancel at a moment's notice.

In universities, as well as in state and city governments, a group of individuals may assume control of the publishing program, many times discontinuing what has been published previously: at the university level the literature of a favorite group of authors, or at a research institution the political and philosophical orientation of a group of researchers may be promoted more than others; and at the state level, the personal interests or preferences of the bureaucrat assigned to the post of overseeing what is published takes priority over quality or previous commitment. Whatever is politically desirable at the time often determines the publishing program. For example, recently a university commissioned a political appointee to direct the writing of the official biography of the PRI governors of the state. Local politicians also influence what is published by the state, frequently sponsoring publications of friends, or commissioning friends to produce books. For many journals the government may be the most significant sponsor, and when the source of funding is reduced or cut, such as resulted from the recent directive from the central government to stop spending, many journals disappear.

Inflation and the peso fluctuation are felt more profoundly in the northern states as they are directly influenced by what happens to the monetary exchanges on the other side of the border. Most of the supplies, tools, and machinery used for printing come from the United States rather than from the interior of Mexico. Therefore, the best made plans for a publication program can be totally devastated by a rapid decrease in the value of the peso. The status of *zona libre* helps somewhat to alleviate this very serious problem by reducing the import taxes that otherwise would have to be paid to bring materials into the country.

In spite of these problems, the publishing industry in northern Mexico is becoming well established and is flourishing.

There are number of successful acquisitions and exchange programs in northern Mexico. There is no substitute for being at the right place at the right time in doing acquisitions work in northern Mexico. Since there is very little concerted effort to publicize and organize the publishing industry in the northern states, even the most valuable books are often found by chance. Since few copies are printed, a title becomes a rare item very quickly. A case in point is the recently published *Vision histórica de la frontera norte de Mexico*, a three-volume work about the history of the U.S.-Mexico border. The bound copies or *ediciones de lujo* are now very hard to find.

The best approach by far is still the personal visit and the personal contact. We have learned that the best way to acquire materials continues to be to visit the place and to purchase or obtain in exchange what you find right then and there and take it with you or ship it through the *paqueteria* service of the bus companies. In these personal contacts, be assertive, convincing, generous, and, at the same time, culturally sensitive and linguistically proficient, and very willing to do the actual searching for documents oneself. For example, this is particularly true in obtaining government documents like *periódicos oficiales* from depositories located in prisons.

Use services such as Hispanic Books Bulletin, or others that are located near the border. Major book distributors located in Mexico City or Guadalajara receive little information about what is published in the northern states and, therefore, cannot be depended upon to collect materials published in limited numbers in areas that are difficult and expensive to reach, e.g., Cronista de la Ciudad de Parra).

I believe that acquisitions for northern Mexico must be done through fieldwork if one is serious about truly collecting the bibliographic output of the country. Some acquisitions work can be done sitting in an office, going through catalogs, and dreaming about what these places look like; but there is no substitute for the experience and knowledge that one gains through fieldwork.

II. Regional Organizations: Documents and Other Publications

29. Organizaciones internacionales de América Latina: Recursos bibliográficos y su adquisición con relación especial a la República Federal de Alemania

Sabine Zehrer

El interés europeo en la integración latinoamericana

Los esfuerzos de la República Federal de Alemania por lograr la integración europea están estrechamente ligados con los de los demás países europeos. Más aún, estos esfuerzos y los intereses nacionales de Alemania no pueden separarse de los de Europa. Debido a la presión del mercado mundial y de las grandes potencias, Europa se ve obligada a impulsar no sólo la integración económica sino también la integración política. Huelga decir que esta situación despierta la disposición de ocuparse de desarrollos similares en otros continentes. De ahí el interés de los países europeos por la integración de América Latina y por sus respectivas organizaciones internacionales.

Un paso decisivo en el camino de una mayor unificación lo representó la creación de la Comunidad Económica Europea en 1958. Los seis países miembros de la Comunidad Económica Europea de Carbón y del Acero de aquel entonces estipularon en los Tratados de Roma los siguientes objetivos: ajuste del desarrollo económico de sus países miembros, expansión continua y equilibrada de sus economías, elevación del nivel de vida en general y, finalmente, la creación de un mercado común con estrechas relaciones entre los países miembros. [1] Junto al hecho de que en los últimos treinta años se haya alcanzado ya un alto grado de interdependencia económica, sobre todo en el sector agrícola, es digno de mencionar que se haya logrado también un notable acercamiento político entre los países miembros de la Comunidad Europea. Este acercamiento no se limita exclusivamente a la colaboración de órganos estatales. Es más, cada individuo es llamado a tener conciencia de su europeidad al elegir directamente a los diputados del Parlamento Europeo, al hacer uso de su derecho de libre circulación dentro de Europa o al pasar las fronteras sin ser controlado. Los ejemplos señalados muestran que Europa ha avanzado ya un buen trecho en el camino hacia su unificación. No obstante, la

Editor's Note: Translated from the German by Jutta Seeger.

Comunidad Europea no deja de correr ciertos peligros. Una que otra vez surgen serias diferencias, sobre todo en cuanto a cuestiones económicas. Sin embargo, la necesidad de una estrecha colaboración a trascendido a la conciencia pública.

Es por ello que el interés de los europeos ha de dirigirse a un continente donde la idea de una unificación se remonta ya a los principios del siglo XIX. Hay que preguntarse hasta qué punto esta idea se hizo realidad y cuáles son los desarrollos y los cambios a lo largo de más de 150 años.

Desde el punto de vista europeo, la integración de América Latina parece ser más viable que la de Europa, tratándose en este caso de un continente cuya población desciende principalmente de sólo dos naciones, la portuguesa y la española. Cabría pensar que la mentalidad y el patrimonio cultural común deben ofrecer las mejores condiciones para lograr un acercamiento político. Estas ideas, sin embargo, descuidan el hecho de que ya en la época colonial se formó uno que otro territorio a semejanza de estado. En cuanto a la América hispánica se desarrollaron dependencias individuales de la corona española, de Sevilla y de Cádiz. [2] Estas iban transformándose en sociedades estatales con características propias de acuerdo con su situación económico-geográfica, su topografía y la influencia continua de su población indígena. Las ideas y el afán de Simón Bolívar de lograr con las guerras de la independencia no sólo el desprendimiento de la corona sino también la unificación política del continente, [3] tampoco podían detener la división en estados individuales. Al desprendimiento de los países ibéricos de origen en el siglo XIX siguió inmediatamente la formación definitiva de los estados nacionales latinoamericanos. Sólo a principios del siglo XX se intensificaron nuevamente los esfuerzos por crear la unidad política latinoamericana. Causa exterior fue la creciente presión económica y política de EEUU sobre el subcontinente latinoamericano. [4] Los esfuerzos de unificación hallaron su expresión concreta en la fundación de diversas organizaciones internacionales latinoamericanas como por ejemplo la ALADI, el Grupo Andino o el MCCA. Por regla general, estas organizaciones no se implantaron la tarea de impulsar la integración política de la región sino primeramente la integración económica. [5] Siguiendo este camino, empero, y una vez lograda la meta primordial de dichas organizaciones —la estrecha colaboración económica— sería factible construir sobre esta base, y en un futuro lejano, el destino político de América Latina. [6] La integración latinoamericano no ha alcanzado todavía un grado tan alto como la europea. Dada la estrecha interdependencia de la economía mundial, es de importancia e interés para la economía, la política y la investigación en Europa observar si y de qué modo las organizaciones internacionales latinoamericanas de orientación esencialmente económica llegan a convertirse también en la fuerza motriz para la integración política de este subcontinente.

Publicaciones de las organizaciones internacionales de América Latina y las instituciones de investigación en la República Federal de Alemania

En la República Federal de Alemania existen un gran número de instituciones que se ocupan de América Latina. Aunque Alemania no tuvo un vínculo especial con el continente latinoamericano ni en cuanto a la historia de su descubrimiento ni en lo que se refiere a la conquista o la colonización, dispone de la mayoría de las instituciones de investigación sobre América Latina en Europa. [7] Esto se explica por el hecho de que las relaciones culturales entre América Latina y Alemania han sido estrechas por tradición. Después de haberse publicado *Voyages aux régions equinoxiales de Nouveau Continent* de Alexander von Humboldt, el interés alemán por el continente desconocido alcanza en el siglo XIX su punto culminante. Esta obra, gracias a su novedosa representación, dio fuertes impulsos a artistas, científicos y escritores. Y esto en una época en que en Alemania expandieron la ciencia y la investigación, ganando una importancia cada vez mayor. Por de pronto, la investigación sobre América Latina se concentró en las ciencias naturales y, particularmente, en las geociencias. Luego siguieron las disciplinas históricas de los llamados estudios americanísticos y, finalmente, las demás ciencias humanísticas. [8] Hoy en día, el *Handbuch der deutschen Lateinamerikaforschung* (manual de estudios alemanes sobre América Latina) recopila en su registro de personas el mayor número de científicos en el campo de las ciencias políticas y sociales, seguidas por las ciencias naturales, la etnología y la historia. [9]

Instituciones de investigación importantes en universidades alemanas son el Instituto Iberoamericano de Investigaciones Científicas de la Universidad de Hamburgo, el Instituto Latinoamericano de la Universidad Libre de Berlín y la Sección de América Latina de la Universidad de Erlangen-Nuremberg. Otros centros de Gießen, Bonn, Munster, Breme, Bamberg, Augsburgo, Maguncia, Frankfort-del-Meno y Colonia. Entre las más importantes instituciones para los estudios latinoamericanos fuera de las universidades se cuentan el Instituto Ibero-Americano en Berlín, el Instituto Arnold Bergstraesser en Friburgo y el Instituto de Estudios Iberoamericanos en Hamburgo. Además existe un gran número de instituciones que se ocupan a nivel mundial de determinadas disciplinas incluyendo, desde luego, los

estudios latinoamericanos. De este grupo merece mención especial el
Instituto de Economía Mundial de la Universidad de Kiel y el Instituto
Max Planck de Derecho Público Comparado y Derecho Internacional
en Heidelberg.

Los centros de estudios latinoamericanos señalados muestran el
gran espacio que ocupa este ramo de la ciencia en la República Federal
de Alemania. En ello, le cabe a las organizaciones latinoamericanas
internacionales un papel preponderante. Estas organizaciones que
influencian directamente el desarrollo político y económico del
continente revisten particular interés para la investigación y la
enseñanza. Teniendo en cuenta que al subdividir los estudios
latinoamericanos según ramos especiales, las ciencias políticas y
sociales ocupan el primer plano. Se pone de relieve que tanto las
publicaciones editadas por las organizaciones latinoamericanas
internacionales como las que se ocupan de ellas son de significancia
fundamental para el trabajo científico de las universidades e
instituciones de investigación.

Recursos bibliográficos

No existe una bibliografía completa que abarca las obras de todas
las organizaciones internacionales latinoamericanas o las publicaciones
que se ocupan de ellas. Por lo contrario, llama la atención que los
registros que pretenden dar una vista general de las publicaciones sobre
la integración de América Latina subrayan ya en el título o en el
prólogo que no son completos. Bien se limitan a publicaciones
aparecidas en cierto período de referencia o constituyen inventarios de
los fondos que poseen las diversas bibliotecas de las obras editadas por
las organizaciones internacionales o publicaciones que versan sobre
éstas.

En cambio, entre los manuales hay uno que otro título que puede
servir al bibliotecario como primer recurso. Existen registros que
indican todas las organizaciones internacionales del mundo y otros que
se limitan a las de América Latina. Por lo general, informan sobre la
estructura y las finalidades de la organización respectiva y muchas veces
citan sus publicaciones más importantes.

Bibliografías sobre organizaciones internacionales

La *International Bibliography: Publications of Intergovernmental
Organizations* ofrece la mejor vista general sobre la documentación y
las posibilidades de adquisición de la literatura recientemente publicada
por las organizaciones internacionales. La bibliografía no está
completa, ya que sólo indica aquellos títulos avisados a la oficina de la

International Bibliography que edita este registro. Contiene las publicaciones de una serie de organizaciones internacionales de América Latina y ordena la material alfabéticamente según grandes grupos de materias. Los títulos se explican por anotaciones breves. Normalmente el precio está indicado. La literatura se hace asequible mediante un índice de materias y de títulos. Las organizaciones están indicadas en un registro alfabético que incluye también las direcciones para la adquisición de todas las obras publicadas por ellas.

Además existen algunas bibliografías que contienen las publicaciones de las organizaciones internacionales de América Latina y las obras que se ocupan de ellas. No pretenden estar completas. Estas bibliografías son de fecha más antigua y registran la literatura publicada en los años 50 hasta los 70. Ya que en este período se fundaron muchas de las organizaciones internacionales de América Latina, estas bibliografías tienen cierta vigencia aún hoy día.

La *Bibliografía selectiva sobre integración* registra por orden alfabético la literatura primaria y secundaria de las organizaciones internacionales, especialmente de las de América Latina. La bibliografía se basa en los fondos del servicio de documentación del Instituto. Incluye monografías y revistas e indica, además, los documentos publicados por las organizaciones internacionales de América Latina. Dispone de un índice de autores y en el apéndice figura una lista alfabética de aquellas revistas que publican regularmente artículos sobre cuestiones de integración.

El *Indice de artículos sobre materias jurídicas institucionales y políticas de las publicaciones periódicas del INTAL, 1965-1985* recopila por materias en orden alfabético los artículos sobre el tema de la integración latinoamericana aparecidos por el INTAL. Cada título está anotado brevemente. A modo de guía, el tomo contiene una lista de descriptores por orden alfabético y un registro de autores.

En "Investigaciones sobre integración en el mundo contemporáneo: fuentes disponibles", Marco Antonio Díaz Poblete recopila 447 monografías y artículos de revista que se ocupan de las organizaciones internacionales. La bibliografía está subdividida temáticamente en publicaciones sobre la teoría de integración, las organizaciones en Europa y las en América Latina.

La bibliografía *Regionalismus und regionale Integration. Bibliographie 1970-1980. Afrika, Karibik, Lateinamerika, Südostasien* es un inventario de la literatura asequible en las bibliotecas de Berlín a este tema. La bibliografía está clasificada según las regiones indicadas en el título. Sin seguir otra subdivisión temática, las monografías y los artículos de revista están enlistados por orden alfabético.

Bibliografías sobre organizaciones individuales

Grupo Andino.—Existen algunas bibliografías sobre organizaciones individuales. Un importante recurso bibliográfico lo constituyen también los catálogos publicados por la OEA y la ONU para la venta de sus publicaciones.

La *Bibliografía anotada sobre aspectos políticos de la integración andina* de Javier Alcalde de Cardoza recopila en siete grupos de materias 254 monografías y artículos de revista referentes al "Grupo Andino". Cada título está anotado brevemente. Además, la bibliografía dispone de un registro de autores.

La *Bibliografía sobre integración subregional andina* contiene 478 títulos sobre la integración de los países andinos entregados a la Biblioteca de la Junta del Acuerdo de Cartagena en Lima hasta abril de 1977. Se registran monografías, artículos y notas bibliográficas ordenados según el "thesaurus" de la biblioteca. Cada título está anotado brevemente. Los autores están registrados por orden alfabético.

El *Catálogo, publicaciones seleccionadas para los Centros de Referencia del Acuerdo de Cartagena* contiene 335 documentos publicados por los órganos del "Grupo Andino". Cada documento está anotado brevemente. Se trata de fondos recopilados en las bibliotecas que pertenecen al red de información de la Junta del Acuerdo de Cartagena. El catálogo está ordenado por materias y contiene un índice respectivo, además de un registro de autores y otro de documentos ordenado temática y cronológicamente. Al final del volumen se encuentra un registro de las instituciones pertenecientes al red de información.

Mercado Común Centroamericano.—La "Bibliografía sobre el Mercado Común Centroamericano" de Eduardo Lizano abarca monografías y artículos de revista sobre la integración de América Central publicados hasta 1977. Los títulos aparecen por orden alfabético. No se indican publicaciones periódicas.

Organización de los Estados Americanos.—Los *Documentos oficiales de la Organización de los Estados Americanos: Lista general de documentos,* que se publican anualmente, recopilan los documentos editados en el año corriente por la Organización de Estados Americanos (OEA). Los documentos están agrupados según las subdivisiones de la OEA que los editan. En estos grupos aparecen por orden cronológico. Además, se publica anualmente el *Catálogo de publicaciones de la OEA* en el que figuran los títulos suministrables. Este catálogo está ordenado según materias. La *Bibliography of Books and Articles in Periodicals on the Organization of American States* abarca monografías y artículos de revista sobre la OEA. Dispone de un registro alfabético de las monografías y de los artículos, respectivamente. Se indican los fondos de la Columbia Memorial Library of Congress y los títulos pertinentes del National Union Catalogue de la Library of Congress.

Organización de las Naciones Unidas.—En las bibliografías aparecidas generalmente en cuanto a la literatura sobre la Organización de las Naciones Unidas (ONU), figura también la literatura primaria y secundaria para la Comisión Económica para América Latina (CEPAL), una suborganización de la ONU que se ocupa de las cuestiones económicas de América Latina. Entre ellas, la bibliografía publicada por Klaus Hüfner y Jens Naumann, *The United Nations System: International Bibliography*, es de gran utilidad. Recopila en cinco volúmenes las monografías y los artículos aparecidos entre 1945 y 1975. Está subdividida según la clase de literatura respectiva: artículos de revista, 1945-1975, monografías, 1945-1965 y artículos en tomos colectivos, 1965-1975. Ya que los títulos están ordenados según materias y, además, se hacen asequibles por un registro de autores incluido al final de cada volumen, la literatura referente a la CEPAL es de fácil acceso. Para las publicaciones editadas por la CEPAL, *The Complete Guide to the United Nations Sales Publications, 1946-1978* de Mary Eva Birchfield es muy recomendable. En el volumen I la literatura aparecida entre 1976 y 1978 está ordenada según la suborganización editora de la ONU. En el volumen II, la literatura se hace asequible por un índice de materias, de títulos y de números de venta, respectivamente. Las publicaciones actuales de la CEPAL están recopiladas en el *Catalogue of United Nations Publications: An Official Guide to United Nations Publications in Print, 1985*. Este catálogo aparece anualmente, está ordenado según 17 grupos temáticos y dispone de un índice de títulos y de materias, respectivamente.

Esta breve exposición de bibliografías sobre las organizaciones internacionales de América Latina prueba que para este campo existe sólo poca, y en parte anquilosada, literatura. Por consiguiente, las bibliografías y los recursos bibliográficos de aquellos países en los cuales las organizaciones internacionales tienen su sede, constituyen un medio importante para obtener acceso a estas publicaciones.

Manuales

Los manuales en los que figuran las organizaciones internacionales constituyen un buen instrumento de trabajo para el bibliotecario encargado de la adquisición de las publicaciones editadas por o sobre estas organizaciones. Entre éstos, también los manuales menos voluminosos indican las organizaciones más importantes, ofrecen una vista general sobre sus finalidades y su estructura y registran sus publicaciones más importantes.

En este campo, el *Yearbook of International Organizations* es el manual más voluminoso e importante. En el volumen I, las organizaciones están ordenadas y registradas según 13 grupos de materias. Se indican la fecha de su fundación, su denominación en todas las lenguas oficiales, su organización precursora, sus tareas, su estructura, sus actividades y por regla general, las publicaciones editadas por la organización respectiva. Contiene un índice por orden alfabético de las organizaciones. El volumen II ordena las organizaciones según países y añade un índice respectivo. En el volumen III las organizaciones están ordenadas según materias con un índice correspondiente. Además, este volumen dispone de un registro por orden alfabético de las publicaciones de aquellas organizaciones que se indican en el volumen I.

El manual *South America, Central America and the Caribbean* ofrece en tres partes una vista general sobre la política, la economía y la historia de América Latina y ofrece, además, estadísticas fundamentales. La primera parte presenta los problemas básicos del continente. La segunda parte registra y describe primeramente las suborganizaciones de la ONU que tienen un vínculo especial con América Latina. Luego siguen las organizaciones internacionales más importantes de América Latina por orden alfabético. Se describen su fundación, estructura y función y se registran las publicaciones más importantes de las organizaciones respectivas. La tercera parte contiene descripciones breves ordenadas según puntos de vista históricos, económicos y políticos. El manual *The Europa— Yearbook: A World Survey*, publicado por la misma editorial, es una versión más amplia, vale decir a nivel mundial, de *South America, Central America and the Caribbean*. Los datos sobre América Latina y sus organizaciones internacionales son en gran parte idénticos.

El *Politisches Lexikon Lateinamerika* informe de modo comprimido, preciso y actual sobre la situación política en América Latina. En la primera y segunda parte se describen 32 estados latinoamericanos independientes y, además, los territorios dependientes de Francia, Gran Bretaña, los Países Bajos y los EEUU. En la tercera parte sigue, por orden alfabético, la descripción de las organizaciones internacionales de América Latina, indicándose también la literatura secundaria y primaria.

El *Lexikon Dritte Welt* es una obra de consulta que informa sobre cuestiones económicas y políticas del Tercer Mundo y que está ordenado según voces guía, nombres de países y voces guía sistemáticas. Las organizaciones latinoamericanas más importantes se describen indicándose la correspondiente literatura secundaria.

El *Latin American Political Dictionary* es un manual sobre temas políticos de América Latina. En un capítulo, "International Law and Organization", se explican las organizaciones internacionales de América Latina y la terminología respectiva. Sigue un registro de voces guía al final del volumen.

NOTAS

1. *Yearbook of International Organizations, 1986/87* (München: Saur, 1986), Vol. 1, DD 0665g.

2. Manfred Mols, "Europäische Bemerkungen zur lateinamerikanischen Integration", *Beiträge zur Soziologie und Sozialkunde Lateinamerikas* 17:39 (1980).

3. Celson J. da Silva, *Regionale Integration in einer Dependenzsituation. Der Fall Lateinamerikas* (Heidelberg: Esprint, 1980), p. 39.

4. León Enrique Bieber, *Der Konsolidierungsprozeß lateinamerikanischer Nationalstaaten und die Bemühungen um die Herstellung der Einheit Lateinamerikas seit 1880* (Berlín, 1978), p. 39.

5. "Tratado de Montevideo 1980, Art. 2 (ALADI), Acuerdo de Cartagena 1969, Art. 1 (Grupo Andino), Tratado General de Integración Económica Centroamericana 1960, Art. 2 (MCCA)", *Ordenamiento de Integración*, 2 vols. (Buenos Aires: Instituto para la Integración de América Latina, 1986).

6. Raúl Prebisch, *Change and Development: Latin America's Great Task*. Report submitted to the Interamerican Development Bank (Washington, DC, 1970), p. 168.

7. Carmelo Mesa-Lago, *Latin American Studies in Europe* (Pittsburgh, PA: Center for Latin American Studies, 1979), p. 15.

8. Gustav Siebenmann, "Sprache und Literatur", *Deutsche Iberoamerika-Forschung in den Jahren 1930-1980* (Berlín: Colloquium, 1987), p. 12.

9. Renate Ferno und Wolfgang Grenz, *Handbuch der deutschen Lateinamerika-Forschung* (Bonn: Deutscher Akademischer Austauschdienst, 1980), pp. 105-386.

BIBLIOGRAFÍA

Bibliografías y catálogos

Bibliografía selectiva sobre integración. Buenos Aires: Instituto para la Integración de América Latina, 1977.

Bibliografía sobre integración subregional andina. Lima: Junta del Acuerdo de Cartagena, 1977.

Bibliography of Books and Articles in Periodicals on the Organization of American States. Washington, DC: Organization of American States, 1977.

Cardoza, Javier Alcalde. *Bibliografía anotada sobre aspectos políticos de la integración andina.* Lima: Junta del Acuerdo de Cartagena, 1978.

Catálogo de publicaciones de la OEA 1986-1987. Washington, DC: Organización de los Estados Americanos, 1986.

Catálogo, publicaciones seleccionadas para los Centros de Referencia del Acuerdo de Cartagena, 1985.

Catalogue of United Nations Publications: An Official Guide to United Nations Publications in Print, 1985. New York: United Nations Department of Conference Services Publishing Division, 1986.

The Complete Guide to the United Nations Sales Publications, 1946-1978. 2 vols. Compiled and edited by Mary Eva Birchfield. Berlin: de Gruyter, 1982.

Díaz Poblete, Marco Antonio. "Investigaciones sobre integración en el mundo contemporáneo: fuentes disponibles". *Revista de Derecho Publico* 5-6 (julio-diciembre 1966), 60-74.

Documentos oficiales de la Organización de los Estados Americanos. Lista general de documentos, vol. 25, 1984. Washington, DC: Organización de los Estados Americanos. (Vol. 1, 1959)

Hufner, Klaus, y Jens Naumann. *The United Nations System: International Bibliography.* München: Dokumentation.
Learned Journals and Monographs, 1945-1965. 1976.
Learned Journals, 1965-1970. 1977.
Learned Journals, 1971-1975. 1977.
Monographs and Articles in Collective Volumes, 1965-1970. 1978.
Monographs and Articles in Collective Volumes, 1971-1975. 1979.

Indice de artículos sobre materias jurídicas institucionales y políticas de las publicaciones periódicas del INTAL, 1965-1985. Buenos Aires: Instituto para la Integración de América Latina, 1985.

International Bibliography: Publications of Intergovernmental Organizations. Vol. 11. New York: UNIPUB, 1983.

Lizano Fait, Eduardo. "Bibliografía sobre el Mercado Común Centroamericano". *Estudios Sociales Centroamericanos* 8 (1979), 271-330.

Regionalismus und regionale Integration. Bibliographie 1970-1980. Afrika, Karibik, Lateinamerika, Südostasien. Ed. Günther Doeker. Frankfurt: Lang, 1981.

Manuales

The Europa—Yearbook 1987: A World Survey. London: Europa Publications, 1987.

Lexikon Dritte Welt, Länder, Organisationen, Theorien, Begriffe, Personen. Ed. Dieter Nohlen. Hamburg: Rowholt Taschenbuch, 1984.

Politisches Lexikon Lateinamerika. Ed. Peter Waldmann. München: Beck, 1982.

Rossi, Ernst E. *The Latin American Political Dictionary.* Oxford: ABC-Clio, 1980.

South America, Central America and the Caribbean. 2d. ed. London: Europa Publications, 1987.

Yearbook of International Organizations. 23d ed. München: Saur, 1986.

30. Documents of the Latin American Regional Organizations on Banking and Finance

Patricio Aranda-Coddou

I have outlined the documents of the Latin American regional organizations on banking and finance and divided the material into four areas: Caribbean, Central America, South America, and Latin America. The appendix contains a directory of addresses and telephone numbers of some of the organizations listed.

I. Caribbean Area

A. Caribbean Development Bank (CDB)
1. Establishment
Agreement of October 18, 1969, 712 UNTS 217.
2. Functions
a. To contribute to the harmonious economic growth and development of the member countries.
b. To promote economic integration and cooperation among those countries, having special and urgent regard to the needs of the less developed countries.
3. Structure
a. Board of Governors is highest policy-making organ, and elects its own Chairman.
b. Board of Directors is the executive organ subject to the provisions of the Agreement and the Board of Governors' policies.
c. The President is the chief executive officer and Chairman of the Board of Directors.
4. Language
English
5. Membership
Anguilla, Antigua and Barbuda, Bahamas, Barbados, Belize, British Virgin Islands, Cayman Islands, Colombia, Dominica, Grenada, Guyana, Jamaica, Mexico, Monserrat, St. Kitts and Nevis, St. Lucia, St. Vincent and the Grenadines, Trinidad and Tobago, Turks and Caicos Islands, and Venezuela.

Nonregional members: Canada, France, and the United
Kingdom.

6. General Publications

Annual Report

Summary of Proceedings of Annual Meetings of Board of
Governors

Statements by the President

Financial Policies

Guidelines for Procurement

Special Development Fund Rules

Sector Policy Papers:

  Agriculture

  Development Finance Corporations

  Electric Power

  Housing

  Industry and Tourism

  Transportation

  Water and Sewerage

Newsletters

Basic Information

Caribbean Development Bank: its purposes, role, and
functions.

B. Eastern Caribbean Central Bank (ECCB)

1. Establishment

Agreement of July 5, 1983.

2. Functions

a. To regulate the availability of money and credit.

b. To promote and maintain monetary stability.

c. To promote credit and exchange conditions and a
sound financial structure conducive to the members'
balanced growth and development.

d. To promote actively the economic development of the
territories of the participating governments.

3. Structure

a. The Monetary Council is the highest policymaker.

b. The Board of Directors is the primary executive organ
and general administrator. The Governor and Deputy
Governor are the chief executive officers.

4. Language

English

5. Membership
Antigua and Barbuda, Dominica, Grenada, Monserrat, St. Kitts and Nevis, St. Lucia, St. Vincent and the Grenadines.

6. General Publications
Annual Report
Quarterly Economic and Finance Review
Commercial Banking

II. Central America Area

A. Central American Bank for Economic Integration (CABEI)/ Banco Centroamericano de Integración Económica (BCIE)

1. Establishment
Agreement of December 13, 1960; 455 UNTS 203.

2. Functions
    a. To implement the economic integration and the balanced economic growth of the member countries.
    b. To invest in regional infrastructure projects; in long-term investment projects in regional industries; in coordinated agricultural projects to improve, expand, or substitute agricultural activities for the establishment of a regional Central American supply system.
    c. To support Central American free trade objectives by financing enterprises that need to expand or modernize their operations; projects to finance services necessary for the functioning of the Common Market; and other productive projects to create economic coordination among the member countries and to increase Central American trade: the Central American Fund for Economic Integration (CAFEI); The Social Development Fund, established by the Board of Governors on January 14, 1975.

3. Structure
Highest authority is the Board of Governors.
Executive organs: Board of Directors. The President is the chief executive officer.

4. Language
Castilian.

5. Membership
Costa Rica, El Salvador, Guatemala, Honduras, Nicaragua.

     6. <u>General Publications</u>
       Annual Report
       Revista de la Integración y el Desarollo de Centroamérica.

B. **Central American Monetary Council/Consejo Monetario Centroamericano**
   1. <u>Establishment</u>
      Agreement for the establishment of a Central American Monetary Union, February 24, 1964, replaced by the Central American Monetary Agreement of October 24, 1974.
   2. <u>Functions</u>
      To promote the coordination of monetary, credit, and exchange policies of members.
   3. <u>Structure</u>
      The Council is formed by the presidents of the central banks of the member countries. The same countries' central banks appoint alternate representatives. The Executive Secretary is the executive officer charged with carrying on policies established by the Council, and under the provisions of the Agreement.
   4. <u>Membership</u>
      Members are the central banks of Costa Rica, El Salvador, Guatemala, Honduras, Nicaragua.
   5. <u>Language</u>
      Castilian (also known as Spanish)
   6. <u>General Publications</u>
      Annual Report
      Boletín Estadístico
      Centro América: Balanza de Pagos
   7. <u>Other Structures</u>
      a. Central American Clearinghouse/Cámara de Compensación Centroamericana.
      b. Central American Stabilization Fund/Fondo Centroamericano de Estabilización Monetaria (FOCEM).

III. South America Area

A. Financial Fund for the Plata Basin Development/Fondo Financiero Para El Desarollo de la Cuenca del Plata (FONOPLATA)

1. Establishment
   Articles of Agreement of June 12, 1974, executed under the
   Treaty for the Plata Basin Development, April 23, 1969,
   875 UNTS 3.
2. Functions
   To finance studies, projects, and programs aimed at
   promoting the development and integration of the Plata
   Basin.
3. Structure
   Board of Governors is highest decision maker. Executive
   Board of Directors. Executive Secretary.
4. Membership
   Argentina, Bolivia, Brazil, Paraguay, Uruguay.
5. Language
   Castilian
6. General Publications
   Annual Report

IV. Latin America

A. Center for Latin American Monetary Studies/Centro de
   Estudios Monetarios Latinoamericanos (LEMLA)/Centre
   d'Études Monetaires Latino-américaines (CEMLA)
   1. Establishment
      Agreement of September 1952.
   2. Functions
      a. To promote knowledge of monetary and banking
         matters in Latin America.
      b. To train central bank personnel.
      c. To undertake and publish research in the matter.
   3. Structure
      Assembly of members. Governing Board, comprised of
      Bank of Mexico and four other members and the Director.
      Assembly serves as Permanent Secretariat for the Meetings
      of Central Bank Governors of the American Continent and
      of Latin America and Spain.
   4. Membership
      51 members. The 29 members are the Central Banks of
      Argentina, The Bahamas, Barbados, Belize, Bolivia, Brazil,
      Chile, Colombia, Costa Rica, Cuba, Dominican Republic,
      East Caribbean Community, Ecuador, El Salvador,
      Guatemala, Guyana, Haiti, Honduras, Jamaica, Mexico,
      Netherlands Antilles, Nicaragua, Paraguay, Peru, Suriname,

Trinidad and Tobago, Uruguay, Venezuela, and the National Banking Commission of Panama. The 22 cooperating members include the UN Economic Commission for Latin America and the Caribbean; international and regional financial institutions, such as the Inter-American Development Bank, the Central American Bank for Economic Integration, the Andean Reserve Fund, and the Latin American Export Bank; non-Latin American central banks, e.g., Canada, France, Philippines, Portugal, Spain, the United States; bank supervising agencies; individual government development banks or agencies; national banking associations.

5. Languages
Castilian, Portuguese, English.

6. General Publications
Boletín (bimonthly)
Monetaria (quarterly)
Seminarios (materials presented at technical seminars)
Wide range of monographs.

B. Inter-American Development Bank (IDB)/Banco Interamericano de Desarollo (BID)/Banque interaméricaine de développement (BID)

1. Establishment
Agreement of April 8, 1959, 10 UST 3029, 389 UNTS 69.

2. Functions
a. To promote investment of public and private capital.
b. To cooperate with and provide technical assistance to members in setting up development plans: Inter-American Investment Corporation, November 19, 1984; Social Progress Trust Fund; Venezuelan Trust Fund.

3. Structure
Board of Governors, Executive Board, President.

4. Membership
44 member countries: Argentina, Austria, The Bahamas, Barbados, Belgium, Bolivia, Brazil, Canada, Chile, Colombia, Costa Rica, Denmark, Dominican Republic, Ecuador, El Salvador, Finland, France, Federal Republic of Germany, Guatemala, Guyana, Haiti, Honduras, Israel, Italy, Jamaica, Japan, Mexico, Netherlands, Nicaragua, Norway, Panama, Paraguay, Peru, Portugal, Spain, Suriname, Sweden, Switzerland, Trinidad and Tobago,

United Kingdom, United States, Uruguay, Venezuela, Yugoslavia.
5. Languages
Castilian, English, French, Portuguese.
6. General Publications
Annual Report
Economic and Social Progress in Latin America (annual)
Proceedings of the Meetings of the Board of Governors (annual)
IDB News (monthly)

C. Institute for Latin American Integration/Instituto para la Integración Latinoamericana (INTAL)
1. Publications
Integración Latinoamericana (monthly)
The Latin American Integration Process (annual)
Hoja de Situación (quarterly)
Boletín de Proyectos (bimonthly)

D. Latin American Association of Development Financing Institutions/Asociación Latinoamericana de Instituciones Financieras de Desarrollo (ALIDE)
1. Establishment
Agreement of January 24, 1968.
2. Functions
   a. To promote cooperation among members.
   b. To establish flow of information between members.
   c. To encourage studies on problems of common interest.
3. Structure
General Assembly.
Executive Committee.
Secretary General.
4. Membership
143 active members, 18 members and 21 collaborating member banks, finance institutions and international organizations of 24 Latin American countries and 5 European countries: Argentina, Aruba, Barbados, Bolivia, Brazil, Colombia, Costa Rica, Chile, Cuba, Dominican Republic, Ecuador, El Salvador, Guatemala, Haiti, Honduras, Mexico, Nicaragua, Panama, Paraguay, Peru, Puerto Rico, Suriname, Uruguay, Venezuela, Federal Republic of Germany, Portugal, Spain, United Kingdom, Yugoslavia.

5. Languages
   Castilian, English, French.
6. General Publications
   Annual Report of ALIDE
   Bulletin (bimonthly)
   Proceedings of Annual Meetings of the General Assembly
   Latin American Directory of Development Financing Institutions
   Publications of Technical Meetings
   Education and Training Program
   Abstract Services (*Resúmenes Informativos*)
   Relatory of the Yearly Governor's Assembly
   Brief News Monthly Bulletin (*Alide Noticias*)

E. Latin American Export Bank/Banco Latinoamericano de Exportaciones (BLADEX)
   1. Establishment
      Organized in January 1978 as a corporation under Panamanian law.
   2. Functions
      a. To promote and finance exports of Latin American and Caribbean member countries.
      b. To obtain and provide additional short- and medium-term export finance credit for products of Latin American origin.
   3. Structure
      Shareholders assembly, Board of Directors, Executive Vice President.
   4. Membership
      22 member countries: Argentina, Barbados, Bolivia, Brazil, Chile, Colombia, Costa Rica, Dominican Republic, Ecuador, El Salvador, Guatemala, Haiti, Honduras, Jamaica, Mexico, Nicaragua, Panama, Paraguay, Peru, Trinidad and Tobago, Uruguay, Venezuela. Shareholders are: (1) 22 central banks and official financial institutions of member countries; (2) 218 regional commercial and investment banks in which the majority interest is controlled by residents; (3) 27 international banks and security dealers from outside the region; and (4) the International Finance Corporation (IFC).
   5. Languages
      English, Castilian.

6. General Publications
   Newsletter
   Quarterly Report
   Annual Report
   Regional Report

APPENDIX

Directory of Latin American Regional Organizations
on Banking and Finance

1. Caribbean Development Bank
   (CDB)
   P.O. Box 408 Wildey
   St. Michael, Barbados
   Tel: (809) 426-1152
   Cable: CARIBANK
   Telex: WB 2287

2. Center for Latin American Monetary
   Studies/Centro de Estudios Mone-
   tarios Latinoamericanos (CEMLA)/
   Centre d'études monétaires latino-
   américaines (CEMLA)
   Durango Num. 54
   Delegación Cuauhtemoc
   México, D.F. 06700
   Tel: 533-03-00
   Cable: CEMLA
   Telex: 01771229 CEMLME

3. Central American Bank for
   Economic Integration (CABEI)/
   Banco Centroamericano de
   Integración Económica (BCIE)
   Apartado Postal 772
   Tegucigalpa, D.C.
   Honduras
   Tel: 22-2230 to 39
   Cable: BANCADIE

4. Central American Monetary
   Council/Consejo Monetario
   Centroamericano
   Edificio Banco Crédito Agrícola
   de Cartago, 4° Piso
   Apartado Postal 5438
   San José, 1.000, Costa Rica
   Tel: 33-60-44, 23-48-90
   Cable: CONMONECA
   Telex: 2234 COMOCA

5. Eastern Caribbean Central Bank
   (ECCB)
   P.O. Box 89
   Basseterre
   St. Kitts
   St. Christopher and Nevis
   Tel: 2537/38
   Cable: CENTRAL BANK
            STKITTS
   Telex: 6828 ECCB SKB KC

6. Financial Fund for the Plata Basin
   Development/Fondo Financiero para
   el Desarrollo de la Cuenca del Plata
   (FONPLATA)
   España 31
   Casilla Correo 47
   Sucre, Bolivia
   Tel: 30311, 25293, 23888
   Cable: FONPLATA
   Telex: 2260 FOPLATA BV

7. Inter-American Development Bank
    (IDB)/Banco Interamericano de
    Desarrollo (BID)/Banque inter-
    américaine de développement (BID)
    1300 New York Avenue, N.W.
    Washington, DC 20577
    Tel: (202) 623-1000
    Cable: INTAMBANC

8. Latin American Association of
    Development Financing Institutions/
    Asociación Latinoamericana de Insti-
    tuciones Financieras de Desarrollo
    (ALIDE)
    Paseo de la República 3211
    P.O. Box 3988
    Lima 100, Peru
    Tel: 422-400
    Cable: ALIDE
    Telex: 21037 PE ALIDE

9. Latin American Export Bank/Banco
    Latinoamericano de Exportaciones
    (BLADEX)
    Office Address:
      Calle 50 & Aquilino Dela Cuardia
      El Dorado
      Panama City
      Republic of Panama
    Postal Address:
      P.O. Box 6-1497
      El Dorado
      Panama City, Panama
    Tel: 636766
    Cable: BLADEX
    Telex: 2240 TRT
              2356 INTEL
    Telefax: 69-63-33

31. Latin American Economic Integration: Documentary and Auxiliary Research Sources

Thomas H. Reynolds

The history, process, organization, and effects of regional and subregional economic integration in Latin America present a picture only slightly less confused and murky than that of the systematization and availability of their documentation. I discuss more than a dozen organizations, most of them interrelated and some of them successor organs of earlier failed efforts. As a further modifying factor, one must be aware of a studied inconsistency in nomenclature: some organizations are known optionally by their English or south official names and acronyms, others only by the Spanish version, and a few by a constantly shifting alphabetic arrangement. [1] Finally, for one organization, the Andes Group, there is no universally accepted nomenclature. [2]

It is difficult to decide just where to start in any discussion of Latin American integration since economic cannot really be separated from political. Much of Latin America was integrated between the early sixteenth and early nineteenth centuries. Spain had effectively consolidated all of the Western Hemisphere land mass from Mexico south into two vast administrative divisions, with Portuguese Brazil excepted. The nineteenth-century independence movements in South America resulted in the creation of economically, socially, and politically disparate national entities beyond any semblance of potential for integration. Central America, including southern Mexico, might have proved a more fertile region for organized integration. Except for a brief period, the Real Audiencia de los Confines de Guatemala y Honduras unified this large area under a single government, currency, and economic system from 1542 to 1821. This was succeeded by a Central American Federation that was, however, unable to impose any sort of unity on its portion of the disintegrating Spanish Empire.

Author's Note: I am most indebted to my colleague, Stefan A. Riesenfeld of the School of Law, University of California, Berkeley, who has permitted me to make use of material from a section titled "The New Regionalism with Special Emphasis on the European Economic Community," part of a work that is in preparation for publication.

Local nationalism, emerging economic differences, incapacity of politicians, and fear of the Mexican Empire accentuated the nationalistic impulse in these small nations.

Latin American and Caribbean integration in the twentieth century owes less to colonial history and more to recent economic history than is first realized. The vast and complex field of economic integration has been impelled and accelerated, while at the same time being overshadowed, by the recurring problems attendant on recovery from cyclical economic catastrophes. The series of crashes, depressions, and recessions that we in the North seemingly overcome have had devastating and lasting effect in the South. Since the 1930s, these economic crises have blighted the entire continent and subcontinent; little blips on our economic indicator have become vast chasms on their charts. Continuing downward spirals have affected all but the uppermost sectors of Latin American society.

The immediate postwar years were a time for optimism in Latin America; economic integration was regarded as a solution to many of the area's problems. In the late 1940s, a more homogeneous United Nations (albeit recognizing U.S. hegemony in Latin America) and its Economic Commission for Latin America, spurred by its dynamic leader Raul Prebisch, initiated a series of major efforts at integration on various levels. The economic system has now been greatly altered—for the worse. The picture of integration, along with the various attendant institutions, has also been greatly altered, although to rather little effect.

The economic crisis in Latin America in the 1980s is the most severe in fifty years; it is affecting all nations, to with differing degrees of severity. Indeed, some of the developed nations, though outwardly more secure, are actually less so, laboring under the time bomb of international debt. While inexorably tied to the international economy and affected to an extraordinary degree by economic swings and adjustments, the single universal characteristic is massive public and private debt.

After thirty years of at least semiformal efforts at regional integration, the nations of Latin America remain mired in debt and saddled with stagnant and grossly inefficient and undercapitalized economies. While we discuss integration, we should be aware of movements aimed at dis-integration—insofar as it is possible to de-stabilize something that was never stable in the first place. What has happened? Why have we gotten here?

In the century and a half preceding World War II, Latin America was in the British sphere of influence, sterling was a controlling and constant factor, and laissez-faire policies prevailed in manufacturing and exporting. With the collapse of the international markets during the Great Depression, the nations of Latin America withdrew from the international system and moved to isolation and protectionism. At the same time, their governments moved toward achieving substantial roles in the control and direction and planning of their economies. By the 1950s, under the impetus of the Bretton Woods Agreement, it was recognized that public institutions, both national and international, were (or should be) controlling; what had commenced in the 1940s was continued and expanded.

Latin American states or groups have approached the possibility of integration via two avenues and under two different sets of economic influences. The old development model of the optimistic 1950s reoriented by Dr. Prebisch and encouraged by the U.N.'s Economic Commission for Latin America was to place the economies within the framework of an international division of labor, with peripheral economies producing and exporting food and raw materials and central economies producing manufactured and capital goods. The emphasis was on improving agricultural and industrial production, along with infrastructure and conditions of life. This was to be accomplished through economic integration.

By the 1970s the monetarist approach of liberalizing markets in money, goods, services, and labor, combined with a new openness in trade and the promotion of private rather than state mechanisms, began to dominate. In the abstract, this may have seemed a good idea, but it was far from the answer to the challenges facing South America, a region caught in a vicious cycle of the need to constantly increase production in order to service the ever-increasing debt. The reappearance of the private financial markets, a weakened dollar, and the need to invest OPEC surpluses contributed to economic fluidity. Currently, resulting increased economic growth and expansion of industrial bases have begun to permit many domestic sectors to satisfy demand for consumer goods locally. New development strategies are affecting integration. Chronic nonobservance of commitments undertaken within agreements, coupled with a lack of political will, has led to new forms of cooperation based on specific actions, covenants, and projects, often among a few jurisdictions.

Currently, we can anticipate some resurgence and emphasis on coordinated economic activity in Latin America. Cut off from access to external financing, domestic investment must be increased and capital repatriation must be encouraged. The monetarist regimes of the 1970s and their cadres of technocrats, long committed to transnational banks and their manipulation of the international debt structure, are now being displaced. This will optimally be combined with the opening up of opportunity and continued democratization of society and control of inflation. It is clearly essential that regional unity be strengthened so that Latin America can better influence international economic events.

Latin America—as a region or collection of countries—has never operated well within the GATT system. The response, early on, was "economic integration" in the form of free trade areas and customs unions. Free trade areas are created by bilateral or multilateral agreements removing or reducing tariff or nontariff barriers between or among nations without affecting the customs duties or quotas of these nations in their trade relations with those outside the area. Customs unions, conversely, not only remove the barriers to interunion trade but also provide for common tariffs and quotas. The modern, and by far the most successful, model of a regional organization based on a "common market" and customs union is the European Economic Community. Indeed, to varying degrees, all the regional organizations we discuss have taken the EEC as the example in form, if not always in actual powers and effect.

Other factors should be borne in mind: integration can be a loose type of cooperation or a more intense form of concerted action. All schemes involve the giving up of some degree of national sovereignty by participating member states; it is in this degree that there is both the greatest danger and the greatest opportunity for success. One economist paints a rather bleak picture of the situation in the late 1980s: "In short, the national and international financial world gives the impression of a mine field in which the chief protagonist—banks, international financial institutions, governments—are venturing with more equipment in the way of experience and devices to detect and temporarily defuse the mines and to look after the wounded when they stumbled against one." [3]

There are so many components of the picture of economic integration that it is difficult to pick any point of reference as a starting position. Perhaps it is best to discard a few at the beginning.

The Pact of Bogotá of 1948 represented the culmination of a century's effort to achieve viable mechanisms for dispute settlement within the Americas. [4] This effort, intended to supersede and replace treaties, aimed to compile and unify the diverse mechanisms of a dozen agreements dating back to 1889. The goal was to create a means within the OAS for settlement of disputes, prior to recourse to U.N. organs. Ratified by thirteen states with operative sections in force, it plays a negligible role, and recourse to provisions of the pact has been infrequent. Dispute settlement can be an important part of economic relations, and all OAS members are bound by Arts. 23-26 of the Charter to settle disputes peacefully, but the Pact of Bogotá is not the answer.

The Latin American Parliament is a fragile reflection of the European Parliament and was created in a "noninstitutionalized" form in 1964. It has met annually as a glorified regional debating society and has had eight joint meetings with its European counterpart. Recent changes in its juridical composition warrant increased attention, and it now may take on a more important role in certain aspects of economic integration. Its goals of increasing democracy and enforcing nonintervention and self-determination and the general tenets of the NIEO are essential foundations for economic integration. It has now been "institutionalized," and its documentation may become worthy of attention. [5]

Moving on to more influential institutions, the all-embracing Latin American Economic System, known by its Spanish acronym SELA, is perhaps the broadest based, almost an umbrella grouping of the major Latin American economic entities. It is concerned with overall economic development and with regional financial cooperation, but it is limited to "consulting, coordination, cooperation and economic and social promotion." It can best be viewed as a regional forum for activities leading to the formulation of common positions and strategies vis-à-vis third countries, groups of countries, or international forums. SELA was created in 1975 and its conventions came into force in 1976. [6] All Central and South American states as well as most Caribbean nations are members. It has a fairly sophisticated institutional structure. Its supreme organ, the Consejo Latinoamericano, holds *Reuniones ordinarias* in different locations, sets general policy, and issues a series of *Decisiones*. The Secretariado Permanente, seated in Caracas, is the technical-administrative organ; it both carries out the directives of the Consejo and supports and facilitates the work of the dozen or more Comités de Acción which are established to achieve development programs in specific areas of interest and which then often lead to negotiating positions. [7] SELA is also viable enough to produce regular informative publications of a nondocumentary nature. They are usually possible to obtain on subscription and are more useful and manageable than the documentation series. [8]

The first and largest effort at creation of a free trade area was the Asociación Latinoamericano de Libre Comercio (ALALC) which was created by the Treaty of Montevideo of 1960, the result of a decade of effort by Dr. Prebisch and ECLA. [9] The objectives of the treaty were the creation of a free trade zone (over a period of twelve years) with establishment of norms to apply to all. The intentions were to maximize production and the coordination of development plans; foster commerce among member states and the rest of the word; and, finally, to create formulas and conditions that will adapt production (of goods and manufactures) to new avenues of commerce. In effect, the treaty mandated the gradual creation of a Latin American Common Market. This was an enormous, unwieldy and, in the long run, overambitious undertaking; ALALC aimed at establishment of a free trade area by means of mandatory annual interregional tariff reductions by member states until the zero level was reached at a fixed date. The member states, for political and economic reasons, were consistently unable to comply with their obligations under the agreement (a not atypical situation in the Latin American integration process), and the dates were postponed. By the late 1970s, it became apparent that the 1960 legal and institutional framework within which ALALC operated was insufficient to achieve the goals. The members of ALALC then set to work to develop and create a more dynamic system, one of similar form but possessed of more effective mechanisms and institutions. The amorphous goals and ideas of ALALC were reworked and redirected when in 1980 the Asociación Latinoamericana de Integración (ALADI) was created by the second Treaty of Montevideo. [10]

The new ALADI has constituted an "area of economic preferences" in its region, mandating the promotion of interregional trade, economic complementation, and market expansion by economic cooperation. The Association has moved forward with renewed dynamism and by 1987 had established Regional Tariff Preferences along with a number of discrete, partial agreements. ALADI, the continuation of the juridical personality of ALADI, describes three tiers of membership: lesser developed states, Bolivia, Ecuador, Paraguay; those in an intermediate stage, Chile, Colombia, Peru, Uruguay, Venezuela; and those more developed, Argentina, Brazil, Mexico.

The documentation and institutions of the two associations can be regarded as single units in sequences. Everything remained in similar format with consistent documentary tendencies, albeit with slight shifts in nomenclature. ALADI is governed by its supreme organ, the Consejo de Ministros de Relaciones Exteriores, which is more effective than its predecessor of the same name. The Conferencia de Evaluación y Convergencia, the continuing body of experts and technocrats, is considerably more powerful than ALALC's Conferencia de las Partes

Contratantes, especially in maintaining general political control and oversight of the integration process. The Comité de Representantes is the permanent political body with greater scope and effect than the earlier Comité Ejecutivo Permanente. The Secretaría Permanente is a more exact continuation in form and function from ALALC to ALADI. The documentation of the institutions and various suborgans of the Association are not easily obtainable, but descriptions of all documents and full text of the most important are available to the diligent subscriber. [11]

A most important source for documentation and information on Latin American integration is to be found in the enormous range of publications of the Banco Interamericano del Desarrollo and its Instituto para la Integración de América Latina, usually cited by its Spanish acronym BID/INTAL. The Inter-American Development Bank, along with the U.N., has been the moving nonnational force for economic integration in Latin America. Its publications, both serial and monographic, are essential. [12]

Moving north and, literally, skipping over the Andes and the Grupo Andino, the next major regional organization to be described is the Central American Common Market. As mentioned, this area has the longest history of unified development coupled with, ultimately, the least appealing results. This institution was another product of ECLA's strategy of separating economics from politics and bringing about gradual integration without regard for earlier efforts at integration. The Central American Common Market (CACM), in effect a Central American customs union, commenced with a treaty of economic association known as the Tripartite Treaty among Guatemala, El Salvador, and Honduras in early 1960. This was superseded by the General Treaty of Central American Economic Integration signed at Managua 13 December 1960. [13] The original signatories, Guatemala, El Salvador, Honduras, and Nicaragua, were joined two years later by Costa Rica.

After about four years of very real movement toward integration on all fronts, the process began to deteriorate rapidly. The uniform tariff regulations were put aside, as it became apparent that the member states, or their political leaders, harbored heightened mutual distrust. The national legislatures would ratify only those instruments that benefited themselves and would ignore their other obligations. In the surge for advancing industrial growth, Honduras, in particular, felt left out. The almost absurd "Soccer War" between Honduras and El Salvador in 1969 signaled further decay. The same year, Nicaragua imposed, unilaterally, consumption taxes on many goods, and in 1971

Honduras imposed external tariffs on all goods, including exports of its neighbors. In effect, the real effort at economic integration in Central America, relatively dynamic in the 1960s, has faltered by the 1980s. Intraregional trade has greatly increased, but the Central American Common Market itself has failed to achieve any sort of acceptance within the political/constitutional structure of the member states, at least at present.

In this atmosphere of revolution, intervention, and even outright warfare, the institutions of the CACM have continued to function and even flourish. There may be some confusion as to these organs, since two of the most important were also created as part of the Organization of Central American States (ODECA). [14] The major institutions of the CACM are: Consejo Económico Centroamericano, which is the supreme organ and is composed of the Ministers of Economy of the member states (also provided by ODECA), the Consejo Ejecutivo Centroamericano (again also an ODECA organ), which consists of a permanent delegate from each state. These two councils area assisted by the administrative organ, the Secretaria Permanente del Tratado General de Integracíon Económica Centroamericana (SIECA) which is surprisingly effective, given the parlous circumstances under which it exists. The CACM does without several of the rather grand organs created for ODECA, such as the regular Meeting of Heads of State and a Conference of Ministers of Foreign Affairs and even a (revived) Central American Court of Justice. SIECA has been productive of the usual range of documents, always difficult to obtain in official format but at least ascertainable in more regularly distributed publications. [15] A final official source for documentation may be found in a few series published by the Banco Centroamericano de Integración Económica (BCIE) which was also created by the Treaty of Managua. [16] A good bibliography, including documentation of the Central American region, has been published by the Columbus Memorial Library. [17]

As proof, however, that the CACM still retains some viability, the institutions, functioning serenely in chaos, have been engaged in promoting a reactivation of the integration process. A draft treaty for a Central American Economic and Social Community was finalized in March 1976. Known as the Tratado Marco, it is more sophisticated than the 1960 treaty and aims at creation of vigorous institutions that would integrate all aspects of Central American economic life: a free trade area, a customs union, establishment of common industrial policies, harmonization of fiscal and financial policies, and implementation of common programs for social and economic development. Whereas the draft treaty has languished unratified, movement toward integration is now evidenced by the signing of the Agreement of Esquipulas of 25 May 1986 which provides for a new Central American Customs Union and proposes a Central American Parliament. [18]

A final important regional economic system is at work in the Caribbean area, basically the English-speaking Caribbean territories and nations. The Caribbean area can now be divided up into distinct, although sometimes overlapping groups: long-independent states, Cuba, Haiti, Dominican Republic; U.S. territories, Puerto Rico, Virgin Islands; former British colonies; former French colonies; former Dutch colonies. We are concerned with efforts at economic interpretation among the former British colonies, now a number of island nations and the States of Belize and Guyana on the mainland. [19]

The first efforts at Caribbean integration, both administrative and economic, were weak and ineffectual, with confused lines of authority from the ever-diminishing colonial powers. The British-inspired West Indies Federation (1958-1963) [20] interrupted the decay of the even more fragile Caribbean Commission (1946-1961). The Caribbean Free Trade Association (CARIFTA) was created in 1968. [21] and an East Caribbean Common Market Agreement was established the same year. [22] Neither of these organizations was particularly effective nor could they be regarded as valuable sources of documentation. [23]

Caribbean economic integration was substantially revised in 1973 with the Treaty of Chaguaramas [24] which established the Caribbean Community and Common Market (CARICOM). It absorbed CARIFTA and created much more than a trade organization, aiming to establish a true common market for cooperation in agricultural and industrial production, as well as in general economic, political, financial, and monetary matters. The broad goals of general economic integration and functional cooperation in sectors of transport, education, and health are possible of some degree of achievement; the announced desire for coordination in foreign policy may be more difficult. The Community recognizes two stages of development: "More developed" countries Barbados, Bahamas (a party to the Community but not to the Common Market), Guyana, Jamaica, Trinidad and Tobago; the remaining eight states are recognized as "lesser developed." CARICOM produces a reasonably accessible set of documentation. It is much more "institutionalized" than CARIFTA with international legal status for its two principal organs, the Conference of Heads of Government (for the Community) and the Common Market Council (for the Common Market). The Secretariat, seated at Georgetown, Guyana, is the principal administrative organ for both. [25]

The Organization of East Caribbean States (OECS) in effect revived the East Caribbean Common Market, which had been absorbed in 1973 by CARICOM. It was established in 1981 and covers the lesser developed states of Antigua, Dominica, Grenada, Monserrat, St. Kitts and Nevis, St. Lucia, St. Vincent, and the Grenadines. [26] This organization has, to date, produced very little in the form of available documentation. [27]

The economic arm of CARICOM, the Caribbean Development Bank, designed to be the financial and lending agency, has been more active (or accessible) in its publishing program. [28]

Two smaller Latin American regional organizations remain to be discussed. The Cuenca del Plata or the La Plata Basin has been the source and cause of another economic organization. Created by the Treaty of Brasilia in 1969, it is very slowly emerging as a regional grouping of marginal effectiveness. [29] It was created to serve certain interests of the five nations, parts of whose territories form the La Plata River basin. It is now recognized as a subregional entity within ALADI, governed by an ambiguous treaty and existing in a purposely weakened condition because its two most powerful members, Argentina and Brazil, wish it that way. The organization has no international legal personality itself, although its secretariat, the CIC, does. It is an organization concerned with all aspects of the landmass of the basin (e.g., 100 percent of the territory of Paraguay, but only 19 percent of the territory of Brazil). Its mission is to foster regional cooperation, as opposed to economic integration, in manners such as promoting identification of areas of common interest, making surveys, drafting agreements, and giving at least lip service to utilizing and conserving natural resources and the environment. Its two principal organs, the Reunión de Ministros de Relaciones Exteriores and the Comité Intergubernamental Coordinador (CIC), along with various ad hoc Grupos de Expertos, must produce documents, but if this is the case, they have not made their way to North America. Its development organ and financial organ FONPLATA, seated in Sucre, Bolivia, also has its own legal personality. The effect of both sectors of the organization in the scheme of Latin American economic integration has been negligible.

Amazon cooperation is the latest cooperative effort to be established in Latin America. As the Cuenca del Plata covers the landmass draining into the River Plata, so this treaty on Amazon cooperation aimed to cover the territories of eight nations draining into the Amazon basin. [30] Here the goal was more nationally oriented, to result ultimately in the full integration and incorporation into the respective economies of the areas of the member states that are in the Amazon basin. Also stated were the goals of preserving the environment and utilizing natural resources sensibly. No documentation has been discovered from the organization's two institutions, the Reunión de Cancilleres de los Países Miembros and the Secretaría pro tempore.

The United Nations, through its Economic Commission for Latin America and the Caribbean, hereinafter referred to either as ECLAC or its Spanish acronym CEPAL, has, of course, played a major and forceful role in providing expertise and impetus for Latin American economic integration. The range of U.N. documentation is beyond the scope of this study, although some mention should be made of certain series that, in themselves, can be used as sources for documentation of regional organizations. [31]

A few sources, albeit "secondary," are essential in providing the researcher or librarian with citations to documents or extensive reprints of legislation or decisions (or highly respectable English translations of these guideposts) in the continuing saga of Latin American economic integration and development. Various Spanish-language publications are cited, a few more continue to be published, and the user should be aware of them. [32]

The vast range of U.S.-based secondary sources for information on this subject is not within the scope of this paper. Dozens of academic or institution-related journals and annals contain excellent articles and invaluable material for the scholar and researcher. This is an ever-shifting bibliographical field and access is through the normal published indexes. A useful chronology—on a continuing basis—is to be found in the University of Miami's *Inter-American Law Review*. Two publications connected with U.S. international legal societies, *International Legal Materials* and *Inter-American Legal Materials*, absolutely must be available in any collection that aims to provide even basic support for study or research on Latin American economic integration. [33]

The next few years will prove a watershed period, both in the continuing development of Latin American economic integration and in providing concrete evidence of the willingness and ability of the governments of the various member states to make the hard economic, political, and social decisions necessary to achieve effective economic planning and integration. This is a region consisting of three giant economic powers, six medium-grade states in varying stages of development, and, finally, some twenty smaller states, almost all of extreme economic fragility. The original organizations of the 1960s,

ALALC and CARIFTA, were rather traditional intergovernmental agencies, loosely associated and given over to discussion rather than decision. Their more effective counterparts, actual "community type" organizations in Central America and the Andean Group, at least had more coherent and potentially activist instruments in place. The former has failed of achievement because of geopolitical dissension; the latter has never reached its goals owing to serious economic, rather than national, rivalries.

The 1980s have now witnessed major restructurings of all the organizations. The Caribbean area has moved toward the community format. ALALC's transformation to ALADI now includes "como objectivo a larga plazo el establecimiento, en forma gradual y progresiva, de un mercado común latinoamericano."[34] ALADI has given further evidence of its determination by the creation of actual community institutions that are not dissimilar from those of the European Communities. The Andean Group, which is, in practice and effect, by far the closest to a true supranational organization, continues to give evidence of operational life and achievement, but it is at present also on the precipice. The Venezuelan Congress has consistently been reluctant to recognize the supranational characteristics of the Cartagena Agreement. The Andean Court of Justice has now been faced with serious suits and countersuits by Venezuela and Ecuador; if they eventually come to a contentious decision, the court itself may become the instrument of Andean disintegration.

In 1992, the European Community is destined to become a single, massive economic market. The goodwill and support embodied in the Lomé treaties should provide some breathing space and cushion for the Caribbean states. The cutting off of European markets, combined with continuing economic stagnation, presents a picture of increasingly negative economic phenomena. The dependent relationship of Latin America with the industrialized economies in all matters—trade, technology, and finance—combined with high unemployment, unequal distribution, and heterogeneity in production bodes ill for this enormous region.

These few years prior to the 1992 deadline are all that remain for the nations of Latin America to strengthen their organs of regional unity so that the region, or regions, can better influence international economic events, rather than, as now, merely respond to situations created by others. While some experienced observers remain optimistic, remarking that

América Latina ha estado actuando sectorialmente, particularmente en los campos de la cooperación económica y financiera, creando instituciones y compromisos recíprocos de diversa naturaleza de contenido tanto regional como subregional, cuyo balance es positivo si vizualizemos nuestra tangible cohesión económico-técnica del presente, comparada con la realidad de hace dos décadas. [35]

Another student of the region urges more austere development, writing that "regional cooperation depends on the will of the countries of Latin America and the Caribbean, because the region already has the institutions and experience which can serve as valuable instruments for efforts of this kind aimed at strengthening regional cooperation and seeking a dynamic source of growth within the region itself." [36]

The situation will only become more desperate, unless the political will is strengthened and viable forms of economic integration are in place for the 1990s. A more realistic (and pessimistic) appraisal is offered by SELA:

Las economías de los países de América Latina y el Caribe continúan enfrentando serias dificultades. Las expectativas de recuperación que se habían forjado en la región como consecuencia del comportamiento positivo del producto y el comercio en 1984, se desvanecieron en 1985. Las perspectivas para 1986 son poco halagadoras. Los problemas del endeudamiento externo siguen gravitando negativamente en el desarrollo latinoamericano. El comercio de la región, incluido el comercio intra-regional, ha perdido dinamismo. [37]

The history of economic integration in Latin America presents a picture of accomplishment second only to that of the European Communities. But this is a distant second, indeed, only ahead of regional nondevelopments in Africa or Southeast Asia. Without true integration on a European model, the outlook is calamitous. Just as we study history to avoid the mistakes of the past, we must collect and maintain, as best we can, the documentation and exegesis, often only runes, of this important endeavor. The prospect is bleak, certainly short term, for dynamic achievement, but the creation of usable and worthwhile collections will be challenge enough for librarians and scholars.

NOTES

1. ALALC and ALADI consistently represent the Spanish form of Asociación Latinoamericana de Libre Comercio and Asociación Latinoamericana de Integración; occasionally they are referred to as LAFTA and LAIA, but are not so described here; SELA, Sistema Económico Latinoamericano, is frequently referred to as the Latin American Economic System, but never by an English acronym; the various Caribbean organizations are almost invariably of English nomenclature; the Central American

Common Market or Mercado Común Centroamericana is equally described as CACM or MCCA, but its organs are referred to exclusively by the Spanish acronyms. The United Nations Economic Commission for Latin America, ECLA, is also known by its Spanish acronym CEPAL; for the sake of consistency, and because the Caribbean is now included, it is referred to as ECLA or ECLAC.

2. Libraries and issuing agencies alike refer to the Andes Group as the Grupo Andino, Junta del Acuerdo de Cartagena, Andean Pact Nations, Andean Pact, Board of the Acuerdo de Cartagena, and so on. Grupo Andino seems the simplest and most comprehensive form.

3. O. Sunkel, "Past, Present and Future of the International Economic Crisis," in A. Gauhar, ed., *Regional Integration: The Latin American Experience* (London, 1985), p. 20.

4. Bogotá, American Treaty on Pacific Settlement, 30 April 1948, 30 *UNTS* 55 (1949); *Inter-American Peace Treaties and Conventions* (Washington, DC, 1972), p. 60.

5. Lima, Treaty of Institutionalization of the Latin American Parliament, 16 November 1987, 27 *International Legal Materials (ILM)* 430 (1988). Its 18 signatories represent almost all the nations of Central and South America.

6. Panama, 17 October 1975, 15 *ILM* 1081 (1976), convention establishing the Latin American Economic System.

7. The Consejo's *Decisiones* appear as SELA document CL/I—; the Secretariado is responsible for all documentation, both its own, e.g., *(Primero-) Informe anual* 1977, and the studies of the various action committees, all appearing either as SP/CL or SP/RCLA. The documentary symbols for the committees are further acronyms, e.g., Comité de Acción sobre Seguridad Alimentaria, CASAR, becomes SP/CL/CASAR.

8. *SELA en Acción*, no. 1 (1977), Caracas, Secretariado Permanente, is the *Boletín* of the Secretariat; an English edition *SELA in Action* is also issued; *SELA Noticias*, no. 1 (1980), Caracas, Secretariado, is more a newsletter; a new periodical has also commenced, *Capítulos de SELA*, no. 1 (1983), Caracas, Secretariado.

9. Tratado de Montevideo de 18 febrero 1960. See Inter-American Institute of International Legal Studies, *Instruments of Economic Integration in Latin America and the Caribbean*, 2d ed., 2 vols. (Dobbs Ferry: Oceana, 1975), the best single source for reliable English translations of all Latin American economic treaties and documents through 1974.

10. Tratado de Montevideo de 12 agosto 1980 establishing ALADI or LAIA (the Latin American Integration Association), 20 *ILM* 672 (1981). For the best analysis, see F. Morales, ed., *ALADI: comentarios preliminares al Tratado de Montevideo de 1980* (Santiago: Jurídica, 1981).

11. It is not easy to rank what is a fairly diverse body of official or quasi-official literature in any comprehensive system: *Síntesis ALALC* (vols. 1-15) (nos. 1-137) (1965-1980), Montevideo, ALALC, and its continuance, *Síntesis ALADI* no. 1 (1981), Montevideo, ALADI, are essential sources for major documents and documentary references. *ALALC Boletín* nos. 1-135/136 (1964-1980), Montevideo, Centro de Estadísticas Nacionales, and the current *Boletín ALADI*, nos. 137/138 (1980), Montevideo, Centro de Estadísticas, are valuable for trade and development information. The new *Síntesis ALADI* now publishes annually a version variously described as "Extraordinaria," "Separata," or "Edición especial" containing useful documentary compilations. These have been issued by the Secretaria since 1983. *LAFTA's Newsletter*, nos. 1-54 (1968-1980) (title varies considerably, but numbering remains constant),

Montevideo, ALALC, has been continued, after a hiatus, by *Newsletter/ALADI*, no. 1 (1984), a useful source for news and references; it appears in both Spanish and English editions. *Anuario ALALC: Grupo Andino: SIECA*, nos. 1-14, 196?-1978/79, Buenos Aires, ALALC, continued by *Anuario ALADI; Grupo Andino: SIECA*, no. 15 (1982/83), Panama, Organización Latinoamericana de Integración, is an important semiofficial source. Most legal documents for ALALC can be found in *Estructura jurídica vigente de la ALALC*, 2d ed., Montevideo, ALALC, 1977-78, 4 vols. in 2. This compilation contains all treaties and major decisions and citations to or digests of the remainder. This is included only in part (for foreign investment) by *Régimen jurídico de las inversiones extranjeras en los países de la ALADI*, Buenos Aires, BID/INTAL, 1985 (it also includes the Grupo Andino). ALADI continues the earlier practice of issuing official documents in mimeographed (or even flimsier) format. These are difficult to obtain and maintain; the important ones invariably appear in the bulletins, or are absorbed in looseleaf publications.

    12. *Derecho de la Integración: revista jurídica latinoamericana*, nos. 1-33 (1967-1979), Buenos Aires, INTAL, was an outstanding publication containing scholarly studies, documents, news, information and national legislation. *Revista de la Integración: económica, política, sociológica*, nos. 1-19/20 (1967-1975), Buenos Aires, INTAL, is its equivalent in related fields. *Boletín de Información Legal*, nos. 1-70 (1973-1979), Buenos Aires, INTAL (nos. 1-4 had title *Síntesis de Información* . . .) had brief reports on legal activities. *Boletín de la Integración*, nos. 1-119/120 (1965-1975), Buenos Aires, INTAL, was invaluable for brief yet informative coverage of all aspects of Latin American integration. *Integración Latinoamericana*, año 1, no. 1 (1976), Buenos Aires, INTAL, continues the *Boletín* and the *Revista* and absorbed the *Boletín de Información Legal* and is now the one, essential source. The Institute's other excellent serial is *El Proceso de Integración en América Latina en* . . ., 1968/1971, Buenos Aires, INTAL (an English edition has been issued since 1976, but not consistently). This yearbook contains comprehensive reportage, region by region, as well as survey articles. The Bank's two major annual reports should not be overlooked: *Informe Anual/Annual Report*, 1st (1960), Washington, DC, 1961, and its *Economic and Social Progress in Latin America: Annual Report*, 1st (1972), Washington, DC, 1972 (continuing its *Social Progress Trust Fund: Annual Report*, 1st-5th (1961-1965) and *Socioeconomic Progress in Latin America*, 6th-11th (report), (1966-1971). The Institute has now published the best single source for the official texts of all instruments dealing with Latin American and Caribbean integration: *Ordenamiento jurídico de la integración económica regional en América Latina*, 2 vols. (Buenos Aires: INTAL, 1986).

    13. *Convenios centroamericanos de integración económica*, 2 vols. (Guatemala: SIECA, 1963-64), is an excellent compilation of documents; English translations are contained in *Instruments of Economic Integration*, n. 9, above).

    14. ODECA, whose stated goals are to comprise "an economic-political community which aspires to the integration of Central America," was created by the Charter of San Salvador, adopted 14 October 1951 and revised at Panama 12 December 1962. ODECA plays, at most, a peripheral role in Central American economic integration, and it has been effective primarily in the settlement of a few boundary disputes.

    15. The Consejo Económico has issued its *Actas* (basically resolutions) in mimeographed form since 1961; the Consejo Ejecutivo also issues its resolutions as *Actas* in similar format since 1962. SIECA issues two serial publications, easily obtained, which reprint all important documents, or at least provide authoritative synopses: *Carta*

informativa—SIECA, no. 1 (1961), Guatemala, SIECA; *Cuadernos de la SIECA*, no. 1 (1976), Guatemala, SIECA (which often devotes an entire issue to a single theme). A useful annual is sponsored by SIECA, *Reunión de organismos de integración y cooperación de América Latina*, 1st (1981), Guatemala, SIECA; Lima, Junta del Acuerdo de Cartagena. SIECA has published *Integración en cifras*, 1972, Guatemala, although it appears to have lapsed.

16. *Carta informativa*, año 1, no. 1 (1967), Tegucigalpa, 1967 (mimeographed), and *Memoria de labores*, no. 1 (1961/62), Tegucigalpa.

17. *Central American Common Market: A Selected Bibliography 1975 to the Present*, Ellen G. Schaffer, comp., Documentation and Information Ser. no. 4 (Washington, DC: OAS, Columbus Memorial Library, 1981).

18. *Carta informativa—SIECA*, no. 303 (1987).

19. Francophone Caribbean nations and the Dutch states of the Netherlands Antilles and Aruba have been greatly affected by the several conventions of the European Communities, first the two Youndé Conventions and now the continuing series of Lomé conventions. These are designed to assist the ACP (African, Caribbean, Pacific) nations in their economic development. Now, with the United Kingdom's participation in the EEC, the entire Caribbean area may be established in a more favorable development and aid position than the rest of Latin America. Major economic sacrifices may be imposed on the Caribbean states in connection with the Lomé policies, and these will have an even harsher effect after the 1992 single European market is achieved, but a substantial economic cushion is nevertheless already in place. The accession of Spain and Portugal to the Treaty of Rome in 1986 may also have serious negative economic implications for their traditional trading partners in Latin America.

20. *West Indies Gazette* (Port of Spain), 1958-1962.

21. *Instruments of Economic Integration* (see n. 9, above), 7 *ILM* 935 (1968).

22. Reprinted in 20 *ILM* 1176 (1981).

23. CARIFTA issued press (or news) releases from its seat at Georgetown, 1968-1973.

24. Treaty Establishing the Caribbean Community (and Annex creating the Caribbean Common Market), Chaguramas, Trinidad and Tobago, 4 July 1973; *Instruments of Economic Integration* (see n. 9, above) 12 *ILM* 1033 (1973).

25. *CARICOM Bulletin*, no. 1 (1978), Georgetown, The Secretariat, is the best source for documentary information; *CARICOM Secretary-General's Report* (1974-1982), and its successor *Report of the Secretary-General of the Caribbean Community* (1983), Georgetown, is also an essential source. *CARICOM Bibliography*, vol. 1, Georgetown, Caribbean Community Secretariat Library (etc.), 1977, is extremely useful as a listing of official and national publications. Two other unofficial sources are invaluable for the access they provide to documentation in this area: One is *Caribbean Yearbook of International Relations*, (vol. 1), 1975, Leyden etc., Sijthoff etc., 1976. Although falling very far behind in publication, its section "Selected Documents" is essential. The other is *Caribbean Law Librarian*, vol. 1 (1984), Jamaica, Caribbean Association of Law Libraries, which contains good articles and references to national legislation.

26. Treaty establishing the Organization of East Caribbean States, Basseterre, St. Kitts, 18 June 1981, 20 *ILM* 1166 (1981).

27. *Trade Digest (OECS)*, vol. 1 (1979/1982), St. Johns, Antigua, Economic Affairs Secretariat; and *Report of Activities (OECS)*, no. 1 (1983/1984), St. Johns, OECS Secretariat.

28. *CDB News*, vol. 1, no. 1 (1983), St. Michael, Barbados, The Bank, is a useful quarterly information bulletin; The Caribbean Development Bank also issues its official *Annual Report* (1970), Bridgetown etc., and *Annual Meeting of the Board of Governors: Summary of Proceedings*, 1st (1971), Bridgetown etc.

29. Tratado de Cuenca del Plata, Brasília, 23 abril 1969, 8 *ILM* 905 (1969).

30. Tratado de Cooperación Amazónica, Brasília, 3 julio 1978, 17 *ILM* 1045 (1978).

31. *Report to the Economic and Social Council*, 1st (1948/49), New York, Santiago de Chile, which appears in the U.N.'s official records series; *Economic Survey of Latin America and the Caribbean*, 1948, Santiago de Chile; *CEPAL Review*, no. 1 (1976), Santiago de Chile, (Spanish edition, *Revista de la CEPAL*), an excellent source for documentary references and information, as was the predecessor publication, *Economic Bulletin for Latin America*, vols. 1-20 (1956-1975), New York etc. Two irregular series are also of great utility for the researcher in this field; although mostly of a monographic nature, they shed considerable light on regional economic activities and documentation: *Cuadernos de la CEPAL*, no. 1 (1981), Santiago de Chile, and *Estudios y Informes de la CEPAL*, no. 1 (1980), Santiago de Chile.

32. *Mercado Común América Latina*, nos. 1-21 (1959-1962), Montevideo, Mercado Común América Latina, continued by *Mercado Común América Latina*, no. 22 (1963), Mexico, Mercado Común de América Latina, and *Revista de la Integración Centroamericana*, nos. 1-19 (1971-1976), Tegucigalpa, Banco Centroamericano de Integración Económica, continued by *Revista de la Integración y el Desarrollo de Centroamérica*, no. 1 (1979), Tegucigalpa, Banco Centroamericano de Integración Económica.

33. *University of Miami Inter-American Law Review*, vol. 1 (1969), Coral Gables, University of Miami School of Law (title varies: vols. 1-15 [1969-1984], *Lawyer of the Americas*). This review contains a brief chronology/reports, usually two or three times a year, on activities of Latin American organizations. The better report, dealing with regional economic developments, is no longer published: "Latin American Economic Integration" appeared regularly in vols. 1-12 (1969-1981), compiled by such well-known scholars as F. V. García-Amador and F. Orrego Vicuña. The section "Regional and International Activities," which continues, and has been edited since 1970 by I. Zanotti, is basically focused on OAS activities. *International Legal Materials*, vol. 1 (1962), Washington, DC, American Society of International Law, is simply indispensable as the most current, comprehensive, and reliable source for English translations of official documents, decisions, and legislation of international organizations and decisional bodies, including those in Latin America. *Inter-American Legal Materials*, vol. 1, no. 1 (1983), Chicago, American Bar Association, Section of International Law and Practice, Inter-American Law Committee (vol. 1 complete in one issue), vol. 2 (1985) is substantially oriented to business interests with national legislation on foreign investment and international debt, but it can be regarded as a possible source for documentation of regional organizations.

34. Tratado de Montevideo, Art. 1 (see n. 10, above).

35. P. Herrera. *América Latina, desarrollo y integración* (Santiago de Chile, 1986), p. 265.

36. N. González, "Reactivation and Development," 30 *CEPAL Review* 13 (1986).

37. "Notas sobre la situación económica de América Latina y el contexto internacional," in *Relaciones económicas internacionales de América Latina* (Lima, 1987), p. 59, a position paper prepared by the SELA secretariat.

32. The Grupo Andino and Its Documents

Igor I. Kavass

History and Purposes of the Grupo Andino

The Grupo Andino (also known as the Andean Common Market [or ANCOM], Acuerdo de Cartagena, and the Andean Pact) is an organization for the economic integration of the five South American countries located in the central and northern parts of the massive Andean mountain range. The present members of the organization are Bolivia, Colombia, Ecuador, Peru, and Venezuela. Originally, when the Grupo Andino was established by means of a treaty known as the Cartagena Agreement (Acuerdo de Cartagena) in 1969, Chile was one of the founding members, whereas Venezuela abstained from joining the organization until 1973. As Chile began to develop a more flexible foreign trade and investment policy in the middle 1970s than was acceptable to the other Grupo Andino countries, it gradually withdrew from the organization's activities, and finally ceased to be a member in late 1976.

The fundamental purposes of the Grupo Andino are to forge stronger economic links among its member countries, to establish a common trade and investment policy toward the outside world, to integrate the individual markets of the member countries, and by all of these means to create a new economic entity in the world market which would be able to compete successfully with the United States, the European Economic Community countries, and the emerging economic giants of the Far East. On the whole, it has not been successful in the achievement of these ends. Agreements have not always been easy to reach. While the countries of the Grupo Andino have significant areas of shared interests, there are also major diversities in individual country goals, positive, economic development, and social growth. The general political environment in South America is more tumultuous than in the United States. Handing over the reins of government, even when it is the result of an election rather than a coup d'état, frequently involves a radical reorientation of a country's policies, both internal and external. Negotiations for common actions among countries are difficult to complete in such a political environment, and even more difficult to

337

enforce once agreement has been reached. Progress has therefore been very slow. The detailed technical implementations of specific policies have frequently been made irrelevant by quite unexpected and serious changes in world and regional economic conditions. Nevertheless, the Grupo Andino has been able to survive if not for other reasons than the realization among its members that they cannot risk going on alone. The economic risks, as indeed can be seen now in the case of Chile, are too unpredictable and quite serious. For these reasons the member countries have been prepared to be flexible and pragmatic in their objectives as long as they can preserve the framework of the system created by the Cartagena Agreement.

The objectives of the Cartagena Agreement were reaffirmed and expanded in the Cartagena Mandate, signed by the presidents of the five countries during the celebration of the tenth anniversary of the Grupo Andino in 1979. The Cartagena Mandate states expressly that Andean integration "constitutes an historical, political, geopolitical, economic, and sociological necessity" for the ultimate achievement of Latin American unity. Thus, for the first time the aims of the Grupo Andino were broadened by extending them to areas of political as well as economic cooperation. To this end the Cartagena Mandate proposed the formation of an Andean Council of Foreign Relations, and this body was set up later in 1979. The Cartagena Mandate recommended also the creation of a regional court or tribunal to assure compliance and uniformity with the Cartagena Agreement and with the subsequent protocols or other agreements pertaining thereto.

In July 1983 the presidents of the member countries met again and signed the so-called Caracas Declaration which recognized that quite often the economic interests of the individual countries are incompatible and that the development of common policies requires a better understanding of these differences and a greater flexibility in solutions. To this end, the Caracas meeting established a permanent Andean Business Consultative Council.

As the Grupo Andino approaches its twentieth anniversary, it remains a viable and relatively vigorous organization with an aptitude for flexibility as its major element for survival. The secret is that its member countries cannot really do without it. While they have constantly complained about the inefficiencies of a common economic program and frequently failed to agree on many fundamental issues, they must seek common ground as a means to overcome the disadvantages of large world trade imbalances and the resulting ever-increasing foreign debt loads each country must bear. Except for Chile, they have never gone so far as to sever their links with one another within the Grupo Andino framework.

Unwilling to demolish the idea of a common economic policy, the member countries of the Grupo Andino have adopted the opposite approach of saving the organization by whatever means are politically acceptable and economically beneficial to them all. For example, they have broadened their participatory base through the creation of many subsidiary organs as links for intraregional dialogue and negotiations, many of them in specialized economic fields. Lately, they have also been willing to formulate more general economic policies which grant the individual member countries greater discretion in their application within the respective jurisdictions. The Quito Protocol of May 12, 1987, as the most recent amending and reaffirming agreement concerning the Grupo Andino, is illustrative of this trend.

Structure and Organization

The Grupo Andino came into existence by virtue of the Cartagena Agreement of May 26, 1969. The agreement not only spelled out the purposes and goals of the organization, it created also several principal organs entrusted with the formulation of detailed policies and their implementation. A number of subsequent agreements, mostly referred to as protocols, contain amendments and modifications to the schema created by the Cartagena Agreement (the Quito Protocol of May 12, 1987, being the latest of these). The Cartagena Agreement with the subsequent protocols constitutes the primary legal source for the Grupo Andino and its activities.

The three main organs of the Grupo Andino are the Commission, the Board (Junta), and the court.

The Commission, located in Lima, Peru, consists of the representatives of all five member countries. Its functions are predominantly of a legislative character. Its legislative measures are known as decisions which, subject to the terms of the Cartagena Agreement and subsequent protocols, are generally binding throughout the territory of the Grupo Andino.

The Board consists of three members appointed by the unanimous decision of the Commission for periods of three years. The Board is also located in Lima, Peru. In effect, the Board is the administrative headquarters of the Grupo Andino, with a large staff housed in a multistory building close to the center of Lima. The Board makes resolutions that deal predominantly with administrative matters and are subject to the decisions of the Commission. The Commission and the Board are assisted in their work by a large number of councils and committees performing consultative work in a variety of specialized areas.

In 1979, on the occasion of the tenth anniversary of the Grupo Andino, the member countries agreed in a special treaty to establish an Andean Court of Justice. Consisting of one judge from each member country with a rotating president, this court has operated since 1984. It is located in Quito, Ecuador. Entrusted with the observance of the Cartagena Agreement, the subsequent protocols and other agreements, and the decisions and resolutions thereunder, the Andean Court of Justice has so far issued three opinions.

In the Quito Protocol of May 12, 1987, the member countries agreed to created an Andean Parliament, the result of approximately ten years of negotiations. They reaffirmed also the existence of the Andean Business Consultative Council and decided to create an Andean Labor Council.

In conjunction with the Grupo Andino the member countries have established several associated organizations. For example, there are an Andean Reserve Fund, located in Bogotá, Colombia, and an Andean Development Corporation with its headquarters in Caracas, Venezuela.

Information and Official Sources

Tracking the decision-making process as well as other actions of the Grupo Andino is not easy. There is no official information service to report on its access in a comprehensive and timely manner. At one time the Board published a monthly magazine entitled *Grupo Andino: Carta informativa oficial de la Junta del Acuerdo de Cartagena*, which provided news about current projects, programs, and actions (though with some delay and rather selectively). For a while there was even an attempt to put out an English version of this publication. The *Grupo Andino* ceased publication in early 1986 for lack of funds. Despite several announcements of its revival, it has not reappeared. The Board also publishes a *Gaceta oficial del Acuerdo de Cartagena*. This is where formal announcements appear, and where the texts of the official documents (e.g., agreements among the member countries, decisions of the Commission, the resolutions of the Board, etc.) are first published. The trouble is that the *Gaceta* comes out irregularly. Arranging subscriptions to it is incredibly difficult. Subscriptions are unreliable and lapse without notice.

This writer has tried to set up subscriptions for the main Grupo Andino serial publications for three years. He has corresponded in Spanish with different offices of the Board in Lima. Sometimes he had to write several times to the same offices before he received replies.

Frequently, these replies simply asked him to write to another person in another office, presumably in the same building. At one time, he thought that the subscriptions were finally established, only to be advised in a subsequent letter that the particular series had ceased to be published. Payments had been made for them, and that is another story, because it took the best part of a year to establish the place where the payments had to be made, the method of payment, and the exact amount. The writer is now trying to re-establish a subscription for the *Gaceta* because, without any explanation, it stopped arriving about a year ago.

The best information sources about the activities of the Grupo Andino are commercial:

Aside from the major newspapers in the member countries, which are quite good in publishing full reports about the latest developments in the Spanish language, an excellent timely source is the Andean Group series of the *Latin American Regional Reports*, published by Latin American Newsletters Ltd. in London. Full text of this publication is available in computerized form on NEXIS.

Another good source is Business Latin America, one of the series of the large and expensive Business International information system.

A timely and reliable publication in Spanish about all Latin American regional organizations, including the Grupo Andino, is the monthly magazine *Integración Latinoamericana*. Edited and published by the prestigious Instituto para la Integración de América Latina (INTAL) in Buenos Aires, Argentina, it is frequently more perceptive than other services in identifying the developments within the Grupo Andino that are worthy of note.

More selective in its news about the Grupo Andino is *Business America*, a monthly magazine of the United States Department of Commerce.

Equally selective, as well as late in coming, are the *University of Miami Inter-American Law Review* (formerly *Lawyer of the Americas* and the *International Financial Law Review*, published in London by Euromoney Publications.

Much more unpredictable is the *Andean Reporter*, supposed to be published by the Peruvian Times S.A. in Lima, Peru. It began in 1975, but the last available issues in the United States are for 1981, although this periodical is still listed as current in Ulrich's catalog and other periodicals lists.

Researchers in Latin America know that information does not come easily and frequently depends on contacts. They usually identify one or two government departments or agencies in their countries which gather information on the Grupo Andino in a systematic manner. Rather than search through newspaper files or look for publications that may not be available because libraries and documentation centers in Latin America are poor, they rely on information on these institutions.

Research cannot depend entirely on current information alone. Frequently, the study of a particular topic requires analysis of the appropriate treaties and protocols, as well as Commission decisions, Board resolutions, or other official documents. Strange as it may seem, such texts are also not always easily accessible. For example, I have been searching without success for the text of the Quito Protocol, signed on May 12, 1987, for months. The text will eventually be published in several sources, even translated into English, but it takes time.

The older documents are accessible quite easily:

The best source in Spanish is the *Ordenamiento Jurídico del Acuerdo de Cartagena*, published by the Board of the Cartagena Agreement in 1982. It consists of six volumes: one volume containing the text of the Cartagena Agreement and all of the other treaties, protocols, etc., through 1982; four volumes of the Commission's decisions arranged chronologically from 1969 to 1982; and one volume of the Board's resolutions for the same period of time. It is unfortunate that this excellent set of documents is not being updated.

Another good source for the earlier documents is the multivolume *Historia documental del Acuerdo de Cartagena*, published in 1974 by INTAL (the publisher of *Integración Latinoamericano*, mentioned above).

All texts of the protocols and agreements, decisions, and other documents are, of course, published in the *Gaceta oficial del Acuerdo de Cartagena*, but the difficulties of obtaining copies of this elusive publication have already been noted.

A better source for the more important recent documents in Spanish is the *Integración Latinoamericana*.

In English the more important earlier documents may be found collected in such books as Francisco García-Amador's *The Andean Legal Order* (Oceana Publications, 1978).

English translations of recent documents are published selectively—perhaps too selectively—in *International Legal Materials* (the

American Society of International Law) and now also in *Inter-American Legal Materials* (issued by the International Legal Section of the American Bar Association).

Of course, for those who read Spanish, a convenient and very timely source for the most recent of the important documents are the major national newspapers of the Grupo Andino member countries. They invariably publish the full texts of the major agreements and decisions. Some of the recent documents, such as the highly important Commission Decision No. 220, which liberalized the Grupo Andino regime for foreign investments, are also published either in Spanish or English or both in specialized journals like the *ICSID Review: Foreign Investment Law Journal*.

For more detailed research it may be necessary to examine background materials, *trauvaux repertoires*, and what is usually referred to among lawyers as "legislative histories." The Grupo Andino headquarters in Lima actually prepares and preserves records of important meetings. Working and project papers as well as other documents of this nature are also produced in mimeograph form and kept by the headquarters. Their distribution, however, is very limited, highly selective, and quite erratic. I am not aware of a complete set of such documents available anywhere in the United States.

In 1984 the Andean Court of Justice began its work in Quito, Ecuador. The court has issued random publications in the form of small booklets, pamphlets, or bulletins, but it has no regular series for the publication of its decisions or other business. The three or four decisions it has handed down so far are available solely in mimeograph form. Better sources for the texts of such decisions are the newspapers of the member countries. The court has also tried to start a newsletter under the name *Noticias del Tribunal de Justicia del Acuerdo de Cartagena*. The first issue, consisting of four pages, came out in May 1986. The writer has not received any later issues and he does not know whether anything has been published since May 1986, though he is supposed to be on the mailing list.

Even more adventurous and unpredictable is gaining access to the laws of the member countries dealing with the implementation of the Cartagena Agreement, the subsequent protocols, and the Commission decisions. The original texts of those laws must be sought in the official gazettes and other legislative publication series of each country. At one time in the 1970s the Board commenced publication of a series known as the Leyes económicos de los países miembros. This ambitious project never really got off the ground. The individual issues, intended to be triennial, came out irregularly, and in 1982 or thereabouts this series presumably ceased to be published.

The best access to the laws of the member countries is achieved by examining articles on particular topics of Grupo Andino development in law reviews. Some of the authors are very good at performing the pioneering work of seeking out and identifying the relevant laws so that at least that part of information retrieval work need not be replicated. It is unfortunate that there is no service that tracks on a regular basis the laws of the member countries pertaining to the Grupo Andino and its activities. It is a serious gap in the already meager documentation base which makes research on any subject relating to the Grupo Andino difficult.

Other Publications

The original plans for the development of research and publication projects of the Grupo Andino were very ambitious. Trying to emulate the highly prolific European Economic Community, the member countries expected the headquarters of the Grupo Andino to become a major investigating and research center for economic integration activities in South America. It was intended that the headquarters would gather and publish all kinds of economic, social, and other data, and serve as a base for scholars working in the fields of economic integration and the development of related theories and policies.

At one time or another the Grupo Andino began to publish several journals of statistical data such as *Económica Andina, Boletín Mensual de Indicadores Económicos del Grupo Andino,* and *Comercio Exterior.* Some of these journals (e.g., *Económica Andina* and *Comercio Exterior*) have now completely ceased publication. Others appear late and irregularly. There has been a substantial reduction in the publication of serious research information or statistical data. What is published presently is primarily in the form of monographs or pamphlets, frequently without any serious content. They are mainly publicity or prestige publications without much substantive merit. The official explanation for the curtailment of publication activities is insufficient funds. Perhaps this is true. But a more likely reason is the indifference of the Grupo Andino officials, who do not find the creation of an efficient publishing system a sufficiently important or professionally rewarding activity.

Books and Articles about the Grupo Andino

Given that the idea of economic integration and a common market was accepted in principle as a fundamental premise of economic survival as long ago as the late 1960s, very little has been written about the Grupo Andino in general. Most analysis, in Spanish as well as other languages, is specialized. It deals with narrow topics that happen to be of immediate interest. Much of the English-language research, especially articles in law reviews, is concerned with the regulation of foreign investments in the Grupo Andino countries (the controversial Commission Decision No. 24). It is expected that this trend will continue as scholars begin to analyze the new Decision No. 220, which liberalizes the policy on foreign investment, and the implementing member country legislation.

Spanish-language literature is more diverse. It addresses foreign investment to some extent, but it emphasizes issues such as the regulation of trade between the member countries, development allocations and directives within the region, external and internal tariffs, and other aspects of economic integration.

The Grupo Andino has become a different entity from what it was during its first decade. Opinions about integration have matured, limits thereto have been recognized, and objectives are more realistic. These changes are clearly visible in the current scholarly literature about the Grupo Andino. What is missing right now are publications, either books or articles, which would present a comprehensive view of today's Grupo Andino and its current importance to the member countries and to the rest of Latin America. It would be worthwhile for scholars to take a careful look at the impact of the Grupo Andino on trade and economy generally and to explore whether implementation of the Cartagena Agreement was worth all the effort.

Development of a Grupo Andino Research Collection

It is not easy to develop a collection of materials supportive of research in the Grupo Andino area. In the first place, the publications of the Grupo Andino itself are not easily accessible. At one time there was a publication office at the headquarters in Lima which issued publication lists periodically. No lists seem to have appeared lately. The latest such list, known as *El Catálogo: Publicaciones seleccionados para los Centros de Referencia del Acuerdo de Cartagena*, was published in Lima in 1985. But even as it was received a notice followed hard on its trail to announce that many of the publications mentioned therein were "suspended" for lack of funds. Short of visiting the headquarters of the Grupo Andino in Lima, it is impossible to ascertain what series are in existence and whether they can be subscribed to easily. It is also difficult to determine the status of other publications.

The point is that much of the valuable information exists in the form of mimeographed or typed material, is known to very few people, is not described in any bibliography, and is not cataloged or even indexed. Access is very difficult. There are many different locales for publication aside from the Lima headquarters—for example, the Andean Court of Justice has published some works from its permanent location in Quito. Many of the court's important studies and records are available only in typed form. The publications of the Andean Development Corporation are issued from Caracas, and the publications of the other associate organizations issue from their respective headquarters without any knowledge thereof at the Grupo Andino headquarters in Lima.

Secondary literature about the Grupo Andino is not easy to gather either. The periodical writings are scattered throughout many different journals in several disciplines; monographic works come in different languages from a variety of publishers in different countries. Obviously, building an information and research collection for the Grupo Andino is a generally frustrating experience. It is hardly the same as developing a collection of reference and research sources for the European Common Market where the problem, if it may be called that, is the abundance of materials and accessibility of information. Information is a privileged commodity in Latin America!

The appendix contains a selected bibliography on the Grupo Andino including treaties, decisions, other binding documents, recent publications issued by them, and recent books and articles about them.

APPENDIX
A Selected Bibliography on the Grupo Andino

Treaties, Decisions, and Other Binding Documents
Documents in Spanish

Texts of treaties, decisions, and other binding documents in the Spanish language may be found in the *Gaceta Oficial del Acuerdo de Cartagena* as well as in INTAL's *Integración Latinoamericano*. The more important documents are also published as books or pamphlets by the Junta del Acuerdo de Cartagena in Lima. Some of the documents are also reprinted in collections or as appendixes in monographs.

English Translations of Present Documents

Agreement Establishing the Andean Council, done at Lima, November 12, 1979, *International Legal Materials* 19 (1980), 612-614.

Agreement Establishing Andean Development Corporation (Bolivia-Chile-Colombia-Ecuador-Peru-Venezuela), signed February 7, 1968, *International Legal Materials* 8 (1969), 940-958.

Andean Subregional Integration Agreement (Bolivia-Chile-Colombia-Ecuador-Peru), signed May 26, 1969 (name later changed to Agreement of Cartagena, entered into force October 16, 1969) *International Legal Materials* 8 (1969), 910-939.

Decision 24: Andean Foreign Investment Code, Codified Text of November 30, 1976, *International Legal Materials*, 16 (1977), 138-158. [Earlier versions at *International Legal Materials* 10 (1971), 152-172, *International Legal Materials* 11 (1972), 126-146, and Modifications at *International Legal Materials* 10 (1971), 1065-1066.

Decision 46: Standard Code on Multinational Enterprises and the Regulations with Regard to Subregional Capital, December 9-18, 1971, *International Legal Materials* 11 (1972), 357-372.

Decision 47: Regulations Concerning State Participation in Mixed Companies, December 9-18, 1971, *International Legal Materials* 11 (1972), 373.

Decision 48: Regulations Concerning the Treatment of Investments made by the Andean Development Corporation, December 9-18, 1971, *International Legal Materials* 11 (1972), 374.

Decision 84: Decision on the Bases for a Subregional Technology Policy, June 5, 1974, *International Legal Materials* 13 (1974), 1478-1489.

Decision 85: Decision on Industrial Property, June 5, 1974, *International Legal Materials* 13 (1974), 1489-1499.

Decision 102: Decision Terminating the Membership of Chile, October 30, 1976, noted at *International Legal Materials* 16 (1976), 1585.

Decisions 124 and 125: Specifying International Financial Institutions and Foreign Development Corporations as Neutral Capital under the Foreign Investment Code, December 16, 1977, *International Legal Materials* 17 (1978), 394-395.

Decision 169: Commission Decision on Andean Multinational Enterprises, March 16-18, 1982, *International Legal Materials* 21 (1982), 542-546.

Decision 184: Statute of the Court of Justice of the Cartagena Agreement, August 19, 1983, *International Legal Materials* 23 (1984), 422-441.

Decision 220: Andean Codes on the Treatment of Foreign Capital and on Trademarks, Patents, Licenses, and Royalties, *International Legal Materials* 3 (1987), 169-182.

Decision 220: Commission of the Cartagena Agreement Decision No. 220, *ICSID Review: Foreign Investment Law Journal* 2 (1987), 519-530.

Lima Protocol Amending Cartagena Agreement, done at Lima October 30, 1976; entered into force April 25, 1979, *International Legal Materials* 16 (1977), 235-241. Protocol approved by Ecuador, December 21, 1976, and by Peru, December 7, 1976, noted at *International Legal Materials* 16 (1977), 765.

Memorandum of Understanding between the United States of America and the Andean Group: For Effective Cooperation in Areas of Trade, Financing, Science and Technology, and Development of Industry, Agriculture and Infrastructure, Done at Washington, November 21, 1979, *International Legal Materials* 19 (1980), 4-10.

Treaty Creating Andean Reserve Fund, done at Caracas, November 12, 1976; entered into force June 8, 1978, *International Legal Materials* 18 (1979), 1191-1202.

Treaty Creating Court of Justice, done at Cartagena, May 28, 1979, *International Legal Materials* 18 (1979), 1203-1210.

Treaty Establishing the Andean Parliament, done at La Paz, October 25, 1979, *International Legal Materials* 19 (1980), 269-272.

Recent Books and Pamphlets Published by the Grupo Andino

Andueza Acuña, José Guillermo. *El Tribunal del Pacto Andino.* Quito: El Tribunal, 1986. (Publicaciones del Tribunal/Estudios; 3).

Cadenas Berthier, Tesalio, and Eva Morales. *Estudio sobre régimen de compras estatales en Venezuela.* [S.l.]: Junta del Acuerdo de Cartagena, 1987. (Jun/dic 1056).

Carmona Estanga, Pedro, et al. *Estrategias de desarrollo e integración en el Grupo Andino: Del seminario realizado en Lima en agosto de 1984.* Lima: Junta del Acuerdo de Cartagena, 1985.

Daavila Andrade, Oswaldo. *El Grupo Andino: Hacia una integración distinta.* Lima: Junta del Acuerdo de Cartagena, 1985.

Doria Medina, Samuel, Juan Antonio Morales, and Rolando Morales. *Estudio nacional sobre el sector servicios: Bolivia*. La Paz: Junta del Acuerdo de Cartagena, 1987. (Serie: Financiamiento).

El derecho de la integración: En el Grupo Andino, la CEE, el CAME y la ALADI. Lima: Junta del Acuerdo de Cartagena, 1983.

El Grupo Andino en transición: Un nuevo estilo de integración. Lima: Junta del Acuerdo de Cartagena, 1985.

El mercado ampliado: Anotaciones sobre su formación en el Grupo Andino—Bolivia, Colombia, Ecuador, Perú, Venezuela. Lima: Junta del Acuerdo de Cartagena, 1982. (Publicaciones de la Junta. Estudios; 1).

El sector agropecuario en el mercado ampliado. Lima: Junta del Acuerdo de Cartagena, 1982.

Estadística agropecuario andino, 1970-1980. Lima: Junta del Acuerdo de Cartagena, 1982.

Estrategia del sector agropecuario. Lima: Junta del Acuerdo de Cartagena, 1984.

Estrategia del sector comercial. Lima: Junta del Acuerdo de Cartagena, 1984.

Estrategia del sector de ciencia y tecnología. Lima: Junta del Acuerdo de Cartagena, 1984.

Estrategia del sector de integración física: Transportes y comunicaciones. Lima: Junta del Acuerdo de Cartagena, 1984.

Estrategia del sector industrial. Lima: Junta del Acuerdo de Cartagena, 1984.

Estrategia en el sector de las relaciones económicas externas. Lima: Junta del Acuerdo de Cartagena, 1984.

Estrategia en el sector del financiamiento: Inversiones y pagos. Lima: Junta del Acuerdo de Cartagena, 1984.

Guía para el establecimiento de empresas multinacionales andinas. Lima: Junta del Acuerdo de Cartagena, 1984.

Indicadores de los países del Grupo Andino. Lima: Junta del Acuerdo de Cartagena, 1985.

Integración democracia y participación. Lima: Junta del Acuerdo de Cartagena, 1985.

Introducción al derecho comunitario andino. Quito: Tribunal de Justicia del Acuerdo de Cartagena, 1985.

La deuda externa en el Grupo Andino. Lima: Junta del Acuerdo de Cartagena, 1984.

La programación industrial: Consideraciones sobre la programación industrial conjunta en el Grupo Andino—Bolivia, Colombia, Ecuador, Perú, Venezuela. Lima: Junta del Acuerdo de Cartagena, 1982. (Publicaciones de la Junta. Estudios; 2).

Mandato de Cartagena. Lima: Junta del Acuerdo de Cartagena, 1982.

Marchán Carrasco, Cornelia. *Estudio nacional sobre el sector servicios: Ecuador.* Quito: Junta del Acuerdo de Cartagena, 1987.

Márquez, Guillermo. *Estudio nacional sobre el sector servicios: Venezuela.* Caracas: Junta de la Acuerdo de Cartagena, 1987. (Serie: Financiamiento, No. 13).

Mecanismos de la integración andina. Lima: Junta del Acuerdo de Cartagena, 1982.

Montenegro, Walter. *La comunidad andina: Bolivia, Colombia, Ecuador, Perú, Venezuela.* Lima: Junta del Acuerdo de Cartagena, 1983.

Para nosotros la patria es América. Lima: Junta del Acuerdo de Cartagena, 1983.

Para nosotros la patria es América: Reflexiones sobre la integración andina. Lima: Junta del Acuerdo de Cartagena, 1983.

Poppe, Hugo E. *Disposiciones jurídicas vigentes en el Tribunal de Justicia del Acuerdo de Cartagena.* Quito: Tribunal de Justicia del Acuerdo de Cartagena, 1985.

Por una visión del desarrollo latinoamericano con autodeterminación, democracia y paz. Lima: Junta del Acuerdo de Cartagena, 1984.

Primer seminario andino de información sobre transferencia de tecnología. Lima: Junta del Acuerdo de Cartagena, 1983.

Programa subregional de apoyo a la pequeña y mediana industria. Lima: Junta del Acuerdo de Cartagena, 1984.

Seguridad alimentaria en el Grupo Andino. Lima: Junta del Acuerdo de Cartagena, 1985.

Sistema andino de integración, 1969-1984. Lima: Junta del Acuerdo de Cartagena, 1985.

Sistema andino José Celestino Mutis sobre la agricultura, seguridad alimentaria y conservación del ambiente. Lima: Junta del Acuerdo de Cartagena, 1983.

Tesauro de términos de la integración subregional andino: biblioteca de la Junta de la Acuerdo de Cartagena. 3d ed. Lima: Junta del Acuerdo de Cartagena, 1983.

Tribunal de Justicia del Acuerdo de Cartagena. Proyecto de Protocolo Modificatorio del Tratado que crea el Tribunal de Justicia del Acuerdo de Cartagena y exposición de motivos. Quito: Tribunal de Justicia del Acuerdo de Cartagena, February 1986. Mimeo, 34 l.

Villate Paris, Alberto. *Estudio nacional sobre el sector servicios: Colombia.* Bogotá: Junta del Acuerdo de Cartagena, 1987. (Serie: Financiamiento, No. 10).

Recent Books on the Grupo Andino

Actitudes y opinión de sectores sociales sobre el Acuerdo de Cartagena, Bolivia. La Paz: Universidad Católica Boliviana, 1983.

Ballesteros Mejía, Javier, ed. *Lecturas sobre el sector externo de la economía colombiana: Selección de documentos.* Bogotá, D.E.: Facultad de Ciencias Económicas y Administrativas, Pontificia Universidad Javeriana, 1982.

Betancur, Belisario. *El consenso de Cartagena: Cumbre latinoamericana de cancilleres y ministros de hacienda; The Cartagena Consensus: Latin American Summit Meeting of Foreign Ministers and Finance Ministers.* Cartagena: Rostro Cultura Tolima, 1984. (Text of the Colombian President's address).

Chaparro, Alfonzo, J. *Manual de integración andino.* 4th ed. Caracas: Monte Avila Editores, 1978.

Comercio exterior del Ecuador con los países de ALADI y Grupo Andino, 1976-1981. Quito: Ministerio de Industria, Comercio e Integración, Departamento de Estadística de la Dirección de Planificación, 1982.

Durieux, Jean, et al. *El Pacto Andino, América Latina y la Comunidad Económica Europea en los años 1980: Del coloquio realizado en Bruselas en mayo de 1983.* Buenos Aires: Instituto para la Integración de América Latina, 1984.

Ehrhardt, Waltraud. *Entwicklung durch Integration?: Peru im Andenpakt.* Frankfurt-am-Main: Lang, 1982.

El Proceso de integración en América Latina en 1982. Buenos Aires: Instituto para la Integración de América Latina, Banco Interamericano de Desarrollo, 1983.

García-Amador, Francisco V. *The Andean Legal Order: A New Community Law.* Dobbs Ferry, NY: Oceana Publications, Inc., 1978. (Published for the Inter-American Institute of International Legal Studies, this book is the most comprehensive work in the English language on the legal structure of the Grupo Andino.)

Golbert, Albert S., and Yenny Nun. "Latin American Laws and Institutions." In *Latin American Economic Integration*: Part II, *Major Regional Integration Efforts—The Andean Pact.* New York, NY: Praeger, 1982. Pp. 261-276.

Herrera, Beatriz. *Grupo Andino & COMECON: Crítica a la integración económica.* Lima: Editorial Pensamiento Crítico, 1982.

Leon de Labarea, Alba Ivonne. *Introducción al estudio de la integración económica y al Acuerdo Subregional Andino.* Maracaibo: Universidad del Zulia, Instituto de Filosofía del Derecho, 1985.

Misas Arango, Gabriel. *Empresas multinacionales y Pacto Andino: Regulaciones andinas al capital multinacional y el patrón de acumulación en Colombia.* Bogotá: Fines: Editorial Oveja Negra, 1983.

Núñez del Arco, José, et al., eds. *The Economic Integration Process of Latin America in the 1980s: Papers Presented at a Seminar Sponsored by the Inter-American Development Bank, September 22-23, 1982.* Washington, DC: Inter-American Development Bank, 1984.

Puyana de Palacios, Alicia. *Economic Integration among Unequal Partners: The Case of the Andean Group.* New York, NY: Pergamon Press, 1982.

Sáchia, Luis Carlos, et al. *El Tribunal de Justicia del Acuerdo de Cartagena.* Buenos Aires: Instituto para la Integración de América Latina, Banco Interamericano de Desarrollo, 1985.

Sanders, Thomas Griffin. *Whither the Andean Pact?* Indianapolis, IN: Universities Field Staff International, 1985. (UFSI Reports, 1985, No. 1 South America.)

Urriza, Manuel. *El empresariado venezolano y el Pacto Andino: Historia de posición de Fedecámaras.* Caracas: Universidad Simón Bolívar, Instituto de Altos Estudios de América Latina, 1984.

Viatsos, Constantine V. *The Role of Transnational Enterprises in Latin American Economic Integration Efforts: Who Integrated, and with Whom, How, and for Whose Benefit?: Summary: Study prepared for UNCTAD Secretariat.* New York, NY: United Nations, 1983.

Recent Articles about the Grupo Andino

Acuerdo de Cartagena, Junta. "Evaluación del programa de reactivación y examen de la situación actual del proceso de integración económica subregional andino (Primera Parte)," *Integración Latinoamericana* 78 (1983), 72-74

Acuerdo de Cartagena, Junta. "Evaluación del programa de reactivación y examen de la situación actual del proceso de la integración económica subregional andino (Segunda Parte)," *Integración Latinoamericana* 79 (1983), 53-58.

Aguirre, Carlos et al. "Integración andina: Hacia un nuevo estilo de gestión tecnológica," *Integración Latinoamericana* 87 (1984), 49-53.

Alcalde Cardoza, Javier. "Hacia una caracterización de los negociaciones en el Acuerdo de Cartagena," *Integración Latinoamericana* 71 (1982), 28-47.

"Andean Pact Seeks EEC Investment: Survey of Country Moves Since Decision 24 Was Scrapped," *Latin American Regional Report: Andean Group* (September 3, 1987), 4-5.

Andueza, José Guillermo. "Aplicación directa del ordenamiento jurídico del Acuerdo de Cartagena," *Integración Latinoamericana* 98 (1985), 3-13 .

Aninat del Solar, Augusto. "Modalidades de complementación industrial en la integración económica regional: Experiencias y proposiciones," *Integración Latinoamericana* 114 (1986), 7-21.

Aragao, José María. "Sistemas de pagos latinoamericanos," *Integración Latinoamericana* 94 (1984), 3-28.

Bitar, Sergio. "La inversión estadounidense en el Grupo Andino," *Integración Latinoamericana* 98 (1985), 42-49 .

Camacho Omiste, Edgar. "Cooperación e integración en el sector de los servicios entre los países miembros del Grupo Andino," *Integración Latinoamericana* 125 (1987), 32-51.

Cárdenas, José Corsino. "Discurso en el acto de toma de posesión de la Presidencia Ejecutiva de la Corporación Andina de Fomento: Quito, 10 de diciembre de 1981," *Integración Latinoamericana* 72 (1982), 78-81.

Carmona Estranga, Pedro. "Acuerdo de Cartagena: Trece años de un proceso de integración: 1982," *Integración Latinoamericana* 79 (1983), 77-81.

Chatterjee, S. K. "The Andean Multinational Enterprises," *The Company Lawyer* 7 (1986), 47-52 .

Cherol, Rachelle L., and José Núñez del Arco. "Andean Multinational Enterprises: A New Approach to Multinational Investment in the Andean Group," *Journal of Common Market Studies* 21 (1983), 409-428.

Cherol, Rachelle L., and José Núñez del Arco. "Empresas multinacionales andinas: Un nuevo enfoque de la inversión multinacional en el Grupo Andino," *Integración Latinoamericana* 73 (1982), 42-54.

Cherol, Rachelle L., and José Núñez del Arco. "Empresas multinacionales andinas: Un nuevo enfoque de la inversión multinacional en el Grupo Andino," *International Lawyer* 17 (1983), 309-332.

Conesa, Eduardo R. "Integración latinoamericana y el Pacto Andino en el decenio de 1980," *Integración Latinoamericana* 81 (1983), 27-37.

Figueredo P., Reinaldo. "Comercio internacional y las políticas para el establecimiento del mercado subregional andino," *Integración Latinoamericana* 98 (1985), 14-31.

Fuentes, Alfredo L., and Guillermo E. Perry. "Participación de los países de menor desarrollo económico relativo en la integración económica subregional andina," *Integración Latinoamericana* 110 (1986), 24-35.

Grosse, Robert. "Codes of Conduct for Multinational Enterprises," *Journal of World Trade Law* 16 (1982), 414-433.

Halperin, Marcelo. "Aspectos jurídicos de la seguridad alimentaria en el proceso de integración regional," *Integración Latinoamericana* 87 (1984), 42-45.

Horton, Scott. "Peru and ANCOM: A Study in the Disintegration of a Common Market," *Texas International Law Journal* 17 (1982), 39-61.

Hubène, Cécile. "Aspectos jurídicos de las relaciones entre la Comunidad Europea y el Grupo Subregional Andino," *Integración Latinoamericana* 68 (1982), 71-81.

Keener, E. Barlow. "The Andean Common Market Court of Justice: Its Purpose, Structure, and Future," *Emory Journal of International Dispute Resolutions* 2 (1987), 39-71.

Leavy, James. "Andean Pact Policy,' *International Financial Law Review*, 7:3 (1988), 36-39

Leavy, James. "Latin American Laws on Transfers of Technology," *Inter-American Legal Materials* 3 (1987), 353-492.

Leavy, James. "Legal Memoranda: Colombia: VI. Trade Policy, Redefinition of Goods of National Origin," *The University of Miami Inter-American Law Review* 17 (1986), 699-700

Lindow, Herbert A. "The Andean Pact Relaunched: Implications for the United States," *Business America* 10 (1987), 12.

Mace, Gordon. "Andean Pact: From the Common Market to the Integration System," in *Latin America and Caribbean Contemporary Record*, Jack W. Hopkins, ed. Vol. 1 (1981-82). Pp. 182-190.

"Management Alert. Andean Pact: Another Round of Talks Set," *Business Latin America* 152 (May 11, 1987).

"Management Alert. Andean Pact: Timing on ANCOM Rules," *Business Latin America* 160 (May 18, 1987).

Mateo, Fernando. "Alternativas instrumentales para la complementación industrial argentino-andina," *Integración Latinoamericana* 81 (1983), 10-26.

Morawetz, David. "Destino del miembro menos desarrollado dentro de un esquema de países de menor desarrollo: Bolivia en el Grupo Andino," *Integración Latinoamericana* 69 (1982), 4-20.

O'Leary, Timothy F. "The Andean Common Market and the Importance of Effective Dispute Resolution Procedures," *International Tax and Business Lawyer* 2 (1984), 101-128.

Palacios Maldonado, Carlos. "Bilateralismo versus multilateralismo en el Grupo Andino: Un falso dilema," *Integración Latinoamericana* 120 (1987), 40-50.

Palomino Roedel, José. "Tratamiento especial en favor de Bolivia y Ecuador en el Acuerdo de Cartagena," *Integración Latinoamericana* 69 (1982), 21-33.

Paz Cafferata, Julio. "Aplicación de regímenes de cláusulas de salvaguardia en el Grupo Andino," *Integración Latinoamericana* 129 (1987), 25-41.

Pierola, Nicolás de. "The Andean Court of Justice," *Emory Journal of International Dispute Resolution* 2 (1987), 11-37.

"Postscript. Andean Group: Trade," *Latin American Regional Reports: Andean Group* 8 (October 8, 1987).

"Postscript. Andean Pact: Setback to Agreement," *Latin American Regional Reports: Andean Group* 7 (April 9, 1987).

Rangifo, Ramiro. "The Check in the Andean Pact Countries That Have Adopted the INTAL Model: The Colombian Experience," *Arizona Journal of International and Comparative Law* (1987), 21-37.

Salazar Santos, Felipe. "Personalidad jurídica internacional de la organización creada por el Acuerdo del Cartagena," *Integración Latinoamericana* 84 (1983), 19-43.

Serrate, Oscar. "Políticas y mecanismos para el desarrollo industrial integrado en el Grupo Andino," *Integración Latinoamericana* 98 (1985), 32-41.

Thornton, Michael G. "Since the Breakup: Development and Divergences in ANCOM's and Chile's Foreign Investment Codes," *Hastings International and Comparative Law Review* 7 (1983), 239-272.

Torres, Jorge A. "Financiamiento a las exportaciones no indicionales en el mercado andino," *Integración Latinoamericana* 114 (1986), 22-34.

Vega Castro, Jorge. "Análises de la evaluación y las perspectivas de la integración andina," *Integración Latinoamericana* 87 (1984), 15-25.

Vendrell, Francesc J. "Nuevo régimen jurídico de las empresas multinacionales andinas," *Integración Latinoamericana* 40 (1983), 23-33.

"Venezuela's Fedecámaras Forces Delay in Signing of Andean Pact," *Latin American Regional Reports: Andean Group*, 1 (March 5, 1987).

Zelada Castedo, Alberto. "Cooperación política en el Grupo Andino," *Integración Latinoamericana* 83 (1983), 30-48.

Zelada Castedo, Alberto. "Cuestiones jurídicas e institucionales en el desarrollo de las relaciones externas del Grupo Andino," *Integración Latinoamericana* 92 (1984), 49-52.

Zelada Castedo, Alberto. "Posibles enmiendas del Acuerdo de Cartagena," *Integración Latinoamericana* 106 (1985), 3-20.

Zelada Castedo, Alberto. "Principio de no discriminación y la reglas del 'Standstill' en el Acuerdo de Cartagena," *Integración Latinoamericana* 90 (1984), 34-47.

Zelada Castedo, Alberto. "Proyecto de reglamento del régimen sobre cláusulas de Salvaguardia," *Integración Latinoamericana* 104 (1985), 61-64.

Zelada Castedo, Alberto. "Tratado que crea el Tribunal Andino de Justicia: Sus consecuencias en el ordenamiento jurídico del Acuerdo de Cartagena," *Integración Latinoamericana* 89 (1984), 49-54.

III. Subnational Official Publications

33. Official Publications at the Subnational Level

Laurence Hallewell

The term "nation state" embraces enormous disparities of population, area, wealth, and publishing activity. The 1,274 acres of the two islands of Sark with their 420 inhabitants are held by their feudal lords as a direct fief of Elizabeth II as heiress of William, Duke of Normandy, outside the United Kingdom, outside the European Common Market, and without even any effective administrative links with the other Channel Islands. I do not know whether this is enough to make Sark an independent sovereign state in international law, but the Vatican City with only twice Sark's population on one tenth its area, certainly is one. At the other end of the scale are China, with its 1,100 million inhabitants, and the Soviet Union, with more than 8 million square miles. Within Latin America the range is almost as great. Brazil, from which most of the examples in this paper are drawn, has close to 150 million people on 3.3 million square miles. Saint Christopher-Nevis, the Hemisphere's smallest ministate, has 45,000 inhabitants on barely a hundred square miles. Common sense might lead one to suppose that convenience, efficiency, and economy would combine to limit administration in the world's smaller sovereignties to the national level, but common sense is a poor guide to political arrangements. Saint Christopher-Nevis is in fact a federation, and one that has already lost one constituent member, the tiny island of Anguilla, which broke away and obtained restitution of its former colonial status, out of fear of excessive central control by the federal authorities on St. Kitts. A megastate, on the other hand, will often have subnational units that are as extensive, as populous, and as wealthy as many a normal-sized independent country. The state of São Paulo in Brazil, for instance, is comparable in area, population, and GDP with the Kingdom of Spain. And the powers of its government are almost commensurate. Until the 1930s São Paulo, ran its own army, incurred its own foreign debt, subsidized its own exports, levied customs duties on goods from neighboring states, and sometimes printed its own money. In 1932 it actually went to war with the rest of Brazil. It still runs its own state bank and its own "national" airline. To such international inequalities must be added disparities within each nation. A Brazilian *municipio* may number its citizens in millions—or in hundreds. It may have a dozen administrative *secretarias* or more, each with its own well-equipped printing and publishing department; or, the entire municipal apparatus may consist of just the *prefeito* and a part-time secretary, who would be fortunate to have access to a manual typewriter and a primitive wax-stencil duplicator.

Nations differ in the number of levels in their governmental structure, and again there is little correlation with overall size. Brazil has only two levels below the national: states and municipios. Chile is one tenth as big (11 million people in 300,000 square miles) but has three levels: region, province, and commune.

Nor is the size or the number of subnational units any guide to the extent and nature of their powers, and hence the importance of what they publish. In France, for instance, higher education is a matter for the central government in Paris. In the German Federal Republic it is the concern of the individual *Länder*. In Brazil there is an overlap of federal and state power in this field, with some public universities provided and funded by the federation, others by the local state authorities. Indeed one cannot even generalize that the federal universities are the more prestigious: the top university overall is USP, and the most outstanding graduate programs are at UNICAMP, both state institutions.

Such differences have little logic, but are rather the fortuitous outcome of each nation's peculiar political history. The Swiss Confederation is the classic case of extreme concentration of power at the subgovernmental (cantonal) level, despite being a relatively small country, a mere 220 miles across. The Republic of Chile in contrast stretches across forty degrees of latitude—eleven times as far—but is a model of a centralized polity, the lone star on its flag proclaiming its unitary constitution. But formal structures may be belied by actual practice, as in the case of the Estados Unidos Mexicanos, where states' rights are effectively circumscribed by the all-pervasive PRI and the power of the presidential office. And all may change over time. The nineteenth-century shifts between union and federation in Argentina and Colombia are older examples. The twentieth-century history of Spain is a more recent one. Some national histories present, overall, a long-term tendency toward greater centralization (the United States, for instance), or away from it (e.g., the Commonwealth Caribbean [1]). Other countries seem to suffer chronic oscillation: witness Brazil's successive changes of pace or direction in 1824, 1836, 1889, 1930, 1937, 1945, 1967, 1985. . . . [2]

Apart from this question of the variable importance and quantity of subnational level official publishing, the problems involved in acquiring it are basically the same as those faced in acquiring national government publications—only much more so! As products of administrative fiat, output is determined by bureaucratic norms, not commercial ones. Print runs are what the budget permits, not what the market needs. So supply of any title is either excessive or (more often) inadequate. "Publication" itself is frequently an ill-defined concept. Availability of what is neither clearly confidential, reserved for internal use, nor avowedly propagandist, devised for wide public consumption, will often depend on the persistence of the individual librarian seeking it, and on the caution or sloth, courage or irresponsibility, of the individual bureaucrat in possession of it. As with publication, the situation is similar with respect to price. This too may bear no relation to any commercial principle. Items may be free, whether for ideological reasons or from poor financial control, or they may be highly priced from a calculated policy to restrict circulation. A civil servant's ignorance of what to charge may even be his reason for refusal to make something available.

Distribution is unlikely to be well organized, at least in the case of the smaller or less affluent authorities. The publishing agent may lack any established sales office. I recall wasting a whole day visiting the widely scattered administrative buildings of a certain city council department in a vain attempt to locate the office from which its annual report emanated. If there is a sales office, it may only be geared to cope with over-the-counter sales for cash. There may be no procedure to deal with foreign checks or currency, or the paperwork involved may be too horrendous for the official to contemplate. Placing orders through book dealers is seldom a satisfactory alternative. It is a time-consuming chore for them, especially if they have to have a representative go to a sales office away from the city where they are located, and the cost of such time and effort may make the material impossibly expensive. Some agencies have a policy, especially if the material is gratis, of allowing only one copy per customer: hardly a method of business acceptable to a book dealer. Not only are dealer discounts almost unheard of, but there is sometimes a refusal to sell at all to anyone recognized as being in the commercial book trade: a bookseller is seen as someone trying to make an illegal profit by reselling government-produced goods at above their official price.

Sometimes no copies of an edition will be available for sale. The publishing agency will have distributed them all to a predetermined readership, although this may possibly include some copies for library exchange partners. I once attended a meeting between a Brazilian library school faculty and the local state secretary for education and culture regarding his publishing program of works by local literary authors. The copies that had not been donated to members of the state legislature and other local worthies had been sent out unsolicited to the state's public libraries. Unfortunately, in that very impoverished part of northeastern Brazil, most upstate public libraries are little more than bare and primitive reading rooms serving almost exclusively as convenient refuges where the less advantaged schoolchildren can go to do their homework. This state secretary had gone to visit some of these "public libraries" a few months after distributing his books. He found that none of them had ever had their pages opened, and he addressed us most eloquently on his poor *livros virgens* and what their inviolate condition implied about the utility of public libraries.

A further obstacle to the acquisition of subnational official publications is the almost total lack of information about them. Budgets are limited, so catalogs are seen as the first expense to be saved. I was frustrated at one sales office to find that the only list of the agency's publications was a much soiled and dog-eared sequence of typed sheets tied to the counter by a length of string. My request that I untie the list and take it next door to photocopy it was denied because the sales would have had to be suspended till I returned.

Government publishers are usually either ignorant of legal deposit laws or they mistakenly believe them to apply only to the commercial book trade. Hence, this material never reaches the national library or other copyright deposit center, and so does not get included in the national bibliography. Bibliographers of national government publications leave it out (even when they know it exists) because it does not emanate from the central government. Book trade bibliographies omit the material because they are not trade publications. Now and again publications of special subject interest may get recorded in national subject bibliographies, but seldom while they are still in print. Even within the local government administration itself, it may well be that no one is keeping track. Thanks in part to the greater flexibility of modern printing and documentary reproduction techniques, not only may each department of a given government be a law unto itself with respect to publishing, but the various sections of the same department may be producing material without any of them sharing the knowledge of what they are about.

Despite such problems of bibliographic control, some subnational official publishing does become fairly well known. In the field of Brazilian literature, for example, there are the literary supplements of the official gazettes of Brazil's two biggest state governments. Minas Gerais's *Suplemento literario* has long been respected, even outside

Brazil, as one of the country's leading journals of literary criticism. São Paulo,'s similar *D.O.: leitura* is becoming almost as famous. Those cases apart, however, it is only too easy to solve the problem by ignoring such intractable material entirely (something many libraries are doing already!). The very lack of bibliographic control means that many of our users will never hear of the material, anyway. Indeed, if we do collect it, we have to accept the necessary consequential task of bringing it to our patrons' attention. Nevertheless, few sources can provide more detailed or up-to-date information about a specific geographical area than the publications of its own local government. It should also be borne in mind that the international agreements that have existed for many years now for the exchange of official publications between governments (and provide some sort of excuse for their neglect on the librarian's part) relate solely and exclusively to national-level publications. Foreign, state, and municipal publications have to be collected by the efforts of individual libraries if they are to be obtained and made available at all.

Any acquisition policy needs also to be flexible, to cope with the vagaries of government publishing policies, which can change totally in quality and quantity from one administration to the next. The output of the Brazilian state of Amazonas, for instance, was almost negligible until 1964 when it was transformed by the new governor, Ferreira Reis, into one of the most active official presses in the whole country, only to lapse again on the end of his mandate in 1967 to its former torpor. [3] It should also be realized that not everything bearing the imprint of a state or local government press is necessarily an official publication. The managers of official presses often seek printing commissions from outsiders in order to keep their organizations fully employed, and in order to generate income for their employing authority during idle time.

NOTES

1. See Laurence Hallewell, "West Indian Official Publishing, and U.K. Official Publishing on the West Indies, before Independence, and after," in *Twenty Years of Latin American Librarianship: Final Report and Working Papers of the XXIst SALALM, Bloomington, IN, 1976* (Austin, TX: SALALM Secretariat, 1978), pp. 201-221.

2. General Golbery, the theorist of the 1967-1985 military regime, believed in a "natural" long-term rhythm in Brazilian politics from decentralization (and democracy) to centralization (and military rule) and back again, ad infinitum.

3. See Laurence Hallewell, *O livro no Brasil, sua história* (São Paulo: T. A. Queiroz, and Editora de Universidade de São Paulo, 1985), pp. 529, 531.

34. Documents and Publications of the Government of President Miguel de la Madrid

Flor de María Hurtado

Carlos María de Bustamante, a distinguished historian of Mexico's Independence, defines archives as "the wealth and guarantee of a nation's property." Since the colonial period, the creation of archives in Mexico has been linked to the task of governing. The oldest and most valuable archives are those that were originally administrative archives of municipalities, regions, and different state agencies. In our tradition, archives are not only a place where the historical information essential to understanding Mexico's development is gathered, but also an indispensable organizational tool for ordering and evaluating accumulated data. Progressively building up such archives should therefore be a national priority.

Upon taking office, President Miguel de la Madrid established the Centro de Documentación de la Gestión Gubernamental 1982-1988 (Government Action Documentation Center) under the Unidad de la Crónica Presidencial, in order to maintain a record of the activities of his administration, to provide a source where present and future generations may go to learn about his government's difficulties and accomplishments, and, more immediately, to set up a study center where documents and publications produced by the federal public sector may be used and consulted by researchers, journalists, and the public at large.

The concept guiding the establishment of the documentation center was based on four premises:

1. Definition of the source of materials.
2. Determination of the type of materials.
3. Establishment of a mechanism to ensure the identification and continuous delivery of such material.
4. Definition of an organizational and processing procedure for immediate retrieval.

The source of documents was defined on the basis of the agencies that comprise federal public administration: the eighteen Secretaries of State, the two Attorney Generals' Offices, the Department of the Federal District, and the Presidency of the Republic. For publications and newspaper material, the universe was expanded to include the Congress of the Union, political parties, certain State and academic publications, and certain material from commercial publishing houses.

The documentation center was essentially an administrative archive, founded on the archival principle that the value of public documents lies not only in the information that they provide, but also in their capacity to faithfully reflect the organization and operations of the government agency that produced them. It was therefore decided to compile documents by group rather than individually and to carry out related follow-up. The full meaning of the information included in each document could thus be obtained by relating it to data in other documents that refer to the same activity.

According to this criterion, the bylaws, organizational manuals, and records of the agencies of the Federal Executive Branch were analyzed in order to obtain a list of significant nonconfidential documents that reflect the internal work of administrative units up to the level of general directors. Thus, the type of documents to be gathered would include:

Regulatory documents (organizational manuals, procedural manuals, and bylaws, etc.).

Programming and budgetary documents (the public account, budgetary programs, work programs, labor reports, etc.).

Legal documents.

Statements of high-level public officials (secretaries and undersecretaries of State).

Conventions, agreements, and coordination bases.

Statistical studies and indices.

Publications and posters.

Photographic and audiovisual documents.

For purposes of locating, obtaining, and ensuring the continuous delivery of material, a mechanism was established to make government agencies responsible for the quality and quantity of material to be sent to the documentation center. An official was designated by the head of each agency to request documents within their entities and to compile, select, and deliver them. These officials decide whether the material provided actually describes the internal work in their areas; they do not leave decisions regarding the importance of a document in the hands of an infinite maelstrom of officials.

The Centro de Documentación de la Gestión is divided into three sections: documents, publications and newspapers, and videotapes. The material is channeled to the different sections according to its general classification and, within each section, it is organized according to source.

Organizing the material in this manner allows for the document section to preserve the different organizational structures of an agency during a specific period and to make the changes required, if restructuring takes place, without removing the documents from the area that produced them, even when there is an operational change in the agency. Thus, if one office merges with another as a result of restructuring, the documents produced by the office that disappears in the merger are not lost, nor are they added to those of the office into which it is incorporated. In this way, information on both the final structure and the previous structures of an office remains available. Such is the case, for example, with the Secretariat of Health, which began the de la Madrid administration with a structure that was eventually changed to reduce its areas by 29 percent during the first five years.

The publications and newspaper section comprise seven collections:

1. A newspaper library that holds the thirteen major national newspapers, approximately 150 magazine titles, and a collection of articles on Mexico published in foreign newspapers, weekly publications, and magazines.
2. Publications of the agencies of the federal public administration (monographs, series, and brochures).
3. Publications of the Congress of the Union.
4. State governors' annual reports from 1982 to 1988.
5. Publications of academic institutions on topics related to the de la Madrid administration.
6. Commercial publications on topics related to de la Madrid's administration.
7. Publications of political parties.

The material is organized by source. The same system is used to organize the cassettes (Beta, VHS, and 3/4), which contain special editions of the most significant activities of government agencies. There is also a video collection of the most important activities of President de la Madrid.

A documentation center serves its purpose when it is open to the general public as a source of information for society as a whole. Providing this kind of service required a processing system that would allow material to be retrieved rapidly and efficiently.

With the assistance of computer technicians, a program was written to identify different kinds of documents in five different ways (institution, topic, place, person, and date). Each document can also have up to five subject definitions to increase access to the information. In order to assign codes, a list of approximately 400 subject areas was developed and codes were given to each administrative area. Publications were classified and cataloged according to the Dewey decimal system. It was decided to publish quarterly catalogs to publicize the material compiled.

The results of this project, initiated five years ago, are satisfactory. The document section has approximately 35,000 documents from different agencies of the Federal Executive Branch, of which 80 percent have been cataloged and 60 percent have been microfilmed. The publications section has 7,000 volumes, of which 60 percent have been processed. The magazine collections, with 150 titles, have practically no gaps. Material may be consulted in the Center using a tested system that facilitates retrieval through nineteen document catalogs and nine publication catalogs.

Apart from the initial objectives of the documentation center, two special collections have been compiled, one containing documents and publications from the election campaign of President Miguel de la Madrid and the other consisting of material on the September 1985 earthquakes. The latter includes official documents and publications, as well as documents produced by earthquake victim groups, political parties, unions, academic centers, and international assistance organizations, among others.

At present, the Centro de Documentación de la Gestión Gubernamental 1982-1988 offers researchers, public servants, and other interested individuals a wealth of official fielded material and nonofficial material that is unique in its field. It is hoped that this information will become part of the historical record of the de la Madrid administration. Thus it will enable future generations of public servants to program their government actions on the basis of well-documented experience and will facilitate the research efforts of scholars interested in studying this period in Mexican history.

35. Survey of Subnational Official Publications from Latin America and the Caribbean

Eudora Loh and David Rozkuszka

This survey was designed to identify collections of Latin American and Caribbean subnational official publications in the United States, and to determine the concerns of librarians related to these collections. Subnational official publications are government publications from state/provincial/departmental, regional, and local/city jurisdictions.

The survey was conducted from April 15 to May 20, 1988. Questionnaires were mailed to more than 200 U.S. personal members of SALALM. In total, 31 individual responses were received representing 26 institutions. Of the 26, 17 were institutions identified by *A Directory of Latin American Studies in the United States* (David B. Bray and Richard E. Greenleaf. New Orleans, LA: Roger Thayer Stone Center for Latin American Studies, Tulane University, 1986) as having a strong commitment to Latin American studies (11 of 22 total in group I, "strongest commitment"; and 6 of 21 total in Group II, "large commitment"). The remaining 9 were in Group III or were not included in the *Directory* (e.g., the Library of Congress).

Half (13) of the responding institutions reported that they do make a deliberate effort to collect foreign official publications. In some instances, there was a conflict between stated intent to collect and actual achieved level of collecting; in other instances, there was no intention to collect, but some country holdings were reported anyway. This follows the fundamental law of surveys that there is great disparity between one's theoretical commitment and one's actual commitment.

It is noteworthy that all but one of the responding institutions that collect subnational official publications enter them into a national bibliographic utility. Some institutions are also using local systems (e.g., LC Link Project, GLADIS, MELVYL, ORION). All except two make them available through interlibrary loan.

Survey of Subnational Official Publications by Country

Subnational official publications are collected from the following jurisdictions. (Please check as appropriate):

A   State/province/department
B   Capital state only
C   Regional groupings (e.g., interstate bodies)
D   Local/cities
E   Capital city only
F   No subnational documents collected

Key to OCLC Symbols

AZS	Arizona State University	LRU	Tulane University
CLU	University of California, Los Angeles	OUN	Ohio University, Athens
		PUL	Princeton University
CUY	University of California, Berkeley	STF	Stanford University
		TJC	Vanderbilt University
DLC	Library of Congress	UIU	University of Illinois, Champaign-Urbana
HLS	Harvard University		
IUL	Indiana University	YUS	Yale University
IXA	University of Texas, Austin	ZCU	Columbia University

Country	A	B	C	D	E
Latin America (in general)	HLS, IXA, UIU		IXA, UIU	HLS, IXA, UIU	
Caribbean (in general)	HLS, IXA, UIU		IXA, UIU	HLS, IXA, UIU	
Anguilla					
Antigua & Barbuda					DLC
Argentina	AZS, CLU, DLC, OUN, PUL, STF, YUS		OUN, PUL, STF	CLU, OUN, PUL	DLC, STF
Bahamas					
Barbados					
Belize	LRU, OUN			OUN	CUY
Bermuda					
Bolivia	OUN, PUL, YUS			OUN, PUL	DLC, STF

Country	A	B	C	D	E
Brazil	CLU, DLC, IUL, OUN, PUL, STF, TJC, YUS		CUY, OUN, PUL, STF	CLU, DLC, OUN, PUL, STF	
Cayman Islands					
Chile	OUN, PUL, STF		OUN, STF	DLC, OUN, STF	PUL
Colombia	CLU, DLC, OUN, STF, TJC	PUL	STF	CLU, DLC, OUN, PUL, STF	
Costa Rica	CUY, LRU, OUN				DLC, PUL, STF
Cuba	DLC, OUN, PUL, STF			DLC, OUN, PUL, STF	
Dominica					DLC
Dominican Republic	OUN				DLC, PUL
Ecuador	OUN	PUL		DLC, OUN, PUL	STF
El Salvador	LRU, OUN	PUL			CUY, DLC, PUL, STF
Falkland Islands					
Grenada					DLC
Guatemala	CUY, LRU, OUN, TJC			OUN	CUY, DLC, PUL, STF
Guyana					DLC
Haiti	OUN	PUL		OUN	DLC, PUL
Honduras	CUY, LRU, OUN				DLC, PUL, STF
Jamaica					DLC
Mexico	AZS, CLU, CUY, DLC, IUL, OUN, PUL, STF, TJC, YUS		OUN, PUL, STF	CLU, DLC, LRU, OUN, PUL	CUY
Montserrat					DLC

Country	A	B	C	D	E
Netherlands Antilles	DLC				DLC
Nicaragua	CUY, LRU, OUN, PUL		OUN, PUL	OUN, PUL	DLC, STF
Panama	CUY, LRU, ZCU		ZCU	OUN, ZCU	DLC, PUL, STF
Paraguay	OUN			PUL	DLC, STF
Peru	AZS, OUN, PUL, STF, YUS		PUL	OUN, PUL, STF	DLC
St. Christopher-Nevis					DLC
St. Lucia					DLC
St. Vincent					DLC
Suriname	OUN				DLC
Trinidad & Tobago					DLC, PUL
Uruguay	OUN	PUL			CLU, DLC, PUL, STF
Venezuela	CLU, DLC, OUN, PUL, STF, YUS		CUY, PUL, STF	PUL, STF, OUN	DLC
Virgin Islands, British					

IV. Marginalized Peoples and Ideas

36. Documenting Brazil's Political and Social Movements, 1966-1986: The Library of Congress Experience

Lygia Maria F. C. Ballantyne

Background

In 1984, the Library of Congress Acquisitions Office in Rio de Janeiro began a systematic effort to identify, locate, and approach a group of noncommercial publishing sources whose production might be of interest to scholars engaged in studying Brazilian grass-roots sociopolitical movements.

The effort was an attempt of the office to document better the activities and ideas of a segment of Brazilian society—the organized rural and urban poor—which in 1984, after twenty years of military rule, had participated prominently in the nationwide campaign for free elections. The campaigns for Diretas Ja (Direct Elections, Now) was itself a popular movement of unprecedented magnitude which brought to the streets of every capital masses of people demanding free elections and a return to democratic rule.

While ultimately unsuccessful in bringing about a direct presidential election, these mammoth public demonstrations hastened the political transition initiated under Presidents Geisel (1975-1980) and Figueiredo (1980-1985) and permitted the inauguration, in March 1985, of the first civilian government to rule the country after a generation of military regime.

Throughout this decade of transition there was a gradual widening of politic freedoms, especially freedom of the press. The media were permitted to resume coverage of the political scene, including the activities of mass-oriented political pressure groups at the national, state, and local levels.

It was toward the written output of these groups that the Library of Congress Rio Office directed its collecting activities, in an effort to cover their views, long suppressed, on old issues, and to document attitudes on new issues that emerged from the shadows onto the political stage.

For example, the long-suppressed debate over land reform in Brazil resurfaced with intensity amidst new outbreaks of violence in the countryside. Urban issues and problems such as overpopulation, lack of adequate infrastructure of services, substandard housing, organized crime, homelessness, abandoned children, and drugs gained increasing urgency. The environmental cost of unrestrained rapid industrial and agricultural development which had been official policy since the 1950s began to be questioned. Finally, the enormous social debt in health, education, housing, and income distribution which the country had accumulated during the years of the "economic miracle" was brought before the nation's consciousness.

The Popular Groups

Against this backdrop, our collecting effort began to identify the popular organizations and to seek their publications. We defined our target as any political, labor, community, or religious entity devoted to furthering the causes of the country's underrepresented and underserved classes and minority groups.

The spectrum was very wide. It included seven groups (the Bibliographic Notes contain sources covering the subjects discussed):

1.   The traditional Marxist parties and their splinter groups, which have been clandestine for much of Brazil's modern history most recently throughout the period of military domination, 1964-1985. [1]

2.   Rural and urban labor unions and their central organizations, the Confederação Nacional dos Trabalhadores na Agricultura (CONTAG), Central Unica dos Trabalhadores (CUT), and Confederação Geral dos Trabalhadores (CGT), which are increasingly active in politics as well. [2]

3. The Partido dos Trabalhadores (PT), a militant workers party, which grew out of the autoworkers union of the State of São Paulo and CUT, and which has been gaining in political importance with every new election. [3]

4. A variety of urban groups struggling for better social services, such as neighborhood organizations, slum-dwellers and squatter-rights' associations, consumers' leagues, and environmental protection advocates. [4]

5. The human rights and minority defense groups (including the women's movement, gay rights, Indian and black organizations), which seek equal treatment under law, better employment opportunities, and greater participation in national politics. [5]

6. Information centers that collect data, conduct research, disseminate information, and provide technical training and education in support of social reform. [6]

7. Groups, operating under the liberal wing of the Catholic Church, whose activities overlap those of the previously mentioned organizations. These include the Comunidades Eclesiais de Base (CEBs), the Comissões Pastorais da Terra (CPTs), and the well-known Conferencia Nacional dos Bispos do Brasil (CNBB).

Their Publications

From the early days of our collecting effort it became evident that the new sources we were tapping were producing a body of literature much weightier than we had suspected. It was also clear that these publications would not easily fit conventional methods of bibliographic control. Special handling was required, and we decided to treat the materials as a collection. [7]

One characteristic of these publications is their generally instructional tone: they seek to reach the masses, educate them as to their rights, and organize them into self-help and political pressure groups. In pursuit of these goals, several approaches are reflected in the collection which may be grouped into four overall categories:

1. Analytical literature: results of field research, situation analysis, statistical reports, and studies of issues and facts generally produced by the research and documentation centers.

2. Prescriptive literature: textbooks, civic education manuals, political platforms, calls for action, pastoral letters, sermons, resolutions of congresses, models for unions' statutes, guides for holding prayer meetings.

3. Informative literature: church bulletins, independent news services, newsletters, house organs, newspaper coverage services, collections of clippings or dossiers on specific issues or facts, bibliographies, catalogs of publications, explanations of government policies, legislation of interest to the groups, and how-to and self-help guides.

4. Creative literature: retellings of biblical stories in the context of Liberation Theology, songbooks, poems, dramatizations of events and of situations affecting the groups.

Geographically, all regions and almost all states of Brazil are represented in the collection. As would be expected, a sizable group of materials come from areas where the popular movements have already demonstrated their strength or have been long established (for example, the State of São Paulo, and Rio's poor suburbs, the *baixada fluminense*), and from areas of chronic tension or where armed conflicts have erupted in the past (the Northeast, Amazon's Araguaia region). [8]

These materials are profusely illustrated with original drawings, photographs, and cartoons; some are in popular verse. Their style and vocabulary reflect their geographic regions or origin. Quality of the printed materials varies widely from mimeographed sheets and amateurishly produced bulletins to sophisticated newspapers and good-quality printed pamphlets, many of which have been run off on the commercial presses of the three major Catholic publishers (Vozes, Paulinas, and Loyola).

As for span of coverage, most of the materials acquired dated from the 1980s. However, we obtained many titles published as far back as the mid-sixties, when the first Comunidades Eclesiais de Base were established in Brazil. The materials attest to the unique role the Catholic Church has played in Brazil during the past twenty years—its quiet reformist-oriented, educational, and organizing efforts at the grass-roots level, as well as its open condemnation of human rights abuses. [9]

The publications also document the gradual liberalization of the regime, the emergence of new political parties, the strengthening of the independent labor movement, the reestablishment of direct elections for governorships, the transition to civil rule in 1985, and the election of a Constitutional Assembly in October 1986.

Organizing the Collection

In consultation with the Library of Congress, we in Rio decided that a chronological arrangement, within broad subject categories, would show this material best, giving the researcher a sense of perspective and change.

The major themes suggested themselves from the start: land reform, human rights, political issues, labor concerns, religion and theology. We later expanded these five original subject groups by separating materials dealing specifically with the situation of women, blacks, and Indians, and by creating special groups to cover urban matters and education and communication issues.

Some overlap of subjects could not be avoided. For instance, one could argue that the whole collection is about human rights, and not only the specific topics Human and Minority Rights, Blacks, Indians, and Women. Similarly, the researcher studying the role of the Catholic Church in Brazil will find materials of interest relating to the Church in all ten subject categories from Agrarian Reform to Women.

Within each subject group, pamphlets were arranged by date of publication, followed by serials arranged alphabetically by title. Each subject group is preceded by a Contents List describing the pamphlets and serials included, in the order in which they were microfilmed.

In addition, the Rio office prepared an Author, a Title, and a Publisher Index describing the whole collection, which was filmed in the first reel. In all, the Brazil's Popular Groups collection contains 2,271 items and is expected to occupy 27 reels of microfilm.

Importance of the Collection

In collecting, organizing, indexing, and filming this material, the Library of Congress is making accessible to a much wider community a body of primary source material in areas that are of considerable interest to scholarship.

In Brazil, historians and political and social scientists are producing increasing numbers of serious studies that focus on the activities of the organized popular groups. Also increasing is the number of research centers and academic programs dedicated to the study of minority groups and political and social movements. This trend is documented in Brazilian dissertation catalogs, bibliographies, and social science indexes which are full of references indicating that the academic community has found in the popular movements of the past twenty-five years a fascinating object of investigation. [10]

It is notable that many of these scholarly or analytical studies are being conducted by researchers who are themselves closely identified with the causes that have ignited the popular movements. Moreover, some of the more interesting analyses are coming from within the ranks of the Brazilian Catholic Church, whose association with Liberation Theology inspired and guided these movements.

The popular materials that we began collecting in 1984 complemented the scholarly studies that we were also acquiring, by supplying the human voices and faces and the real-life problems that were behind the object of study.

This particular collection effort also illuminated the relationships between the Brazilian popular organizations as well as their counterparts in other Latin American countries and their "first world" supporters. For example, the Brazilian material contained many references to titles similar to those being issued elsewhere in Latin America. Focusing on this area, I have compiled the references to serial publications issued in countries other than Brazil, and prepared two preliminary checklists: one on women and feminist organizations, with 111 entries and the other on the alternative press in Latin America, including 189 titles issued by popular organizations of every type. [11]

The volume, variety, and widespread geographic distribution of these publications are measures of the mobilization of the poor and marginalized segments of Latin American society. These lists, which were compiled almost entirely from references found in the Brazilian materials, could easily be doubled in size if a systematic research were to be undertaken.

In Brazil alone, these segments comprise millions of people—perhaps the majority of the population—and are evidence that they feel they were denied the benefits of the so-called economic miracle that propelled the country to the position of eighth largest economy in the non-Communist world. Traditionally underrepresented or excluded from the nation's decision-making process throughout modern Brazilian history, these groups have recently made great strides toward organizing themselves to press for inclusion in the political equation.

One of the salient questions currently asked regarding the future of this huge country is whether these groups will be successfully incorporated into the mainstream or whether they will continue to be underserved, underrepresented, alienated, and marginalized, and, if so, what the consequences will be. These documents, we believe, may assist scholars who are focusing on these issues.

BIBLIOGRAPHIC NOTES

1. For a review and analysis of the parties, splinter groups, and other clandestine left-wing organizations during the military period see Jacob Gorender, *Combate nas Trevas: a esquerda brasileira das ilusões perdidas à luta armada* (São Paulo: Atica, 1987), 255 pp.

2. A survey of the Brazilian labor movement, including statistics, political tendencies, and biographical sketches, accompanied by pictures, of the major union leaders, appears in "Quem comanda os sindicatos," *Exame*, October 30, 1985, pp. 36-42.

3. Ibid.

4. Some of these urban groups, and their causes, are studied in:

   a. Movimentos populares no Brasil: III Semana de Estudos Maria Augusta Albano, Rio de Janeiro, 27 a 31 de maio de 1985, Coleção Temas Sociais/CBCISS, no. 19 (Rio de Janeiro: Centro Brasileiro de Cooperação e Intercambio de Serviços Sociais-CBCISS, 1985), 119 pp.

   b. Pedro Roberto Jacobi, "Movimentos sociais urbanos no Brasil," *BIB—Boletim Informativo e Bibliográfico de Ciências Sociais*, 9 (1980), 22-30.

   c. Lucio Kowarick, "Movimentos urbanos no Brasil contemporáneo: uma análise da literatura," *Revista Brasileira de Ciências Sociais*, 1:3 (February 1987), 38-50.

   d. Renato Raul Boschi, *A arte da associação: política de base e democrácia no Brasil* (Rio de Janeiro: Instituto Universitário de Pesquisas do Rio de Janeiro; São Paulo: Vértice, 1987).

     e. Eduardo J. Viola, "O movimento ecológico no Brasil (1974-1986): do ambientalismo à ecopolítica," *Revista Brasileira de Ciências Sociais,* 1:3 (February 1987), 5-26. Traces the history of the ecological movement in Brazil, its phases, tendencies, and major fronts of action. Includes a description of the birth of the Partido Verde and an extensive bibliography.

     5. *a.* A directory and a profile of black organizations in Brazil appear in Caetana Damasceno, Micenio Santos, e Sonia Giacomini, *Catálogo de entidades de movimento negro no Brazil, precedido de um perfil das entidades dedicadas a questão do negro no Brazil,* Comunicações do ISER, 29, (Rio de Janeiro: Instituto de Estudos da Religião, Programa Religião e Negritude Brasileira, 1988), 89 pp. Lists 573 groups, 80 percent of which are located in four states (40 percent in São Paulo, 22 percent in Rio de Janeiro, 10 percent in Minas Gerais, and 8 percent in Bahia). Includes a list of publications issued by these groups.

     b. Lidia Izabel da Luz, "Fontes de informação sobre populações indígenas no Brasil," in *A questão indígena na sala de aula: subsídios para professores de 1º e 2º graus,* Aracy Lopes da Silva, org., prefácio, Frei Betto (São Paulo, Brasiliense: Comissão Pro-Indio, 1987), pp. 219-253. Lists the historical, contemporary, literary, and analytical bibliography about Indians, as well as videos and films, museums, Indian groups, and other organizations that defend the rights of the Indian nations. Titles listed are available from publishers or vendors. Includes an extensive list of Brazilian social science journals that publish material on Indians.

     6. *a.* For a list of such centers, including their addresses, areas of interest, services, collections, and publications, see "Diretório de Centros de Documentação em Movimentos Sociais" (São Paulo, Centro de Estudos de Cultura Contemporánea, 1985), 37 leaves, mimeo.

     b. *Entidades cristãs de comunicação social no Brasil* (São Paulo, Paulinas, 1986), 199 pp. A directory of Christian (mostly Catholic) communication agencies, including documentation centers, news services, publishers, printers, periodicals, radio and television producers and stations, video and film procedures, and training centers.

     c. *Centros de documentação alternativos: algumas questões,* 2a ed., Memória/CEDI, v. 1, no. 7 (Rio de Janeiro: Centro Ecuménico de Documentação e Informação, 1984), 26 leaves. Describes the mission, organization, and services rendered by the documentation centers identified with the popular movements. Includes a useful table comparing the different types of centers and a discussion of their philosophy.

     d. Seminario de Documentação Alternativa, 1st, Rio de Janeiro, 1984, *Relatório* (Rio de Janeiro: Centro Ecuménico de Documentação e Informação, Setor de Documentação, 1985); (Memoria/CEDI, v. 2, no. 10, Nov. 1985), Circulação Interna. The major issues discussed during this seminar were: What types of sources to give priority within the documentation centers; what to collect and what to discard; what techniques to use to process the materials; how the centers should exchange publications and information. The report includes descriptions of the major activities and philosophies of a dozen centers that participated in the seminar.

     e. Pedro Pontual, "Algumas reflexões sobre o papel e atuação dos centros de assessoria, pesquisa e educação popular na conjuntura brasileira" (São Paulo, Centro de Educação Popular do Instituto Sedes Sapientiae, 1985); (Documento/CEPIS, no. 1), 10 pp., mimeo. An analysis of the historical development of these popular centers, their role and activities, as well as the major issues and policies presently confronting them.

     f. Justino Alves Lina, "SEDIPO/Serviço de Documentação e Informação Popular: a informação a serviço das organizações populares," *Revista Brasileira de*

Biblioteconomia e Documentação, 19:1/4 (dez. 1986), 32-49. Describes one of the most important and active centers serving the popular movements in the northeast of the country, maintained by the Catholic Church in Recife.

　　g. "10 anos de CEDI: serviços as igrejas e movimentos populares, 1974-1984," *Tempo e Presençá*, 192 (junho/julho 1984). Describes ten years of activities—major programs, philosophy, library services, and publishing output—of the most important research and documentation center linked to the Protestant Church. Includes an account of the financing of the organization.

　　h. "No CPV, a primeira distribuidora de publicações populares," in *Comunicação Popular e Alternativa no Brasil*, Regina Festa e Carlos Eduardo Lins da Silva, orgs. (São Paulo: Paulinas, 1986), pp. 184-189. São Paulo's Centro Pastoral Vergueiro, maintained by the Catholic Church, is not only the first distributor of popular publications, but probably the largest in the country. The article describes its beginnings as a documentation center, publisher, and clearinghouse for the distribution of other centers' publications, includes some hard-to-find statistics about the subject.

　　7. Some interesting studies of popular publications are contained in:

　　a. Frei Betto, "Comunicação popular e igreja," in *Comunicação Popular e Alternativa no Brasil*, pp. 99-117. A detailed look at the functioning of the Comunidades Eclesiais de Base, especially at the nature of their internal communication process. Describes the See-Judge-Act method practiced inside the communities, their communications with the Church as an institution, and the written and oral documentation produced by members of the community.

　　b. Regina Festa, "Movimentos sociais, comunicação popular e alternativa," in *Comunicação Popular e Alternativa no Brasil*, pp. 9-30. Traces the development of the popular media from 1968 to 1983, and its relationship to the publications and the major actors in the establishment of popular or alternative means of communication.

　　c. Ismar de Oliveira Soares, "Os periódicos editados pela igreja no Brazil," in *Puebla/Brasil: comunicação, um estudo crítico*, Clarencio Neotti, org. (São Paulo, Loyola, 1981), pp. 104-114. Contains statistical data and lists of periodicals published by the Catholic Church in Brazil.

　　d. Clarencio Neotti, "Editoras católicas no Brasil," in *Puebla/Brasil: comunicação, um estudo crítico*, pp. 122-128.

　　8. *a.* In the Baixada Fluminense (1240 km2, pop. 2,650,000), there are 500 Comunidades Eclesiais de Base (CEBs) and 300 neighborhood associations, according to Orivaldo Perin, "Baixada Fluminense reage e cobra promessas políticas," *Jornal do Brasil*, July 12, 1987, 1º caderno, p. 14.

　　b. The State of São Paulo has 6,800 CEBs and one of the poor neighborhoods on the outskirts of São Paulo has 129 CEBs, according to Augusto Ferreira Neto and Sebastião Garcia, *Desenvolvimento comunitário: princípios para a ação* (Rio de Janeiro: Bloch), 207 pp.

　　c. Gustavo Correia de Camargo, "O avanço dos progressistas," in *Parlamento: Revista de Política*, 74 (1986), 16-18. Reports on the Brazilian Bishops' 24th General Assembly (Itaici, São Paulo, April 1986), states that the Church estimates the CEBs involve 4.5 million people, in groups of thirty, spread throughout the whole country.

　　9. The role of the Catholic Church in Brazil in the past twenty years and the Church/State relationship are discussed in:

　　a. A igreja nas bases em tempo de transição (1974-1985), Paulo Krischke e Scott Mainwaring, orgs. (Porto Alegre: L&PM; São Paulo: CEDEC, 1986), 208 pp.

b.   *Parlamento: Revista de Política*, 74 (1986). Whole issue on the Brazilian Catholic Church.

c.   Leonardo Boff, *Igreja, carisma e poder: ensaios de eclesiologia militante* (Petrópolis: Vozes, 1981), 249 pp.

d.   Fernando Bastos de Avila, *Igreja e estado no Brazil: perspectivas e prospectivas* (São Paulo: Loyola, 1987).

e.   Marcos de Castro, *A igreja e o autoritarismo*, prefácio de Frei Betto, *A igreja vista por dentro* (Rio de Janeiro: J. Zahar, 1985), 95 pp. Brasil, os anos do autoritarismo: analise, balanço, perspectivas.

f.   Ivo Lesbaupin, "A igreja e os movimentos populares urbanos," *Religião e Sociedade*, 5 (1980).

g.   Anna Luiza Salles Souto, "Movimentos populares e suas formas de organização ligadas à igreja," *Ciências Sociais Hoje*, 2 (1983), 63-95.

10.   Official (i.e., government) interest in the issues and problems behind social mobilization has also increased, especially in states like São Paulo and Rio de Janeiro. For an interesting perspective on government analysis and action directed at such problems, particularly in urban areas, see the quarterly *São Paulo em Perspectiva: Revista de Fundação SEADE*, 1–:1– (April/June 1987–).

11.   The following bibliographies are useful for the study of political and social movements in Brazil:

a.   Centro Informação Mulher, *Catálogo 1985* (São Paulo: CIM, 1986), 192 pp. Lists 1519 books and pamphlets, 680 periodical articles, and 400 serial titles on women.

b.   *Movimentos sociais urbanos: levantamento bibliográfico*, CEDEC documentção, 6 (São Paulo: Centro de Estudos de Cultura Contemporánea, 1985), 79 leaves.   A catalog of CEDEC's collection on this subject, including references to articles found in 27 major journals, daily newspapers, monographic series, and papers presented to seminars.

c.   Lucio Kowarcik, "Movimentos urbanos no Brasil contemporáneo: uma análise da literatura (see n. 4*c* above). Reviews 69 studies on the subject.

d.   Elimar Pinheiro do Nascimento, "Movimentos sociais urbanos no Nordeste: menos que um balanço crítico, mais que uma resenha," in *Rural urbano: movimentos sociais para alem de uma dicotomia a rural urbano* (Recife: Lider, 1985), pp.. 22-31. Lists 27 studies.

e   Renato Raul Boschi, *A arte da associação: política de base e democrácia no Brasil* (see n. 4*d*, above). Lists 71 studies by Brazilian authors in its extensive bibliography.

11.   *a.*   Lygia Maria F. C. Ballantyne, "The Alternative Press in Latin America: A Checklist of Current Serials" (see chap. 39, below).

b.   _____ . "Women in Latin America: A Checklist of Current Serials" (see chap. 40, below).

37. Catholic Literature of Popular Religiosity, Clerical Activism, and the Catholic Church's Social Role

Rafael E. Tarragó

Because of the size of the Roman Catholic Church's professed membership and the influence that members of its hierarchy still exercise in some Latin American countries, the Catholic Church is hardly a marginalized group in Latin America. If one looks at the subject matter of the research being done on Latin America, however, it becomes evident that research on the Church is indeed marginal. In terms of the nature of such research, most is historical, or refers to the hierarchy of the Church, to the Church as an institution-power contender, or to the activities of religious orders. While it is true that there recently has been a proliferation of studies on Liberation Theology, and grass-roots developments such as the base communities (*comunidades eclesiais de base/comunidades eclesiásticas de base*), the social role of the Church can be termed a marginalized subject of research.

I do not attempt to survey the history of this social role, which some authors have traced back to Father Las Casas' campaign for the human rights of native Americans at the time of the conquests by the Castilians. Nor do I analyze present developments throughout Latin America. The subject of this presentation is humbler: to give an overview of the various types of bibliographic materials on the subject, and to note the perspectives from which it is approached by different sectors within the Catholic Church—because the Catholic Church is a big house with many rooms.

The term "social role" here means concern for social justice—with social issues like divorce and abortion ruled out. This concern in the Catholic Church in Latin America started from the top. In contemporary times we find its origins right after the issuing of the encyclical (letter) "Rerum novarum" by Pope Leo XIII in 1891. The most recent papal encyclical is "On Social Concern," by Pope John Paul II, issued in December of 1987. After World War II , the development of Christian Democratic parties gave to this concern a political base, but it was not until the 1950s, with the promotion of Catholic Action that Catholic laity began to take an active part in the promotion of social justice "as Catholics." What we see today is part of a long process, not something that happened overnight.

The bibliographic material includes official groups like the Latin American Bishops' Council, theological ideologies such as those illustrated by publications of proliberation theology entities like the Centro de Estudios y Publicaciones and, from a more traditional theological angle, by the Facultad Teológica de Lima. Various research institutes produce working papers or serial publications analyzing the subject from the point of view of the social sciences, such as the ISER in Rio de Janeiro. Other institutes study grass roots groups within the Church, or publish materials for consciousness raising. Then there is ephemera published by the grass roots groups themselves. During a recent visit to six Latin American countries, I observed the variety of the bibliographic materials produced by various Catholic groups, and the wide spectrum of perspectives within the Catholic literature on social justice. The following are some of my findings:

The Conferencia Episcopal Latinoamericana (Latin American Bishops' Council) has its headquarters in Bogotá, Colombia, where it publishes a wide variety of materials as well as its official proclamations, a bulletin, and the proceedings of its conferences (the latest one was held at Puebla, Mexico, in 1979). These publications are essential for the study of the social role of the Catholic Church in Latin America, but they represent only an "official voice."

Several institutes throughout Latin America publish materials of a socio- or politicotheological nature. The Centro de Investigaciones y Educación Popular (CINEP) in Bogotá publishes a numbered series of working papers of that nature, as well as pamphlets for social-consciousness raising, some of them in comic book format. The Instituto Bartolomé de las Casas in Lima publishes the bimonthly *Páginas*, and a series of working papers. In Brazil, the Instituto de Estudos da Religião in Rio publishes a monograph series and a journal. In Chile, the Instituto Latinoamericano de Doctrina y Estudios Sociales publishes working papers. Not all of these centers are in capital cities. In Peru, the Centro de Estudios Teológicos de la Amazonia (CETA) in Iquitos is located in a less than central location.

The Centro de Estudios y Publicaciones (CEP) in Lima is a publishing entity dedicated to the publication of Liberation Theology and of works in the social sciences related to the Church and her social role in Latin America. CEP issues catalogs of their publications. The Brazilian equivalent of the CEP is Editora Vozes. This publishing entity has an impressive catalog of titles by Brazilian theologians and social scientists interested in the social role of the Church, as well as translations from the Spanish of works by Spanish Americans. Another important publisher of works on this topic is Editora Paz e Terra in São Paulo.

A very important information source for the study of the social role of Catholics in Latin America is the Secretariado Latinoamericano Pax Romana—MIE-JECI in Lima. This documentation center has been collecting materials on the involvement of Catholics (mainly student movements) in social issues in Latin America since 1967. They do not publish, but upon request they will photocopy materials in their collection.

Some Catholic institutions involved in social action do publish. One example is the Vicaria de la Solidaridad in Santiago de Chile, an association that works in behalf of human rights in Chile. The Vicaria publishes a monthly bulletin. Many grass roots groups publish bulletins and newsletters which, although difficult to monitor, are very important for understanding the operation and ideologies of groups that are becoming increasingly important in the political life of their countries, and in the life of the Roman Catholic Church. A selected list of institutions and publishers is given in the appendix below.

APPENDIX
Selected Institutes and Publishers

Centro de Estudios Teológicos de la Amazonia (CETA)
Putumayo 355
Iquitos, Peru

Centro de Estudios y Publicaciones (CEP)
Jirón Lampa 808
Oficina 601
Apartado 6118
Lima 100, Peru

Centro de Investigaciones y Educación Popular (CINEP)
Carriera 5a, no. 33A-08
Bogotá, Colombia

Instituto Bartolomé de las Casas
Ricardo Quentin #763
Rimac
Lima, Peru

Instituto de Estudos da Religião
Largo de Machado 21
Rio de Janeiro: R.J., Brazil

Instituto Latinoamericano de Doctrina y Estudios Sociales
Almirante, Barroso 6
Casilla 26-D
Santiago, Chile

Secretariado Latinoamericano Pax Romana—MIE-JECI
Belisario Flores
Apartado 140330
Lima, Peru

Vicaria de la Solidaridad
Plaza de Armas #444, 2° piso
Casilla 1444-6 Correo 21
Santiago, Chile

Editora Vozes
Rua Frei Luis 100
25600 Petropolis, RJ, Brazil

38. Resources and Collection Development Strategies of Social and Political Fringe Organizations

Angela M. Carreño

This paper draws upon the experience of persons from a number of activist organizations of the solidarity type and from small private research organizations. By means of a combination of correspondence, telephone calls, and on-site visits, I have pulled together information on some centers and their strategies for collecting elusive material on new social movements in Latin America. My own experience as a reference librarian and bibliographer has been frustrating when it comes to providing coverage for topics related to new social movements, despite the fact that I have a pretty wide safety net with the New York Public Library and the Columbia Libraries within a commuting distance of five miles. The frustration led me to take a closer look at the wealth of information provided by some of the smaller, often overlooked centers, particularly the ones in New York. The centers I chose to look at all maintain a library of sorts.

In this paper I discuss briefly what I mean by new social movements and describe the library and publication activities of a few centers, including some of their strategies for identifying and acquiring material outside the standard trade networks.

By new social movements I mean sociopolitical, religious, labor, human rights, and minority grass roots organizations formed since 1970. These groups would include: workers' associations organizing independent of and even in opposition to traditional trade union structures and political parties; squatter movements and neighborhood councils springing up in virtually all the large cities; the base level communities within the Catholic Church; indigenous associations appearing autonomously on the political scene; women's associations and feminist groups; human rights committees converting themselves into focal points of social communication and consciousness; coalitions for the defense of regional traditions and interest; and a patchwork of self-help groups among unemployed and poor people.

The new social movements attract a great deal of attention from social scientists and policy makers. Major newspapers in the United States routinely carry articles on groups such as the Miskito Indian, the

Mothers of the Plaza, or the Sendero Luminoso. Some of these new social movements are seen as having contributed to the erosion of military rule in several Latin American countries. They may inhibit or foster a more democratic political culture in the future. Clearly they are significant to social scientists today, and will be studied by historians in the future.

For a basic understanding of a particular social movement, information is needed on its public policy impact (significant vs. weak), social base (popular class or middle sectors), and size. Also necessary is a social, cultural, political, and economic context in which the movement operates, preferably at a regional or local level. Finally, information is needed on the movement's leadership, activities, stated goals, and vision of society and social transformation.

The hows and wheres of this sort of information are bewildering. Identifying and collecting potentially valuable sources on new social movements are challenges that few research libraries can consistently meet. The information is typically unpublished or quasi-published material that cannot be obtained through the usual bookselling channels, and is rarely incorporated into the large databases or standard reference sources. Many publications are even issued clandestinely, and important publishing activity occurs among exile and solidarity groups outside the country involved. Occasional papers, working papers, organizational documents and minutes, preprints, transcripts from media programs, texts of speeches, annual reports, conference proceedings and papers presented at learned meetings are all examples of what may form this critical body of information.

In 1987 I wrote, telephoned, and visited a number of activist organizations of the solidarity type and a few small research organizations. All of them, I assumed, focused a lot of energy on identifying and acquiring material outside standard trade networks. They had, I guessed, the formal and informal networks in place to facilitate the collection of this material. My purpose was threefold. One, I was interested in their strategies for identifying and acquiring material on political and social fringe movements. Two, I was interested in what makes their collections unique and helps to fill gaps in the research libraries. And, three, I was interested in whether they published materials on political and social fringe movements.

Sixteen centers were contacted (see Appendix). In New York I personally visited the Center for Migration Studies, the Center for Cuban Studies, the Research Institute for the Study of Man, the North American Congress on Latin America, and the Ecumenical Committee on the Andes.

The Center for Migration Studies Library includes approximately 18,000 books; 250 periodicals; 115 newsletters; 35 newspapers; press dossiers; conference proceedings; foreign and U.S. government documents; and vertical file materials. All the material relates to sociodemographic, historical, economic, political, legislative, and pastoral aspects of international migration and refugee movements. It receives documents daily from around the globe via a network of contacts established and maintained through: (1) its two journals, *International Migration Review* and *Migration World*, and (2) the sponsorship of, and participation in, a host of national and international conferences. Further, CMS Library maintains regular exchange agreements with most major specialized libraries and research centers in Latin America. I counted 28, but this is a conservative estimate. The Center also benefits from a network of affiliated Centers for Migration Studies, including the ones in São Paulo, and Buenos Aires. The Center publishes five to seven texts annually which range from conference proceedings, oral histories, and scholarly monographs to bibliographies and organization directories. Two recent publications and a forthcoming one are of particular interest: *Refugees: Holdings of the Center for Migration Studies Library/Archives*; *A Directory of International Migration Study Centers, Research Programs and Library Resources*; and *When Borders Don't Divide: Labor Migration and Refugee Movement in the Americas*, edited by Patricia R. Pessar.

The Research Institute for the Study of Man has an outstanding library collection for the Caribbean area. The collection includes a wide range of scholarly publications. There are more than 20,000 volumes, extensive reprint files, a comprehensive collection of West Indian periodicals, official documents, conference proceedings, and dissertations. The geographic areas covered include Surinam, French Guiana, Guyana, Belize, Bermuda, the Bahamas, and the islands of the Antillean Archipelago, with the exception of the Spanish-speaking territories. An important corollary of regular library activities has been the generation of specialized bibliographies. Lambros Comitas, the Director of the Institute, has prepared the West Indies ethnology sections of the *Handbook of Latin American Studies*, and produced a standard reference tool, *The Complete Caribbeana*, a four-volume bibliographic guide to scholarly literature on the Caribbean. A glance through this bibliography gives an idea of the breadth and depth of the collection. In addition, I have obtained a list of periodical titles and recent acquisitions lists. In the New York area, many of these periodicals are only available at the Institute. In the acquisitions lists, the two sections "Social Classes and Groups," and "Reprints, Pamphlets, etc." are of particular interest.

The Center for Cuban Studies maintains the Lourdes Casal Library. The Library includes books, journals, and newspapers, vertical files, graphics, and photographic archives. There is an emphasis on the post-1959 period. The classification schedule of the vertical files includes the subjects "Popular Power," "Human Rights," "Exiles and Solidarity Groups," "Agrarian Struggles," "Agrarian Workers," "Non-Agricultural Workers," and "Women." The Center's publications catalog gives an idea of recent library acquisitions. The catalog contains an excellent list of Cuban films available for sale. The Center organizes special-interest and professional visits to Cuba on a regular basis. These trips are used for maintaining contacts, and for acquiring material. The Center publications include the bimonthly *Cuba Update*, the more specialized and occasional *Cuba in Focus*, and bibliographic lists.

The library of the Ecumenical Committee on the Andes, or ECO-Andes, was founded in 1983. Sister Bernadette Desmond maintains the library with volunteer help. The objective of ECO-Andes is to educate the U.S. public by presenting social justice issues of the Andean Region from the perspective of the poor in those countries, particularly through its bimonthly publication *Andean Focus*. Sister Bernadette lived in Peru for more than twenty years, has an extensive network of contacts in Ecuador, Peru, and Bolivia, and regularly receives information from her contacts. The key people in her network of contacts are men and women who worked in missions in the Andean region, missioners home on leave, and people currently in missions in the region. In the U.S. she works closely with what she calls the faith community. This would include organizations such as the Washington Office on Latin America (WOLA), the Maryknoll Sisters, and the Interchurch Committee on Human Rights. She collects information from and on women's groups, human rights groups, worker associations, community organizations, and violent movements such as the Sendero Luminoso. The library includes periodicals, newsletters, a small collection of monographs, and vertical file material. The most useful reference tool for her purposes is the *Informativo Mensual de la Asociación Nacional de Centros de Investigación, Promoción Social y Desarrollo*. The *Informativo Mensual* follows the activities of Centers primarily in the Andean region.

When I visited the North American Congress on Latin America, I was informed that its library would be put into storage. NACLA would continue to publish the journal, but the library would be inaccessible.

Facing severe funding shortages, the journal operation moved to smaller quarters near Columbia University. Fortunately, NACLA has now found a public space for their library collection at Borinquen, a Puerto Rican Center. The impact of the separation of the journal operation from the library collection is yet to be determined. Clearly, however, the journal was used as a tool for the generation of new acquisitions. Most of the serials arrived on exchange for the journal, the vertical file was based on topics covered in the journal, and gifts arrived mainly from people familiar with the journal.

The Data Center is a user-supported, public-interest library. It gets its funds from individual and organizational annual memberships; sale of publications, corporate profiles; grants; and sliding-scale charges for various computer and file searches. Their primary aim is to provide information critical to those "working for reform." The Data Center Library receives more than 350 newspapers and periodicals representing a broad range of political perspectives. The publications are received, clipped, filed, and made available to the public by a staff of eleven. The Latin American material is organized by country with subcategories for "Human and Political Rights," "Political Parties and Movements," "Social Groups and Classes," and "Social Issues.' A significant portion of this material is made available in research libraries through subscriptions to the Center's clipping services: *Information Services Latin America* and *Central America Monitor*.

Human Rights Internet alerted me to the fact that a substantial portion of their material is available on microfiche from the Inter Documentation Company in Switzerland. Human Rights Internet serves as an unofficial depository for the documentation produced by nongovernmental human rights organizations throughout the world. They have published a directory for Latin American organizations which gives some idea of their coverage.*

Finally I would like to present verbatim excerpts from two letters which portray the enormity of the task. One is from William Ratliff, Curator for Latin America, Hoover Institution on War, Revolution and Peace, and the other is from Caese Linda Levo, Librarian, Canada-Latin America Resource Centre, Toronto.

---

*Larie S. Wiseberg and Harry M. Scoble, eds., *Human Rights Directory: Latin America, Africa, Asia* (Washington, DC: Human Rights Internet, 1981).

Hoover Institution

"1. Most of Latin America has an abundance of nontrade literature and ephemera (posters, throwaways, etc.); the quantity is particularly great just now in Central America. For collecting this kind of material on a regular basis we rely heavily on our vendor in San José, Costa Rica, named Fred Morgner (Literatura de Vientos Tropicales, AP. 186, Codigo 1017, San José 2,000). Fred is from the States, but has lived in San José for some years now, first working for another bookdealer and then going out on his own. He has proven to be very resourceful in acquiring publications produced by both mainstream and obscure political and other groups, including such underground revolutionary organizations as the FMLN in El Salvador.

"In order to obtain materials of a nonstandard nature, I have found it useful to establish personal contacts in Mexico, Costa Rica, Panama, and some other countries in the region and beyond. These contacts have been made and/or cultivated during trips to the region, which were devoted partly to research and partly to library work. Since my return to the Hoover Institution full time about 18 months ago, I have been to the Caribbean once, South America once, Mexico twice, and Central America/Panama twice. These contacts are especially valuable for gathering politically sensitive items such as circulars and placards released during protest meetings and street demonstrations.

"2. Apart from pamphlets, specialized newspapers and books, we try to collect all forms of political ephemera, including posters, placards, circulars as well as video and cassette recordings. This may be done on a piecemeal basis or through the acquisition of collections that contain standard publications and specialized materials.

"3. Given the special nature (and format) of such nonstandard library materials, their cataloging and preservation pose some problems. In anticipation of building up our film library on Central and South America, we are consulting with the Stanford Media Librarian about the equipment we need for preserving and screening films that come in different formats. Nondescript and otherwise difficult-to-classify items are sent to the Hoover Archives, where they are stored in optimal environmental conditions. For example, posters are photographed, encapsulated in plastic and then cataloged by general subject area (e.g., Nicaragua, El Salvador). Major self-contained collections, like our recently acquired one on the Mexican Communist Party, are housed in cataloged folders and boxes in the Archives.

"Non-fragile materials that can be cataloged are incorporated into our general holdings, usually as pamphlets in a general subject area.

"4. The Hoover Institution microfilms and sells some serials and newspapers from Latin America—particularly Cuba—but the press does not publish nonstandard materials related to political and social fringe."

Canada-Latin America Resource Centre

"The CLARC was incorporated in 1985 to maintain and make available to the public the large collection of material gathered together by the Latin American Working Group over its 20 years of existence. It has been acquired in a rather ad hoc fashion and maintained similarly. But it is still the largest collection of its kind in Canada and is remarkably well organized and accessible, all things considered.

"We certainly operate in the category of 'materials outside standard trade networks.' What is amazing is that there are so many other networks that do exist. They have been developed because the standard sources cannot service the needs of specialized library collections. We do order items that are reviewed in periodicals that focus on Third World and development issues. Most of these periodicals are from small, independent organizations throughout the world. Examples are ISIS in Rome (a resource and documentation centre on the international women's movement), the Latinoamerica Press in Lima (a church based weekly) and Third World Resources (a quarterly from the Data Centre in Oakland, CA).

"The type of material that you are writing about is exactly the material that we recognize as our richest resource. We try to obtain primary source material from grass roots organizations like women, trade unions, human rights, and church based groups. Because LAWG is a non-profit, independent organization with a very limited budget— much of the material from Latin America is obtained on an exchange basis. LAWG sends it publications instead of cash for a subscription. Many of these arrangements have been made over the years as a result of travels by LAWG members to other centres in Latin America. But we continue to initiate this arrangement whenever we learn of new publications.

"We have also collected publications produced by the refugee/ solidarity committees in Canada, the U.S., and to some extent Europe. We recognize that this material is a valuable testament for future researchers.

"Because of our commitment to make this material available, individuals and institutions have started to donate material to the library. We are now continually receiving periodicals from the Inter-

Church Committee on Human Rights in Latin America (ICCHRLA) here in Toronto. They receive many important primary documents from Latin American church and human rights groups. These donations are both wonderful and problematic. They raise the issues of space and preservation which we are now grappling with. We are now looking for funding that will enable us to microfiche the collection and store our bulging archives offsite. We are also investigating the joys of computerization to make the control of the material easier as well as more widely accessible."

APPENDIX
Organizations Surveyed

1.   Canada-Latin America Resource Centre, Latin American Working Group, P.O. Box 2207, Sta. P, Toronto, Ontario M5S2T2, Canada   Tel. 416-533-4221

2.   Center for Cuban Studies, 124 W. 23rd Street, New York, NY 10011 Tel. 212-685-9038

3.   Center for Hemispheric Affairs (American Enterprise Institute), 1150 Seventeenth Street NW, Washington, DC 20036   Tel. 202-862-5800

4.   Center for Migration Studies Library, 209 Flagg Place, Staten Island, NY 10304 Tel. 212-351-8800

5.   Central America Research Institute, 2700 Bancroft Way, Berkeley, CA 94704 Tel. 415-843-5041

6.   Central America Resource Center, P.O. Box 2327, Austin, TX 78768   Tel. 512-476-9841

7.   Children of the Americas/Niños de las Américas, P.O. Box 21707, Santa Barbara, CA 93121   Tel. 805-963-2189.

8.   Data Center, 464 19th Street, Oakland, CA 94612   Tel. 415-835-4692

9.   Ecumenical Committee on the Andes, 198 Broadway, Rm. 302, New York, NY 10038   Tel. 212-964-6730.

10.   Guatemala News and Information Bureau, P.O. Box 28594, Oakland, CA 94604 Tel. 415-835-0810

11.   Hoover Institution on War, Revolution and Peace, Stanford University, Stanford, CA 94305   Tel. 415-497-1754

12.   Human Rights Internet, 1338 G Street SE, Washington, DC 20003 Tel. 202-543-9200

13.   New York CIRCUS, P.O. Box 37, Times Square Station, New York, NY 10108 Tel. 212-663-8112

14.   Nicaragua Information Center, P.O. Box 1004, Berkeley, CA 94701 Tel. 415-549-1387

15.   North American Congress on Latin America (see the latest issue of NACLA's journal for a current address and telephone number).

16.   The Research Institute for the Study of Man, 162 E. 78th Street, New York, NY 10021   Tel. 212-535-8448

39. The Alternative Press in Latin America: A Checklist of Current Serials

Lygia Maria F. C. Ballantyne

This list includes serials published by sociopolitical, religious, labor, human rights, and minority grass-roots organizations in Latin America, or by their supporters in Europe and the United States.

It was compiled largely from references found in some 2,271 publications issued in Brazil by similar grass-roots organizations which the Library of Congress Rio de Janeiro Office acquired, organized, and indexed, and which the Library's Photoduplication Service microfilmed. (A full description of this microfilm collection is contained in my "Documenting Brazil's Political and Social Movements, 1966-1986: The Library of Congress Experience," chap. 36, above.)

This list includes both serials and monographic series reported as current. No attempt was made to confirm titles and addresses, nor to be exhaustive.

La Abeja
CEPAM
Apartado Postal 182c, Sucursal 15
Quito, Ecuador

Al Margen
Bimonthly
Grupo de Autoconciencia de Lesbianas Feministas/GALF
Casilla Postal 11890
Lima 11, Peru

Gays; Women

ALER Informa
Quarterly
Asociación Latinoamericana de Educación Radiofónica/ALER
Atahualpa 427
Casilla de Correo 4639-A
Quito, Ecuador

Education and communication

Amanecer
Centro Ecuménico Antonio Valdiviesco
Al. Sur 1206 Apartado 3205
Managua, Nicaragua

Religion and theology

Amanecer Indio
Confederación de las Nacional-
idades Indígenas de la Amazonia
Ecuatoriana
Apartado Postal 41-80
Quito, Ecuador

Indians

Amazona
Colectivo de Lesbianas del
FHAR
Frente Homosexual de Acción
Revolucionaria
México, D.F., Mexico

Gays; women

Americas Watch
36 W 44th Street
New York, NY 10036, USA

Human rights; political issues

Amerindia
Centro de Estudios Teológicos
de la Amazonia/CETA
Putumayo 355, Apartado 145
Iquitos, Peru

Also available from Conselho
Indigenista Missionario, Brazil

Indians

**Balance Semestral de la
Situación**
Centro de Documentación de
Honduras/CEDOH
Apartado Postal 1882
Tegucigalpa, Honduras

Human rights

Barricada Internacional
Frente Sandinista de Liberación
Nacional
Managua, Nicaragua

Political issues

**Bibliografía Teológica
Comentada**
Instituto Superior de Estudios
Teológicos/ISEDET
Camacua 282
Buenos Aires 1406, Argentina

Religion and theology

La Bocina
Monthly
Fondo Ecuatoriano Populorum
Progressio/FEPP
Mariano Reyes 228
Quito, Ecuador

Religion and theology

Boina Blanca 1984–
3 issues per year
Editorial Boina Blanca
Viamonte 1345, 2. piso B
Buenos Aires, Argentina

"Símbolo radical para la unión
nacional."

Political issues

Boletim/CEHILA
Comissão de Estudos de
História da Igreja na América
Latina/CEHILA
Caixa Postal 14543
Rio de Janeiro, RJ 22412, Brazil

Religion and theology

Boletín del MOVIP, 1986–
Movimiento por la Vida y la
Paz/MOVIP
Julian Alvarez 2797
Buenos Aires, Argentina
Human rights

Boletín Documentación
Centro de Promoción del
Laicado "Ricardo Bacherer"
Casilla de Correo 11199
La Paz, Bolivia
Religion and theology

Boletín Informativo/CEDOH
Centro de Documentación de
Honduras
Apartado Postal 1882
Tegucigalpa DC, Honduras
Political and social news and
analysis.
Political issues

Boletín Informativo/PAI
Publicaciones Amnistía
Internacional/PAI
Apartado Postal 6306-1000
San José, Costa Rica
Human rights

**Boletín Nacional de las CEBs
de México**
México, D.F., Mexico
Religion and theology

Boletín Teológico, 1980–
Fraternidad Teológica
Latinoamericana
Cuernavaca, Morelos, Mexico
Religion and theology

**Boletín/Centro de Promoción
Humana Integral**
Centro de Promoción Humana
Integral
Apartado Postal 118
Santo Domingo, Dominican
Republic
Human rights

**Boletín/Comisión Andina de
Juristas**
Los Sauces 285
Lima 27, Peru
Human rights

**Boletín/Comisión Nacional de
Promoción y Protección de los
Derechos Humanos**
Comisión Nacional de Promo-
ción y Protección de los
Derechos Humanos/CNPDH
Managua, Nicaragua
Human rights

**Boletín/Comité pro Justicia y
Paz de Guatemala**
Comité pro Justicia y Paz de
Guatemala
México, D.F., Mexico
Human rights; Political issues

**Boletín/Consejo de Iglesias
Evangélicas Metodistas de
América Latina**
Consejo de Iglesias Evangélicas
Metodistas de América Latina
La Paz, Bolivia
Religion and theology

Brecha
Comisión para la Defensa de
los Derechos Humanos en
Centroamérica/CODEHUMA
Paseo de los Estudiantes
Apartado Postal 189
San José, Costa Rica

Human rights

La Cacerola
Monthly
Fundación de Defensa del
Consumidor
Casilla de Correo 179-C
Quito, Ecuador

Consumer issues

Caminos
Bimonthly
Centro Cristiano de
Promoción y Servicios/CEPS
Av. Tacna 685, of. 91
Lima 100, Peru

Religion and theology

La Canasta
Asepade Apato. 444
Tegucigalpa, Honduras
22-3608

CEAAL Informativo
Consejo de Educación de
Adultos de América Latina
Diagonal Oriente 1604
Casilla de Correo 6257
Santiago 22, Chile

Education and communication

CEDIQ
Monthly
Centro de Información Obispado
de Quilmes
Belgrano 230-1876 Bernal
Buenos Aires, Argentina

Religion and theology

CEMEDIM
Centro de Estudios de los Medios
de Difusión Masiva
Calle 23, 452 Apartado 6646
Habana 4, Cuba

Education and communication

Central America Report, 1974–
Weekly
Inforpress Centroamericana
9 calle "A" 3-56, Zona 1
Guatemala, Guatemala
29432

Analytical reports on the region's
economic and political scene.

Political issues

Central American Update
P.O. Box 22077 Station P
Toronto, Ontario, Canada M53 2T2

Political issues

Centro América, 1981–
Annual
Inforpress Centroamericana
9 calle "A" 3-56, Zona 1
Guatemala, Guatemala
29432

Includes chronology, charts, and
maps.

Political issues

**Centro Regional de Informa-
ciones Ecuménicas**
Centro Regional de Informa-
ciones Ecuménicas
Yosemite 45
Col. Napoles 03810
México, D.F., Mexico

Religion and theology

**CH/Boletín Informativo
Honduras**
Monthly
Centro de Documentación de
Honduras/CEDOH
Apartado Postal 1882
Tegucigalpa, Honduras

Political issues

Chamiza
Corporación Ecuatoriana para el
Desarrollo de la Comunicación
Casilla 906-A
Quito, Ecuador

No. 15: "Feminismo y educación
popular."

Education and communication

La Chicharra
19 West 21st Street, 2nd floor
New York, NY, USA

Political issues

Christian Aid News
Christian Aid
P.O. Box 1
London SW9 8BH, England

Religion and theology

Church in the World
Catholic Institute for International Relations/CIIR
22 Coleman Fields
London N17AF, England

Religion and theology

CIDHAL Noticias
Quarterly
Centro de Investigaciones y
Desarrollo Humano de América
Latina/CIDHAL
Orozco Y Berra 27, int. 6
México, D.F., Mexico

Economic and social
development

CIIR Newsletter
Catholic Institute for International Relations/CIIR
22 Coleman Fields
London N17AF, England

Religion and theology

CODEH
Comité para la Defensa de los
Derechos Humanos en
Honduras
Apartado Postal 1256
Tegucigalpa, D.C., Honduras

Human rights

Combat
Bimonthly
P.O. Box 5035
Spanga 5 S-163 05, Sweden

Political issues

Comunicación América Latina
Quarterly
Asociación Católica Latino-
americana para la Radio y la
Televisión
Estados Unidos 2057
Buenos Aires 1227, Argentina

Education and communication

Comunicación América Latina
Quarterly
Organizaciones Cristianas de
Comunicación de América
Latina/OCIC
Quito, Ecuador

Education and communication

Comunicado
Comisión para la Defensa de los
Derechos Humanos en Centro
América
Apartado Postal 189, Paseo de
los Estudiantes
San José, Costa Rica

Human rights

**Comunicado/Comité pro Justicia
y Paz de Guatemala**
Comité pro Justicia y Paz de
Guatemala
Mexico, D.F., Mexico

Human rights

Conscience
Bimonthly
Catholics for a Free Choice/
CFFC

2008 17th Street, N.W.
Washington, DC 20009, USA

Includes articles on the Church
in Latin America.

Religion and theology

Contact
Bimonthly
World Council of Churches
Comisión Médica Cristiana
150, Route de Fernay
Geneva 1211 20, Switzerland

Religion and theology

**Coordinadora de Ayuda a
Refugiados Guatemaltecos**
Secretaría de Ayuda a
Refugiados Guatemaltecos
Casilla Postal 06760
México, D.F., Mexico

Human rights

Correo del Sur
Weekly
Casilla Postal 62000
Cuernavaca, Morelos, Mexico

Linked to the Catholic Church.
News and opinions.

Religion and theology

Crisalida
Grupo Orgullo Homosexual de
Liberación/Gohl
Apartado Postal 1-1693
Guadalajara, Jalisco, Mexico

Gays

Cristianismo y Sociedad
Quarterly
Cristianismo y Sociedad
Apartado Postal 20-656
México, D.F., Mexico

Published by Acción Social
Ecuménica Latinoamericana/
ASEL.

Religion and theology

**Cuadernos de Comunicación
Alternativa**
Centro de Integración de
Medios de Comunicación Alter-
nativa/CIMCA
Apartado Postal 5828
La Paz, Bolivia

Education and communication

**Cuadernos de Derechos
Humanos. Serie América Latina**
Quarterly
Movimiento de Jóvenes y
Estudiantes para las Naciones
Unidas/ISMUN
Fed. Univ. de Movimientos
Estudiantiles Cristianos
27, chemin des Crets-de-Pregny
Geneva, Switzerland

Human rights

**Cuadernos de Pensamiento
Propio**
Semimonthly
Instituto de Investigaciones
Económicas y Sociales/INIES
Apartado Postal C-16
Managua, Nicaragua

Economic and social
development

Cultura Popular, 1976–
Consejo Evangélico Latino
Americano de Educación
Cristiana
Lima, Peru

Religion and theology

**De Ambiente: Informativo de
Lesbianas y Homosexuales**
Colectivo de Orgullo Gay
Bogotá, Colombia

Gays

Derechos del Hombre
Liga Argentina de Derechos del
Hombre
Corrientes 1785, 2. C2
Casilla Postal 1042
Buenos Aires, Argentina

Human rights

Derechos del Pueblo
Comisión Ecuménica de
Derechos del Pueblo
Casilla Postal 720-A
Quito, Ecuador

Human rights

Desde las Bases
Centro Ecuménico de Educación
Popular/CEDEPO
Combate de los Pozos 730
Buenos Aires 1222, Argentina

Education and communication

Diferentes, 1984–
Buenos Aires, Argentina

Gays

DIM—Diálogo Indígena Misionero
Conferencia Episcopal Paraguaya
Equipo Nacional de Misiones
Alberdi, 782
Casilla de Correo 1436
Asunción, Paraguay

Religion and theology; Indians

Documento de Trabajo
Consejo de Educación de Adultos de América Latina/ CEAAL
Casillas 6257
Santiago, Chile

Education and communication

Dossie IDOC
IDOC
Via Santa Maria dell'Anima 30
Roma 00186, Italy

Education and communication

Educación Popular en América Latina
Educación Popular en América Latina
Casilla de Correo 116-Sucursal 34(B)
Buenos Aires, Argentina

Education and communication

Entendido: Revista Mensual de Sexualidades
Caracas, Venezuela

Envío
Monthly
Instituto Histórico Centro-americano
Apartado A-194
Managua, Nicaragua

Linked to the Catholic Church

Religion and theology

Espérance des Pauvres
Monthly
Espérance des Pauvres
Rue des Dominicains, 11-13
Mons 7000, Belgium

Religion and theology

Ethnies: Droits de l'Homme et Peuples Autochtones, 1985–
Quarterly
Survival International (France)
28 rue Saint Guilhaume
Paris 75007, France
222-35930

No.1/2: "La question amér-indienne en Guyanne française."

Indians

Extracta
Centro de Investigación y Promoción Amazónica/CIPA
Lima, Peru

Faim et Développement Magazine
Monthly
Comité Catholique Contre la
Faim et Pour le Développement
4, rue Jean Lantier
Paris 75001, France

Economic and social
development

FHAR Informa
Frente Homosexual de Acción
Revolucionaria/FHAR
México, D.F., Mexico

Gays; Political issues

Fidelidad
Grupo Fidelidad
México, D.F., Mexico

Gays

Foi et Développement
Monthly
Centre Lebret
39, boul. Saint Germain
Paris 75005, France

Economic and social
development

Furia
Colectivo Furia
No address given
Chile

Gaceta de la FITPAS
Federación Internacional de
Trabajadores de las Plantaciones
Agrícolas e Similares
Rue Necker 17
Geneva 1201, Switzerland

Labor and laboring classes

Gay: Tubreviaro Samizdat
San Martín, Argentina

Gays

Golondrina
Monthly
Centro de Mujeres Chilenas
Exiliadas
No addresses given
San José, Costa Rica

Political issues; Gays

Grito do Nordeste
Animação dos Cristãos no Meio
Rural/ACR
Rua do Giriquiti, 48
Recife, PE 50.000, Brazil

Linked to the Catholic Church

Agrarian reform; Human rights

Guazapa
Weekly
Centro de Ediciones "Guazapa"
San Salvador, El Salvador

Hacia Nuestra Liberación
Unidad Nicaragüense Opositora
San José, Costa Rica

Political issues

Hasta Encontrarlos
Bimonthly
Federación Latinoamericana de
Asociaciones de Familiares de
Detenidos–Desaparecidos/
FEDEFAM
Carmelitas 1010-A
Apartado Postal 2444
Caracas, Venezuela

Human rights

HC—Heraldo Cristiano
Bimonthly
Iglesia Presbiteriana Reformada
en Cuba
Salud, 222
Habana 2, Cuba
Religion and theology

Homosexuales
Frente de Liberación Homo-
sexual de la Argentina
Buenos Aires, Argentina
Gays

Human Rights Watch
36 West 44th Street
New York, NY 10036, USA
Human rights

**ICIA/Información Católica
Iberoamericana**
Semimonthly
Comisión Episcopal de Misiones
y Cooperación entre las Iglesias
de la Conferencia Episcopal
Española
C/Anastro 1
Madrid 28033, Spain
766-5500
Religion and theology

Ideas y Acción
Bimonthly
FAU, Campaña Mundial Contra
el Hambre
Acción Pro Desarrollo
Via Terme di Caracalla
Roma 00100, Italy

ISSN 0251-1908
Economic and social
development

IDOC International Bulletin
Monthly
IDOC International
Via Santa Maria dell'Anima, 30
Roma 06186, Italy

Issued also in Italian

Education and communication;
Religion and theology

Iglesias—CENCOS
Monthly
Centro Nacional de Comunica-
ción Social/CENCOS
Medellín 33, Col. Roma
Casilla Postal 06700
México, D.F., Mexico

Religion and theology

Index on Censorship
39 c Highbury Place
London N5 1QP, England

Human rights

Informador Guerrillero
Bimonthly
Ejército Guerrillero de los
Pobres/EGP
Unidid Revolucionaria Nacional
Guatemalteca/URNG
Guatemala

Political issues

**Informativo/Secretariado Latino-
Americano de Grupos
Homosexuales**
SLAGH, c/o GGB
Caixa Postal 2552
Salvador, Bahia 40.000, Brazil

Gays

Informativo Andino
Comisión Andina de Juristas
Los Sauces 285
Lima 27, Peru

Human rights

Informativo CELATS/ALAETS
Quarterly
Centro Latinoamericano de
Trabajo Social, Asociación
Latinoamericana de Escuelas de
Trabajo Social
Jr. Vanderghen, 351
Lima 18, Peru

Economic and social
development

Informativo Signos
Biweekly
Centro de Estudios y
Publicaciones/CEP
Instituto Bartolomé de las Casas
Lima, Peru

Linked to the Catholic Church

Human rights; Religion and
theology

Informe "R"
Monthly
Centro de Documentación e
Información/CEDOIN
Calle Ayacucho, 320—5. piso
Casilla de Correos 20194
La Paz, Bolivia

Independent political and
economic analysis

Political issues

Informe Anual/CCIM
Comisión Católica Internacional
de Migración/CCIM
37-39 rue de Vermont
Geneva 1211, Switzerland

Migration

**Informe de Actividades/
ASOFAMD**
Annual
Asociación de Familiares de
Detenidos Desaparecidos y
Mártires por la Liberación
Nacional/ASOFAMD
La Paz, Bolivia

Human rights

**Informe Mensual/Arzobispado
de Santiago**
Monthly
Arzobispado de Santiago
Vicaría de la Solidaridad
Santiago, Chile

Human rights

INFORMEDH
Movimiento Ecuménico por los
Derechos Humanos
Buenos Aires, Argentina

Human rights

Inforpress Centroamericana,
1972–
Weekly
Inforpress Centroamericana
9a. calle "A", 3-56
Guatemala Zona 1, Guatemala
29-432

Analytical reports on the
region's political and economic
situation.

Political issues

Intercambio: Educación y
Desarrollo
FAO, Campaña Mundial contra
el Hambre
Via Terme di Caracalla
Roma 00100, Italy

Economic and social development

Jornal Indígena
União das Nações Indígenas/
UNI
Rua Ministro Godoy, 1484,
sala 57
São Paulo, SP 05015, Brazil

Indians

Justice and Service News
Monthly
World Council of Churches

150 Route de Ferney
Geneva 1211 20, Switzerland

Human rights

Latinamerica Press
Weekly
Latinamerica Press
Apartado Postal 5594
Lima 100, Peru

Independent news service

Education and communication

Liaisons Latino-Américaines
Monthly
Liaisons Latino-Américaines
28, rue Eugene-Millon
Paris 75015, France

Information bulletin on the
churches of Latin America

Religion and theology

Lleguemos, 1985–
Grupo de Periodismo, Sindicato
de Trabajadoras Domésticas/
SINTRASEDOM
Apartado Aéreo 1880
Bogotá, Colombia

Labor and laboring classes;
Women

Lorenza Abimanay
Centro de Educación Popular/
CEDEP
La Isla 416 y Cuba
Casilla Postal 1171
Quito, Ecuador

Education and communication

Luchemos
Quarterly
Federación Campesina Latino-
americana
Apartado 1422
Caracas 1010-A, Venezuela

Political issues; Labor and
laboring classes

Madres de Plaza de Mayo
Las Madres de Plaza de Mayo
Hipólito Yrigoyen, 1441
Buenos Aires 1089, Argentina

Human rights; Women

Manuela Ramos
Monthly
Movimiento Manuela Ramos
Av. Bolivia 921–Bena
Casilla Postal 11176
Lima, Peru

Political issues; Women

**Mapuche: Boletín Promoción
Desarrollo Indígena**
Obra Indígena Iglesia Metodista
Argentina

Indians; Religion and theology

Micaela, 1981–
Bimonthly
Asociación Latinoamericana de
Mujeres/ALAM
Box 5099
Spanga 16305, Sweden

Political issues; Women

Migraciones
World Council of Churches
Secretaría de Migraciones
150, route de Ferney
Geneva 12111 20, Switzerland

Migration

Movimiento Sindical Mundial
Federação Sindical Mundial
Rua dos Eucaliptos, 10-3, Esq.o.
Apartado 176 – Cova de
Piedade
Lisboa, Portugal

Labor and laboring classes

Mujer, 1985–
Centro de Orientación de la
Mujer Obrera/COMO
Calles Ejido y Brasil
Ciudad Juárez, Chihuahua
Mexico
24747

Labor and laboring classes;
Women

Mujer Adelante
Monthly
Movimiento Feminista
Hermanas Mirabal
Dominican Republic
No address given

Political issues; Women

Mujer Combatiente
Monthly
Grupo Femenino "8 de Marzo"
Apartado Aéreo 40009
Bucaramanga, Colombia

Political issues; Women

Mujeres del Continente contra la Intervención
Frente Continental de Mujeres/ FCM
Apartado Postal 847
Managua, Nicaragua

Political issues; Women

Mujeres del Mundo Entero
Quarterly
Federación Democrática
Mundial de Mujeres/FEDIM
Unter den Linden 13
Berlin 1080, GDR

Political issues; Women

Nicaragua Hoy
San José, Costa Rica

Political issues

Nosotras
Movimiento Feminista
"El Pozo"
Jirón Quilca 431
Lima, Peru

Political issues; Women

Nosotras (Madrid)
Colectivo Feminista Lesbianas
de Madrid
Apartado de Correos 16108
Madrid, Spain

Gays; Women

Nosotras (Mexico)
Bimonthly
Mujeres en Acción Sindical/ MAS
Palma Norte 402, Desp. 12,
Centro
México, D.F., Mexico

Labor and laboring classes;
Women

Noticias de Argentina
Secretaría de Relaciones Internacionales del Peronismo
Revolucionario
Calle Brasil 1682
Buenos Aires, Argentina

Political issues

Noticias de Guatemala
Monthly
Noticias de Guatemala
Apartado Postal 20-209
México 01000, D.F., Mexico

Political issues

Noticias de Latino-América Documentos
Bimonthly
Service Européen Universitaries
Latinoaméricains
Rue de Suede, 41
Brussels 1060, Belgium

Education and communication

Nuestra Voz
Quarterly
Alianza de Mujeres
Costarricenses
Apartado Postal 6851
San José, Costa Rica

Political issues; Women

Nuestro Cuerpo
Colectivo Mariposas Negras del
Frente Homosexual de Acción
Revolucionaria/FHAR
México, D.F., Mexico

Gays; Women

Nuevo Ambiente
Grupo Lambda de Liberación
Homosexual
Apartado Postal 73-130
México, D.F., Mexico

Gays

8 Días
Weekly
ACEP-WACC
Apartado Postal 136
Cartago 7050, Costa Rica

Opinión Popular
Movimiento Nacional
Revolucionario/MNR
San José, Costa Rica

Political issues

El Otro
Medellín, Colombia

Gays

Pa Fuera
Comunidad de Orgullo Gay
San Juan, Costa Rica

Gays

Páginas
Monthly
Centro de Estudios y
Publicaciones/CEP
Instituto Bartolomé de las Casas
Lima, Peru

Linked to the Catholic Church.

Human rights; Religion and
theology

Paraguay Watch
Bimonthly
Paraguay Watch
P.O. Box 21128
Washington, DC 20009, USA

Political issues

Pasos
Departamento Ecuménico de
Investigaciones/DEI
San José, Costa Rica

Religion and theology

Pastoral Popular
Centro Ecuménico "Diego de
Medellín"
Casilla de Correos 386-V
Santiago 21, Chile

Religion and theology

Paz y Justicia, 1983–
Buenos Aires, Argentina

Human rights

Paz y Liberación
Quarterly
P.O. Box 600063
Houston, TX 77260, USA

Text in English, Spanish, and Portuguese.

Gays

PCR Información: Reports and Background Papers
World Council of Churches
Programme to Combat Racism
150, route de Ferney
P.O. Box 66
Geneva 1211 20, Switzerland
(022) 91-6111

Human rights

Perspectivas Reformadas
Alianza Reformada Mundial
150, route de Ferney
Geneva 1211 20, Switzerland
(022) 91-6111
No. 156, April 1986: "Voces de América Latina."

Religion and theology

Política Sexual
Frente Homosexual de Acción Revolucionaria/FHAR
México, D.F., Mexico

Gays; Political issues

La Prensa Sindical, 1986–
Posta restante C.I.1, 403, 338-2
Montevideo, Uruguay

Labor and laboring classes

Puebla, 1978–
5 issues per year
Editora Vozes
Caixa Postal 90023
Petrópolis, RJ 25600, Brazil

Religion and theology

Pueblo
CONAMUP
México, D.F., Mexico

Rápidas
Consejo Latinoamericano de Iglesias/CLAI
Casilla de Correos 85-22
Quito, Ecuador
238-220

Religion and theology

Red Mundial de Mujeres para los Derechos Reproductivos
Women's Global Network on Reproductive Rights
P.O. Box 4098
Amsterdam 1009 AB, Netherlands

Human rights; Women

La Red
Asociación de Defensa y Capacitación and Instituto de Defensa Legal
Av. 6 de agosto 589, oficina 307
Lima 11, Peru

Human rights

Revista CEPAE
Bimonthly
Centro de Planificación y Acción
Ecuménica/ECPAE
Benito Monción, 213
Santo Domingo, Dominican
Republic

Religion and theology

**Revista Chilena de Derechos
Humanos**
Academia de Humanismo
Cristiano
Catedral 1063 – 5. piso
Santiago, Chile

Human rights

**Revista de la Asamblea
Permanente por los Derechos
Humanos**
Buenos Aires, Argentina

Human rights

Ríos de Sanidad
Asociación La Iglesia de Dios/
ALIDD
Calle Miralla 453
Buenos Aires, Argentina
642-9298

A Pentecostal denomination.

Religion and theology

**Rulpa Dungun = Transmitir la
Palabra**
Monthly
Casa de la Mujer Mapuche
San Martin 433
Temuco, Chile

Indians; Women

SADEC Lettre
Quarterly
Santé, Développement,
Cultures/SADEC
14, rue Saint Benoit
Paris 75006, France

Economic and social
development

Salud y Sociedad
Movimiento Nacional por un
Sistema Integrado de Salud
Buenos Aires, Argentina

Economic and social
development

SEDOI Documentación
Monthly
Servicio de Documentación e
Información/SEDOI
Instituto de Cultura Religiosa
Superior
Rodríguez Peña 1054
Buenos Aires 1020 B, Argentina
44-2972

Linked to the Catholic Church.

Religion and theology

Selección Informativa/CEDEP
Semimonthly
Centro Ecuménico de Docu-
mentación, Estudios y
Publicaciones/CEDEP
Pedernera 1291
San José, Mendoza 5519
Argentina

Religion and theology

Serie Cronologías
Centro de Documentación de
Honduras/CEDOH
Apartado Postal 1882
Tegucigalpa, Honduras

Political issues

**Serie Documentos/Amnistía
Internacional**
Publicaciones Amnistía Inter-
nacional/PAI
Apartado Aéreo 6306-1000
San José, Costa Rica

Human rights

Servir: Teología y Pastoral
Quarterly
Servir
Apartado Postal 334
Jalapa 9100, Veracruz, Mexico

Religion and theology

SI Annual Review
Survival International
29 Craven Street
London WC2N 5NT, England
(01) 839-3267

"For the rights of threatened
tribal peoples."

Indians

Sin Fronteras
P.O. Box 1551
Denver, CO 80201, USA

Gays

SINTRASEDOM
Monthly
Sindicato de Trabajadoras
Domésticas/ SINTRASEDOM
Apartado Aéreo 1880
Bogotá, Colombia

Labor and laboring classes;
Women

**SIR Servicio de Informaciones
Religiosas**
Monthly
SIR
Camacua 282
Buenos Aires 1406, Argentina
ISSN 0326-6702

Religion and theology

Solidarios
Bimonthly
Consejo de Fundaciones
Americanas de Desarrollo
Apartado Postal 620
Santo Domingo, Dominican
Republic

Economic and social
development

Somos
Frente de Liberación
Homosexual de la Argentina
Comunidad de Orgullo Gay
San Juan, Puerto Rico

Gays

Somos (Managua)
Bimonthly
Asociación de Mujeres
Nicaragüenses "Luisa Amanda
Espinoza"
Rep. San Juan, 2 y media
cuadras al S.O.
Managua, Nicaragua

Political issues; Women

Sucede en la Iglesia
Monthly
Centro de Promoción Rural
Casilla de Correos 9934
Guayaquil, Ecuador
304-172

Religion and theology

Survival International News
Quarterly
Survival International
29 Craven Street
London WC2n 5NT, England
(01) 839-3267

"For the rights of threatened
tribal peoples."

Indians

Temas
Consejo Latinoamericano de
Iglesias/CLAI
Santiago, Chile

Religion and theology

**Testimonios sobre la Represión
y la Tortura, 1984–**
Familiares de Desaparecidos y
Detenidos por Razones Políticas
Riobamba 34, planta baja
Buenos Aires, Argentina

Human rights

Trabajadora
Secretaría de la Mujer de las
Comisiones Obreras de España
Fernández de la Hoz, 12
Madrid 28010, Spain

Labor and laboring classes;
Women

**El Trueno: Periódico para
Comunidades Nativas de la
Amazonia Peruana**
Monthly
Centro Amazónico de Antropo-
logía y Aplicación Práctica
Av. Gonzales Prada 626
Apartado Postal 111-66
Lima 14, Peru
61-5223

Indians

Tu Voz, Mujer
Bimonthly
Comité de Defensa de los
Derechos de la Mujer/CODEM
Cochrane 1012, 1er piso
Concepción, Chile

Political issues; Women

ULAJE Comparte
Quarterly
Unión Latinoamericana de
Juventudes Ecuménicas/ULAJE
Jr. Tungasuca, 274 - 2. piso
Apartado Postal 11621
Lima, Peru
52-5961

Religion and theology

Um Outro Olhar, 1987–
Quarterly
Grupo de Ação Lésbica
Feminista/GALF
Caixa Postal 62618
São Paulo, SP 01295, Brazil

Gays; Women

Unamus, 1985–
Unión Nacional de Mujeres
Guatemaltecas/UNAMG
Guatemala
No address given

Political issues; Women

Unión Femenina
Comité Femenino de la
Empresa de Teléfonos de
Bogotá
Apartado Aéreo 7860
Bogotá, Colombia

Political issues; Women

Urgent Action Bulletin
Survival International
29 Craven Street
London WC2N 5NT, England

Indians

Vamos
Centro de Defesa dos Direitos
Humanos
Av. Almirante Barroso, 774–
Centro
Caixa Postal 93
João Pessoa, PB, Brazil

Human rights

Venceremos
Monthly
Unión de Mujeres Campesinas
Casilla de Correo 760-A
Quito, Ecuador

Labor and laboring classes;
Women

Ventana Gay
Apartado Aéreo 43.593
Bogotá 1, Colombia

Gays

**Víspera: Boletín de Análisis del
Movimiento Popular Social
Cristiano**
Víspera
2350 San Francisco de los Ríos
Apartado Postal 117
San José, Costa Rica

Vivar
Semimonthly
Grupo de Reflexión "Vivir" en
Defensa de la Vida y la
Dignidad Humana
Apartado Postal 270071
Lima 27, Peru
23-7790

Human rights

**Y Que!: Boletín para la Comuni-
dad Homosexual/Lesbiana**
Tijuana, Baja California, Mexico

Gays

40. Women in Latin America: A Checklist of Current Serials

Lygia Maria F. C. Ballantyne

This list includes serials currently published by women and feminist groups in Latin America, and by European and American organizations which are supportive of the Latin American women's movement.

It was compiled largely from bibliographic references found in some 58 women's serial publications issued in Brazil, which the Library of Congress Rio de Janeiro Office acquired as part of its "Brazil Popular Groups Collections." (This collection, recently microfilmed by the Library of Congress, is described in my "Documenting Brazil's Political and Social Movements, 1966-1986: The Library of Congress Experience," chap. 36, above.)

Because most of the periodicals issued by Brazilian women's groups are included in the microfilm collection mentioned above and are, therefore, available to researchers, only a few Brazilian titles are described in the present list. This list covers both serials and monographic series reported as current. As the list was compiled from secondary sources only, no effort was made to confirm the accuracy of the information.

Alfonsina
Galanternik Comunicaciones
Callao 1121, 3er piso
Buenos Aires, Argentina
42-5381

Alternativa Feminista
Catamarca 970
Buenos Aires, Argentina

Amazona
Colectivo de Lesbianas del
FHAR
Frente Homosexual de Acción
Revolucionaria
México, D.F., Mexico

Boleticam
Centro Acción de Mujeres/
CAM
Velez 1919 y Carchi
Apartado Postal 10201
Guayaquil, Ecuador

Boletín de D.I.M.A.
Derechos Iguales para la Mujer
Argentina/DIMA
Sarmiento 1169, 6to. C.
Buenos Aires 1041, Argentina

Boletín FMC
Federación de Mujeres Cubanas
Habana, Cuba

Boletín Internacional de AMES
Bimonthly
Asociación Mujeres de
El Salvador
Apartado Postal 20134
México, D.F., Mexico

Boletina Chilena
Bimonthly
Movimiento de Emancipación de
la Mujer Chilena/MEMCH
No address given

La Boletina
Red Nacional de Mujeres
Maclovio Herrera 455
Colima, mexico

Brujas, 1982–
Biannual
Centro de Estudios e Investiga-
ciones Sobre la Mujer
Apartado Postal 49105
Medellín, Colombia

Brujas, 1983–
Asociación Trabajo y Estudio
Sobre la Mujer
Calle Venezuela 1286
Buenos Aires, Argentina

La Cacerola, 1984–
Quarterly
Grupo de Estudios Sobre la
Condición de la Mujer/
GRECMU
Casilla de Correo 10587
Montevideo, Uruguay

Carta Trimestral
Red de la Mujer de Grupos
Populares
Apartado Postal 4240
Caracas, Venezuela

CEPA—Mujer
Bimonthly
Centro Ecuatoriano de Promo-
ción y Acción de la Mujer/
CEPAM

**Colección Comunicación Alter-
nativa de la Mujer**
Instituto Latinoamericano de
Estudios Transnacionales/ILET
Unidad de Comunicación Alter-
nativa de la Mujer
Casilla 16637
Santiago 9, Chile

Comai
Bimonthly
Taller Salud del Colectivo
Feminista COMAI
Estación Metropol Shopping
Center
Apartado 2172
Hato Rey 00919, Puerto Rico

Compañeras
Quarterly
Centro Mujeres para el Diálogo
Apartado Postal 19493
Mixcoac 03910, Mexico

Cotidiano Mujer
Colectivo Editorial Mujer
Jackson 1270, Apto. SS 101
Montevideo, Uruguay
40-3709

Cuadernos Culturales
Centro de Documentación Sobre
la Mujer/CENDOC Mujer
Av. Arenales 2626 - 3er. piso,
Lince
Lima 14, Peru

**Cuadernos de Divulgación
(INDESO Mujer)**
Instituto de Estudios Jurídico-
Sociales de la Mujer
Montevideo, 2303
Rosario 2000, Argentina

Cuadernos de Liberación y Vida
Agrupación Mujeres de Viña del
Mar/AMUDEVI
6 Oriente 1141
Viña del Mar, Chile

Cuadernos de Nueva Mujer
Casilla Postal 3224
Quito, Ecuador
52-3835

Documentos Sobre la Mujer,
1987–
Quarterly
Centro de Investigación de la
Realidad de América Latina/
CIRA
Ciudad Jardín A-22
Apartado Postal 814
Managua, Nicaragua

Enfoques de Mujer, 1986–
Grupo de Estudios de la Mujer
Paraguaya/GEMPA
Eligio Ayala 973
Asunción, Paraguay

Especial Mujer
Quarterly
Instituto Latinoamericano de
Estudios Transnacionales/ILET
Unidad de Comunicación
Alternativa de la Mujer
Casilla 16637
Santiago 9, Chile

Each issue treats a special
subject of interest to women

Eva de la Manzana
Grupo Autónomo de Mujeres
Evas
Recalde 282
Quito, Ecuador

Fem, 1976–
Bimonthly
Colectivo de Mujeres FEM
Av. Mexico 761, Col. Progreso,
Tizapan
México 20, D.F., Mexico

Each issue treats a different
subject in depth

Femina Sapiens, 1982–
Apartado Aéreo 25922
Bogotá, Colombia

Feminaria, 1988–
Catálogos S.R.L.
Av. Independencia 1860
1225 Buenos Aires, Argentina

Golondrina
Monthly
Centro de Mujeres Chilenas
Exiliadas
No address given
San José, Costa Rica

Grupo Mujer
Grupo Mujer
Arica 1074, 4. piso, of. 2
Chiclayo, Peru

Informe Mulher
Conselho Nacional dos Direitos
da Mulher
Edifício do Ministério da
Justiça—5o. andar, sala 505
Brasília, D.F. 70.064, Brazil

Ixquic
Monthly
Centro de Investigación de la
Mujer en Guatemala
Apartado Postal 27008
C.P. 06760
Mexico, D.F., Mexico

Lleguemos, 1985–
Grupo de Periodismo, Sindicato
de Trabajadoras Domésticas/
SINTRASEDOM
Apartado Aéreo 1880
Bogotá, Colombia

Lucha Feminista
Acción Femenina
Santo Domingo, Dominican
Republic
6899903

Madres de Plaza de Mayo
Las Madres de Plaza de Mayo
Hipólito Yrigoyen, 1441
Buenos Aires 1089, Argentina

La Mala Vida
Colectivo Feminista La Conjura
Apartado Postal 47659
Caracas 1041, Venezuela

Manuela Ramos
Monthly
Movimiento Manuela Ramos
Av. Bolivia 921 – Bena
Casilla Postal 11176
Lima, Peru

La Manzana, 1983–
Mujeres en Lucha
Apartado Postal 11739
Lima 11, Peru
62-3287

María, Cosas de Mujeres
Colectivo de Feministas de
Monterrey
Pirandello 425, Sendero de
San Jerónimo
Monterrey, Nuevo León, Mexico

María, Liberación del Pueblo
Monthly
María, Liberación del Pueblo
Av. Morelos, 714
Apartado Postal 158-B
Cuernavaca 62190, Morelos
Mexico

Publication for women from the
barrios

Micaela, 1981–
Bimonthly
Asociación Latinoamericana de
Mujeres/ALAM
Box 5099
Spanga 16305, Sweden

**Movimiento Hacia una Nueva
Mujer**
Renato Descartes 368
Urbanización La Novia
Trujillo, Peru

MUDE Informativo
Quarterly
Mujeres en Desarrollo/MUDE
Apartado 325
Santo Domingo, Dominican
Republic

Mujer, 1985–
Centro de Orientación de la
Mujer Obrera/COMO
Calles Ejido y Brasil
Ciudad Juárez, Chihuahua
Mexico
24747

Mujer (San José), 1980–
Monthly
Centro Feminista de Informa-
ción y Acción/CEFEMINA
Apartado Postal 949
San José, Costa Rica

Mujer/Fempress
Monthly
Instituto Latinoamericano de
Estudios Transnacionales/ILET
Unidad de Comunicación Alter-
nativa de la Mujer
Casilla 16637
Santiago 9, Chile

Mujer Adelante
Monthly
Movimiento Feminista
Hermanas Mirabel
Dominican Republic
No address given

Mujer Combatiente
Monthly
Grupo Femenino "8 de Marzo"
Apartado Aéreo 40009
Bucaramanga, Colombia

La Mujer Feminista
Unión de Mujeres Feministas
Apartado Correos 311
Madrid, Spain

Mujer Mujer, 1985–
Quarterly
Grupo "Mujer Mujer"
Arzobispo Merino 270, Apt. 1
Santo Domingo, Dominican
Republic

Mujer y Actualidad
Monthly
Federación de Asociaciones
Femeninas Hondureñas/FAFH
Av. Juan Lindo
Tegucigalpa, Honduras

Mujer y Educación, 1987–
Colectivo Mujer y Educación
7a. Línea 1247 – 4o. piso
Santiago, Chile

Mujer y Sociedad
Monthly
Organización de Mujeres "Mujer
y Sociedad"
J. Trujillo 678
Magdalena del Mar
Lima, Peru

La Mujer (Quito)
Bimonthly
Instituto de Estudios de la
Familia
Robles 840
Quito, Ecuador

Mujeres
Galiano 264, entre Neptuno y
Concordia
Habana 2, Cuba

Mujeres (Buenos Aires)
Sindicato Gráfico Argentino
Balcarce 236–2 p.
Buenos Aires, Argentina

Mujeres (Madrid)
Instituto de la Mujer
Ministerio de la Cultura
Almagro 36 – 2a. planta
Madrid 28019, Spain
41-05112

**Mujeres (Partido Justicialista,
Buenos Aires), 1987–**
Partido Justicialista, Secretaría
de la Mujer
Ayacucho 915
Buenos Aires, Argentina

Mujeres (San José), 1987–
Bimonthly
Servicio Especial de la Mujer
Latinoamericana/SEMLA
Paseo de los Estudiantes
Apartado Postal 70
San José, Costa Rica

Mujeres (Santo Domingo)
Monthly
Círculo Feminista
Apartado Postal 2793
Santo Domingo, Dominican
Republic

Mujeres (Tegucigalpa)
Tegucigalpa, Honduras

Mujeres de Lucha
Monthly
Círculos Femeninos Populares
Apartado Postal 21078
Caracas 1020-A, Venezuela

**Mujeres del Continente Contra
la Intervención**
Frente Continental de Mujeres/
FCM
Apartado Postal 847
Managua, Nicaragua

Mujeres del Mundo Entero
Quarterly
Federación Democrática
Mundial de Mujeres/FEDIM
Unter den Linden 13
Berlin 1080, GDR

Mujeres en Acción
Isis Internacional
Via San Saba 5, Interno 1
Roma 000153, Italy

Mujeres en Movimiento, 1986–
Pedernera 504
El Palomar 1684
Buenos Aires, Argentina

Mujeres Organizándonos, 1983–
Instituto de la Mujer Peruana
Agrupación Feminista María de
Jesús Alvarado
Av. Arequipa 343, of. 1
Lima, Peru

Mujeres Populares del Cuzco
Asociación Amauta-Cusco
Apartado Postal 982
Cuzco, Peru

Each issue discusses a specific
theme

Mulher
Conselho Estadual da Condição
Feminina
Rua Estados Unidos 346
São Paulo, SP 01427, Brazil

Mulher e Saúde
Associação de Mulheres de
Mato Grosso
Rua Baltazar Navarro 231
Cuiabá, MT 78000, Brazil

Mulher Libertação
Quarterly
Movimento de Libertação da
Mulher
Caixa Postal 285
Lins, SP 16400, Brazil

Linked to the Catholic Church's
Pastoral da Mulher
Marginalizada

Mulheres, 1978–
Av. Duque de Laiole, 111 – 4o.
Lisboa, Portugal

Mulherio
Bimonthly
Nucleo de Comunicação
"Mulherio"
Rua Amalia de Noronha 268
Pinheiros
São Paulo, SP 05410, Brazil
(011) 212-9052

Nos/otras
Quarterly
Centro de Estudios de la Mujer
Purísima 353
Santiago, Chile

Nosotras
Movimiento Feminista "El
Pozo"
Jirón Quilca 431
Lima, Peru

Nosotras (Madrid)
Colectivo Feminista Lesbianas
de Madrid
Apartado de Correos 16108
Madrid, Spain

Nosotras (Mexico)
Bimonthly
Mujeres en Acción
Sindical/MAS
Palma Norte 402, Desp. 12,
Centro
México, D.F., Mexico

Noticias de la Mujer
Monthly
Centro Dominicano Estudios y
Educación/CEDEE
Apartado Postal 20307
Santo Domingo, Dominican Republic

Nuestra Voz
Quarterly
Alianza de Mujeres
Costarricenses
Apartado Postal 6851
San José, Costa Rica

Nuestro Cuerpo
Colectivo Mariposas Negras del
Frente Homosexual de Acción
Revolucionaria/FHAR
México, D.F., Mexico

Persona
Quarterly
Organización Feminista
Argentina
Pena 2214
P.O. "B"
Buenos Aires 1126, Argentina

Prensa de Mujeres
Buenos Aires, Argentina

Presença da Mulher
Editora Liberdade Mulher Ltda.
Rua dos Bororós, 5 – 1o. andar
São Paulo, SP 01320, Brazil

Quehaceres
Bimonthly
Centro de Investigación para la
Acción Femenina/CIPAF
Benigno Filomeno de Rojas 305
Santo Domingo, Dominican
Republic

**Red de Salud de las Mujeres
Latinoamericanas y del Caribe**
ISIS Internacional
Casilla 2067, Correo Central
Santiago, Chile
49-0271

**Red Mundial de Mujeres para
los Derechos Reproductivos**
Women's Global Network on
Reproductive Rights
P.O. Box 4098
Amsterdam 1009 AB
Netherlands

Redes de Comunicación
Centro de la Mujer, Colegio
Regional de Aguadilla
Universidad de Puerto Rico
Ramey, Puerto Rico

Monographic, analytical series

**Rulpa Dungun = Transmitir la
Palabra**
Monthly
Casa de la Mujer Mapuche
San Martín 433
Temuco, Chile

Ser Mujer
Quarterly
Asociación Uruguaya de Planifi-
cación Familiar e Investigaciones
Sobre Reproducción Humana/
AUPFIRH
Casilla de Correo 10634
Montevideo, Uruguay

Serie Mujeres
Movimiento Feminista
"Creatividad y Cambio"
J.R. Quilca 431
Lima, Peru

Pamphlets on specific themes

Serie Mujeres Nuevas
Movimiento Feminista
"Creatividad y Cambio"
J.R. Quilca 431
Lima, Peru

Serie Prostitución
Movimiento Feminista
"Creatividad y Cambio"
J.R. Quilca 431
Lima, Peru

Sexo Finalmente Explícito
Monthly
Casa da Mulher, Coletivo
Feminista
Rua Cosme Velho
Rio de Janeiro, RJ, Brazil

SINTRASEDOM
Monthly
Sindicato de Trabajadoras
Domésticas/SINTRASEDOM
Apartado Aéreo 1880
Bogotá, Colombia

Somos (Managua)
Bimonthly
Asociación de Mujeres
Nicaragüenses "Luisa Amanda
Espinoza"
Rep. San Juan, 2 y media
cuadras al S.O.
Managua, Nicaragua

**Taller de Mujeres Latino-
americanas**
a/c CIMADE
176, rue de Grenelle
Paris 75007, France

La Tortuga, 1982–
Monthly
Asociación Cultural
"La Tortuga"
Jr. Huancavelica 470, of. 408
Lima, Peru

Trabajadora
Secretaría de la Mujer de las
Comisiones Obreras de España
Fernández de la Hoz, 12
Madrid 28010, Spain

**La Tribuna: Boletín Trimestral
Sobre la Mujer y el Desarrollo**
Centro de la Tribuna Inter-
nacional de la Mujer
777 United Nations Plaza
New York, NY 10017, USA

Tu Voz, Mujer
Bimonthly
Comité dc Defensa de los
Derechos de la Mujer/CODEM
Cochrane 1012, 1er piso
Concepción, Chile

Um Outro Olhar, 1987–
Quarterly
Grupo de Ação Lésbica
Feminista/GALF
Caixa Postal 62618
São Paulo, SP 01295, Brazil

Unamus, 1985–
Unión Nacional de Mujeres
Guatemaltecas/UNAMG
Guatemala
No address given

Unión Femenina
Comité Femenino de la
Empresa de Teléfonos de
Bogotá
Apartado Aéreo 7860
Bogotá, Colombia

Vamos Mujer
Monthly
Comité de Defensa de los
Derechos de la Mujer/CODEM
Casilla de Correos 5216,
Correo 3
Santiago, Chile

Venceremos
Monthly
Unión de Mujeres Campesinas
Casilla de Correo 760-A
Quito, Ecuador

**Ventana: Una Visión Diferente
de la Mujer**
Irregular
Grupo Feminista "Ventana"
Apartado 117, San Pedro
Montes de Oca
San José, Costa Rica

Viva!
Monthly
Centro de la Mujer Peruana
Parque Hernán Velarde
Lima 100, Peru

La Voz de la Mujer, 1980–
Monthly
Instituto de Promoción y
Educación Popular/IPIP
Apartado Postal 16
Chimbote, Peru

Voz de Mujer
Apartado Postal 579
Morelos 62000
Cuernavaca, Morelos, Mexico

Women's Watch
International Women's Rights
Action Watch
University of Minnesota
301 19th Ave. South
Minneapolis, MN 55455, USA

Women's World
Quarterly
Women's International Cross-
Cultural Exchange/WICCE
P.O. Box 2471
Geneva 2 1211, Switzerland

Part Four

Meeting the Automation Challenge

I. Automated Systems: Six Perspectives from Librarians and Vendors

41. Automation and Latin American Acquisitions: An Acquisitions Manager's Perspective

Dana D'Andraia

An academic library acquisitions manager needs to look in two opposite and external directions as well as manage internal acquisitions functions and activities. In a sense, the acquisitions manager acts as a middleman between the publisher or vendor and the selector. More specifically, in the present context, the acquisitions manager is the middleman and, it is to be hoped, the expediter, between the Latin American bibliographer and the Latin American vendor.

In my experience as an acquisitions librarian, however, I have been very aware of the high level of knowledge, interest, and involvement in the acquisitions function by Latin American bibliographers. And I believe there is a much finer line between collection development activities and acquisitions activities in the collecting of Latin American library materials than, for instance, in domestic or Western European materials collection development. It is common for Latin Americanists to develop and maintain contact with Latin American vendors. It is not unknown for a fully planned and arranged-for approval or blanket order to be presented to the acquisitions manager without the latter's prior awareness that a program was even in the works. Such a gift can prove successful, or extremely troublesome, depending on the situation. But by and large, this arrangement has worked well for the three parties concerned. Vendors are accustomed to conducting their business with library personnel in a certain way. Latin American bibliographers build a network of connections and personal relationships which helps them stay current in their field, and the acquisitions librarians are able to tap the bibliographer's knowledge in helping to acquire materials for the library as expeditiously as possible.

Enter into this equation the automation of acquisitions functions. This revolution, which swept most academic library acquisitions departments only a few years ago, made acquisitions managers very busy during the planning and implementing stages. When it surfaced, however, the same basic relationships still existed: the acquisitions manager was still a middleman between the vendor and the selector, with the new added prospect of being able to provide increased service to the bibliographer, and the boon of better business practices to the vendor. Has this happened in terms of Latin American acquisitions?

Let's first take a look at the effect on the vendors of automating acquisitions. I will make a few points or suggestions, and fully concede there may be more. It has often been said that one of the results of automating acquisitions, besides generally improving the quality of our purchase orders and speeding up the payment process, is that the acquisitions librarian begins to demand more from the vendor. For domestic vendors, this translates into concrete and costly expectations, such as the electronic transmission of orders and invoicing by tape cartridge. We expect our materials vendors to work with our systems vendor in developing and supporting the product that makes this possible. We spend a lot of money with our main domestic vendors, and we expect them to pay the cost of the automated service. For most of us, our Latin American acquisitions represent much less "business"— if you will. But we are accustomed to spending more in terms of labor per transaction. For example, we expect to be invoiced in any way the vendor chooses, as was the case before automation, and we expect to be able to handle it. But changes do occur in the relationship between Latin American vendor and the library upon automating acquisitions.

Let's take the matter of appearances. Automating acquisitions means that purchase orders, claim forms, and cancellation notices will look different from the way they looked with a manual system. How many acquisitions managers thought to (or were able to) send samples of the new forms to the vendors they use, including all the Latin American vendors who, from the acquisitions point of view, may not figure very large in the picture? To be fair to acquisitions librarians, it is not uncommon to have 600 or more vendors in the vendor files. The new forms might be deceptively similar. That is, a purchase order, a claim request, and a cancellation notice for the same book are printed on the same basic form and are identical to each other with the exception of a few words. One expensive and frustrating result of this is the extra labor and expense for both vendor and library when a claim or cancellation crosses in the mail with its shipment and is mistaken for a new order by the vendor, resulting in duplication. The ease of claiming on an automated system increases the possibility of this happening. With a manual acquisitions system, claiming is rarely maintained on schedule, and is usually the first activity to be sacrificed in times of high activity or crisis. Automated, your acquisitions department is probable claiming more and with greater frequency. Confusion may not always be avoidable, but the acquisitions manager needs to be aware that old and well-established customs and ways of conducting business are being changed, without forewarning, over long distances, and in two different languages. Yes, most Latin American materials vendors will conduct business in English. That is another expectation the acquisitions manager probably has, and there is even less provision for attempting to communicate in the vendor's language when a greater percentage of the acquisitions department's correspondence is produced automatically and mailed without further examination or consideration. It may be that it remains for the bibliographer, even more than before, to maintain much of the human touch that characterized the business of acquiring Latin American materials for our academic libraries.

On the other side of the coin, the personal relationship the Latin American bibliographer develops with the vendor can cause problems for the acquisitions manager. An automated system usually provides accessible, quantifiable information about vendor performance. Adding the qualifiable information readily obtainable from acquisitions staff who have day-to-day experience with a vendor's performance, the acquisitions manager can build good cases for using or not using various vendors. The authority for vendor selection varies from library to library, but when a selector insists that orders be sent to a particular vendor when better alternatives have been identified in the acquisitions process, internal conflict is bound to emerge. The acquisitions manager is accountable for acquiring the material that has been selected in the most cost effective manner possible. This includes ensuring that staff time and labor are used efficiently.

Automating acquisitions has little effect on the various problems inherent in acquiring library materials from Latin America, and while the expectations we have regarding Latin American vendors may be less than the demands we place on domestic vendors, there is an area in which the Latin American vendors have a very legitimate request to make of us. Because of the high incidence of theft in the Latin American mail and the forging of checks, many vendors have requested special payment practices—from concealing the payment check in several thicknesses of letter paper and handwriting the envelope, to paying a domestic bank account and simultaneously notifying the vendor that payment has been processed. Acquisitions managers need to do their best to comply with these requests although they may not have control over their institution's check cutting and mailing procedure. At the least, they need to ensure that payment processing under an automated system is not less flexible than a manual process. The system should have the capability of alerting the operator during the payment process when the vendor being paid has particular exigencies or requirements.

And now, looking in the opposite direction, and one much closer to the acquisitions manager's own department, what is the effect of automating acquisitions on the Latin American collection development process? Recently I informally polled Latin American bibliographers working in five of the fifteen academic libraries generally considered to have the largest Latin American collections. As indicated in the 1987 edition of *The Automation Inventory of Research Libraries,** all but one of the fifteen libraries is making use of some form of automated acquisitions. Some are planning or already using their second generation of automated systems. I asked these five Latin American bibliographers two sorts of questions: What kind of management information is available to you now that acquisitions operations are automated? And how does this relate to the service the acquisitions department is providing? While I was interested in the strengths and limitations of the various systems, I was more interested in the use of the system in the internal library environment in terms of the relationship between the acquisitions department and the Latin American bibliographer.

A common denominator among those responsible for developing a very large Latin American collection seems to be control over a budget. All other factors, such as reporting structure, type of system, and years automated were quite disparate, even among the five with whom I spoke. For all these bibliographers, therefore, budgetary information is especially meaningful. Many responses to my questions were similar even though not all of these bibliographers had been consulted when the system was being planned for their library. All receive management reports containing acquisitions information, but the reports may not be provided by the acquisitions department. Rather a systems office may be responsible for providing reports and programming requested changes. The reports themselves vary in scope and sophistication. While the lack of certain reports was noted,

---

*Maxine K. Sitts, ed., *The Automation Inventory of Research Libraries, 1987* (Washington, DC: Office of Management Studies, Association of Research Libraries, 1987).

generally satisfaction was expressed, and most felt they were getting most of the information they need to do their jobs. Most have an informal, rather than a formal, mechanism for making changes in the reports they are getting, which seemed to be a satisfactory arrangement, and all felt the information received was useful.

As an acquisitions librarian I was most interested in the responses to the following four-part question: When you have requested acquisitions information that you were not getting, did you ever receive these answers: The information can't be provided because: (1) of system limitations; (2) we don't have the time; (3) it would cost too much; (4) it would be too complicated. I heard five different combinations of answers, including one all yes to the four reasons, and one all no. Seemingly, the age of the system being used was not a factor, nor was the system itself, because people with the same system answered differently.

Everyone I spoke with cited benefits they recognized and enjoyed with an automated acquisitions system. Information is quicker and better in quality; flexible fund structures and customized reports ensure that the different areas of the Latin American collection are being supported as they should; frequent budget reports help ensure the budget is spent appropriately; and library users benefit directly by having access to acquisitions and in-process information—to name some of them. On the negative side, there is the realization that an automated acquisitions system does not solve all problems, and the reality of the system may be less than the expectations one had been led to believe. Also, much trepidation is felt about changing from an old familiar system to one that will do things differently, and some things perhaps not as well.

The bibliographers I spoke with (and I would like to express my thanks to those who spent their time and thought on the telephone with me) seemed to have reasonable, realistic, and informed outlooks concerning the services and information that can be expected from acquisitions. The experiences of these bibliographers may or may not be similar to the experiences of bibliographers in libraries with smaller, less influential Latin American collections, and in which the competition for resources may be fiercer. The group was too small, and my method was too informal, to arrive at generalizations. But I would like to conclude with some observations based on these conversations, and based on my own experience.

Both the acquisitions manager and the bibliographer can help promote the good management of acquisitions in an automated environment. Besides managing the acquisitions function, the acquisitions manager should provide meaningful information in an understandable format and in a timely manner to the bibliographer. The acquisitions manager should involve representatives from collection development to the extent possible in the planning or upgrading of the system. A dialog should be maintained, whether formal or informal, to keep information and reports current with what is needed. Needs change, so the acquisitions manager should periodically describe in nonjargon language reports which are available, but not being used, and which may have been forgotten. The acquisitions manager should also listen carefully when a report is requested. The information that is needed may be different from what is available on the report being requested. An alternative may be available that will meet the bibliographer's needs better.

Bibliographers need to keep in mind that material and vendor selection are but the first step in the acquisitions process. Manual or automated, the acquisitions process still consists of order preparation and placement, records management, receiving, payment processing, and appropriate distribution and in-process control to avoid the lost-in-the-library syndrome. Requests for special services and reports have to be weighed against other requests, and perhaps scheduled at a time less convenient than desired. Automated does not mean automatic, or error free, or inexpensive. The capabilities of the system may exceed the ability of an organization to take advantage of them. Resources vary among libraries, and the information sought may be unobtainable owing to too few terminals, cost, time, or low priority from an administrative point of view—not because of system limitation. Bibliographers need to hold up their end of the dialog between acquisitions and collection development. They should be involved in the implementing and upgrading of the system as it relates to their needs, but not expect to know the ins and outs of the system as well as do the acquisitions librarians. Thus, when a report is requested, it is important to explain the context of the request. The more information acquisitions managers have, the better they can evaluate requests against other demands and determine the appropriate and more efficient course of action.

Automated acquisitions are here to stay. Systems vary in sophistication and ease of use. Even so, a return to manual operation is far less likely than a move to a second generation of automation. While automating acquisitions alters some of the traditional relationships as well as provides significant improvements, the fundamental concept of the acquisitions manager as the middleman between bibliographer and vendor remains.

42. Implementing Automated Acquisitions Systems: A Systems Librarian's Perspective

John Waiblinger

Implementation of any automated library system involves a complex and multifaceted set of activities that ideally should include the input and involvement of as much of a library's staff as possible. Implementation is an ongoing process that requires continuing review of how operations and procedures are affected, changed, and enhanced through the application of automation technology. Equally important is the need to plan for the retrieval and evaluation of the wealth of extractable management information an automated system finally makes possible.

This paper focuses on the facet of the implementation process that is probably of most interest to bibliographers/selectors and one that requires their active involvement and input into the automation process: the ability to produce meaningful collection development and other management reports capable of enhancing the information base upon which collection decisions and evaluations are made.

This is a critical developmental area because there are significant limitations in the online interface and the information it provides. This statement does not in any way downplay the magnitude of improvement achieved by putting the On Order File online for everyone to view, efficiencies of operations achieved in the Acquisitions Department, the ability to update budget information instantaneously, and so on. It is simply that once these immediate efficiencies and enhancements have been achieved, much more should be made available in terms of summarized collection development, problem, and other management information that is not readily retrievable on a one-by-one order look-up basis online. One needs the ability to scan the entire Acquisitions database and all of the thousands of order records and information contained therein to extract and summarize specific desired information in a usable format.

In this area, the Systems Office needs to work closely with the bibliographers/selectors in identifying their informational needs. It is System Office's job to design the programs and methods for extracting the information. It is the users' responsibility to articulate clearly their informational needs. I address briefly some of those management information areas and some of the issues involved in getting meaningful and usable data.

The most important information that should be extractable from an automated acquisitions system is detailed and sophisticated collection development information that identifies for any specified subject area or program how much money is being expended to support that area and how many items, and what kinds of items, that support represents. The sophistication with which this kind of information can be collected is heavily dependent on how the budget structure is set up. Setting up the budget structure to simply coincide with fund allocations alone is not sufficient to also allow extraction of detailed collection-specific information. What is required is a budget structure that tracks both allocation information for an item AND in addition tracks which specific part (or parts) of the collection the item was purchased to support. These two broad areas of required information are often not mutually compatible and, therefore, cannot be tracked on the basis of assigning a single budget fund to the item.

This dilemma is best clarified by providing some specific examples of problem areas: For example, if the library is using approval plans, it is necessary to track the total part of the book fund that has been allocated to each approval plan. Items received on the approval plan must be recorded as payments against the approval plan budget allocations. But, recording only this level of information provides no data on which specific collection areas the items purchased on approval are supporting. Use of endowment funds presents a similar problem when the endowment has been established to support more than a single, specific area of the library's collections. Another problematic area is when a bibliographer is given a "programmatic-type budget" to administer (some examples of these at USC are the AUL for Collection Development's Discretionary Fund, Special Collections Rare Books Fund, GPO Depository, Latin American). Again in this situation, the allocation information required for tracking funds does not provide detail on the specific subject area of the collection the item will support.

What is required in each of these examples is the ability to track for a single item two different pieces of information. Collection of both pieces of information is provided through the use of an "On-Behalf-Of" strategy for assigning multiple accounts to a single item. Our system allows the ability not only to assign an "Apply" Account to any item that is used by the system to reflect the account against which the "real" dollars are spent but also to assign "On-Behalf-Of" information that does not affect real dollars in the system, but does provide the required collection development information. Therefore, an item purchased on the Yankee Press Approval Plan is actually paid for against the proper fund (Yankee Press Approval Budget) but can also be tagged informationally with a Subject Fund (i.e., Ethnic Studies Budget) even though that account has not been actually charged for the item. This design structure allows us not only to produce information and reports on actual expenditures by account but also to produce equally important detailed specific collection development reports. Bibliographers/selectors, therefore, receive information on how much was actually expended against their actual fund allocations and also information on what was expended "On-Behalf-Of" their funds, including information against which account such an "On-Behalf-Of" was actually paid (i.e., approval, discretionary). Thus, bibliographers/selectors are provided with the full picture on each area of their collection responsibilities.

Establishing such an account structure involves considerable planning. The appropriate level of specific collection detail desired must be determined. The account structure itself needs to be designed in a way that facilitates easy and logical assignment of this information to a given order record. Those allocated accounts that by nature require supplemental assignment of "On-Behalf-Of" information must be clearly identified. Most critical is the need for all the bibliographers/selectors to clearly understand the design, purpose, and function of the accounting structure. It is the selector's responsibility to assign all of the necessary account information at the time of ordering an item—both the account that will actually pay for the items and any desired supplementary "On-Behalf-Of" collection detail. Unless the bibliographers/selectors have been actively involved in understanding the accounting structure's design and function in the automated system, they will not be able to fulfill this responsibility. Again, it is the Systems Office's responsibility to provide the explanation of how the system works and what its capabilities are; it is the user's responsibility to identify the kinds of information and level of detail they require. Only through a joint effort and involvement can the system be set up in a way that meets the library's full informational needs.

In addition the kind of collection development information described above, there are many other categories of information available in the automated system that need to be pulled out and presented in a usable format. Again, identification of this information can only be determined by the users of the system. Identification of the information that needs to be extracted should be done on a careful and selective basis. Otherwise, it is all too easy to find oneself buried in a mass of printouts that become meaningless owing to the sheer volume of information presented.

In identifying desirable reports, three factors should be considered. Consider what actual use the extracted information will be put to and narrow the focus accordingly. Decide carefully whether a listing of all individual orders meeting a selected criteria is necessary or whether summarized information is all that is really required. It can make the difference between a one-page report and a report that is hundreds of pages long! Finally, consider how frequently the information is required—is it required every month or is a quarterly, biannual, or annual report sufficient? Keeping these three factors in mind when requesting information will help prevent information overload.

At USC we are still in the process of identifying all of the possible information residing in our Geac Acquisitions System that we would like to extract in usable format. The Systems Office is working with the bibliographers/selectors to develop usable and meaningful reports. After considerable discussion we have developed the following initial reports:

A monthly summary collection development report that lists for each "subject' account the total number of real orders/expenditures charged to that account. Additionally, the report lists all "On-Behalf-Of" orders/expenditures for the account and groups them by the account against which the item was actually paid. Currently, individual order detail is provided with this report; the need for this detail is being reviewed.

Monthly "RUSH" order reports listing individual order detail sorted by "subject" account on all RUSHes received during the current month and a cumulative listing of all RUSHes outstanding greater than 30 days.

Monthly cancellations reports listing individual order detail sorted by "subject" account on all orders canceled during the month. This is also provided on an annual basis, summarizing all canceled orders for the year.

A biannual "outstanding orders" report listing individual order detail sorted by "subject" acts committed but not yet received. This is printed once in January and again after year-end closing to show all orders carried forward as commitments into the new fiscal year.

Work continues on identifying other desirable informational reports.

In conclusion, one of the prime benefits derived from automating the acquisitions process is the wealth of extractable information residing in the system that can help contribute to enhancing the intellectual tasks required in the area of collection development and management. This can only be accomplished through a cooperative effort between the Systems Office and the end users of the automated system.

43. The System Vendor's Perspective

Virginia Rodes

Innovative Interfaces has been a library automation vendor since 1978. The system includes acquisitions, serials control, and online catalog and circulation functions which can be purchased separately, but which are fully integrated.

Currently installed and operating in nearly one hundred libraries throughout North America, the system is very easy to learn and to use, since all appropriate choices are on each menu screen. Each screen is clear and concise, eliminating the need for a separate "help" function.

The following examples illustrate the kinds of management information available to administrators, bibliographers, collection management staff, in addition to technical service specialists by describing the INNOVACQ system. Customized reports are produced by a report generator and statistical package capable of identifying any subset of the database and combining any of the values in any data element in a fully Boolean fashion, on demand at any time. The resulting records can be sorted into any sequence and then listed with any or all data elements displaying, or be counted by, any of the values in any of the fixed-length data fields.

Here are some of the reports the Latin American bibliographer can produce without going to the acquisitions or systems librarian:

1. All reports are in US dollars, for easy comparison. Up to forty foreign currency conversion rates can be stored in the system, so that both new orders and invoice payments record accurate US dollar amounts for fund encumbrances and expenditures. The rates can be changed easily, as often as desired, to keep up with changes in the foreign currency market. If these rates are kept current, the balance in each fund will be accurate.

2. Each library can set a "percentage of appropriations spent" limit, so that you are warned, whenever placing orders, if the fund balance limit is below the amount you are encumbering. In addition to seeing this in traditional columnar display, you can graph any of the fund report data and see the amount spent as a solid bar and the amount encumbered as a shaded bar, as shown in figure 1.

3. A standard system supports 600 funds, each of which can have up to seven subfunds. Each fund is identified by a unique five-character code which is keyed into order records. When an estimated amount is also keyed into the order record, the system automatically and instantly encumbers that fund by that amount. During invoice processing, the price is verified, the fund amount is automatically disencumbered, and the payment added to the expenditure column for the fund. If an order is canceled, INNOVACQ automatically disencumbers it. Latin American bibliographers might choose to group funds by country, with regional subtotals.

4. Fund reports can be produced at any point in time for each fund, fund group, or all funds. Displayed or printed are appropriations for a FY, expenditures YTD, encumbrances YTD, and either the free balance or cash balance (unencumbered balance). a "fund" can be only books, with another "fund" for continuations or one "fund" by country or language, with subfunds for books, continuations, and so on.

    As shown in figure 2, the single fund display includes all information: amounts in each category, totals, and percentage calculations.

5. Another kind of report drawn from fund information is the Fund Activity Report, much like a checking account statement; one is produced for each fund. It shows the balance in the account at the

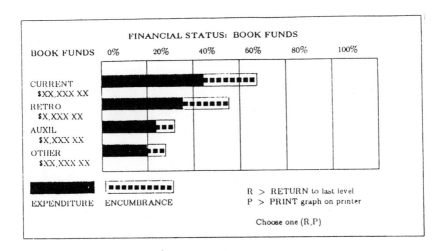

Figure 1

beginning of the accounting period, all charges made since that time, and concludes with the current balance. Charges are listed title by title, so that a fund manager can readily see exactly how much was paid for each item. This report, besides providing useful information for the fund manager, serves as an "audit trail," documenting in print every change made to the fund's balance. It can also verify the balance which the system keeps for each fund as each invoice is posted.

Note in figure 3 that two new orders (lien no. 6179 and 6297) have been recorded, while one invoice (voucher no. 805615) has been paid. The total at the bottom of the encumbrance column includes the minus amount, but the new encumbrances total shown at the bottom of the listing does not.

These Fund Activity Reports can either be displayed on the screen or printed for a single fund or for all funds on the system.

```
              FINANCIAL STATUS:   BOOK FUNDS

   CURRENT          APPROP.     EXPEND.     ENCUMB.     FREE BAL.

1 > APPROVAL        $xxxx.xx    $xxx.xx     $xxx.xx     $xxxx.xx
2 > BLANKET          xx.xx       x.xx        xx.xx        .xx
3 > STANDING         xxx.xx      xx.xx       xx.xx       xx.xx
4 > SERIALS          x.xx        x.xx        x.xx        x.xx
5 > ONE-TIME         x.xx        x.xx        x.xx        x.xx


        Total       $xx,xxx.xx·  $xxx.xx     $xxx.xx     $xxxx.xx
```

```
                  FINANCIAL STATUS:   BOOK FUNDS

   Fund name          American Pubs.
   Fund code          ameap
   Note1
   Note2

   Approp $10,000.00  Expend $5,000.00        Encumb $3,000.00
                      Free balance $2,000.00

   Expenditures by subfund:

   REG $x.xx  x%      STAND ORD         $x.xx  x%   ITEM S.O. $x.xx  x%
   APP $x.xx  x%      SUBSCRIP          $x.xx  x%
   External fund # O   xx,   Codes 1, 2, 3:    "u", "x", " "

   R  >  To RETURN to last level

   Choose one (R)
```

Figure 2

xxxxx FUND ACTIVITY REPORT, page heading			
PREVIOUS BALANCE	APPROPRIATION	EXPENDITURE	ENCUMBRANCE
$6,698.10	$8,500.00	$50.73	$1,751.17
CURRENT ACTIVITY - - -			

	PONUM	TITLE		
6179	1095730	Directory of natural hi	$0.00	$9.42
6297	1097003	Stedman's Medical dicti	$0.00	$80.00
805615	1029010	Physiological ecology o	$40.00	-$40.00
SUBTOTAL =			$0.00 $40.00	$49.42
CURRENT BAL = $6648.68		$8,500.00	$90.73	$1,800.59

1 payments listed above averaging $40.00
There are 2 new encumbrances listed above total $89.42,
   and average $44.71

Figure 3

6. If responsible for selecting and obtaining materials, keep one eye
    on titles, another on money, and your third eye on vendors! The
    Vendor Performance Report shows everything that happens to
    orders placed in a certain time period—including receipts, claims,
    cancellations received outside that time period, a list of invoices
    paid to each vendor, the number of orders claimed or canceled,
    with a percentage of the total, the average delivery time, and so on
    (see fig. 4).

7. In contrast, the vendor activity report shows all activity within a
    certain time period. This also serves as a record of technical
    services activity with each vendor (see fig. 5).

8. The system is very flexible and allows the user to create all sorts of
    lists from any subset of the database sorted in any order. For
    example, title ordered within a certain time period by price, or
    titles received within a certain time period by call number, etc.

9. In addition to lists, statistical reports can be created using any
    subset of the database. For example, type of material sorted by
    language. The possibilities are endless.

```
    ***   Vendor : bna   ***              ***   STATISTICS   ***


            Vendor Performance w orders of 07-01-85 — 05-01-86
                    Serials included, All order types
                 These statistics calculated on 05-06-86

                    Orders      :      1098
                    Claims      :        30
            Orders claimed      :        24      Percent Claimed      :    2%
            Orders canceled     :        18      Percent Canceled     :    1%
            Orders received     :      1019      Avg. weeks to deliver :   4
                 Amount paid    :   $17,745.09
                 Open orders    :        61
        Amount of open orders   :     $865.20
        # of copies received    :      1103

    105 Invoices in invoice file

    I > Display INVOICES
    R > RETURN to previous screen
```

FULL FORMAT — Second Screen

```
    ***   Vendor code : bna   ***        ***   Invoices 1-3 out of 3   ***
```

NO.	INV.NO.	AMT.	INV.DATE	PD.DATE	VOUCHER	#ITEMS
1	12454	$165.74	08/02/83	09/08/83	805880	4
2	15839	$366.86	08/05/84	09/08/83	805881	13

FULL FORMAT — Third Screen

Figure 4

10. Other features include being able to add desiderata or OP titles to the database, with status 1, which means that they go through the title check for duplicates in the system, but are not in queue to print purchase orders and no fund encumbrance is made until the status is changed to "on order." They are, in effect, on hold, but ready to go.

Online interfaces are in use all over the country between INNOVACQ and all major approval vendors, so that bibliographic and invoice information is transmitted electronically in conjunction with approval shipments, eliminating the need to re-key and thus eliminating many errors. Tape interfaces are used in a similar fashion between all major US serials vendors and INNOVACQ.

CODE	CLAIM CYCLE	NO. OF ORDER	NO. OF CLAIM	NO. OF CNCEL	NO. OF REC'T	TOT.AMT. ORDERS	TOT.AMT. INVOICES
bna	u	154	1	16	133	$1500 00	$1330 00
bnas	u	169	1	0	206	$400 35	$575 49
bobbs	a	100	0	5	50	$1000 00	$745 37
bor	a	200	27	0	0	$759 00	$0 00
bow	u	50	0	0	20	$279 50	$107 64

F > Browse FORWARD
B > Browse BACKWARD

STATISTICAL FORMAT

CODE	ALT. CODE	VENDOR's NAMES AND ADDRESSES
bna		Blackwell North America, Inc. 6024 S.W. Jean Road Bldg. G Lake Oswego, Oregon 97034
bnas		BNA Search Service 6024 S.W. Jean Road I Lake Oswego, Oregon
bobbs		Bobbs Merrill Co., Inc. Subs of Howard W. Sai 4 W. 58th Street New York, N.Y. 10019

F - Browse FORWARD
B - Browse BACKWARD

ADDRESS FORMAT

There are xxx vendors in the vendor file

CODE : bna	NAME :	Blackwell North America, Inc.
CODE : bnas	NAME :	BNA/Search Service
CODE : bobbs	NAME :	Bobbs Merrill Co., Inc.
CODE : bor	NAME :	Borgo Press
CODE : bow	NAME :	Bowker Press
CODE : brl	NAME :	E.J. Brill
CODE : bro	NAME :	Brockhaus of Stuttgart
CODE : broud	NAME :	Broude Brothers Limited
CODE : brown	NAME :	William C. Brown Co.
CODE : bst	NAME :	Boise State College
CODE : bso	NAME :	Biblioteca Siglo de Oro

F - Browse FORWARD
B - Browse BACKWARD

BRIEF FORMAT

Figure 5

C1001801 Last updated: 07-31-85 Created: 03-25-85 Revision: 26						
AUTHOR	United States. Supreme Court					
TITLE	Decisions of the U.S. Supreme Court					
CALL #	KP101 .W4 LOCATIONS res					
NOTE	Photocopy title page					

Boxes 8 - 28 of 52

Win 84	Spr 84	Sum 84	Fal 84	Win 85	Spr 85	Sum 85
ARRIVED	ARRIVED	ARRIVED	ARRIVED	CLAIM1	LATE	EXPECTED
01/15/84	04/15/83	07/15/84	10/15/84	07/31/85	04/15/85	07/15/85
8:1 1	8.2 1	8 3 1	8:4 1	9:1 1	9:2 1	9:3 1
Fal 85	Win 86	Spr 86	Sum 86	Fal 86	Win 86	Spr 87
E	E	E	E	E	E	E
10/15/85	01/15/86	04/15/86	07/15/86	10/15/86	01/15/87	04/15/87
9:4	10:1	10:2	10.3	10.4	11:1	11:2
Sum 87	Fal 87	Win 88	Spr 88	Sum 88	Fal 88	Win 89
E	E	E	E	E	E	E
07/15/87	10/15/87	01/15/88	04/15/88	07/15/88	10/15/88	04/15/87
11:3	11:4	12:1	12:2	12:3	12:4	13:1

Figure 6

Anyone searching in INNOPAC (online catalog) can also see what has been ordered, what is in process, and which serial issue is the last received when INNOPAC is integrated with INNOVACQ. Features such as searching another library's database are also available. This could be used to help make selection decisions about expensive items which other institutions may also have considered purchasing.

The system makes it easy for the bibliographer to order any type of material, while helping to manage appropriations and collections effectively at the same time (see fig. 6).

44. A Computer Saga: The U.S. Book Dealer's Perspective

Howard L. Karno

I decided to computerize my business in 1982. It seemed the obvious solution to the exasperating problem of retyping titles again and again from catalog to catalog. Also, it promised an end to the rows of file boxes containing the 3 X 5 cards and their bibliographic data. In addition, the possibility of quoting titles on any subject by the mere touch of a few buttons seemed incredibly attractive.

Several articles had appeared in the *AB Bookman's Weekly* about the ease of converting to a computer-based inventory and cataloging operation. Nothing to it. Just purchase some hardware (but only after selecting the proper software) and away you go. The articles advised attending a computer orientation class before making the leap. So I went to an all-day meeting at the local community college. Three hours of RAM, bytes, formatting, etc., and I was ready. Well not really. I realized that the main task was to find the proper software and the employee to run it. At the time there were no programs on the market, at least to my knowledge. So I decided that I would approach the computer sales houses with my requirements. What I wanted was to store in memory some 15,000 titles with access via author, title, and several subject fields. "No problem," the computer folks said, "just take a database program and modify it for your particular needs." Great, now who was going to do it? That was the rub. Some months passed, and "Gracias a Díos," I read in the *AB* of a program specifically written for the antiquarian bookseller. Called Book Ease, it was the work of Marc Younger in New York. His system is based on the Ashton-Tate DB2 program and used a DOS 2.0. I didn't and still don't know what that is all about, but I have employees who do. Anyway, after some very trying moments with computer sales companies, who promised the moon and delivered very little and very wrong, we eventually became operational in early 1983.

It has not always been an easy road. The lack of adequate support from the hardware suppliers is still an irritant. Either they go out of business or they ignore you. At present we are having a backup problem which has not yet been resolved after five months. Operator

449

error almost lost us some 1,500 titles, but a special recovery program saved the majority. And there have been some lengthy down times. We have had three computers over the five years. We started out with a Corona PC, a 27 Megabyte Great Lakes hard disc, the biggest then available, and a NEC 3550 printer. Now all that remains of the original system is the printer, which although reliable is quite slow by today's standards. The Corona burned up at the shop of a Corona dealer who claimed it wasn't his fault, and eventually the hard disc—after storing more than 18,000 titles—ran out of capacity. When the Corona gave up the ghost we bought an ITT Xtra which still gives good service. However, the lure of a faster machine with vastly increased memory led to the purchase of a Fountain AT turbo with 65 megabytes memory. The DOS is 3.3 for those of you who care about these things. I should mention that the software package has been updated to some extent, but is still based on the DB2, although there are modifications available using the DB3. Among the various software programs we use are Smart Key which speeds up operations, Smart Print which provides accents and foreign language corrections, and MultiMate for word processing.

What has this all meant as far as productivity and ease of operation? Our average catalog is now about 10 to 12 pages, contains approximately 150 to 200 titles, and weighs 1 to 2 ounces. With mostly new and some recycled items we issue around four each month versus the one per month prior to computerization (although it must be admitted the older catalogs were substantially larger). This is achieved more inexpensively as far as time spent in adding entries is concerned. Mailing labels and quotas take only a few minutes. However, several functions are not utilized. The number of copies for each title is noted, but we don't enter the prices paid, nor the supplier. We have the capability of invoicing, addressing envelopes or labels, and automatically removing sold titles from the inventory in the same operation, but we don't. We have the capability of storing asked-for titles and printing want lists from the computer. Instead, this is done by typewriter. Finally, we have not installed a modem nor have we networked various work stations. Expense is one reason. Inertia is another.

Apparently, there is an effort at present to encourage dealers to purchase space on a title-by-title basis in a common data bank. However, since most of our sales are institutional we are more interested in reaching libraries than in selling to other dealers. Thanks to computerization we can provide librarians bibliographically detailed lists on a variety of subjects. But, ideally, the next step is utilization of the modem by which the library selector can electronically search our inventory. This capability is, hopefully, not too far off in the future.

Most if not all small business computer systems are extremely reliable, as are the numerous user-friendly software programs. Therefore, while it is true that the task of starting from scratch to train personnel to enter large inventories is foreboding, given the present state and cost of computers, it is difficult to deny the value of computers for the antiquarian bookseller.

45. La perspectiva de un librero latinoamericano

Martín García Cambeiro

A principios de 1985, comenzamos a pensar en la necesidad de incorporar una computadora, que nos ayudara en determinadas tareas, que en ese entonces estaban superando nuestra capacidad de trabajo. Fue así que en septiembre del mismo año adquirimos una Personal Computer Hewlett Packard con 15 megabytes de capacidad de almacenamiento en disco y comenzamos a desarrollar un software, ya que en Buenos Aires no existía un programa similar al necesitado.

A los pocos meses comenzamos a obtener buenos resultados, pero también a darnos cuenta que las posibilidades de automatización son ilimitadas, y lo que comenzó como una ayuda para determinados trabajos de rutina (facturación, catálogos, etc.) se convirtió en un elemento requerido para el resto de las tareas.

La computadora quedaba superada y a principios de 1987 tuvimos que tomar una decisión, o nos limitábamos a las posibilidades disponibles o invertíamos en un equipo varias veces más costoso que la computadora personal disponible. En abril de ese mismo año incorporamos un Computador Hewlett Packard 250, con una capacidad de almacenamiento en disco de 65 megabytes.

Rápidamente nos dimos cuenta que el equipo adquirido debía ser complementado con un importante software, y para desarrollarlo organizamos un equipo de bibliotecarios, analistas en computación, mi hermano Marcelo y yo.

Del análisis, decidimos crear una base de datos, como corazón de la librería y a partir de la cual, manejaríamos los servicios (approval plan, catálogos estadísticas, suscripciones, guía de seriadas, listas de agotados, compras automáticas, canje automático, etc.). Así lo hicimos y en febrero de este año comenzamos a incorporar información analizada e indizada exclusivamente por un equipo de tres bibliotecarios profesionales contratados definitivamente para desarrollo y mantenimiento de la base; esta contiene 15 campos distintos, todos de posible consulta, que además de los más comunes como autor, título, editor, colección, etc., incluye keywords, países relacionados con la obra, coverage, sexo del autor, alcance temporal, origen del editor (gubernamental o privado), etc.; y con una capacidad actual de más de 100.000 libros.

La base de datos sería el origen de los servicios, que en épocas de restricciones presupuestarias deberían orientarse a colaborar con el bibliotecario y como consecuencia del mejor servicio, permitimos crecer en épocas de crisis.

En octubre próximo recibiremos un Computador Hewlett Packard 3000 con 150 megabytes de almacenamiento y cuatro terminales porque, debido al crecimiento de la librería y lo ambicioso del proyecto, tuvimos la misma opción antes mencionada, o limitábamos el proyecto o continuábamos invirtiendo.

Los servicios desarrollados han sido:

1. Catálogos especiales a pedido con información registrada en la base de datos.
2. Estadísticas generales de todo tipo.
3. Registro de todos los libros comprados por cada biblioteca (y por lo tanto los no comprados) para la elaboración de informes y estadísticas que permitan hacer compras adicionales o simplemente conocer la colección incorporada a través del informe recibido.
4. Cincuenta catálogos automáticos distintos, dentro de los cuales elegir el que corresponde a cada biblioteca por sus intereses. Con esto intentamos facilitar la tarea del bibliotecario, generalmente superado por la enorme información recibida.
5. Sistema automático de adquisiciones por medio del cual luego de ingresada una orden de compra, automáticamente la computadora revisa su existencia en stock y, en caso contrario, le asigna una orden de compra al primer de cinco distribuidores posibles que podemos asignar a cada editorial. Pasados los 15 días, las órdenes que no han sido recibidas, se reúnen en un informe generado automáticamente y debemos decidir algunas de las siguientes opciones:
   a. prorrogar el plazo de vencimiento
   b. transferir la orden a alguno de los otros 4 distribuidores posibles
   c. considerar que el libro está agotado y por esta razón será incluido en listados especiales de búsqueda que preveemos serán distribuidos a colegas de todo el país.

Finalmente, también a las órdenes por libros agotados le asignamos fecha de vencimiento, pasada la cual serán incluidos en un informe a cada biblioteca cancelándolas con opción a reactivarla por un período adicional.

6. Nuevos Approval Plan Sistemas 1 y 2, que debido al tiempo escaso de exposición me limitaré a decir que creemos que por sus beneficios cambiará el concepto convencional de Approval Plan en América Latina y que está basado en la enorme información semanal y mensual enviada al bibliotecario para que éste pueda controlar la sección y hacer compras adicionales sin riesgos de duplicación.

7. Desarrollo de canjes basados en nuestra Base de Datos, única en Argentina por sus características. Estamos formando una red de canjes con universidades, institutos y otros editores del interior del país con publicaciones fuera del circuito comercial, enviándoles información bibliográfica muy elaborada y complementándola con nuestra capacidad de proveer los libros seleccionados. A las ventajas mencionadas para esta clase de editores debe agregarse que muchas veces nuestro canje es su única posibilidad de recibir libros.

8. Stock computarizado. Hemos comenzado a registrar nuestro stock en la computadora. A partir de 1989 cada libro recibido en nuestro depósito será incluido, y años anteriores serán paulatinamente registrados. Al igual que las bibliotecas que comienzan a automatizarse sabemos que será un trabajo de años y por ello hemos decidido dar prioridad a las mejores obras de todos los años. Como resultado podremos elaborar catálogos especiales con los mejores libros en cada tema.

9. Guía de seriadas argentinas clasificadas por título y por tema y que incluirá comentarios de cada seriada. En 1986 publicamos una guía elaborada con nuestra primera computadora y en 1989 publicaremos la nueva edición preparada por bibliotecarios profesionales.

10. Programa automático de suscripciones.

Algunos servicios no han sido mencionados por falta de tiempo y otros aún están en estudio, pero lo importante a destacar es que continuamos desarrollando sistemas especializados en la atención a bibliotecas. Para finalizar queremos aprovechar la oportunidad para agradecer a todos los bibliotecarios que han confiado en nuestros servicios, así como también a nuestro padre Fernando que durante 25 años construyó las bases que hicieron posible el proyecto iniciado.

46. A Bibliographer's Perspective

Charles S. Fineman

Though it is certainly pure coincidence, I find that my position in this section (last after dealers and representatives of computer firms) somehow symbolizes where many bibliographers and collection management librarians have "spoken" when it came to conceiving and installing computer systems in libraries: last. Coming last frequently means one can benefit from the mistakes of those who have preceded, but it also usually means one's concerns have not been properly taken into account. While I incline toward the view that selectors have entered the systems dialog late, and that their libraries have been poorly served because of this, I am nevertheless optimistic about the future and hope to suggest that there are indeed things we can do within our libraries and across institutional lines to improve the situation.

I speak not only as a Latin American and Caribbean bibliographer; my institution now has a B.A.-level certificate program in Latin American and Caribbean studies, and I select materials for that program and the ongoing program of faculty seminars, but, as Humanities Bibliographer, I also have selection responsibilities for most languages and literatures (except Slavic and African); linguistics; philosophy; radio, TV, film, dance, and theater; journalism and direct marketing; library science; and Jewish Studies. This long list of subject responsibilities means I need to have very good information on what I am selecting for the collections and what it costs.

My library developed NOTIS and has been successful of late in marketing this remarkable software system to many libraries in North America and also to a few in South America. There are many fine features to NOTIS but, as currently implemented at Northwestern, there is no programmatic means for any selector to keep track of his or her selections at the point that makes the most sense for a bibliographer, namely, the moment of submitting an order. It was against such a background, and with the need to have certain collection management data at his disposal, that my predecessor, Ross W. Atkinson, now the AUL for collection management at Cornell

University, set up the HUM BIB programs which the Humanities Bibliographer at Northwestern has been using since the early 1980s. Without Ross's hard work and dedication to this problem, little of what I am saying today would be possible, so it is a very pleasant duty to acknowledge a debt of gratitude to him.

Running off the university computing center's (and not the library's) computer, and constructed using a simple social sciences data package, the HUM BIB system allows the bibliographer to receive, on a quarterly basis, statistics regarding all monographic purchases submitted to the acquisitions department. When an order is submitted, the bibliographer must note (manually; it is important to state again that this system is not at present integrated with NOTIS) the fund number used, the subject (there is tracking of close to thirty different subjects, from primary English literature to secondary German literature to linguistics and Latin American [Spanish-language] and Latin American [Portuguese-language]), the source of the original citation (e.g., a dealer's list; a national bibliography; miscellaneous review; faculty request) and the price (either a firm price in a foreign currency or an estimate in U.S. dollars). At the end of each quarter of the fiscal year, a run is made and analyses are produced whereby the bibliographer can see the number of orders per discipline; the average price per title in a given discipline; the average price by country of origin; the value of orders submitted using a certain fund number; and so on.

To be sure, HUM BIB was a stopgap system devised when a librarian needed to gather statistics about his collecting activity and found that the library system could not generate them. Since the system that emerged is not integrated with the library's system, the bibliographer cannot submit an order or authorize payment for a book in a shipment without HUM BIB pad in hand, ready to jot down four pieces of coded information for each and every selection. But this is better than nothing. The bibliographer is better equipped than most of his colleagues to compose annual or occasional reports that provide data to library management on trends in selection and prices, collection needs, and how they are (or are not) being met.

Selectors in the system quickly realized that combinations of good guesswork plus labor-intensive, manually maintained "systems" were, in the last analysis, counterproductive, and a librarywide task force was convened to reach agreement on the data elements needed for all facets of collection management, the best way to work these elements into the existing integrated system, and the most efficient way to generate reports that would be useful to both selectors and administrator/

managers. I was a member of that task force, which included representatives from the systems office, acquisitions, preservation, and other interested departments.

This task force realized that some information it was seeking already existed in many of the bibliographic records the library generated; manipulation of these data required programming so the elements could be "unfrozen" and help generate reports. In other cases, however, the information was not being collected or it was not clear that there was space in the existing records to track it. In the end, the task force saw that simply stating which elements were needed was a difficult job, indeed, one that required various departments and divisions to compromise a bit on territory.

Has the report of this task force made it easier for a selector to keep track of collecting practice? Unfortunately not. To date, several years after the submission of the task force's final report, library administration has still not acted on any of its recommendations and selectors are still coping (admirably) with a disparate array of different, all manually maintained, home-grown "systems." Everyone is aware that this is not the best situation, yet progress toward realizing something better is painfully slow.

Why has this been the case? I would point out that the origins of NOTIS (and the same can be said, in general terms, of other similar local systems) lie in technical processing, an area of library work which, early on, saw that computers had to be applied to cope with the growing complexities of work in that area. Technical processing departments had, in their hands, physical objects, books, and items in other media, around which they could construct their data. Bibliographers and collection developers, since they concerned themselves with a much earlier stage of processing, did not, and therein lay the problem. As one of my first supervisors put it, bibliographers deal with symbolic representations of books (namely, citations, blurbs, advertisements, and reviews), only at a much later stage with the books themselves. And, owing to this abstract nature of a bibliographer's job, it has been difficult for selectors to have their concerns factored into thinking about systems.

I said at the beginning of this paper that I was optimistic about the ability of collection developers to have their concerns about management data translated into actual programmatic action in local library computer networks. As library management is obliged to provide more and more detailed reports about how money is spent on collections, it too is coming to see that centralized data collection must be an institutional, not just an individual bibliographer's, concern.

However, before selectors achieve this, they will have to have a very thorough understanding of the system their library has so the wheel need not be reinvented. It will require bibliographers to learn more than they probably ever wanted to know about the structure of bibliographic records and about the report-writing capabilities of any member of programs or subprograms. But, in the end, it will be worth it. And there are hints (picked up earlier this spring at the ACRL/WESS conference in Florence) that our counterparts in Western Europe as well have begun to apply themselves to this problem, with a view toward possibly incorporating elements relevant to collections into the structure of bibliographic records as we now know them. If we work together within our libraries, across institutions, and even across borders, I am convinced we bibliographers, though we have entered the dialog about systems at a comparatively late date, will contribute much to the dialog and come away with much that we can apply with intelligence and skill to our tasks of developing research library collections.

II. Database Coverage of Frontiers, Borders, and Hinterlands

47. Databases in the Humanities and Social Sciences: An Update and Review of Border Research

Peter Stern

In 1988 the online revolution is already twenty-five years old. The first online databases were developed in the 1960s under government contract: Lockheed developed DIALOG for NASA, while Systems Development Corporation developed the ORBIT system to put the National Library of Medicine's enormous database of medical references online, the system now available through MEDLARS.

Through the intervening decades the online database has been developed into an information storing and processing industry which has become an essential part of medical, legal, engineering, scientific, and business research. While DIALOG remains the premier database vendor, it has been joined and challenged, albeit unsuccessfully, for preeminence by BRS, ORBIT, WilsonLine, Questelle, NYT, MDC, and Westlaw. Profits have matched the expansions of available searchable databases. Hard figures are surprisingly difficult to find, but an estimate for online usage in 1980 was 5 million searches carried out at a cost of $75 million. [1] In 1982 sixty-nine databases generated more than $100,000 each per year, and that number grew to eighty in 1983. [2] Those figures are certainly now far out of date; one researcher quotes a DIALOG official as recently claiming one-half billion dollars in revenue from online searches annually. It would be safe and conservative to estimate that revenues from online searches far exceed a billion dollars per year in this country.

The number and comprehensive nature of databases is also expanding. DIALOG at last count was offering 340 databases for end-user searching. The *North American Online Directory* for 1987 lists more than one thousand databases, and 133 vendors of databases. [3] One recent estimate put the number of commercially available databases at 500, and the number of noncommercially available numeric files at ten times that number! [4] The problem then, is not scarcity of online resources but their utilization in Latin American studies research.

In this paper I ask three questions: What databases are available and suitable for historical, and specifically frontier-oriented research?

Are researchers in the humanities and social sciences using the electronic technologies available to them in their work? And, finally, what is the prospectus for future developments in Latin American databases?

Databases suitable for Latin American-oriented research have been the subject of two previous SALALM papers.[5] Basically the types of databases are two: databases which are subject or discipline oriented and which happen to have information pertaining to Latin America, and those specifically created for use by Latin Americans and Latin Americanists. Among the former are familiar names in the humanities and social sciences: *Historical Abstracts, PAIS* and *PAIS Foreign Language Index, Social Sciences Index, Social Science Citation Index,* and *Arts and Humanities Citation Index, Dissertations Abstracts, MLA International Bibliography, Psychological Abstracts,* and *Sociological Abstracts.* All are still in print as bibliographic guides, but online database searching obviously affords the scholar extremely rapid, if expensive, searching of a bibliography in its entirety. In the past few years, a number of interesting current affairs databases have joined the familiar list: *BBC Summary of World Broadcasts, National Newspaper Index, Magazine Index, Newspaper Abstracts,* and *National Newspaper Index,* as well as full-text retrieval of a number of magazines and daily newspapers.[6] However, the overwhelming majority of online databases are scientific or business in orientation. This does not rule out their use by Latin American researchers, but it remains a basic economic fact that the greatest profitability lies in these sectors.

One example of a nonsocial science or humanities database is AGRICOLA (Agricultural On-Line Access), the computerized database of the United States National Agricultural Library. A foreign database covering much of the same ground is CAB (Commonwealth Agricultural Bureau) of the United Kingdom. Both databases contain bibliographic references on food and human nutrition, forestry, and rural sociology. CAB in particular has an abstract, World Agricultural Economics and Rural Sociology Abstracts (now Rural Development Abstracts), and a Leisure, Recreation, and Tourism Abstract, which can be used to retrieve information on Caribbean and Latin American tourism. Other nonstandard but possibly relevant databases include AGRIS International (an important FAO source for Third World agricultural information), Food Science and Technology Abstracts, BIS Informat World Business, Foreign Traders Index, Agribusiness, Coffeeline, Foreign Trade and Economic Abstracts, Aquaculture, Aquatic Sciences and Fisheries Abstracts, Environmental Bibliography (particularly useful in researching rain forest ecosystems and their destruction), GPO Monthly Catalog, NTIS reports, and many others. In fact, nearly all but the most technical databases available through commercial vendors could be utilized in some aspect of Latin American subject research.

Beyond the vast commercial database industry are the databases designed by Latin Americans themselves or subject-dedicated databases, many not available through any commercial system. These include Central American Update and Latin American Debt Chronicle, both produced by the Latin American Institute at the University of New Mexico, available not through DIALOG or BRS but on NewsNet. Another interesting experiment, temporarily in commercial limbo, is FRANCIS: Social Sciences (Amerique Latine), produced by the Centre Nationale de la Recherche Scientifique, Centre de Documentation Sciences Humaines. A bibliographical compilation of French and continental research on Latin America, its print counterpart is the *Bulletin Bibliographique Amerique Latine*; it is available through Questelle. [7]

Many databases exist only as tape loads on a mainframe at an academic or governmental institution, unavailable through any dial-up access. The AID Economic and Social Data Bank is a good example of the database unavailable to the scholar who cannot travel to where the information is stored. Veenstra and Posner include many such databases in their list: Balance of Payment and Directory of Trade Data Tapes from the International Monetary Fund, Capital Markets Data System of the World Bank, Foreign Production Supply and Demand data from the Foreign Agricultural Service, HRAF (Human Relations Area File) tapes, and others. [8] Libraries are now seeking to add MRDFs (machine-readable data files) to their collections; while dial-up access to many is just a matter of time, others will not be made available to the scholar except on-site for the foreseeable future.

A 1984 survey of Latin American databases showed that commercially available online databases and offline local site databases roughly parallel those existing in the United States in terms of subjects and compiling agencies. For example, paralleling AGRICOLA and CAB is AGRINTER (Sistema Interamericano de Información Agricola) in Costa Rica, compiled by the Inter-American Centre for Agricultural Documentation, Information and Communication. ALERTA is based at the Center for Scientific and Humanistic Information at UNAM in Mexico City; it is primarily a current-awareness service covering some 6,000 journals, but is only on-site. BIREME (Bibliotec Regional de Medicina) is a subsystem of MEDLINE for Brazil. CEPAL, the Economic Commission for Latin

America, runs a number of machine-readable databases with economic and social planning information. [9] Many of the Latin American databases are on-site MRDFs only; whether they will be made available for dial-up access may depend largely on economic factors.

One of the greatest obstacles to expanded use of online database searching is cost; since commercial databases operate for profit, the costs of running even a modest search tend to deter researchers in the humanities, and to a lesser degree in the social sciences, from using online bibliographies. Both libraries and the information industry itself are aware of these trends, but there is no consensus on how to resolve the dilemma. [10] One interesting development that leapfrogs this economic bottleneck is the direct acquisition by academic libraries of databases. Tapes are loaded onto mainframe computers, and the database can be accessed through library terminals in the same manner as the online catalog. The University of California at Berkeley now offers MEDLINE searching by library end-users through its MELVYL system. (There are some problems, however, in terms of hardware costs; MEDLINE occupies 4.5 gigabytes of memory, which requires a substantial investment in new storage and processing equipment.) The most relevant database to frontier or border investigation, UCLA's BorderLine, can be searched through UCLA's ORION online catalog. BorderLine's bibliographical database contains more than 9,000 records on the U.S.-Mexican border. Subjects treated include U.S.-Mexican relations, transborder immigration, history, political science, economics, urbanization and city planning, commerce and trade, rural and agricultural development, communications and mass media, language and linguistics, religion and mythology, literature and the arts. [11] Dial-up access to databases on academic mainframes and CD-ROM technology may offer a way out of the economic dilemma the commercial database vendor presents to the academic researcher.

With the proliferation of available databases and online services one would assume that the Latin American researcher is happily swamped with electronic alternatives to standard bibliographic research techniques. The reality, I believed, is markedly different. There is a significant gap between resources available online and their utilization by faculty, students, and researchers. I would assert as a historian who has earned a doctorate within the last three years, that new electronic research methods have barely begun to have an effect upon traditional graduate education in most humanities disciplines; as a librarian, that the majority of faculty are either strongly resistant to technical change, or simply ignorant of the many electronic alternatives available to them online.

Why is the humanities and social sciences community so reluctant to utilize these available technologies, especially when their counterparts in the "hard" sciences have so readily embraced them? I believe that there are a number of reasons for this resistance. One of the most serious obstacles to wider utilization of online searching is cost. Researchers in the physical sciences, many of whom think little of spending $50 each week to keep current on their field's literature online, usually have research funds to allay the costs of searching. Humanities scholars lack access to this type of consistent funding. This economic fact of life is one of the reasons a survey of database use among academics concluded that "it is clear that a strong demand for databases by faculty end-users does not yet exist." [12] Another obstacle to database use in history is problems inherent in the discipline itself. Many databases have backfiles dating back only to the mid-1970s; others do not provide for searching by historical period. Unless indexing and abstracting is done carefully, the imprecision of historical vocabulary can defeat categorization, and make the citation unretrievable. [13]

Furthermore, it has been suggested that humanists are suspicious of and hostile to technology and its allegedly dehumanizing effects. [14] As the PC replaces the typewriter, this theory is rapidly losing any validity. But many scholars who do utilize computers in their writing are still totally ignorant about online databases and electronic bibliographic retrieval. When one of the foremost young Mexicanists in the country informs me that he has never heard of DIALOG or of the concept of the online bibliography, I know that the librarian's most essential task at this point is dissemination of information. Rapid changes in technology usually far outstrip societal, or in this case, academic, response. The adoption of new research technologies in the last bastion of holdouts, the humanities researchers, will be a laborious process. Proposals to discuss new research technologies in the Committee on Latin American History of the AHA and the Latin American Studies Association have met, until quite recently, with a disinterested response. [15] There is, of course, a vigorous minority of social sciences and humanities researchers who have enthusiastically embraced these new research technologies. A survey printed in *History Microcomputer Review* (itself proof of a growing acceptance of the PC among the most traditional of social sciences researchers) demonstrated that use of the personal computer as an analytical and word-processing tool was widespread. [16] The survey concluded, however, that use of the computer in classroom instruction was still limited; database searching was not even addressed.

Another technological innovation is the telecommunications network, utilized by scholars to exchange information rapidly by electronic means. Exchange of conference papers, research materials, joint writing projects, and job information can be facilitated by use of "electronic bulletin boards": examples of such networks include Bitnet, CarNet, PeaceNet, and ScholarNet, the latter established expressly by and for humanities and social sciences scholars at North Carolina State University. [17]

What, then, are the prospects for Latin Americanists in the online revolution? Although use of commercial bibliographic databases is bound to increase slowly, I believe that costs, inherent problems with coverage and retrospective backfiles, and ingrained resistance to change will combine to prevent full utilization of the online database by academic researchers. What will increase, however, is the compilation and availability of extremely area- or discipline-specific databases, many of which will be accessible outside the present commercial vendor system. Examples of success databases already in existence are Central America Update, Latin American Debt Chronicle, and BorderLine. The last is basically a bibliographic database; the first two are current-awareness bulletins, their information culled from domestic and foreign news services. [18]

A third and very different database is the Documentary Relations of the Southwest (DRSW) Project, at the University of Arizona. This is a primary materials database; citations to thousands of documents relating to the Spanish borderlands have been entered in a database, searchable by a number of criteria, including subject and geographical descriptors. Judith Rowe claimed that in the future many types of research data for the social sciences would be available only in machine-readable form [19]; at the time I thought her prediction wildly unrealistic, but projects like the DRSW indicate that she may be right.

Several other promising developments may aid the scholar willing to come to terms with new research technologies. Every major research library's catalog is now automated, and many are available through a dial-up system, giving the scholar with a PC and modem instant access to his or her library. RLIN, the online catalog of RLG, forms a "super catalog" of some fifteen million items, searchable by author, title, and LC subject heading. RLIN is conducting an outreach program to train scholars to search its catalog directly, without the intermediary aid of the librarian; dial-up access to RLIN is already available. And CR-ROM technology may ultimately replace the online database. An example from our own field is illustrative of its potential. SALALM in the early '80s urged that the *Hispanic American Periodicals*

Index (HAPI) be put online; a proposal to do so through RLIN collapsed when the network demanded that *HAPI* subsidize its costs.

CD-ROM technology (of which the commercial vendors profess not to be afraid) may enable smaller and narrowly subject-specific databases to be made available in a compact form suitable for end-user searching. CD-ROM databases available in academic libraries may ultimately enable scholars to avoid the high costs of online searching.

A "quick and dirty" search carried out on a library bibliographic database, RLIN, and ten databases on DIALOG confirmed the utility of electronic research on border studies. Combining the search term "Latin America with frontier# (truncated), border# (truncated), and hinter# (truncated), retrieved 32 "hits" on RLIN; they ranged from the general (John Alexander Mackay, *Christianity on the Frontier*, a general work on religion in Latin America), to the specific (Alistair Hennessy, *The Frontier in Latin American History*). Most were "frontier studies" only in the abstract; for example, Luella N. Dambaugh, *The Coffee Frontier in Brazil*, or Christine A. Horak, *The Formation of Public Policy on the Amazonian Frontier*. Since we are comfortable with the most elastic and general definition of "frontier" in the first place, we can hardly blame catalogers for not being more rigorous in their application of the term. Replacing "Latin America" with Mexic# (truncated) fetched 326 "hits." The citations ranged from history to economics to demographics, including straight history, both Mexican and United States, anthropology, a study of southwest border trade, a conference on technology and culture on the border, an examination of births in two Texas border areas, a book on urbanization of Tijuana, and one on *maquiladores* and migration—confirming that "frontier" studies are multidisciplinary in nature.

A search of social and physical sciences and humanities databases on DIALOG turned up an interesting mix of citations (with the usual false drops). Running the same search strategy on *Historical Abstracts* retrieved a mixed bag of results. "Agricultural Colonization in Rondonia, Brazil," "The Venezuela-Guyana Border Dispute," were typical of straightforward interpretations of terms like "border," "frontier," and "hinterland"; there were also more abstract citations, like "The Fourth North American Frontier," an examination of foreign policy options for the U.S. in Latin America, and "'Peripheral' cities as Cultural Arenas (Russia, Austria, Latin America)." The same search strategy in *America: History and Life* retrieved 14 citations, most on U.S.-Latin American relations, with a few false drops on the American (U.S.) frontier.

But running the same search in nonhistorical files yielded fascinating results; in Population Bibliography, 39 citations; in Geobase, 30 hits; in CAB Abstracts, 33. Population Bibliography was especially fruitful, with articles on contraception and health care, and clandestine labor circulation on the U.S.-Mexican border, resettlement, new urban development, and land reform in Latin America, and Amazonian colonization. "The Borderland as Extended Community" examined migration across frontiers in the context of U.S.-Mexican political and cultural relations. CAB (Commonwealth Agricultural Bureau) has two subfiles of particular interest, Nutrition Abstracts and Rural Development Abstracts; citations retrieved included social and economic aspects of malaria control on the Amazon frontier; ecosystem disturbance in the Amazonian rain forests, commodity production in the Peruvian sierra in the last century, and a comparison of the economic dynamics of pioneer areas in Nicaragua and Brazil.

The same search yielded significantly poorer results in databases like PAIS International, Economic Literature Index, and MLA Bibliography. The relevant hit in MLA was "Images North and South of the Border: The United States and Latin America Today and Tomorrow," in *Hispania: A Journal Devoted to the Interests of the Teaching of Spanish and Portuguese*. Hits in PAIS tended to be of the "agricultural" or "economic frontier in . . ." variety; one article was on Miami as "banking's frontier town" in close proximity to Latin America. One of the best results was obtained with Dissertation Abstracts; 55 citations were retrieved, all but a few relevant. Although the results of the search were not discouraging, better results were obtained by combining country-specific descriptors with the search terms on borders, frontiers, and hinterlands. Nevertheless, one immediately apparent problem is that the very terms used to describe frontiers are so elastic that they can be utilized in nearly any situation.

Technology has placed at the disposal of the researcher a staggering amount of information, but humanities, and to a lesser degree social sciences, scholars have been resistant to change in traditional research methods. The librarian, whose education has become increasingly technical, has the opportunity to act as the interface between the brave new world and the academic. It is essential that professional organizations like SALALM play a role in technological education. In 1986 a professor of English wrote:

> Databases of humanistic materials are already beginning to alter the way researchers interact with the objects of their studies. As a younger generation becomes increasingly familiar with them, the basic nature of humanistic research may be changed. Even without any central control or even communication among its sectors, this new development is

significant; if the components can be co-ordinated, a type of scholarly research may emerge unlike anything known since modern academic norms were established. We have already crossed the divide between research by index card and research by electronic database. [20]

Here the key phrase is "if the components can be co-ordinated." As a discrete area study, Latin America is ideal for such a coordinated effort; it is my hope that SALALM will take a leading role in closing the scholar-technology gap.

NOTES

1. Hugh Lock, ed., *An Introduction to Electronic Publishing: A Snapshot of the Early 1980s* (Oxford: Learned Information, 1983), p. 16.

2. Martha E. Williams, "Useage and Revenue Data for the *On-Line Industry,*" *On-Line Review* 9:3 (June 1985), 205-210.

3. *The North American Online Directory* (New York, NY: R. R. Bowker Company, 1987).

4. Trudi Bellardo and Judy Stephenson, "The Use of Online Numeric Databases in Academic Libraries: A Report of a Survey," *Journal of Academic Librarianship* 12:3 (1986), 152.

5. John G. Veenstra, "Data Bases Relating to Latin American Studies," *Library Resources on Latin America: New Perspectives for the 1980s*, SALALM XXV (Madison, WI: SALALM Secretariat, 1981), pp. 307-312; John G. Veenstra and Marjorie Posner, "A Directory of Data Bases in Latin America," *Latin American Economic Issues: Information Needs and Sources*, SALALM XXVI (Madison, WI: SALALM Secretariat, 1984), pp. 183-205.

6. Harold Colson, a social sciences bibliographer at the Auburn University Library, has produced a directory, "Online Databases for Latin American Studies Research."

7. Ibid.

8. See Veenstra and Posner, "A Directory of Databases in Latin America."

9. Ibid.

10. Michael T. Nelson, "High Database Prices and Their Impact on Information Access: Is There a Solution?" *Journal of Academic Librarianship* 13:3 (1987), 158-162.

11. BorderLine handout; BorderLine is available at terminals throughout the UCLA campus, and at the San Diego State University Library, the University of New Mexico Library, and the library at the University of Texas, Austin. Fields can be searched by author, title, series, added descriptive fields, LC subject heading, or classification code number. BorderLine will also be released in print form; for further information, contact Barbara Valk, Coordinator of Bibliographic Development, UCLA Latin American Center, University of California, Los Angeles, CA 90024.

12. Christine L. Borgman et al., "University Faculty Use of Computerized Databases: An Assessment of Needs and Resources," *On-Line Review* 9:4 (August 1985), 318.

13. Richard W. Slatta, "Historians and Telecommunications," *History Microcomputer Review* (Fall 1986), 25-26.

14. Scott D. Stebelman, "On-Line Searching and the Humanities: Relevance, Resistance, and Marketing Strategies," in *National On-Line Meeting: Proceedings, 1981*, Martha E. Williams and Thomas H. Hogan, eds. (Medford, NJ: Learned Information, 1981), p. 445.

15. A workshop at the 1988 LASA meeting, "Electronic Research and Communications in Latin American Studies" resulted in a proposal for the establishment of a permanent task force on new research and networking technologies.

16. Lawrence H. Douglas, "Computers and Historians: The Results of Two National Surveys," *History Microcomputer Review* 2:1 (1986), 16-18.

17. Richard W. Slatta, "ScholarNet: Telecommunications for the Humanities and Social Sciences," *The Social Studies Teacher* 8:2 (February/March 1987).

18. Central America Update and Latin American Debt Chronicle are produced by the staff of the Latin American Institute at the University of New Mexico. Shortwave and verbal radio broadcasts from Latin America, as well as print media originating in Latin America and the United States, are monitored daily by the LADB staff, which uses these sources to prepare both journalistic and analytical articles. Dr. Nelson Valdes is LADB director and associate professor of sociology at the University of New Mexico; Dr. Barbara Kohl is LADB managing editor. Update and Chronicle are published in both electronic and print formats. The electronic version is published twice weekly and is accessible via the commercial system NewNet and the noncommercial system Bitnet. Diskettes of back issues are available. Print copies of both newsletters are published weekly, available from the LADB: Latin American Institute, 801 Yale Blvd. NE, University of New Mexico, Albuquerque, NM 87131.

19. Judith S. Rowe, "Primary Data for Historical Research: New Machine-Readable Sources," *RQ* 21:4 (Summer 1982), 352-353.

20. Joseph Raben, "Databases for the Humanities," *Scholarly Publishing* 18:1 (October 1986), 23.

48. Latin American Studies Online: Status and Outlook

Harold Colson

The widespread availability of online information storage and retrieval systems has eased the research process for investigators in many academic and professional fields. Containing massive varieties of bibliographic, textual, and numeric information, computerized databases offer quantitative and qualitative advances in the ability of researchers to identify and gather relevant background resources. For example, chemistry specialists routinely use the comprehensive Chemical Abstracts Service database to sift through millions of scientific journal articles for studies on specific compounds. Medical personnel around the world depend on the equally massive MEDLARS bibliographic file produced by the National Library of Medicine. Likewise, journalists access the NEXIS, VU/TEXT, and DataTimes systems to retrieve and display current newspaper articles and newswire reports on particular topics. Although search costs vary considerably, among the leading databases, many queries pay for themselves by eliminating or reducing time spent paging through conventional indexing and abstracting products. Indeed, most online systems enable searchers to generate customized retrieval sets that cannot be produced using counterpart printed sources. Moreover, numerous files are not distributed in printed form, so their information assets are available only to persons or institutions with appropriate online access capabilities.

Existing database resources offer fairly good support to the Latin American studies field. Although the online arena is dominated by scientific and business files, coverage of social sciences and humanities disciplines has improved to the point that powerful databases now cover all standard Latin American studies specialties, including history, literature, political science, sociology, economics, and anthropology. Indeed, there are hundreds of bibliographic, textual, and numeric files that provide at least some treatment of Latin American topics. Fortunately, the busy subject specialist need not come to grips with all of these potential sources, for two dozen or so basic files can handle most social sciences and humanities queries on Latin America. The majority of the key Latin American studies sources are general databases that contain substantial amounts of information on the region. Nearly all of these files are computerized versions of familiar indexing and abstracting products like *Historical Abstracts, Social Sciences Citation Index, Humanities Index,* and *MLA International Bibliography.* Because of their broad scope and utility, these basic databases should be familiar to searchers who tap DIALOG, BRS, and Wilsonline. The other pertinent sources are regional databases that treat only Latin American affairs. Reflecting their narrow coverage, these area files are carried by specialized vendors like NEXIS, NewsNet, and QUESTEL. Most regional databases are numeric or textual works.

This article surveys the principal area databases that support Latin American studies research. Most attention is devoted to the files that reside on the major commercial database systems, but some consideration is given to the resources which are produced in Latin America or which are distributed outside usual vendor channels. Of course, very few Latin American searches can be fully satisfied by the handful of available regional files. For the most part, only scientific disciplines are blessed with reasonably comprehensive core databases, so queries in social sciences and humanities fields generally call for the use of multiple files. Given the multidisciplinary character of area studies scholarship and the limited power of existing regional databases, the various general files are especially crucial tools for achieving adequate search coverage of Latin America. Nevertheless, the largely textual and numeric area files offer substantial varieties of information that cannot be extracted from the predominantly bibliographic general databases. [1]

Commercial Files

The only bibliographic file devoted exclusively to Latin American studies research is contained in Francis QUESTEL. Known as Amérique Latine, this database corresponds to the printed *Bulletin Bibliographique Amérique Latine* produced by Centre National de la Recherche Scientifique (Paris). Amérique Latine contains a few thousand citations to articles, books, reports, theses, and conference papers produced in France and other French-speaking countries. Updated once a year, this file offers retrospective listings back to 1980. Its value derives from its unmatched coverage of current French social sciences and humanities scholarship on Latin America. France is one of the leading European centers of research on Latin America, but very little of the French literature is cited by other commercial databases.

Most of the works found in Amérique Latine are written in French (85 percent) or Spanish (13 percent), so searchers must make appropriate language adjustments in their query statements. Title, descriptor, and abstract fields offer ample targets for subject searches. Because *Bulletin Bibliographique Amérique Latine* is held by very few American libraries, Amérique Latine make this substantial body of important research literature much more accessible to the domestic Latin Americanist community. [2]

The largest and oldest regional database is Latin American Newsletters (NEXIS), which offers full-text access to a number of the respected serial publications of the London-based Latin American Newsletters, Ltd. Included in this file are computerized versions of *Latin American Weekly Report*, *Latin American Regional Reports: Mexico and Central America*, *Latin American Regional Reports: Southern Cone*, *Latin American Regional Reports: Andean Group*, *Latin American Regional Reports: Caribbean*, *Latin American Regional Reports: Brazil*, and *Latin American Commodities Report*. Students and researchers have long depended on these newsletters for their informative and balanced reports of current political, military, diplomatic, economic, financial, and social developments throughout Latin America. Typical articles contain between 150 and 1,200 words. Because the corresponding print works are not accompanied by any cumulative indexing, the Latin American Newsletters database is a most welcome addition to the online menu, as anyone who has ever had to search scores of individual issues of *Latin American Weekly Report* will readily attest. Portions of this weekly file date back to 1967.

Two relatively new specialized databases are Central America Update (NewsNet) and Latin American Debt Chronicle (NewsNet). Both of this textual files are produced by the Latin American Data Base, a nonprofit entity of the Latin American Institute of the University of New Mexico. Latin American Data Base personnel monitor newswires, newspapers, and radio broadcasts to produce timely (twice a week) summaries and analyses of contemporary Latin American affairs. Most articles range between 100 and 400 words in length. Typical sources include Associated Press, Reuters, United Press International, Agence France-Presse, Deutsche Presse-Agentur, Prensa Latina (Cuba), *Excelsior*, *The Washington Post*, and *The New York Times*. As its name suggests, Central America Update follows economic, trade, political, security, and human rights developments throughout the volatile Central American region. Latin American Debt Chronicle, on the other hand, traces political, economic, and financial aspects of the ongoing external debt crisis in Latin America.

Both files extend back through 1986. Paper, electronic (via Bitnet), and diskette subscriptions are also available.

A few other source databases also focus on Latin America. Produced and distributed by the WEFA Group of Bala Cynwyd, Pennsylvania, Monthly Latin America and Latin America Forecast contain thousands of monthly and annual time-series compilations of macroeconomic data. Current, historical, and forecast figures for Argentina, Bolivia, Brazil, Chile, Colombia, Ecuador, Mexico, Peru, Uruguay, and Venezuela are recorded. Two related numeric files are Latin American Historical Data Base and Latin American Forecast Data Base, both of which are produced by the WEFA Group and distributed by the Uni-Coll Corporation (Philadelphia). These files provide monthly and annual time-series listings of major national economic indicators for Argentina, Brazil, Chile, Colombia, Venezuela, and Mexico. Political Risks: South America (NewsNet) is a textual file that discusses and forecasts political, economic, and social conditions in Argentina, Bolivia, Brazil, Chile, Colombia, Ecuador, Peru, Uruguay, and Venezuela. The companion Political Risks: North & Central America (NewsNet) treats Costa Rica, the Dominican Republic, El Salvador, Guatemala, Haiti, Honduras, Jamaica, Mexico, Nicaragua, and Panama. Providing analytical narratives along with background statistics, these files represent online versions of printed business risk assessments produced by Frost & Sullivan, Inc. Online updates are made on an annual basis. [3]

Noncommercial Sources

This survey of major online sources of information on Latin America would not be complete without some discussion of the relevant files that exist outside the standard commercial database systems. Although these noncommercial resources lack the convenience of the vendor files, they do offer many unique and valuable sets of bibliographic, textual, and numeric data for Latin American studies research. For example, several libraries in the United States and Mexico have cooperated to develop the BorderLine bibliographic file of books and other materials on the United States-Mexico border region. This file is loaded on the ORION library information system of the University of California, Los Angeles. [4] Many universities, research centers, and government agencies in Latin America have likewise created useful bibliographic and numeric databases. Some examples of these kinds of sources include the Centro de Información Científica y Humanística files of the Universidad Nacional Autónoma de México (Mexico City), the Latin American

Population Documentation System files of the Latin American Demographic Center (Santiago), the Information and Documentation Service files of the UNESCO Regional Center for Higher Education in Latin America and the Caribbean (Caracas), and the Banco de Dados files of the Fundação Getúlio Vargas (Rio de Janeiro). [5] Furthermore, certain educational and policy groups in the United States operate electronic bulletin board and messaging systems devoted to Latin American issues. One such service is the Central America Resource Network of Stanford, California. Known as CARNet, this electronic system offers numerous specialized news and information products, including the aforementioned Central America Update from the University of New Mexico. CARNet is a service of the San Francisco-based PeaceNet system. [6]

Assessment and Outlook

Online searchers who take full advantage of available databases should be able to achieve satisfactory results on many Latin American queries. Nevertheless, existing online products do not eliminate the need to consult standard print resources, for only a small portion of the reference works regularly used by Latin American studies specialists are now available in database form. Although one cannot reasonably expect all key sources to be computerized, the Latin American studies searcher must face two rather significant database gaps. Despite the current wave of popular, media, business, and government attention to hemispheric affairs, the Latin American field still lacks the convenience and power of a good area studies file along the lines of Mideast File (DIALOG) or Middle East: Abstracts and Index (DIALOG). [7] No databases from Latin America are now being distributed by the major commercial vendors. [8]

One immediate consequence of the current Latin American studies database environment is the frequent need to utilize multiple files. Of course, this condition will probably never disappear, for only some fantastic megafile could carry the myriad newspapers, newswires, newsletters, magazines, journals, books, dissertations, technical reports, and government publications that discuss Latin American affairs. A less apparent but more detrimental handicap stems from the fact that existing files provide generally weak coverage of works produced by Latin American publishers. Certain subject files do treat foreign periodicals, but relatively few articles from Latin America are found on available commercial databases. Because nearly all of these articles are drawn from academic journals, coverage of Latin American newspapers and magazines is virtually nonexistent. The book situation is only slightly better, for even the massive LC MARC and RLIN databases provide just partial coverage of Latin American monographs.

These substantial coverage problems would diminish if *Hispanic American Periodicals Index* and the *Handbook of Latin American Studies* were available online. Produced by the UCLA Latin American Center, *HAPI* treats around 250 specialized journals published in North America, Latin America, and Europe. Retrospective coverage reaches back to 1970. Edited by the Hispanic Division of the Library of Congress, *HLAS* identifies and discusses the latest social sciences and humanities scholarship on Latin America. Thousands of books, articles, and other publications are covered in each volume. (First published in 1935, the series has by now cited some 280,000 works.) Despite the substantial and unique contributions made by these two works, neither one has reached the national online circuit. The UCLA Latin American Center attempted to distribute the machine-readable *HAPI* file (featuring some 120,000 entries) via a commercial system or bibliographic utility, but unfavorable market projections and prohibitive startup fees doomed these efforts. [9] The Library of Congress has likewise begun to computerize *HLAS* operations, but the resulting bibliographic file will be limited to the local MUMS catalog network. According to the *HLAS* production staff, there are no current plans to distribute the work as a commercial database. Considering the *HAPI* experience, however, it seems unlikely that *HLAS* would be very attractive to market-conscious vendor executives anyway. Because Latin American databases probably hold even less market potential, area specialists will have to seek access to various noncommercial resources in order to obtain full bibliographic, textual, and numeric coverage of Latin American affairs.

NOTES

1. Some discussion of pertinent general files is provided by Harold Colson, "Searching Latin America Online: Social Sciences and Humanities," *Database Searcher*, June 1988, pp. 20-24. Two leading directories of available files are the *Directory of Online Databases* (New York, NY: Cuadra/Elsevier, 1979–) and the *Encyclopedia of Information Systems and Services* (Detroit, MI: Gale, 1978–). Helpful professional periodicals include *Database* (Weston, CT: Online, 1978–), *Online* (Weston, CT: Online, 1977–), *Information Today* (Medford, NJ: Learned Information, 1984–), *Online Access* (Chicago, IL: Online Access, 1987–), *Database Searcher* (Westport, CT: Meckler, 1987–), and *Link-Up* (Medford, NJ: Learned Information, 1985–).

2. Searching OCLC and RLIN indicates that only sixteen large U.S. libraries hold *Bulletin Bibliographique Amérique Latine*. These libraries are unlikely to cancel their subscriptions because Amérique Latine is available on QUESTEL, so the online database complements rather than undercuts the print product.

3. More recent Frost & Sullivan country information is provided by the weekly F&S Political Risk Newsletter (NewsNet). Other political risk databases are S. J. Rundt World Risk Analysis (I. P. Sharp) and International Investment Monitor (Profile). NewsNet also offers Opportunities for Investment/Latin America, a full-text business file that identifies goods and services needed by Latin American companies and agencies.

4. Access by outside users is available on a fee basis. The BorderLine staff can also generate offline prints for outside researchers. More information on the BorderLine project is presented in Barbara G. Valk, "Third World Databases and the New Information Age," *Latin American Masses and Minorities: Their Images and Realities*, SALALM XXX (Madison, WI: SALALM Secretariat, 1987), pp. 514-518. A similar Chicano database is being developed by the Chicano Studies Library of the University of California, Berkeley. The file producer intends to allow dial-up searches by remote users.

5. Of course, gaining direct access to a separate foreign database may be a somewhat difficult (but not impossible) undertaking. Fortunately, some Latin American database producers sell their machine-readable tapes, enabling purchasers to establish local files on mainframe computers. Moreover, a few Latin American databases are now being distributed in CD-ROM format. For example, a Mexico City company named Multiconsult is beginning to market a variety of Universidad Nacional Autónoma de México information products on CD-ROM. Among the projected offerings are LIBRUNAM (UNAM library holdings catalog), CLASE (Latin American social sciences and humanities journals index), PERIODICA (Latin American science and technology journals index), and BIBLAT (foreign journals index).

For more information on Latin American database systems, consult *Latin American Economic Issues: Information Needs and Sources*, SALALM XXVI (Madison, WI: SALALM Secretariat; Los Angeles: UCLA Latin American Center, 1984); Nancy Green-Maloney, "The Development of Online Information in Latin America: A Perspective," *International On-Line Information Meeting* (9th, 1985), 121-130; Enzo Molino, "On-Line Databases in Mexico," *Information Development* 2 (April 1986), 93-98; Tefko Saracevic, Gilda Maria Braga, Alvaro Quijano Solís, "Information Systems in Latin America," *Annual Review of Information Science and Technology* 14 (1979), 249-282; Marietta Daniels Shepard, "Information Systems and Library Automation in Latin America," *Advances in Librarianship* 13 (1984), 151-184; *The Transfer of Scholarly, Scientific and Technical Information between North and South America*, Victor Rosenberg and Gretchen Whitney, eds. (Metuchen, NJ: Scarecrow Press, 1986); and United Nations Economic Commission for Latin America and the Caribbean, *Microcomputers and Bibliographic Information Systems in Latin America: Problems, Experiences, and Projections* (Santiago: CEPAL, 1984).

6. The mailing address for CARNet is P.O. Box 2348, Stanford, California 94309. PeaceNet can be reached at 3228 Sacramento Street, San Francisco, California 94115.

7. An area studies database for Latin America is being created by the North-South Center of the University of Miami under a grant from the Department of State. Patterned after Mideast File, INFO-SOUTH is supposed to constitute "a comprehensive, multiphase information service designed to provide the fullest possible range of access for

government, academic, and business users to information in print and broadcast media regarding contemporary Latin America, especially information on social, political, and economic issues that is difficult or impossible to obtain in a timely fashion within the United States." Final decisions regarding file contents and access modes have not yet been made.

8. A Centro de Información Científica y Humanística database used to be available on QUESTEL. Known as BIBLAT, this file was dropped in January 1988. Likewise, NewsNet no longer carries NPD Mexico Daily News Briefs, a North American file which translated and summarized articles from selected Mexican periodicals.

9. According to *HAPI* editor Barbara Valk, some consideration is now being given to the production of a CD-ROM version of the index.

49. A Bibliographic Database for the Study of South American Border Regions

Patricia Wade

An important first step in the organization of a South American borderlands project has been the creation of a bibliography, or bibliographic database, of materials pertaining to border regions in South America.

This project was carried out at the University of California, Los Angeles, from 1985 to 1987 under the direction of Jorge Reina Schement, then a professor at UCLA's Graduate School of Library and Information Science. The materials were gathered and selected by Sylvia Mariscal, a research assistant at UCLA's Latin American Center, who was also responsible for creating the database structure and for inputting the information into the database.

The result of these efforts was a prototype bibliographic database containing 478 entries pertaining to border regions in South America. It is hoped that as the overall research project progresses, this prototype will be expanded and developed into a useful support tool and a means for scholars to share bibliographic information with other participants in the project.

In this paper I describe features of the bibliographic database as it exists now, including the various features of Notebook II, the software program used to create and manage the database, the possible changes in the existing database, and possibilities for future development.

The database now focuses on four key regions: Lower Orinoco Valley; Itaipu; Patagonia/Tierra del Fuego/Straits of Magellan; and the Brazil/Peru, Central Andean Piedmont. Central America and Mexico have been excluded. In keeping with the interdisciplinary nature of the project, the scope of the database is quite broad. A wide range of topics and academic disciplines are represented including political science, economics, business, finance, archaeology, anthropology, and history. Virtually no subject area has been consciously excluded, although some areas may be more thoroughly represented than others.

The database contains a variety of publication types—books, periodical articles, government documents—written in several different languages. There are no limitations regarding publication date. Both old and new items are represented.

The citations for the items currently included in the database were collected from a variety of different sources, including UCLA's main card catalog at the University Research Library, UCLA's online public catalog ORION, UC's MELVYL Catalog, the *Hispanic American Periodicals Index* (*HAPI*), the *Handbook of Latin American Studies*, and the *Social Sciences Index*.

Each item in the database is represented by a record. Each record currently consists of nine fields. These fields represent a mixture of bibliographic information and subject information. The first field is the Keyname, a unique identifying number for each record. The next five fields represent the basic elements of bibliographic description: (1) Author (corporate or personal), (2) Title, (3) Publisher and publication date (for periodicals, the title of the periodical is entered as the publisher), (4) Collation (for books this includes number of pages and indication of bibliographies, illustrations, maps, etc.; for periodical articles this includes volume number, issue number, date, and pages), and (5) Series title and number. The seventh field contains the Library of Congress subject headings assigned to the item. The eighth field is designated as a "notes" field. This has been used to provide annotations for some of the items. At this point, the only records containing annotations are those taken from the *Handbook of Latin American Studies*. This information has been taken from the annotations provided by the *Handbook* and modified. Each of these annotations is followed by the acronym HLAS in parentheses to indicate the source of information for the annotation. The ninth field contains a "classification code number." The bibliography has a numeric classification scheme. Numbers correspond to the principal areas of growing frontier contact, such as 1 Iguasu; 2 Lower Orinoco; 3 Southern Andes Magellan; 4 Brazil-Peru, Central Andean Piedmont. Six other regions have been identified as being of possible interest for future study. Other classification numbers represent important concepts or issues common to all border regions (e.g., ecology, integration).

No specific style manual was chosen for the presentation of the bibliographic information, but the format closely resembles that suggested by the *Chicago Manual of Style*. The bibliography has been entered into Notebook II, which is a database management program designed specifically for handling text. It allows the user to create databases consisting of individual records containing any kind of text. These databases can then be searched, reordered, and manipulated in many different ways. Since Notebook II is designed specifically for text rather than numerical data, it is suitable for use with bibliographic information. The bibliography can thus be presented in any order based on the information contained in each field. For example, it can be arranged in alphabetical order by author or title. It can be ordered by publication date. Items can be grouped together geographically based on the classification codes. In other words, tailor-made bibliographies based on the contents of the database can be created.

There are currently three kinds of subject access to the database: Library of Congress subject headings, classification codes (geographic or border concept), and title keywords. This allows several approaches to isolating items appropriate to a researcher's needs. It is intended that these three types of subject access—two controlled and one free text—work together to provide adequate subject access to the database.

Future Development

The frontier database is still in its beginning stages. It is off to a good start, but needs editing and proofreading. Furthermore, if it is to develop further, it is necessary to take a close look at the information contained in each record and at the overall structure of the database in order to evaluate its usefulness as a shared research tool. Is all of the necessary information there? Are there additional points of access or fields that should be added? Has the record structure been designed to make optimum use of the search capabilities provided by the Notebook II program? Additionally, it is important to consider broader questions such as how this database can be developed, distributed, and managed in a way in which it can be shared by the scholars participating in the research project.

Behind any changes or additions to the database should be the question of whether the information and the way that it is arranged and accessed is actually meeting the needs of the people who will be using it. This will always be tempered by the technical limitations of software and hardware and the practical limitations of time and money. No matter how hard one tries to foresee all possible uses and problems, there will always be errors and miscalculations. The only way to really know what is needed is to plan as carefully as possible, and to always maintain flexibility as much as possible. I believe that this bibliographic database in its current state represents a basis for the formation of a useful bibliographic tool for scholarly research.

I have numerous details about ways to improve the system, but they are beyond the scope of this paper. Those interested may contact me.

About the Authors

FERNANDO ALEGRÍA is a poet from Chile and Professor of Spanish at Stanford University.

PATRICIO ARANDA-CODDOU is Law Librarian at the International Monetary Fund.

GEORGINA ARTEAGA CARLEBACH is Librarian at the Centro Regional de Información y Documentación en Salud, Facultad de Medicina, Universidad Autónoma de Nuevo León.

MARTA STIEFEL AYALA is at the Institute for Border Studies at San Diego State University.

LYGIA MARIA F. C. BALLANTYNE is currently Assistant Chief, Overseas Operation Division of the Library of Congress. At the time of the conference she was serving as Field Director of the Library of Congress Office in Rio.

SUSAN SHATTUCK BENSON is Senior Specialist, Development of Libraries, Archives and Mass Media, Department of Cultural Affairs of the Organization of American States.

DAVID BLOCK is Latin American Librarian at Cornell University.

WILLIAM H. BOLIN is Senior Research Fellow at the University of California, Los Angeles and retired Vice-Chairman of the Bank of America.

WOODROW BORAH is Professor Emeritus at the University of California, Berkeley, where he was the Abraham D. Shepard Professor in History and Communications.

JAMES M. BREEDLOVE is Curator for Latin American and Iberian Collections at Stanford University.

ELLEN H. BROW is currently Basque Studies Librarian at the University of Nevada at Reno. At the time of the conference she was Book Selector for Ibero-America at Harvard University.

ANGELA M. CARREÑO is Librarian for Latin American Studies at New York University's Bobst Library.

HAROLD COLSON is Public Services and Collection Development Librarian at the International Relations and Pacific Studies Library of the University of California, San Diego.

PAULA HATTOX COVINGTON is Latin American and Iberian Studies Bibliographer and Lecturer in Latin American Studies at Vanderbilt University. She served as President of SALALM for 1987-88.

DANA D'ANDRAIA is Head of Acquisitions at the Library of the University of California, Irvine.

CARL W. DEAL is Director of Library Collections at the University of Illinois Libraries at Urbana-Champaign.

CHARLES S. FINEMAN is Humanities Bibliographer at Northwestern University Library.

JUDY GANSON is Assistant University Librarian for Technical Services at the University of Southern California

MARTÍN GARCÍA CAMBEIRO is with Latin American Books and Serials in Buenos Aires.

MARK L. GROVER is Latin American Studies Bibliographer at Brigham Young University.

HELEN LADRÓN DE GUEVARA COX is Director of the Library Institute of the Universidad de Guadalajara.

LAURENCE HALLEWELL is Ibero-American Bibliographer at the University of Minnesota Libraries in Minneapolis.

J. NOÉ HERRERA C. is with Libros de Colombia y Latino-América in Bogotá.

LAWRENCE A. HERZOG is Associate Professor, Department of Mexican American Studies, San Diego State University. At the time of the conference he was Coordinator and Assistant Professor of Urban Studies and Planning at the University of California, San Diego.

FLOR DE MARÍA HURTADO is Directora, Centro de Documentación de la Gestión Gubernamental 1982-1988 in Mexico City.

HOWARD L. KARNO is an Antiquarian Bookdealer with Howard Karno Books.

IGOR I. KAVASS is Professor of Law and Director, Law Library, Vanderbilt University.

LUIS LEAL is a literary critic and poet and Professor of Spanish at the University of California, Santa Barbara.

EUDORA LOH is Foreign Documents Librarian at the University of California, Los Angeles.

SHEILA A. MILAM is Latin American Cataloger at Arizona State University in Tempe.

CARMEN MEURER MURICY is Chief, Acquisitions Section of the Library of Congress Office in Rio.

THOMAS NIEHAUS is Director, Latin American Library, Tulane University.

RICHARD F. PHILLIPS is Team Leader of Romance Languages Cataloging at Princeton University Library.

THOMAS H. REYNOLDS is Associate and Foreign Law Librarian at the University of California, Berkeley.

BARBARA J. ROBINSON is Curator of the Boeckmann Collection at the Doheny Library, University of Southern California.

VIRGINIA RODES is with Innovative Interfaces, Inc.

DAVID ROZKUSZKA is Foreign Document Librarian at Stanford University Libraries.

A. J. R. RUSSELL-WOOD is Chairman, Department of History, Johns Hopkins University.

URSULA SCHADLICH SCHÖNHALS is Coordinador-General of the Biblioteca Nacional in Santiago.

RICHARD W. SLATTA is Associate Professor of History at North Carolina State University, Raleigh.

GABRIELA SONNTAG-GRIGERA is currently with San Diego State University—Imperial Valley Campus. At the time of the conference she was Librarian for the American Community Schools in Buenos Aires.

PETER STERN is Latin American Librarian, University of Florida Libraries, Gainesville.

RAFAEL E. TARRAGÓ is Bibliographer for Latin American Studies, University of Notre Dame.

NORMAN J. W. THROWER is Professor, Department of Geography, University of California, Los Angeles.

PATRICIA WADE is Information Services Librarian, St. Mary's College Library. At the time of the conference she was Reference-Instructional Librarian at the University of California, Los Angeles.

RONALD J. WASOWSKI is Assistant Professor, Department of Earth Sciences, University of Notre Dame.

JOHN WAIBLINGER is Head, Bibliographic Information Services, at the University of Southern California Library.

GAYLE ANN WILLIAMS is currently Bibliographer for Spain, Latin America, and Portugal at the University of Georgia Libraries. At the time of the conference she was Iberoamerican Cataloger at the University of New Mexico.

SABINE ZEHRER is Librarian for Latin American Law, Ibero-Amerikanisches Institut Preussischer Kulturbesitz, Berlin.

Program of Substantive Panels and Workshops

Monday, June 6

8:00-5:00   Committee Meetings

7:30-10:00   Executive Board

Tuesday, June 7

9:00-9:45   Opening Session

James D. Hart, Director, The Bancroft Library, University of California, Berkeley

Iván Jaksic, Program Coordinator, Center for Latin American Studies, University of California, Berkeley

Paula Covington, President, SALALM, Vanderbilt University

James M. Breedlove, Curator, Latin American and Iberian Collections, Stanford University Libraries

Dan C. Hazen, Librarian for Latin America, Spain and Portugal, University of California, Berkeley

Richard D. Woods, Trinity University, Chair, José Toribio Medina Award

Rapporteur General, *Charles S. Fineman*, Northwestern University

10:15-12:00   Theme Panel 1

Borders and Frontiers in the Americas: A Multidisciplinary Overview of Research Trends, Issues and Themes

Chair, *Paul Ganster*, Institute for Regional Studies of the Californias, San Diego State University

Richard W. Slatta, North Carolina State University: "Historical Frontier Imagery in the Americas"

Lawrence A. Herzog, University of California, San Diego: "The United States-Mexico Border Region in Comparative Human Geographical Perspective"

William H. Bolin, UCLA Latin American Center: "'Nose to Nose in Nowhere': Organizing to Study the Penetration of South America's Empty Borderlands"

Patricia Wade, University of California, Los Angeles: "A Bibliographic Database for the Study of South American Border Regions"

Rapporteur, *Carol Walton*, University of Florida

1:15-3:15   Theme Panel 2

Regional Organizations in Latin America and the Caribbean as Instrumentalities of Solving Transborder Problems: Documents and Other Publications

Chair, *Igor Kavass*, Vanderbilt University

Sabine Zehrer, Ibero-Amerikanisches Institut: "Organizaciones internacionales de América Latina"

Thomas L. Welch, Organization of American States: "The Organization of American States and Its Documentation"

Patricio Aranda-Coddou, International Monetary Fund: "The Documents of the Latin American Regional Organizations on Banking and Finance"

Thomas H. Reynolds, University of California, Berkeley: "Latin American Regional Organizations: Documentary and Auxiliary Research Sources"

Igor I. Kavass, Vanderbilt University: "The Grupo Andino and Its Documents"

Rapporteur, *Pamela Howard*, Arizona State University

3:45-5:15   Panel

Frontier, Border, and Hinterlands Resources: Case Studies

Chair, *Reynaldo Ayala*, Institute for Border Studies, San Diego State University—Imperial Valley Campus

Carmen Meurer Muricy, Library of Congress Office, Rio: "Acquiring Publications from the Amazon: Issues and Sources"

J. Noé Herrera C., Libros de Colombia y Latino-América: "Colombia (editorialmente): Un país de fronteras en papel. . . y sin papel"

Gabriela Sonntag-Grigera, Asociación Escuelas Lincoln, Buenos Aires: "Establishing Exchange Programs with Argentine Institutions"

Marta Stiefel Ayala, San Diego State University—Imperial Valley: "Acquisitions and Exchanges on the Mexican Side of the United States-Mexico Border"
Rapporteur, *Angela Carreño,* New York University

Wednesday, June 8
9:00-10:30 Theme Panel 3

Historical and Geographical Perspectives of Frontiers and Hinterlands

Chair, *Walter V. Brem, Jr.,* University of California, Berkeley

A. J. R. Russell-Wood, Johns Hopkins University: "Frontiers in Colonial Brazil: Reality, Myth and Metaphor"

Hilgard O'Reilly Sternberg, University of California, Berkeley: "Contemporary Frontiers in the Brazilian Amazon"

Ronald J. Wasowski, University of Notre Dame, and *Norman J. W. Thrower,* University of California, Los Angeles: "Cartographic and Image Resources for Research on the United States-Mexico Borderlands"

Rapporteur, *Donald L. Gibbs,* University of Texas at Austin

11:00-12:30 Panel

On the Frontier with Automated Systems: Six Perspectives from Librarians and Vendors

Chair, *Barbara Robinson,* University of Southern California

Dana D'Andraia, University of California, Irvine: "Automation and Latin American Acquisitions: An Acquisitions Manager's Perspective"

John Waiblinger, University of Southern California: "Implementing Automated Acquisitions Systems: A Systems Librarian's Perspective"

Virginia Rodes, Innovative Interfaces, Inc.: "The System Vendor's Perspective"

Howard L. Karno, Howard Karno Books: "A Computer Saga: The U.S. Book Dealer's Perspective"

Martín García Cambeiro, Librería/Editorial Fernando García: "The Latin American Book Dealer's Perspective"

Charles S. Fineman, Northwestern University: "The Bibliographer's Perspective"

Rapporteur, *Tamara Brunnschweiler,* Michigan State University

2:00-3:30   Panel

SALALM and the Columbian Quincentenary: Echoes of the Past, Reflections on the Future

Chair, *Laura Gutiérrez-Witt*, University of Texas at Austin

Ludwig Lauerhass, Jr., University of California, Los Angeles

Allan Metz, University of Illinois, Urbana

Russ T. Davidson, University of New Mexico

A. J. R. Russell-Wood, Johns Hopkins University

David Block, Cornell University

Rapporteur, *Patricia Wade*, University of California, Los Angeles

2:00-3:30   Workshop

Subnational Official Publications: Problems and Prospects

Chair, *Eudora I. Loh*, University of California, Los Angeles

Lawrence Hallewell, University of Minnesota: "Official Publications at the Subnational Level"

Flor de María Hurtado, Centro de Documentación de la Gestión Gubernamental, Presidencia de la República: "Documentos y publicaciones del Gobierno del Presidente Miguel de la Madrid"

Eudora Loh, University of California, Los Angeles, and *W. David Rozkuszka*, Stanford University: "Survey on Subnational Official Publications from Latin America and the Caribbean"

4:00-5:30   Workshop

Town Meeting: Medium-Range Agenda for SALALM

Dan C. Hazen, University of California, Berkeley

Deborah L. Jakubs, Duke University

Rapporteur, *Rachel B. Miller*, University of Kansas

4:00-5:30   Panel

Cataloging Backlogs and Institutional Cooperation: Past, Present, and Future

Chair, *Laura D. Loring*, University of Southern California

Gayle Ann Williams, University of New Mexico: "No Bibliographer Is an Island: Cataloging and Collection Development of Latin Americana"

Richard F. Phillips, Princeton University: "Innovations in Cataloging at Princeton University"

Sheila A. Milam, Arizona State University: "Sweeping Out the Bibliographic Closet: Cataloging the Arrearage at Arizona State University"

Judy Ganson, University of Southern California: "An Administrator Looks at Cooperative Cataloging"

Respondent, *Thomas Niehaus*, Tulane University

Rapporteur, *Carol A. Evans*, Jamestown College

Thursday, June 9

8:30-10:00 Theme Panel 4

Historical Dimensions of the Frontier

Chair, *David Block*, Cornell University

David Block, Cornell University: "Themes and Sources for Missionary History in Hispanic America"

Peter Stern, University of Florida: "Sons (and Grandsons) of Bolton: The Development of Borderlands Historiography"

Woodrow Borah, University of California, Berkeley: "Commentary"

Rapporteur, *César Rodríguez*, Yale University

10:30-12:00 Workshop

Workshop on Marginalized Peoples and Ideas, I

Chair, *Peter T. Johnson*, Princeton University

Lygia Maria F. C. Ballantyne, Library of Congress Office, Rio: "Documenting Brazil's Political and Social Movements, 1966-1986: The Library of Congress Experience"

Margaret H. Johnson, The British Library

Lygia F. C. Ballantyne, Library of Congress Office, Rio

Peter T. Johnson, Princeton University

Fred Morgner, Literatura de Vientos Tropicales: "Evaluating Acquisitions Methods: Book Dealers, Blanket Orders and Field Trips"

10:30-12:00 Panel

Reaching Out Across Borders: Sharing Knowledge and Resources

Chair, *Iliana L. Sonntag*, San Diego State University

Mark L. Grover, Brigham Young University: "The 'Strange Career' of Latin American Librarianship in the United States"

Helen Ladrón de Guevara Cox, Universidad de Guadalajara: "Cooperation among Libraries: A Mexican Proposal"

Ursula Schadlich Schönhals, Biblioteca Nacional, Santiago, Chile: "La Biblioteca Nacional de Chile y sus colecciones patrimoniales"

Susan Shattuck Benson, Organization of American States: "Pooling Resources: The OAS Programs for Library and Archives Development in the 1980s"

Rapporteur, *Cecilia Botero*, University of Florida

3:15-5:15   Theme Panel 5 (Stanford)

Welcome to Stanford

David C. Weber, Director, Stanford University Libraries

George A. Collier, Director, Center for Latin American Studies, Stanford University

Literatura Fronteriza

Chair, Roberto G. Trujillo, Stanford University

Fernando Alegría, Stanford University: "Unos cuantos frailes y unos pocos burros"

Luis Leal, University of California, Santa Barbara: "La Frontera: Imágenes literarias y realidad social"

Rapporteur, *Lynn M. Shirey*, Harvard University

Friday, June 10

8:30-10:00 Workshop

Workshop on Marginalized Peoples and Ideas, II

Chair, *Peter Stern*, University of Florida

Valerie Sandoval Mwalilino, Schomburg Center for Research in Black Culture, New York Public Library: "Collecting Documentation on the Black Experience in the Americas"

Rafael E. Tarragó, Notre Dame University: "Catholic Literature of Popular Religiosity, Clerical Activism, and the Catholic Church's Social Role"

Angela M. Carreño, New York University: "Social and Political Fringe Movements: Resources and Collection Development Strategies of Activist, Solidarity-Type Organizations"

8:30-10:00   Workshop

Workshop on Bibliographic Instruction

Chair, *Laurence Hallewell*, University of Minnesota
Robert McNeil, The Bodleian Library
Maria Segura Hoopes, University of Arizona
Pauline P. Collins, University of Massachusetts
Anne Hartness, University of Texas at Austin

8:30-10:00   Workshop

Workshop on Cataloging

Chair, *Richard F. Phillips*, Princeton University
Georgina Arteaga Carlebach, Universidad Autónoma de Nuevo León: "ARUDSI--Primera red de bibliotecas en Mexico"
Rapporteur, *Peter S. Bushnell*, University of Florida

10:30-12:00   Panel

Building Latin American Research Collections

Chair and Introduction, *Barbara J. Robinson*, University of Southern California
Ludwig Lauerhass, Jr., University of California, Los Angeles: "Collectors, Book Barons, Libraries and the California Vision of Latin America"
Carl W. Deal, University of Illinois, Urbana: "Latin American Collections: Criteria for Major Status"
Thomas Niehaus, Tulane University: "Methods of Collecting: Latin American Library Materials"
Ellen H. Brow, Harvard University: "Exploring the Third Bank of the River: Deciding What to Collect for a Research Library"
James M. Breedlove: "Cooperative Development of Latin American Collections: The Stanford/Berkeley Experience"
Rapporteur, *Sara Sánchez*, University of Miami

1:30-3:00   Panel

Border and Frontier Regions in the Context of Principal National Publishing Trends

Chair, *S. Lief Adelson*, Books from Mexico
S. Lief Adelson, Books from Mexico: "Regional Publishing in Mexico"

Alfredo Montalvo, Editorial Inca: "Publishing Trends in the
Andean Region"
Alfonso Vijil, Libros Latinos: "Central America"
Werner Guttentag, Editorial Los Amigos del Libro:
"Bolivian Publishing"
Juan Ignacio Risso, Librería Linardi y Risso: "Publishing in
Uruguay"
Rapporteur, *María Otero-Boisvert*, University of Nevada

1:30-3:00   Panel

Database Coverage of Frontiers, Borders, and Hinterlands

Chair, *Walter V. Brem, Jr.*, University of California,
Berkeley
Peter Stern: "Databases in the Humanities and Social
Sciences: An Update and Review of Border Research"
Harold Colson: "Latin American Studies Online: Status
and Outlook"
María del Consuelo Tuñón R.: "Bases de datos en México:
perspectivas fronterizas"

3:30-5:30   Closing Session

5:30-6:30   Executive Board